Principles of Information Security

Fourth Edition

Principles of Information Security
Fourth Edition

Michael E. Whitman, *Ph.D., CISM, CISSP*

Herbert J. Mattord, *CISM, CISSP*
Kennesaw State University

COURSE TECHNOLOGY
CENGAGE Learning

Australia • Brazil • Japan • Korea • Mexico • Singapore • Spain • United Kingdom • United States

COURSE TECHNOLOGY
CENGAGE Learning™

Principles of Information Security,
Fourth Edition
Michael E. Whitman and
Herbert J. Mattord

Vice President Editorial, Career Education & Training Solutions: Dave Garza

Director of Learning Solutions: Matthew Kane

Executive Editor: Steve Helba

Managing Editor: Marah Bellegarde

Product Manager: Natalie Pashoukos

Development Editor: Lynne Raughley

Editorial Assistant: Jennifer Wheaton

Vice President Marketing, Career Education & Training Solutions: Jennifer Ann Baker

Marketing Director: Deborah S. Yarnell

Senior Marketing Manager: Erin Coffin

Associate Marketing Manager: Shanna Gibbs

Production Manager: Andrew Crouth

Content Project Manager: Brooke Greenhouse

Senior Art Director: Jack Pendleton

Manufacturing Coordinator: Amy Rogers

Technical Edit/Quality Assurance: Green Pen Quality Assurance

Library of Congress Control Number: 2010940654

ISBN-13: 978-1-111-13821-9

ISBN-10: 1-111-13821-4

Course Technology
20 Channel Center
Boston, MA 02210
USA

Cengage Learning is a leading provider of customized learning solutions with office locations around the globe, including Singapore, the United Kingdom, Australia, Mexico, Brazil, and Japan. Locate your local office at: **international.cengage.com/region**.

Cengage Learning products are represented in Canada by Nelson Education, Ltd.

For your lifelong learning solutions, visit **course.cengage.com**

Purchase any of our products at your local college store or at our preferred online store **www.cengagebrain.com**.

Printed in the United States of America
1 2 3 4 5 6 7 8 9 14 13 12 11 10

Brief Table of Contents

Table of Contents

Preface

As global networks expand the interconnection of the world's information systems, the smooth operation of communication and computing solutions becomes vital. However, recurring events such as virus and worm attacks and the success of criminal attackers illustrate the weaknesses in current information technologies and the need to provide heightened security for these systems.

When attempting to secure their existing systems and networks, organizations must draw on the current pool of information security practitioners. But to develop more secure computing environments in the future, these same organizations are counting on the next generation of professionals to have the correct mix of skills and experience to anticipate and manage the complex information security issues that are sure to arise. Thus, improved texts with supporting materials, along with the efforts of college and university faculty, are needed to prepare students of technology to recognize the threats and vulnerabilities in existing systems and to learn to design and develop the secure systems needed in the near future.

The purpose of *Principles of Information Security, Fourth Edition*, is to fill the need for a quality academic textbook that surveys the discipline of information security. While there are dozens of quality publications on information security and assurance that are oriented to the practitioner, there is a dearth of textbooks that provide the student with a balanced introduction to both security management and the technical components of security. By creating a book specifically from the perspective of the discipline of information systems, we hope to close this gap. Further, there is a clear need for criminal justice, political science, accounting information systems, and other disciplines to gain a clear understanding of the principles of information security, in order to formulate interdisciplinary solutions for systems vulnerabilities. The essential tenet of this textbook is that information security in the modern organization is a problem for management to solve, and not one that technology alone can address. In other words, the information security of an organization has important economic consequences, for which management will be held accountable.

Approach

Principles of Information Security, Fourth Edition, provides a broad review of the entire field of information security, background on many related elements, and enough detail to facilitate an understanding of the topic as a whole. The book covers the terminology of the field, the history of the discipline, and strategies for managing an information security program.

Structure and Chapter Descriptions

Principles of Information Security, Fourth Edition, is structured to follow a model called the security systems development life cycle (or SecSDLC). This structured methodology can be used to implement information security in an organization that has little or no formal information security measures in place. SecSDLC can also serve as a method for improving established information security programs. The SecSDLC provides a solid framework very similar to that used in application development, software engineering, traditional systems analysis and design, and networking. This textbook's use of a structured methodology is intended to provide a supportive but not overly dominant foundation that will guide instructors and students through an examination of the various components of the information domains of information security. To serve this end, the book is organized into seven sections and twelve chapters.

Section I—Introduction
Chapter 1—Introduction to Information Security
The opening chapter establishes the foundation for understanding the broader field of information security. This is accomplished by defining key terms, explaining essential concepts, and providing a review of the origins of the field and its impact on the understanding of information security.

Section II—Security Investigation Phase
Chapter 2—The Need for Security
Chapter 2 examines the business drivers behind the information security analysis design process. It examines current organizational and technological security needs, and emphasizes and builds on the concepts presented in Chapter 1. One principle concept presented here is that information security is primarily a management issue, rather than a technological one. To put it another way, the best practices within the field of information security involve applying technology only after considering the business needs.

The chapter also examines the various threats facing organizations and presents methods for ranking these threats (in order to assign them relative priority) that organizations can use when they begin their security planning process. The chapter continues with a detailed examination of the types of attacks that could result from these threats, and how these attacks could impact the organization's information systems. The chapter also provides a further discussion of the key principles of information security, some of which were introduced in Chapter 1: confidentiality, integrity, availability, authentication and identification, authorization, accountability, and privacy.

Finally, the chapter explains the concept and tenets of software assurance, and provides insight into the newly developing common body of knowledge in software assurance, along with several "deadly security sins" of software development.

Chapter 3—Legal, Ethical, and Professional Issues in Information Security

In addition to being a fundamental part of the SecSDLC investigation process, a careful examination of current legislation, regulation, and common ethical expectations of both national and international entities provides important insights into the regulatory constraints that govern business. This chapter examines several key laws that shape the field of information security, and presents a detailed examination of the computer ethics that those who implement security must adhere to. Although ignorance of the law is no excuse, it's considered better than negligence (that is, knowing the law but doing nothing to comply with it). This chapter also presents several legal and ethical issues that are commonly found in today's organizations, as well as formal and professional organizations that promote ethics and legal responsibility.

Section III—Security Analysis
Chapter 4—Risk Management

Before the design of a new information security solution can begin, the information security analysts must first understand the current state of the organization and its relationship to information security. Does the organization have any formal information security mechanisms in place? How effective are they? What policies and procedures have been published and distributed to the security managers and end users? This chapter describes how to conduct a fundamental information security assessment by describing the procedures for identifying and prioritizing threats and assets, and the procedures for identifying what controls are in place to protect these assets from threats. The chapter also provides a discussion of the various types of control mechanisms and identifies the steps involved in performing the initial risk assessment. The chapter continues by defining risk management as the process of identifying, assessing, and reducing risk to an acceptable level and implementing effective control measures to maintain that level of risk. The chapter concludes with a discussion of risk analysis and the various types of feasibility analyses.

Section IV—Logical Design
Chapter 5—Planning for Security

Chapter 5 presents a number of widely accepted security models and frameworks. It examines best business practices and standards of due care and due diligence, and offers an overview of the development of security policy. This chapter details the major components, scope, and target audience for each of the levels of security policy. This chapter also explains data classification schemes, both military and private, as well as the security education training and awareness (SETA) program. The chapter examines the planning process that supports business continuity, disaster recovery, and incident response; it also describes the organization's role during incidents and specifies when the organization should involve outside law enforcement agencies.

Section V—Physical Design

Author's Note: The material in this section is sequenced to introduce students of information systems to the information security aspects of various technology topics. If you are not familiar with networking technology and the TCP/IP protocol, the material in Chapters 6, 7, 8, and 9 may prove difficult. Students who do not have a grounding in network protocols should prepare for their study of the chapters in this section by reading a chapter or two from a networking textbook on the TCP/IP protocol.

Chapter 6—Security Technology: Firewalls and VPNs Chapter 6 provides a detailed overview of the configuration and use of technologies designed to segregate the organization's systems from the insecure Internet. This chapter examines the various definitions and categorizations of firewall technologies and the architectures under which firewalls may be deployed. The chapter continues with a discussion of the rules and guidelines associated with the proper configuration and use of firewalls. Chapter 6 also discusses remote dial-upsServices, and the security precautions necessary to secure this access point for organizations still deploying this older technology. The chapter continues with a presentation of content filtering capabilities and considerations. The chapter concludes with an examination of technologies designed to provide remote access to authorized users through virtual private networks.

Chapter 7—Security Technology: Intrusion Detection, Access Control, and Other Security Tools Chapter 7 continues the discussion of security technologies by examining the concept of the intrusion, and the technologies necessary to prevent, detect, react, and recover from intrusions. Specific types of intrusion detection and prevention systems (IDPSs)—the host IDPS, network IDPS, and application IDPS—and their respective configurations and uses are also presented and discussed. The chapter continues with an examination of the specialized detection technologies that are designed to entice attackers into decoy systems (and thus away from critical systems) or simply to identify the attackers' entry into these decoy areas, which are known as honey pots, honey nets, and padded cell systems. Also examined are trace-back systems, which are designed to track down the true address of attackers who were lured into decoy systems. The chapter continues with a detailed examination of some of the key security tools information security professionals can use to examine the current state of their organization's systems, and to identify any potential vulnerabilities or weaknesses that may exist in the systems or the organization's overall security posture. The chapter concludes with a discussion of access control devices commonly deployed by modern operating systems, and new technologies in the area of biometrics that can provide strong authentication to existing implementations.

Chapter 8—Cryptography Chapter 8 continues the section on security technologies with a presentation of the underlying foundations of modern cryptosystems, as well as a discussion of the architectures and implementations of those cryptosystems. The chapter begins with an overview of the history of modern cryptography, and a discussion of the various types of ciphers that played key roles in that history. The chapter also examines some of the mathematical techniques that comprise cryptosystems, including hash functions. The chapter extends this discussion by comparing traditional symmetric encryption systems with more modern asymmetric encryption systems. The chapter also examines the role of asymmetric systems as the foundation of public-key encryption systems. Also covered in this chapter are the cryptography-based protocols used in secure communications; these include protocols such as SHTTP, SMIME, SET, SSH, and several others. The chapter then provides a discussion of steganography, and its emerging role as an effective means of hiding information. The chapter concludes by revisiting those attacks on information security that are specifically targeted at cryptosystems.

Chapter 9—Physical Security A vital part of any information security process, physical security is concerned with the management of the physical facilities, the implementation of physical access control, and the oversight of environmental controls. From designing a secure data center to assessing the relative value of guards and watchdogs to resolving the technical issues involved in fire suppression and power conditioning, physical security involves a wide range of special considerations. Chapter 9 examines these considerations by factoring in the various physical security threats that modern organizations face.

Section VI—Implementation

Chapter 10—Implementing Security The preceding chapters provided guidelines for how an organization might design its information security program. Chapter 10 examines the elements critical to *implementing* this design. Key areas in this chapter include the bull's-eye model for implementing information security and a discussion of whether an organization should outsource the various components of an information security program. Change management, program improvement, and additional planning for the business continuity efforts are also discussed.

Chapter 11—Personnel Security The next area in the implementation stage addresses people issues. Chapter 11 examines both sides of the personnel coin: security personnel and security of personnel. It examines staffing issues, professional security credentials, and the implementation of employment policies and practices. The chapter also discusses how information security policy affects, and is affected by, consultants, temporary workers, and outside business partners.

Section VII—Maintenance and Change

Chapter 12—Information Security Maintenance Last and most important is the discussion on maintenance and change. Chapter 12 presents the ongoing technical and administrative evaluation of the information security program that an organization must perform to maintain the security of its information systems. This chapter explores ongoing risk analysis, risk evaluation, and measurement, all of which are part of risk management. The special considerations needed for the varieties of vulnerability analysis needed in the modern organization are explored from Internet penetration testing to wireless network risk assessment. The chapter and the book conclude with coverage of the subject of digital forensics.

Features

Here are some features of the book's approach to the topic of information security:

Information Security Professionals Common Bodies of Knowledge—Because the authors hold both the Certified Information Security Manager (CISM) and Certified Information Systems Security Professional (CISSP) credentials, those knowledge domains have had an influence in the design of the text. Although care was taken to avoid producing another certification study guide, the author's backgrounds ensure that the book's treatment of information security integrates, to some degree, much of the CISM and CISSP Common Bodies of Knowledge (CBK).

Chapter Scenarios—Each chapter opens with a short story that features the same fictional company as it encounters information security issues commonly found in real-life organizations. At the end of each chapter, there is a brief follow-up to the opening story and a set of discussion questions that provide students and instructors opportunities to discuss the issues that underlie the story's content.

Offline and Technical Details Boxes—Interspersed throughout the textbook, these sections highlight interesting topics and detailed technical issues, giving the student the option of delving into various information security topics more deeply.

Hands-On Learning—At the end of each chapter, students find a Chapter Summary and Review Questions as well as Exercises, which give them the opportunity to examine the information security arena outside the classroom. In the Exercises, students are asked to research, analyze, and write responses to questions that are intended to reinforce learning objectives and deepen their understanding of the text.

New to this Edition

- Enhanced section on Security Models and Standards, including access control models, Bell-LaPadula, Biba, and others, as well as enhanced coverage of NIST and ISO standards
- Information on security governance adds depth and breadth to the topic
- Provides coverage on the newest laws and a host of identity theft bills
- Addresses the methods and results of systems certification and accreditation in accordance with federal guidelines

Additional Student Resources

To access additional course materials including CourseMate, please visit www.cengagebrain. com. At the CengageBrain.com home page, search for the ISBN of your title (from the back cover of your book) using the search box at the top of the page. This will take you to the product page where these resources can be found.

CourseMate

The CourseMate that accompanies *Principles of Information Security, Fourth Edition* helps you make the grade.

CourseMate includes:

- An interactive eBook, with highlighting, note taking and search capabilities
- Interactive learning tools including:
  - Quizzes
  - Flashcards

- PowerPoint slides
- Glossary
- and more!

CourseMate

- Printed Access Code (ISBN 1-1111-3824-9)
- Instant Access Code (ISBN 1-1111-3825-7)

Instructor Resources

Instructor Resources CD

A variety of teaching tools have been prepared to support this textbook and to enhance the classroom learning experience:

Electronic Instructor's Manual—The Instructor's Manual includes suggestions and strategies for using this text, and even suggestions for lecture topics. The Instructor's Manual also includes answers to the Review Questions and suggested solutions to the Exercises at the end of each chapter.

Solutions—The instructor resources include solutions to all end-of-chapter material, including review questions and exercises.

Figure Files—Figure files allow instructors to create their own presentations using figures taken from the text.

PowerPoint Presentations—This book comes with Microsoft PowerPoint slides for each chapter. These are included as a teaching aid to be used for classroom presentation, to be made available to students on the network for chapter review, or to be printed for classroom distribution. Instructors can add their own slides for additional topics they introduce to the class.

Lab Manual—Course Technology has developed a lab manual to accompany this and other books: *The Hands-On Information Security Lab Manual* (ISBN 0-619-21631-X). The lab manual provides hands-on security exercises on footprinting, enumeration, and firewall configuration, as well as a number of detailed exercises and cases that can serve to supplement the book as laboratory components or as in-class projects. Contact your Course Technology sales representative for more information.

ExamView—ExamView®, the ultimate tool for objective-based testing needs. ExamView® is a powerful objective-based test generator that enables instructors to create paper, LAN- or Web-based tests from testbanks designed specifically for their Course Technology text. Instructors can utilize the ultra-efficient QuickTest Wizard to create tests in less than five minutes by taking advantage of Course Technology's question banks, or customize their own exams from scratch.

WebTUTOR™

WebTUTOR™ for Blackboard is a content rich, web-based teaching and learning aid that reinforces and clarifies complex concepts while integrating into your Blackboard course. The WebTUTOR™ platform also provides rich communication tools for instructors and students, making it much more than an online study guide. Features include PowerPoint presentations, practice quizzes, and more, organized by chapter and topic. Whether you want to Web-enhance your class, or offer an entire course online, WebTUTOR™ allows you to focus on what you do best, teaching.

- Instructor Resources CD (ISBN: 1-1111-3822-2)
- WebTUTOR™ on Blackboard (ISBN: 1-1116-4104-8)

CourseMate

Principles of Information Security, Fourth Edition includes CourseMate, a complement to your textbook. CourseMate includes:

- An interactive eBook
- Interactive teaching and learning tools including:
  - Quizzes
  - Flashcards
  - PowerPoint slides
  - Glossary
  - and more
- Engagement Tracker, a first-of-its-kind tool that monitors student engagement in the course

To access these materials online, visit http://login.cengage.com.

CourseMate

- Printed Access Code (ISBN 1-1111-3824-9)
- Instant Access Code (ISBN 1-1111-3825-7)

Author Team

Michael Whitman and Herbert Mattord have jointly developed this text to merge knowledge from the world of academic study with practical experience from the business world.

Michael Whitman, Ph.D., CISM, CISSP is a Professor of Information Security in the Computer Science and Information Systems Department at Kennesaw State University, Kennesaw, Georgia, where he is also the Coordinator of the Bachelor of Science in Information Security and Assurance degree and the Director of the KSU Center for Information Security Education (*infosec.kennesaw. edu*). Dr. Whitman is an active researcher in Information Security, Fair and Responsible Use Policies, Ethical Computing and Information Systems Research Methods. He currently teaches graduate and undergraduate courses in Information Security, and Contingency Planning. He has published articles in the top journals in his field, including *Information Systems Research, Communications of the ACM, Information and Management, Journal of International Business Studies,* and *Journal of Computer Information Systems.* He is a member of the Information

Systems Security Association, the Association for Computing Machinery, and the Association for Information Systems. Dr. Whitman is also the co-author of *Management of Information Security, Principles of Incident Response and Disaster Recovery, Readings and Cases in the Management of Information Security, The Guide to Firewalls and Network Security*, and *The Hands-On Information Security Lab Manual*, all published by Course Technology. Prior to his career in academia, Dr. Whitman was an Armored Cavalry Officer in the United States Army.

Herbert Mattord, M.B.A., CISM, CISSP completed 24 years of IT industry experience as an application developer, database administrator, project manager, and information security practitioner before joining the faculty as Kennesaw State University in 2002. Professor Mattord is the Operations Manager of the KSU Center for Information Security Education and Awareness (*infosec.kennesaw.edu*), as well as the coordinator for the KSU department of Computer Science and Information Systems Certificate in Information Security and Assurance. During his career as an IT practitioner, he has been an adjunct professor at Kennesaw State University, Southern Polytechnic State University in Marietta, Georgia, Austin Community College in Austin, Texas, and Texas State University: San Marcos. He currently teaches undergraduate courses in Information Security, Data Communications, Local Area Networks, Database Technology, Project Management, Systems Analysis & Design, and Information Resources Management and Policy. He was formerly the Manager of Corporate Information Technology Security at Georgia-Pacific Corporation, where much of the practical knowledge found in this textbook was acquired. Professor Mattord is also the co-author of *Management of Information Security, Principles of Incident Response and Disaster Recovery, Readings and Cases in the Management of Information Security, The Guide to Firewalls and Network Security*, and *The Hands-On Information Security Lab Manual*, all published by Course Technology.

Acknowledgments

The authors would like to thank their families for their support and understanding for the many hours dedicated to this project, hours taken away, in many cases, from family activities. Special thanks to Dr. Carola Mattord. Her reviews of early drafts and suggestions for keeping the writing focused on the students resulted in a more readable manuscript.

Contributors

Several people and organizations have also contributed materials that were used in the preparation of this textbook, and we thank them for their contributions:

- John W. Lampe—Contributed draft content on several topics in the area of cryptography
- The National Institute of Standards and Technology is the source of many references, tables, figures and other content used in many places in the textbook

Reviewers

We are indebted to the following individuals for their respective contributions of perceptive feedback on the initial proposal, the project outline, and the chapter-by-chapter reviews of the text:

- Lonnie Decker, Davenport University-Midland
- Jeffrey Smith, Park University
- Dale Suggs, Campbell University

Special Thanks

The authors wish to thank the editorial and production teams at Course Technology. Their diligent and professional efforts greatly enhanced the final product:

- Natalie Pashoukos, Product Manager
- Lynne Raughley, Developmental Editor
- Steve Helba, Executive Editor
- Brooke Greenhouse, Content Project Manager

In addition, several professional and commercial organizations and individuals have aided the development of the textbook by providing information and inspiration, and the authors wish to acknowledge their contribution:

- Charles Cresson Wood
- Our colleagues in the Department of Computer Science and Information Systems, Kennesaw State University

Our Commitment

The authors are committed to serving the needs of the adopters and readers of this book. We would be pleased and honored to receive feedback on the textbook and its supporting materials. You can contact us through Course Technology, via e-mail at mis@course.com.

Foreword

Information security is an art, not a science, and the mastery of information security requires a multi-disciplinary knowledge of a huge quantity of information, experience, and skill. You will find much of the necessary information here in this book as the authors take you through the subject in a security systems development life cycle using real-life scenarios to introduce each topic. The authors provide the experience and skill of many years of real life experience, combined with their academic approach, to provide a rich learning experience that they expertly present in this book. You have chosen the authors and the book well.

Since you are reading this book, you are most likely working toward a career in information security or at least have some serious information security interest. You must anticipate that just about everybody hates the constraints that your work of increasing security will put upon them, both the good guys and the bad guys—except for malicious hackers that love the security you install as a challenge to be beaten. I concentrate on fighting the bad guys in security because when security is developed against bad guys it also applies to accidents and errors, but when developed against accidental problems, it tends to be ineffective against enemies acting with intent.

I have spent 35 years of my life working in a field that most people hate but still found it exciting and rewarding working with computers and pitting my wits against malicious people. Security controls and practices include logging on, using passwords, encrypting vital information, locking doors and drawers, motivating stakeholders to support security, and installing pipes to spray water down on your fragile computers in case of fire. These are means of protection that have no benefit except rarely when adversities occur. Good security is when nothing bad happens, and when nothing bad happens, who needs security. So why do we engage in security? Now-a-days we do it because the law says that we must do it like we are required to use seat belts and air bags—especially if we deal with the personal information of others, electronic money, intellectual property, and keeping ahead of the competition.

There is great satisfaction knowing that your employer's information, communications, systems, and people are secure, and getting paid a good salary, being the center of attention in emergencies, and knowing that you are matching your wits against the bad guys all make up for the downsides of your work. It is no job for perfectionists, because you will almost never be fully successful, and there will always be vulnerabilities that you aren't aware of or that you haven't fixed yet. The enemy has a great advantage over us. He has to find only one vulnerability and one target to attack in a known place, electronically or physically while we must defend from potentially millions of enemies' attacks against all of our assets and vulnerabilities that are no longer in one computer room but are spread all over the world by wire and now by air. It's like playing a game in which you don't know your opponents and where they are, what they are doing, why they are doing it, and are changing the rules as they play. You must be highly ethical, defensive, secretive, and cautious about bragging about the great security that you are employing that might tip off the enemy. Enjoy the few successes that you experience for you will not even know about some of them.

There is a story that describes the kind of war you are entering into. A small country inducted a young man into their ill-equipped army. They had no guns; so they issued a broom to the new recruit for training purposes. In basic training, the young man asked, "What do I do with this broom?"

They took him out to the rifle range and told him to pretend it is a gun, aim it at the target, and go, bang, bang, bang. He did that. Then they took him out to bayonet practice, and he said, "What do I do with this broom?"

They said, "pretend it is a gun with a bayonet on it and go stab, stab, stab."

He did that also. Then the war started, they still didn't have guns; so the young man found himself out on the front line with enemy soldiers running toward him across a field, and all he had was his trusty broom. So he could only do what he was trained to do, aimed the broom at the enemy soldiers, and said, "bang, bang, bang." Some of the enemy soldiers fell down, but many kept coming. Some got so close that he had to go stab, stab, stab, and some more enemy soldiers fell down. However, There was one stubborn enemy soldier (there is always one in these stories) running toward him. He said, "bang, bang, bang," but to no effect. The enemy continued to get closer. He got so close that the recruit had to go stab, stab, stab, but it still had no effect. In fact, the enemy soldier ran right over the recruit, left him lying in the dirt, and broke his broom in half. However, as the enemy soldier ran by, the recruit heard the enemy muttering under his breath, "tank, tank, tank."

I tell this story at the end of my many lectures on computer crime and security to impress on my audience that if you are going to win against crime, you must know the rules, and it is the criminal who is making up his secret rules as he goes along. This makes winning very difficult.

When I was lecturing in Rio De Janeiro, a young lady performed simultaneous translation into Portuguese for my audience of several hundred people, all with earphones clapped over their ears. In such situations, I have no idea what my audience is hearing, and after telling my joke nobody laughed. They just sat there with puzzled looks on their faces. After the lecture, I asked the translator what had happened. She had translated tank, tank, tank into water tank, water tank, water tank. I and the recruit were both deceived that time.

Three weeks later, I was lecturing to an audience of French bankers at the George V Hotel in Paris. I had a bilingual friend listen to the translation of my talk. The same thing happened as in Rio. Nobody laughed. Afterwards, I asked my friend what had happened. He said, "You will never believe this, but the translator translated tank, tank, tank into merci, merci, merci (thanks)." Even in telling the joke I didn't know the rules to the game.

Remember that when working in security, you are in a virtual army defending your employer and stakeholders from their enemies, and from your point of view they will probably think and act irrationally, but from their perspective they are perfectly rational with serious personal problems to solve and gains to be made by violating your security. You are no longer a techie with the challenging job of installing technological controls in systems and networks. Most of your work should be assisting potential victims to protect themselves from information adversities and dealing with your smart but often irrational enemies even though you rarely see or even get close to them. I spent a major part of my security career hunting down computer criminals and interviewing them and their victims trying to obtain knowledge from them to do a better job of defending from their attacks. You, likewise, should also use every opportunity to seek them out and get to know them. This experience gives you great cachet as a real and unique expert even with only minimal exposure to a few enemies.

Comprehensiveness is an important part of the game you play for real stakes because the enemy will likely seek the easiest way to attack the vulnerabilities and assets that you haven't fully protected yet. For example, one of the most common threats is endangerment of assets that means putting information assets in harm's way, yet I rarely find it on threat lists. Endangerment is also one of the most common mistakes that security professionals make. You must be thorough, meticulous, document everything (in case your competence is questioned and to meet the requirements of the Sarbanes—Oxley Law), and keep the documents safely locked away. Be careful and document so that when an adversity hits and you lose the game, you will have proof of having been diligent in spite of the loss. Otherwise, your career could be damaged, or at least your effectiveness will be diminished. For example, if the loss is due to management failing to give you an adequate budget and support for the security that you know that you need, you must have documented that before the incident occurs. Don't brag about how great your security is, because it can always be beaten. Keep, expand, and use every-day check lists of everything—threats, vulnerabilities, assets, key potential victims and suspects of wrongdoing, security supporters and those that don't bother with security, attacks, enemies, criminal justice resources, auditors, regulators, and legal council. To assist your stakeholders that are the real defenders of their information and systems in managing their security, you must identify what they must protect and measure the real extent of their security. And make sure that those to whom you report and higher management understand the nature of your job and its limitations.

You will have a huge collection of sensitive passwords to do your job. Use the best possible passwords to set a good example, write them down, and keep the list safely in your wallet next to your credit card. Know as much about the systems and networks in your organization as possible and have access to the expert people that know the rest. Make good friends of the local and national criminal justice people, your organization's lawyers, insurance risk managers, human resources people, talent, facilities managers and auditors. Audit is one of the most powerful controls that your organization has. Remember that people hate security and must be properly motivated with penalties and rewards to make it work. Seek ways to make security invisible or transparent to stakeholders, yet effective. Don't recommend or install controls or practices that they won't support, because they will beat you every time by making it look like the controls are effective but are not—a situation worse than no security at all.

One of the most exciting parts of the job is the insight you gain about the inner workings and secrets of your organization and its culture that you must thoroughly understand. As an information security consultant, I was privileged to learn about the culture and secrets of more then 250 of the largest international corporations throughout the world. I had the opportunity to interview and advise the most powerful business giants if even for only a few minutes of their valuable time. You should always be ready to use the five minutes that you get with them once every year or so as your silver bullet to use with top management for the greatest benefit of their security. Carefully learn the limits of their security appetites. Know the nature of the business whether it is a government department or a hotly competitive business. I once found myself in a meeting with the board of directors intensely and seriously discussing and suppressing my snickering about the protection of their greatest trade secret, the manufacturing process of their new disposable diapers.

Finally, we come to the last important bit of advice. Be trustworthy and develop mutual trust among your peers. Your most important objectives are not risk reduction and increased security; they are diligence to avoid negligence, exceeding compliance with all of the laws and standards and auditors, and enablement when security becomes a competitive or a budget issue. To achieve these objectives, you must develop a trusting exchange of the most sensitive security intelligence among your peers in your and other security people's organizations so that you know where your organization stands in protection relative to them. You need to know what the generally accepted current security solutions are and especially those used in your competitors' businesses or other related organizations. Therefore, you need to exchange this highly sensitive information among your peers. If the information exchanged is exposed, it could ruin your and others' careers as well as be a disaster for your or their organizations. Your personal and ethical performance must be spotless, and you must protect your reputation at all costs. Pay particular attention to the ethics section of this book. You must be discrete and careful by testing and growing the ongoing peer trust to facilitate the sharing of sensitive security information. I recommend that you join the Information Systems Security Association and become professionally certified as soon as you are qualified. My favorite is to be a Certified Information Systems Security Professional (CISSP) offered by the International Information Systems Security Certification Consortium.

Donn B. Parker, CISSP
Los Altos, California

chapter 1

Introduction to Information Security

Do not figure on opponents not attacking; worry about your own lack of preparation.

BOOK OF THE FIVE RINGS

For Amy, the day began like any other at the Sequential Label and Supply Company (SLS) help desk. Taking calls and helping office workers with computer problems was not glamorous, but she enjoyed the work; it was challenging and paid well. Some of her friends in the industry worked at bigger companies, some at cutting-edge tech companies, but they all agreed that jobs in information technology were a good way to pay the bills.

The phone rang, as it did on average about four times an hour and about 28 times a day. The first call of the day, from a worried user hoping Amy could help him out of a jam, seemed typical. The call display on her monitor gave some of the facts: the user's name, his phone number, the department in which he worked, where his office was on the company campus, and a list of all the calls he'd made in the past.

"Hi, Bob," she said. "Did you get that document formatting problem squared away?"

"Sure did, Amy. Hope we can figure out what's going on this time."

"We'll try, Bob. Tell me about it."

"Well, my PC is acting weird," Bob said. "When I go to the screen that has my e-mail program running, it doesn't respond to the mouse or the keyboard."

"Did you try a reboot yet?"

"Sure did. But the window wouldn't close, and I had to turn it off. After it restarted, I opened the e-mail program, and it's just like it was before—no response at all. The other stuff is working OK, but really, really slowly. Even my Internet browser is sluggish."

"OK, Bob. We've tried the usual stuff we can do over the phone. Let me open a case, and I'll dispatch a tech over as soon as possible."

Amy looked up at the LED tally board on the wall at the end of the room. She saw that there were only two technicians dispatched to deskside support at the moment, and since it was the day shift, there were four available.

"Shouldn't be long at all, Bob."

She hung up and typed her notes into ISIS, the company's Information Status and Issues System. She assigned the newly generated case to the deskside dispatch queue, which would page the roving deskside team with the details in just a few minutes.

A moment later, Amy looked up to see Charlie Moody, the senior manager of the server administration team, walking briskly down the hall. He was being trailed by three of his senior technicians as he made a beeline from his office to the door of the server room where the company servers were kept in a controlled environment. They all looked worried.

Just then, Amy's screen beeped to alert her of a new e-mail. She glanced down. It beeped again—and again. It started beeping constantly. She clicked on the envelope icon and, after a short delay, the mail window opened. She had 47 new e-mails in her inbox. She opened one from Davey Martinez, an acquaintance from the Accounting Department. The subject line said, "Wait till you see this." The message body read, "Look what this has to say about our managers' salaries..." Davey often sent her interesting and funny e-mails, and she failed to notice that the file attachment icon was unusual before she clicked it.

Her PC showed the hourglass pointer icon for a second and then the normal pointer reappeared. Nothing happened. She clicked the next e-mail message in the queue. Nothing happened. Her phone rang again. She clicked the ISIS icon on her computer desktop to activate the call management software and activated her headset. "Hello, Tech Support, how can I help you?" She couldn't greet the caller by name because ISIS had not responded.

"Hello, this is Erin Williams in receiving."

Amy glanced down at her screen. Still no ISIS. She glanced up to the tally board and was surprised to see the inbound-call-counter tallying up waiting calls like digits on a stopwatch. Amy had never seen so many calls come in at one time.

"Hi, Erin," Amy said. "What's up?"

"Nothing," Erin answered. "That's the problem." The rest of the call was a replay of Bob's, except that Amy had to jot notes down on a legal pad. She couldn't dispatch the deskside support team either. She looked at the tally board. It had gone dark. No numbers at all.

Then she saw Charlie running down the hall from the server room. He didn't look worried anymore. He looked frantic.

Amy picked up the phone again. She wanted to check with her supervisor about what to do now. There was no dial tone.

LEARNING OBJECTIVES:

Upon completion of this material, you should be able to:

- Define information security
- Recount the history of computer security, and explain how it evolved into information security
- Define key terms and critical concepts of information security
- Enumerate the phases of the security systems development life cycle
- Describe the information security roles of professionals within an organization

Introduction

James Anderson, executive consultant at Emagined Security, Inc., believes information security in an enterprise is a "well-informed sense of assurance that the information risks and controls are in balance." He is not alone in his perspective. Many information security practitioners recognize that aligning information security needs with business objectives must be the top priority.

This chapter's opening scenario illustrates that the information risks and controls are not in balance at Sequential Label and Supply. Though Amy works in a technical support role and her job is to solve technical problems, it does not occur to her that a malicious software program, like a worm or virus, might be the agent of the company's current ills. Management also shows signs of confusion and seems to have no idea how to contain this kind of incident. If you were in Amy's place and were faced with a similar situation, what would you do? How would you react? Would it occur to you that something far more insidious than a technical malfunction was happening at your company? As you explore the chapters of this book and learn more about information security, you will become better able to answer these questions. But before you can begin studying the details of the discipline of information security, you must first know the history and evolution of the field.

The History of Information Security

The history of information security begins with **computer security**. The need for computer security—that is, the need to secure physical locations, hardware, and software from threats—arose during World War II when the first mainframes, developed to aid computations for communication code breaking (see Figure 1-1), were put to use. Multiple levels of security were implemented to protect these mainframes and maintain the integrity of their data. Access to sensitive military locations, for example, was controlled by means of badges, keys, and the facial recognition of authorized personnel by security guards. The growing need to maintain national security eventually led to more complex and more technologically sophisticated computer security safeguards.

During these early years, information security was a straightforward process composed predominantly of physical security and simple document classification schemes. The primary threats to security were physical theft of equipment, espionage against the products of the systems, and sabotage. One of the first documented security problems that fell outside these categories occurred in the early 1960s, when a systems administrator was working on an MOTD

Earlier versions of the German code machine Enigma were first broken by the Poles in the 1930s. The British and Americans managed to break later, more complex versions during World War II. The increasingly complex versions of the Enigma, especially the submarine or *Unterseeboot* version of the Enigma, caused considerable anguish to Allied forces before finally being cracked. The information gained from decrypted transmissions was used to anticipate the actions of German armed forces. "Some ask why, if we were reading the Enigma, we did not win the war earlier. One might ask, instead, when, if ever, we would have won the war if we hadn't read it."[1]

Figure 1-1 The Enigma

Source: Courtesy of National Security Agency

(message of the day) file, and another administrator was editing the password file. A software glitch mixed the two files, and the entire password file was printed on every output file.[2]

The 1960s

During the Cold War, many more mainframes were brought online to accomplish more complex and sophisticated tasks. It became necessary to enable these mainframes to communicate via a less cumbersome process than mailing magnetic tapes between computer centers. In response to this need, the Department of Defense's Advanced Research Project Agency (ARPA) began examining the feasibility of a redundant, networked communications system to support the military's exchange of information. Larry Roberts, known as the founder of the Internet, developed the project—which was called ARPANET—from its inception. ARPANET is the predecessor to the Internet (see Figure 1-2 for an excerpt from the ARPANET Program Plan).

The 1970s and 80s

During the next decade, ARPANET became popular and more widely used, and the potential for its misuse grew. In December of 1973, Robert M. "Bob" Metcalfe, who is credited

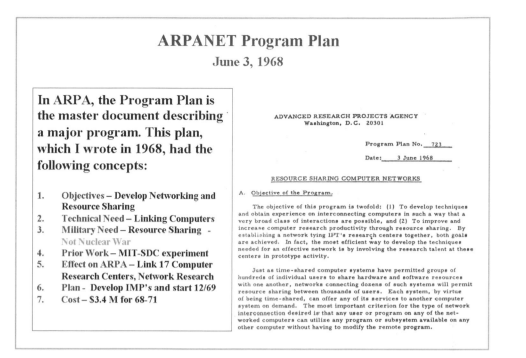

Figure 1-2 Development of the ARPANET Program Plan[3]

Source: Courtesy of Dr. Lawrence Roberts

with the development of Ethernet, one of the most popular networking protocols, identified fundamental problems with ARPANET security. Individual remote sites did not have sufficient controls and safeguards to protect data from unauthorized remote users. Other problems abounded: vulnerability of password structure and formats; lack of safety procedures for dial-up connections; and nonexistent user identification and authorization to the system. Phone numbers were widely distributed and openly publicized on the walls of phone booths, giving hackers easy access to ARPANET. Because of the range and frequency of computer security violations and the explosion in the numbers of hosts and users on ARPANET, network security was referred to as network insecurity.[4] In 1978, a famous study entitled "Protection Analysis: Final Report" was published. It focused on a project undertaken by ARPA to discover the vulnerabilities of operating system security. For a timeline that includes this and other seminal studies of computer security, see Table 1-1.

The movement toward security that went beyond protecting physical locations began with a single paper sponsored by the Department of Defense, the Rand Report R-609, which attempted to define the multiple controls and mechanisms necessary for the protection of a multilevel computer system. The document was classified for almost ten years, and is now considered to be the paper that started the study of computer security.

The security—or lack thereof—of the systems sharing resources inside the Department of Defense was brought to the attention of researchers in the spring and summer of 1967. At that time, systems were being acquired at a rapid rate and securing them was a pressing concern for both the military and defense contractors.

Date	Documents
1968	Maurice Wilkes discusses password security in *Time-Sharing Computer Systems*.
1973	Schell, Downey, and Popek examine the need for additional security in military systems in *"Preliminary Notes on the Design of Secure Military Computer Systems."*[5]
1975	The Federal Information Processing Standards (FIPS) examines Digital Encryption Standard (DES) in the *Federal Register*.
1978	Bisbey and Hollingworth publish their study "Protection Analysis: Final Report," discussing the Protection Analysis project created by ARPA to better understand the vulnerabilities of operating system security and examine the possibility of automated vulnerability detection techniques in existing system software.[6]
1979	Morris and Thompson author "Password Security: A Case History," published in the Communications of the Association for *Computing Machinery* (ACM). The paper examines the history of a design for a password security scheme on a remotely accessed, time-sharing system.
1979	Dennis Ritchie publishes "On the Security of UNIX" and "Protection of Data File Contents," discussing secure user IDs and secure group IDs, and the problems inherent in the systems.
1984	Grampp and Morris write "UNIX Operating System Security." In this report, the authors examine four "important handles to computer security": physical control of premises and computer facilities, management commitment to security objectives, education of employees, and administrative procedures aimed at increased security.[7]
1984	Reeds and Weinberger publish "File Security and the UNIX System Crypt Command." Their premise was: "No technique can be secure against wiretapping or its equivalent on the computer. Therefore no technique can be secure against the systems administrator or other privileged users ... the naive user has no chance."[8]

Table 1-1 Key Dates for Seminal Works in Early Computer Security

In June of 1967, the Advanced Research Projects Agency formed a task force to study the process of securing classified information systems. The Task Force was assembled in October of 1967 and met regularly to formulate recommendations, which ultimately became the contents of the Rand Report R-609.[9]

The Rand Report R-609 was the first widely recognized published document to identify the role of management and policy issues in computer security. It noted that the wide utilization of networking components in information systems in the military introduced security risks that could not be mitigated by the routine practices then used to secure these systems.[10] This paper signaled a pivotal moment in computer security history—when the scope of computer security expanded significantly from the safety of physical locations and hardware to include the following:

- Securing the data
- Limiting random and unauthorized access to that data
- Involving personnel from multiple levels of the organization in matters pertaining to information security

MULTICS Much of the early research on computer security centered on a system called Multiplexed Information and Computing Service (MULTICS). Although it is now obsolete, MULTICS is noteworthy because it was the first operating system to integrate security into its core functions. It was a mainframe, time-sharing operating system developed in the mid-1960s by a consortium of General Electric (GE), Bell Labs, and the Massachusetts Institute of Technology (MIT).

In mid-1969, not long after the restructuring of the MULTICS project, several of its developers (Ken Thompson, Dennis Ritchie, Rudd Canaday, and Doug McIlro) created a new operating system called UNIX. While the MULTICS system implemented multiple security levels and passwords, the UNIX system did not. Its primary function, text processing, did not require the same level of security as that of its predecessor. In fact, it was not until the early 1970s that even the simplest component of security, the password function, became a component of UNIX.

In the late 1970s, the microprocessor brought the personal computer and a new age of computing. The PC became the workhorse of modern computing, thereby moving it out of the data center. This decentralization of data processing systems in the 1980s gave rise to networking—that is, the interconnecting of personal computers and mainframe computers, which enabled the entire computing community to make all their resources work together.

The 1990s

At the close of the twentieth century, networks of computers became more common, as did the need to connect these networks to each other. This gave rise to the Internet, the first global network of networks. The Internet was made available to the general public in the 1990s, having previously been the domain of government, academia, and dedicated industry professionals. The Internet brought connectivity to virtually all computers that could reach a phone line or an Internet-connected local area network (LAN). After the Internet was commercialized, the technology became pervasive, reaching almost every corner of the globe with an expanding array of uses.

Since its inception as a tool for sharing Defense Department information, the Internet has become an interconnection of millions of networks. At first, these connections were based on de facto **standards**, because industry standards for interconnection of networks did not exist at that time. These de facto standards did little to ensure the security of information though as these precursor technologies were widely adopted and became industry standards, some degree of security was introduced. However, early Internet deployment treated security as a low priority. In fact, many of the problems that plague e-mail on the Internet today are the result of this early lack of security. At that time, when all Internet and e-mail users were (presumably trustworthy) computer scientists, mail server authentication and e-mail encryption did not seem necessary. Early computing approaches relied on security that was built into the physical environment of the data center that housed the computers. As networked computers became the dominant style of computing, the ability to physically secure a networked computer was lost, and the stored information became more exposed to security threats.

2000 to Present

Today, the Internet brings millions of unsecured computer networks into continuous communication with each other. The security of each computer's stored information is now contingent on the level of security of every other computer to which it is connected. Recent years have seen a growing awareness of the need to improve information security, as well as a realization that information security is important to national defense. The growing threat of cyber attacks have made governments and companies more aware of the need to defend the computer-controlled control systems of utilities and other critical infrastructure. There is also growing concern about nation-states engaging in information warfare, and the possibility that business and personal information systems could become casualties if they are undefended.

What Is Security?

In general, **security** is "the quality or state of being secure—to be free from danger."[11] In other words, protection against adversaries—from those who would do harm, intentionally or otherwise—is the objective. National security, for example, is a multilayered system that protects the sovereignty of a state, its assets, its resources, and its people. Achieving the appropriate level of security for an organization also requires a multifaceted system.

A successful organization should have the following multiple layers of security in place to protect its operations:

- **Physical security**, to protect physical items, objects, or areas from unauthorized access and misuse
- **Personnel security**, to protect the individual or group of individuals who are authorized to access the organization and its operations
- **Operations security**, to protect the details of a particular operation or series of activities
- **Communications security**, to protect communications media, technology, and content
- **Network security**, to protect networking components, connections, and contents
- **Information security**, to protect the confidentiality, integrity and availability of information assets, whether in storage, processing, or transmission. It is achieved via the application of policy, education, training and awareness, and technology.

The Committee on National Security Systems (CNSS) defines information security as the protection of information and its critical elements, including the systems and hardware that use, store, and transmit that information.[12] Figure 1-3 shows that information security includes the broad areas of information security management, computer and data security, and network security. The CNSS model of information security evolved from a concept developed by the computer security industry called the C.I.A. triangle. The **C.I.A. triangle** has been the industry standard for computer security since the development of the mainframe. It is based on the three characteristics of information that give it value to organizations: confidentiality, integrity, and availability. The security of these three characteristics of information is as important today as it has always been, but the C.I.A. triangle model no longer adequately addresses the constantly changing environment. The threats to the confidentiality, integrity, and availability of information have evolved into a vast collection of events, including accidental or intentional damage, destruction, theft, unintended or unauthorized modification, or other misuse from human or nonhuman threats. This new environment of many constantly evolving threats has prompted the development of a more robust model that addresses the complexities of the current information security environment. The expanded model consists of a list of critical characteristics of information, which are described in the next

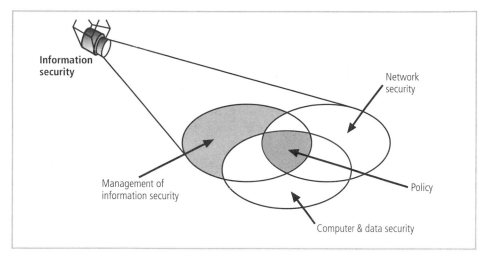

Figure 1-3 Components of Information Security

Source: Course Technology/Cengage Learning

section. C.I.A. triangle terminology is used in this chapter because of the breadth of material that is based on it.

Key Information Security Concepts

This book uses a number of terms and concepts that are essential to any discussion of information security. Some of these terms are illustrated in Figure 1-4; all are covered in greater detail in subsequent chapters.

- **Access:** A subject or object's ability to use, manipulate, modify, or affect another subject or object. Authorized users have legal access to a system, whereas hackers have illegal access to a system. Access controls regulate this ability.

- **Asset:** The organizational resource that is being protected. An asset can be logical, such as a Web site, information, or data; or an asset can be physical, such as a person, computer system, or other tangible object. Assets, and particularly information assets, are the focus of security efforts; they are what those efforts are attempting to protect.

- **Attack:** An intentional or unintentional act that can cause damage to or otherwise compromise information and/or the systems that support it. Attacks can be active or passive, intentional or unintentional, and direct or indirect. Someone casually reading sensitive information not intended for his or her use is a passive attack. A hacker attempting to break into an information system is an intentional attack. A lightning strike that causes a fire in a building is an unintentional attack. A direct attack is a hacker using a personal computer to break into a system. An indirect attack is a hacker compromising a system and using it to attack other systems, for example, as part of a botnet (slang for robot network). This group of compromised computers, running software of the attacker's choosing, can operate autonomously or under the attacker's direct control to attack systems and steal user information or conduct distributed denial-of-service attacks. Direct attacks originate from the threat itself. Indirect attacks originate from a compromised system or resource that is malfunctioning or working under the control of a threat.

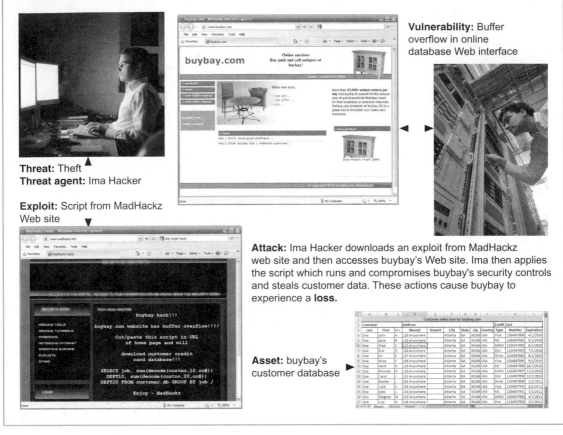

Figure 1-4 Information Security Terms

Source: Course Technology/Cengage Learning

- **Control, safeguard,** or **countermeasure:** Security mechanisms, policies, or procedures that can successfully counter attacks, reduce risk, resolve vulnerabilities, and otherwise improve the security within an organization. The various levels and types of controls are discussed more fully in the following chapters.

- **Exploit:** A technique used to compromise a system. This term can be a verb or a noun. Threat agents may attempt to exploit a system or other information asset by using it illegally for their personal gain. Or, an exploit can be a documented process to take advantage of a vulnerability or exposure, usually in software, that is either inherent in the software or is created by the attacker. Exploits make use of existing software tools or custom-made software components.

- **Exposure:** A condition or state of being exposed. In information security, exposure exists when a vulnerability known to an attacker is present.

- **Loss:** A single instance of an information asset suffering damage or unintended or unauthorized modification or disclosure. When an organization's information is stolen, it has suffered a loss.

- **Protection profile** or **security posture:** The entire set of controls and safeguards, including policy, education, training and awareness, and technology, that the organization implements (or fails to implement) to protect the asset. The terms are sometimes used interchangeably with the term *security program*, although the security program often comprises managerial aspects of security, including planning, personnel, and subordinate programs.

- **Risk:** The probability that something unwanted will happen. Organizations must minimize risk to match their **risk appetite**—the quantity and nature of risk the organization is willing to accept.

- **Subjects** and **objects:** A computer can be either the **subject** of an attack—an agent entity used to conduct the attack—or the **object** of an attack—the target entity, as shown in Figure 1-5. A computer can be both the subject and object of an attack, when, for example, it is compromised by an attack (object), and is then used to attack other systems (subject).

- **Threat:** A category of objects, persons, or other entities that presents a danger to an asset. Threats are always present and can be purposeful or undirected. For example, hackers purposefully threaten unprotected information systems, while severe storms incidentally threaten buildings and their contents.

- **Threat agent:** The specific instance or a component of a threat. For example, all hackers in the world present a collective threat, while Kevin Mitnick, who was convicted for hacking into phone systems, is a specific threat agent. Likewise, a lightning strike, hailstorm, or tornado is a threat agent that is part of the threat of severe storms.

- **Vulnerability:** A weaknesses or fault in a system or protection mechanism that opens it to attack or damage. Some examples of vulnerabilities are a flaw in a software package, an unprotected system port, and an unlocked door. Some **well-known vulnerabilities** have been examined, documented, and published; others remain latent (or undiscovered).

Critical Characteristics of Information

The value of information comes from the characteristics it possesses. When a characteristic of information changes, the value of that information either increases, or, more commonly, decreases. Some characteristics affect information's value to users more than others do. This can depend on circumstances; for example, timeliness of information can be a critical factor, because information loses much or all of its value when it is delivered too late. Though information security professionals and end users share an understanding of the characteristics of

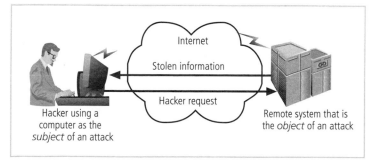

Figure 1-5 Computer as the Subject and Object of an Attack

Source: Course Technology/Cengage Learning

information, tensions can arise when the need to secure the information from threats conflicts with the end users' need for unhindered access to the information. For instance, end users may perceive a tenth-of-a-second delay in the computation of data to be an unnecessary annoyance. Information security professionals, however, may perceive that tenth of a second as a minor delay that enables an important task, like data encryption. Each critical characteristic of information—that is, the expanded C.I.A. triangle—is defined in the sections below.

Availability Availability enables authorized users—persons or computer systems—to access information without interference or obstruction and to receive it in the required format. Consider, for example, research libraries that require identification before entrance. Librarians protect the contents of the library so that they are available only to authorized patrons. The librarian must accept a patron's identification before that patron has free access to the book stacks. Once authorized patrons have access to the contents of the stacks, they expect to find the information they need available in a useable format and familiar language, which in this case typically means bound in a book and written in English.

Accuracy Information has **accuracy** when it is free from mistakes or errors and it has the value that the end user expects. If information has been intentionally or unintentionally modified, it is no longer accurate. Consider, for example, a checking account. You assume that the information contained in your checking account is an accurate representation of your finances. Incorrect information in your checking account can result from external or internal errors. If a bank teller, for instance, mistakenly adds or subtracts too much from your account, the value of the information is changed. Or, you may accidentally enter an incorrect amount into your account register. Either way, an inaccurate bank balance could cause you to make mistakes, such as bouncing a check.

Authenticity Authenticity of information is the quality or state of being genuine or original, rather than a reproduction or fabrication. Information is authentic when it is in the same state in which it was created, placed, stored, or transferred. Consider for a moment some common assumptions about e-mail. When you receive e-mail, you assume that a specific individual or group created and transmitted the e-mail—you assume you know the origin of the e-mail. This is not always the case. **E-mail spoofing**, the act of sending an e-mail message with a modified field, is a problem for many people today, because often the modified field is the address of the originator. Spoofing the sender's address can fool e-mail recipients into thinking that messages are legitimate traffic, thus inducing them to open e-mail they otherwise might not have. Spoofing can also alter data being transmitted across a network, as in the case of user data protocol (UDP) packet spoofing, which can enable the attacker to get access to data stored on computing systems.

Another variation on spoofing is **phishing**, when an attacker attempts to obtain personal or financial information using fraudulent means, most often by posing as another individual or organization. Pretending to be someone you are not is sometimes called *pretexting* when it is undertaken by law enforcement agents or private investigators. When used in a phishing attack, e-mail spoofing lures victims to a Web server that does not represent the organization it purports to, in an attempt to steal their private data such as account numbers and passwords. The most common variants include posing as a bank or brokerage company, e-commerce organization, or Internet service provider. Even when authorized, pretexting does not always lead to a satisfactory outcome. In 2006, the CEO of Hewlett-Packard

Corporation, Patricia Dunn, authorized contract investigators to use pretexting to "smokeout" a corporate director suspected of leaking confidential information. The resulting firestorm of negative publicity led to Ms. Dunn's eventual departure from the company.[13]

Confidentiality
Information has **confidentiality** when it is protected from disclosure or exposure to unauthorized individuals or systems. Confidentiality ensures that *only* those with the rights and privileges to access information are able to do so. When unauthorized individuals or systems can view information, confidentiality is breached. To protect the confidentiality of information, you can use a number of measures, including the following:

- Information classification
- Secure document storage
- Application of general security policies
- Education of information custodians and end users

Confidentiality, like most of the characteristics of information, is interdependent with other characteristics and is most closely related to the characteristic known as privacy. The relationship between these two characteristics is covered in more detail in Chapter 3, "Legal and Ethical Issues in Security."

The value of confidentiality of information is especially high when it is personal information about employees, customers, or patients. Individuals who transact with an organization expect that their personal information will remain confidential, whether the organization is a federal agency, such as the Internal Revenue Service, or a business. Problems arise when companies disclose confidential information. Sometimes this disclosure is intentional, but there are times when disclosure of confidential information happens by mistake—for example, when confidential information is mistakenly e-mailed to someone *outside* the organization rather than to someone *inside* the organization. Several cases of privacy violation are outlined in Offline: Unintentional Disclosures.

Other examples of confidentiality breaches are an employee throwing away a document containing critical information without shredding it, or a hacker who successfully breaks into an internal database of a Web-based organization and steals sensitive information about the clients, such as names, addresses, and credit card numbers.

As a consumer, you give up pieces of confidential information in exchange for convenience or value almost daily. By using a "members only" card at a grocery store, you disclose some of your spending habits. When you fill out an online survey, you exchange pieces of your personal history for access to online privileges. The bits and pieces of your information that you disclose are copied, sold, replicated, distributed, and eventually coalesced into profiles and even complete dossiers of yourself and your life. A similar technique is used in a criminal enterprise called **salami theft**. A deli worker knows he or she cannot steal an entire salami, but a few slices here or there can be taken home without notice. Eventually the deli worker has stolen a whole salami. In information security, salami theft occurs when an employee steals a few pieces of information at a time, knowing that taking more would be noticed—but eventually the employee gets something complete or useable.

Integrity
Information has **integrity** when it is whole, complete, and uncorrupted. The integrity of information is threatened when the information is exposed to corruption,

Offline
Unintentional Disclosures

In February 2005, the data aggregation and brokerage firm ChoicePoint revealed that it had been duped into releasing personal information about 145,000 people to identity thieves during 2004. The perpetrators used stolen identities to create obstensibly legitimate business entities, which then subscribed to ChoicePoint to acquire the data fraudulently. The company reported that the criminals opened many accounts and recorded personal information on individuals, including names, addresses, and identification numbers. They did so without using any network or computer-based attacks; it was simple fraud.[14] While the the amount of damage has yet to be compiled, the fraud is feared to have allowed the perpetrators to arrange many hundreds of instances of identity theft.

The giant pharmaceutical organization Eli Lilly and Co. released the e-mail addresses of 600 patients to one another in 2001. The American Civil Liberties Union (ACLU) denounced this breach of privacy, and information technology industry analysts noted that it was likely to influence the public debate on privacy legislation.

The company claimed that the mishap was caused by a programming error that occurred when patients who used a specific drug produced by the company signed up for an e-mail service to access support materials provided by the company. About 600 patient addresses were exposed in the mass e-mail.[15]

In another incident, the intellectual property of Jerome Stevens Pharmaceuticals, a small prescription drug manufacturer from New York, was compromised when the FDA released documents the company had filed with the agency. It remains unclear whether this was a deliberate act by the FDA or a simple error; but either way, the company's secrets were posted to a public Web site for several months before being removed.[16]

damage, destruction, or other disruption of its authentic state. Corruption can occur while information is being stored or transmitted. Many computer viruses and worms are designed with the explicit purpose of corrupting data. For this reason, a key method for detecting a virus or worm is to look for changes in file integrity as shown by the size of the file. Another key method of assuring information integrity is **file hashing**, in which a file is read by a special algorithm that uses the value of the bits in the file to compute a single large number called a **hash value**. The hash value for any combination of bits is unique. If a computer system performs the same hashing algorithm on a file and obtains a different number than the recorded hash value for that file, the file has been compromised and the integrity of the information is lost. Information integrity is the cornerstone of information systems, because information is of no value or use if users cannot verify its integrity.

File corruption is not necessarily the result of external forces, such as hackers. Noise in the transmission media, for instance, can also cause data to lose its integrity. Transmitting data on a circuit with a low voltage level can alter and corrupt the data. Redundancy bits and check bits can compensate for internal and external threats to the integrity of information. During each transmission, algorithms, hash values, and the error-correcting codes ensure the integrity of the information. Data whose integrity has been compromised is retransmitted.

Utility The **utility** of information is the quality or state of having value for some purpose or end. Information has value when it can serve a purpose. If information is available, but is not in a format meaningful to the end user, it is not useful. For example, to a private citizen U.S. Census data can quickly become overwhelming and difficult to interpret; however, for a politician, U.S. Census data reveals information about the residents in a district, such as their race, gender, and age. This information can help form a politician's next campaign strategy.

Possession The **possession** of information is the quality or state of ownership or control. Information is said to be in one's possession if one obtains it, independent of format or other characteristics. While a breach of confidentiality always results in a breach of possession, a breach of possession does not always result in a breach of confidentiality. For example, assume a company stores its critical customer data using an encrypted file system. An employee who has quit decides to take a copy of the tape backups to sell the customer records to the competition. The removal of the tapes from their secure environment is a breach of possession. But, because the data is encrypted, neither the employee nor anyone else can read it without the proper decryption methods; therefore, there is no breach of confidentiality. Today, people caught selling company secrets face increasingly stiff fines with the likelihood of jail time. Also, companies are growing more and more reluctant to hire individuals who have demonstrated dishonesty in their past.

CNSS Security Model

The definition of information security presented in this text is based in part on the CNSS document called the National Training Standard for Information Systems Security Professionals NSTISSI No. 4011. (See *www.cnss.gov/Assets/pdf/nstissi_4011.pdf*. Since this document was written, the NSTISSC was renamed the Committee on National Security Systems (CNSS)—see *www.cnss.gov*. The library of documents is being renamed as the documents are rewritten.) This document presents a comprehensive information security model and has become a widely accepted evaluation standard for the security of information systems. The model, created by John McCumber in 1991, provides a graphical representation of the architectural approach widely used in computer and information security; it is now known as the **McCumber Cube**.[17] The McCumber Cube in Figure 1-6, shows three dimensions. If extrapolated, the three dimensions of each axis become a $3 \times 3 \times 3$ cube with 27 cells representing areas that must be addressed to secure today's information systems. To ensure system security, each of the 27 areas must be properly addressed during the security process. For example, the intersection between technology, integrity, and storage requires a control or safeguard that addresses the need to use *technology* to protect the *integrity* of information while in *storage*. One such control might be a system for detecting host intrusion that protects the integrity of

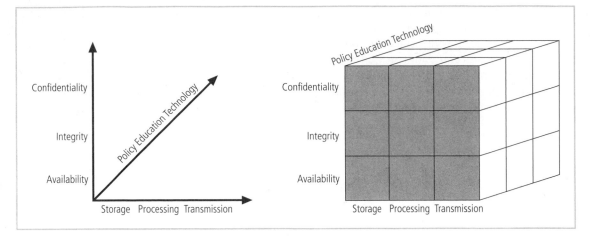

Figure 1-6 The McCumber Cube[18]

Source: Course Technology/Cengage Learning

information by alerting the security administrators to the potential modification of a critical file. What is commonly left out of such a model is the need for guidelines and policies that provide direction for the practices and implementations of technologies. The need for policy is discussed in subsequent chapters of this book.

Components of an Information System

As shown in Figure 1-7, an **information system (IS)** is much more than computer hardware; it is the entire set of software, hardware, data, people, procedures, and networks that make possible the use of information resources in the organization. These six critical components enable information to be input, processed, output, and stored. Each of these IS components has its own strengths and weaknesses, as well as its own characteristics and uses. Each component of the information system also has its own security requirements.

Software

The software component of the IS comprises applications, operating systems, and assorted command utilities. Software is perhaps the most difficult IS component to secure. The exploitation of errors in software programming accounts for a substantial portion of the attacks on information. The information technology industry is rife with reports warning of holes, bugs, weaknesses, or other fundamental problems in software. In fact, many facets of daily life are affected by buggy software, from smartphones that crash to flawed automotive control computers that lead to recalls.

Software carries the lifeblood of information through an organization. Unfortunately, software programs are often created under the constraints of project management, which limit time, cost, and manpower. Information security is all too often implemented as an afterthought, rather than developed as an integral component from the beginning. In this way, software programs become an easy target of accidental or intentional attacks.

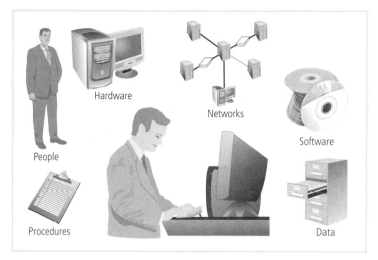

Figure 1-7 Components of an Information System

Source: Course Technology/Cengage Learning

Hardware

Hardware is the physical technology that houses and executes the software, stores and transports the data, and provides interfaces for the entry and removal of information from the system. Physical security policies deal with hardware as a physical asset and with the protection of physical assets from harm or theft. Applying the traditional tools of physical security, such as locks and keys, restricts access to and interaction with the hardware components of an information system. Securing the physical location of computers and the computers themselves is important because a breach of physical security can result in a loss of information. Unfortunately, most information systems are built on hardware platforms that cannot guarantee any level of information security if unrestricted access to the hardware is possible.

Before September 11, 2001, laptop thefts in airports were common. A two-person team worked to steal a computer as its owner passed it through the conveyor scanning devices. The first perpetrator entered the security area ahead of an unsuspecting target and quickly went through. Then, the second perpetrator waited behind the target until the target placed his/her computer on the baggage scanner. As the computer was whisked through, the second agent slipped ahead of the victim and entered the metal detector with a substantial collection of keys, coins, and the like, thereby slowing the detection process and allowing the first perpetrator to grab the computer and disappear in a crowded walkway.

While the security response to September 11, 2001 did tighten the security process at airports, hardware can still be stolen in airports and other public places. Although laptops and notebook computers are worth a few thousand dollars, the information contained in them can be worth a great deal more to organizations and individuals.

Data

Data stored, processed, and transmitted by a computer system must be protected. Data is often the most valuable asset possessed by an organization and it is the main target of intentional attacks. Systems developed in recent years are likely to make use of database management systems. When done properly, this should improve the security of the data and the application. Unfortunately, many system development projects do not make full use of the database management system's security capabilities, and in some cases the database is implemented in ways that are less secure than traditional file systems.

People

Though often overlooked in computer security considerations, people have always been a threat to information security. Legend has it that around 200 B.C. a great army threatened the security and stability of the Chinese empire. So ferocious were the invaders that the Chinese emperor commanded the construction of a great wall that would defend against the Hun invaders. Around 1275 A.D., Kublai Khan finally achieved what the Huns had been trying for thousands of years. Initially, the Khan's army tried to climb over, dig under, and break through the wall. In the end, the Khan simply bribed the gatekeeper—and the rest is history. Whether this event actually occurred or not, the moral of the story is that people can be the weakest link in an organization's information security program. And unless policy, education and training, awareness, and technology are properly employed to prevent people from accidentally or intentionally damaging or losing information, they will remain the weakest link. Social engineering can prey on the tendency to cut corners and the common-place nature of human error. It can be used to manipulate the actions of people to obtain access information about a system. This topic is discussed in more detail in Chapter 2, "The Need for Security."

Procedures

Another frequently overlooked component of an IS is procedures. Procedures are written instructions for accomplishing a specific task. When an unauthorized user obtains an organization's procedures, this poses a threat to the integrity of the information. For example, a consultant to a bank learned how to wire funds by using the computer center's procedures, which were readily available. By taking advantage of a security weakness (lack of authentication), this bank consultant ordered millions of dollars to be transferred by wire to his own account. Lax security procedures caused the loss of over ten million dollars before the situation was corrected. Most organizations distribute procedures to their legitimate employees so they can access the information system, but many of these companies often fail to provide proper education on the protection of the procedures. Educating employees about safeguarding procedures is as important as physically securing the information system. After all, procedures are information in their own right. Therefore, knowledge of procedures, as with all critical information, should be disseminated among members of the organization only on a need-to-know basis.

Networks

The IS component that created much of the need for increased computer and information security is networking. When information systems are connected to each other to form local area networks (LANs), and these LANs are connected to other networks such as the Internet, new security challenges rapidly emerge. The physical technology that enables network functions is becoming more and more accessible to organizations of every size. Applying the traditional tools of physical security, such as locks and keys, to restrict access to and interaction with the hardware components of an information system are still important; but when computer systems are networked, this approach is no longer enough. Steps to provide network security are essential, as is the implementation of alarm and intrusion systems to make system owners aware of ongoing compromises.

Balancing Information Security and Access

Even with the best planning and implementation, it is impossible to obtain perfect information security. Recall James Anderson's statement from the beginning of this chapter, which emphasizes the need to balance security and access. Information security cannot be absolute: it is a process, not a goal. It is possible to make a system available to anyone, anywhere, anytime, through any means. However, such unrestricted access poses a danger to the security of the information. On the other hand, a completely secure information system would not allow anyone access. For instance, when challenged to achieve a TCSEC C-2 level security certification for its Windows operating system, Microsoft had to remove all networking components and operate the computer from only the console in a secured room.[19]

To achieve balance—that is, to operate an information system that satisfies the user and the security professional—the security level must allow reasonable access, yet protect against threats. Figure 1-8 shows some of the competing voices that must be considered when balancing information security and access.

Because of today's security concerns and issues, an information system or data-processing department can get too entrenched in the management and protection of systems. An imbalance can occur when the needs of the end user are undermined by too heavy a focus on protecting and administering the information systems. Both information security technologists and end users must recognize that both groups share the same overall goals of the organization—to ensure the data is available when, where, and how it is needed, with

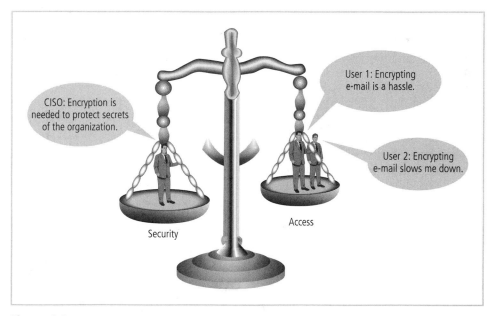

Figure 1-8 Balancing Information Security and Access

Source: Course Technology/Cengage Learning

minimal delays or obstacles. In an ideal world, this level of availability can be met even after concerns about loss, damage, interception, or destruction have been addressed.

Approaches to Information Security Implementation

The implementation of information security in an organization must begin somewhere, and cannot happen overnight. Securing information assets is in fact an incremental process that requires coordination, time, and patience. Information security can begin as a grassroots effort in which systems administrators attempt to improve the security of their systems. This is often referred to as a **bottom-up approach**. The key advantage of the bottom-up approach is the technical expertise of the individual administrators. Working with information systems on a day-to-day basis, these administrators possess in-depth knowledge that can greatly enhance the development of an information security system. They know and understand the threats to their systems and the mechanisms needed to protect them successfully. Unfortunately, this approach seldom works, as it lacks a number of critical features, such as participant support and organizational staying power.

The **top-down approach**—in which the project is initiated by upper-level managers who issue policy, procedures and processes, dictate the goals and expected outcomes, and determine accountability for each required action—has a higher probability of success. This approach has strong upper-management support, a dedicated champion, usually dedicated funding, a clear planning and implementation process, and the means of influencing organizational culture. The most successful kind of top-down approach also involves a formal development strategy referred to as a systems development life cycle.

For any organization-wide effort to succeed, management must buy into and fully support it. The role played in this effort by the champion cannot be overstated. Typically, this champion is an executive, such as a chief information officer (CIO) or the vice president of information technology (VP-IT), who moves the project forward, ensures that it is properly managed, and pushes for acceptance throughout the organization. Without this high-level support, many mid-level administrators fail to make time for the project or dismiss it as a low priority. Also critical to the success of this type of project is the involvement and support of the end users. These individuals are most directly affected by the process and outcome of the project and must be included in the information security process. Key end users should be assigned to a developmental team, known as the joint application development team (JAD). To succeed, the JAD must have staying power. It must be able to survive employee turnover and should not be vulnerable to changes in the personnel team that is developing the information security system. This means the processes and procedures must be documented and integrated into the organizational culture. They must be adopted *and promoted* by the organization's management.

The organizational hierarchy and the bottom-up and top-down approaches are illustrated in Figure 1-9.

The Systems Development Life Cycle

Information security must be managed in a manner similar to any other major system implemented in an organization. One approach for implementing an information security system in

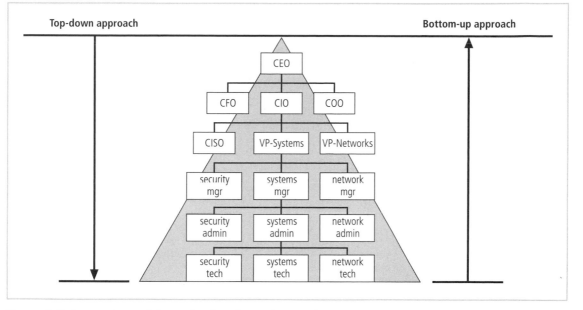

Top-down approach   Bottom-up approach

Figure 1-9 Approaches to Information Security Implementation

Source: Course Technology/Cengage Learning

an organization with little or no formal security in place is to use a variation of the systems development life cycle (SDLC): the security systems development life cycle (SecSDLC). To understand a *security* systems development life cycle, you must first understand the basics of the method upon which it is based.

Methodology and Phases

The **systems development life cycle (SDLC)** is a methodology for the design and implementation of an information system. A **methodology** is a formal approach to solving a problem by means of a structured sequence of procedures. Using a methodology ensures a rigorous process with a clearly defined goal and increases the probability of success. Once a methodology has been adopted, the key milestones are established and a team of individuals is selected and made accountable for accomplishing the project goals.

The traditional SDLC consists of six general phases. If you have taken a system analysis and design course, you may have been exposed to a model consisting of a different number of phases. SDLC models range from having three to twelve phases, all of which have been mapped into the six presented here. The **waterfall model** pictured in Figure 1-10 illustrates that each phase begins with the results and information gained from the previous phase.

At the end of each phase comes a structured review or reality check, during which the team determines if the project should be continued, discontinued, outsourced, postponed, or returned to an earlier phase depending on whether the project is proceeding as expected and on the need for additional expertise, organizational knowledge, or other resources.

Once the system is implemented, it is maintained (and modified) over the remainder of its operational life. Any information systems implementation may have multiple iterations as the cycle is repeated over time. Only by means of constant examination and renewal can

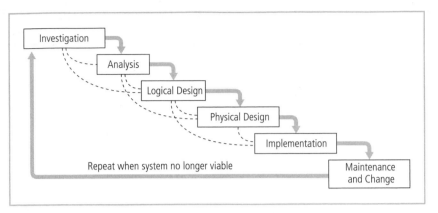

Figure 1-10 SDLC Waterfall Methodology

Source: Course Technology/Cengage Learning

any system, especially an information security program, perform up to expectations in the constantly changing environment in which it is placed.

The following sections describe each phase of the traditional SDLC.[20]

Investigation

The first phase, investigation, is the most important. What problem is the system being developed to solve? The investigation phase begins with an examination of the event or plan that initiates the process. During the investigation phase, the objectives, constraints, and scope of the project are specified. A preliminary cost-benefit analysis evaluates the perceived benefits and the appropriate levels of cost for those benefits. At the conclusion of this phase, and at every phase following, a feasibility analysis assesses the economic, technical, and behavioral feasibilities of the process and ensures that implementation is worth the organization's time and effort.

Analysis

The analysis phase begins with the information gained during the investigation phase. This phase consists primarily of assessments of the organization, its current systems, and its capability to support the proposed systems. Analysts begin by determining what the new system is expected to do and how it will interact with existing systems. This phase ends with the documentation of the findings and an update of the feasibility analysis.

Logical Design

In the logical design phase, the information gained from the analysis phase is used to begin creating a systems solution for a business problem. In any systems solution, it is imperative that the first and driving factor is the business need. Based on the business need, applications are selected to provide needed services, and then data support and structures capable of providing the needed inputs are chosen. Finally, based on all of the above, specific technologies to implement the physical solution are delineated. The logical design is, therefore, the blueprint for the desired solution. The logical design is implementation independent, meaning that it contains no reference to specific technologies, vendors, or products. It addresses, instead, how the proposed system will solve the problem at hand. In this stage, analysts generate a number of alternative solutions, each with corresponding strengths and weaknesses, and costs and benefits, allowing for a general comparison of available options. At the end of this phase, another feasibility analysis is performed.

Physical Design

During the physical design phase, specific technologies are selected to support the alternatives identified and evaluated in the logical design. The selected components are evaluated based on a make-or-buy decision (develop the components in-house or purchase them from a vendor). Final designs integrate various components and technologies. After yet another feasibility analysis, the entire solution is presented to the organizational management for approval.

Implementation

In the implementation phase, any needed software is created. Components are ordered, received, and tested. Afterward, users are trained and supporting documentation created. Once all components are tested individually, they are installed and tested as a system. Again a feasibility analysis is prepared, and the sponsors are then presented with the system for a performance review and acceptance test.

Maintenance and Change

The maintenance and change phase is the longest and most expensive phase of the process. This phase consists of the tasks necessary to support and modify the system for the remainder of its useful life cycle. Even though formal development may conclude during this phase, the life cycle of the project continues until it is determined that the process should begin again from the investigation phase. At periodic points, the system is tested for compliance, and the feasibility of continuance versus discontinuance is evaluated. Upgrades, updates, and patches are managed. As the needs of the organization change, the systems that support the organization must also change. It is imperative that those who manage the systems, as well as those who support them, continually monitor the effectiveness of the systems in relation to the organization's environment. When a current system can no longer support the evolving mission of the organization, the project is terminated and a new project is implemented.

Securing the SDLC

Each of the phases of the SDLC should include consideration of the security of the system being assembled as well as the information it uses. Whether the system is custom and built from scratch, is purchased and then customized, or is commercial off-the-shelf software (COTS), the implementing organization is responsible for ensuring it is used securely. This means that each implementation of a system is secure and does not risk compromising the confidentiality, integrity, and availability of the organization's information assets. The following section, adapted from NIST Special Publication 800-64, rev. 1, provides an overview of the security considerations for each phase of the SDLC.

Each of the example SDLC phases [discussed earlier] includes a minimum set of security steps needed to effectively incorporate security into a system during its development. An organization will either use the general SDLC described [ear-lier] or will have developed a tailored SDLC that meets their specific needs. In either case, NIST recommends that organizations incorporate the associated IT security steps of this general SDLC into their development process:

Investigation/Analysis Phases

- *Security categorization—defines three levels (i.e., low, moderate, or high) of potential impact on organizations or individuals should there be a breach of security (a loss of confidentiality, integrity, or availability). Security categorization standards assist organizations in making the appropriate selection of security controls for their information systems.*

- *Preliminary risk assessment—results in an initial description of the basic security needs of the system. A preliminary risk assessment should define the threat environment in which the system will operate.*

Logical/Physical Design Phases

- *Risk assessment—analysis that identifies the protection requirements for the system through a formal risk assessment process. This analysis builds on the initial risk assessment performed during the Initiation phase, but will be more in-depth and specific.*

- *Security functional requirements analysis—analysis of requirements that may include the following components: (1) system security environment (i.e., enterprise information security policy and enterprise security architecture) and (2) security functional requirements*

- *Security assurance requirements analysis—analysis of requirements that address the developmental activities required and assurance evidence needed to produce the desired level of confidence that the information security will work correctly and effectively. The analysis, based on legal and functional security requirements, will be used as the basis for determining how much and what kinds of assurance are required.*

- *Cost considerations and reporting—determines how much of the development cost can be attributed to information security over the life cycle of the system. These costs include hardware, software, personnel, and training.*

- *Security planning—ensures that agreed upon security controls, planned or in place, are fully documented. The security plan also provides a complete characterization or description of the information system as well as attachments or references to key documents supporting the agency's information security program (e.g., configuration management plan, contingency plan, incident response plan, security awareness and training plan, rules of behavior, risk assessment, security test and evaluation results, system interconnection agreements, security authorizations/ accreditations, and plan of action and milestones).*

- *Security control development—ensures that security controls described in the respective security plans are designed, developed, and implemented. For information systems currently in operation, the security plans for those systems may call for the development of additional security controls to supplement the controls already in place or the modification of selected controls that are deemed to be less than effective.*

- *Developmental security test and evaluation—ensures that security controls developed for a new information system are working properly and are effective. Some types of security controls (primarily those controls of a non-technical nature) cannot be tested and evaluated until the information system is deployed—these controls are typically management and operational controls.*

- *Other planning components—ensures that all necessary components of the development process are considered when incorporating security into the life cycle. These components include selection of the appropriate contract type, participation by all necessary functional groups within an organization, participation by the certifier and accreditor, and development and execution of necessary contracting plans and processes.*

Implementation Phase

- *Inspection and acceptance—ensures that the organization validates and verifies that the functionality described in the specification is included in the deliverables.*

- *System integration—ensures that the system is integrated at the operational site where the information system is to be deployed for operation. Security control settings and switches are enabled in accordance with vendor instructions and available security implementation guidance.*

- *Security certification—ensures that the controls are effectively implemented through established verification techniques and procedures and gives organization officials confidence that the appropriate safeguards and countermeasures are in place to protect the organization's information system. Security certification also uncovers and describes the known vulnerabilities in the information system.*

- *Security accreditation—provides the necessary security authorization of an information system to process, store, or transmit information that is required. This authorization is granted by a senior organization official and is based on the verified effectiveness of security controls to some agreed upon level of assurance and an identified residual risk to agency assets or operations.*

Maintenance and Change Phase

- *Configuration management and control—ensures adequate consideration of the potential security impacts due to specific changes to an information system or its surrounding environment. Configuration management and configuration control procedures are critical to establishing an initial baseline of hardware, software, and firmware components for the information system and subsequently controlling and maintaining an accurate inventory of any changes to the system.*

- *Continuous monitoring—ensures that controls continue to be effective in their application through periodic testing and evaluation. Security control monitoring (i.e., verifying the continued effectiveness of those controls over time) and reporting the security status of the information system to appropriate agency officials is an essential activity of a comprehensive information security program.*

- *Information preservation—ensures that information is retained, as necessary, to conform to current legal requirements and to accommodate future technology changes that may render the retrieval method obsolete.*

- *Media sanitization—ensures that data is deleted, erased, and written over as necessary.*

- *Hardware and software disposal—ensures that hardware and software is disposed of as directed by the information system security officer.*

Adapted from Security Considerations in the Information System Development Life Cycle.[21]

It is imperative that information security be designed into a system from its inception, rather than added in during or after the implementation phase. Information systems that were designed with no security functionality, or with security functions added as an afterthought, often require constant patching, updating, and maintenance to prevent risk to the systems and information. It is a well-known adage that "an ounce of prevention is worth a pound of cure." With this in mind, organizations are moving toward more security-focused development approaches, seeking to improve not only the functionality of the systems they have in place, but consumer confidence in their products. In early 2002, Microsoft effectively suspended development work on many of its products while it put its OS developers, testers, and program managers through an intensive program focusing on secure software development. It also delayed release of its flagship server operating system to address critical security issues. Many other organizations are following Microsoft's recent lead in putting security into the development process.

The Security Systems Development Life Cycle

The same phases used in the traditional SDLC can be adapted to support the implementation of an information security project. While the two processes may differ in intent and specific activities, the overall methodology is the same. At its heart, implementing information security involves identifying specific threats and creating specific controls to counter those threats. The SecSDLC unifies this process and makes it a coherent program rather than a series of random, seemingly unconnected actions. (Other organizations use a risk management approach to implement information security systems. This approach is discussed in subsequent chapters of this book.)

Investigation

The investigation phase of the SecSDLC begins with a directive from upper management, dictating the process, outcomes, and goals of the project, as well as its budget and other constraints. Frequently, this phase begins with an **enterprise information security policy (EISP)**, which outlines the implementation of a security program within the organization. Teams of responsible managers, employees, and contractors are organized; problems are analyzed; and the scope of the project, as well as specific goals and objectives and any additional constraints not covered in the program policy, are defined. Finally, an organizational feasibility analysis is performed to determine whether the organization has the resources and commitment necessary to conduct a successful security analysis and design. The EISP is covered in depth in Chapter 5 of this book.

Analysis

In the analysis phase, the documents from the investigation phase are studied. The development team conducts a preliminary analysis of existing security policies or programs, along with that of documented current threats and associated controls. This phase also includes an analysis of relevant legal issues that could affect the design of the security solution. Increasingly, privacy laws have become a major consideration when making decisions about information systems that manage personal information. Recently, many states have implemented legislation making certain computer-related activities illegal. A detailed understanding of these issues is vital. Risk management also begins in this stage. **Risk management** is the process of identifying, assessing, and evaluating the levels of risk facing the organization, specifically the threats to the organization's security and to the information stored and processed by the organization. Risk management is described in detail in Chapter 4 of this book.

Logical Design

The logical design phase creates and develops the blueprints for information security, and examines and implements key policies that influence later decisions. Also at this stage, the team plans the incident response actions to be taken in the event of partial or catastrophic loss. The planning answers the following questions:

- Continuity planning: How will business continue in the event of a loss?
- Incident response: What steps are taken when an attack occurs?
- Disaster recovery: What must be done to recover information and vital systems immediately after a disastrous event?

Next, a feasibility analysis determines whether or not the project should be continued or be outsourced.

Physical Design

The physical design phase evaluates the information security technology needed to support the blueprint outlined in the logical design generates alternative solutions, and determines a final design. The information security blueprint may be revisited to keep it in line with the changes needed when the physical design is completed. Criteria for determining the definition of successful solutions are also prepared during this phase. Included at this time are the designs for physical security measures to support the proposed technological solutions. At the end of this phase, a feasibility study determines the readiness of the organization for the proposed project, and then the champion and sponsors are presented with the design. At this time, all parties involved have a chance to approve the project before implementation begins.

Implementation

The implementation phase in of SecSDLC is also similar to that of the traditional SDLC. The security solutions are acquired (made or bought), tested, implemented, and tested again. Personnel issues are evaluated, and specific training and education programs conducted. Finally, the entire tested package is presented to upper management for final approval.

Maintenance and Change

Maintenance and change is the last, though perhaps most important, phase, given the current ever-changing threat environment. Today's information security systems need constant

Phases	Steps common to both the systems development life cycle and the security systems development life cycle	Steps unique to the security systems development life cycle
Phase 1: Investigation	• Outline project scope and goals • Estimate costs • Evaluate existing resources • Analyze feasibility	• Management defines project processes and goals and documents these in the program security policy
Phase 2: Analysis	• Assess current system against plan developed in Phase 1 • Develop preliminary system requirements • Study integration of new system with existing system • Document findings and update feasibility analysis	• Analyze existing security policies and programs • Analyze current threats and controls • Examine legal issues • Perform risk analysis
Phase 3: Logical Design	• Assess current business needs against plan developed in Phase 2 • Select applications, data support, and structures • Generate multiple solutions for consideration • Document findings and update feasibility analysis	• Develop security blueprint • Plan incident response actions • Plan business response to disaster • Determine feasibility of continuing and/or outsourcing the project
Phase 4: Physical Design	• Select technologies to support solutions developed in Phase 3 • Select the best solution • Decide to make or buy components • Document findings and update feasibility analysis	• Select technologies needed to support security blueprint • Develop definition of successful solution • Design physical security measures to support techno logical solutions • Review and approve project
Phase 5: Implementation	• Develop or buy software • Order components • Document the system • Train users • Update feasibility analysis • Present system to users • Test system and review performance	• Buy or develop security solutions • At end of phase, present tested package to management for approval
Phase 6: Maintenance and Change	• Support and modify system during its useful life • Test periodically for compliance with business needs • Upgrade and patch as necessary	• Constantly monitor, test, modify, update, and repair to meet changing threats

Table 1-2 SDLC and SecSDLC Phase Summary

monitoring, testing, modification, updating, and repairing. Applications systems developed within the framework of the traditional SDLC are not designed to anticipate a software attack that requires some degree of application reconstruction. In information security, the battle for stable, reliable systems is a defensive one. Often, repairing damage and restoring information is a constant effort against an unseen adversary. As new threats emerge and old threats evolve, the information security profile of an organization must constantly adapt to prevent threats from successfully penetrating sensitive data. This constant vigilance and security can be compared to that of a fortress where threats from outside as well as from within must be constantly monitored and checked with continuously new and more innovative technologies.

Table 1-2 summarizes the steps performed in both the systems development life cycle and the security systems development life cycle. Since the security systems development life cycle is based on the systems development life cycle, the steps in the cycles are similar, and thus those common to both cycles are outlined in column 2. Column 3 shows the steps unique to the security systems development life cycle that are performed in each phase.

Security Professionals and the Organization

It takes a wide range of professionals to support a diverse information security program. As noted earlier in this chapter, information security is best initiated from the top down. Senior management is the key component and the vital force for a successful implementation of an information security program. But administrative support is also essential to developing and executing specific security policies and procedures, and technical expertise is of course essential to implementing the details of the information security program. The following sections describe the typical information security responsibilities of various professional roles in an organization.

Senior Management

The senior technology officer is typically the **chief information officer (CIO)**, although other titles such as vice president of information, VP of information technology, and VP of systems may be used. The CIO is primarily responsible for advising the chief executive officer, president, or company owner on the strategic planning that affects the management of information in the organization. The CIO translates the strategic plans of the organization as a whole into strategic information plans for the information systems or data processing division of the organization. Once this is accomplished, CIOs work with subordinate managers to develop tactical and operational plans for the division and to enable planning and management of the systems that support the organization.

The **chief information security officer (CISO)** has primary responsibility for the assessment, management, and implementation of information security in the organization. The CISO may also be referred to as the manager for IT security, the security administrator, or a similar title. The CISO usually reports directly to the CIO, although in larger organizations it is not uncommon for one or more layers of management to exist between the two. However, the recommendations of the CISO to the CIO must be given equal, if not greater, priority than other technology and information-related proposals. The placement of the CISO and supporting security staff in organizational hierarchies is the subject of current debate across the industry.[22]

Information Security Project Team

The information security **project team** should consist of a number of individuals who are experienced in one or multiple facets of the required technical and nontechnical areas. Many of the same skills needed to manage and implement security are also needed to design it. Members of the security project team fill the following roles:

- **Champion:** A senior executive who promotes the project and ensures its support, both financially and administratively, at the highest levels of the organization.
- **Team leader:** A project manager, who may be a departmental line manager or staff unit manager, who understands project management, personnel management, and information security technical requirements.
- **Security policy developers:** People who understand the organizational culture, existing policies, and requirements for developing and implementing successful policies.
- **Risk assessment specialists:** People who understand financial risk assessment techniques, the value of organizational assets, and the security methods to be used.
- **Security professionals:** Dedicated, trained, and well-educated specialists in all aspects of information security from both a technical and nontechnical standpoint.
- **Systems administrators:** People with the primary responsibility for administering the systems that house the information used by the organization.
- **End users:** Those whom the new system will most directly affect. Ideally, a selection of users from various departments, levels, and degrees of technical knowledge assist the team in focusing on the application of realistic controls applied in ways that do not disrupt the essential business activities they seek to safeguard.

Data Responsibilities

The three types of data ownership and their respective responsibilities are outlined below:

- **Data owners:** Those responsible for the security and use of a particular set of information. They are usually members of senior management and could be CIOs. The data owners usually determine the level of data classification (discussed later), as well as the changes to that classification required by organizational change. The data owners work with subordinate managers to oversee the day-to-day administration of the data.
- **Data custodians:** Working directly with data owners, data custodians are responsible for the storage, maintenance, and protection of the information. Depending on the size of the organization, this may be a dedicated position, such as the CISO, or it may be an additional responsibility of a systems administrator or other technology manager. The duties of a data custodian often include overseeing data storage and backups, implementing the specific procedures and policies laid out in the security policies and plans, and reporting to the data owner.
- **Data users:** End users who work with the information to perform their assigned roles supporting the mission of the organization. Everyone in the organization is responsible for the security of data, so data users are included here as individuals with an information security role.

Communities of Interest

Each organization develops and maintains its own unique culture and values. Within each **organizational culture**, there are communities of interest that develop and evolve. As defined here, a **community of interest** is a group of individuals who are united by similar interests or values within an organization and who share a common goal of helping the organization to meet its objectives. While there can be many different communities of interest in an organization, this book identifies the three that are most common and that have roles and responsibilities in information security. In theory, each role must complement the other; in practice, this is often not the case.

Information Security Management and Professionals

The roles of information security professionals are aligned with the goals and mission of the information security community of interest. These job functions and organizational roles focus on protecting the organization's information systems and stored information from attacks.

Information Technology Management and Professionals

The community of interest made up of IT managers and skilled professionals in systems design, programming, networks, and other related disciplines has many of the same objectives as the information security community. However, its members focus more on costs of system creation and operation, ease of use for system users, and timeliness of system creation, as well as transaction response time. The goals of the IT community and the information security community are not always in complete alignment, and depending on the organizational structure, this may cause conflict.

Organizational Management and Professionals

The organization's general management team and the rest of the resources in the organization make up the other major community of interest. This large group is almost always made up of subsets of other interests as well, including executive management, production management, human resources, accounting, and legal, to name just a few. The IT community often categorizes these groups as users of information technology systems, while the information security community categorizes them as security subjects. In fact, this community serves as the greatest reminder that all IT systems and information security objectives exist to further the objectives of the broad organizational community. The most efficient IT systems operated in the most secure fashion ever devised have no value if they are not useful to the organization as a whole.

Information Security: Is it an Art or a Science?

Given the level of complexity in today's information systems, the implementation of information security has often been described as a combination of art and science. System technologists, especially those with a gift for managing and operating computers and computer-based systems, have long been suspected of using more than a little magic to keep the systems running and functioning as expected. In information security such technologists are sometimes called *security artisans*.[23] Everyone who has studied computer systems can appreciate the anxiety most people feel when faced with complex technology. Consider the inner workings of the computer: with the mind-boggling functions of the transistors in a CPU, the interaction of the various digital devices, and the memory storage units on the circuit boards, it's a miracle these things work at all.

Security as Art

The administrators and technicians who implement security can be compared to a painter applying oils to canvas. A touch of color here, a brush stroke there, just enough to represent the image the artist wants to convey without overwhelming the viewer, or in security terms, without overly restricting user access. There are no hard and fast rules regulating the installation of various security mechanisms, nor are there many universally accepted complete solutions. While there are many manuals to support individual systems, there is no manual for implementing security throughout an entire interconnected system. This is especially true given the complex levels of interaction among users, policy, and technology controls.

Security as Science

Technology developed by computer scientists and engineers—which is designed for rigorous performance levels—makes information security a science as well as an art. Most scientists agree that specific conditions cause virtually all actions in computer systems. Almost every fault, security hole, and systems malfunction is a result of the interaction of specific hardware and software. If the developers had sufficient time, they could resolve and eliminate these faults.

The faults that remain are usually the result of technology malfunctioning for any one of a thousand possible reasons. There are many sources of recognized and approved security methods and techniques that provide sound technical security advice. Best practices, standards of due care, and other tried-and-true methods can minimize the level of guesswork necessary to secure an organization's information and systems.

Security as a Social Science

A third view to consider is information security as a social science, which integrates some of the components of art and science and adds another dimension to the discussion. Social science examines the behavior of individuals as they interact with systems, whether these are societal systems or, as in this context, information systems. Information security begins and ends with the people inside the organization and the people that interact with the system, intentionally or otherwise. End users who need the very information the security personnel are trying to protect may be the weakest link in the security chain. By understanding some of the behavioral aspects of organizational science and change management, security administrators can greatly reduce the levels of risk caused by end users and create more acceptable and supportable security profiles. These measures, coupled with appropriate policy and training issues, can substantially improve the performance of end users and result in a more secure information system.

Selected Readings

- *Beyond Fear* by Bruce Schneier, 2006, Springer-Verlag, New York. This book is an excellent look at the broader areas of security. Of special note is Chapter 4, Systems and How They Fail, which describes how systems are often implemented and how they might be vulnerable to threats and attacks.

- *Fighting Computer Crime* by Donn B. Parker, 1983, Macmillan Library Reference.

- *Seizing the Enigma: The Race to Break the German U-Boats Codes, 1939–1943* by David Kahn, 1991, Houghton Mifflin.

- Glossary of Terms Used in Security and Intrusion Detection by SANS Institute. This can be accessed online at *www.sans.org/resources/glossary.php*.

- RFC 2828–Internet Security Glossary from the Internet RFC/STD/FYI/BCP Archives. This can be accessed online at *www.faqs.org/rfcs/rfc2828.html*.

Chapter Summary

- Information security evolved from the early field of computer security.

- Security is protection from danger. There are a number of types of security: physical security, personal security, operations security, communications security, national security, and network security, to name a few.

- Information security is the protection of information assets that use, store, or transmit information from risk through the application of policy, education, and technology.

- The critical characteristics of information, among them confidentiality, integrity, and availability (the C.I.A. triangle), must be protected at all times; this protection is implemented by multiple measures (policies, education training and awareness, and technology).

- Information systems are made up of six major components: hardware, software, data, people, procedures, and networks.

- Upper management drives the top-down approach to security implementation, in contrast with the bottom-up approach or grassroots effort, whereby individuals choose security implementation strategies.

- The traditional systems development life cycle (SDLC) is an approach to implementing a system in an organization and has been adapted to provide the outline of a security systems development life cycle (SecSDLC).

- The control and use of data in the organization is accomplished by

  - Data owners—responsible for the security and use of a particular set of information

  - Data custodians—responsible for the storage, maintenance, and protection of the information

  - Data users—work with the information to perform their daily jobs supporting the mission of the organization

- Each organization has a culture in which communities of interest are united by similar values and share common objectives. The three communities in information security are general management, IT management, and information security management.

- Information security has been described as both an art and a science, and also comprises many aspects of social science.

Review Questions

1. What is the difference between a threat agent and a threat?

2. What is the difference between vulnerability and exposure?

3. How is infrastructure protection (assuring the security of utility services) related to information security?

4. What type of security was dominant in the early years of computing?

5. What are the three components of the C.I.A. triangle? What are they used for?

6. If the C.I.A. triangle is incomplete, why is it so commonly used in security?

7. Describe the critical characteristics of information. How are they used in the study of computer security?

8. Identify the six components of an information system. Which are most directly affected by the study of computer security? Which are most commonly associated with its study?

9. What system is the father of almost all modern multiuser systems?

10. Which paper is the foundation of all subsequent studies of computer security?

11. Why is the top-down approach to information security superior to the bottom-up approach?

12. Why is a methodology important in the implementation of information security? How does a methodology improve the process?

13. Which members of an organization are involved in the security system development life cycle? Who leads the process?

14. How can the practice of information security be described as both an art and a science? How does security as a social science influence its practice?

15. Who is ultimately responsible for the security of information in the organization?

16. What is the relationship between the MULTICS project and the early development of computer security?

17. How has computer security evolved into modern information security?

18. What was important about Rand Report R-609?

19. Who decides how and when data in an organization will be used or controlled? Who is responsible for seeing that these wishes are carried out?

20. Who should lead a security team? Should the approach to security be more managerial or technical?

Exercises

1. Look up "the paper that started the study of computer security." Prepare a summary of the key points. What in this paper specifically addresses security in areas previously unexamined? *RAND REPORT R-609*

2. Assume that a security model is needed for the protection of information in your class. Using the CNSS model, examine each of the cells and write a brief statement on how you would address the three components occupying that cell.

3. Consider the information stored on your personal computer. For each of the terms listed, find an example and document it: threat, threat agent, vulnerability, exposure, risk, attack, and exploit.

4. Using the Web, identify the chief information officer, chief information security officer, and systems administrator for your school. Which of these individuals represents the data owner? Data custodian?

5. Using the Web, find out more about Kevin Mitnick. What did he do? Who caught him? Write a short summary of his activities and explain why he is infamous.

Case Exercises

The next day at SLS found everyone in technical support busy restoring computer systems to their former state and installing new virus and worm control software. Amy found herself learning how to install desktop computer operating systems and applications as SLS made a heroic effort to recover from the attack of the previous day.

Questions:

1. Do you think this event was caused by an insider or outsider? Why do you think this?

2. Other than installing virus and worm control software, what can SLS do to prepare for the next incident?

3. Do you think this attack was the result of a virus or a worm? Why do you think this?

Endnotes

1. *Bletchley Park—Home of the Enigma machine.* Accessed 15 April 2010 from *http://churchwell.co.uk/bletchley-park-enigma.htm.*

2. Peter Salus. "Net Insecurity: Then and Now (1969–1998)." *Sane '98 Online.* 19 November 1998. Accessed 26 March 2007 from *www.nluug.nl/events/sane98/aftermath/salus.html.*

3. Roberts, Larry. "Program Plan for the ARPANET." Accessed 26 March 2007 from *www.ziplink.net/~lroberts/SIGCOMM99_files/frame.htm.*

4. Roberts, Larry. "Program Plan for the ARPANET." Accessed 8 February 2007 from *www.ziplink.net/~lroberts/SIGCOMM99_files/frame.htm.*

5. Schell, Roger R., Downey, Peter J., and Popek, Gerald J. *Preliminary Notes on the Design of Secure Military Computer System.* January 1973. File, MCI-73-1, ESD/ AFSC, Hanscom AFB, Bedford, MA 01731.

6. Bisbey, Richard, Jr., and Hollingsworth, Dennis. *Protection Analysis: Final Report.* May 1978. Final report, ISI/SR-78-13, USC/Information Sciences Institute, Marina Del Rey, CA 90291.

7. Grampp, F. T., and Morris, R. H. "UNIX Operating System Security." *AT&T Bell Laboratories Technical Journal* 63, no. 8 (1984): 1649–1672.

8. Peter Salus. "Net Insecurity: Then and Now (1969–1998)." *Sane '98 Online.* 19 November 1998. Accessed 26 March 2007 from *www.nluug.nl/events/sane98/after-math/salus.html.*

9. Willis Ware. "Security Controls for Computer Systems: Report of Defense Science Board Task Force on Computer Security." *Rand Online.* 10 October 1979. Accessed 8 February 2007 from *www.rand.org/pubs/reports/R609-1/R609.1.html.*

10. Willis Ware. "Security Controls for Computer Systems: Report of Defense Science Board Task Force on Computer Security." *Rand Online.* 10 October 1979. Accessed 8 February 2004 from *www.rand.org/publications/R/R609.1/R609.1.html.*

11. Merriam-Webster. "security." *Merriam-Webster Online.* Accessed 8 February 2007 from *www.m-w.com/dictionary/security.*

12. National Security Telecommunications and Information Systems Security. *National Training Standard for Information Systems Security (Infosec) Professionals.* 20 June 1994. File, 4011. Accessed 8 Feb 2007 from *www.cnss.gov/Assets/pdf/nstissi_4011. pdf.*

13. Lemos, R. "HP's pretext to spy," *Security Focus Online.* Accessed 21 June 2007 from *www.securityfocus.com/brief/296.*

14. "ChoicePoint Data Theft Affected Thousands." *Wall Street Journal* (Eastern edition). 22 February 2005. New York, 1.

15. Dash, J. "ACLU Knocks Eli Lilly for Divulging E-Mail Addresses," *Computerworld* 35, no. 28 (9 July 2001): 6.

16. CyberCrime Staff. "FDA Flub." *G4.* Accessed 8 February 2007 from *www.g4tv.com/ techtvvault/features/39450/FDA_Flub.html.*

17. Wikipedia. "The McCumber Cube." Accessed 16 February 2007 from *http://en.wiki-pedia.org/wiki/McCumber_cube.*

18. McCumber, John. "Information Systems Security: A Comprehensive Model." Proceedings of the 14th National Computer Security Conference, National Institute of Standards and Technology, Baltimore, MD, October 1991.

19. Microsoft. "C2 Evaluation and Certification for Windows NT (Q93362)." *Microsoft Online.* 1 November 2006. Accessed 25 January 2007 from *http://support.microsoft. com/default.aspx?scid=kb;en-us;93362.*

20. Adapted from Sandra D. Dewitz. *Systems Analysis and Design and the Transition to Objects.* 1996. New York: McGraw Hill Publishers, 94.

21. Grance, T., Hash, J., and Stevens, M. *Security Considerations in the Information System Development Life Cycle.* NIST Special Publication 800-64, rev. 1. Accessed 16 February 2007 from *http://csrc.nist.gov/publications/nistpubs/800-64/NIST-SP800-64.pdf.*

22. Mary Hayes. "Where The Chief Security Officer Belongs." *InformationWeek* no. 877 (25 February 2002): 38.

23. D. B. Parker. *Fighting Computer Crime.* 1998. New York: Wiley Publishing, 189.

chapter 2

The Need for Security

Our bad neighbor makes us early stirrers,
Which is both healthful and good husbandry.
WILLIAM SHAKESPEARE (1564–1616),
KING HENRY, IN HENRY V, ACT 4, SC. 1, L. 6-7.

Fred Chin, CEO of sequential label and supply, leaned back in his leather chair and propped his feet up on the long mahogany table in the conference room where the SLS Board of Directors had just adjourned their quarterly meeting.

"What do you think about our computer security problem?" he asked Gladys Williams, the company's chief information officer, or CIO. He was referring to last month's outbreak of a malicious worm on the company's computer network.

Gladys replied, "I think we have a real problem, and we need to put together a real solution, not just a quick patch like the last time." Eighteen months ago, the network had been infected by an employee's personal USB drive. To prevent this from happening again, all users in the company were banned from using USB drives.

Fred wasn't convinced. "Can't we just add another thousand dollars to the next training budget?"

Gladys shook her head. "You've known for some time now that this business runs on technology. That's why you hired me as CIO. I have some experience at other firms and I've been researching information security, and my staff and I have some ideas to discuss with you. I've asked Charlie Moody to come in today to talk about it. He's waiting to speak with us."

When Charlie joined the meeting Fred said, "Hello, Charlie. As you know, the Board of Directors met today. They received a report on the expenses and lost production from the worm outbreak last month, and they directed us to improve the security of our technology. Gladys says you can help me understand what we need to do about it."

"To start with," Charlie said, "instead of setting up a computer security solution, we need to develop an information security program. We need a thorough review of our policies and practices, and we need to establish an ongoing risk management program. There are some other things that are part of the process as well, but these would be a good start."

"Sounds expensive," said Fred.

Charlie looked at Gladys, then answered, "Well, there will be some extra expenses for specific controls and software tools, and we may have to slow down our product development projects a bit, but the program will be more of a change in our attitude about security than a spending spree. I don't have accurate estimates yet, but you can be sure we'll put cost-benefit worksheets in front of you before we spend any money."

Fred thought about this for a few seconds. "OK. What's our next step?"

Gladys answered, "First, we need to initiate a project plan to develop our new information security program. We'll use our usual systems development and project management approach. There are a few differences, but we can easily adapt our current models. We'll need to appoint or hire a person to be responsible for information security."

"Information security? What about computer security?" asked Fred.

Charlie responded, "Information security includes computer security, plus all the other things we use to do business: procedures, data, networks, our staff, and computers."

"I see," Fred said. "Bring me the draft project plan and budget in two weeks. The audit committee of the board meets in four weeks, and we'll need to report our progress."

LEARNING OBJECTIVES:

Upon completion of this material, you should be able to:

- Demonstrate that organizations have a business need for information security
- Explain why a successful information security program is the responsibility of both an organization's general management and IT management
- Identify the threats posed to information security and the more common attacks associated with those threats, and differentiate *threats* to the information within systems from *attacks* against the information within systems
- Describe the issues facing software developers, as well as the most common errors made by developers, and explain how software development programs can create software that is more secure and reliable

Introduction

Unlike any other information technology program, the primary mission of an information security program is to ensure that systems and their contents remain the same. Organizations expend hundreds of thousands of dollars and thousands of man-hours to maintain their information systems. If threats to information and systems didn't exist, these resources could be used to improve the systems that support the information. However, attacks on information systems are a daily occurrence, and the need for information security grows along with the sophistication of such attacks.

Organizations must understand the environment in which information systems operate so that their information security programs can address actual and potential problems. This chapter describes this environment and identifies the threats it poses to organizations and their information.

Business Needs First

Information security performs four important functions for an organization:

1. Protecting the organization's ability to function
2. Enabling the safe operation of applications running on the organization's IT systems
3. Protecting the data the organization collects and uses
4. Safeguarding the organization's technology assets

Protecting the Functionality of an Organization

Both general management and IT management are responsible for implementing information security that protects the organization's ability to function. Although many business and government managers shy away from addressing information security because they perceive it to be a technically complex task, in fact, implementing information security has more to do with *management* than with *technology*. Just as managing payroll has more to do with management than with mathematical wage computations, managing information security has more to do with policy and its enforcement than with the technology of its implementation. As the noted information security author Charles Cresson Wood writes,

> *In fact, a lot of [information security] is good management for information technology. Many people think that a solution to a technology problem is more technology. Well, not necessarily... So a lot of my work, out of necessity, has been trying to get my clients to pay more attention to information security as a management issue in addition to a technical issue, information security as a people issue in addition to the technical issue.*[1]

Each of an organization's communities of interest must address information security in terms of business impact and the cost of business interruption, rather than isolating security as a technical problem.

Enabling the Safe Operation of Applications

Today's organizations are under immense pressure to acquire and operate integrated, efficient, and capable applications. A modern organization needs to create an environment that safeguards these applications, particularly those that are important elements of the organization's infrastructure—operating system platforms, electronic mail (e-mail), and instant messaging (IM) applications. Organizations acquire these elements from a service provider or they build their own. Once an organization's infrastructure is in place, management must continue to oversee it, and not relegate its management to the IT department.

Protecting Data that Organizations Collect and Use

Without data, an organization loses its record of transactions and/or its ability to deliver value to its customers. Any business, educational institution, or government agency operating within the modern context of connected and responsive services relies on information systems. Even when transactions are not online, information systems and the data they process enable the creation and movement of goods and services. Therefore, protecting *data in motion* and *data at rest* are both critical aspects of information security. The value of data motivates attackers to steal, sabotage, or corrupt it. An effective information security program implemented by management protects the integrity and value of the organization's data.

Safeguarding Technology Assets in Organizations

To perform effectively, organizations must employ secure infrastructure services appropriate to the size and scope of the enterprise. For instance, a small business may get by using an e-mail service provided by an ISP and augmented with a personal encryption tool. When an organization grows, it must develop additional security services. For example, organizational growth could lead to the need for public key infrastructure (PKI), an integrated system of software, encryption methodologies, and legal agreements that can be used to support the entire information infrastructure.

Chapter 8 describes PKI in more detail, but for now know that PKI involves the use of digital certificates to ensure the confidentiality of Internet communications and transactions. Into each of these digital certificates, a certificate authority embeds an individual's or an organization's public encryption key, along with other identifying information, and then cryptographically signs the certificate with a tamper-proof seal, thus verifying the integrity of the data within the certificate and validating its use.

In general, as an organization's network grows to accommodate changing needs, more robust technology solutions should replace security programs the organization has outgrown. An example of a robust solution is a firewall, a mechanism that keeps certain kinds of network traffic out of a private network. Another example is caching network appliances, which are devices that store local copies of Internet content, such as Web pages that are frequently accessed by employees. The appliance displays the cached pages to users, rather than accessing the pages from the server each time.

Threats

Around 500 B.C., the Chinese general Sun Tzu Wu wrote *The Art of War*, a military treatise that emphasizes the importance of knowing yourself as well as the threats you face.[2] To protect your organization's information, you must (1) know yourself; that is, be familiar with the information to be protected and the systems that store, transport, and process it; and (2) know the threats you face. To make sound decisions about information security, management must be informed about the various threats to an organization's people, applications, data, and information systems. In the context of information security, a **threat** is an object, person, or other entity that presents an ongoing danger to an asset.

To investigate the wide range of threats that pervade the interconnected world, researchers have interviewed practicing information security personnel and examined information security literature. While the categorizations may vary, threats are relatively well researched and, consequently, fairly well understood. There is wide agreement that the threat from external sources increases when an organization connects to the Internet. The number of Internet users continues to grow; about 26 percent of the world's 6.8 billion people—that is, 1.7 billion people—have some form of Internet access. Figure 2-1 shows Internet usage by continent.

The Computer Security Institute (CSI) Computer Crime and Security Survey is a representative study. The 2009 CSI study found that 64 percent of organizations responding to the survey suffered malware infections, with only 14 percent indicating system penetration by an outsider. Organizations reported losses of approximately $234,244 per respondent, down from an all-time high of more than $3 million in 2001. The figures haven't topped

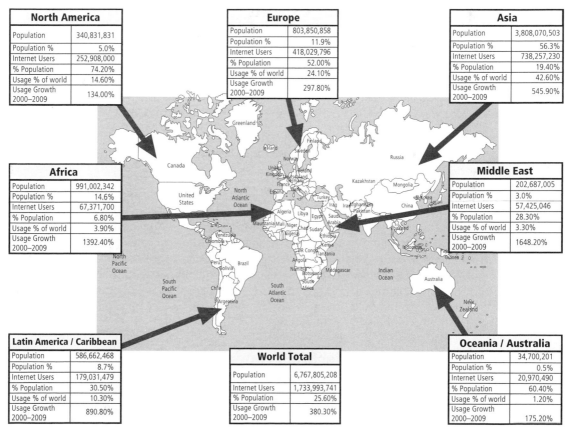

North America

Population	340,831,831
Population %	5.0%
Internet Users	252,908,000
% Population	74.20%
Usage % of world	14.60%
Usage Growth 2000–2009	134.00%

Europe

Population	803,850,858
Population %	11.9%
Internet Users	418,029,796
% Population	52.00%
Usage % of world	24.10%
Usage Growth 2000–2009	297.80%

Asia

Population	3,808,070,503
Population %	56.3%
Internet Users	738,257,230
% Population	19.40%
Usage % of world	42.60%
Usage Growth 2000–2009	545.90%

Africa

Population	991,002,342
Population %	14.6%
Internet Users	67,371,700
% Population	6.80%
Usage % of world	3.90%
Usage Growth 2000–2009	1392.40%

Middle East

Population	202,687,005
Population %	3.0%
Internet Users	57,425,046
% Population	28.30%
Usage % of world	3.30%
Usage Growth 2000–2009	1648.20%

Latin America / Caribbean

Population	586,662,468
Population %	8.7%
Internet Users	179,031,479
% Population	30.50%
Usage % of world	10.30%
Usage Growth 2000–2009	890.80%

World Total

Population	6,767,805,208
Internet Users	1,733,993,741
% Population	25.60%
Usage Growth 2000–2009	380.30%

Oceania / Australia

Population	34,700,201
Population %	0.5%
Internet Users	20,970,490
% Population	60.40%
Usage % of world	1.20%
Usage Growth 2000–2009	175.20%

Figure 2-1 World Internet Usage[3]

Source: Course Technology/Cengage Learning

	Category of Threat	Examples
1.	Compromises to intellectual property	Piracy, copyright infringement
2.	Software attacks	Viruses, worms, macros, denial of service
3.	Deviations in quality of service	ISP, power, or WAN service issues from service providers
4.	Espionage or trespass	Unauthorized access and/or data collection
5.	Forces of nature	Fire, flood, earthquake, lightning
6.	Human error or failure	Accidents, employee mistakes
7.	Information extortion	Blackmail, information disclosure
8.	Missing, inadequate, or incomplete	Loss of access to information systems due to disk drive failure without proper backup and recovery plan organizational policy or planning in place
9.	Missing, inadequate, or incomplete controls	Network compromised because no firewall security controls
10.	Sabotage or vandalism	Destruction of systems or information
11.	Theft	Illegal confiscation of equipment or information
12.	Technical hardware failures or errors	Equipment failure
13.	Technical software failures or errors	Bugs, code problems, unknown loopholes
14.	Technological obsolescence	Antiquated or outdated technologies

Table 2-1   Threats to Information Security[4]

$500,000 since 2005. Overall, the survey indicates that security is improving. The number of organizations declining to outsource security has climbed from 59 percent in 2008 to 71 percent in 2009.[5]

The categorization scheme shown in Table 2-1 consists of fourteen general categories that represent clear and present dangers to an organization's people, information, and systems.[6] Each organization must prioritize the threats it faces, based on the particular security situation in which it operates, its organizational strategy regarding risk, and the exposure levels at which its assets operate. Chapter 4 covers these topics in more detail. You may notice that many of the threat examples in Table 2-1 (i.e., acts or failures) could be listed in more than one category. For example, theft performed by a hacker falls into the category "theft," but is also often accompanied by defacement actions to delay discovery and thus may also be placed in the category of "sabotage or vandalism."

Compromises to Intellectual Property

Many organizations create, or support the development of, intellectual property (IP) as part of their business operations (you will learn more about IP in Chapter 3). Intellectual property is defined as "the ownership of ideas and control over the tangible or virtual representation of those ideas. Use of another person's intellectual property may or may not involve royalty payments or permission, but should always include proper credit to the source."[7] Intellectual property can be trade secrets, copyrights, trademarks, and patents. The unauthorized appropriation

Offline
Violating Software Licenses

Adapted from "Bootlegged Software Could Cost Community College"[8]

By Natalie Patton, *Las Vegas Review Journal*, September 18, 1997.

Ever heard of the software police? The Washington-based Software Publishers Association (SPA) copyright watchdogs were tipped off that a community college in Las Vegas, Nevada was using copyrighted software in violation of the software licenses. The SPA spent months investigating the report. Academic Affairs Vice President Robert Silverman said the college was prepared to pay some license violation fines, but was unable to estimate the total amount of the fines. The college cut back on new faculty hires and set aside over 1.3 million dollars in anticipation of the total cost.

The audit was intensive, examining every computer on campus, including faculty machines, lab machines, and the college president's computer. Peter Beruk, SPA's director of domestic antipiracy cases, said the decision to audit a reported violation is only made when there is overwhelming evidence to win a lawsuit, as the SPA has no policing authority and can only bring civil actions. Most of the investigated organizations settle out of court, agreeing to pay the fines, to avoid costly court battles.

The process begins with an anonymous tip, usually from an individual inside the organization. Of the hundreds of tips the SPA receives each week, only a handful are selected for onsite visits. If the audited organizations have license violations they are required to destroy illegal copies, repurchase software they wish to keep (at double the retail price), and pay the proper licensing fees for the software that was used illegally.

In this case, the community college president suggested the blame for the community college's violations belonged to faculty and students who may have downloaded illegal copies of software from the Internet or installed software on campus computers without permission. Some of the faculty suspected that the problem lay in the qualifications and credibility of the campus technology staff. The president promised to put additional staff and rules in place to prevent a reoccurrence of such license violations.

of IP constitutes a threat to information security. Employees may have access privileges to the various types of IP, and may be required to use the IP to conduct day-to-day business.

Organizations often purchase or lease the IP of other organizations, and must abide by the purchase or licensing agreement for its fair and responsible use. The most common IP breach is the unlawful use or duplication of software-based intellectual property, more commonly known as **software piracy**. Many individuals and organizations do not purchase software as mandated by the owner's license agreements. Because most software is licensed to a particular purchaser, its use is restricted to a single user or to a designated user in an organization. If the user copies the program to another computer without securing another license or transferring the license, he or she has violated the copyright. The Offline, *Violating Software Licenses*, describes a classic case of this type of copyright violation. Software licenses are strictly enforced by a number of regulatory and private organizations, and software publishers use several control mechanisms to prevent copyright infringement. In addition to the laws against software piracy, two watchdog organizations investigate allegations of software abuse: the Software & Information Industry Association (SIIA) at *www.siia.net*, formerly known as the Software Publishers Association, and the Business Software Alliance (BSA) at *www.bsa.org*. A BSA survey in May 2006 revealed that as much as a third of all software in use globally is pirated. Additional details on these organizations and how they operate to protect IP rights are provided in Chapter 3.

A number of technical mechanisms—digital watermarks and embedded code, copyright codes, and even the intentional placement of bad sectors on software media—have been used to enforce copyright laws. The most common tool, a license agreement window that usually pops up during the installation of new software, establishes that the user has read and agrees to the license agreement.

Another effort to combat piracy is the online registration process. Individuals who install software are often asked or even required to register their software to obtain technical support or the use of all features. Some believe that this process compromises personal privacy, because people never really know exactly what information is obtained from their computers and sent to the software manufacturer.

Deliberate Software Attacks

Deliberate software attacks occur when an individual or group designs and deploys software to attack a system. Most of this software is referred to as **malicious code** or **malicious software**, or sometimes **malware**. These software components or programs are designed to damage, destroy, or deny service to the target systems. Some of the more common instances of malicious code are viruses and worms, Trojan horses, logic bombs, and back doors.

Prominent among the history of notable incidences of malicious code are the denial-of-service attacks conducted by Mafiaboy (mentioned earlier) on Amazon.com, CNN.com, ETrade.com, ebay.com, Yahoo.com, Excite.com, and Dell.com. These software-based attacks lasted approximately four hours, and are reported to have resulted in millions of dollars in lost revenue.[9] The British Internet service provider Cloudnine is believed to be the first business "hacked out of existence" in a denial-of-service attack in January 2002. This attack was similar to denial-of-service attacks launched by Mafiaboy in February 2000.[10]

Virus A computer **virus** consists of segments of code that perform malicious actions. This code behaves very much like a virus pathogen that attacks animals and plants, using the cell's own replication machinery to propagate the attack beyond the initial target. The code attaches itself to an existing program and takes control of that program's access to the targeted computer. The virus-controlled target program then carries out the virus's plan by replicating itself into additional targeted systems. Many times users unwittingly help viruses get into a system. Opening infected e-mail or some other seemingly trivial action can cause anything from random messages popping up on a user's screen to the complete destruction of entire hard drives of data. Just as their namesakes are passed among living bodies, computer viruses are passed from machine to machine via physical media, e-mail, or other forms of computer data transmission. When these viruses infect a machine, they may immediately scan the local machine for e-mail applications, or even send themselves to every user in the e-mail address book.

One of the most common methods of virus transmission is via e-mail attachment files. Most organizations block e-mail attachments of certain types and also filter all e-mail for known viruses. In earlier times, viruses were slow-moving creatures that transferred viral payloads through the cumbersome movement of diskettes from system to system. Now, computers are networked, and e-mail programs prove to be fertile ground for computer viruses unless suitable controls are in place. The current software marketplace has several established vendors, such as Symantec Norton Anti-Virus and McAfee VirusScan, that provide applications to assist in the control of computer viruses.

Among the most common types of information system viruses are the **macro virus**, which is embedded in automatically executing macro code used by word processors, spread sheets, and database applications, and the **boot virus**, which infects the key operating system files located in a computer's boot sector.

Worms Named for the Tapeworm in John Brunner's novel *The Shockwave Rider*, a **worm** is a malicious program that replicates itself constantly, without requiring another program environment. Worms can continue replicating themselves until they completely fill available resources, such as memory, hard drive space, and network bandwidth. Read the Offline on Robert Morris and the worm he created to learn about the damage a worm can cause. Code Red, Sircam, Nimda ("admin" spelled backwards), and Klez are examples of a class of worms that combines multiple modes of attack into a single package. Figure 2-2 shows sample e-mails containing the Nimda and Sircam worms. These newer worm variants contain multiple exploits that can use any of the many predefined distribution vectors to programmatically distribute the worm (see the section on polymorphism later in this chapter for more details). The Klez virus, shown in Figure 2-3, delivers a double-barreled payload: it has an attachment that contains the worm, and if the e-mail is viewed on an HTML-enabled

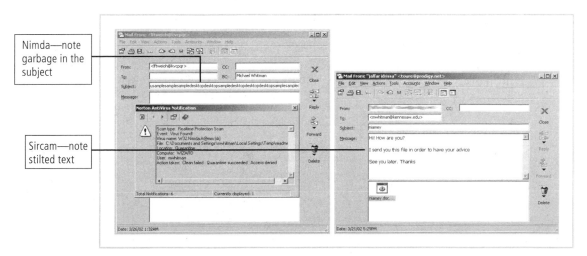

Figure 2-2 Nimda and Sircam Viruses

Source: Course Technology/Cengage Learning

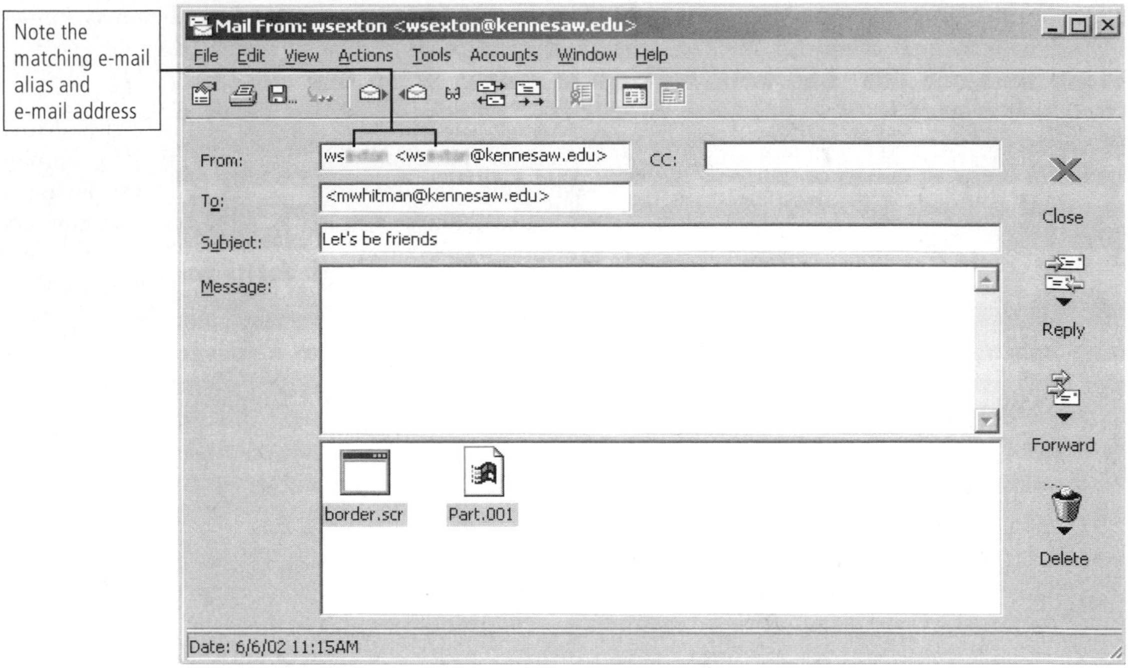

Note the matching e-mail alias and e-mail address

Figure 2-3 Klez Virus

Source: Course Technology/Cengage Learning

browser, it attempts to deliver a macro virus. News-making attacks, such as MS-Blaster, MyDoom, and Netsky, are variants of the multifaceted attack worms and viruses that exploit weaknesses in the leading operating systems and applications.

The complex behavior of worms can be initiated with or without the user downloading or executing the file. Once the worm has infected a computer, it can redistribute itself to all e-mail addresses found on the infected system. Furthermore, a worm can deposit copies of itself onto all Web servers that the infected system can reach, so that users who subsequently visit those sites become infected. Worms also take advantage of open shares found on the network in which an infected system is located, placing working copies of the worm code onto the server so that users of those shares are likely to become infected.

Trojan Horses Trojan horses are software programs that hide their true nature and reveal their designed behavior only when activated. Trojan horses are frequently disguised as helpful, interesting, or necessary pieces of software, such as readme.exe files often included with shareware or freeware packages. Unfortunately, like their namesake in Greek legend, once Trojan horses are brought into a system, they become activated and can wreak havoc on the unsuspecting user. Figure 2-4 outlines a typical Trojan horse attack. Around January 20, 1999, Internet e-mail users began receiving e-mail with an attachment of a Trojan horse program named Happy99.exe. When the e-mail attachment was opened, a brief multimedia program displayed fireworks and the message "Happy 1999." While the fireworks display was running, the Trojan horse program was installing itself into the user's system. The program continued to propagate itself by following up every e-mail the user sent with a second e-mail to the same recipient that contained the Happy99 Trojan horse program.

Offline
Robert Morris and the Internet Worm[11]

In November of 1988, Robert Morris, Jr. made history. He was a postgraduate student in at Cornell, who had invented a self-propagating program called a worm. He released it onto the Internet, choosing to send it from MIT to conceal the fact that the worm was designed and created at Cornell. Morris soon discovered that the program was reproducing itself and then infecting other machines at a speed much faster than he had envisaged. There was a bug.

Finally, many of machines across the U.S. and the world stopped working or became unresponsive. When Morris realized what was occurring he reached out for help. Contacting a friend at Harvard, they sent a message to system administrators at Harvard letting them know what was going on and giving guidance on how to disable the worm. But, since the networks involved were jammed from the worm infection, the message was delayed to the point it had no effect. It was too little too late. Morris' worm had infected many computers including academic institutions, military sites, and commercial concerns. The cost estimate for the infection and the aftermath was estimated at roughly $200 per site.

The worm that Morris created took advantage of flaws in the sendmail program. It was a widely known fault that allowed debug features to be exploited, but few organizations had taken the trouble to update or patch the flaw. Staff at The University of California at Berkeley and MIT had copies of the program and reverse-engineered them determine how it functioned. The teams of programmers worked nonstop and, after about twelve hours, devised a method to slow down the infection. Another method was also discovered at Purdue and widely published. Ironically, the response was hampered by the clogged state of the email infrastructure caused by the worm. After a few days, things slowly started to regain normalcy and everyone wondered where this worm had originated. Morris was identified in a article in the New York Times as the author, even though it was not confirmed at that time.

Morris was convicted under the Computer Fraud and Abuse Act and was sentenced to a fine, probation, community service, and court costs. His appeal was rejected in March of 1991.

Back Door or Trap Door A virus or worm can have a payload that installs a **back door** or **trap door** component in a system, which allows the attacker to access the system at will with special privileges. Examples of these kinds of payloads include Subseven and Back Orifice.

Polymorphic Threats One of the biggest challenges to fighting viruses and worms has been the emergence of polymorphic threats. A **polymorphic threat** is one that over time

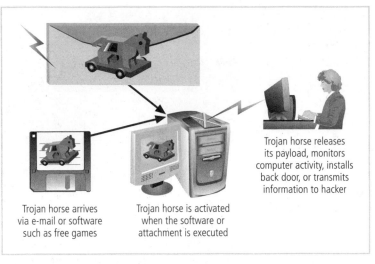

Figure 2-4 Trojan Horse Attack

Source: Course Technology/Cengage Learning

changes the way it appears to antivirus software programs, making it undetectable by techniques that look for preconfigured signatures. These viruses and worms actually evolve, changing their size and other external file characteristics to elude detection by antivirus software programs.

Virus and Worm Hoaxes As frustrating as viruses and worms are, perhaps more time and money is spent on resolving **virus hoaxes**. Well-meaning people can disrupt the harmony and flow of an organization when they send group e-mails warning of supposedly dangerous viruses that don't exist. When people fail to follow virus-reporting procedures, the network becomes overloaded, and much time and energy is wasted as users forward the warning message to everyone they know, post the message on bulletin boards, and try to update their antivirus protection software.

A number of Internet resources enable individuals to research viruses to determine if they are fact or fiction. For the latest information on real, threatening viruses and hoaxes, along with other relevant and current security information, visit the CERT Coordination Center at *www.cert.org*. For a more entertaining approach to the latest virus, worm, and hoax information, visit the Hoax-Slayer Web site at *www.hoax-slayer.com*.

Deviations in Quality of Service

An organization's information system depends on the successful operation of many interdependent support systems, including power grids, telecom networks, parts suppliers, service vendors, and even the janitorial staff and garbage haulers. Any one of these support systems can be interrupted by storms, employee illnesses, or other unforeseen events. Deviations in quality of service can result from incidents such as a backhoe taking out a fiber-optic link for an ISP. The backup provider may be online and in service, but may be able to supply only a fraction of the bandwidth the organization needs for full service. This degradation of service is a form of **availability disruption**. Irregularities in Internet service, communications, and power supplies can dramatically affect the availability of information and systems.

Internet Service Issues In organizations that rely heavily on the Internet and the World Wide Web to support continued operations, Internet service provider failures can considerably undermine the availability of information. Many organizations have sales staff and telecommuters working at remote locations. When these offsite employees cannot contact the host systems, they must use manual procedures to continue operations.

When an organization places its Web servers in the care of a Web hosting provider, that provider assumes responsibility for all Internet services as well as for the hardware and operating system software used to operate the Web site. These Web hosting services are usually arranged with an agreement providing minimum service levels known as a **Service Level Agreement (SLA)**. When a service provider fails to meet the SLA, the provider may accrue fines to cover losses incurred by the client, but these payments seldom cover the losses generated by the outage.

Communications and Other Service Provider Issues Other utility services can affect organizations as well. Among these are telephone, water, wastewater, trash pickup, cable television, natural or propane gas, and custodial services. The loss of these services can impair the ability of an organization to function. For instance, most facilities require water service to operate an air-conditioning system. Even in Minnesota in February, air-conditioning systems help keep a modern facility operating. If a wastewater system fails, an organization might be prevented from allowing employees into the building.

Power Irregularities Irregularities from power utilities are common and can lead to fluctuations such as power excesses, power shortages, and power losses. This can pose problems for organizations that provide inadequately conditioned power for their information systems equipment. In the United States, we are supplied 120-volt, 60-cycle power usually through 15 and 20 amp circuits. When voltage levels **spike** (experience a momentary increase), or **surge** (experience a prolonged increase), the extra voltage can severely damage or destroy equipment. Equally disruptive are power shortages from a lack of available power. A momentary low voltage or **sag**, or a more prolonged drop in voltage, known as a **brownout**, can cause systems to shut down or reset, or otherwise disrupt availability. Complete loss of power for a moment is known as a **fault**, and a more lengthy loss as a **blackout**. Because sensitive electronic equipment—especially networking equipment, computers, and computer-based systems—are vulnerable to fluctuations, controls should be applied to manage power quality. With small computers and network systems, quality power-conditioning options such as surge suppressors can smooth out spikes. The more expensive uninterruptible power supply (UPS) can protect against spikes and surges as well as against sags and even blackouts of limited duration.

Espionage or Trespass

Espionage or trespass is a well-known and broad category of electronic and human activities that can breach the confidentiality of information. When an unauthorized individual gains access to the information an organization is trying to protect, that act is categorized as espionage or trespass. Attackers can use many different methods to access the information stored in an information system. Some information gathering techniques are quite legal, for example, using a Web browser to perform market research. These legal techniques are called, collectively, **competitive intelligence**. When information gatherers employ techniques that cross the threshold of what is legal or ethical, they are conducting **industrial espionage**. Many countries considered allies of the United States engage in industrial espionage against

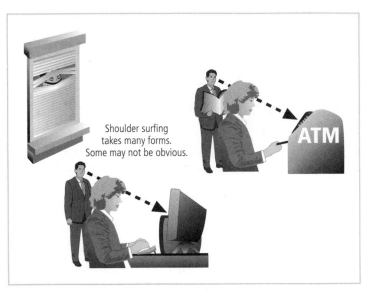

Figure 2-5 Shoulder Surfing

Source: Course Technology/Cengage Learning

American organizations. When foreign governments are involved, these activities are considered espionage and a threat to national security. Some forms of espionage are relatively low tech. One example, called **shoulder surfing**, is pictured in Figure 2-5. This technique is used in public or semipublic settings when individuals gather information they are not authorized to have by looking over another individual's shoulder or viewing the information from a distance. Instances of shoulder surfing occur at computer terminals, desks, ATM machines, on the bus or subway where people use smartphones and tablet PCs, or other places where a person is accessing confidential information. There is unwritten etiquette among professionals who address information security in the workplace. When someone can see another person entering personal or private information into a system, the first person should look away as the information is entered. Failure to do so constitutes not only a breach of etiquette, but an affront to privacy as well as a threat to the security of confidential information.

Acts of **trespass** can lead to unauthorized real or virtual actions that enable information gatherers to enter premises or systems they have not been authorized to enter. Controls sometimes mark the boundaries of an organization's virtual territory. These boundaries give notice to trespassers that they are encroaching on the organization's cyberspace. Sound principles of authentication and authorization can help organizations protect valuable information and systems. These control methods and technologies employ multiple layers or factors to protect against unauthorized access.

The classic perpetrator of espionage or trespass is the hacker. **Hackers** are "people who use and create computer software [to] gain access to information illegally."[12] Hackers are frequently glamorized in fictional accounts as people who stealthily manipulate a maze of computer networks, systems, and data to find the information that solves the mystery or saves the day. Television and motion pictures are inundated with images of hackers as heroes or heroines. However, the true life of the hacker is far more mundane (see Figure 2-6). In the

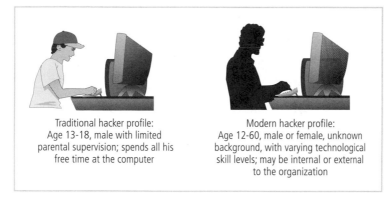

Traditional hacker profile:
Age 13-18, male with limited
parental supervision; spends all his
free time at the computer

Modern hacker profile:
Age 12-60, male or female, unknown
background, with varying technological
skill levels; may be internal or external
to the organization

Figure 2-6 Hacker Profiles

Source: Course Technology/Cengage Learning

real world, a hacker frequently spends long hours examining the types and structures of the targeted systems and uses skill, guile, or fraud to attempt to bypass the controls placed around information that is the property of someone else.

There are generally two skill levels among hackers. The first is the **expert hacker**, or **elite hacker**, who develops software scripts and program exploits used by those in the second category, the novice or **unskilled hacker**. The expert hacker is usually a master of several programming languages, networking protocols, and operating systems and also exhibits a mastery of the technical environment of the chosen targeted system. As described in the Offline section, Hack PCWeek expert hackers are extremely talented individuals who usually devote lots of time and energy to attempting to break into other people's information systems.

Once an expert hacker chooses a target system, the likelihood that he or she will successfully enter the system is high. Fortunately for the many poorly protected organizations in the world, there are substantially fewer expert hackers than novice hackers.

Expert hackers, dissatisfied with attacking systems directly, have turned their attention to writing software. These programs are automated exploits that allow novice hackers to act as **script kiddies**—hackers of limited skill who use expertly written software to attack a system—or **packet monkeys**—script kiddies who use automated exploits to engage in distributed denial-of-service attacks (described later in this chapter). The good news is that if an expert hacker can post a script tool where a script kiddie or packet monkey can find it, then systems and security administrators can find it, too. The developers of protection software and hardware and the service providers who keep defensive systems up to date also keep themselves informed of the latest in exploit scripts. As a result of preparation and continued vigilance, attacks conducted by scripts are usually predictable and can be adequately defended against.

In February 2000, a juvenile hacker named Mafiaboy, who was responsible for a series of widely publicized denial-of-service attacks on prominent Web sites, pled guilty to 56 counts of computer mischief and was sentenced to eight months in juvenile detention, and to pay $250 to charity.[13] His downfall came from his inability to delete the system logs that tracked his activity, and his need to brag about his exploits in chat rooms.

On September 20, 1999, PCWeek did the unthinkable: It set up two computers, one Linux-based, one Windows NT-based, and challenged members of the hacking community to be the first to crack either system, deface the posted Web page, and claim a $1000 reward. Four days later the Linux-based computer was hacked. Figure 2-7 shows the configuration of the *www.hackpcweek.com* Web site, which is no longer functional. The article below provides the technical details of how the hack was accomplished not by a compromise of the root operating system, but by the exploitation of an add-on CGI script with improper security checks.

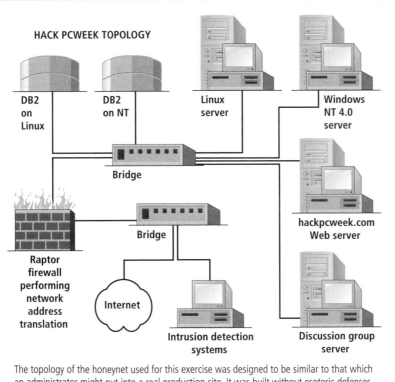

HACK PCWEEK TOPOLOGY

DB2 on Linux

DB2 on NT

Linux server

Windows NT 4.0 server

Bridge

Raptor firewall performing network address translation

Bridge

Internet

Intrusion detection systems

hackpcweek.com Web server

Discussion group server

The topology of the honeynet used for this exercise was designed to be similar to that which an administrator might put into a real production site. It was built without esoteric defenses, sticking to standard firewall and network approaches.

Figure 2-7 Hack PCWeek Configuration

Source: Course Technology/Cengage Learning

In just under 20 hours, the hacker, known as JFS and hailing from Gibraltar (a.k.a the Rock), used his advanced knowledge of the Common Gateway Interface protocol (CGI) to gain control over the target server. He began as most attackers do, with a standard port scan, finding only the HTTP port 80 open. A more detailed analysis of the web servers revealed no additional information.

"Port scanning reveals TCP-based servers, such as telnet, FTP, DNS, and Apache, any of which are potential access points for an attacker. Further testing revealed that most of the potentially interesting services refused connections, with Jfs speculating that TCP wrappers was used to provide access control. The Web server port, 80/TCP, had to be open for Web access to succeed. JFS next used a simple trick. If you send GET X HTTP/1.0 to a Web server, it will send back an error message (unless there is a file named X) along with the standard Web server header. The header contains interesting facts, such as the type and version or the Web server, and sometimes the host operating system and architecture... As the header information is part of the Web server standard, you can get this from just about any Web server, including IIS."

Web Citation (from Cached page: http://cc.bingj.com/cache.aspx?q=JFS+hack+PC +week&d=4567500289476568&mkt=en-US&setlang=en-US&w=a53e4143,65aaf858; accessed November 6, 2010)

He then methodically mapped out the target, starting with the directory server, using the publicly offered WWW pages. He identified commercial applications and scripts. Since he had learned nothing useful with the networking protocol analyses, he focused on vulnerabilities in the dominant commercial application served on the system, PhotoAds. He was able to access the source code as it was offered with the product's sale. With this knowledge JFS was able to find, identify and look at the environment configuration script, but little else.

Not stopping, JFS started his effort to exploit known server-side vulnerabilities such as the use of script includes and mod_PERL embedded commands. When that did not pan out with his first attempt, he kept on, trying this process out with every field to find that a PERL regexp was in place to filter out most input before it was processed. JFS was able to locate just one user-assigned variable that wasn't being screened properly for malformed content. This single flaw encouraged him to keep up his effort.

JFS had located an ENV variable in the HTTP REFERER that was left unprotected. He first tried to use it with a server-side include or mod_PERL embedded command to launch some code of his choosing. Too bad for him that these services were not configured on the machine.

JFS continued to poke and prod though the system configuration, looking specifically for vulnerabilities in the PhotoAds CGI scripts. As he turned his attention he began looking at open() and system() calls. Dead end.

JFS tried post commands, but it stripped out one of the necessary components of the hack string, the % sign making the code fail to function. He then tried uploading files, but the file name variable was again being filtered by a regexp, and they were

(continued)

just placed into a different directory and renamed anyway. He tried and eventually gave up getting around the rename function.

After extensive work to create a C-based executable and smuggle it into the server, constantly battling to minimize the file size to the 8, 190 byte size restriction imposed on the get command, JFS hit another dead end, and turned his attention to gaining root access.

"Using the bugtraq service, he found a cron exploit for which patches hadn't been applied. He modified the hack to get a suidroot. This got him root access—and the ability to change the home page to the chilling: "This site has been hacked. JFS was here".[14]

Game over.

There are other terms for system rule breakers that may be less familiar. The term **cracker** is now commonly associated with an individual who *cracks* or removes software protection that is designed to prevent unauthorized duplication. With the removal of the copyright protection, the software can be easily distributed and installed. The terms hacker and cracker in current usage denote criminal intent.

A **phreaker** hacks the public telephone network to make free calls or disrupt services. Phreakers grew in fame in the 1970s when they developed devices called blue boxes that enabled free calls from pay phones. Later, red boxes were developed to simulate the tones of coins falling in a pay phone, and finally black boxes emulated the line voltage. With the advent of digital communications, these boxes became practically obsolete. Even with the loss of the colored box technologies, phreakers continue to cause problems for all telephone systems.

The most notorious hacker in recent history is Kevin Mitnick, whose history is highlighted in the previous Offline.

Forces of Nature

Forces of nature, *force majeure*, or acts of God can present some of the most dangerous threats, because they usually occur with very little warning and are beyond the control of people. These threats, which include events such as fires, floods, earthquakes, and lightning as well as volcanic eruptions and insect infestations, can disrupt not only the lives of individuals but also the storage, transmission, and use of information. Some of the more common threats in this group are listed here.

- **Fire:** In this context, usually a structural fire that damages a building housing computing equipment that comprises all or part of an information system, as well as smoke damage and/or water damage from sprinkler systems or firefighters. This threat can usually be mitigated with fire casualty insurance and/or business interruption insurance.

- **Flood:** An overflowing of water onto an area that is normally dry, causing direct damage to all or part of the information system or to the building that houses all or part of the information system. A flood might also disrupt operations through interruptions in

Among the most notorious hackers to date is Kevin Mitnick. The son of divorced parents, Kevin Mitnick grew up in an unremarkable middle-class environment. Kevin got his start as a phreaker with a local group of juvenile enthusiasts. Eventually this group expanded their malicious activities and began to target computer companies. After attacking and physically breaking into the Pacific Bell Computer Center for Mainframe Operations, the group was arrested when a former girlfriend of one of the members turned them in. A 17-year-old, Mitnick was convicted of the destruction of data and theft of equipment, and sentenced to three months in juvenile detention and a year's probation.

Mitnick spent the next few years sharpening his hacking and phreaking skills and surviving run-ins with the police. He was arrested again in 1983 at the University of Southern California, where he was caught breaking into Pentagon computers over ARPANET. He received six months in another juvenile prison. He disappeared a few years later, after a warrant was issued for his arrest for breaking into a credit agency computer database. In 1987, he was eventually convicted of using illegal telephone cards and sentenced to 36 months probation. His next hacking battle pitched him against the FBI. His knowledge of the telephone system frustrated their efforts to apprehend him until his best friend turned him in. His unusual defense of computer addiction resulted in a one-year prison sentence and six months counseling. By 1992, it seemed that Mitnick had reverted to a relatively normal life until an episode of illegal database use was traced back to him. After an FBI search of his residence, he was charged with illegally accessing a phone company's computer and associating with a former criminal associate. But this time Kevin Mitnick disappeared before his trial.[15]

In 1995, he was finally tracked down and arrested. Because he was a known flight risk, he was held without bail for nearly five years, eight months of it in solitary confinement. Afraid he would never get to trial, he eventually pleaded guilty to wire fraud, computer fraud, and intercepting communications. He is now free on probation and was required, until January 2003, to get permission to travel or use any technology. His newest job is on the lecture circuit, where he speaks out in support of information security and against hacking.[16]

access to the buildings that house all or part of the information system. This threat can sometimes be mitigated with flood insurance and/or business interruption insurance.

- **Earthquake:** A sudden movement of the earth's crust caused by the release of stress accumulated along geologic faults or by volcanic activity. Earthquakes can cause direct damage to all or part of the information system or, more often, to the building that houses it, and can also disrupt operations through interruptions in access to the buildings that house all or part of the information system. This threat can sometimes be mitigated with specific casualty insurance and/or business interruption insurance, but is usually a separate policy.

- **Lightning:** An abrupt, discontinuous natural electric discharge in the atmosphere. Lightning usually directly damages all or part of the information system an/or its power distribution components. It can also cause fires or other damage to the building that houses all or part of the information system, and disrupt operations by interfering with access to the buildings that house all or part of the information system. This threat can usually be mitigated with multipurpose casualty insurance and/or business interruption insurance.

- **Landslide or mudslide:** The downward sliding of a mass of earth and rock directly damaging all or part of the information system or, more likely, the building that houses it. Land- or mudslides also disrupt operations by interfering with access to the buildings that house all or part of the information system. This threat can sometimes be mitigated with casualty insurance and/or business interruption insurance.

- **Tornado or severe windstorm:** A rotating column of air ranging in width from a few yards to more than a mile and whirling at destructively high speeds, usually accompanied by a funnel-shaped downward extension of a cumulonimbus cloud. Storms can directly damage all or part of the information system or, more likely, the building that houses it, and can also interrupt access to the buildings that house all or part of the information system. This threat can sometimes be mitigated with casualty insurance and/or business interruption insurance.

- **Hurricane or typhoon:** A severe tropical cyclone originating in the equatorial regions of the Atlantic Ocean or Caribbean Sea or eastern regions of the Pacific Ocean (typhoon), traveling north, northwest, or northeast from its point of origin, and usually involving heavy rains. These storms can directly damage all or part of the information system or, more likely, the building that houses it. Organizations located in coastal or low-lying areas may experience flooding (see above). These storms may also disrupt operations by interrupting access to the buildings that house all or part of the information system. This threat can sometimes be mitigated with casualty insurance and/or business interruption insurance.

- **Tsunami:** A very large ocean wave caused by an underwater earthquake or volcanic eruption. These events can directly damage all or part of the information system or, more likely, the building that houses it. Organizations located in coastal areas may experience tsunamis. Tsunamis may also cause disruption to operations through interruptions in access or electrical power to the buildings that house all or part of the information system. This threat can sometimes be mitigated with casualty insurance and/or business interruption insurance.

- **Electrostatic discharge (ESD):** Usually, static electricity and ESD are little more than a nuisance. Unfortunately, however, the mild static shock we receive when walking across a carpet can be costly or dangerous when it ignites flammable mixtures and damages costly electronic components. Static electricity can draw dust into clean-room environments or cause products to stick together. The cost of ESD-damaged electronic devices and interruptions to service can range from only a few cents to several millions of dollars for critical systems. Loss of production time in information processing due to ESD impact is significant. While not usually viewed as a threat, ESD can disrupt information systems, but it is not usually an insurable loss unless covered by business interruption insurance.

- **Dust contamination:** Some environments are not friendly to the hardware components of information systems. Because dust contamination can shorten the life of information systems or cause unplanned downtime, this threat can disrupt normal operations.

Since it is not possible to avoid force of nature threats, organizations must implement controls to limit damage, and they must also prepare contingency plans for continued operations, such as disaster recovery plans, business continuity plans, and incident response plans.

Human Error or Failure

This category includes acts performed without intent or malicious purpose by an authorized user. When people use information systems, mistakes happen. Inexperience, improper training, and the incorrect assumptions are just a few things that can cause these misadventures. Regardless of the cause, even innocuous mistakes can produce extensive damage. For example, a simple keyboarding error can cause worldwide Internet outages:

> In April 1997, the core of the Internet suffered a disaster. Internet service providers lost connectivity with other ISPs due to an error in a routine Internet router-table update process. The resulting outage effectively shut down a major portion of the Internet for at least twenty minutes. It has been estimated that about 45 percent of Internet users were affected. In July 1997, the Internet went through yet another more critical global shutdown for millions of users. An accidental upload of a corrupt database to the Internet's root domain servers occurred. Since this provides the ability to address hosts on the net by name (i.e., eds.com), it was impossible to send e-mail or access Web sites within the .com and .net domains for several hours. The .com domain comprises a majority of the commercial enterprise users of the Internet.[17]

One of the greatest threats to an organization's information security is the organization's own employees. Employees are the threat agents closest to the organizational data. Because employees use data in everyday activities to conduct the organization's business, their mistakes represent a serious threat to the confidentiality, integrity, and availability of data—even, as Figure 2-8 suggests, relative to threats from outsiders. This is because employee mistakes can easily lead to the following: revelation of classified data, entry of erroneous data, accidental deletion or modification of data, storage of data in unprotected areas, and failure to protect information. Leaving classified information in unprotected areas, such as on a desktop, on a Web site, or even in the trash can, is as much a threat to the protection of the information as is the individual who seeks to exploit the information, because one person's carelessness can create a vulnerability and thus an opportunity for an attacker. However, if someone damages or destroys data on purpose, the act belongs to a different threat category.

Much human error or failure can be prevented with training and ongoing awareness activities, but also with controls, ranging from simple procedures, such as requiring the user to type a critical command twice, to more complex procedures, such as the verification of commands by a second party. An example of the latter is the performance of key recovery actions in PKI systems. Many military applications have robust, dual-approval controls built in.

Figure 2-8 Acts of Human Error or Failure

Source: Course Technology/Cengage Learning

Some systems that have a high potential for data loss or system outages use expert systems to monitor human actions and request confirmation of critical inputs.

Information Extortion

Information extortion occurs when an attacker or trusted insider steals information from a computer system and demands compensation for its return or for an agreement not to disclose it. Extortion is common in credit card number theft. For example, Web-based retailer CD Universe was the victim of a theft of data files containing customer credit card information. The culprit was a Russian hacker named Maxus, who hacked the online vendor and stole several hundred thousand credit card numbers. When the company refused to pay the $100,000 blackmail, he posted the card numbers to a Web site, offering them to the criminal community. His Web site became so popular he had to restrict access.[18]

Another incident of extortion occurred in 2008 when pharmacy benefits manager Express Scripts, Inc. fell victim to a hacker who demonstrated that he had access to seventy-five customer records and claimed to have access to millions. The perpetrator demanded an undisclosed amount of money. The company notified the FBI and offered a $1 million reward for the arrest of the perpetrator. Express Scripts notified the affected customers, as required by various state information breach notification laws. Express Scripts was obliged to pay undisclosed expenses for the notifications, as well as for credit monitoring services that the company was required by some state laws to buy for its customers.[19]

Missing, Inadequate, or Incomplete Organizational Policy or Planning

Missing, inadequate, or incomplete organizational policy or planning makes an organization vulnerable to loss, damage, or disclosure of information assets when other threats lead to attacks. Information security is, at its core, a management function. The organization's executive leadership is responsible for strategic planning for security as well as for IT and business functions—a task known as governance.

Missing, Inadequate, or Incomplete Controls

Missing, inadequate, or incomplete controls—that is, security safeguards and information asset protection controls that are missing, misconfigured, antiquated, or poorly designed or managed—make an organization more likely to suffer losses when other threats lead to attacks.

For example, if a small organization installs its first network using small office/home office (SOHO) equipment (which is similar to the equipment you might have on your home network) and fails to upgrade its network equipment as it becomes larger, the increased traffic can affect performance and cause information loss. Routine security audits to assess the current levels of protection help to ensure the continuous protection of organization's assets.

Sabotage or Vandalism

This category of threat involves the deliberate sabotage of a computer system or business, or acts of vandalism to either destroy an asset or damage the image of an organization. These acts can range from petty vandalism by employees to organized sabotage against an organization.

Although not necessarily financially devastating, attacks on the image of an organization are serious. Vandalism to a Web site can erode consumer confidence, thus diminishing an organization's sales and net worth, as well as its reputation. For example, in the early hours of July 13, 2001, a group known as Fluffi Bunni left its mark on the front page of the SysAdmin, Audit, Network, Security (SANS) Institute, a cooperative research and education organization. This event was particularly embarrassing to SANS Institute management, since the Institute provides security instruction and certification. The defacement read, "Would you really trust these guys to teach you security?"[20]

There are innumerable reports of hackers accessing systems and damaging or destroying critical data. Hacked Web sites once made front-page news, as the perpetrators intended. The impact of these acts has lessened as the volume has increased. The Web site that acts as the clearinghouse for many hacking reports, *Attrition.org*, has stopped cataloging all Web site defacements, because the frequency of such acts has outstripped the ability of the volunteers to keep the site up to date.[21]

Compared to Web site defacement, vandalism within a network is more malicious in intent and less public. Today, security experts are noticing a rise in another form of online vandalism, **hacktivist** or **cyberactivist** operations, which interfere with or disrupt systems to protest the operations, policies, or actions of an organization or government agency. For example, in November 2009, a group calling itself "anti-fascist hackers" defaced the Web site of holocaust denier and Nazi sympathizer David Irving. They also released his private e-mail correspondence, secret locations of events on his speaking tour, and detailed information about people attending those events, among them members of various white supremacist organizations. This information was posted on the Web site WikiLeaks, an organization that publishes sensitive and classified information provided by anonymous sources.[22]

Figure 2-9 illustrates how Greenpeace, a well-known environmental activist organization, once used its Web presence to recruit cyberactivists.

A much more sinister form of hacking is **cyberterrorism**. Cyberterrorists hack systems to conduct terrorist activities via network or Internet pathways. The United States and other governments are developing security measures intended to protect the critical computing and communications networks as well as the physical and power utility infrastructures.

> *In the 1980s, Barry Collin, a senior research fellow at the Institute for Security and Intelligence in California, coined the term "cyberterrorism" to refer to the convergence of cyberspace and terrorism. Mark Pollitt, special agent for the FBI, offers a working definition: "Cyberterrorism is the premeditated, politically motivated attacks against information, computer systems, computer programs, and data which result in violence against noncombatant targets by subnational groups or clandestine agents."[23]*

Figure 2-9 Cyber Activists Wanted

Source: Course Technology/Cengage Learning

Cyberterrorism has thus far been largely limited to acts such as the defacement of NATO Web pages during the war in Kosovo. Some industry observers have taken the position that cyberterrorism is not a real threat, and instead is merely hype that distracts from the more concrete and pressing information security issues that do need attention.[24]

However, further instances of cyberterrorism have begun to surface. According to Dr. Mudawi Mukhtar Elmusharaf at the *Computer Crime Research Center*, "on Oct. 21, 2002, a distributed denial-of-service (DDOS) attack struck the 13 root servers that provide the primary road-map for all Internet communications. Nine servers out of these thirteen were jammed. The problem was taken care of in a short period of time."[25] While this attack was significant, the results were not noticeable to most users of the Internet A news report shortly after the attack noted that "the attack, at its peak, only caused 6 percent of domain name service requests to go unanswered [...and the global] DNS system normally responds almost 100 percent of the time."[26]

Theft

The threat of **theft**—the illegal taking of another's property, which can be physical, electronic, or intellectual—is a constant. The value of information is diminished when it is copied without the owner's knowledge.

Physical theft can be controlled quite easily by means of a wide variety of measures, from locked doors to trained security personnel and the installation of alarm systems. Electronic theft, however, is a more complex problem to manage and control. When someone steals a physical object, the loss is easily detected; if it has any importance at all, its absence is noted. When electronic information is stolen, the crime is not always readily apparent. If thieves are clever and cover their tracks carefully, no one may ever know of the crime until it is far too late.

Technical Hardware Failures or Errors

Technical hardware failures or errors occur when a manufacturer distributes equipment containing a known or unknown flaw. These defects can cause the system to perform outside of expected parameters, resulting in unreliable service or lack of availability. Some errors are terminal—that is, they result in the unrecoverable loss of the equipment. Some errors are intermittent, in that they only periodically manifest themselves, resulting in faults that are not easily repeated, and thus, equipment can sometimes stop working, or work in unexpected ways. Murphy's Law (and yes, there really was a Murphy) says that if something can possibly go wrong, it will.[27] In other words, it's not *if* something will fail, but *when*.

One of the best-known hardware failures is that of the Intel Pentium II chip (similar to the one shown in Figure 2-10), which had a defect that resulted in a calculation error under certain circumstances. Intel initially expressed little concern for the defect, stating that it would take an inordinate amount of time to identify a calculation that would interfere with the reliability of the results. Yet within days, popular computing journals were publishing a simple calculation (the division of 4195835 by 3145727 by a spreadsheet) that determined whether an individual's machine contained the defective chip and thus the floating-point operation bug. The Pentium floating-point division bug (FDIV) led to a public relations disaster for Intel that resulted in its first-ever chip recall and a loss of over $475 million. A few months later, disclosure of another bug, known as the Dan-0411 flag

Figure 2-10 Pentium II Chip

Source: Course Technology/Cengage Learning

erratum, further eroded the chip manufacturer's public image.[28] In 1998, when Intel released its Xeon chip, it also had hardware errors. Intel said, "All new chips have bugs, and the process of debugging and improving performance inevitably continues even after a product is in the market."[29]

Technical Software Failures or Errors

Large quantities of computer code are written, debugged, published, and sold before all their bugs are detected and resolved. Sometimes, combinations of certain software and hardware reveal new bugs. These failures range from bugs to untested failure conditions. Sometimes these bugs are not errors, but rather purposeful shortcuts left by programmers for benign or malign reasons. Collectively, shortcut access routes into programs that bypass security checks are called trap doors and can cause serious security breaches.

Software bugs are so commonplace that entire Web sites are dedicated to documenting them. Among the most often used is Bugtraq, found at *www.securityfocus.com*, which provides up-to-the-minute information on the latest security vulnerabilities, as well as a very thorough archive of past bugs.

Technological Obsolescence

Antiquated or outdated infrastructure can lead to unreliable and untrustworthy systems. Management must recognize that when technology becomes outdated, there is a risk of loss of data integrity from attacks. Management's strategic planning should always include an analysis of the technology currently in use. Ideally, proper planning by management should prevent technology from becoming obsolete, but when obsolescence is manifest, management must take immediate action. IT professionals play a large role in the identification of probable obsolescence.

Recently, the software vendor Symantec retired support for a legacy version of its popular antivirus software, and organizations interested in continued product support were obliged to upgrade immediately to a different antivirus control software. In organizations where IT personnel had kept management informed of the coming retirement, these replacements were made more promptly and at lower cost than at organizations where the software was allowed to become obsolete.

Attacks

An **attack** is an act that takes advantage of a vulnerability to compromise a controlled system. It is accomplished by a **threat agent** that damages or steals an organization's information or physical asset. A **vulnerability** is an identified weakness in a controlled system, where controls are not present or are no longer effective. Unlike threats, which are always present, attacks only exist when a specific act may cause a loss. For example, the *threat* of damage from a thunderstorm is present throughout the summer in many places, but an *attack* and its associated risk of loss only exist for the duration of an actual thunderstorm. The following sections discuss each of the major types of attacks used against controlled systems.

Malicious Code

The **malicious code** attack includes the execution of viruses, worms, Trojan horses, and active Web scripts with the intent to destroy or steal information. The state-of-the-art malicious code attack is the polymorphic, or multivector, worm. These attack programs use up to six known attack vectors to exploit a variety of vulnerabilities in commonly found information system devices. Perhaps the best illustration of such an attack remains the outbreak of Nimda in September 2001, which used five of the six vectors to spread itself with startling speed. TruSecure Corporation, an industry source for information security statistics and solutions, reports that Nimda spread to span the Internet address space of 14 countries in less than 25 minutes.[30] Table 2-2 lists and describes the six categories of known attack vectors.

Other forms of malware include covert software applications—bots, spyware, and adware—that are designed to work out of sight of users or via an apparently innocuous user action. A **bot** (an abbreviation of robot) is "an automated software program that executes certain commands when it receives a specific input. Bots are often the technology used to implement Trojan horses, logic bombs, back doors, and spyware."[31] **Spyware** is "any technology that aids in gathering information about a person or organization without their knowledge. Spyware is placed on a computer to secretly gather information about the user and report it. The various types of spyware include (1) a Web bug, a tiny graphic on a Web site that is referenced within the Hypertext Markup Language (HTML) content of a Web page or e-mail to collect information about the user viewing the HTML content; (2) a tracking cookie, which is placed on the user's computer to track the user's activity on different

Vector	Description
IP scan and attack	The infected system scans a random or local range of IP addresses and targets any of several vulnerabilities known to hackers or left over from previous exploits such as Code Red, Back Orifice, or PoizonBox.
Web browsing	If the infected system has write access to any Web pages, it makes all Web content files (.html, .asp, .cgi, and others) infectious, so that users who browse to those pages become infected.
Virus	Each infected machine infects certain common executable or script files on all computers to which it can write with virus code that can cause infection.
Unprotected shares	Using vulnerabilities in file systems and the way many organizations configure them, the infected machine copies the viral component to all locations it can reach.
Mass mail	By sending e-mail infections to addresses found in the address book, the infected machine infects many users, whose mail-reading programs also automatically run the program and infect other systems.
Simple Network Management Protocol (SNMP)	By using the widely known and common passwords that were employed in early versions of this protocol (which is used for remote management of network and computer devices), the attacking program can gain control of the device. Most vendors have closed these vulnerabilities with software upgrades.

Table 2-2 Attack Replication Vectors

Web sites and create a detailed profile of the user's behavior."[32] **Adware** is "any software program intended for marketing purposes such as that used to deliver and display advertising banners or popups to the user's screen or tracking the user's online usage or purchasing activity."[33] Each of these hidden code components can be used to collect information from or about the user which could then be used in a social engineering or identity theft attack.

Hoaxes

A more devious attack on computer systems is the transmission of a virus hoax *with a real virus attached*. When the attack is masked in a seemingly legitimate message, unsuspecting users more readily distribute it. Even though these users are trying to do the right thing to avoid infection, they end up sending the attack on to their coworkers and friends and infecting many users along the way.

Back Doors

Using a known or previously unknown and newly discovered access mechanism, an attacker can gain access to a system or network resource through a back door. Sometimes these entries are left behind by system designers or maintenance staff, and thus are called trap doors.[34] A trap door is hard to detect, because very often the programmer who puts it in place also makes the access exempt from the usual audit logging features of the system.

Password Crack

Attempting to reverse-calculate a password is often called **cracking**. A cracking attack is a component of many dictionary attacks (to be covered shortly). It is used when a copy of the Security Account Manager (SAM) data file, which contains hashed representation of the user's password, can be obtained. A password can be hashed using the same algorithm and compared to the hashed results. If they are the same, the password has been cracked.

Brute Force

The application of computing and network resources to try every possible password combination is called a **brute force attack**. Since the brute force attack is often used to obtain passwords to commonly used accounts, it is sometimes called a **password attack**. If attackers can narrow the field of target accounts, they can devote more time and resources to these accounts. That is one reason to always change the manufacturer's default administrator account names and passwords.

Password attacks are rarely successful against systems that have adopted the manufacturer's recommended security practices. Controls that limit the number of unsuccessful access attempts allowed per unit of elapsed time are very effective against brute force attacks.

Dictionary

The **dictionary attack** is a variation of the brute force attack which narrows the field by selecting specific target accounts and using a list of commonly used passwords (the dictionary) instead of random combinations. Organizations can use similar dictionaries to disallow passwords during the reset process and thus guard against easy-to-guess passwords. In addition, rules requiring numbers and/or special characters in passwords make the dictionary attack less effective.

Denial-of-Service (DoS) and Distributed Denial-of-Service (DDoS)

In a **denial-of-service** (DoS) attack, the attacker sends a large number of connection or information requests to a target (see Figure 2-11). So many requests are made that the target system becomes overloaded and cannot respond to legitimate requests for service. The system may crash or simply become unable to perform ordinary functions. A **distributed denial-of-service** (DDoS) is an attack in which a coordinated stream of requests is launched against a target from many locations at the same time. Most DDoS attacks are preceded by a preparation phase in which many systems, perhaps thousands, are compromised. The compromised machines are turned into **zombies**, machines that are directed remotely (usually by a transmitted command) by the attacker to participate in the attack. DDoS attacks are the most difficult to defend against, and there are presently no controls that any single organization can apply. There are, however, some cooperative efforts to enable DDoS defenses among groups of service providers; among them is the Consensus Roadmap for Defeating Distributed Denial of Service Attacks.[35] To use a popular metaphor, DDoS is considered a weapon of mass destruction on the Internet.[36] The MyDoom worm attack of early 2004 was intended to be a DDoS attack against *www.sco.com* (the Web site of a vendor of a UNIX operating system) that lasted from February 1, 2004 until February 12, 2004. Allegedly, the

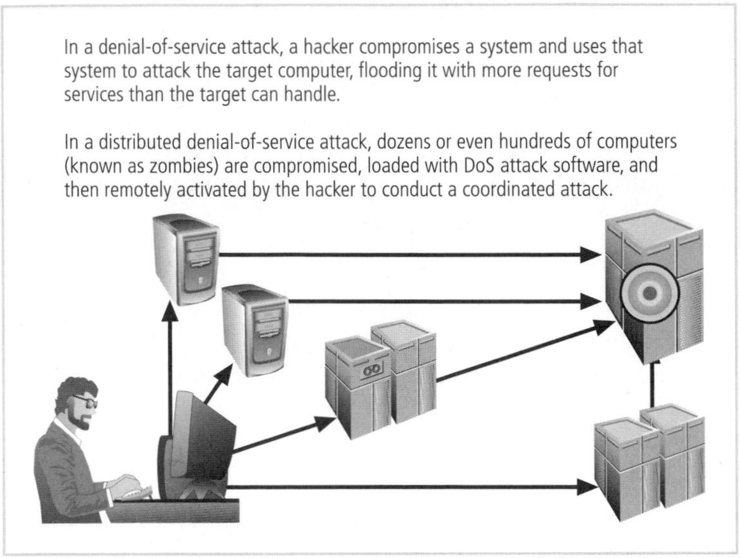

In a denial-of-service attack, a hacker compromises a system and uses that system to attack the target computer, flooding it with more requests for services than the target can handle.

In a distributed denial-of-service attack, dozens or even hundreds of computers (known as zombies) are compromised, loaded with DoS attack software, and then remotely activated by the hacker to conduct a coordinated attack.

Figure 2-11 Denial-of-Service Attacks

Source: Course Technology/Cengage Learning

attack was payback for the SCO Group's perceived hostility toward the open-source Linux community.[37]

Any system connected to the Internet and providing TCP-based network services (such as a Web server, FTP server, or mail server) is vulnerable to DoS attacks. DoS attacks can also be launched against routers or other network server systems if these hosts enable (or turn on) other TCP services (e.g., echo).

Spoofing

Spoofing is a technique used to gain unauthorized access to computers, wherein the intruder sends messages with a source IP address that has been forged to indicate that the messages are coming from a trusted host. To engage in IP spoofing, hackers use a variety of techniques to obtain trusted IP addresses, and then modify the packet headers (see Figure 2-12) to insert these forged addresses.[38] Newer routers and firewall arrangements can offer protection against IP spoofing.

Man-in-the-Middle

In the well-known **man-in-the-middle** or **TCP hijacking attack**, an attacker monitors (or sniffs) packets from the network, modifies them, and inserts them back into the network. This type of attack uses IP spoofing to enable an attacker to impersonate another entity on the network. It allows the attacker to eavesdrop as well as to change, delete, reroute, add, forge, or divert data.[39] A variant of TCP hijacking, involves the interception of an encryption key exchange, which enables the hacker to act as an invisible man-in-the-middle—that is, an eavesdropper—on encrypted communications. Figure 2-13 illustrates these attacks by showing how a hacker uses public and private encryption keys to intercept messages. You will learn more about encryption keys in Chapter 8.

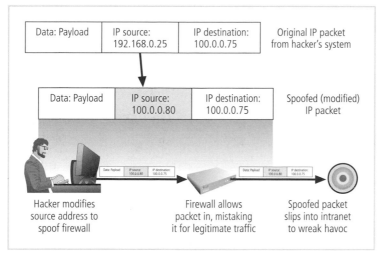

Figure 2-12 IP Spoofing

Source: Course Technology/Cengage Learning

Spam

Spam is unsolicited commercial e-mail. While many consider spam a trivial nuisance rather than an attack, it has been used as a means of enhancing malicious code attacks. In March 2002, there were reports of malicious code embedded in MP3 files that were included as attachments to spam.[40] The most significant consequence of spam, however, is the waste of computer and human resources. Many organizations attempt to cope with the flood of spam by using e-mail filtering technologies. Other organizations simply tell the users of the mail system to delete unwanted messages.

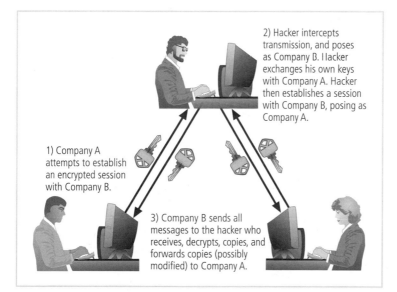

Figure 2-13 Man-in-the-Middle Attack

Source: Course Technology/Cengage Learning

Mail Bombing

Another form of e-mail attack that is also a DoS is called a **mail bomb**, in which an attacker routes large quantities of e-mail to the target. This can be accomplished by means of social engineering (to be discussed shortly) or by exploiting various technical flaws in the Simple Mail Transport Protocol (SMTP). The target of the attack receives an unmanageably large volume of unsolicited e-mail. By sending large e-mails with forged header information, attackers can take advantage of poorly configured e-mail systems on the Internet and trick them into sending many e-mails to an address chosen by the attacker. If many such systems are tricked into participating in the event, the target e-mail address is buried under thousands or even millions of unwanted e-mails.

Sniffers

A **sniffer** is a program or device that can monitor data traveling over a network. Sniffers can be used both for legitimate network management functions and for stealing information. Unauthorized sniffers can be extremely dangerous to a network's security, because they are virtually impossible to detect and can be inserted almost anywhere. This makes them a favorite weapon in the hacker's arsenal. Sniffers often work on TCP/IP networks, where they're sometimes called **packet sniffers**.[41] Sniffers add risk to the network, because many systems and users send information on local networks in clear text. A sniffer program shows all the data going by, including passwords, the data inside files—such as word-processing documents—and screens full of sensitive data from applications.

Social Engineering

In the context of information security, **social engineering** is the process of using social skills to convince people to reveal access credentials or other valuable information to the attacker. There are several social engineering techniques, which usually involve a perpetrator posing as a person higher in the organizational hierarchy than the victim. To prepare for this false representation, the perpetrator may have used social engineering tactics against others in the organization to collect seemingly unrelated information that, when used together, makes the false representation more credible. For instance, anyone can check a company's Web site, or even call the main switchboard to get the name of the CIO; an attacker may then obtain even more information by calling others in the company and asserting his or her (false) authority by mentioning the CIO's name. Social engineering attacks may involve individuals posing as new employees or as current employees requesting assistance to prevent getting fired. Sometimes attackers threaten, cajole, or beg to sway the target.

Another social engineering attack called the advance-fee fraud (AFF), and internationally known as the 4-1-9 fraud, is named after a section of the Nigerian penal code. The perpetrators of 4-1-9 schemes often name fictitious companies, such as the Nigerian National Petroleum Company. Alternatively, they may invent other entities, such as a bank, government agency, or a nongovernmental organization. See Figure 2-14 for a sample letter from this type of scheme. This scam is notorious for stealing funds from credulous individuals, first by requiring that people who wish to participate in the proposed money-making venture send money up front, and then by soliciting an endless series of fees. These 4-1-9 schemes are even suspected to involve kidnapping, extortion, and murder, and they have, according to the Secret Service, bilked over $100 million from unsuspecting Americans lured into

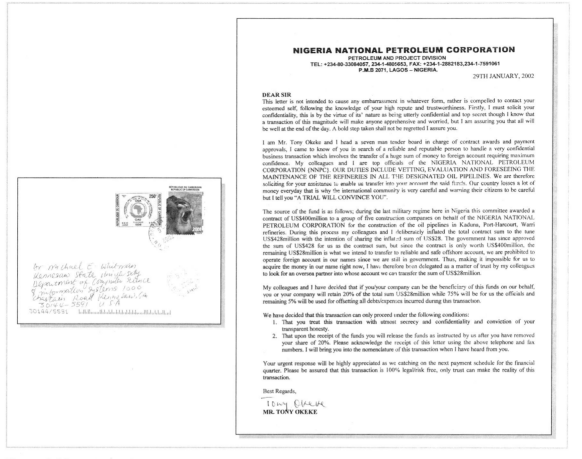

Figure 2-14 Example of a Nigerian 4-1-9 Fraud

Source: Course Technology/Cengage Learning

disclosing personal banking information. For more information, go to www.ftc.gov/bcp/edu/pubs/consumer/alerts/alt117.shtm.

The infamous hacker Kevin Mitnick (whose exploits are detailed in an Offline section in this chapter) once stated:

> *People are the weakest link. You can have the best technology; firewalls, intrusion-detection systems, biometric devices...and somebody can call an unsuspecting employee. That's all she wrote, baby. They got everything.*[42]

Phishing There are many other attacks that involve social engineering. One such is described by The Computer Emergency Response Team/Coordination Center (CERT/CC):

> *CERT/CC has received several incident reports concerning users receiving requests to take an action that results in the capturing of their password. The request could come in the form of an e-mail message, a broadcast, or a telephone call. The latest ploy instructs the user to run a "test" program, previously*

installed by the intruder, which will prompt the user for his or her password. When the user executes the program, the user's name and password are e-mailed to a remote site. These messages can appear to be from a site administrator or root. In reality, they may have been sent by an individual at a remote site, who is trying to gain access or additional access to the local machine via the user's account.[43]

While this attack may seem crude to experienced users, the fact is that *many* e-mail users have fallen for these tricks (refer to CERT Advisory CA-91.03). These tricks and similar variants are called phishing attacks. **Phishing** is an attempt to gain personal or financial information from an individual, usually by posing as a legitimate entity. Phishing attacks gained national recognition with the AOL phishing attacks that were widely reported in the late 1990s, in which individuals posing as AOL technicians attempted to get logon credentials from AOL subscribers. The practice became so widespread that AOL added a warning to all official correspondence that no one working at AOL would ever ask for password or billing information.

A variant is **spear phishing**, a label that applies to any highly targeted phishing attack. While normal phishing attacks target as many recipients as possible, a spear phisher sends a message that appears to be from an employer, a colleague, or other legitimate correspondent, to a small group or even one specific person. This attack is sometimes used to target those who use a certain product or Web site.

Phishing attacks use three primary techniques, often in combination with one another: URL manipulation, Web site forgery, and phone phishing. In URL manipulation, attackers send an HTML embedded e-mail message, or a hyperlink whose HTML code opens a forged Web site. For example, Figure 2-15 shows an e-mail that appears to have come from Regions Bank. Phishers usually use the names of large banks or retailers, ones that potential targets are more likely to have accounts with. In Figure 2-15 the link appears to be to RegionsNetOnline. But the HTML code actually links the user to a Web site in Poland, which only looks like it belongs to the bank. This is a very simple example; many phishing

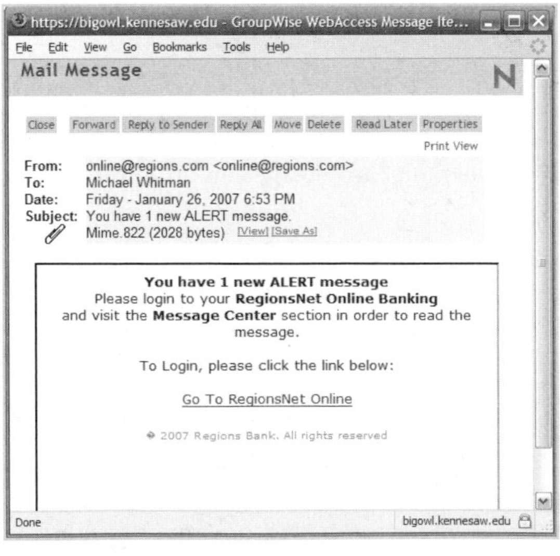

Figure 2-15 Phishing Example: Lure

Source: Course Technology/Cengage Learning

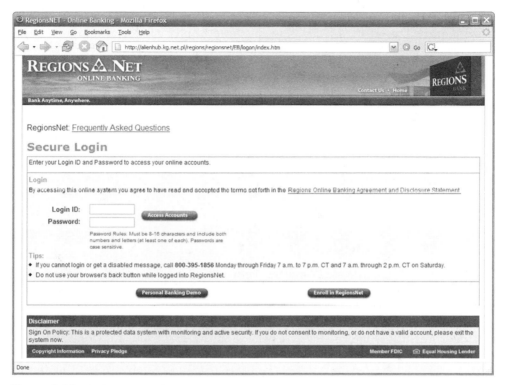

Figure 2-16 Phishing Example Fake Web Site

Source: Course Technology/Cengage Learning

attackers use very sophisticated simulated Web sites in their e-mails, usually copied from actual Web sites. Some of the companies more commonly used in phishing attacks are AOL, Bank of America, Microsoft, and Wachovia.

In the forged Web site in Figure 2-16, the page looks legitimate; indeed, when users click on either of the bottom two buttons—*Personal Banking Demo* or *Enroll in RegionsNet*, they are directed to the authentic bank Web page. The *Access Accounts* button, however, links to another simulated page that looks just like the real bank login Web page. When victims type their banking ID and password the attacker records that information and displays a message that the Web site is now offline. The attackers can use the recorded credentials to perform transactions, including funds transfers, bill payments, or loan requests.

Phone phishing is pure social engineering. The attacker calls a victim on the telephone and pretends to be someone they are not (a practice sometimes called pretexting) in order to gain access to private or confidential information such as health or employment records or financial information. They may impersonate someone who is known to the potential victim only by reputation.

Pharming

Pharming is "the redirection of legitimate Web traffic (e.g., browser requests) to an illegitimate site for the purpose of obtaining private information. Pharming often uses Trojans, worms, or other virus technologies to attack the Internet browser's address bar so that the valid URL typed by the user is modified to that of the illegitimate Web site. Pharming may also exploit the Domain Name System (DNS) by causing it to transform the legitimate host name into the invalid site's IP address; this form of pharming is also known as **DNS cache poisoning**."[44]

Timing Attack

A **timing attack** explores the contents of a Web browser's cache and stores a malicious cookie on the client's system. The cookie (which is a small quantity of data stored by the Web browser on the local system, at the direction of the Web server) can allow the designer to collect information on how to access password-protected sites.[45] Another attack by the same name involves the interception of cryptographic elements to determine keys and encryption algorithms.[46]

Secure Software Development

Systems consist of hardware, software, networks, data, procedures, and people using the system. Many of the information security issues described in this chapter have their root cause in the software elements of the system. Secure systems require secure, or at least securable, software. The development of systems and the software they use is often accomplished using a methodology, such as the systems development life cycle (SDLC). Many organizations recognize the need to include planning for security objectives in the SDLC they use to create systems, and have put in place procedures to create software that is more able to be deployed in a secure fashion. This approach to software development is known as software assurance, or SA.

Software Assurance and the SA Common Body of Knowledge

As you learned in Chapter 1, organizations are increasingly working to build security into the systems development life cycle, to prevent security problems before they begin. A national effort is underway to create a common body of knowledge focused on secure software development. The U.S. Department of Defense (DoD) launched a Software Assurance Initiative in 2003. This initial process was led by Joe Jarzombek and was endorsed and supported by the Department of Homeland Security (DHS), which joined the program in 2004. This program initiative resulted in the publication of the Secure Software Assurance (SwA) Common Body of Knowledge (CBK).[47] A working group drawn from industry, government, and academia was formed to examine two key questions:

1. What are the engineering activities or aspects of activities that are relevant to achieving secure software?

2. What knowledge is needed to perform these activities or aspects?

Based on the findings of this working group, and a host of existing external documents and standards, the SwA CBK was developed and published to serve as a guideline. While this work has not yet been adopted as a standard or even a policy requirement of government agencies, it serves as a strongly recommended guide to developing more secure applications.

The SwA CBK, which is a work in progress, contains the following sections:

- Nature of Dangers
- Fundamental Concepts and Principles

- Ethics, Law, and Governance
- Secure Software Requirements
- Secure Software Design
- Secure Software Construction
- Secure Software Verification, Validation, and Evaluation
- Secure Software Tools and Methods
- Secure Software Processes
- Secure Software Project Management
- Acquisition of Secure Software
- Secure Software Sustainment.[48]

The following sections provides insight into the stages that should be incorporated into the software SDLC.

Software Design Principles

Good software development should result in a finished product that meets all of its design specifications. Information security considerations are a critical component of those specifications, though that has not always been true. Leaders in software development J. H. Saltzer and M. D. Schroeder note that

> *The protection of information in computer systems [...and] the usefulness of a set of protection mechanisms depends upon the ability of a system to prevent security violations. In practice, producing a system at any level of functionality that actually does prevent all such unauthorized acts has proved to be extremely difficult. Sophisticated users of most systems are aware of at least one way to crash the system, denying other users authorized access to stored information. Penetration exercises involving a large number of different general-purpose systems all have shown that users can construct programs that can obtain unauthorized access to information stored within. Even in systems designed and implemented with security as an important objective, design and implementation flaws provide paths that circumvent the intended access constraints. Design and construction techniques that systematically exclude flaws are the topic of much research activity, but no complete method applicable to the construction of large general-purpose systems exists yet...[49]*

This statement could be about software development in the early part of the 21st century, but actually dates back to 1975, before information security and software assurance became critical factors for many organizations. In this same article, the authors provide insight into what are now commonplace security principles:

- *Economy of mechanism: Keep the design as simple and small as possible.*
- *Fail-safe defaults: Base access decisions on permission rather than exclusion.*
- *Complete mediation: Every access to every object must be checked for authority.*
- *Open design: The design should not be secret, but rather depend on the possession of keys or passwords.*

- *Separation of privilege: Where feasible, a protection mechanism should require two keys to unlock, rather than one.*

- *Least privilege: Every program and every user of the system should operate using the least set of privileges necessary to complete the job.*

- *Least common mechanism: Minimize mechanisms (or shared variables) common to more than one user and depended on by all users.*

- *Psychological acceptability: It is essential that the human interface be designed for ease of use, so that users routinely and automatically apply the protection mechanisms correctly.*[50]

Many of these topics are discussed in the following sections and in later chapters of this text.

Software Development Security Problems

Some software development problems that result in software that is difficult or impossible to deploy in a secure fashion have been identified as "deadly sins in software security."[51] These twenty problem areas in software development (which is also called software engineering) were originally categorized by John Viega, upon request of Amit Youran, who at the time was the Director of the Department of Homeland Security's National Cyber Security Division. These problem areas are described in the following sections.

Buffer Overruns Buffers are used to manage mismatches in the processing rates between two entities involved in a communication process. A **buffer overrun** (or **buffer overflow**) is an application error that occurs when more data is sent to a program buffer than it is designed to handle. During a buffer overrun, an attacker can make the target system execute instructions, or the attacker can take advantage of some other unintended consequence of the failure. Sometimes this is limited to a denial-of-service attack. In any case, data on the attacked system loses integrity.[52] In 1998, Microsoft encountered the following buffer overflow problem:

> *Microsoft acknowledged that if you type a res:// URL (a Microsoft-devised type of URL) which is longer than 256 characters in Internet Explorer 4.0, the browser will crash. No big deal, except that anything after the 256th character can be executed on the computer. This maneuver, known as a buffer overrun, is just about the oldest hacker trick in the book. Tack some malicious code (say, an executable version of the Pentium-crashing FooF code) onto the end of the URL, and you have the makings of a disaster.*[53]

Command Injection Command injection problems occur when user input is passed directly to a compiler or interpreter. The underlying issue is the developer's failure to ensure that command input is validated before it is used in the program. Perhaps the simplest example involves the Windows command shell:

```
@echo off
set /p myVar="Enter the string>"
set someVar=%myVar%
echo %somevar%
```

These simple commands ask the user to provide a string and then simply set another variable to the value and then display it. However, an attacker could use the command chaining character "&" to append other commands to the string the user provides (Hello&del*.*).[54]

Cross-site Scripting Cross site scripting (or XSS) occurs when an application running on a Web server gathers data from a user in order to steal it. An attacker can use weaknesses in the Web server environment to insert commands into a user's browser session, so that users ostensibly connected to a friendly Web server are, in fact, sending information to a hostile server. This allows the attacker to acquire valuable information, such as account credentials, account numbers, or other critical data. Often an attacker encodes a malicious link and places it in the target server, making it look less suspicious. After the data is collected by the hostile application, it sends what appears to be a valid response from the intended server.[55]

Failure to Handle Errors What happens when a system or application encounters an scenario that it is not prepared to handle? Does it attempt to complete the operation (reading or writing data or performing calculations)? Does it issue a cryptic message that only a programmer could understand? Or does it simply stop functioning? Failure to handle errors can cause a variety of unexpected system behaviors. Programmers are expected to anticipate problems and prepare their application code to handle them.

Failure to Protect Network Traffic With the growing popularity of wireless networking comes a corresponding increase in the risk that wirelessly transmitted data will be intercepted. Most wireless networks are installed and operated with little or no protection for the information that is broadcast between the client and the network wireless access point. This is especially true of public networks found in coffee shops, bookstores, and hotels. Without appropriate encryption (such as that afforded by WPA), attackers can intercept and view your data.

Traffic on a wired network is also vulnerable to interception in some situations. On networks using hubs instead of switches, any user can install a packet sniffer and collect communications to and from users on that network. Periodic scans for unauthorized packet sniffers, unauthorized connections to the network, and general awareness of the threat can mitigate this problem.

Failure to Store and Protect Data Securely Storing and protecting data securely is a large enough issue to be the core subject of this entire text. Programmers are responsible for integrating access controls into, and keeping secret information out of, programs. Access controls, the subject of later chapters, regulate who, what, when, where, and how individuals and systems interact with data. Failure to properly implement sufficiently strong access controls makes the data vulnerable. Overly strict access controls hinder business users in the performance of their duties, and as a result the controls may be administratively removed or bypassed.

The integration of secret information—such as the "hard coding" of passwords, encryption keys, or other sensitive information—can put that information at risk of disclosure.

Failure to Use Cryptographically Strong Random Numbers Most modern cryptosystems, like many other computer systems, use random number generators. However, a decision support system using random and pseudo-random numbers for Monte Carlo method forecasting does not require the same degree of rigor and the same need for true randomness as a system that seeks to implement cryptographic procedures. These "random" number generators use a mathematical algorithm, based on a seed value and another other system component (such as the computer clock) to simulate a random number. Those who understand the workings of such a "random" number generator can predict particular values at particular times.

Format String Problems Computer languages often are equipped with built-in capabilities to reformat data while they're outputting it. The formatting instructions are usually written as a "format string." Unfortunately, some programmers may use data from untrusted sources as a format string.[56] An attacker may embed characters that are meaningful as formatting directives (e.g., %x, %d, %p, etc.) into malicious input; if this input is then interpreted by the program as formatting directives (such as an argument to the C printf function), the attacker may be able to access information or overwrite very targeted portions of the program's stack with data of the attacker's choosing.[57]

Neglecting Change Control Developers use a process known as **change control** to ensure that the working system delivered to users represents the intent of the developers. Early in the development process, change control ensures that developers do not work at cross purposes by altering the same programs or parts of programs at the same time. Once the system is in production, change control processes ensure that only authorized changes are introduced and that all changes are adequately tested before being released.

Improper File Access If an attacker changes the expected location of a file by intercepting and modifying a program code call, the attacker can force a program to use files other than the ones the program is supposed to use. This type of attack could be used to either substitute a bogus file for a legitimate file (as in password files), or trick the system into running a malware executable. The potential for damage or disclosure is great, so it is critical to protect not only the location of the files but also the method and communications channels by which these files are accessed.

Improper Use of SSL Programmers use Secure Sockets Layer (SSL) to transfer sensitive data, such as credit card numbers and other personal information, between a client and server. While most programmers assume that using SSL guarantees security, unfortunately they more often than not mishandle this technology. SSL and its successor, Transport Layer Security (TLS), both need certificate validation to be truly secure. Failure to use Hypertext Transfer Protocol Secure (HTTPS), to validate the certificate authority and then validate the certificate itself, or to validate the information against a certificate revocation list (CRL), can compromise the security of SSL traffic.

Information Leakage One of the most common methods of obtaining inside and classified information is directly or indirectly from an individual, usually an employee. The World War II military poster warned that "loose lips sink ships," emphasizing the risk to naval deployments from enemy attack should the sailors, marines, or their families disclose the movements of these vessels. It was a widely-shared fear that the enemy had civilian operatives waiting in bars and shops at common Navy ports of call, just waiting for the troops to drop hints about where they were going and when. By warning employees against disclosing information, organizations can protect the secrecy of their operation.

Integer Bugs (Overflows/Underflows) Although paper and pencil can deal with arbitrary numbers of digits, the binary representations used by computers are of a particular fixed length. For example, adding 1 to 32,767 should produce 32,768, but in computer arithmetic with 16-bit signed integers, the result is –32,768. An underflow can occur when, for example, you subtract 5 from negative 32,767, which returns the incorrect result +32,764, because the largest negative integer that can be represented in 16 bits is negative 32,768.

> **Integer bugs** *fall into four broad classes: overflows, underflows, truncations, and signedness errors. Integer bugs are usually exploited indirectly—that is, triggering an integer bug enables an attacker to corrupt other areas of memory, gaining control of an application.[58] The memory allocated for a value could be exceeded, if that value is greater than expected, with the extra bits written into other locations. The system may then experience unexpected consequences, which could be miscalculations, errors, crashing or other problems. Even though integer bugs are often used to build a buffer overflow or other memory corruption attack, integer bugs are not just a special case of memory corruption bugs.[59]*

Race Conditions A race condition is a failure of a program that occurs when an unexpected ordering of events in the execution of the program results in a conflict over access to the same system resource. This conflict does not need to involve streams of code inside the program, since current operating systems and processor technology automatically break a program into multiple threads that can be executed simultaneously. If the threads that result from this process share any resources, they may interfere with each other.[60]

A race condition occurs, for example, when a program creates a temporary file, and an attacker is able to replace it between the time it is created and the time it is used. A race condition can also occur when information is stored in multiple memory threads if one thread stores information in the wrong memory location, by accident or intent.

SQL Injection SQL injection occurs when developers fail to properly validate user input before using it to query a relational database. For example, a fairly innocuous program fragment expects the user to input a user ID and then perform a SQL query against the USERS table to retrieve the associated name:

```
Accept USER-ID from console;
SELECT USERID, NAME FROM USERS WHERE USERID = USER-ID;
```

This is very straightforward SQL syntax and, when used correctly, displays the userid and name. The problem is that the string accepted from the user is passed directly the SQL database server as part of the SQL command. What if an attacker enters the string "JOE OR 1=1"? This string includes some valid SQL syntax that will return all rows from the table where either the user id is "JOE" or "1=1." Since one is always equal to one, the system returns all user ids and names. The possible effects of this "injection" of SQL code of the attacker's choosing into the program are not limited to improper access to information—what if the attacker included SQL commands to drop the USERS table, or even shut down the database?[61]

Trusting Network Address Resolution The Domain Name System (DNS) is a function of the World Wide Web that converts a URL (Uniform Resource Locator) like *www.course.com* into the IP address of the Web server host. This distributed model is vulnerable to attack or "poisoning." DNS cache poisoning involves compromising a DNS server and then changing the valid IP address associated with a domain name into one which the attacker chooses, usually a fake Web site designed to obtain personal information or one that accrues a benefit to the attacker, for example, redirecting shoppers from a competitor's Web site. It is usually more sinister, for example, a simulated banking site used for a phishing attack that harvests online banking information.

How does someone get this fake information into the DNS server? Aside from a direct attack against a root DNS server, most attempts are made against organizational primary and secondary DNS servers, local to the organization and part of the distributed DNS system. Other attacks attempt to compromise the DNS servers further up the DNS distribution mode—those of Internet service providers or backbone connectivity providers. The DNS relies on a process of automated updates which can be exploited. Attackers most commonly compromise segments of the DNS by either attacking the name of the nameserver and substituting their own DNS primary name server, by incorrectly updating an individual record, or by responding before an actual DNS can. In the last type of attack, if the attacker discovers a delay in a name server (or can introduce one, as in a denial of service attack) they can set up another server to respond as if it were the actual DNS server, before the real DNS server can. The client accepts the first set of information it receives and is directed to that IP address.

Unauthenticated Key Exchange One of the biggest challenges in private key systems, which involve two users sharing the same key, is securely getting the key to the other party. Sometimes an "out of band" courier is used, but other times a public key system, which uses both a public and private key, is used to exchange the key. But what if the person who receives a key that was copied onto a USB device and shipped doesn't really work for the company, but was simply expecting that particular delivery and intercepted it? The same scenario can occur on the Internet, where an attacker writes a variant of a public key system and places it out as "freeware," or corrupts or intercepts the function of someone else's public key encryption system, perhaps by posing as a public key repository.

Use of Magic URLs and Hidden Forms HTTP is a stateless protocol where the computer programs on either end of the communication channel cannot rely on a guaranteed delivery of any message. This makes it difficult for software developers to track a user's exchanges with a Web site over multiple interactions. Too often sensitive state information is simply included in a "magic" URL (for example, the authentication ID is passed as a parameter in the URL for the exchanges that will follow) or included in hidden form fields on the HTML page. If this information is stored as plain text, an attacker can harvest the information from a magic URL as it travels across the network, or use scripts on the client to modify information in hidden form fields. Depending on the structure of the application, the harvested or modified information can be used in spoofing or hijacking attacks, or to change the way the application operates (for example, if an item's price is kept in a hidden form field, the attacker could arrange to buy that item for $.01).[62]

Use of Weak Password-Based Systems Failure to require sufficient password strength, and to control incorrect password entry, is a serious security issue. Password policy

It is estimated that to brute force crack a password, a computer will need to perform a maximum of n^k operations (n^k), where n is the length of the character set and k is the length of the password. On average it will only need to perform half that amount.

Using a standard alphabet set (case *in*sensitive) without numbers or special characters = 26 characters in set, on an average 2008-era dual-core PC performing 30,000 MIPS (million instructions per second):

Password Length	Maximum Number of Operations (guesses)	Maximum Time to Crack
8	208,827,064,576	7.0 seconds
9	5,429,503,678,976	3.0 minutes
10	141,167,095,653,376	1.3 hours
11	3,670,344,486,987,780	34.0 hours
12	95,428,956,661,682,200	36.8 days
13	2,481,152,873,203,740,000	2.6 years
14	64,509,974,703,297,200,000	68.2 years
15	1,677,259,342,285,730,000,000	1,772.9 years
16	43,608,742,899,428,900,000,000	46,094.1 years

Using an extended data set with case sensitive letters (upper and lower case), numbers, and 20 special characters = 82 characters in set, on the same 2008-era dual-core PC:

Password Length	Maximum Number of Operations (guesses)	Maximum Time to Crack
8	2,044,140,858,654,980	18.9 hours
9	167,619,550,409,708,000	64.7 days
10	13,744,803,133,596,100,000	14.5 years
11	1,127,073,856,954,880,000,000	1,191.3 years
12	92,420,056,270,299,900,000,000	97,687.4 years
13	7,578,444,614,164,590,000,000,000	8,010,363.4 years
14	621,432,458,361,496,000,000,000,000	656,849,799.6 years
15	50,957,461,585,642,700,000,000,000,000	53,861,683,563.4 years
16	4,178,511,850,022,700,000,000,000,000,000	4,416,658,052,197.2 years

Table 2-3 Password Power

can specify the number and type of characters, the frequency of mandatory changes, and even the reusability of old passwords. Similarly, a system administrator can regulate the permitted number of incorrect password entries that are submitted and further improve the level of protection. Systems that do not validate passwords, or store passwords in easy-to-access locations, are ripe for attack. As shown in Table 2-3, the strength of a password determines its ability to withstand a brute force attack. Using non-standard password components (like the 8.3 rule—at least 8 characters, with at least one letter, number, and non-alphanumeric character) can greatly enhance the strength of the password.

Poor Usability Employees prefer doing things the easy way. When faced with an "official way" of performing a task and an "unofficial way"—which is easier—they prefer the easier method. The only way to address this issue is to only provide one way—the secure way! Integrating security and usability, adding training and awareness, and ensuring solid controls all contribute to the security of information. Allowing users to default to easier, more usable solutions will inevitably lead to loss.

Selected Readings

- The journal article "Enemy at the Gates: Threats to Information Security" by Michael Whitman was published in *Communications of the ACM* in August 2003 and can be found on pages 91–96. An abstract is available from the ACM Digital Library at *www.acm.org*. Journal access may be available through your local library.

- *The Art of War* by Sun Tzu. Many translations and editions are widely available, both print and online.

- 24 *Deadly Sins of Software Security—Programming Flaws and How to Fix Them* by M. Howard, D. LeBlanc, and J. Viega is published by McGraw-Hill/Osborne Publishing.

- "The 14th Annual CSI Computer Crime and Security Survey: Executive Summary," published in December 2009 by Robert Richardson, the Executive Director of CSI, can be downloaded from *www.gocsi.com*.

Chapter Summary

- Information security performs four important functions:
  - Protecting an organization's ability to function
  - Enabling the safe operation of applications implemented on the organization's IT systems
  - Protecting the data an organization collects and uses
  - Safeguarding the technology assets in use at an organization

- To make sound decisions about information security, management must be informed about threats to its people, applications, data, and information systems.

- Threats or dangers facing an organization's people, information, and systems fall into the following fourteen general categories:

- Replace list with:
  - Compromises to intellectual property
  - Deliberate software attacks
  - Deviations in quality of service
  - Espionage or trespass
  - Forces of nature
  - Human error or failure

- Information extortion
- Missing, inadequate, or incomplete organizational policy or planning
- Missing, inadequate, or incomplete controls
- Sabotage or vandalism
- Theft
- Technical hardware failures or errors
- Technical software failures or errors
- Technological obsolescence

■ An attack is a deliberate act that takes advantage of a vulnerability to compromise a controlled system. It is accomplished by a threat agent that damages or steals an organization's information or physical asset. A vulnerability is an identified weakness in a controlled system, where controls are not present or are no longer effective.

■ Software assurance (SA)—a discipline within the area of computer security—attempts to identify the activities involved in creating secure systems.

■ Poor software development practices can introduce significant risk but by developing sound development practices, change control and quality assurance into the process, overall software quality and the security performance of software can be greatly enhanced.

Review Questions

1. Why is information security a management problem? What can management do that technology cannot?

2. Why is data the most important asset an organization possesses? What other assets in the organization require protection?

3. Which management groups are responsible for implementing information security to protect the organization's ability to function?

4. Has the implementation of networking technology created more or less risk for businesses that use information technology? Why?

5. What is information extortion? Describe how such an attack can cause losses, using an example not found in the text.

6. Why do employees constitute one of the greatest threats to information security?

7. What measures can individuals take to protect against shoulder surfing?

8. How has the perception of the hacker changed over recent years? What is the profile of a hacker today?

9. What is the difference between a skilled hacker and an unskilled hacker (other than skill levels)? How does the protection against each differ?

10. What are the various types of malware? How do worms differ from viruses? Do Trojan horses carry viruses or worms?

11. Why does polymorphism cause greater concern than traditional malware? How does it affect detection?

12. What is the most common form of violation of intellectual property? How does an organization protect against it? What agencies fight it?

13. What are the various types of *force majeure*? Which type might be of greatest concern to an organization in Las Vegas? Oklahoma City? Miami? Los Angeles?

14. How does technological obsolescence constitute a threat to information security? How can an organization protect against it?

15. Does the intellectual property owned by an organization usually have value? If so, how can attackers threaten that value?

16. What are the types of password attacks? What can a systems administrator do to protect against them?

17. What is the difference between a denial-of-service attack and a distributed denial-of-service attack? Which is more dangerous? Why?

18. For a sniffer attack to succeed, what must the attacker do? How can an attacker gain access to a network to use the sniffer system?

19. What methods does a social engineering hacker use to gain information about a user's login id and password? How would this method differ if it were targeted towards an administrator's assistant versus a data-entry clerk?

20. What is a buffer overflow, and how is it used against a Web server?

Exercises

1. Consider the statement: an individual threat agent, like a hacker, can be a factor in more than one threat category. If a hacker hacks into a network, copies a few files, defaces the Web page, and steals credit card numbers, how many different threat categories does this attack fall into?

2. Using the Web, research Mafiaboy's exploits. When and how did he compromise sites? How was he caught?

3. Search the Web for the "The Official Phreaker's Manual." What information contained in this manual might help a security administrator to protect a communications system?

4. The chapter discussed many threats and vulnerabilities to information security. Using the Web, find at least two other sources of information on threat and vulnerabilities. Begin with *www.securityfocus.com* and use a keyword search on "threats."

5. Using the categories of threats mentioned in this chapter, as well as the various attacks described, review several current media sources and identify examples of each.

Case Exercises

Soon after the board of directors meeting, Charlie was promoted to Chief Information Security Officer, a new position that reports to the CIO, Gladys Williams, and that was created to provide leadership for SLS's efforts to improve its security profile.

Questions:

1. How do Fred, Gladys, and Charlie perceive the scope and scale of the new information security effort?

2. How will Fred measure success when he evaluates Gladys' performance for this project? How will he evalute Charlie's performance?

3. Which of the threats discussed in this chapter should receive Charlie's attention early in his planning process?

Endnotes

1. Levine, Daniel S. "One on One with Charles Cresson Wood of InfoSecurity Infrastructure." *Techbiz Online*. 12 October 2001. Accessed 1 March 2010 from *www.sanfrancisco.bizjournals.com/sanfrancisco/stories/2001/10/15/newscolumn7.html*.

2. Sun-Tzu. "The Principles of Warfare—The Art of War," Chapter Three: Planning Attacks. Accessed 1 March 2010 from *www.sonshi.com/sun3.html*.

3. Internet World Stats. "Internet Usage Statistics: The Internet Big Picture, World Internet Users and Population Stats." Accessed 24 February 2010 from *www.internetworldstats.com/stats.htm*.

4. Whitman, Michael. "Enemy at the Gates: Threats to Information Security." *Communications of the ACM*, 46, no. 8 (August 2003), pp. 91–96.

5. Richardson, R. "14th Annual CSI Computer Crime and Security Survey: Executive Summary." December 2009. Accessed 2 February 2010 from *www.gocsi.com*

6. Whitman, Michael. "Enemy at the Gates: Threats to Information Security." *Communications of the ACM*, 46, no. 8 (August 2003), pp. 91–96.

7. FOLDOC. "Intellectual Property." *FOLDOC Online*. 27 March 1997. Accessed 1 March 2010 from *http://foldoc.org/index.cgi?query=intellectual+property*.

8. Patton, Natalie. "Bootlegged Software Could Cost Community College." *Las Vegas Review Journal Online*. 18 September 1997. Accessed 1 March 2010 from *www.lvrj.com/lvrj_home/1997/Sep-18-Thu-1997/news/6072867.html*.

9. Hopper, D. Ian. "'Mafiaboy' Faces up to 3 Years in Prison." *CNN.com Online*. 19 April 2000. Accessed 1 March 2010 from *archives.cnn.com/2000/TECH/computing/04/19/dos.charges/index.html*.

10. Warner, Bernhard. "Internet Firm Hacked Out of Business." *Tech Update Online*. 1 February 2002. Accessed 1 March 2002 from *http://news.zdnet.com/2100-10532_22-296698.html*.

11. Kehoe, Brendan P. *Zen and the Art of the Internet*, 1st Edition. January 1992. Accessed 1 March 2010 from *www.cs.indiana.edu/docproject/zen/zen-1.0_10.html#SEC91*.

12. Merriam-Webster. "hackers." *Merriam-Webster Online*. Accessed 1 March 2010 from *www.merriam-webster.com/dictionary/hacker*.

13. Rosencrance, Linda. "Teen Hacker 'Mafiaboy' Sentenced." *ComputerWorld Online*. Accessed 1 March 2010 from *www.computerworld.com/securitytopics/security/story/0,10801,63823,00.html*.

14. Chowdhry, Pankaj. "The Gibraltar Hack: Anatomy of a Break-in." *PCWeek* 16, no. 41 (1999): pp. 1, 22.

15. Excerpt from *Takedown*. "Kevin Mitnick." *Takedown Online*. Accessed 1 Mar 2010 from *www.takedown.com/bio/mitnick1.html*.

16. Mitnick, Kevin. *The Art of Deception: Controlling the Human Element of Security*. 2002. Wiley.

17. Kennedy, James T. "Internet Intricacies: Don't Get Caught in the Net." *Contingency Planning & Management* 3, no.1, p. 12.

18. "Rebuffed Internet Extortionist Posts Stolen Credit Card Data." *CNN Online*. 10 January 2000. Accessed 1 March 2010 from *http://attrition.org/dataloss/2000/01/cduniv01.html*.

19. Consumer Affairs. Help Net Security. "Express Scripts Extortion Scheme Widens." 30 September 2009. Accessed 15 April 2010 from *www.consumeraffairs.com/news04/2009/09/express_scripts_breach.html*.

20. Attrition.org. "Commentary." Accessed 1 March 2010 from *http://attrition.org/security/commentary/sans.html*

21. Costello, Sam. "Attrition.org Stops Mirroring Web Site Defacements." *ComputerWorld Online*. 22 May 2001. Accessed 1 March 2010 from *www.computerworld.com/securitytopics/ security/story/0,10801,60769,00.html*.

22. Infoshop News. "Fighting the Fascists Using Direct Action Hacktivism." 28 March 2010. Accessed 15 April 2010 from *http://news.infoshop.org/article.php?story=20100328011601751*.

23. Denning, Dorothy E. "Activism, Hacktivism, and Cyberterrorism: The Internet as a Tool for Influencing Foreign Policy." *Info War Online*. 4 February 2000. Accessed 1 March 2010 from *www.iwar.org.uk/cyberterror/resources/denning.htm*.

24. RKnake, Robert K. *Cyberterrorism Hype v. Fact*. Council on Foreign Relations. Accessed 1 March 2010 from *www.cfr.org/publication/21434/cyberterrorism_hype_v_fact.html*.

25. Elmusharaf, M. "Cyber Terrorism: The New kind of Terrorism." *Computer Crime Research Center Online*. 8 April 2004. Accessed 1 March 2010 from *www.crimeresearch.org/articles/CyberTerrorismnewkindTerrorism/*.

26. Lemos, R. "Assault on Net servers fails" *C|Net News.com*. October 22, 2002. Accessed 1 March 2010 from *news.com.com/Assault+on+Net+servers+fails/2100-1001_3-963005.html*.

27. "Murphy's Laws Site." Accessed 1 March 2010 from *www.murphys-laws.com/*.

28. Wolfe, Alexander "Intel Preps Plan to Bust Bugs in Pentium MPUs." *Electronic Engineering Times* no. 960 (June 1997): p. 1.

29. Taylor, Roger. "Intel to Launch New Chip Despite Bug Reports." *Financial Times* (London), no. 25 (June 1998), p. 52.

30. Trusecure. "Trusecure Successfully Defends Customers Against Goner Virus." *Trusecure Online*. 18 December 2001. Accessed 1 March 2010 from *www.findarticles.com/p/articles/mi_m0EIN/is_2001_Dec_18/ai_80877835*.

31. Redwine Samuel T., Jr. (Editor). *Software Assurance: A Guide to the Common Body of Knowledge to Produce, Acquire, and Sustain Secure Software Version 1.1.* US Department of Homeland Security, September 2006.

32. Redwine Samuel T., Jr. (Editor). *Software Assurance: A Guide to the Common Body of Knowledge to Produce, Acquire, and Sustain Secure Software Version 1.1.* US Department of Homeland Security, September 2006.

33. Redwine Samuel T., Jr. (Editor). *Software Assurance: A Guide to the Common Body of Knowledge to Produce, Acquire, and Sustain Secure Software Version 1.1.* US Department of Homeland Security, September 2006.

34. SANS Institute. "Back Door NSA Glossary of Terms Used in Security and Intrusion Detection." *SANS Institute Online.* Accessed 1 March 2010 from *www.sans.org/resources/glossary.php.*

35. SANS Institute. "Consensus Roadmap for Defeating Distributed Denial of Service Attacks: A Project of the Partnership for Critical Infrastructure Security." *SANS Institute Online.* 23 February 2000. Accessed 1 March 2010 from *www.sans.org/dosstep/roadmap.php.*

36. Brooke, Paul. "DDoS: Internet Weapons of Mass Destruction." *Network Computing* 12, no. 1 (January 2001): p. 67.

37. Trend Micro. "WORM_MYDOOM.A." Accessed 1 March 2010 from *www.trend micro.com/vinfo/virusencyclo/default5.asp?VName=WORM_MYDOOM.A.*

38. Webopedia. "IP spoofing." *Webopedia Online.* 4 June 2002. Accessed 1 March 2010 from *www.webopedia.com/TERM/I/IP_spoofing.html.*

39. Bhansali, Bhavin Bharat. "Man-In-The-Middle Attack: A Brief." *SANS Institute Online.* 16 February 2001. Accessed 1 March 2010 from *www.giac.org/practical/gsec/Bhavin_Bhansali_GSEC.pdf.*

40. Pearce, James. "Security Expert Warns of MP3 Danger." *ZDNet News Online.* 18 March 2002. Accessed 1 March 2010 from *zdnet.com.com/2100-1105-861995.html.*

41. Webopedia. "sniffer." *Webopedia Online.* 5 February 2002. Accessed 1 March 2010 from *http://www.webopedia.com/TERM/s/sniffer.html.*

42. Abreu, Elinor. "Kevin Mitnick Bares All." *Network WorldFusion News Online.* 28 September 2000. Accessed 1 March 2010 from *www.nwfusion.com/news/2000/0928mitnick.html.*

43. CERT Advisory CA-1991-03 Unauthorized Password Change Requests Via Email Messages.

44. Redwine, Samuel T., Jr. (Editor). *Software Assurance: A Guide to the Common Body of Knowledge to Produce, Acquire, and Sustain Secure Software Version 1.1.* US Department of Homeland Security, September 2006.

45. Princeton University. "Standard Feature of Web Browser Design Leaves Opening For Privacy Attacks." *Science Daily Online.* 8 December 2000. Accessed 1 March 2010 from *www.sciencedaily.com/releases/2000/12/001208074325.htm.*

46. Hachez, Gaël, Koeune, François, and Quisquater, Jean-Jacques. "Timing attack: What can be achieved by a powerful adversary?" Proceedings of the 20th Symposium on Information Theory in the Benelux, May 1999, 63–70.

47. Redwine, Samuel T., Jr. (Editor). *Software Assurance: A Guide to the Common Body of Knowledge to Produce, Acquire, and Sustain Secure Software Version 1.1.* US Department of Homeland Security, September 2006.

48. Redwine, Samuel T., Jr. (Editor). *Software Assurance: A Guide to the Common Body of Knowledge to Produce, Acquire, and Sustain Secure Software Version 1.1.* US Department of Homeland Security, September 2006.

49. Saltzer, J. H., and Schroeder, M. D. "The protection of information in computer systems," *Proceedings of the IEEE*, vol. 63, no. 9 (1975), pp. 1278–1308, Accessed 1 March 2010 from *http://cap-lore.com/CapTheory/ProtInf/*

50. Martin, J. *Security, Accuracy, and Privacy in Computer Systems.* Englewood Cliffs, NJ: Prentice Hall, 1973. (I-A1, SFR) I

51. Howard, M., LeBlanc, D., and Viega, J. *19 Deadly Sins of Software Security–Programming Flaws and How to Fix them.* 2005. New York: McGraw-Hill/Osborne.

52. Webopedia. "buffer overflow." *Webopedia Online.* 29 July 2003. Accessed 1 March 2010 from *www.webopedia.com/TERM/b/buffer_overflow.html.*

53. Spanbauer, Scott. "Pentium Bug, Meet the IE 4.0 Flaw." *PC World* 16, no. 2 (February 1998): 55.

54. Austin, Richard. Conversations on the *19 Deadly Sins of Software Security–Programming Flaws and How to Fix Them.* 28 February 2007.

55. *cgisecurity.com* "The Cross Site Scripting FAQ." Accessed 1 March 2010 from *www.cgisecurity.com/articles/xss-faq.shtml.*

56. Wheeler, D. "Write It Secure: Format Strings and Locale Filtering." Accessed 1 March 2010 from *www.dwheeler.com/essays/write_it_secure_1.html.*

57. Austin, Richard. Conversations on *19 Deadly Sins of Software Security–Programming Flaws and How to Fix Them.* 28 February 2007.

58. Brumley, D., Tzi-cker, C., Johnson, R., Lin, H., and Song, D. "RICH: Automatically Protecting Against Integer-Based Vulnerabilities." Accessed 1 March 2010 from *www.cs.berkeley.edu/.../efficient_detection_integer-based_attacks.pdf.*

59. Brumley, D., Tzi-cker, C., Johnson, R., Lin, H., and Song, D. "RICH: Automatically Protecting Against Integer-Based Vulnerabilities." Accessed 1 March 2010 from *www.cs.berkeley.edu/.../efficient_detection_integer-based_attacks.pdf.*

60. Wheeler, D. A. "Secure programmer: Prevent race conditions." IBM. Accessed 1 March 2010 from *www-128.ibm.com/developerworks/linux/library/l-sprace.html>*

61. Austin, Richard. *Conversations on the 19 Deadly Sins.* 28 February 2007.

62. Austin, Richard. *Conversations on the 19 Deadly Sins.* 28 February 2007.

chapter 3

Legal, Ethical, and Professional Issues in Information Security

In civilized life, law floats in a sea of ethics.

EARL WARREN, CHIEF JUSTICE OF
THE UNITED STATES, 12 NOVEMBER 1962

Henry Magruder made a mistake—he left a CD at the coffee station. Later, when Iris Majwubu was topping off her mug with fresh tea, hoping to wrap up her work on the current SQL code module before it was time to go home, she saw the unlabeled CD on the counter. Being the helpful sort, she picked it up, intending to return it to the person who'd left it behind.

Expecting to find perhaps the latest device drivers, or someone's work from the development team's office, Iris slipped the disk into the drive of her computer and ran a virus scan on its contents before opening the file explorer program. She had been correct in assuming the CD contained data files, and lots of them. She opened a file at random: names, addresses, and Social Security numbers appeared on her screen. These were not the test records she expected; they looked more like critical payroll data. Concerned, she found a readme.txt file and opened it. It read:

Jill, see files on this disc. Hope they meet your expectations. Wire money to account as arranged. Rest of data sent on payment.

Iris realized that someone was selling sensitive company data to an outside information broker. She looked back at the directory listing and saw that the files spanned the range of every department at Sequential Label and Supply—everything from customer lists to shipping invoices. She saw one file that appeared to contain the credit card numbers of every Web customer the company supplied. She opened another file and saw that it only contained about half of the relevant data. Whoever did this had split the data into two parts. That made sense: payment on delivery of the first half.

Now, who did this belong to? She opened up the file properties option on the readme.txt file. The file owner was listed as "hmagruder." That must be Henry Magruder, the developer two cubes over in the next aisle. Iris pondered her next action.

LEARNING OBJECTIVES:

Upon completion of this material, you should be able to:

- Describe the functions of and relationships among laws, regulations, and professional organizations in information security
- Differentiate between laws and ethics
- Identify major national laws that affect the practice of information security
- Explain the role of culture as it applies to ethics in information security

Introduction

As a future information security professional, you must understand the scope of an organization's legal and ethical responsibilities. The information security professional plays an important role in an organization's approach to managing liability for privacy and security risks. In the modern litigious societies of the world, sometimes laws are enforced in civil courts, where large damages can be awarded to plaintiffs who bring suits against organizations. Sometimes these damages are punitive—assessed as a deterrent. To minimize liability and reduce risks from electronic and physical threats, and to reduce all losses from legal action, information security practitioners must thoroughly understand the current legal environment, stay current with laws and regulations, and watch for new and emerging issues. By educating the management and employees of an organization on their legal and ethical obligations and the proper use of information technology and information security, security professionals can help keep an organization focused on its primary objectives.

In the first part of this chapter, you learn about the legislation and regulations that affect the management of information in an organization. In the second part, you learn about the ethical issues related to information security, and about several professional organizations with established codes of ethics. Use this chapter as both a reference to the legal aspects of information security and as an aide in planning your professional career.

Law and Ethics in Information Security

In general, people elect to trade some aspects of personal freedom for social order. As Jean-Jacques Rousseau explains in *The Social Contract, or Principles of Political Right*[1], the rules the members of a society create to balance the individual rights to self-determination against the needs of the society as a whole are called *laws*. **Laws** are rules that mandate or prohibit certain behavior; they are drawn from **ethics**, which define socially acceptable behaviors. The key difference between laws and ethics is that laws carry the authority of a governing body, and ethics do not. Ethics in turn are based on **cultural mores**: the fixed moral attitudes or customs of a particular group. Some ethical standards are universal. For example, murder, theft, assault, and arson are actions that deviate from ethical and legal codes throughout the world.

Organizational Liability and the Need for Counsel

What if an organization does not demand or even encourage strong ethical behavior from its employees? What if an organization does not behave ethically? Even if there is no breach of criminal law, there can still be liability. **Liability** is the legal obligation of an entity that extends beyond criminal or contract law; it includes the legal obligation to make **restitution**, or to compensate for wrongs committed. The bottom line is that if an employee, acting with or without the authorization of the employer, performs an illegal or unethical act that causes some degree of harm, the employer can be held financially liable for that action. An organization increases its liability if it refuses to take measures known as due care. **Due care** standards are met when an organization makes sure that every employee knows what is acceptable or unacceptable behavior, and knows the consequences of illegal or unethical actions. **Due diligence** requires that an organization make a valid effort to protect others and continually maintains this level of effort. Given the Internet's global reach, those who could be injured or wronged by an organization's employees could be anywhere in the world. Under the U.S. legal system, any court can assert its authority over an individual or organization if it can establish **jurisdiction**—that is, the court's right to hear a case if a wrong is committed in its territory or involves its citizenry. This is sometimes referred to as **long arm jurisdiction**—the long arm of the law extending across the country or around the world to draw an accused individual into its court systems. Trying a case in the injured party's home area is usually favorable to the injured party.[2]

Policy Versus Law

Within an organization, information security professionals help maintain security via the establishment and enforcement of policies. These **policies**—guidelines that describe acceptable and unacceptable employee behaviors in the workplace—function as organizational laws, complete with penalties, judicial practices, and sanctions to require compliance. Because these policies function as laws, they must be crafted and implemented with the same care to ensure that they are complete, appropriate, and fairly applied to everyone in the workplace. The difference between a policy and a law, however, is that ignorance of a policy is an acceptable defense. Thus, for a policy to become enforceable, it must meet the following five criteria:

- Dissemination (distribution)—The organization must be able to demonstrate that the relevant policy has been made readily available for review by the employee. Common dissemination techniques include hard copy and electronic distribution.

- Review (reading)—The organization must be able to demonstrate that it disseminated the document in an intelligible form, including versions for illiterate, non-English reading, and reading-impaired employees. Common techniques include recordings of the policy in English and alternate languages.

- Comprehension (understanding)—The organization must be able to demonstrate that the employee understood the requirements and content of the policy. Common techniques include quizzes and other assessments.

- Compliance (agreement)—The organization must be able to demonstrate that the employee agreed to comply with the policy through act or affirmation. Common techniques include logon banners, which require a specific action (mouse click or keystroke) to acknowledge agreement, or a signed document clearly indicating the employee has read, understood, and agreed to comply with the policy.

- Uniform enforcement—The organization must be able to demonstrate that the policy has been uniformly enforced, regardless of employee status or assignment.

Only when all of these conditions are met can an organization penalize employees who violate the policy without fear of legal retribution.

Types of Law

Civil law comprises a wide variety of laws that govern a nation or state and deal with the relationships and conflicts between organizational entities and people. **Criminal law** addresses activities and conduct harmful to society, and is actively enforced by the state. Law can also be categorized as private or public. **Private law** encompasses family law, commercial law, and labor law, and regulates the relationship between individuals and organizations. **Public law** regulates the structure and administration of government agencies and their relationships with citizens, employees, and other governments. Public law includes criminal, administrative, and constitutional law.

Relevant U.S. Laws

Historically, the United States has been a leader in the development and implementation of information security legislation to prevent misuse and exploitation of information and information technology. The implementation of information security legislation contributes to a more reliable business environment, which in turn, enables a stable economy. In its global leadership capacity, the United States has demonstrated a clear understanding of the importance of securing information and has specified penalties for people and organizations that breach U.S. civil statutes. The sections that follow present the most important U.S. laws that apply to information security.

General Computer Crime Laws

There are several key laws relevant to the field of information security and of particular interest to those who live or work in the United States. The **Computer Fraud and Abuse Act of 1986 (CFA Act)** is the cornerstone of many computer-related federal laws and enforcement efforts. It was amended in October 1996 by the **National Information Infrastructure Protection Act of 1996**, which modified several sections of the previous act and increased the penalties for selected crimes. The punishment for offenses prosecuted under this statute varies from fines to imprisonment up to 20 years, or both. The severity of the penalty depends on the value of the information obtained and whether the offense is judged to have been committed:

1. For purposes of commercial advantage

2. For private financial gain

3. In furtherance of a criminal act

The previous law, along with many others, was further modified by the **USA PATRIOT Act of 2001,** which provides law enforcement agencies with broader latitude in order to combat terrorism-related activities. In 2006, this act was amended by the **USA PATRIOT Improvement and Reauthorization Act,** which made permanent fourteen of the sixteen expanded powers of the Department of Homeland Security and the FBI in investigating terrorist activity. The act also reset the date of expiration written into the law as a so-called *sunset clause* for certain wiretaps under the Foreign Intelligence Surveillance Act of 1978 (FISA), and revised many of the criminal penalties and procedures associated with criminal and terrorist activities.[3]

Another key law is the **Computer Security Act of 1987.** It was one of the first attempts to protect federal computer systems by establishing minimum acceptable security practices. The National Bureau of Standards, in cooperation with the National Security Agency, is responsible for developing these security standards and guidelines.

Privacy

Privacy has become one of the hottest topics in information security at the beginning of the 21st century. Many organizations are collecting, swapping, and selling personal information as a commodity, and many people are looking to governments for protection of their privacy. The ability to collect information, combine facts from separate sources, and merge it all with other information has resulted in databases of information that were previously impossible to set up. One technology that was proposed in the past was intended to monitor or track private communications. Known as the Clipper Chip, it used an algorithm with a two-part key that was to be managed by two separate government agencies, and it was reportedly designed to protect individual communications while allowing the government to decrypt suspect transmissions.[4] This technology was the focus of discussion between advocates for personal privacy and those seeking to enable more effective law enforcement. Consequently, this technology was never implemented by the U.S. government.

In response to the pressure for privacy protection, the number of statutes addressing an individual's right to privacy has grown. It must be understood, however, that **privacy** in this context is not absolute freedom from observation, but rather is a more precise "state of being free from unsanctioned intrusion."[5] To help you better understand this rapidly evolving issue, some of the more relevant privacy laws are presented here.

Privacy of Customer Information
Some regulations in the U.S. legal code stipulate the responsibilities of common carriers (organizations that process or move data for hire) to protect the confidentiality of customer information, including that of other carriers. The **Privacy of Customer Information Section** of the common carrier regulation states that any proprietary information shall be used explicitly for providing services, and not for any marketing purposes, and that carriers cannot disclose this information except when necessary to provide their services. The only other exception is when a customer requests the disclosure of information, and then the disclosure is restricted to that customer's information only. This law does allow for the use of aggregate information, as long as the same information is provided to all common carriers and all carriers possessing the information engage in fair competitive business practices. **Aggregate information** is created by combining pieces of non-private data—often collected during software updates and via cookies—that when combined may violate privacy.

While common carrier regulation regulates public carriers in order to protect individual privacy, the **Federal Privacy Act of 1974** regulates government agencies and holds them accountable if they release private information about individuals or businesses without permission. The following agencies, regulated businesses, and individuals are exempt from some of the regulations so that they can perform their duties:

- Bureau of the Census
- National Archives and Records Administration
- Congress
- Comptroller General
- Federal courts with regard to specific issues using appropriate court orders
- Credit reporting agencies
- Individuals or organizations that demonstrate that information is necessary to protect the health or safety of that individual

The **Electronic Communications Privacy Act of 1986** is a collection of statutes that regulates the interception of wire, electronic, and oral communications. These statutes work in conjunction with the **Fourth Amendment of the U.S. Constitution**, which protects individuals from unlawful search and seizure.

The **Health Insurance Portability and Accountability Act Of 1996 (HIPAA)**, also known as the **Kennedy-Kassebaum Act**, protects the confidentiality and security of health care data by establishing and enforcing standards and by standardizing electronic data interchange. HIPAA affects all health care organizations, including doctors' practices, health clinics, life insurers, and universities, as well as some organizations that have self-insured employee health programs. HIPAA specifies stiff penalties for organizations that fail to comply with the law, with fines up to $250,000 and/or 10 years imprisonment for knowingly misusing client information. Organizations were required to comply with the act by April 14, 2003.[6]

How does HIPAA affect the field of information security? Beyond the basic privacy guidelines, the act requires organizations to use information security mechanisms, as well as policies and procedures, to protect health care information. It also requires a comprehensive assessment of information security systems, policies, and procedures where health care information is handled or maintained. Electronic signatures have become more common, and HIPAA provides guidelines for the use of these signatures based on security standards that ensure message integrity, user authentication, and nonrepudiation. There is no specification of particular security technologies for each of the security requirements, only that security must be implemented to ensure the privacy of the health care information.

The privacy standards of HIPAA severely restrict the dissemination and distribution of private health information without documented consent. The standards provide patients with the right to know who has access to their information and who has accessed it. The standards also restrict the use of health information to the minimum necessary for the health care services required.

HIPAA has five fundamental principles:

1. Consumer control of medical information
2. Boundaries on the use of medical information
3. Accountability for the privacy of private information

4. Balance of public responsibility for the use of medical information for the greater good measured against impact to the individual

5. Security of health information

> *Best known for its allocation of $787 million to stimulate the U.S. economy, the American Recovery and Reinvestment Act of 2009 (ARRA) includes new legisla-tion that broadens the scope of HIPAA and gives HIPAA investigators direct, monetary incentives to pursue violators. The HIPAA-specific parts of ARRA are found in the Health Information Technology for Economic and Clinical Health Act (HITECH), which Congress included in the overall ARRA legislation. HITECH broadens the scope of HIPAA to cover all business associates of Health Care Organizations (HCOs). This means that any accounting firm, legal firm, IT consultancy, or other business partner of an HCO must comply with HIPAA security mandates to protect PHI.*

> *Effective February 2010, organizations face the same civil and legal penalties that doctors, hospitals, and insurance companies face for violating the HIPAA Privacy Rule. HITECH not only changes how fines will be levied, it also raises the upper limit on the fines that can be imposed. An HCO or business partner who violates HIPAA may have to pay fines reaching as high as $1.5 million per calendar year. In addition, private citizens and lawyers can now sue to collect fines for security breaches. Overall, HITECH considerably increases the potential financial liability of any organization that mishandles the PHI that passes through its IT infrastructure.*

> *The HITECH Act also includes new data breach notification rules that apply to HCOs and business partners. If an employee discovers a PHI security breach, the employee's organization has only 60 days in which to notify each individual whose privacy has been compromised. If the organization is unable to contact ten or more of the affected individuals, it must either report the security breach on its Web site or issue a press release about the breach to broadcast and print media. If the breach affects 500 or more individuals, the organization must addi-tionally notify the Security of the HHS, along with major media outlets. The HHS will then report the breach on its own Web site.[7]*

The **Financial Services Modernization Act** or **Gramm-Leach-Bliley Act of 1999** contains a number of provisions focusing on facilitating affiliation among banks, securities firms, and insurance companies. Specifically, this act requires all financial institutions to disclose their privacy policies on the sharing of nonpublic personal information. It also requires due notice to customers, so that they can request that their information not be shared with third par-ties. In addition, the act ensures that the privacy policies in effect in an organization are both fully disclosed when a customer initiates a business relationship, and distributed at least annually for the duration of the professional association.

See Table 3-1 for a summary of information security-related laws.

Identity Theft Related to the legislation on privacy is the growing body of law on iden-tity theft. The Federal Trade Commission (FTC) describes identity theft as "occurring when someone uses your personally identifying information, like your name, Social Security num-ber, or credit card number, without your permission, to commit fraud or other crimes."[8] The FTC estimates that perhaps as many as nine million Americans are faced with identity

Area	Act	Date	Description
Telecommunications	Telecommunications Deregulation and Competition Act of 1996—Update to Communications Act of 1934 (47 USC 151 et seq.)	1934	Regulates interstate and foreign telecommunications (amended 1996 and 2001)
Freedom of information	Freedom of Information Act (FOIA)	1966	Allows for the disclosure of previously unreleased information and documents controlled by the U.S. government
Privacy	Federal Privacy Act of 1974	1974	Governs federal agency use of personal information
Copyright	Copyright Act of 1976—Update to U.S. Copyright Law (17 USC)	1976	Protects intellectual property, including publications and software
Cryptography	Electronic Communications Privacy Act of 1986 (Update to 18 USC)	1986	Regulates interception and disclosure of electronic information; also referred to as the Federal Wiretapping Act
Access to stored communications	Unlawful Access to Stored Communications (18 USC 2701)	1986	Provides penalties for illegally accessing stored communications (such as e-mail and voicemail) stored by a service provider
Threats to computers	Computer Fraud and Abuse Act (also known as Fraud and Related Activity in Connection with Computers) (18 USC 1030)	1986	Defines and formalizes laws to counter threats from computer-related acts and offenses (amended 1996, 2001, and 2006)
Federal agency information security	Computer Security Act of 1987	1987	Requires all federal computer systems that contain classified information to have security plans in place, and requires periodic security training for all individuals who operate, design, or manage such systems
Trap and trace restrictions	General prohibition on pen register and trap and trace device use; exception (18 USC 3121 et seq.)	1993	Prohibits the use of electronic "pen registers" and trap and trace devices without a court order
Criminal intent	National Information Infrastructure Protection Act of 1996 (update to 18 USC 1030)	1996	Categorizes crimes based on defendant's authority to access a protected computer system and criminal intent
Trade secrets	Economic Espionage Act of 1996	1996	Prevents abuse of information gained while employed elsewhere
Personal health information protection	Health Insurance Portability and Accountability Act of 1996 (HIPAA)	1996	Requires medical practices to ensure the privacy of personal medical information
Encryption and digital signatures	Security and Freedom through Encryption Act of 1997	1997	Affirms the rights of persons in the United States to use and sell products that include encryption and to relax export controls on such products
Intellectual property	No Electronic Theft Act Amends 17 USC 506(a)—copyright infringement, and 18 USC 2319—criminal infringement of copyright (Public Law 105-147)	1997	Amends copyright and criminal statues to provide greater copyright protection and penalties for electronic copyright infringement

Table 3-1   Key U.S. Laws of Interest to Information Security Professionals

Area	Act	Date	Description
Copy protection	Digital Millennium Copyright Act (update to 17 USC 101)	1998	Provides specific penalties for removing copyright protection from media
Identity theft	Identity Theft and Assumption Deterrence Act of 1998 (18 USC 1028)	1998	Attempts to instigate specific penalties for identity theft by identifying the individual who loses their identity as the true victim, not just those commercial and financial credit entities who suffered losses
Banking	Gramm-Leach-Bliley Act of 1999 (GLB) or the Financial Services Modernization Act	1999	Repeals the restrictions on banks affiliating with insurance and securities firms; has significant impact on the privacy of personal information used by these industries
Terrorism	USA PATRIOT Act of 2001 (update to 18 USC 1030)	2001	Defines stiffer penalties for prosecution of terrorist crimes
Accountability	Sarbanes-Oxley Act of 2002 (SOX) or Public Company Accounting Reform and Investor Protection Act	2002	Enforces accountability for executives at publicly traded companies; this law is having ripple effects throughout the accounting, IT, and related units of many organizations
Spam	Controlling the Assault of Non-Solicited Pornography and Marketing Act of 2003 CAN-SPAM Act (15 USC 7701 et seq.)	2003	Sets the first national standards for regulating the distribution of commercial email; the act includes mobile phone spam as well
Fraud with access devices	Fraud and Related Activity in Connection with Access Devices (18 USC 1029)	2004	Defines and formalizes law to counter threats from counterfeit access devices like ID cards, credit cards, telecom equipment, mobile or electronic serial numbers, and the equipment that creates them
Terrorism and extreme drug trafficking	USA PATRIOT Improvement and Reauthorization Act of 2005 (update to 18 USC 1030)	2006	Renews critical sections of the USA PATRIOT Act

Table 3-1 Key U.S. Laws of Interest to Information Security Professionals (continued)

theft each year. Many people, among them perhaps you or someone you know have been affected by some form of identity theft.[9] Organizations can also be victims of identity theft by means of URL manipulation or DNS redirection, as described in Chapter 2. In May of 2006, President Bush signed an executive order creating the Identity Theft Task Force, which on April 27, 2007 issued a strategic plan to improve efforts of the government and private organizations and individuals in combating identity theft. The U.S. FTC now oversees efforts to foster coordination among groups, more effective prosecution of criminals engaged in these activities, and methods to increase restitution made to victims.[10]

While numerous states have passed identity theft laws, at the federal level the primary legislation is the **Fraud and Related Activity in Connection with Identification Documents, Authentication Features, and Information** (Title 18, U.S.C. § 1028), which criminalizes creation, reproduction, transfer, possession, or use of unauthorized or false identification documents or document-making equipment. The penalties for such offenses range from 1 to 25 years in prison, and fines as determined by the courts.

The FTC recommends that people take the following four steps when they suspect they are victims of identity theft:

1. Report to the three dominant consumer reporting companies that your identity is threatened so that they may place a fraud alert on your record. This informs current and potential creditors to follow certain procedures before taking credit-related actions.

2. If you know which accounts have been compromised, close them. If new accounts are opened using your identity without your permission, you can obtain a document template online that may be used to dispute these new accounts. The FTC offers a comprehensive identity theft site to provide guidance, tools, and forms you might need at *www.ftc.gov/bcp/edu/microsites/idtheft*.

3. Register your concern with the FTC. There is a form to register a complaint at the FTC's identity theft site.

4. Report the incident to either your local police or police in the location where the identity theft occurred. Use your copy of the FTC ID Theft complaint form to make the report. Once your police report has been filed, be sure to get a copy or acquire the police report number.[11]

Export and Espionage Laws

To meet national security needs and to protect trade secrets and other state and private assets, several laws restrict which information and information management and security resources may be exported from the United States. These laws attempt to stem the theft of information by establishing strong penalties for these crimes.

To protect American ingenuity, intellectual property, and competitive advantage, Congress passed the **Economic Espionage Act** in 1996. This law attempts to prevent trade secrets from being illegally shared.

The **Security and Freedom through Encryption Act of 1999** provides guidance on the use of encryption and provides protection from government intervention. The acts include provisions that:

- Reinforce an individual's right to use or sell encryption algorithms, without concern for regulations requiring some form of key registration. Key registration is the storage of a cryptographic key (or its text equivalent) with another party to be used to break the encryption of data. This is often called "key escrow."

- Prohibit the federal government from requiring the use of encryption for contracts, grants, and other official documents and correspondence.

- State that the use of encryption is not probable cause to suspect criminal activity.

- Relax export restrictions by amending the Export Administration Act of 1979.

- Provide additional penalties for the use of encryption in the commission of a criminal act.

As illustrated in Figure 3-1, the distribution of many software packages is restricted to approved organizations, governments, and countries.

U.S. Copyright Law

Intellectual property is a protected asset in the United States. The U.S. copyright laws extend this privilege to the published word, including electronic formats. Fair use allows copyrighted materials to be used to support news reporting, teaching, scholarship, and a number of

Figure 3-1 Export and Espionage

Source: Course Technology/Cengage Learning

similar activities, as long as the use is for educational or library purposes, is not for profit, and is not excessive. As long as proper acknowledgement is provided to the original author of such works, including a proper description of the location of source materials (citation), and the work is not represented as one's own, it is entirely permissible to include portions of someone else's work as reference. For more detailed information on copyright regulations, visit the U.S. Copyright Office Web site at *www.copyright.gov*.

Financial Reporting

The **Sarbanes-Oxley Act of 2002** is a critical piece of legislation that affects the executive management of publicly traded corporations and public accounting firms. This law seeks to improve the reliability and accuracy of financial reporting, as well as increase the accountability of corporate governance, in publicly traded companies. Penalties for non-compliance range from fines to jail terms. Executives working in firms covered by this law seek assurance on the reliability and quality of information systems from senior information technology managers. In turn, IT managers are likely to ask information security managers to verify the confidentiality and integrity of those information systems in a process known in the industry as sub-certification.

Freedom of Information Act of 1966 (FOIA)

The **Freedom of Information Act** allows any person to request access to federal agency records or information not determined to be a matter of national security. Agencies of the federal government are required to disclose any requested information on receipt of a written request. This requirement is enforceable in court. Some information is, however, protected from disclosure, and the act does not apply to state or local government agencies or to private businesses or individuals, although many states have their own version of the FOIA.

State and Local Regulations

In addition to the national and international restrictions placed on organizational use of computer technology, each state or locality may have a number of its own applicable laws and regulations. Information security professionals must therefore understand state laws and regulations and ensure that the organization's security policies and procedures comply with those laws and regulations.

For example, in 1991 the state of Georgia passed the **Georgia Computer Systems Protection Act,** which seeks to protect information, and which establishes penalties for the use of information technology to attack or exploit information systems.

International Laws and Legal Bodies

It is important for IT professionals and information security practitioners to realize that when their organizations do business on the Internet, they do business globally. As a result, these professionals must be sensitive to the laws and ethical values of many different cultures, societies, and countries. While it may be impossible to please all of the people all of the time, dealing with the laws of other states and nations is one area where it is certainly *not* easier to ask for forgiveness than for permission.

A number of different security bodies and laws are described in this section. Because of the political complexities of the relationships among nations and the differences in culture, there are currently few international laws relating to privacy and information security. The laws discussed below are important, but are limited in their enforceability. The American Society of International Law is one example of an American institution that deals in international law (see *www.asil.org*).

Council of Europe Convention on Cybercrime

The Council of Europe adopted the **Convention on Cybercrime** in 2001. It created an international task force to oversee a range of security functions associated with Internet activities for standardized technology laws across international borders. It also attempts to improve the effectiveness of international investigations into breaches of technology law. This convention has been well received by advocates of intellectual property rights because it emphasizes prosecution for copyright infringement. However, many supporters of individual rights oppose the convention because they think it unduly infringes on freedom of speech and threatens the civil liberties of U.S. residents.

While thirty-four countries attended the signing in November 2001, only twenty-nine nations, including the United States, have ratified the Convention as of April 2010. The United States is technically not a "member state of the council of Europe" but does participate in the Convention.

As is true with much complex international legislation, the Convention on Cybercrime lacks any realistic provisions for enforcement. The overall goal of the convention is to simplify the acquisition of information for law enforcement agencies in certain types of international crimes. It also simplifies the extradition process. The convention has more than its share of skeptics, who see it as an overly simplistic attempt to control a complex problem.

Agreement on Trade-Related Aspects of Intellectual Property Rights

The **Agreement on Trade-Related Aspects of Intellectual Property Rights** (TRIPS), created by the World Trade Organization (WTO) and negotiated over the years 1986–1994, introduced intellectual property rules into the multilateral trade system. It is the first significant international effort to protect intellectual property rights. It outlines requirements for governmental oversight and legislation of WTO member countries to provide minimum levels of protection for intellectual property. The WTO TRIPS agreement covers five issues:

- How basic principles of the trading system and other international intellectual property agreements should be applied
- How to give adequate protection to intellectual property rights
- How countries should enforce those rights adequately in their own territories
- How to settle disputes on intellectual property between members of the WTO
- Special transitional arrangements during the period when the new system is being introduced[12]

Digital Millennium Copyright Act (DMCA)

The **Digital Millennium Copyright Act** (DMCA) is the American contribution to an international effort by the World Intellectual Properties Organization (WIPO) to reduce the impact of copyright, trademark, and privacy infringement, especially when accomplished via the removal of technological copyright protection measures. This law was created in response to the 1995 adoption of **Directive 95/46/EC** by the European Union, which added protection for individuals with regard to the processing of personal data and the use and movement of such data. The United Kingdom has implemented a version of this law called the **Database Right**, in order to comply with Directive 95/46/EC.

The DMCA includes the following provisions:

- Prohibits the circumvention protections and countermeasures implemented by copyright owners to control access to protected content
- Prohibits the manufacture of devices to circumvent protections and countermeasures that control access to protected content
- Bans trafficking in devices manufactured to circumvent protections and countermeasures that control access to protected content
- Prohibits the altering of information attached or imbedded into copyrighted material
- Excludes Internet service providers from certain forms of contributory copyright infringement

Ethics and Information Security

Many Professional groups have explicit rules governing ethical behavior in the workplace. For example, doctors and lawyers who commit egregious violations of their professions' canons of conduct can be removed from practice. Unlike the medical and legal fields, however, the information technology field in general, and the information security field in particular, do not

Offline
The Ten Commandments of Computer Ethics[13]

From The Computer Ethics Institute

1. Thou shalt not use a computer to harm other people.

2. Thou shalt not interfere with other people's computer work.

3. Thou shalt not snoop around in other people's computer files.

4. Thou shalt not use a computer to steal.

5. Thou shalt not use a computer to bear false witness.

6. Thou shalt not copy or use proprietary software for which you have not paid.

7. Thou shalt not use other people's computer resources without authorization or proper compensation.

8. Thou shalt not appropriate other people's intellectual output.

9. Thou shalt think about the social consequences of the program you are writing or the system you are designing.

10. Thou shalt always use a computer in ways that ensure consideration and respect for your fellow humans.

have a binding code of ethics. Instead, professional associations—such as the Association for Computing Machinery (ACM) and the Information Systems Security Association—and certification agencies—such as the International Information Systems Security Certification Consortium, Inc., or (ISC)[2]—work to establish the profession's ethical codes of conduct. While these professional organizations can prescribe ethical conduct, they do not always have the authority to banish violators from practicing their trade. To begin exploring some of the ethical issues particular to information security, take a look at the Ten Commandments of Computer Ethics in the nearby Offline.

Ethical Differences Across Cultures

Cultural differences can make it difficult to determine what is and is not ethical—especially when it comes to the use of computers. Studies on ethics and computer use reveal that people of different nationalities have different perspectives; difficulties arise when one nationality's ethical behavior violates the ethics of another national group. For example, to Western cultures, many of the ways in which Asian cultures use computer technology is software piracy.[14] This ethical conflict arises out of Asian traditions of collective ownership, which clash with the protection of intellectual property. Approximately 90 percent of all software is created in the United States. Some countries are more relaxed with intellectual property copy restrictions than others.

A study published in 1999 examined computer use ethics of eight nations: Singapore, Hong Kong, the United States, England, Australia, Sweden, Wales, and the Netherlands.[15] This study selected a number of computer-use vignettes (see the Offline titled The Use of Scenarios in Computer Ethics Studies) and presented them to students in universities in these eight nations. This study did not categorize or classify the responses as ethical or unethical. Instead, the responses only indicated a degree of ethical sensitivity or knowledge about the performance of the individuals in the short case studies. The scenarios were grouped into three categories of ethical computer use: software license infringement, illicit use, and misuse of corporate resources.

Software License Infringement The topic of software license infringement, or piracy, is routinely covered by the popular press. Among study participants, attitudes toward piracy were generally similar; however, participants from the United States and the Netherlands showed statistically significant differences in attitudes from the overall group. Participants from the United States were significantly less tolerant of piracy, while those from the Netherlands were significantly more permissive. Although other studies have reported that the Pacific Rim countries of Singapore and Hong Kong are hotbeds of software piracy, this study found tolerance for copyright infringement in those countries to be moderate, as were attitudes in England, Wales, Australia, and Sweden. This could mean that the individuals surveyed *understood* what software license infringement was, but felt either that their use was not piracy, or that their society permitted this piracy in some way. Peer pressure, the lack of legal disincentives, the lack of punitive measures, and number of other reasons could a explain why users in these alleged piracy centers disregarded intellectual property laws despite their professed attitudes toward them. Even though participants from the Netherlands displayed a more permissive attitude toward piracy, that country only ranked third in piracy rates of the nations surveyed in this study.

Illicit Use The study respondents unilaterally condemned viruses, hacking, and other forms of system abuse. There were, however, different degrees of tolerance for such activities among the groups. Students from Singapore and Hong Kong proved to be significantly more tolerant than those from the United States, Wales, England, and Australia. Students from Sweden and the Netherlands were also significantly more tolerant than those from Wales and Australia, but significantly less tolerant than those from Hong Kong. The low overall degree of tolerance for illicit system use may be a function of the easy correspondence between the common crimes of breaking and entering, trespassing, theft, and destruction of property and their computer-related counterparts.

Misuse of Corporate Resources The scenarios used to examine the levels of tolerance for misuse of corporate resources each presented a different degree of noncompany use of corporate assets without specifying the company's policy on personal use of company resources. In general, individuals displayed a rather lenient view of personal use of company equipment. Only students from Singapore and Hong Kong view personal use of company equipment as unethical. There were several substantial differences in this category, with students from the Netherlands revealing the most lenient views. With the exceptions of those from Singapore and Hong Kong, it is apparent that many people, regardless of cultural background, believe that unless an organization explicitly forbids personal use of its computing resources, such use is acceptable. It is interesting to note that only participants among the two Asian samples, Singapore and Hong Kong, reported generally intolerant attitudes toward personal use of organizational computing resources. The reasons behind this are unknown.[16]

Adapted from "Cross-National Differences in Computer-Use Ethics":

By Michael E. Whitman, Anthony M. Townsend, and Anthony R. Hendrickson,

The Journal of International Business Studies.

The following vignettes can be used in an open and frank discussion of computer ethics. Review each scenario carefully and respond to each question using the following statement, choosing the description you feel most appropriate: *I feel the actions of this individual were (very ethical / ethical / neither ethical nor unethical / unethical / very unethical).* Then, justify your response.

Ethical Decision Evaluation

Note: These scenarios are based on published works by Professor Whitman and Professor Paradice.

1. A scientist developed a theory that required proof through the construction of a computer model. He hired a computer programmer to build the model, and the theory was shown to be correct. The scientist won several awards for the development of the theory, but he never acknowledged the contribution of the computer programmer.

   The scientist's failure to acknowledge the computer programmer was:

2. The owner of a small business needed a computer-based accounting system. One day, he identified the various inputs and outputs he felt were required to satisfy his needs. Then he showed his design to a computer programmer and asked the programmer if she could implement such a system. The programmer knew she could implement the system because she had developed much more sophisticated systems in the past. In fact, she thought this design was rather crude and would soon need several major revisions. But she didn't say anything about her thoughts, because the business owner didn't ask, and she hoped she might be hired to implement the needed revisions.

   The programmer's decision not to point out the design flaws was:

3. A student found a loophole in the university computer's security system that allowed him access to other students' records. He told the system administrator about the loophole, but continued to access others' records until the problem was corrected two weeks later.

   The student's action in searching for the loophole was:

   The student's action in continuing to access others' records for two weeks was:

   The system administrator's failure to correct the problem sooner was:

4. A computer user called a mail-order software company to order a particular accounting system. When he received his order, he found that the store had accidentally sent him a very expensive word-processing program as well as the accounting package that he had ordered. The invoice listed only the accounting package. The user decided to keep the word-processing package.

   The user's decision to keep the word-processing package was:

5. A programmer at a bank realized that he had accidentally overdrawn his checking account. He made a small adjustment in the bank's accounting system so that his account would not have the additional service charge assessed. As soon as he deposited funds that made his balance positive again, he corrected the bank's accounting system.

   The programmer's modification of the accounting system was:

6. A computer programmer enjoyed building small computer applications (programs) to give his friends. He would frequently go to his office on Saturday when no one was working and use his employer's computer to develop applications. He did not hide the fact that he was going into the building; he had to sign a register at a security desk each time he entered.

   The programmer's use of the company computer was:

7. A computer programmer built small computer applications (programs) in order to sell them. This was not his main source of income. He worked for a moderately sized computer vendor. He would frequently go to his office on Saturday when no one was working and use his employer's computer to develop applications. He did not hide the fact that he was going into the building; he had to sign a register at a security desk each time he entered.

   The programmer's use of the company computer was:

8. A student enrolled in a computer class was also employed at a local business part-time. Frequently her homework in the class involved using popular word-processing and spreadsheet packages. Occasionally she worked on her homework on the office computer at her part-time job, on her coffee or meal breaks.

   The student's use of the company computer was:

   If the student had worked on her homework during "company time" (not during a break), the student's use of the company computer would have been:

9. A student at a university learned to use an expensive spreadsheet program in her accounting class. The student would go to the university microcomputer lab and use the software to complete her assignment. Signs were posted in the lab indicating that copying software was forbidden. One day, she decided to copy the software anyway to complete her work assignments at home.

   If the student destroyed her copy of the software at the end of the term, her action in copying the software was:

(continued)

If the student forgot to destroy her copy of the software at the end of the term, her action in copying the software was:

If the student never intended to destroy her copy of the software at the end of the term, her action in copying the software was:

10. A student at a university found out that one of the local computer bulletin boards contained a "pirate" section (a section containing a collection of illegally copied software programs). He subscribed to the board, and proceeded to download several games and professional programs, which he then distributed to several of his friends.

    The student's actions in downloading the games were:

    The student's actions in downloading the programs were:

    The student's actions in sharing the programs and games with his friends were:

11. State College charges its departments for computer time usage on the campus mainframe. A student had access to the university computer system because a class she was taking required extensive computer usage. The student enjoyed playing games on the computer, and frequently had to request extra computer funds from her professor in order to complete her assignments.

    The student's use of the computer to play games was:

12. An engineer needed a program to perform a series of complicated calculations. He found a computer programmer capable of writing the program, but would only hire the programmer if he agreed to share any liability that may result from an error in the engineer's calculations. The programmer said he would be willing to assume any liability due to a malfunction of the program, but was unwilling to share any liability due to an error in the engineer's calculations.

    The programmer's position in this situation is:

    The engineer's position in this situation is:

13. A manager of a company that sells computer-processing services bought similar services from a competitor. She used her access to the competitor's computer to try to break the security system, identify other customers, and cause the system to "crash" (cause loss of service to others). She used the service for over a year and always paid her bills promptly.

    The manager's actions were:

14. One day, a student programmer decided to write a virus program. Virus programs usually make copies of themselves on other disks automatically, so the virus can spread to unsuspecting users. The student wrote a program that caused the microcomputer to ignore every fifth command entered by a user. The student took his program to the university computing lab and installed it on one of the microcomputers. Before long, the virus spread to hundreds of users.

    The student's action of infecting hundreds of users' disks was:

    If the virus program output the message "Have a nice day," then the student's action of infecting hundreds of users' disks would have been:

    If the virus erased files, then the student's action of infecting hundreds of users' files would have been:

Ethics and Education

Attitudes toward the ethics of computer use are affected by many factors other than nationality. Differences are found among individuals within the same country, within the same social class, and within the same company. Key studies reveal that the overriding factor in leveling the ethical perceptions within a small population is education. Employees must be trained and kept aware of a number of topics related to information security, not the least of which are the expected behaviors of an ethical employee. This is especially important in information security, as many employees may not have the formal technical training to understand that their behavior is unethical or even illegal. Proper ethical and legal training is vital to creating an informed, well prepared, and low-risk system user.

Deterring Unethical and Illegal Behavior

There are three general causes of unethical and illegal behavior:

- Ignorance—Ignorance of the law is no excuse; however, ignorance of policy and procedures is. The first method of deterrence is education. This is accomplished by means of designing, publishing, and disseminating organization policies and relevant laws, and also obtaining agreement to comply with these policies and laws from all members of the organization. Reminders, training, and awareness programs keep the policy information in front of the individual and thus better support retention and compliance.

- Accident—Individuals with authorization and privileges to manage information within the organization are most likely to cause harm or damage by accident. Careful planning and control helps prevent accidental modification to systems and data.

- Intent—Criminal or unethical intent goes to the state of mind of the person performing the act; it is often necessary to establish criminal intent to successfully prosecute offenders. Protecting a system against those with intent to cause harm or damage is best accomplished by means of technical controls, and vigorous litigation or prosecution if these controls fail.

Whatever the cause of illegal, immoral, or unethical behavior, one thing is certain: it is the responsibility of information security personnel to do everything in their power to deter these acts and to use policy, education and training, and technology to protect information and systems. Many security professionals understand the technology aspect of protection but underestimate the value of policy. However, laws and policies and their associated penalties only deter if three conditions are present:

- Fear of penalty—Potential offenders must fear the penalty. Threats of informal reprimand or verbal warnings may not have the same impact as the threat of imprisonment or forfeiture of pay.

- Probability of being caught—Potential offenders must believe there is a strong possibility of being caught. Penalties will not deter illegal or unethical behavior unless there is reasonable fear of being caught.

- Probability of penalty being administered—Potential offenders must believe that the penalty will in fact be administered.

Codes of Ethics and Professional Organizations

A number of professional organizations have established codes of conduct or codes of ethics that members are expected to follow. Codes of ethics can have a positive effect on people's judgment regarding computer use.[17] Unfortunately, many employers do not encourage their employees to join these professional organizations. But employees who have earned some level of certification or professional accreditation can be deterred from ethical lapses by the threat of loss of accreditation or certification due to a violation of a code of conduct. Loss of certification or accreditation can dramatically reduce marketability and earning power.

It is the responsibility of security professionals to act ethically and according to the policies and procedures of their employers, their professional organizations, and the laws of society. It is likewise the organization's responsibility to develop, disseminate, and enforce its policies. Following is a discussion of professional organizations and where they fit into the ethical landscape. Table 3-2 provides an overview of these organizations. Many of these organizations offer certification programs that require the applicants to subscribe formally to the ethical codes. Professional certification is discussed in Chapter 11.

Major IT Professional Organizations

Many of the major IT professional organizations maintain their own codes of ethics.

The **Association of Computing Machinery (ACM)** (*www.acm.org*) is a respected professional society that was established in 1947 as "the world's first educational and scientific computing society." It is one of the few organizations that strongly promotes education and provides

Professional Organization	Web Resource Location	Description	Focus
Association of Computing Machinery	*www.acm.org*	Code of 24 imperatives of personal ethical responsibilities of security professionals	Ethics of security professionals
Information Systems Audit and Control Association	*www.isaca.org*	One process area and six subject areas that focus on auditing, information security, business process analysis, and IS planning through the CISA and CISM certifications	Tasks and knowledge required of the information systems audit professional
Information Systems Security Association	*www.issa.org*	Professional association of information systems security professionals; provides education forums, publications, and peer networking for members	Professional security information sharing
International Information Systems Security Certification Consortium (ISC)²	*www.isc2.org*	International Consortium dedicated to improving the quality of security professionals through SSCP and CISSP certifications	Requires certificants to follow its published code of ethics
SANS Institutes Global Information Assurance Certification	*www.giac.org*	GIAC certifications focus on four security areas: security administration, security management, IT audit, and software security, and has standard, gold, and expert levels	Requires certificants to follow its published code of ethics

Table 3-2 **Professional Organizations of Interest to Information Security Professionals**

discounts for student members. The ACM's code of ethics requires members to perform their duties in a manner befitting an ethical computing professional. The code contains specific references to protecting the confidentiality of information, causing no harm (with specific references to viruses), protecting the privacy of others, and respecting the intellectual property and copyrights of others. The ACM also publishes a wide variety of professional computing publications, including the highly regarded *Communications of the ACM*.

The **International Information Systems Security Certification Consortium, Inc. (ISC)^2** (*www.isc2.org*) is a nonprofit organization that focuses on the development and implementation of information security certifications and credentials. The (ISC)^2 manages a body of knowledge on information security and administers and evaluates examinations for information security certifications. The code of ethics put forth by (ISC)^2 is primarily designed for information security professionals who have earned an (ISC)^2 certification, and has four mandatory canons: "Protect society, the commonwealth, and the infrastructure; act honorably, honestly, justly, responsibly, and legally; provide diligent and competent service to principals; and advance and protect the profession."[18] This code enables (ISC)^2 to promote reliance on the ethicality and trustworthiness of the information security professional as the guardian of information and systems.

The **System Administration, Networking, and Security Institute (SANS)** (*www.sans.org*), which was founded in 1989, is a professional research and education cooperative organization with a current membership of more than 156,000 security professionals, auditors, system administrators, and network administrators. SANS offers a set of certifications called the Global Information Assurance Certification, or GIAC. All GIAC-certified professionals are required to acknowledge that certification and the privileges that come from it carry a corresponding obligation to uphold the GIAC Code of Ethics. Those certificate holders that do not conform to this code face punishment, and may lose GIAC certification.

The **Information Systems Audit and Control Association (ISACA)** (*www.isaca.org*) is a professional association that focuses on auditing, control, and security. The membership comprises both technical and managerial professionals. ISACA provides IT control practices and standards, and although it does not focus exclusively on information security, it does include many information security components within its areas of concentration. ISACA also has a code of ethics for its professionals, and it requires many of the same high standards for ethical performance as the other organizations and certifications.

The **Information Systems Security Association (ISSA)** (*www.issa.org*) is a nonprofit society of information security professionals. As a professional association, its primary mission is to bring together qualified information security practitioners for information exchange and educational development. ISSA provides a number of scheduled conferences, meetings, publications, and information resources to promote information security awareness and education. ISSA also promotes a code of ethics, similar in content to those of (ISC)^2, ISACA, and the ACM, whose focus is "promoting management practices that will ensure the confidentiality, integrity, and availability of organizational information resources."[19]

Key U.S. Federal Agencies

A number of key U.S. federal agencies are charged with the protection of American information resources and the investigation of threats to, or attacks on, these resources. These include the Department of Homeland Security (DHS) and the Federal Bureau of Investigation (see Figure 3-2), the National Security Administration, the FBI's Infragard program (see Figure 3–3), and the U.S. Secret Service (see Figure 3-4).

The **Department of Homeland Security (DHS)** was created in 2003 by the Homeland Security Act of 2002, which was passed in response to the events of September 11, 2001. DHS is made up of five directorates, or divisions, through which it carries out its mission of protecting the people as well as the physical and informational assets of the United States. The Directorate of Information and Infrastructure creates and enhances resources used to discover and respond to attacks on national information systems and critical infrastructure. The Science and Technology Directorate is responsible for research and development activities in support of homeland defense. This effort is guided by an ongoing examination of vulnerabilities throughout the national infrastructure, and this directorate sponsors the emerging best practices developed to counter the threats and weaknesses in the system.

Established in January 2001, the **National InfraGard Program** began as a cooperative effort between the FBI's Cleveland Field Office and local technology professionals. The FBI sought assistance in determining a more effective method of protecting critical national information

Figure 3-2 DHS and FBI Home Pages

Source: Course Technology/Cengage Learning

Figure 3-3 Infragard and NSA Home Pages

Source: Course Technology/Cengage Learning

resources. The resulting cooperative, the first InfraGard chapter, was a formal effort to combat both cyber and physical threats. Since then, every FBI field office has established an InfraGard chapter and collaborates with public and private organizations and the academic community to share information about attacks, vulnerabilities, and threats. The National InfraGard Program serves its members in four basic ways:

- Maintains an intrusion alert network using encrypted e-mail
- Maintains a secure Web site for communication about suspicious activity or intrusions
- Sponsors local chapter activities
- Operates a help desk for questions

InfraGard's dominant contribution is the free exchange of information to and from the private sector in the areas of threats and attacks on information resources.

Figure 3-4 The Secret Service Home Page

Source: Course Technology/Cengage Learning

Another key federal agency is the **National Security Agency (NSA)**. The NSA is:

> *the Nation's cryptologic organization. It coordinates, directs, and performs highly specialized activities to protect U.S. information systems and produce foreign intelligence information ... It is also one of the most important centers of foreign language analysis and research within the Government.*[20]

The NSA is responsible for signal intelligence and information system security. The NSA's Information Assurance Directorate (IAD) provides information security "solutions including the technologies, specifications and criteria, products, product configurations, tools, standards, operational doctrine, and support activities needed to implement the protect, detect and report, and respond elements of cyber defense."[21] The IAD also develops and promotes an Information Assurance Framework Forum in cooperation with commercial organizations and academic researchers. This framework provides strategic guidance as well as technical specifications for security solutions. IAD's Common Criteria is a set of standards designed to promote understanding of information security.

Prominent among the NSA's efforts and activities in the information security arena are the Information Security Outreach programs. The NSA recognizes universities that not only offer information security education, but that have also integrated information security philosophies and efforts into the internal operations of the schools. These recognized "Centers of Excellence in Information Assurance Education" receive the honor of displaying the recognition as well as being acknowledged on the NSA's Web site. Additionally, the NSA has a program to certify curricula in information security. The Information Assurance Courseware Evaluation process examines institutional information security courses and provides a three-year accreditation. Graduates of these programs receive certificates that indicate this accreditation.

The **U.S. Secret Service** is an agency within the Department of the Treasury. In addition to its well-known mission of providing protective services for key members of the U.S. government, the Secret Service is also charged with the detection and arrest of any person committing a United States federal offense relating to computer fraud and false identification crimes. This is an extension of the agency's original mission to protect U.S. currency—a logical extension, given that the communications networks of the United States carry more funds than all of the armored cars in the world combined. Protect the networks and protect the data, and you protect money, stocks, and other financial transactions. For more information on the Secret Service, see its Web site (the home page is shown in Figure 3-4).

Selected Readings

- *The Digital Person: Technology and Privacy in the Information Age*, by Daniel Solove. 2004. New York University Press.

- *The Practical Guide to HIPAA Privacy and Security Compliance*, by Kevin Beaver and Rebecca Herold. 2003. Auerbach.

- *When Good Companies Do Bad Things*, by Peter Schwartz. 1999. John Wiley and Sons.

Chapter Summary

- Laws are formally adopted rules for acceptable behavior in modern society. Ethics are socially acceptable behaviors. The key difference between laws and ethics is that laws carry the authority of a governing body and ethics do not.

- Organizations formalize desired behaviors in documents called policies. Policies must be read and agreed to before they are binding.

- Civil law comprises a wide variety of laws that are used to govern a nation or state. Criminal law addresses violations that harm society and are enforced by agents of the state or nation.

- Private law focuses on individual relationships, and public law governs regulatory agencies.

- Key U.S. laws protecting privacy include the Federal Privacy Act of 1974, the Electronic Communications Privacy Act of 1986, and the Health Insurance Portability and Accountability Act of 1996.

- The desire to protect national security, trade secrets, and a variety of other state and private assets has led to several laws restricting what information and information management and security resources may be exported from the United States.

- Intellectual property is recognized as a protected asset in this country. U.S. copyright law extends this privilege to the published word, including electronic media.

- Studies have determined that individuals of differing nationalities have differing perspectives on ethical practices regarding the use of computer technology.

- Deterrence can prevent an illegal or unethical activity from occurring. Deterrence requires significant penalties, a high probability of apprehension, and an expectation of enforcement of penalties.

- As part of an effort to encourage ethical behavior, a number of professional organizations have established codes of conduct or codes of ethics that their members are expected to follow.

- There are a number of U.S. federal agencies responsible for protecting American information resources and investigating threats to, or attacks on, these resources.

Review Questions

1. What is the difference between law and ethics?

2. What is civil law, and what does it accomplish?

3. What are the primary examples of public law?

4. Which law amended the Computer Fraud and Abuse Act of 1986, and what did it change?

5. Which law was specifically created to deal with encryption policy in the United States?

6. What is privacy in an information security context?

7. What is another name for the Kennedy-Kassebaum Act (1996), and why is it important to organizations that are not in the health care industry?

8. If you work for a financial service organization such as a bank or credit union, which 1999 law affects your use of customer data? What other affects does it have?

9. What is the primary purpose of the USA PATRIOT Act?

10. Which 1997 law provides guidance on the use of encryption?

11. What is intellectual property (IP)? Is it afforded the same protection in every country of the world? What laws currently protect it in the United States and Europe?

12. How does the Sarbanes-Oxley Act of 2002 affect information security managers?

13. What is due care? Why should an organization make sure to exercise due care in its usual course of operations?

14. How is due diligence different from due care? Why are both important?

15. What is a policy? How is it different from a law?

16. What are the three general categories of unethical and illegal behavior?

17. What is the best method for preventing an illegal or unethical activity?

18. Of the information security organizations listed that have codes of ethics, which has been established for the longest time? When was it founded?

19. Of the organizations listed that have codes of ethics, which is focused on auditing and control?

20. What can be done to deter someone from committing a crime?

Exercises

1. What does CISSP stand for? Use the Internet to identify the ethical rules CISSP holders have agreed to follow.

2. For what kind of information security jobs does the NSA recruit? Use the Internet to visit its Web page and find out.

3. Using the resources available in your library, find out what laws your state has passed to prosecute computer crime.

4. Using a Web browser go to *www.eff.org*. What are the current top concerns of this organization?

5. Using the ethical scenarios presented in the chapter, finish each of the incomplete statements, and bring your answers to class to compare them with those of your peers.

Case Exercises

Iris called the company security hotline. The hotline was an anonymous way to report any suspicious activity or abuse of company policy, although Iris chose to identify herself. The next morning, she was called to a meeting with an investigator from corporate security, which led to more meetings with others in corporate security, and then finally a meeting with the director of human resources and Gladys Williams, the CIO of SLS.

Questions:

1. Why was Iris justified in determining who the owner of the CD was?

2. Should Iris have approached Henry directly, or was the hotline the most effective way to take action? Why do you think so?

3. Should Iris have placed the CD back at the coffee station and forgotten the whole thing? Explain why that action would have been ethical or unethical.

Endnotes

1. Noone, John B. *Rousseau's Social Contract: A Conceptual Analysis*. Athens: University of Georgia Press, 1981.

2. Alberts, Robert J., Townsend, Anthony M., and Whitman, Michael E. "The Threat of Long-arm Jurisdiction to Electronic Commerce." *Communications of the ACM* 41, no. 12 (December 1998): 15–20.

3. Yeh, B., and Doyle, C. "USA PATRIOT Improvement and Reauthorization Act of 2005: A Legal Analysis" CRS Report for Congress. Accessed 22 February 2007 from *www.fas.org/sgp/crs/intel/RL33332.pdf*.

4. EPIC. "The Clipper Chip." Accessed 6 March 2004 from *www.epic.org/crypto/clipper/.*

5. American Heritage Dictionary. "Privacy." *The American Heritage Dictionary of the English Language Online.* Accessed 22 February 2007 from *www.bartleby.com/61/87/P0568700.html.*

6. HIPAAdvisory. "HIPAA Primer." *HIPAAdvisory Online.* Accessed 31 January 2007 from *www.hipaadvisory.com/REGS/HIPAAprimer.htm.*

7. Proofpoint, HIPAA and Beyond: An Update on Healthcare Security Regulations for Email. WWW Document viewed 6/10/2010 from www.findwhitepapers.com/force-download.php?id=8558.

8. FTC. "About Identity Theft." Accessed 22 February 2007 from *www.ftc.gov/bcp/edu/microsites/idtheft/consumers/about-identity-theft.html.*

9. Ibid.

10. FTC. "The President's Identity Theft Task Force Releases Comprehensive Strategic Plan to Combat Identity Theft." Accessed 25 April 2010 from *www.ftc.gov/opa/2007/04/idtheft.shtm.*

11. FTC. "If You Think Your Identity Has Been Stolen, Here's What To Do." Accessed 22 February 2007 from *www.ftc.gov/bcp/edu/microsites/idtheft/.*

12. WTO. "Understanding the TRIPS Agreement." Accessed 22 February 2007 from *www.wto.org/english/thewto_e/whatis_e/tif_e/agrm7_e.htm.*

13. The Computer Ethics Institute. "The 10 Commandments of Computer Ethics." *CEI Online.* 1992. Accessed 14 April 2007 from *www.brook.edu/its/cei/overview/Ten_Commanments_of_Computer_Ethics.htm.*

14. Inquirer. "Software Piracy in Asia Exposed." *The Inquirer Online.* 27 January 2002. Accessed 14 April 2007 from *www.theinquirer.net/piracy1.htm.*

15. Whitman, Michael E., Townsend, Anthony M., and Hendrickson, Anthony R. "Cross-National Differences in Computer-Use Ethics: A Nine Country Study." *The Journal of International Business Studies* 30, no. 4 (1999): 673–687.

16. Ibid.

17. Harrington, Susan J. "The Effects of Codes of Ethics and Personal Denial of Responsibility on Computer Abuse Judgment and Intentions." *MIS Quarterly* 20, no. 3 (September 1996): 257–278.

18. International Information Systems Security Certification Consortium, Inc. "(ISC)^2 Code of Ethics." *(ISC)^2 Online.* Accessed 14 April 2007 from *www.isc2.org/cgi/content.cgi?category=12.*

19. ISSA. "ISSA Code of Ethics." *ISSA Online.* Accessed 14 April 2007 from *www.issa.org/codeofethics.html.*

20. National Security Agency. *Introduction to NSA/CSS.* Accessed 14 April 2007 from *www.nsa.gov/about/index.cfm.*

21. National Security Agency. *Information Assurance.* Accessed 14 April 2007 from *www.nsa.gov/ia/.*

chapter 4

Risk Management

Once we know our weaknesses, they cease to do us any harm.
G.C. (GEORG CHRISTOPH) LICHTENBERG (1742–1799)
GERMAN PHYSICIST, PHILOSOPHER

Charlie Moody called the meeting to order. The conference room was full of developers, systems analysts, and IT managers, as well as staff and management from sales and other departments.

"All right everyone, let's get started. Welcome to the kick-off meeting of our new project team, the Sequential Label and Supply Information Security Task Force. We're here today to talk about our objectives and to review the initial work plan."

"Why is my department here?" asked the manager of sales. "Isn't security a problem for the IT department?"

Charlie explained, "Well, we used to think so, but we've come to realize that information security is about managing the risk of using information, which involves almost everyone in the company. In order to make our systems more secure, we need the participation of representatives from all departments."

Charlie continued, "I hope everyone read the packets we sent out last week describing the legal requirements we face in our industry and the background articles on threats and attacks. Today we'll begin the process of identifying and classifying all of the information technology risks that face our organization. This includes everything from fires and floods that could disrupt our business to hackers who might try to steal or destroy our data. Once we identify and classify the risks facing our assets, we can discuss how to reduce or eliminate these risks by establishing controls. Which controls we actually apply will depend on the costs and benefits of each control."

"Wow, Charlie!" said Amy Windahl from the back of the room. "I'm sure we need to do it—I was hit by the last attack, just as everyone here was—but we have hundreds of systems."

"It's more like thousands," said Charlie. "That's why we have so many people on this team, and why the team includes members of every department."

Charlie continued, "Okay, everyone, please open your packets and take out the project plan with the work list showing teams, tasks, and schedules. Any questions before we start reviewing the work plan?"

LEARNING OBJECTIVES:

Upon completion of this material, you should be able to:

- Define risk management, risk identification, and risk control
- Describe how risk is identified and assessed
- Assess risk based on probability of occurrence and likely impact
- Explain the fundamental aspects of documenting risk via the process of risk assessment
- Describe the various risk mitigation strategy options
- Identify the categories that can be used to classify controls
- Recognize the existing conceptual frameworks for evaluating risk controls and formulate a cost benefit analysis
- Describe how to maintain and perpetuate risk controls

Introduction

As an aspiring information security professional, you will have a key role to play in risk management. It is the responsibility of an organization's general management to structure the IT and information security functions to defend the organization's information assets—information and data, hardware, software, procedures, networks, and people. The IT community must serve the information technology needs of the entire organization and at the same time leverage the special skills and insights of the information security community. The information security team must lead the way with skill, professionalism, and flexibility as it works with the other communities of interest to balance the usefulness and security of the information system.

In the early days of information technology, corporations used IT systems mainly to gain a definitive advantage over the competition. Establishing a competitive business model, method, or technique enabled an organization to provide a product or service that was superior and created a **competitive advantage**. This earlier model has given way to one in which all competitors have reached a certain level of automation. IT is now readily available to all organizations that make the investment, allowing competitors to react quickly to changes in the market. In this highly competitive environment, organizations cannot expect the implementation of new technologies to provide a competitive lead over others in the industry. Instead, the concept of **competitive disadvantage**—falling behind the competition—has emerged. Effective IT-enabled organizations quickly absorb emerging technologies now, not to gain or maintain competitive advantage, but to avoid loss of market share resulting from an inability to maintain the highly responsive services required in today's marketplaces.

To keep up with the competition, organizations must design and create safe environments in which business processes and procedures can function. These environments must maintain confidentiality and privacy and assure the integrity of organizational data—objectives that are met via the application of the principles of risk management.

This chapter explores a variety of control approaches, and follows with a discussion of how controls can be categorized. The chapter finishes with a section on maintaining effective controls in the modern IT organization.

An Overview of Risk Management

Risk management is the process of identifying risk, as represented by vulnerabilities, to an organization's information assets and infrastructure, and taking steps to reduce this risk to an acceptable level. Each of the three elements in the C.I.A. triangle, introduced in Chapter 1, is an essential part of every IT organization's ability to sustain long-term competitiveness. When an organization depends on IT-based systems to remain viable, information security and the discipline of risk management must become an integral part of the economic basis for making business decisions. These decisions are based on trade-offs between the costs of applying information systems controls and the benefits realized from the operation of secured, available systems.

Risk management involves three major undertakings: risk identification, risk assessment, and risk control. **Risk identification** is the examination and documentation of the security posture of an organization's information technology and the risks it faces. **Risk assessment** is the determination of the extent to which the organization's information assets are exposed or at risk. **Risk control** is the application of controls to reduce the risks to an organization's data and information systems. The various components of risk management and their relationship to each other are shown in Figure 4-1.

An observation made over 2,400 years ago by Chinese General Sun Tzu Wu has direct relevance to information security today.

> *If you know the enemy and know yourself, you need not fear the result of a hundred battles. If you know yourself but not the enemy, for every victory gained you will also suffer a defeat. If you know neither the enemy nor yourself, you will succumb in every battle.*[1]

Consider for a moment the similarities between information security and warfare. Information security managers and technicians are the defenders of information. The many threats discussed in Chapter 2 are constantly attacking the defenses surrounding information assets. Defenses are built in layers, by placing safeguard upon safeguard. The defenders attempt to prevent, protect, detect, and recover from a seemingly endless series of attacks. Moreover, those defenders are legally prohibited from deploying offensive tactics, so the attackers have no need to expend resources on defense. In order to be victorious, you, a defender, must know yourself and know the enemy.

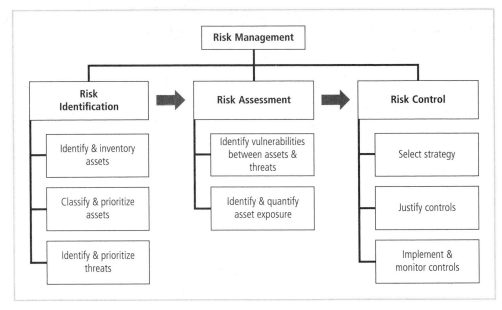

Figure 4-1 Components of Risk Management

Source: Course Technology/Cengage Learning

Know Yourself

First, you must identify, examine, and understand the information and systems currently in place within your organization. This is self-evident. To protect *assets*, which are defined here as information and the systems that use, store, and transmit information, you must know what they are, how they add value to the organization, and to which vulnerabilities they are susceptible. Once you know what you have, you can identify what you are already doing to protect it. Just because a control is in place does not necessarily mean that the asset is protected. Frequently, organizations implement control mechanisms but then neglect the necessary periodic review, revision, and maintenance. The policies, education and training programs, and technologies that protect information must be carefully maintained and administered to ensure that they remain effective.

Know the Enemy

Having identified your organization's assets and weaknesses, you move on to Sun Tzu's second step: Know the enemy. This means identifying, examining, and understanding the *threats* facing the organization. You must determine which threat aspects most directly affect the security of the organization and its information assets, and then use this information to create a list of threats, each one ranked according to the importance of the information assets that it threatens.

The Roles of the Communities of Interest

Each community of interest has a role to play in managing the risks that an organization encounters. Because the members of the information security community best understand the threats and attacks that introduce risk into the organization, they often take a leadership role in addressing risk. Management and users, when properly trained and kept aware of the threats the organization faces, play a part in the early detection and response process.

Management must also ensure that sufficient resources (money and personnel) are allocated to the information security and information technology groups to meet the security needs of the organization. Users work with the systems and the data and are therefore well positioned to understand the value these information assets offer the organization and which assets among the many in use are the most valuable. The information technology community of interest must build secure systems and operate them safely. For example, IT operations ensure good backups to control the risk from hard drive failures. The IT community can provide both valuation and threat perspectives to management during the risk management process.

All of the communities of interest must work together to address all levels of risk, which range from disasters that can devastate the whole organization to the smallest employee mistakes. The three communities of interest are also responsible for the following:

- Evaluating the risk controls
- Determining which control options are cost effective for the organization
- Acquiring or installing the needed controls
- Ensuring that the controls remain effective

It is essential that all three communities of interest conduct periodic management reviews. The first focus of management review is asset inventory. On a regular basis, management must verify the completeness and accuracy of the asset inventory. In addition, organizations must review and verify the threats to and vulnerabilities in the asset inventory, as well as the current controls and mitigation strategies. They must also review the cost effectiveness of each control and revisit the decisions on deployment of controls. Furthermore, managers at all levels must regularly verify the ongoing effectiveness of every control deployed. For example, a sales manager might assess control procedures by walking through the office before the workday starts, picking up all the papers from every desk in the sales department. When the workers show up, the manager could inform them that a fire had been simulated and all of their papers destroyed, and that each worker must now follow the disaster recovery procedures to assess the effectiveness of the procedures and suggest corrections.

Risk Identification

A risk management strategy requires that information security professionals know their organizations' information assets—that is, identify, classify, and prioritize them. Once the organizational assets have been identified, a threat assessment process identifies and quantifies the risks facing each asset.

The components of risk identification are shown in Figure 4-2.

Plan and Organize the Process

Just as with any major information security undertaking, the first step in the Risk Identification process is to follow your project management principles. You begin by organizing a team, typically consisting of representatives of all affected groups. With risk identification, since risk can exist everywhere in the organization, representatives will come from every department from users, to managers, to IT and InfoSec groups. The process must then be planned out, with periodic deliverables, reviews, and presentations to management. Once the project is ready to begin, a meeting like the one Charlie is conducting in the opening case

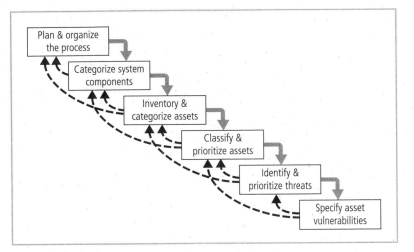

Figure 4-2 Components of Risk Identification

Source: Course Technology/Cengage Learning

Traditional System Components	SesSDLC Components	Risk Management System Components
People	Employees	Trusted employees Other staff
	Nonemployees	People at trusted organizations Strangers
Procedures	Procedures	IT and business standard procedures IT and business sensitive procedures
Data	Information	Transmission Processing Storage
Software	Software	Applications Operating systems Security components
Hardware	System devices and peripherals	Systems and peripherals Security devices
	Networking components	Intranet components Internet or DMZ components

Table 4-1 Categorizing the Components of an Information System

begins. Tasks are laid out, assignments made, and timetables discussed. Only then is the organization ready to actually begin the next step—identifying and categorizing assets.

Asset Identification and Inventory

This iterative process begins with the enumeration of assets, including all of the elements of an organization's system, such as people, procedures, data and information, software, hardware, and networking elements (see Table 4-1). Then, you classify and categorize the assets, adding details as you dig deeper into the analysis. The objective of this process is to establish the relative priority of the assets to the success of the organization.

Table 4-1 compares the categorizations found within a standard information system (people, procedures, data and information, software, and hardware) with those found in an enhanced version, which incorporates risk management and the SecSDLC approach. As you can see, the SecSDLC/risk management categorization introduces a number of new subdivisions:

- People comprise employees and nonemployees. There are two subcategories of employees: those who hold trusted roles and have correspondingly greater authority and accountability, and other staff who have assignments without special privileges. Nonemployees include contractors and consultants, members of other organizations with which the organization has a trust relationship, and strangers.

- Procedures fall into two categories: IT and business standard procedures, and IT and business sensitive procedures. The business sensitive procedures are those that may enable a threat agent to craft an attack against the organization or that have some other content or feature that may introduce risk to the organization. One instance of the loss of a sensitive procedure was the theft of the documentation for the E911 system from Bellsouth.[2] This documentation revealed certain aspects of the inner workings of a critical phone system.

- Data components account for the management of information in all its states: transmission, processing, and storage. These expanded categories solve the problem posed by the term *data*, which is usually associated with databases and not the full range of modalities of data and information used by a modern organization.

- Software components are assigned to one of three categories: applications, operating systems, or security components. Security components can be applications or operating systems, but are categorized as part of the information security control environment and must be protected more thoroughly than other systems components.

- Hardware is assigned to one of two categories: the usual systems devices and their peripherals, and those devices that are part of information security control systems. The latter must be protected more thoroughly than the former, since networking subsystems are often the focal point of attacks against the system; they should be considered as special cases rather than combined with general hardware and software components.

People, Procedures, and Data Asset Identification Identifying human resources, documentation, and data assets is more difficult than identifying hardware and software assets. People with knowledge, experience, and judgment should be assigned the task. As the people, procedures, and data assets are identified, they should be recorded using a reliable data-handling process. Whatever record keeping mechanism you use, be sure it has the flexibility to allow the specification of attributes particular to the type of asset. Some attributes are unique to a class of elements. When deciding which information assets to track, consider the following asset attributes:

- People: Position name/number/ID (avoid names and stick to identifying positions, roles, or functions); supervisor; security clearance level; special skills

- Procedures: Description; intended purpose; relationship to software, hardware, and networking elements; storage location for reference; storage location for update

- Data: Classification; owner, creator, and manager; size of data structure; data structure used (sequential or relational); online or offline; location; backup procedures employed

As you develop the data-tracking process, consider carefully how much data should be tracked and for which specific assets. Most large organizations find that they can only effectively track a few valuable facts about the most critical devices. For instance, a company may only track the IP address, server name, and device type for the mission-critical servers used by the company. They may forego the tracking of more details on all devices and completely forego the tracking of desktop or laptop systems.

Hardware, Software, and Network Asset Identification

Which attributes of hardware, software, and network assets should be tracked? It depends on the needs of the organization and its risk management efforts, as well as the preferences and needs of the information security and information technology communities. You may want to consider including the following asset attributes:

- Name: Use the most common device or program name. Organizations may have several names for the same product. For example, a software product might have a nickname within the company use while it is in development, as well as a formal name used by marketing and vendors. Make sure that the names you choose are meaningful to all the groups that use the information. You should adopt naming standards that do not convey information to potential system attackers. For instance, a server named CASH1 or HQ_FINANCE may entice attackers to take a shortcut to those systems.

- IP address: This can be a useful identifier for network devices and servers, but does not usually apply to software. You can, however, use a relational database and track software instances on specific servers or networking devices. Also note that many organizations use the dynamic host control protocol (DHCP) within TCP/IP that reassigns IP numbers to devices as needed, making the use of IP numbers as part of the asset identification process problematic. IP address use in inventory is usually limited to those devices that use static IP addresses.

- Media access control (MAC) address: MAC addresses are sometimes called electronic serial numbers or hardware addresses. As part of the TCP/IP standard, all network interface hardware devices have a unique number. The MAC address number is used by the network operating system to identify a specific network device. It is used by the client's network software to recognize traffic that it must process. In most settings, MAC addresses can be a useful way to track connectivity. They can, however, be spoofed by some hardware and software combinations.

- Element type: For hardware, you can develop a list of element types, such as servers, desktops, networking devices, or test equipment, to whatever degree of detail you require. For software elements, you may choose to develop a list of types that includes operating systems, custom applications by type (accounting, HR, or payroll to name a few), packaged applications, and specialty applications, such as firewall programs. The needs of the organization determine the degree of specificity. Types may, in fact, be recorded at two or more levels of specificity. Record one attribute that classifies the asset at a high level and then add attributes for more detail. For example, one server might be listed as:
  - DeviceClass = S (server)
  - DeviceOS = W2K (Windows 2000)
  - DeviceCapacity = AS (advanced server)

- Serial number: For hardware devices, the serial number can uniquely identify a specific device. Some software vendors also assign a software serial number to each instance of the program licensed by the organization.

- Manufacturer name: Record the manufacturer of the device or software component. This can be useful when responding to incidents that involve these devices or when certain manufacturers announce specific vulnerabilities.

- Manufacturer's model number or part number: Record the model or part number of the element. This record of exactly what the element is can be very useful in later analysis of vulnerabilities, because some vulnerability instances only apply to specific models of certain devices and software components.

- Software version, update revision, or FCO number: Whenever possible, document the specific software or firmware revision number and, for hardware devices, the current **field change order** (FCO) number. An FCO is an authorization issued by an organization for the repair, modification, or update of a piece of equipment. The equipment is not returned to the manufacturer, but is usually repaired at the customer's location, often by a third party. Documenting the revision number and FCO is particularly important for networking devices that function mainly by means of the software running on them. For example, firewall devices often have three versions: an operating system (OS) version, a software version, and a basic input/output system (BIOS) firmware version. Depending on your needs, you may have to track all three of those version numbers.

- Physical location: Note where this element is located physically. This may not apply to software elements, but some organizations have license terms that specify where software can be used.

- Logical location: Note where this element can be found on the organization's network. The logical location is most useful for networking devices and indicates the logical network where the device is connected.

- Controlling entity: Identify which organizational unit controls the element. Sometimes a remote location's onsite staff controls a networking device, and at other times the central networks team controls other devices of the same make and model. You should try to differentiate which group or unit controls each specific element, because that group may want a voice in how much risk that device can tolerate and how much expense they can sustain to add controls.

Automated Asset Inventory Tools Automated tools can sometimes identify the system elements that make up hardware, software, and network components. For example, many organizations use automated asset inventory systems. The inventory listing is usually available in a database or can be exported to a database for custom information on security assets. Once stored, the inventory listing must be kept current, often by means of a tool that periodically refreshes the data.

When you move to the later steps of risk management, which involve calculations of loss and projections of costs, the case for the use of automated risk management tools for tracking information assets becomes stronger. At this point in the process, however, simple word processing, spreadsheet, and database tools can provide adequate record keeping.

Data Classification and Management Corporate and military organizations use a variety of classification schemes. Many corporations use a **data classification scheme** to help secure the confidentiality and integrity of information.

The typical information classification scheme has three categories: confidential, internal, and external. Information owners are responsible for classifying the information assets for which they are responsible. At least once a year, information owners must review information classifications to ensure the information is still classified correctly and the appropriate access controls are in place.

The information classifications are as follows:

- Confidential: Used for the most sensitive corporate information that must be tightly controlled, even within the company. Access to information with this classification is strictly on a need-to-know basis or as required by the terms of a contract. Information with this classification may also be referred to as "sensitive" or "proprietary."

- Internal: Used for all internal information that does not meet the criteria for the confidential category and is to be viewed only by corporate employees, authorized contractors, and other third parties.

- External: All information that has been approved by management for public release.

As you might expect, the U.S. military classification scheme has a more complex categorization system than that of most corporations. The military is perhaps the best-known user of data classification schemes. In order to maintain the protection of the confidentiality of information, the military has invested heavily in INFOSEC (information security), OPSEC (operations security), and COMSEC (communications security). In fact, many of the developments in data communications and information security are the result of military-sponsored research and development. For most information, the military uses a five-level classification scheme: Unclassified, Sensitive But Unclassified (i.e., For Official Use Only), Confidential, Secret, and Top Secret. Each of these is defined below.[3]

- Unclassified data: Information that can generally be distributed to the public without any threat to U.S. national interests.

- Sensitive But Unclassified data (SBU): "Any information of which the loss, misuse, or unauthorized access to, or modification of might adversely affect U.S. national interests, the conduct of Department of Defense (DoD) programs, or the privacy of DoD personnel." Common SBU categories include For Official Use Only, Not for Public Release, or For Internal Use Only.

- Confidential data: "Any information or material the unauthorized disclosure of which reasonably could be expected to cause damage to the national security. Examples of damage include the compromise of information that indicates strength of ground, air, and naval forces in the United States and overseas areas; disclosure of technical information used for training, maintenance, and inspection of classified munitions of war; revelation of performance characteristics, test data, design, and production data on munitions of war."

- Secret data: "Any information or material the unauthorized disclosure of which reasonably could be expected to cause serious damage to the national security. Examples of serious damage include disruption of foreign relations significantly affecting the national security; significant impairment of a program or policy directly related to the national security; revelation of significant military plans or intelligence operations; compromise of significant military plans or intelligence operations; and compromise of significant scientific or technological developments relating to national security."

- Top Secret data: "Any information or material the unauthorized disclosure of which reasonably could be expected to cause exceptionally grave damage to the national security. Examples of exceptionally grave damage include armed hostilities against the United States or its allies; disruption of foreign relations vitally affecting the national security; the compromise of vital national defense plans or complex cryptologic and communications intelligence systems; the revelation of sensitive intelligence operations; and the disclosure of scientific or technological developments vital to national security." This classification comes with the general expectation of "crib-to-grave" protection, meaning that any individual entrusted with top-secret information is expected to retain this level of confidence for his or her lifetime.

The military also has some specialty classification ratings, such as Personnel Information and Evaluation Reports, to protect related areas of information. Federal agencies such as the FBI and CIA also use specialty classification schemes, like Need-to-Know and Named Projects. Obviously, Need-to-Know allows access to information by individuals who need the information to perform their work. Named Projects are clearance levels based on a scheme similar to Need-to-Know. When an operation, project, or set of classified data is created, the project is assigned a code name, such as Phoenix. Next, a list of authorized individuals is created and assigned to either the Need-to-Know or Named Projects category, and the list is maintained to enable the restriction of access to these categories of material.

Most organizations do not need the detailed level of classification used by the military or federal agencies. However, a simple scheme, such as the following, can allow an organization to protect such sensitive information as marketing or research data, personnel data, customer data, and general internal communications.

- Public: Information for general public dissemination, such as an advertisement or public release.

- For Official Use Only: Information that is not particularly sensitive, but not for public release, such as internal communications.

- Sensitive: Information important to the business that could embarrass the company or cause loss of market share if revealed.

- Classified: Information of the utmost secrecy to the organization, disclosure of which could severely impact the well-being of the organization.

Security Clearances Corresponding to the data classification scheme is the personnel **security clearance** structure. In organizations that require security clearances, each user of data must be assigned a single authorization level that indicates the level of classification he or she is authorized to view. This is usually accomplished by assigning each employee to a named role, such as data entry clerk, development programmer, information security analyst, or even CIO. Most organizations have a set of roles and their associated security clearances. Overriding an employee's security clearance requires that the **need-to-know** standard described earlier be met. In fact, this standard should be met regardless of an employee's security clearance. This extra level of protection ensures that the confidentiality of information is properly maintained.

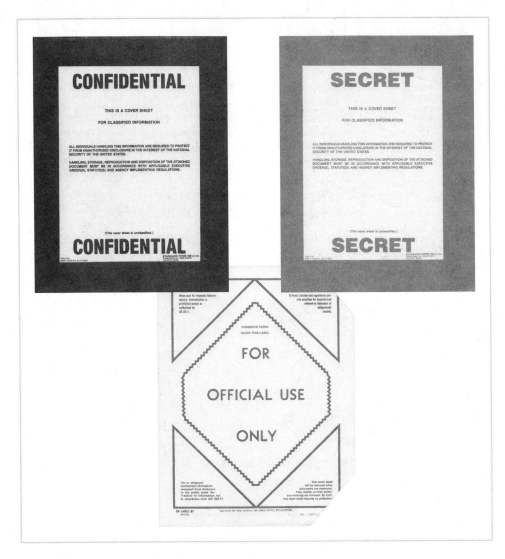

Figure 4-3 Military Data Classification Cover Sheets

Source: Course Technology/Cengage Learning

Management of Classified Data Management of classified data includes its storage, distribution, portability, and destruction. All information that is not unclassified or public must be clearly marked as such; see the examples from the military shown in Figure 4-3. The military also uses color-coordinated cover sheets to protect classified information from the casual observer. In addition, each classified document should contain the appropriate designation at the top and bottom of each page. When classified data is stored, it must be available only to authorized individuals. This usually requires locking file cabinets, safes, or other protective devices for hard copies and systems. When a person carries classified information, it should be inconspicuous, as in a locked briefcase or portfolio.

Figure 4-4 Clean Desk Policy Violation?

Source: Course Technology/Cengage Learning

One control policy that can be difficult to enforce is the clean desk policy. A **clean desk policy** requires that employees secure all information in appropriate storage containers at the end of each day. When copies of classified information are no longer valuable or excess copies exist, proper care should be taken to destroy them, usually after double signature verification, by means of shredding, burning, or transferring to a service offering authorized document destruction. As is evident from the photograph of the desk of one of the authors (Figure 4-4) this type of policy is generally not a requirement in academia! It is important to enforce policies to ensure that no classified information is disposed of in trash or recycling areas. There are individuals who search trash and recycling bins—a practice known as **dumpster diving**—to retrieve information that could embarrass a company or compromise information security.

Classifying and Prioritizing Information Assets

Some organizations further subdivide the categories listed in Table 4-1. For example, the category "Internet components" can be subdivided into servers, networking devices (routers, hubs, switches), protection devices (firewalls, proxies), and cabling. Each of the other categories can be similarly subdivided as needed by the organization.

You should also include a dimension to represent the sensitivity and security priority of the data and the devices that store, transmit, and process the data—that is, a data classification scheme. Examples of data classification categories are confidential, internal, and public. A data classification scheme generally requires a corresponding personnel security clearance structure, which determines the level of information individuals are authorized to view, based on what they need to know.

Any system component classification method must be specific enough to enable determination of priority levels, because the next step in risk assessment is to rank the components. It is also important that the categories be comprehensive and mutually exclusive. *Comprehensive* means that all information assets must fit in the list somewhere, and *mutually exclusive* means that an information asset should fit in only one category. For example, suppose an organization has a public key infrastructure certificate authority, which is a software application that provides cryptographic key management services. Using a purely technical standard, an analysis team could categorize the certificate authority in the asset list of Table 4-1 as software, and within the software category as either an application or a security component. A certificate authority should actually be categorized as a software security component, since it is part of the security infrastructure and must be protected carefully.

Information Asset Valuation

To assign value to information assets for risk assessment purposes, you can pose a number of questions and collect your answers on a worksheet like the one shown in Figure 4-5 for later analysis. Before beginning the inventory process, the organization should determine which criteria can best establish the value of the information assets. Among the criteria to be considered are:

- Which information asset is the most critical to the success of the organization? When determining the relative importance of each asset, refer to the organization's mission

---

System Name: SLS E-Commerce

Date Evaluated: February 2012

Evaluated By: D. Jones

Information assets	Data classification	Impact to profitability
Information Transmitted:		
EDI Document Set 1—Logistics BOL to outsourcer (outbound)	Confidential	High
EDI Document Set 2—Supplier orders (outbound)	Confidential	High
EDI Document Set 2—Supplier fulfillment advice (inbound)	Confidential	Medium
Customer order via SSL (inbound)	Confidential	Critical
Customer service request via e-mail (inbound)	Private	Medium
DMZ Assets:		
Edge router	Public	Critical
Web server #1—home page and core site	Public	Critical
Web server #2—Application server	Private	Critical

Notes: BOL: Bill of Lading
DMZ: Demilitarized Zone
EDI: Electronic Data Interchange
SSL: Secure Sockets Layer

Figure 4-5 Sample Inventory Worksheet

Source: Course Technology/Cengage Learning

statement or statement of objectives to determine which elements are essential, which are supportive, and which are merely adjuncts. For example, a manufacturing company that makes aircraft engines finds that the process control systems controlling the machine tools on the assembly line are of the first order of importance. Although shipping and receiving data-entry consoles are important, they are less critical because alternatives are available or can be easily arranged. Another example is an online organization such as Amazon.com. The Web servers that advertise Amazon's products and receive orders 24 hours a day are critical to the success of the business, whereas the desktop systems used by the customer service department to answer e-mails are less important.

- Which information asset generates the most revenue? You can also determine which information assets are critical by evaluating how much of the organization's revenue depends on a particular asset, or for nonprofit organizations, which are most critical to service delivery. In some organizations, different systems are in place for each line of business or service offering. Which of these plays the biggest role in generating revenue or delivering services?

- Which information asset generates the most profitability? Organizations should evaluate how much of the organization's profitability depends on a particular asset. For instance, at Amazon.com, some servers support the sales operations and other servers support the auction process, while other servers support the customer review database. Which of these servers contribute most to the profitability of the business? Although important, the customer review database server really does not directly add to profitability—at least not to the degree that the sales operations servers do. Note, however, that some services may have large revenue values, but are operating on such thin or nonexistent margins that they do not generate a profit. Nonprofit organizations can determine what percentage of their clientele receives services from the information asset being evaluated.

- Which information asset would be the most expensive to replace? Sometimes an information asset acquires special value because it is unique. If an enterprise still uses a Model-129 keypunch machine, for example, to create special punch card entries for a critical batch run, that machine may be worth more than its cost, since there may no longer be spare parts or service providers available for it. Another example is a specialty device with a long acquisition lead time because of manufacturing or transportation requirements. Such a device has a unique value to the organization. After the organization has identified this unique value, it can address ways to control the risk of losing access to the unique asset. An organization can also control the risk of loss for this kind of asset by buying and storing a backup device.

- Which information asset would be the most expensive to protect? In this case, you are determining the cost of providing controls. Some assets are by their nature difficult to protect. Finding a complete answer to this question may have to be delayed beyond the risk identification phase of the process, because the costs of controls cannot be computed until the controls are identified, and that is a later step in this process. But information about the difficulty of establishing controls should be collected in the identification phase.

- Which information asset would most expose the company to liability or embarrassment if revealed? Almost every organization is aware of its image in the local, national, and international spheres. For many organizations, the compromise of certain assets could prove especially damaging to this image. The image of Microsoft, for example, was tarnished when one of its employees became a victim of the QAZ Trojan capability and the (then) latest version of Microsoft Office was stolen.[4]

When it is necessary to calculate, estimate, or derive values for information assets, consideration might be given to the following:

- Value retained from the cost of creating the information asset: Information is created or acquired at some cost to the organization. The cost can be calculated or estimated. One category of this cost is software development, and another is data collection and processing. Many organizations have developed extensive cost accounting practices to capture the costs associated with the collection and processing of data, as well as the costs of the software development and maintenance activities.

- Value retained from past maintenance of the information asset: It is estimated that for every dollar spent developing an application or acquiring and processing data, many more dollars are spent on maintenance over the useful life of the data or software. Such costs can be estimated by quantifying the human resources used to continually update, support, modify, and service the applications and systems associated with a particular information asset.

- Value implied by the cost of replacing the information: Another important cost associated with the loss or damage to information is the cost associated with replacing or restoring the information. This includes the human resource time needed to reconstruct, restore, or regenerate the information from backups, independent transactions logs, or even hard copies of data sources. Most organizations rely on routine media backups to protect their information, but lost real-time information may not be recoverable from a tape backup, unless journaling capabilities are built into the system process. To replace information in the system, the information may have to be reconstructed, and the data reentered into the system and validated. This restoration can take longer than it took to create the data.

- Value from providing the information: Different from the cost of developing or maintaining the information is the cost of providing the information to the users who need it. This includes the value associated with the delivery of the information via databases, networks, and hardware and software systems. It also includes the cost of the infrastructure necessary to provide access and control of the information.

- Value incurred from the cost of protecting the information: Here is a recursive dilemma: the value of an asset is based in part on the cost of protecting it, while the amount of money spent to protect an asset is based in part on the value of the asset. While this is a seemingly unsolvable circle of logic, it is possible to estimate the value of the protection for an information asset to better understand the value associated with its potential loss. The values listed previously are easy to calculate. This and the following values are more likely to be estimates of cost.

- Value to owners: How much is your Social Security number worth to you? Or your telephone number? It can be quite a daunting task to place a value on information. A market researcher collects data from a company's sales figures and determines that there is a strong market potential for a certain age group with a certain demographic value for a new product offering. The cost associated with the creation of this new information may be small, so how much is it actually worth? It could be worth millions if it successfully defines a new market. The value of information to an organization, or how much of the organization's bottom line is directly attributable to the information, may be impossible to estimate. However, it is vital to understand the overall cost of protecting this information in order to understand its value. Here again, estimating value may be the only method.

- Value of intellectual property: Related to the value of information is the specific consideration of the value of intellectual property. The value of a new product or service to a customer may be unknowable. How much would a cancer patient pay for a cure? How much would a shopper pay for a new type of cheese? What is the value of an advertising jingle? All of these could represent the intellectual property of an organization, yet their valuation is complex. A related but separate consideration is intellectual properties known as trade secrets. These intellectual information assets are so valuable that they are literally the primary assets of some organizations.

- Value to adversaries: How much would it be worth to an organization to know what the competition is up to? Many organizations have departments that deal in competitive intelligence and that assess and estimate the activities of their competition. Even organizations in traditionally not-for-profit sectors can benefit from understanding what is going on in political, business, and competing organizations.

There are likely to be company-specific criteria that may add value to the asset evaluation process. They should be identified, documented, and added to the process. To finalize this step of the information asset identification process, each organization should assign a weight to each asset based on the answers to the chosen questions.

Information Asset Prioritization Once the inventory and value assessment are complete, you can prioritize each asset using a straightforward process known as *weighted factor analysis*, as shown in Table 4-2. In this process, each information asset is assigned a score for each of a set of assigned critical factor. In the example shown in Table 4-2, there are three assigned critical factors and each asset is assessed a score for each of the critical factors. In the example, the scores range from 0.1 to 1.0, which is the range of values recommended by NIST SP800-30, Risk Management for Information Technology Systems,

Information Asset	Criteria 1: Impact to Revenue	Criteria 2: Impact to Profitability	Criteria 3: Impact to Public Image	Weighted Score
Criterion Weight (1-100) Must total 100	30	40	30	
EDI Document Set 1—Logistics BOL to outsourcer (outbound)	0.8	0.9	0.5	75
EDI Document Set 2—Supplier orders (outbound)	0.8	0.9	0.6	78
EDI Document Set 2—Supplier fulfillment advice (inbound)	0.4	0.5	0.3	41
Customer order via SSL (inbound)	1.0	1.0	1.0	100
Customer service request via e-mail (inbound)	0.4	0.4	0.9	55

Table 4-2 **Example of a Weighted Factor Analysis Worksheet**

Notes: EDI: Electronic Data Interchange
       SSL: Secure Sockets Layer

a document published by the National Institute of Standards and Technology. In addition, each of the critical factors is also assigned a weight (ranging from 1 to 100) to show that criteria's assigned importance for the organization.

A quick review of Table 4-2 shows that the customer order via SSL (inbound) data flow is the most important asset on this worksheet with a weighted score of 100, and that the EDI document set 2—supplier fulfillment advice (inbound) is the least critical, with a score of 41.

Identifying and Prioritizing Threats

After identifying and performing the preliminary classification of an organization's information assets, the analysis phase moves on to an examination of the threats facing the organization. As you discovered in Chapter 2, a wide variety of threats face an organization and its information and information systems. The realistic threats must be investigated further while the unimportant threats are set aside. If you assume every threat can and will attack every information asset, the project scope quickly becomes so complex it overwhelms the ability to plan.

The threats to information security that you learned about in Chapter 2 are shown here in Table 4-3.

Each of the threats from Table 4-3 must be examined to assess its potential to endanger the organization. This examination is known as a **threat assessment**. You can begin a threat assessment by answering a few basic questions, as follows:

- Which threats present a danger to an organization's assets in the given environment? Not all threats have the potential to affect every organization. While it is unlikely that

Threat	Example
Compromises to intellectual property	Piracy, copyright infringement
Espionage or trespass	Unauthorized access and/or data collection
Forces of nature	Fire, flood, earthquake, lightning
Human error or failure	Accidents, employee mistakes, failure to follow policy
Information extortion	Blackmail of information disclosure
Missing, inadequate, or incomplete controls	Software controls, physical security
Missing, inadequate, or incomplete organizational policy or planning	Training issues, privacy, lack of effective policy
Quality of service deviations from service providers	Power and WAN quality of service issues
Sabotage or vandalism	Destruction of systems or information
Software attacks	Viruses, worms, macros, denial of service
Technical hardware failures or errors	Equipment failure
Technical software failures or errors	Bugs, code problems, unknown loopholes
Technological obsolescence	Antiquated or outdated technologies
Theft	Illegal confiscation of property

Table 4-3 **Threats to Information Security**[5]

Source: ©2003 ACM, Inc., Included here by permission.

an entire category of threats can be eliminated, such elimination speeds up later steps of the process. (Take a look at the Offline entitled Threats to Information Security to see which threats leading CIOs identified for their organizations.) Once an organization has determined which threats apply, the security team brainstorms for particular examples of threats within each category. These specific threats are examined to determine if any do not apply to the organization. For example, a company with offices on the twelfth floor of a high-rise in Denver, Colorado, is not subject to flooding. Similarly, a firm with an office in Oklahoma City, Oklahoma, should not be concerned with landslides. With this methodology, specific threats may be eliminated because of very low probability.

- Which threats represent the most danger to the organization's information? The degree of danger a threat presents is difficult to assess. Danger may be simply the probability of a threat attacking the organization, or it can represent the amount of damage the threat could create. It can also represent the frequency with which an attack can occur. Since this is a preliminary assessment, the analysis is limited to examining the existing level of preparedness, as well as improving the information security strategy. The results represent a quick overview of the components involved. As you will discover later in this chapter, you can use both quantitative and qualitative measures to rank values. Since information in this case is preliminary, the security team may wish to rank threats subjectively in order of danger. Alternatively, the organization may simply rate each of the threats on a scale of one to five, with one designating threats that are not significant and five designating threats that are highly significant.

- How much would it cost to recover from a successful attack? One of the calculations that guides corporate spending on controls is the cost of recovery operations in the event of a successful attack. At this preliminary phase, it is not necessary to conduct a detailed assessment of the costs associated with recovering from a particular attack. You might find a simpler technique quite sufficient to allow investigators to continue with the process. For example, you could subjectively rank or list the threats based on the cost to recover. Or you could assign a rating for each of the threats on a scale of one to five, with one designating not expensive at all and five designating extremely expensive. You could, if the information were available, assign a raw value to the cost, for example $5 thousand, $10 thousand, or $2 million. In other words, the goal of this phase is to provide a rough assessment of the cost to recover operations should the attack interrupt normal business operations and require recovery.

- Which of the threats would require the greatest expenditure to prevent? Just as in the previous question, another factor that affects the level of danger posed by a particular threat is the cost of protecting the organization against the threat. The cost of protecting against some threats, such as malicious code, are nominal. The cost of protection from forces of nature, on the hand, can be very great. As a result, the amount of time and money invested in protecting against a particular threat is moderated by the amount of time and money required to fully protect against that particular threat. Here again you can begin by ranking, rating, or attempting to quantify the level of effort or expense it would take to defend an asset from a particular threat. The ranking might use the same techniques outlined above in calculating recovery costs. Read the Offline entitled Expenditures for Threats to Information Security to see how some top executives recently handled this issue.

By answering these questions, you establish a framework for the discussion of threat assessment. This list of questions may not cover everything that affects the information security

Offline
Threats to Information Security—Survey of Industry

Portions adapted from "Enemy at the Gates: Threats to Information Security"[6]
By Michael E. Whitman, *Communications of the ACM*, August 2003.

What are the threats to information security according to top computing executives? A study conducted in 2003 and repeated in 2009 asked that very question. Based on the categories of threats presented earlier, over 1000 top computing executives were asked to rate each threat category on a scale of "not significant" to "very significant." The data was converted to a five-point scale with five representing "very significant." CIOs were also asked to identify the top five threats to their organizations. These were converted into weights, with five points for a first place vote and so on to one point for a fifth place vote. The two ratings were combined into a weighted rank and compared to the rankings from 2003, as shown in Table 4-4.

Categories of Threats Ranked by Greatest to Least Threat	2009 Ranking	2003 Ranking
Espionage or trespass	1	4
Software attacks	2	1
Human error or failure	3	3
Missing, inadequate, or incomplete organizational policy or planning	4	—
Missing, inadequate, or incomplete controls	5	—
Theft	6	7
Compromises to intellectual property	7	9
Sabotage or vandalism	8	5
Technical software failures or errors	9	2
Technical hardware failures or errors	10	6
Forces of nature	11	8
Quality of service deviations from service providers	12	10
Technological obsolescence	13	11
Information extortion	14	12

Table 4-4 Weighted Ranks of Threats to Information Security

Another popular study also examines threats to information security. The Computer Security Institute conducts an annual study of computer crime. Table 4-5 shows the results of the CSI/FBI study from the last five years.

Type of Attack or Misuse	2009	2008	2007	2006	2005	2004	2003	2002	2001	2000
Malware infection (renamed 2009)	64%	50%	52%	65%	74%	78%	82%	85%	94%	85%
Laptop or mobile hardware theft or loss	42%	42%	50%	47%	48%	49%	59%	55%	64%	60%
Being fraudulently represented as sender of phishing message	34%	31%	26%	(new in 2007)						
Insider abuse of Internet access or e-mail	30%	44%	59%	42%	48%	59%	80%	78%	91%	79%
Denial of service	29%	21%	25%	25%	32%	39%	42%	40%	36%	27%
Bots within the organization	23%	20%	21%	(new in 2007)						
Financial fraud	20%	12%	12%	9%	7%	8%	15%	12%	12%	11%
Password sniffing	17%	9%	10%	(new in 2007)						
Unauthorized access or privilege escalation by insider	15% (altered in 2009)									
Web site defacement	14%	6%	10%	6%	5%	7%	(new in 2004)			
System penetration by outsider	14% (altered in 2009)									
Exploit of client Web browser	11% (new in 2009)									
Theft of or unauthorized access to PII or PHI due to all other causes	10%	8% (new in 2008)								
Instant Messaging misuse	8%	21%	25% (new in 2007)							
Exploit of wireless network	8%	14%	17%	14%	17%	15% (new in 2004)				
Theft of or unauthorized access to IP due to all other causes	8%	5% (new in 2008)								
Exploit of DNS Server	7%	8%	7% (new in 2007)							
Exploit of user's social network profile	7% (new in 2009)									
Other exploit of public-facing Web site	6% (new in 2009)									

Table 4-5 CSI Survey Results for Types of Attack or Misuse (2000–2009)[7]

(continued)

Type of Attack or Misuse	2009	2008	2007	2006	2005	2004	2003	2002	2001	2000
Theft of or unauthorized access to IP due to mobile device theft or loss	6%	4% (new in 2008)								
Theft of or unauthorized access to PII or PHI due to mobile device theft or loss	6%	8% (new in 2008)								
Extortion or blackmail associated with threat of attack or release of stolen data	3% (new in 2009)									
These categories were replaced or dropped in subsequent years										
Unauthorized access to information		29%	25%	32%	32%	37%	45%	38%	49%	71%
Theft or loss of customer or employee data		17%	17% (new in 2007)							
System penetration		13%	13%	15%	14%	17%	36%	40%	40%	25%
Misuse of public Web applications		11%	9%	6%	5%	10% (new in 2004)				
Theft or loss of proprietary information		9%	8%	9%	9%	10%	21%	20%	26%	20%
Telecommunications fraud		5%	5%	8%	10%	10%	10%	9%	10%	11%
Sabotage		2%	4%	3%	2%	5%	21%	8%	18%	17%
Telecomm eavesdropping							6%	6%	10%	7%
Active wiretap							1%	1%	2%	1%

Table 4-5 CSI Survey Results for Types of Attack or Misuse (2000–2009) (continued)

The number of successful attacks continues the declining trend started in 2001. In the 2004 CSI/FBI study, every surveyed company reported some number of Web site incidents. Most reporting organizations, representing 89 percent of respondents, indicated their organization had from one to five Web site incidents in the previous 12 months. Whether a company catches an attack and is then willing to report the attack is another matter entirely. In any case, the fact is that almost every company has been attacked. Whether or not that attack was successful depended on the company's security efforts.

threat assessment. If an organization has specific guidelines or policies, these should influence the process and require additional questions. This list can be easily expanded to include additional requirements.

Vulnerability Identification

Once you have identified the organization's information assets and documented some criteria for beginning to assess the threats it faces, you then review each information asset for each

Offline
Expenditures for Threats to Information Security

**Portions Adapted from "Enemy at the Gates: Threats to Information Security"[8]
By Michael E. Whitman, *Communications of the ACM*, August 2003.**

The study described earlier also asked top computing executives to determine the priorities for expenditures for threats to information security. The respondents indicated their top five expenditures. These ratings were used to create a rank order of the expenses. The results are presented in Table 4-6.

Ranking of Top Threats Based on Money and Effort Spent to Defend Against or React to the Threat	2009 Ranking	2003 Ranking
Espionage or trespass	1	6
Software attacks	2	1
Missing, inadequate, or incomplete controls	3	—
Theft	4	7
Quality of service deviations by service providers	5	5
Forces of nature	6	10
Sabotage or vandalism	7	8
Technological obsolescence	8	9
Technical software failures or errors	9	3
Technical hardware failures or errors	10	4
Compromises to intellectual property	11	11
Human error or failure	12	2
Missing, inadequate, or incomplete organizational policy or planning	13	—
Information extortion	14	12

Table 4-6 Weighted Ranking of Top Threat-Driven Expenditures

©2003 ACM, Inc. Included here by permission.

threat it faces and create a list of vulnerabilities. What are vulnerabilities? They are specific avenues that threat agents can exploit to attack an information asset. They are chinks in the armor—a flaw or weakness in an information asset, security procedure, design, or control that could be exploited accidentally or on purpose to breach security. For example, suppose the edge router in an organization's DMZ is the asset. The threats to the possible vulnerabilities of this router would be analyzed as shown in Table 4-7.

Now you examine how each of the threats that are possible or likely could be perpetrated, and list the organization's assets and their vulnerabilities. The list is usually long and shows all the vulnerabilities of the information asset. Some threats manifest themselves in multiple ways, yielding multiple vulnerabilities for that threat. The process of listing vulnerabilities is somewhat subjective and depends upon the experience and knowledge of the people creating the list. Therefore, the process works best when groups of people with diverse backgrounds within the organization work iteratively in a series of brainstorming sessions. For instance, the team that reviews the vulnerabilities of networking equipment should include the networking specialists, the systems management team that operates the network, the information security risk specialist, and technically proficient users of the system.

The TVA Worksheet At the end of the risk identification process, you should have a prioritized list of assets and their vulnerabilities. This list serves as the starting point (with its supporting documentation from the identification process) for the next step in the risk management process—risk assessment. Another list prioritizes threats facing the organization based on the weighted table discussed earlier. These two lists can be combined into a threats-vulnerabilities-assets (TVA) worksheet in preparation for the addition of vulnerability and control information during risk assessment.

Table 4-8 shows the placement of assets along the horizontal axis, with the most important asset at the left. The prioritized list of threats are placed along the vertical axis, with the most important or most dangerous threat listed at the top. The resulting grid provides a convenient method of determining the exposure of assets, allowing a simplistic vulnerability assessment. As you begin the risk assessment process, create a list of the TVA triples to facilitate your identification of the severity of the vulnerabilities. For example, between threat 1 and asset 1 there may or may not be a vulnerability. After all, not all threats pose risk to all assets. If a pharmaceutical company's most important asset is its research and development database, and that database resides on a stand-alone network (that is, one that is not connected to the Internet), then there may be no vulnerability to external hackers. If the intersection of threat 1 and asset 1 has no vulnerability, then the risk assessment team simply crosses out that box. It is much more likely, however, that one or more vulnerabilities exist between the two, and as these vulnerabilities are identified, they are categorized as follows:

> T1V1A1—Vulnerability 1 that exists between Threat 1 and Asset 1
> T1V2A1—Vulnerability 2 that exists between Threat 1 and Asset 1
> T2V1A1—Vulnerability 1 that exists between Threat 2 and Asset 1 … and so on.

In the risk assessment phase, the assessment team examines not only the vulnerabilities but also any existing controls that protect the asset or mitigate the losses that may occur. Cataloging and categorizing these controls is the next step in the TVA spreadsheet.

Risk Assessment

Now that you have identified the organization's information assets and the threats and vulnerabilities, you can evaluate the relative risk for each of the vulnerabilities. This process is called

Threat	Possible Vulnerabilities
Compromises to intellectual property	• Copyrighted works developed in-house and stored on Intranet servers can be copied without permission unless the router is configured to limit access from outsiders. • Copyrighted works by others can be stolen; your organization is liable for that loss to the copyright holder.
Espionage or trespass	• This information asset (router) may have little intrinsic value, but other assets protected by this device could be attacked if it does not perform correctly or is compromised.
Forces of nature	• All information assets in the organization are subject to forces of nature, unless suitable controls are provided.
Human error or failure	• Employees or contractors may cause outage if configuration errors are made.
Information extortion	• If attackers bypasses the router or compromises it and enters your network, they may encrypt your data in place. They may not have stolen it, but unless you pay them to acquire the encryption key, it is inert and no longer of value to you.
Missing, inadequate, or incomplete controls	• You are expected to protect the information assets under your stewardship. For example, if you do not add authentication controls to the router, a control that a reasonable and prudent professional would apply, you are responsible if the device is compromised.
Missing, inadequate, or incomplete organizational policy or planning	• You are expected to manage the resources and information assets under your stewardship. A reasonable and prudent manager would develop and use policies and plans for the acquisition, deployment, and operation of a router or any other networking device.
Quality of service deviations from service providers	• Power system failures are always possible. • Unless suitable electrical power conditioning is provided, failure is probable over time. • ISP connectivity failures can interrupt Internet bandwidth.
Sabotage or vandalism	• Internet protocol is vulnerable to denial of service. • This device may be subject to defacement or cache poisoning.
Software attacks	• Internet protocol is vulnerable to denial of service. • Outsider IP fingerprinting activities can reveal sensitive information unless suitable controls are implemented.
Technical hardware failures or errors	• Hardware can fail and cause an outage.
Technical software failures or errors	• Vendor-supplied routing software could fail and cause an outage.
Technological obsolescence	• If this asset is not reviewed and periodically updated, it may fall too far behind its vendor support model to be kept in service.
Theft	• Data has value and can be stolen. Routers are important network devices and the controls they have and help enforce are critical layers in your defense in depth. When data is copied in place you may not know it has been stolen.

Table 4-7 Vulnerability Assessment of a Hypothetical DMZ Router

risk assessment. Risk assessment assigns a risk rating or score to each information asset. While this number does not mean anything in absolute terms, it is useful in gauging the relative risk to each vulnerable information asset and facilitates the development of comparative

	Asset 1	Asset 2	...	...	...	...	...	...	...	...	...	Asset n
Threat 1												
Threat 2												
...												
...												
...												
...												
...												
...												
...												
...												
...												
Threat n												
Priority of Controls	1		2		3		4		5		6	
These bands of controls should be continued through all asset–threat pairs.												

Table 4-8   Sample TVA Spreadsheet

Source: Course Technology/Cengage Learning

ratings later in the risk control process. The major stages of risk assessment are shown in Figure 4-6.

Introduction to Risk Assessment

Figure 4-7 shows the factors that go into the risk-rating estimate for each of the vulnerabilities.

Note that the goal at this point is to create a method for evaluating the relative risk of each of the listed vulnerabilities. Chapter 5 describes methods that determine more accurate and detailed costs of each vulnerability, as well as projected expenses for the variety of controls that can reduce the risk for each of them. For now, use the simpler risk model described in Figure 4-7 to evaluate the risk for each information asset. The following sections itemize the factors that are used to calculate the relative risk for each vulnerability.

Likelihood

Likelihood is the probability that a specific vulnerability will be the object of a successful attack.[9] In risk assessment, you assign a numeric value to likelihood. The National Institute of Standards and Technology recommends in Special Publication 800-30 assigning a number

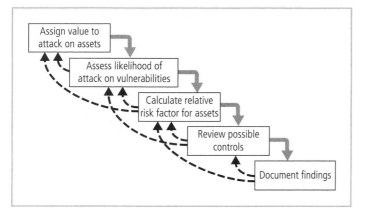

Figure 4-6 Major Stages of Risk Assessment

Source: Course Technology/Cengage Learning

Figure 4-7 Factors of Risk

Source: Course Technology/Cengage Learning

between 0.1 (low) and 1.0 (high). For example, the likelihood of an asset being struck by a meteorite while indoors would be rated 0.1. At the other extreme, receiving at least one e-mail containing a virus or worm in the next year would be rated 1.0. You could also choose to use a number between 1 and 100 (zero is not used, since vulnerabilities with a zero likelihood have been removed from the asset/vulnerability list). Whichever rating system you choose, use professionalism, experience, and judgment—and use the rating model you select consistently. Whenever possible, use external references for likelihood values that have been reviewed and adjusted for your specific circumstances. Many asset/vulnerability combinations have sources for likelihood, for example:

- The likelihood of a fire has been estimated actuarially for each type of structure.

- The likelihood that any given e-mail contains a virus or worm has been researched.

- The number of network attacks can be forecast based on how many assigned network addresses the organization has.

Risk Determination

For the purpose of relative risk assessment, risk *equals* likelihood of vulnerability occurrence *times* value (or impact) *minus* percentage risk already controlled *plus* an element of uncertainty, as illustrated in Figure 4-7. For example:

- Information asset A has a value score of 50 and has one vulnerability. Vulnerability 1 has a likelihood of 1.0 with no current controls. You estimate that assumptions and data are 90 percent accurate.

- Information asset B has a value score of 100 and has two vulnerabilities: Vulnerability 2 has a likelihood of 0.5 with a current control that addresses 50 percent of its risk; vulnerability 3 has a likelihood of 0.1 with no current controls. You estimate that assumptions and data are 80 percent accurate.

The resulting ranked list of risk ratings for the three vulnerabilities is:

- Asset A: Vulnerability 1 rated as $55 = (50 \times 1.0) - 0\% + 10\%$ where
  $55 = (50 \times 1.0) - ((50 \times 1.0) \times 0.0) + ((50 \times 0.0) \times 0.1)$
  $55 = 50 - 0 + 5$

- Asset B: Vulnerability 2 rated as $35 = (100 \times 0.5) - 50\% + 20\%$ where
  $35 = (100 \times 0.5) - ((100 \times 0.5) \times 0.5) + ((100 \times 0.5) \times 0.2)$
  $35 = 50 - 25 + 10$

- Asset B: Vulnerability 3 rated as $12 = (100 \times 0.1) - 0\% + 20\%$ where
  $12 = (100 \times 0.1) - ((100 \times 0.1) \times 0.0) + ((100 \times 0.1) \times 0.2)$
  $12 = 10 - 0 + 2$

Identify Possible Controls

For each threat and its associated vulnerabilities that have residual risk, you must create a preliminary list of potential controls. **Residual risk** is the risk to the information asset that remains even after the application of controls.

As you learned in Chapter 1, controls, safeguards, and countermeasures are terms for security mechanisms, policies, and procedures. These mechanisms, policies, and procedures counter attacks, reduce risk, resolve vulnerabilities, and otherwise improve the general state of security within an organization.

There are three general categories of controls: policies, programs, and technologies. *Policies* are documents that specify an organization's approach to security. There are four types of security policies: general security policies, program security policies, issue-specific policies, and systems-specific policies. The *general security policy* is an executive-level document that outlines the organization's approach and attitude toward information security and relates the strategic value of information security within the organization. This document, typically created by the CIO in conjunction with the CEO and CISO, sets the tone for all subsequent security activities. The *program security policy* is a planning document that outlines the process of implementing security in the organization. This policy is the blueprint for the analysis, design, and implementation of security. *Issue-specific policies* address the specific implementations or applications of which users should be aware. These policies are typically developed to provide detailed instructions and restrictions associated with security issues. Examples include policies for Internet use, e-mail, and access to the building. Finally, *systems-specific policies* address the particular use of certain systems. This could include firewall configuration policies, systems access policies, and other technical configuration areas. *Programs* are activities performed within the organization to improve security. These include security education, training, and awareness programs. Chapter 5 covers all of these policies in detail. Security *technologies* are the technical implementations of the policies defined by the organization. Chapters 6, 7, and 8 present a more detailed description of the various technologies used in security implementations.

One particular approach to control is fundamental to the processes of information security. Access control is often considered a simple function of the information system that uses it. In fact the principles of access control apply to physical control and other kinds of systems unrelated to IT. Access controls are covered in depth in Chapter 6.

Documenting the Results of Risk Assessment

By the end of the risk assessment process, you probably have in hand long lists of information assets with data about each of them. The goal so far has been to identify the information assets that have specific vulnerabilities and list them, ranked according to those most needing protection. In preparing this list, you collected and preserved a wealth of factual information about the assets, the threats they face, and the vulnerabilities they expose. You should also have collected some information about the controls that are already in place. The final summarized document is the ranked vulnerability risk worksheet, a sample of which is shown in Table 4-9. A review of this worksheet shows similarities to the weighted factor analysis worksheet shown in Table 4-2. The worksheet shown in Table 4-9 is organized as follows:

- Asset: List each vulnerable asset.
- Asset Impact: Show the results for this asset from the weighted factor analysis worksheet. In the example, this is a number from 1 to 100.
- Vulnerability: List each uncontrolled vulnerability.
- Vulnerability Likelihood: State the likelihood of the realization of the vulnerability by a threat agent, as noted in the vulnerability analysis step. In the example, the number is from 0.1 to 1.0.
- Risk-Rating Factor: Enter the figure calculated from the asset impact multiplied by likelihood. In the example, the calculation yields a number from 1 to 100.

You may be surprised that the most pressing risk in Table 4-9 lies in the vulnerable mail server. Even though the information asset represented by the customer service e-mail has an impact rating of only 55, the relatively high likelihood of a hardware failure makes it the most pressing problem.

Now that you have completed the risk identification process, what should the documentation package for this process look like? In other words, what are the deliverables from this phase of the project? The process you develop for risk identification should include designating what function the reports serve, who is responsible for preparing the reports, and who reviews them. The ranked vulnerability risk worksheet is the initial working document for the next step in the risk management process: assessing and controlling risk. Table 4-10 shows a sample list of the worksheets that might be prepared by the information security project team. Note that another method of presenting the results of the risk assessment process is given in Chapter 12.

Asset	Asset Impact or Relative Value	Vulnerability	Vulnerability Likelihood	Risk-Rating Factor
Customer service request via e-mail (inbound)	55	E-mail disruption due to hardware failure	0.2	11
Customer order via SSL (inbound)	100	Lost orders due to Web server hardware failure	0.1	10
Customer order via SSL (inbound)	100	Lost orders due to Web server or ISP service failure	0.1	10
Customer service request via e-mail (inbound)	55	E-mail disruption due to SMTP mail relay attack	0.1	5.5
Customer service request via e-mail (inbound)	55	E-mail disruption due to ISP service failure	0.1	5.5
Customer order via SSL (inbound)	100	Lost orders due to Web server denial-of-service attack	0.025	2.5
Customer order via SSL (inbound)	100	Lost orders due to Web server software failure	0.01	1

Table 4-9   Ranked Vulnerability Risk Worksheet

SSL: Secure sockets layer

Deliverable	Purpose
Information asset classification worksheet	Assembles information about information assets and their impact on or value to the organization
Weighted criteria analysis worksheet	Assigns ranked value or impact weight to each information asset
Ranked vulnerability risk worksheet	Assigns ranked value of risk rating for each uncontrolled asset-vulnerability pair

Table 4-10   Risk Identification and Assessment Deliverables

Risk Control Strategies

When organizational management determines that risks from information security threats are creating a competitive disadvantage, they empower the information technology and information security communities of interest to control the risks. Once the project team for information security development has created the ranked vulnerability worksheet, the team must choose one of five basic strategies to control each of the risks that result from these vulnerabilities. The five strategies are defend, transfer, mitigate, accept, and terminate. Table 4-11 recaps the strategies defined here and shows how offer sources of risk management process knowledge refer to them.

Defend

The **defend control strategy** attempts to prevent the exploitation of the vulnerability. This is the preferred approach and is accomplished by means of countering threats, removing vulnerabilities from assets, limiting access to assets, and adding protective safeguards. There are three common methods used to defend:

- Application of policy
- Education and training
- Application of technology

Implementing the Defend Strategy Organizations can mitigate risk to an asset by countering the threats it faces or by eliminating its exposure. It is difficult, but possible, to eliminate a threat. For example, in 2002 McDonald's Corporation, which had been subject to attacks by animal rights cyberactivists, sought to reduce risks by imposing stricter conditions on egg suppliers regarding the health and welfare of chickens.[10] This strategy was consistent with other changes made by McDonald's to meet demands from animal rights activists and improve relationships with these groups.

Another defend strategy is the implementation of security controls and safeguards to deflect attacks on systems and therefore minimize the probability that an attack will be successful. An organization with dial-in access vulnerability, for example, may choose to implement a control or safeguard for that service. An authentication procedure based on a cryptographic technology, such as RADIUS (Remote Authentication Dial-In User Service), or another protocol or product, would provide sufficient control.[11] On the other hand, the organization may choose to eliminate the dial-in system and service to avoid the potential risk (see the terminate strategy later in this chapter).

Transfer

The transfer control strategy attempts to shift risk to other assets, other processes, or other organizations. This can be accomplished by rethinking how services are offered, revising deployment models, outsourcing to other organizations, purchasing insurance, or implementing service contracts with providers. In the popular book *In Search of Excellence,* management consultants Tom Peters and Robert Waterman present a series of case studies of high-performing corporations. One of the eight characteristics of excellent organizations is that they "stick to their knitting ... They stay reasonably close to the business they know."[12] This means that Kodak, a manufacturer of photographic equipment and chemicals, focuses on photographic equipment and chemicals, while General Motors focuses on the design and construction of cars and trucks. Neither company spends strategic energies on the technology of Web site development—for this expertise, they rely on consultants or contractors.

This principle should be considered whenever an organization begins to expand its operations, including information and systems management and even information security. If an organization does not already have quality security management and administration experience, it should hire individuals or firms that provide such expertise. For example, many organizations want Web services, including Web presences, domain name registration, and domain and Web hosting. Rather than implementing their own servers and hiring their own Webmasters, Web systems administrators, and specialized security experts, savvy organizations hire an ISP or a consulting organization to provide these products and services for them. This allows the organization to transfer the risks associated with the management of these complex systems to another organization that has experience in dealing with those risks. A side benefit of specific contract arrangements is that the provider is responsible for disaster recovery, and through service level agreements is responsible for guaranteeing server and Web site availability.

Outsourcing, however, is not without its own risks. The owner of the information asset, IT management, and the information security team must ensure that the disaster recovery requirements of the outsourcing contract are sufficient and have been met *before* they are needed. If the outsourcer fails to meet the contract terms, the consequences may be far worse than expected.

Mitigate

The **mitigate control strategy** attempts to reduce the impact caused by the exploitation of vulnerability through planning and preparation. This approach requires the creation of three types of plans: the incident response plan, the disaster recovery plan, and the business continuity plan. Each of these plans depends on the ability to detect and respond to an attack as quickly as possible and relies on the quality of the other plans. Mitigation begins with the early detection that an attack is in progress and a quick, efficient, and effective response.

Incident Response Plan The actions an organization can and perhaps should take while an incident is in progress should be specified in a document called the incident response (IR) plan. The IR plan provides answers to questions victims might pose in the midst of an incident, such as "What do I do now?" For example, a systems administrator may notice that someone is copying information from the server without authorization, signaling violation of policy by a potential hacker or an unauthorized employee. What should the administrator do first? Whom should he or she contact? What should he or she document? The IR plan supplies the answers. In the event of a serious virus or worm outbreak, the IR plan can be used to assess the likelihood of imminent damage and to inform key decision makers in the various communities of interest (IT, information security, organization management, and users). The IR plan also enables the organization to take coordinated action that is either predefined and specific, or ad hoc and reactive.

Disaster Recovery Plan The most common of the mitigation procedures is the disaster recovery (DR) plan. Although media backup strategies are an integral part of the DR plan, the overall program includes the entire spectrum of activities used to recover from an incident. The DR plan can include strategies to limit losses before and during the disaster. These strategies are fully deployed once the disaster has stopped. DR plans usually include all preparations for the recovery process, strategies to limit losses during the disaster, and detailed steps to follow when the smoke clears, the dust settles, or the floodwaters recede. The DR plan and the IR plan overlap to a degree. In many respects, the DR plan is the subsection of the IR plan that covers disastrous events. The IR plan is also flexible enough to be useful in situations that are near disasters, but that still require coordinated, planned actions. While some DR plan and IR plan decisions and actions are the same, their urgency and outcomes can differ dramatically. The DR plan focuses more on preparations completed before and actions taken after the incident, whereas the IR plan focuses on intelligence gathering, information analysis, coordinated decision making, and urgent, concrete actions.

Business Continuity Plan The business continuity (BC) plan is the most strategic and long term of the three plans. It encompasses the continuation of business activities if a catastrophic event occurs, such as the loss of an entire database, building, or operations center. The BC plan includes planning the steps necessary to ensure the continuation of the organization when the scope or scale of a disaster exceeds the ability of the DR plan to restore operations. This can include preparation steps for activation of secondary data centers, hot sites, or business recovery sites, which you will learn about in detail in Chapter 5. These systems enable the organization to continue operations with minimal disruption of service. Many companies offer DR services as a contingency against disastrous events such as fires, floods, earthquakes, and most natural disasters. Table 4-12 summarizes each of the mitigation plans and supplies examples.

Accept

The **accept control strategy** is the choice to do nothing to protect a vulnerability and to accept the outcome of its exploitation. This may or may not be a conscious business decision. The only industry-recognized valid use of this strategy occurs when the organization has done the following:

- Determined the level of risk
- Assessed the probability of attack
- Estimated the potential damage that could occur from attacks
- Performed a thorough cost benefit analysis
- Evaluated controls using each appropriate type of feasibility
- Decided that the particular function, service, information, or asset did not justify the cost of protection

This strategy is based on the conclusion that the cost of protecting an asset does not justify the security expenditure. For example, suppose it would cost an organization $100,000 per year to protect a server. The security assessment determined that for $10,000 the organization could replace the information contained in the server, replace the server itself, and cover associated recovery costs. In this case, management may be satisfied with taking its chances and saving the money that would normally be spent on protecting this asset. If every vulnerability in the organization is handled by means of acceptance, it may reflect an inability to conduct proactive security activities and an apathetic approach to security in general. It is not acceptable for an organization to adopt a policy that ignorance is bliss and hope to avoid litigation by pleading ignorance of its obligation to protect employee and customer information. It is also unacceptable for management to hope that if they do not try to protect information, the opposition will assume that there is little to be gained by an attack. The risks far outweigh the benefits of this approach. Acceptance as a strategy is often mistakenly chosen based on the "school of fish" justification—that sharks will not come after a small fish in a school of other small fish. But this reasoning can be very risky.

Risk Control Strategy	Categories Used by NIST SP 800-30	Categories Used by ISACA and ISO/IEC 27001	Others
Defend	Research and Acknowledgement	Treat	Self-protection
Transfer	Risk Transference	Transfer	Risk transfer
Mitigate	Risk Limitation and Risk Planning	Tolerate (partial)	Self-insurance (partial)
Accept	Risk Assumption	Tolerate (partial)	Self-insurance (partial)
Terminate	Risk Avoidance	Terminate	Avoidance

Table 4-11 Risk Control Strategy Terminology

Plan	Description	Example	When Deployed	Time Frame
Incident Response Plan	Actions an organization takes during incidents (attacks)	• List of steps to be taken during disaster • Intelligence gathering • Information analysis	As incident or disaster unfolds	Immediate and real-time reaction
Disaster Recovery Plan	Preparations for recovery should a disaster occur; strategies to limit losses before and during disaster; step-by-step instructions to regain normalcy	• Procedures for the recovery of lost data • Procedures for the reestablishment of lost services • Shutdown procedures to protect systems and data	Immediately after the incident is labeled a disaster	Short-term recovery
Business Continuity Plan	Steps to ensure continuation of the overall business when the scale of a disaster exceeds the DR plan's ability to restore operations	• Preparation steps for activation of secondary data centers • Establishment of a hot site in a remote location	Immediately after the disaster is determined to affect the continued operations of the organization	Long-term operation

Table 4-12   Summaries of Mitigation Plans

Terminate

The terminate control strategy directs the organization to avoid those business activities that introduce uncontrollable risks. If an organization studies the risks from implementing business-to-consumer e-commerce operations and determines that the risks are not sufficiently offset by the potential benefits, the organization may seek an alternate mechanism to meet customer needs—perhaps developing new channels for product distribution or new partnership opportunities. By terminating the questionable activity, the organization reduces the risk exposure.

Selecting a Risk Control Strategy

Risk control involves selecting one of the five risk control strategies for each vulnerability. The flowchart in Figure 4-8 guides you through the process of deciding how to proceed with one of the five strategies. As shown in the diagram, after the information system is designed, you query as to whether the protected system has vulnerabilities that can be exploited. If the answer is yes and a viable threat exists, you begin to examine what the attacker would gain from a successful attack. To determine if the risk is acceptable or not, you estimate the expected loss the organization will incur if the risk is exploited.

Some rules of thumb on strategy selection are presented below. When weighing the benefits of the different strategies, keep in mind that the level of threat and value of the asset should play a major role in strategy selection.

Offline
Top 10 Information Security Mistakes Made by Individuals

**Adapted from "Top 10 Security Mistakes"[13]
By Alan S. Horowitz, *Computerworld*, July 9, 2001.**

The following compilation was developed by security experts to represent the mistakes most commonly made by employees—often unknowingly—which put their organization's information assets at risk:

1. Passwords on Post-it notes

2. Leaving unattended computers on

3. Opening e-mail attachments from strangers

4. Poor password etiquette

5. Laptops on the loose (unsecured laptops that are easily stolen)

6. Blabbermouths (people who talk about passwords)

7. Plug and play (technology that enables hardware devices to be installed and configured without the protection provided by people who perform installations)

8. Unreported security violations

9. Always behind the times (the patch procrastinator)

10. Not watching for dangers *inside* the organization

- When a vulnerability (flaw or weakness) exists: Implement security controls to reduce the likelihood of a vulnerability being exercised.

- When a vulnerability can be exploited: Apply layered protections, architectural designs, and administrative controls to minimize the risk or prevent occurrence.

- When the attacker's cost is less than his or her potential gain: Apply protections to increase the attacker's cost (e.g., use system controls to limit what a system user can access and do, thereby significantly reducing an attacker's gain).

- When potential loss is substantial: Apply design principles, architectural designs, and technical and nontechnical protections to limit the extent of the attack, thereby reducing the potential for loss.

Feasibility Studies

Before deciding on the strategy (defend, transfer, mitigate, accept, or terminate) for a specific vulnerability, the organization must explore all the economic and noneconomic consequences of the vulnerability facing the information asset. This is an attempt to answer the question, "What are the actual and perceived advantages of implementing a control as opposed to the actual and perceived disadvantages of implementing the control?"

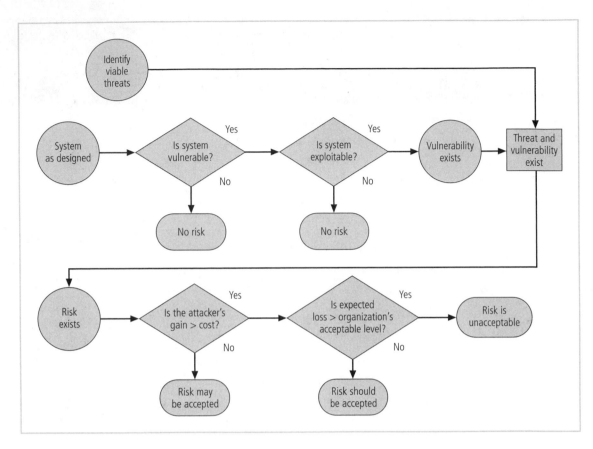

Figure 4-8 Risk Handling Decision Points

Source: Course Technology/Cengage Learning

There are a number of ways to determine the advantage of a specific control. There are also many methods an organization can use to identify the disadvantages of specific controls. The following sections discuss some of the more commonly used techniques for making these choices. Note that some of these techniques use dollar expenses and savings implied from economic cost avoidance, and others use noneconomic feasibility criteria. **Cost avoidance** is the process of preventing the financial impact of an incident by implementing a control.

Cost Benefit Analysis (CBA)

Organizations must consider the economic feasibility of implementing information security controls and safeguards. While a number of alternatives for solving a problem may exist, they may not all have the same economic feasibility. Most organizations can spend only a reasonable amount of time and money on information security, and the definition of reasonable differs from organization to organization and even from manager to manager. Organizations are urged to begin the cost benefit analysis by evaluating the worth of the information assets to be protected and the loss in value if those information assets were compromised by the exploitation of a specific vulnerability. It is only common sense that an organization should not spend more to protect an asset than the asset is worth. The formal decision-making process is called a **cost benefit analysis** or an **economic feasibility study**.

Just as it is difficult to determine the value of information, it is also difficult to determine the cost of safeguards. Some of the items that affect the cost of a control or safeguard include the following:

- Cost of development or acquisition (purchase cost) of hardware, software, and services
- Training fees (cost to train personnel)
- Cost of implementation (cost to install, configure, and test hardware, software, and services)
- Service costs (vendor fees for maintenance and upgrades)
- Cost of maintenance (labor expense to verify and continually test, maintain, and update)

Benefit is the value that an organization realizes by using controls to prevent losses associated with a specific vulnerability. The amount of the benefit is usually determined by valuing the information asset or assets exposed by the vulnerability and then determining how much of that value is at risk and how much risk there is for the asset. A benefit may be expressed as a reduction in the annualized loss expectancy, which is defined later in this chapter.

Asset valuation is the process of assigning financial value or worth to each information asset. Some argue that it is virtually impossible to determine the true value of information and information-bearing assets. Perhaps this is one reason why insurance underwriters currently have no definitive valuation tables for assigning worth to information assets. The value of information differs within organizations and between organizations, depending both on the characteristics of the information and the perceived value of that information. Much of the work of assigning value to assets can draw on the information asset inventory and assessment that was prepared for the risk identification process described earlier in this chapter.

The valuation of assets involves estimation of real and perceived costs associated with design, development, installation, maintenance, protection, recovery, and defense against loss and litigation. These estimates are calculated for every set of information-bearing systems or information assets. Some component costs are easy to determine, such as the cost to replace a network switch or the hardware needed for a specific class of server. Other costs are almost impossible to determine accurately, for example, the dollar value of the loss in market share if information on new product offerings is released prematurely and a company loses its competitive edge. A further complication is the value that some information assets acquire over time that is beyond the **intrinsic value** of the asset under consideration. The higher **acquired value** is the more appropriate value in most cases.

Asset valuation techniques are discussed in more detail earlier in this chapter.

Once an organization has estimated the worth of various assets, it can begin to examine the potential loss that could occur from the exploitation of a vulnerability or a threat occurrence. This process results in the estimate of potential loss per risk. The questions that must be asked here include:

- What damage could occur, and what financial impact would it have?
- What would it cost to recover from the attack, in addition to the financial impact of damage?
- What is the single loss expectancy for each risk?

A **single loss expectancy (SLE)** is the calculation of the value associated with the most likely loss from an attack. It is a calculation based on the value of the asset and the **exposure factor (EF)**, which is the expected percentage of loss that would occur from a particular attack, as follows:

SLE = asset value × exposure factor (EF)

where EF equals the percentage loss that would occur from a given vulnerability being exploited.

For example, if a Web site has an estimated value of $1,000,000 (value determined by asset valuation), and a deliberate act of sabotage or vandalism (hacker defacement) scenario indicates that 10 percent of the Web site would be damaged or destroyed after such an attack, then the SLE for this Web site would be $1,000,000 × 0.10 = $100,000. This estimate is then used to calculate another value, annual loss expectancy, which will be discussed shortly.

As difficult as it is to estimate the value of information, the estimation of the probability of a threat occurrence or attack is even more difficult. There are not always tables, books, or records that indicate the frequency or probability of any given attack. There are sources available for some asset-threat pairs. For instance, the likelihood of a tornado or thunderstorm destroying a building of a specific type of construction within a specified region of the country is available to insurance underwriters. In most cases, however, an organization can rely only on its internal information to calculate the security of its information assets. Even if the network, systems, and security administrators have been actively and accurately tracking these occurrences, the organization's information is sketchy at best. As a result, this information is usually estimated. In most cases, the probability of a threat occurring is usually a loosely derived table indicating the probability of an attack from each threat type within a given time frame (for example, once every 10 years). This value is commonly referred to as the **annualized rate of occurrence (ARO)**. ARO is simply how often you expect a specific type of attack to occur. As you learned earlier in this chapter, many attacks occur much more frequently than every year or two. For example, a successful deliberate act of sabotage or vandalism might occur about once every two years, in which case the ARO would be 50 percent (0.50), whereas some kinds of network attacks can occur multiple times per second. To standardize calculations, you convert the rate to a yearly (annualized) value. This is expressed as the probability of a threat occurrence.

Once each asset's worth is known, the next step is to ascertain how much loss is expected from a single expected attack, and how often these attacks occur. Once those values are established, the equation can be completed to determine the overall lost potential per risk. This is usually determined through an **annualized loss expectancy (ALE)**, which is calculated from the ARO and SLE, as shown here:

ALE = SLE × ARO

Using the example of the Web site that might suffer a deliberate act of sabotage or vandalism and thus has an SLE of $100,000 and an ARO of 0.50, the ALE would be calculated as follows:

ALE = $100,000 × 0.50

ALE = $50,000

This indicates that unless the organization increases the level of security on its Web site, it can expect to lose $50,000 per year, every year. Armed with such a figure, the organization's information security design team can justify expenditure for controls and safeguards and deliver a budgeted value for planning purposes. Note that sometimes noneconomic factors are considered in this process, so that in some cases even when ALE amounts are not huge, control budgets can be justified.

The Cost Benefit Analysis (CBA) Formula In its simplest definition, CBA (or economic feasibility) determines whether or not a particular control is worth its cost. CBAs may be calculated before a control or safeguard is implemented to determine if the control is worth implementing. CBAs can also be calculated after controls have been functioning for a time. Observation over time adds precision to the evaluation of the benefits of the safeguard and the determination of whether the safeguard is functioning as intended. While many techniques exist, the CBA is most easily calculated using the ALE from earlier assessments before the implementation of the proposed control, which is known as ALE(prior). Subtract the revised ALE, estimated based on the control being in place, known as ALE(post). Complete the calculation by subtracting the **annualized cost of the safeguard (ACS)**.

$$CBA = ALE(prior) - ALE(post) - ACS$$

Once controls are implemented, it is crucial to continue to examine their benefits to determine when they must be upgraded, supplemented, or replaced. As Frederick Avolio states in his article "Best Practices in Network Security":

> *Security is an investment, not an expense. Investing in computer and network security measures that meet changing business requirements and risks makes it possible to satisfy changing business requirements without hurting the business' viability.*[14]

Evaluation, Assessment, and Maintenance of Risk Controls

The selection and implementation of a control strategy is not the end of a process; the strategy, and its accompanying controls, must be monitored and reevaluated on an ongoing basis to determine their effectiveness and to calculate more accurately the estimated residual risk. Figure 4-9 shows how this cyclical process is used to ensure that risks are controlled. Note that there is no exit from this cycle; it is a process that continues for as long as the organization continues to function.

Quantatitive Versus Qualitative Risk Control Practices

The many steps described previously were performed using actual values or estimates. This is known as a **quantitative assessment.** However, an organization could decide that it cannot put specific numbers on these values. Fortunately, it is possible to repeat these steps using an evaluation process, called **qualitative assessment,** that does not use numerical measures. For example, instead of placing a value of once every 10 years for the ARO, the organization could list all possible attacks on a particular set of information and rate each by the probability of occurrence. This could be accomplished using scales rather than specific estimates. A sample scale could include none, representing no chance of occurrence, then low, medium,

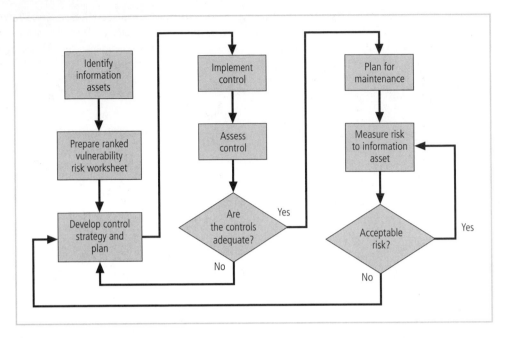

Figure 4-9 Risk Control Cycle

Source: Course Technology/Cengage Learning

high, up to very high, representing almost certain occurrence. Organizations may, of course, prefer other scales: A–Z, 0–10, 1–5, or 0–20. Using scales also relieves the organization from the difficulty of determining exact values. Many of these same scales can be used in any situation requiring a value, even in asset valuation. For example, instead of estimating that a particular piece of information is worth $1 million, you can value information on a scale of 1–20, with 1 indicating relatively worthless information, and 20 indicating extremely critical information, such as a certain soda manufacturer's secret recipe or those eleven herbs and spices of a popular fried chicken vendor.

Benchmarking and Best Practices

Instead of determining the financial value of information and then implementing security as an acceptable percentage of that value, an organization could take a different approach to risk management and look to peer organizations for benchmarks. **Benchmarking** is the process of seeking out and studying the practices used in other organizations that produce results you would like to duplicate in your organization. An organization typically benchmarks itself against other institutions by selecting a measure upon which to base the comparison. The organization then measures the difference between the way it conducts business and the way the other organizations conduct business. The industry Web site Best Practices Online puts it this way:

> *Benchmarking can yield great benefits in the education of executives and the realized performance improvements of operations. In addition, benchmarking can be used to determine strategic areas of opportunity. In general, it is the application of what is learned in benchmarking that delivers the marked and impressive*

results so often noted. The determination of benchmarks allows one to make a direct comparison. Any identified gaps are improvement areas.[15]

When benchmarking, an organization typically uses one of two types of measures to compare practices: metrics-based measures or process-based measures.

Metrics-based measures are comparisons based on numerical standards, such as:

- Numbers of successful attacks
- Staff-hours spent on systems protection
- Dollars spent on protection
- Numbers of security personnel
- Estimated value in dollars of the information lost in successful attacks
- Loss in productivity hours associated with successful attacks

An organization uses numerical standards like these to rank competing organizations with a similar size or market to its own and then determines how it measures up to the competitors. The difference between an organization's measures and those of others is often referred to as a **performance gap**. Performance gaps provide insight into the areas that an organization should work on to improve its security postures and defenses.

The other measures commonly used in benchmarking are **process-based measures**. Process-based measures are generally less focused on numbers and are more strategic than metrics-based measures. For each of the areas the organization is interested in benchmarking, process-based measures enable the organization to examine the activities an individual company performs in pursuit of its goal, rather than the specifics of how goals are attained. The primary focus is the *method* the organization uses to accomplish a particular process, rather than the outcome. In information security, two categories of benchmarks are used: standards of due care and due diligence, and best practices.

For legal reasons, an organization may be forced to adopt a certain minimum level of security, as discussed in Chapter 3. When organizations adopt levels of security for a legal defense, they may need to show that they have done what any *prudent* organization would do in similar circumstances. This is referred to as a **standard of due care**. It is insufficient to implement these standards and then ignore them. The application of controls at or above the prescribed levels and the maintenance of those standards of due care show that the organization has performed due diligence. **Due diligence** is the demonstration that the organization is diligent in ensuring that the implemented standards continue to provide the required level of protection. Failure to maintain a standard of due care or due diligence can open an organization to legal liability, provided it can be shown that the organization was negligent in its application or lack of application of information protection. This is especially important in areas in which the organization maintains information about customers, including medical, legal, or other personal data.

The security an organization is expected to maintain is complex and broad in scope. It may, therefore, be physically impossible to be the "best in class" in any or all categories. Based on the budgets assigned to the protection of information, it may also be financially impossible to provide a level of security equal to organizations with greater revenues. Sometimes organizations want to implement the best, most technologically advanced, most secure levels of protection, but for financial or other reasons they cannot. Such organizations should remember the adage, "Good security now is better than perfect security never."[16] It would also be counterproductive to establish costly, state-of-the-art security in one area, only to leave other areas exposed. Organizations must make sure they have met a reasonable level of security across the board, protecting all information, before beginning to improve individual areas to reach a higher standard, such as best practices.

Security efforts that seek to provide a superior level of performance in the protection of information are referred to as **best business practices** or simply **best practices** or **recommended practices**. Even the standards promoted on the Internet as requests for comments (RFCs) have best practices (see *www.rfc-editor.org/categories/rfc-best.html*). Best security practices are those security efforts that are among the best in the industry, balancing the need for access to information with adequate protection. Best practices seek to provide as much security as possible for information and systems while maintaining a solid degree of fiscal responsibility. Companies deploying best practices may not be the best in every area, but may have established an extremely high quality or successful security effort in one or more areas. Benchmarking best practices is accomplished by means of the metrics-based or process-based measures described earlier. The federal government has established a Web site through which government agencies can share best practices in the area of information security with other agencies (see *http://csrc.nist.gov/groups/SMA/fasp/index.html*). This project is known as the Federal Agency Security Project (FASP). It was the result of

> the Federal Chief Information Officer Council's Federal Best Security Practices (BSP) pilot effort to identify, evaluate, and disseminate best practices for computer information protection and security... The FASP site contains agency policies, procedures, and practices; the CIO pilot BSPs; and a Frequently-Asked-Questions (FAQ) section.[17]

While few commercial equivalents exist, many of the government's BSPs are applicable to the areas of security in both the public and the private sector. The FASP has collected sample policies, strategies, and other practice-related documents, which are presented for use as guidelines.

Even the best business practices are not sufficient for some organizations. These organizations prefer to set the standard by implementing the most protective, supportive, and fiscally responsible standards they can. They strive toward the gold standard. Within best practices, the **gold standard** is a subcategory of practices that are typically viewed as "the best of the best." The gold standard is a defining level of performance that demonstrates one company's industrial leadership, quality, and concern for the protection of information. The implementation of this level of security requires a great amount of support, both in financial and personnel resources. While there is limited public information on best practices, there are virtually no published criteria for the gold standard. The gold standard represents an almost unobtainable level of security. Many vendors claim to offer a gold standard in one product or service, but this is predominantly marketing hype.

You can sometimes get advice about how to select control strategies from government sources. For some organizations that operate in industries that are regulated by governmental agencies, government recommendations are, in effect, requirements. For other organizations, government regulations are excellent sources of information about controlling information security risks.

Applying Best Practices The preceding sections have presented a number of sources you can consider when applying standards to your organization. You can study the documented best practice processes or procedures that have been shown to be effective and are thus recommended by a person or organization and evaluate how they apply to your organization. When considering best practices for adoption, consider the following:

- Does your organization resemble the identified target organization with the best practice under consideration? Is your organization in a similar industry as the target? Keep in mind that a strategy that works well in manufacturing organizations often has little bearing in a nonprofit organization. Does your organization face similar challenges as the target? If your organization has no functioning information security program, a best practice target that assumes you start with a functioning program is not useful. Is your organizational structure similar to the target's? Obviously, a best practice proposed for a small home office setting is not appropriate for a multinational company.

- Are the resources your organization can expend similar to those identified with the best practice? If your approach is significantly limited by resources, it is not useful to submit a best practice proposal that assumes unlimited funding.

- Is your organization in a similar threat environment as that proposed in the best practice? A best practice from months and even weeks ago may not be appropriate for the current threat environment. Think of the best practices for Internet connectivity that are required in the modern organization at the opening of the 21st century and compare them to the best practices of 5 years earlier.

Another source for best practices information is the CERT Web site *(www.cert.org/nav/index_green.html)*, which presents a number of articles and practices. Similarly, Microsoft publishes its security practices on its Web site *(www.microsoft.com/security/default.mspx)*. Microsoft focuses on the following seven key areas for home users:

1. Use antivirus software.
2. Use strong passwords.
3. Verify your software security settings.
4. Update product security.
5. Build personal firewalls.
6. Back up early and often.
7. Protect against power surges and loss.

For the small businesses Microsoft recommends the following:[18]

1. Protect desktops and laptops—Keep software up to date, protect against viruses, and set up a firewall.
2. Keep data safe—Implement a regular backup procedure to safeguard critical business data, set permissions, and use encryption.
3. Use the Internet safely—Unscrupulous Web sites, popups, and animations can be dangerous. Set rules about Internet usage.

4. Protect the network—Remote network access is a security risk you should closely monitor. Use strong passwords and be especially cautious about wireless networks.

5. Protect servers—Servers are the network's command center—protect your servers.

6. Secure business applications—Make sure that software critical to your business operations is fully secure around the clock.

7. Manage desktops and laptops from the server—Without stringent administrative procedures in place, security measures may be unintentionally jeopardized by users.[19]

In support of security efforts, Microsoft offers "The Ten Immutable Laws of Security" as follows:

Law #1: If a bad guy can persuade you to run his program on your computer, it's not your computer anymore.

Law #2: If a bad guy can alter the operating system on your computer, it's not your computer anymore.

Law #3: If a bad guy has unrestricted physical access to your computer, it's not your computer anymore.

Law #4: If you allow a bad guy to upload programs to your Web site, it's not your Web site anymore.

Law #5: Weak passwords trump strong security.

Law #6: A machine is only as secure as the administrator is trustworthy.

Law #7: Encrypted data is only as secure as the decryption key.

Law #8: An out-of-date virus scanner is only marginally better than no virus scanner at all.

Law #9: Absolute anonymity isn't practical, in real life or on the Web.

Law #10: Technology is not a panacea.

Problems with the Application of Benchmarking and Best Practices The biggest problem with benchmarking and best practices in information security is that organizations don't talk to each other. A successful attack is viewed as an organizational failure. Because valuable lessons are not recorded, disseminated, and evaluated, the entire industry suffers. However, more and more security administrators are joining professional associations and societies (such as the Information Systems Security Association), sharing stories, and publishing the lessons learned. Security administrators often submit sanitized versions of attacks (from which details that could identify the targeted organization have been removed) to security journals. Still, most organizations refuse even to acknowledge, much less publicize, the occurrence of successful attacks.

Another problem with benchmarking is that no two organizations are identical. Even if two organizations are producing products or services in the same market, their sizes, compositions, management philosophies, organizational cultures, technological infrastructures, and budgets for security may differ dramatically. Thus, even if these organizations did exchange specific information, it may not apply in other contexts. What organizations seek most are lessons and examples, rather than specific technologies they should adopt, because they know that security is a managerial problem, not a technical one. If it were a technical problem, implementing a certain technology could solve the problem regardless of industry or organizational composition. But in fact, the number and types of variables that affect the security of an organization can differ radically among businesses.

A third problem is that best practices are a moving target. What worked well 2 years ago may be completely worthless against today's threats. Security practices must keep abreast of new threats in addition to the methods, techniques, policies, guidelines, educational and training approaches, and technologies used to combat the threats.

One last issue to consider is that simply researching information security benchmarks doesn't necessarily prepare a practitioner for what to do next. It is said that those who cannot remember the past are condemned to repeat it. In security, those who do not prepare for the attacks of the past see them occur again and again. However, preparing for past threats does not safeguard against new challenges to come.

Baselining An activity related to benchmarking is baselining. A **baseline** is a "value or profile of a performance metric against which changes in the performance metric can be usefully compared."[20] An example is the establishment of the number of attacks per week the organization is experiencing. In the future, this baseline can serve as a reference point to determine if the average number of attacks is increasing or decreasing. **Baselining** is the analysis of measures against established standards. In information security, baselining is the comparison of security activities and events against the organization's future performance. In a sense, baselining can provide the foundation for internal benchmarking. The information gathered for an organization's first risk assessment becomes the baseline for future comparisons. Therefore, it is important that the initial baseline be accurate.

When baselining, it is useful to have a guide to the overall process. The National Institute of Standards and Technology has two publications specifically written to support these activities:

- Security SP 800-27 Rev A Engineering Principles for Information Technology Security (A Baseline for Achieving Security), June 2004

- SP 800-26 Security Self-Assessment Guide for Information Technology Systems, November 2001, and NIST DRAFT Special Publication 800-26, Rev 1: Guide for Information Security Program Assessments and System Reporting Form, August 2005

These documents are available at *csrc.nist.gov/publications/nistpubs/index.html*.

Other Feasibility Studies

Other qualitative approaches that can be used to determine an organization's readiness for any proposed set of controls are operational, technical, and political feasibility analyses. The methods for these feasibility evaluations are discussed in the following sections.

Organizational Feasibility Organizational feasibility analysis examines how well the proposed information security alternatives will contribute to the efficiency, effectiveness, and overall operation of an organization. In other words, the proposed control must contribute to the organization's strategic objectives. Above and beyond their impact on the bottom line, the organization must determine how the proposed alternatives contribute to the business objectives of the organization. Does the implementation align with the strategic planning for the information systems? Or does it require deviation from the planned expansion and management of the current systems? An organization should not invest in technology that alters its fundamental ability to explore certain avenues and opportunities. For example, suppose that a university decides to implement a new firewall without considering the organizational feasibility of this project. Consequently, it takes a few months for the technology group to learn enough about the firewall to completely configure it. Then, a few months after the implementation begins, it is discovered that the firewall in its current configuration does not permit outgoing Web-streamed media. If one of the business goals of the university is the pursuit of distance-learning opportunities, and the firewall prevents the pursuit of that goal, the firewall has failed the organizational feasibility measure and should be modified or replaced.

Operational Feasibility Operational feasibility analysis addresses several key areas not covered in the other feasibility measures. **Operational feasibility** analysis examines user acceptance and support, management acceptance and support, and the overall requirements of the organization's stakeholders. Operational feasibility is also known as **behavioral feasibility**, because it measures the behavior of users. One of the fundamental requirements of systems development is user buy-in. If the users do not accept a new technology, policy, or program, it will fail. Users may not openly oppose a change, but if they do not support a control, they will find ways of disabling or circumventing it, thereby creating yet another vulnerability. One of the most common methods for obtaining user acceptance and support is through user involvement. User involvement can be obtained via three simple steps: communicate, educate, and involve.

Organizations should *communicate* with system users throughout the development of the security program, letting them know that changes are coming. This includes communicating the implementation timetables and schedules, as well as the dates, times, and locations of upcoming briefings and training. Those making the changes should outline the purpose of the proposed changes and explain how these changes will enable everyone to work more securely. In addition, organizations should make efforts to design training to *educate* employees about how to work under the new constraints and avoid any negative impact on performance. One of the most frustrating things for users is the implementation of a program that prevents them from accomplishing their duties, with only a promise of eventual training. Those making changes must also *involve* users by asking them what they want from the new systems and what they will tolerate from the new systems, and by including selected representatives from the various constituencies in the development process. These three basic undertakings— communication, education, and involvement—can reduce *resistance* to change and build *resilience* for change. Resilience is that ethereal quality that allows workers not only to tolerate constant change but also to accept it as a necessary part of their jobs.

Technical Feasibility In addition to the economic costs and benefits of proposed controls, the project team must also consider the technical feasibilities of their design, implementation, and management. Some safeguards, especially technology-based safeguards, are extremely difficult to implement, configure, and manage. **Technical feasibility** analysis examines whether or not the organization has or can acquire the technology necessary to implement and support the proposed control. Does the organization have the hardware and software necessary to support a new firewall system? If not, can it be obtained? Technical feasibility also examines whether the organization has the technological expertise to manage the new technology. Does the organization have a staff qualified (and possibly certified) to install and manage a new firewall system? If not, can staff be spared from their current obligations to attend formal training and education programs to prepare them to administer the new systems? Or must personnel be hired? In the current job environment, how difficult is it to find qualified personnel? These issues must be examined in detail before the acquisition of a new set of controls. Many organizations rush into the acquisition of new safeguards, without completely examining the associated requirements.

Political Feasibility For some organizations, the most important feasibility evaluated may be political. Politics has been defined as the art of the possible.[21] Within organizations, **political feasibility** determines what can and cannot occur based on the consensus and relationships among the communities of interest. The limits placed on an organization's actions or behaviors by the information security controls must fit within the realm of the possible before they can be effectively implemented, and that realm includes the availability of staff resources.

In some cases, resources are provided directly to the information security community under a budget apportionment model. The management and professionals involved in information security then allocate the resources to activities and projects using processes of their own design.

In other organizations, resources are first allocated to the IT community of interest, and the information security team must compete for these resources. In some cases, cost benefit analysis and other forms of justification discussed previously in this chapter are used in an allocation process to make rational decisions about the relative merit of various activities and projects. Unfortunately in some settings, these decisions are politically charged and are not made according to the pursuit of the greater organizational goals.

Another methodology for budget allocation requires the information security team to propose and justify use of the resources for activities and projects in the context of the entire organization. This requires that arguments for information security spending articulate the benefit of the expense for the whole organization, so that members of the organizational communities of interest can understand its value.

Risk Management Discussion Points

Not every organization has the collective will or budget to manage each vulnerability by applying controls; therefore, each organization must define the level of risk it is willing to live with.

Risk Appetite

Risk appetite defines the quantity and nature of risk that organizations are willing to accept as they evaluate the tradeoffs between perfect security and unlimited accessibility. For instance, a financial services company, regulated by government and conservative by nature, may seek to apply every reasonable control and even some invasive controls to protect its information assets. Other, nonregulated organizations may also be conservative by nature, seeking to avoid the negative publicity associated with the perceived loss of integrity from the exploitation of a vulnerability. Thus, a firewall vendor may install a set of firewall rules that are far stricter than normal because the negative consequence of being hacked would be catastrophic in the eyes of its customers. Other organizations may take on dangerous risks through ignorance. The reasoned approach to risk is one that balances the expense (in terms of finance and the usability of information assets) of controlling vulnerabilities against the losses possible if these vulnerabilities were exploited.

As mentioned in Chapter 1, James Anderson, former vice president of information security at Inovant, the world's largest commercial processor of financial payment transactions, believes that information security in today's enterprise is a "well-informed sense of assurance that the information risks and controls are in balance." The key for the organization is to find the balance in its decision-making processes and in its feasibility analyses, therefore assuring that an organization's risk appetite is based on experience and facts and not on ignorance or wishful thinking.

Residual Risk

Even when vulnerabilities have been controlled as much as possible, there is often still some risk that has not been completely removed, shifted, or planned for. This remainder is called residual risk. To express it another way, "residual risk is a combined function of (1) a threat less the effect of threat-reducing safeguards, (2) a vulnerability less the effect of vulnerability-reducing safeguards, and (3) an asset less the effect of asset value-reducing safeguards."[22] Figure 4-10 illustrates how residual risk remains after safeguards are implemented.

The significance of residual risk must be judged within the context of the organization. Although it is counterintuitive, the goal of information security is not to bring residual risk to zero; it is to bring residual risk into line with an organization's comfort zone or risk appetite. If decision makers have been informed of uncontrolled risks and the proper authority groups within the communities of interest have decided to leave residual risk in place, the information security program has accomplished its primary goal.

Documenting Results

The results of risk assessment activities can be delivered in a number of ways: a report on a systematic approach to risk control, a project-based risk assessment, or a topic-specific risk assessment.

When the organization is pursuing an overall risk management program, it requires a systematic report that enumerates the opportunities for controlling risk. This report documents a series of proposed controls, each of which has been justified by one or more feasibility or rationalization approaches. At a minimum, each information asset-threat pair should have a documented control strategy that clearly identifies any residual risk remaining after the proposed strategy has been executed. Furthermore, each control strategy should articulate which of the four fundamental risk-reducing approaches will be used or how they might be combined, and how that should justify the findings by referencing the feasibility studies. Additional preparatory work for project management should be included where available.

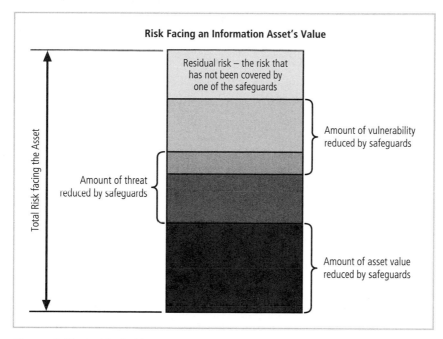

Figure 4-10 Residual Risk

Source: Course Technology/Cengage Learning

Another option is to document the outcome of the control strategy for each information asset-threat pair in an action plan. This action plan includes concrete tasks, each with accountability assigned to an organizational unit or to an individual. It may also include hardware and software requirements, budget estimates, and detailed timelines to activate the project management activities needed to implement the control.

Sometimes a risk assessment is prepared for a specific IT project at the request of the project manager, either because it is required by organizational policy or because it is good project management practice. On some occasions, the project risk assessment may be requested by auditors or senior management if they perceive that an IT project has sidestepped the organization's information security objectives. The project risk assessment should identify the sources of risk in the finished IT system, with suggestions for remedial controls, as well as those risks that might impede the completion of the project. For example, a new application usually requires a project risk assessment at system design time and then periodically as the project evolves toward completion.

Lastly, when management requires details about a specific risk to the organization, risk assessment may be documented in a topic-specific report. These are usually demand reports that are prepared at the direction of senior management and are focused on a narrow area of information systems operational risk. For example, an emergent vulnerability is reported to management, which then asks for a specific risk assessment. A more complete treatment of the process of documenting the results of risk management activities is presented in Chapter 12.

Recommended Risk Control Practices

If an organization seeks to implement a control strategy that requires a budget of $50,000, the planned expenditures must be justified and budget authorities must be convinced to spend up to *$50,000 to protect a particular asset from an identified threat*. Unfortunately, most budget authorities focus on trying to cut a percentage of the total figure to save the organization money. This underlines the importance of developing strong justifications for specific action plans and providing concrete estimates in those plans.

Another factor to consider is that each control or safeguard affects more than one asset-threat pair. If a new $50,000 firewall is installed to protect the Internet connection infrastructure from the threat posed by hackers launching port-scanning attacks, the same firewall may protect this Internet connection infrastructure from other threats and attacks. In addition, the firewall may protect other information assets from other threats and attacks. The chosen controls may in the end be a balanced mixture that provides the greatest value to as many asset-threat pairs as possible. This reveals another facet of the risk management problem: information security professionals manage a dynamic matrix covering a broad range of threats, information assets, controls, and identified vulnerabilities. Each time a control is added to the matrix, it undoubtedly changes the ALE for the information asset vulnerability for which it has been designed, and it also may alter the ALE for other information asset vulnerabilities. To put it more simply, if you put in one safeguard, you decrease the risk associated with all subsequent control evaluations. To make matters even more complex, the action of implementing a control may change the values assigned or calculated in a prior estimate.

Between the impossible task associated with the valuation of information assets and the dynamic nature of the ALE calculations, it's no wonder organizations are looking for a way to implement controls that doesn't involve such complex, inexact, and dynamic calculations. There is an ongoing search for ways to design security architectures that go beyond the direct application of specific controls, in which each is justified for a specific information asset vulnerability, to safeguards that can be applied to several vulnerabilities at once.

Selected Readings

- *Against the Gods: The Remarkable Story of Risk*, by Peter L. Bernstein. 1998. John Wiley and Sons.
- *Information Security Risk Analysis*, Second Edition, by Thomas R. Peltier. 2005. Auerbach.
- *The Security Risk Assessment Handbook: A Complete Guide for Performing Security Risk Assessments*, by Douglas J. Landoll. 2005. CRC Press.

Chapter Summary

- Risk management examines and documents the current information technology security being used in an organization. It is the process of identifying vulnerabilities in an organization's information systems and taking carefully reasoned steps to assure the confidentiality, integrity, and availability of all of the components in the information systems.

- A key component of a risk management strategy is the identification, classification, and prioritization of the organization's information assets.

- The human resources, documentation, and data information assets of an organization are more difficult to identify and document than tangible assets, such as hardware and software.

- After identifying and performing a preliminary classification of information assets, the threats facing an organization should be examined. There are fourteen categories of threats to information security.

- To fully understand each threat and the impact it can have on the organization, each identified threat must be examined through a threat assessment process.

- The goal of risk assessment is the assignment of a risk rating or score that represents the relative risk for a specific vulnerability of a specific information asset.

- Once the vulnerabilities are identified and ranked, the organization must choose a strategy to control the risks resulting from these vulnerabilities. The five control strategies are defend, transfer, mitigate, accept, and avoid.

- The economic feasibility study determines the costs associated with protecting an asset. The formal documentation process of feasibility is called a cost benefit analysis.

- Benchmarking is an alternative method to the economic feasibility analysis that seeks out and studies the practices used in other organizations that produce the results desired in an organization.

- The goal of information security is to reduce residual risk, the amount of risk unaccounted for after the application of controls and other risk management strategies, to an acceptable level.

Review Questions

1. What is risk management? Why is the identification of risks, by listing assets and their vulnerabilities, so important to the risk management process?

2. According to Sun Tzu, what two key understandings must you achieve to be successful in battle?

3. Who is responsible for risk management in an organization? Which community of interest usually takes the lead in information security risk management?

4. In risk management strategies, why must periodic review be a part of the process?

5. Why do networking components need more examination from an information security perspective than from a systems development perspective?

6. What value does an automated asset inventory system have for the risk identification process?

7. What information attribute is often of great value for local networks that use static addressing?

8. Which is more important to the systems components classification scheme: that the asset identification list be comprehensive or mutually exclusive?

9. What's the difference between an asset's ability to generate revenue and its ability to generate profit?

10. What are vulnerabilities? How do you identify them?

11. What is competitive disadvantage? Why has it emerged as a factor?

12. What are the strategies for controlling risk as described in this chapter?

13. Describe the "defend" strategy. List and describe the three common methods.

14. Describe the "transfer" strategy. Describe how outsourcing can be used for this purpose.

15. Describe the "mitigate" strategy. What three planning approaches are discussed in the text as opportunities to mitigate risk?

16. How is an incident response plan different from a disaster recovery plan?

17. What is risk appetite? Explain why risk appetite varies from organization to organization.

18. What is a cost benefit analysis?

19. What is the definition of single loss expectancy? What is annual loss expectancy?

20. What is residual risk?

Exercises

1. If an organization has three information assets to evaluate for risk management, as shown in the accompanying data, which vulnerability should be evaluated for additional controls first? Which one should be evaluated last?

   Data for Exercise 1:

   - Switch L47 connects a network to the Internet. It has two vulnerabilities: it is susceptible to hardware failure at a likelihood of 0.2, and it is subject to an SNMP buffer overflow attack at a likelihood of 0.1. This switch has an impact rating of 90 and has no current controls in place. You are 75 percent certain of the assumptions and data.

   - Server WebSrv6 hosts a company Web site and performs e-commerce transactions. It has a Web server version that can be attacked by sending it invalid Unicode values. The likelihood of that attack is estimated at 0.1. The server has been assigned an impact value of 100, and a control has been implanted that reduces the impact of the vulnerability by 75 percent. You are 80 percent certain of the assumptions and data.

   - Operators use an MGMT45 control console to monitor operations in the server room. It has no passwords and is susceptible to unlogged misuse by the operators. Estimates show the likelihood of misuse is 0.1. There are no controls in place on this asset; it has an impact rating of 5. You are 90 percent certain of the assumptions and data.

2. Using the data classification scheme presented in this chapter, identify and classify the information contained in your personal computer or personal digital assistant. Based on the potential for misuse or embarrassment, what information would be confidential, sensitive but unclassified, or for public release?

3. Suppose XYZ Software Company has a new application development project, with projected revenues of $1,200,000. Using the following table, calculate the

ARO and ALE for each threat category that XYZ Software Company faces for this project.

Threat Category	Cost per Incident (SLE)	Frequency of Occurrence
Programmer mistakes	$5,000	1 per week
Loss of intellectual property	$75,000	1 per year
Software piracy	$500	1 per week
Theft of information (hacker)	$2,500	1 per quarter
Theft of information (employee)	$5,000	1 per six months
Web defacement	$500	1 per month
Theft of equipment	$5,000	1 per year
Viruses, worms, Trojan horses	$1,500	1 per week
Denial-of-service attacks	$2,500	1 per quarter
Earthquake	$250,000	1 per 20 years
Flood	$250,000	1 per 10 years
Fire	$500,000	1 per 10 years

4. How might XYZ Software Company arrive at the values in the above table? For each entry, describe the process of determining the cost per incident and frequency of occurrence.

5. Assume a year has passed and XYZ has improved security by applying a number of controls. Using the information from Exercise 3 and the following table, calculate the post-control ARO and ALE for each threat category listed.

Threat Category	Cost per Incident	Frequency of Occurrence	Cost of Control	Type of Control
Programmer mistakes	$5,000	1 per month	$20,000	Training
Loss of intellectual property	$75,000	1 per 2 years	$15,000	Firewall/IDS
Software piracy	$500	1 per month	$30,000	Firewall/IDS
Theft of information (hacker)	$2,500	1 per 6 months	$15,000	Firewall/IDS
Theft of information (employee)	$5,000	1 per year	$15,000	Physical security
Web defacement	$500	1 per quarter	$10,000	Firewall
Theft of equipment	$5,000	1 per 2 years	$15,000	Physical security
Viruses, worms, Trojan horses	$1,500	1 per month	$15,000	Antivirus
Denial-of-service attacks	$2,500	1 per 6 months	$10,000	Firewall
Earthquake	$250,000	1 per 20 years	$5,000	Insurance/backups
Flood	$50,000	1 per 10 years	$10,000	Insurance/backups
Fire	$100,000	1 per 10 years	$10,000	Insurance/backups

Why have some values changed in the columns Cost per Incident and Frequency of Occurrence? How could a control affect one but not the other?

Assume the values in the Cost of Control column presented in the table are those unique costs directly associated with protecting against that threat. In other words, don't worry about overlapping costs between controls. Calculate the CBA for the planned risk control approach for each threat category. For each threat category, determine if the proposed control is worth the costs.

Case Exercises

As Charlie wrapped up the meeting, he ticked off a few key reminders for everyone involved in the asset identification project.

"Okay, everyone, before we finish, please remember that you should try to make your asset lists complete, but be sure to focus your attention on the more valuable assets first. Also, remember that we evaluate our assets based on business impact to profitability first, and then economic cost of replacement. Make sure you check with me about any questions that come up. We will schedule our next meeting in two weeks, so please have your draft inventories ready."

Questions:

1. Did Charlie effectively organize the work before the meeting? Why or why not? Make a list of the important issues you think should be covered by the work plan. For each issue, provide a short explanation.

2. Will the company get useful information from the team it has assembled? Why or why not?

3. Why might some attendees resist the goals of the meeting? Does it seem that each person invited was briefed on the importance of the event and the issues behind it?

Endnotes

1. Sun Tzu. *The Art of War*, trans. Samuel B. Griffith. Oxford: Oxford University Press, 1988, p. 84.

2. Godwin, Mike. "When Copying Isn't Theft." *Electronic Frontier Foundation Online.* Accessed 16 April 2007 from *www.eff.org/Misc/Publications/Mike_Godwin/phrack_riggs_neidorf_godwin.article.*

3. Department of the Army. *Army Training and Leadership Development AR 350-1.* Accessed 26 February 2007 from *www.army.mil/usapa/epubs/350_Series_Collection_1.html.*

4. Bridis, Ted, and Buckman, Rebecca. "Microsoft Hacked! Code Stolen?" *ZDNet News Online.* 20 March 2004. Accessed 16 April 2007 from zdnet.*com.com/2100-11-525083.html.*

5. Whitman, Michael E. "Enemy at the Gates: Threats to Information Security." *Communications of the ACM*, 46, no. 8 (August 2003): 91–95.

6. Ibid.

7. Gordon, Lawrence A., Loeb, Martin P. Lucyshyn, William and Richardson, Robert. *2006 CSI/FBI Computer Crime and Security Survey.* Accessed 25 April 2006 from *www.gocsi.com.*

8. Whitman, pp. 91–95.

9. National Institute of Standards and Technology. *Risk Management Guide for Information Technology Systems.* SP 800-30. January 2002.

10. Greenberg, Jack M. "Corporate Press Release: First Worldwide Social Responsibility Report." *McDonald's Corporation Online.* 15 April 2002. Accessed 9 May 2010 from *www.csrwire.com/press/press_release/25172-McDonald-s-Issues-First-Worldwide-Social-Responsibility-Report-hjm.*

11. 37th IETF. "Remote Authentication Dial-In User Service (RADIUS) Charter." Proceedings at the 37th IETF meeting, San Jose, California, December 1996. Accessed 26 February 2007 from *www3.ietf.org/proceedings/96dec/charters/radius-charter.html.*

12. Peters, Thomas J., and Waterman, Robert H. *In Search of Excellence: Lessons from America's Best Run Companies.* New York: Harper and Row, 1982.

13. Horowitz, Alan S. "Top 10 Security Mistakes." *Computerworld* 35, no. 28 (9 July 2001): 38.

14. Avolio, Frederick M. "Best Practices in Network Security." *Network Computing* 11, no. 5 (20 March 2000): 60–66.

15. Best Practices, LLC. "What is Benchmarking?" *Best Practices Online.* Accessed 26 February 2007 from *www3.best-in-class.com/bestp/domrep.nsf/pages/716AD479AB1F 512C85256DFF006BD072! OpenDocument.*

16. Avolio, Frederick M. "Best Practices in Network Security." *Network Computing* 11, no. 5 (20 March 2000): 60–66.

17. National Institute of Standards and Technology. *Computer Security Resource Center* June 2002. Accessed 24 April 2007 from *fasp.nist.gov.*

18. The Microsoft Security Response Center. *The Ten Immutable Laws of Security?* July 2002. Accessed 24 April 2007 from *www.microsoft.com/technet/archive/community/columns/security/essays/10imlaws.mspx.*

19. Adapted from Microsoft "Small Business Security Computer Check List" Accessed 26 February 2007 from *www.microsoft.com/smallbusiness/support/checklist/default.mspx.*

20. Carden, Philip. "Network Baselining and Performance Management." *Network Computing Online.* Accessed 24 April 2007 from *www.networkcomputing.com/netdesign/base1.html.*

21. Mann, Thomas. "Politics Is Often Defined as the Art of the Possible." Speech in the Library of Congress, Washington, D.C., 29 May 1945.

22. Gamma Secure Systems Limited. "First Measure Your Risk." *Gamma Online.* 2 January 2002. Accessed 25 April 2007 from *www.gammassl.co.uk/inforisk/.*

chapter 5

Planning for Security

Begin with the end in mind.
STEPHEN COVEY, AUTHOR OF *SEVEN HABITS OF HIGHLY EFFECTIVE PEOPLE*

Charlie Moody flipped his jacket collar up to cover his ears. The spray blowing over him from the fire hoses was icing the cars that lined the street where he stood watching his office building burn. The warehouse and shipping dock were not gone, only severely damaged by smoke and water. He tried to hide his dismay by turning to speak to Fred Chin.

"Look at the bright side," said Charlie. "At least we can get the new servers that we've been putting off."

Fred shook his head. "Charlie, you must be dreaming. We don't have enough insurance for a full replacement of everything we've lost."

Charlie was stunned. The offices were gone, all the computer systems, servers, and desktops were melted slag, and he was going to have to try to rebuild without the resources he needed. At least he had good backups, or so he hoped. He thought hard, trying to remember the last time the off-site backup tapes had been tested.

He wondered where all the network design diagrams were. He knew he could call his network provider to order new circuits as soon as Fred found some new office space. But where were all the circuit specs? The only copy had been in a drawer in his office, the office that wasn't there anymore. This was not going to be fun. He would have to call directory assistance just to get the phone number for his boss, Gladys Williams, the CIO.

Charlie heard a buzzing noise off to his left. He turned to see the flashing numbers of his alarm clock. Relief flooded him as he realized it was just a nightmare; Sequential Label and Supply had not really burned down. He turned on the light to make some notes for himself to go over with his staff later in the morning. Charlie was going to make some changes to the company contingency plans *today*.

LEARNING OBJECTIVES:

Upon completion of this material, you should be able to:

- Define management's role in the development, maintenance, and enforcement of information security policy, standards, practices, procedures, and guidelines
- Describe what an information security blueprint is, identify its major components, and explain how it supports the information security program
- Discuss how an organization institutionalizes its policies, standards, and practices using education, training, and awareness programs
- Explain what contingency planning is and how it relates to incident response planning, disaster recovery planning, and business continuity plans

Introduction

An organization's information security effort succeeds only if it operates in conjunction with the organization's information security policy. An information security program begins with policy, standards, and practices, which are the foundation for the information security architecture and blueprint. The creation and maintenance of these elements require coordinated planning. The role of planning in the modern organization is hard to overemphasize. All but the smallest organizations engage in some planning: strategic planning to manage the allocation of resources and contingency planning to prepare for the uncertainties of the business environment.

Information Security Planning and Governance

Strategic planning sets out the long-term direction to be taken by the whole organization and by each of its component parts. Strategic planning should guide organizational efforts and focus resources toward specific, clearly defined goals. After an organization develops a general strategy, it generates an overall strategic plan by extending that general strategy into strategic plans for major divisions. Each level of each division then translates those plan objectives into more specific objectives for the level below. To execute this broad strategy and turn the general strategy into action, the executive team (sometimes called the C-level of the organization, as in CEO, COO, CFO, CIO, and so on) must first define individual responsibilities. The conversion of goals from one strategic level to the next lower level is perhaps more art than science. It relies on an executive's ability to know and understand the strategic goals of the entire organization, to know and appreciate the strategic and tactical abilities of each unit within the organization, and to negotiate with peers, superiors, and subordinates. This mix of skills helps to achieve the proper balance between goals and capabilities.

Planning Levels

Once the organization's overall strategic plan is translated into strategic plans for each major division or operation, the next step is to translate these plans into tactical objectives that move toward reaching specific, measurable, achievable, and time-bound accomplishments. The process of strategic planning seeks to transform broad, general, sweeping statements into more specific and applied objectives. Strategic plans are used to create tactical plans, which are in turn used to develop operational plans.

Tactical planning focuses on shorter-term undertakings that will be completed within one or two years. The process of tactical planning breaks each strategic goal into a series of incremental objectives. Each objective in a tactical plan should be specific and should have a delivery date within a year of the plan's start. Budgeting, resource allocation, and personnel are critical components of the tactical plan. Although these components may be discussed in general terms at the strategic planning level, the actual resources must be in place before the tactical plan can be translated into the operational plan. Tactical plans often include project plans and resource acquisition planning documents (such as product specifications), project budgets, project reviews, and monthly and annual reports.

Because tactical plans are often created for specific projects, some organizations call this process project planning or intermediate planning. The chief information security officer (CISO) and the security managers use the tactical plan to organize, prioritize, and acquire resources necessary for major projects and to provide support for the overall strategic plan.

Managers and employees use operational plans, which are derived from the tactical plans, to organize the ongoing, day-to-day performance of tasks. An operational plan includes the necessary tasks for all relevant departments, as well as communication and reporting requirements, which might include weekly meetings, progress reports, and other associated tasks. These plans must reflect the organizational structure, with each subunit, department, or project team conducting its own operational planning and reporting. Frequent communication and feedback from the teams to the project managers and/or team leaders, and then up to the various management levels, will make the planning process as a whole more manageable and successful.

Planning and the CISO

The first priority of the CISO and the information security management team is the creation of a strategic plan to accomplish the organization's information security objectives. While each organization may have its own format for the design and distribution of a strategic plan, the fundamental elements of planning share characteristics across all types of enterprises. The plan is an evolving statement of how the CISO and the various elements of the organization will implement the objectives of the information security charter that is expressed in the enterprise information security policy (EISP), which you will learn about later in this chapter.

Information Security Governance

Governance is "the set of responsibilities and practices exercised by the board and executive management with the goal of providing strategic direction, ensuring that objectives are achieved, ascertaining that risks are managed appropriately and verifying that the enterprise's resources are used responsibly."[1] Governance describes the entire process of governing, or controlling, the processes used by a group to accomplish some objective.

Just like governments, corporations and other organizations have guiding documents—corporate charters or partnership agreements—as well as appointed or elected leaders or officers, and planning and operating procedures. These elements in combination provide **corporate governance.** Each operating unit within an organization also has controlling customs, processes, committees, and practices. The information security group's leadership monitors and manages all of the organizational structures and processes that safeguard information. **Information security governance**, then, is the application of the principles of corporate governance—that is, executive management's responsibility to provide strategic direction, ensure the accomplishment of objectives, oversee that risks are appropriately managed, and validate responsible resource utilization—to the information security function.

The governance of information security is a strategic planning responsibility whose importance has grown over recent years. Many consider good information security practices and sound information security governance a component of U.S. homeland security. Unfortunately, information security is all too often regarded as a technical issue when it is, in fact, a management issue. In order to secure information assets, an organization's management must integrate information security practices into the fabric of the organization, expanding corporate governance policies and controls to encompass the objectives of the information security process.

Information security objectives must be addressed at the highest levels of an organization's management team in order to be effective and sustainable. When security programs are designed and managed as a technical specialty in the IT department, they are less likely to be effective. A broader view of information security encompasses all of an organization's information assets, including the knowledge managed by those IT assets.

The value of the information assets of an organization must be protected regardless of how the data within it are processed, stored, or transmitted, and with a thorough understanding of the risks to, and the benefits of, the information assets. According to the Information Technology Governance Institute (ITGI), information security governance includes all of the accountabilities and methods undertaken by the board of directors and executive management to provide strategic direction, establishment of objectives, measurement of progress toward those objectives, verification that risk management practices are appropriate, and validation that the organization's assets are used properly.

Information Security Governance Outcomes
Effective communication among stakeholders is critical to the structures and processes used in governance at every level especially in information security governance. This requires the development of constructive relationships, a common language, and a commitment to the objectives of the organization.

The five goals of information security governance are:

> *Strategic alignment of information security with business strategy to support organizational objectives*

> *Risk management by executing appropriate measures to manage and mitigate threats to information resources*

Resource management by utilizing information security knowledge and infrastructure efficiently and effectively

Performance measurement by measuring, monitoring, and reporting information security governance metrics to ensure that organizational objectives are achieved

Value delivery by optimizing information security investments in support of organizational objectives[2]

Governance Framework In order to effectively implement security governance, the Corporate Governance Task Force (CGTF) recommends that organizations follow an established framework, such as the IDEAL framework from the Carnegie Mellon University Software Engineering Institute. This framework, which is described in the document "Information Security Governance: Call to Action," defines the responsibilities of (1) the board of directors or trustees, (2) the senior organizational executive (i.e., CEO), (3) executive team members, (4) senior managers, and (5) all employees and users. This important document can be found at the Information Systems Audit and Control Association (ISACA) Web site at *www.isaca.org/ContentManagement/ContentDisplay.cfm?ContentID=34997*.

Information Security Policy, Standards, and Practices

Management from all communities of interest, including general staff, information technology, and information security, must make policies the basis for all information security planning, design, and deployment. Policies direct how issues should be addressed and technologies should be used. Policies do not specify the proper operation of equipment or software—this information should be placed in the standards, procedures, and practices of users' manuals and systems documentation. In addition, *policy should never contradict law*, because this can create a significant liability for the organization. For a discussion of this issue, see the Offline box regarding Arthur Andersen.

Quality security programs begin and end with policy.[3] Information security is primarily a management problem, not a technical one, and policy is a management tool that obliges personnel to function in a manner that preserves the security of information assets. Security policies are the least expensive control to execute, but the most difficult to implement *properly*. They have the lowest cost in that their creation and dissemination requires only the time and effort of the management team. Even if the management team hires an outside consultant to help develop policy, the costs are minimal compared to those of technical controls. However, shaping policy is difficult because policy must:

- Never conflict with laws
- Stand up in court, if challenged
- Be properly administered through dissemination and documented acceptance

Definitions

A **policy** is a plan or course of action that conveys instructions from an organization's senior management to those who make decisions, take actions, and perform other duties. Policies are organizational laws in that they dictate acceptable and unacceptable behavior within the

"I obstructed justice," testified David B. Duncan, the former chief outside auditor of Enron Corporation, an American energy company. He told a federal jury that he knew he had committed a crime when he instructed his colleagues at Arthur Andersen LLP to destroy documents as their energy client collapsed. "I instructed people on the engagement team to follow a document-retention policy which I knew would result in the destruction of documents." Duncan was fired by Andersen in January of 2002 after an internal probe revealed that the company shredded documents and deleted Enron-related e-mail messages. He pleaded guilty to a single count of obstruction of justice.[4]

The Enron Corporation was found to have lied about its financial records, specifically about its reported profits. Enron was also accused of many dubious business practices, including concealing financial losses and debts. The depth and breadth of the fraud was so great that at least one executive committed suicide rather than face criminal charges. And one of the company's accounting firms, world-renowned Arthur Andersen Consulting, contributed to the problem by shredding literally tons of financial documents in an attempt to hide the problem. Andersen claimed this was its policy.

Policy that conflicts with law is by definition illegal; therefore following such a policy is a criminal act. In the Enron/Arthur Andersen scandal, people went to jail claiming they had simply followed policy. And they might have gotten away with it, if they actually had followed policy that was being enforced for legitimate and lawful purposes.

The Arthur Andersen policy for document retention stated that staff must keep work papers for 6 years before destroying them, but client-related files, such as correspondence or other records, are only kept "until not useful." Managers and individual partners keeping such material in client folders or other files should "purge" the documents, the policy stated. But in cases of threatened litigation, Andersen staff were not supposed to destroy "related information."[5] A subsequent update to the policy was interpreted as a mandate to shred all but the most basic working papers as soon as possible unless precluded by an order for legal discovery.

And so the shredding party began. A big part of the problem was that the policy was not followed consistently—that is, this shredding began right *after* Arthur Andersen found out that Enron was to be investigated for fraudulent business practices, which indicated that the consulting firm had decided to cover its tracks and those of its business partner.

In the end, people went to jail, one person is dead, thousands of people's lives were disrupted when they became unemployed and/or lost their investment and retirement accounts, a company with a long tradition of integrity and trustworthiness is gone, and everyone made claims they were just following policy.

organization. Like laws, policies define what is right, what is wrong, what the penalties are for violating policy, and what the appeal process is. **Standards**, on the other hand, are more detailed statements of what must be done to comply with policy. They have the same requirements for compliance as policies. Standards may be informal or part of an organizational culture, as in **de facto standards**. Or standards may be published, scrutinized, and ratified by a group, as in formal or **de jure standards**. Finally, practices, procedures, and guidelines effectively explain how to comply with policy. Figure 5-1 shows policies as the force that drives standards, which in turn drive practices, procedures, and guidelines.

Policies are put in place to support the mission, vision, and strategic planning of an organization. The **mission** of an organization is a written statement of an organization's purpose. The **vision** of an organization is a written statement about the organization's goals—where will the organization be in five years? In ten? Strategic planning is the process of moving the organization toward its vision.

The meaning of the term **security policy** depends on the context in which it is used. Governmental agencies view security policy in terms of national security and national policies to deal with foreign states. A security policy can also communicate a credit card agency's method for processing credit card numbers. In general, a security policy is a set of rules that protect an organization's assets. An **information security policy** provides rules for the protection of the information assets of the organization.

Management must define three types of security policy, according to the National Institute of Standards and Technology's Special Publication 800-14 (a publication that is discussed in much greater detail later in this chapter):

1. Enterprise information security policies

2. Issue-specific security policies

3. Systems-specific security policies

For a policy to be effective and thus legally enforceable, it must meet the following criteria:

- Dissemination (distribution)—The organization must be able to demonstrate that the policy has been made readily available for review by the employee. Common dissemination techniques include hard copy and electronic distribution.

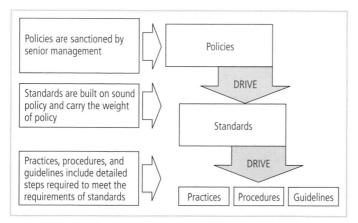

Figure 5-1 Policies, Standards, and Practices

Source: Course Technology/Cengage Learning

- Review (reading)—The organization must be able to demonstrate that it disseminated the document in an intelligible form, including versions for illiterate, non-English reading, and reading-impaired employees. Common techniques include recording the policy in English and other languages.

- Comprehension (understanding)—The organization must be able to demonstrate that the employee understood the requirements and content of the policy. Common techniques include quizzes and other assessments.

- Compliance (agreement)—The organization must be able to demonstrate that the employee agrees to comply with the policy, through act or affirmation. Common techniques include logon banners which require a specific action (mouse click or keystroke) to acknowledge agreement, or a signed document clearly indicating the employee has read, understood, and agreed to comply with the policy.

- Uniform enforcement—The organization must be able to demonstrate that the policy has been uniformly enforced, regardless of employee status or assignment.

Enterprise Information Security Policy (EISP)

An **enterprise information security policy (EISP)** is also known as a general security policy, organizational security policy, IT security policy, or information security policy. The EISP is based on and directly supports the mission, vision, and direction of the organization and sets the strategic direction, scope, and tone for all security efforts. The EISP is an executive-level document, usually drafted by or in cooperation with the chief information officer of the organization. This policy is usually two to ten pages long and shapes the philosophy of security in the IT environment. The EISP usually needs to be modified only when there is a change in the strategic direction of the organization.

The EISP guides the development, implementation, and management of the security program. It sets out the requirements that must be met by the information security blueprint or framework. It defines the purpose, scope, constraints, and applicability of the security program. It also assigns responsibilities for the various areas of security, including systems administration, maintenance of the information security policies, and the practices and responsibilities of the users. Finally, it addresses legal compliance. According to the National Institute of Standards and Technology (NIST), the EISP typically addresses compliance in the following two areas:

1. General compliance to ensure meeting the requirements to establish a program and the responsibilities assigned therein to various organizational components

2. The use of specified penalties and disciplinary action[6]

When the EISP has been developed, the CISO begins forming the security team and initiating the necessary changes to the information security program.

EISP Elements Although the specifics of EISPs vary from organization to organization, most EISP documents should include the following elements:

- An overview of the corporate philosophy on security

- Information on the structure of the information security organization and individuals who fulfill the information security role

- Fully articulated responsibilities for security that are shared by all members of the organization (employees, contractors, consultants, partners, and visitors)
- Fully articulated responsibilities for security that are unique to each role within the organization

The components of a good EISP are shown in Table 5-1.

Issue-Specific Security Policy (ISSP)

As an organization executes various technologies and processes to support routine operations, it must instruct employees on the proper use of these technologies and processes. In general, the **issue-specific security policy**, or **ISSP**, (1) addresses specific areas of technology as listed below, (2) requires frequent updates, and (3) contains a statement on the organization's position on a specific issue.[7] An ISSP may cover the following topics, among others:

- E-mail
- Use of the Internet
- Specific minimum configurations of computers to defend against worms and viruses

Component	Description
Statement of Purpose	Answers the question, "What is this policy for?" Provides a framework that helps the reader to understand the intent of the document. Can include text such as the following: "This document will: • Identify the elements of a good security policy • Explain the need for information security • Specify the various categories of information security • Identify the information security responsibilities and roles • Identify appropriate levels of security through standards and guidelines This document establishes an overarching security policy and direction for our company. Individual departments are expected to establish standards, guidelines, and operating procedures that adhere to and reference this policy while addressing their specific and individual needs."[8]
Information Security Elements	Defines information security. For example: "Protecting the confidentiality, integrity, and availability of information while in processing, transmission, and storage, through the use of policy, education and training, and technology…" This section can also lay out security definitions or philosophies to clarify the policy.
Need for Information Security	Provides information on the importance of information security in the organization and the obligation (legal and ethical) to protect critical information, whether regarding customers, employees, or markets.
Information Security Responsibilities and Roles	Defines the organizational structure designed to support information security within the organization. Identifies categories of individuals with responsibility for information security (IT department, management, users) and their information security responsibilities, including maintenance of this document.
Reference to Other Information Standards and Guidelines	Lists other standards that influence and are influenced by this policy document, perhaps including relevant laws (federal and state) and other policies.

Table 5-1 Components of the EISP[8]

- Prohibitions against hacking or testing organization security controls
- Home use of company-owned computer equipment
- Use of personal equipment on company networks
- Use of telecommunications technologies (fax and phone)
- Use of photocopy equipment

There are a number of approaches to creating and managing ISSPs within an organization. Three of the most common are:

1. Independent ISSP documents, each tailored to a specific issue
2. A single comprehensive ISSP document covering all issues
3. A modular ISSP document that unifies policy creation and administration, while maintaining each specific issue's requirements

The independent ISSP document typically has a scattershot effect. Each department responsible for a particular application of technology creates a policy governing its use, management, and control. This approach may fail to cover all of the necessary issues and can lead to poor policy distribution, management, and enforcement.

The single comprehensive ISSP is centrally managed and controlled. With formal procedures for the management of ISSPs in place, the comprehensive policy approach establishes guidelines for overall coverage of necessary issues and clearly identifies processes for the dissemination, enforcement, and review of these guidelines. Usually, these policies are developed by those responsible for managing the information technology resources. Unfortunately, these policies tend to overgeneralize the issues and skip over vulnerabilities.

The optimal balance between the independent and comprehensive ISSP is the modular ISSP. It is also centrally managed and controlled but is tailored to the individual technology issues. The modular approach provides a balance between issue orientation and policy management. The policies created with this approach comprise individual modules, each created and updated by people responsible for the issues addressed. These people report to a central policy administration group that incorporates specific issues into an overall comprehensive policy.

Table 5-2 is an outline of a sample ISSP, which can be used as a model. An organization should add to this structure the specific details that dictate security procedures not covered by these general guidelines.

The components of each of the major categories presented in the sample issue-specific policy shown in Table 5-2 are discussed below. Even though the details may vary from policy to policy, and some sections of a modular policy may be combined, it is essential for management to address and complete each section.

Statement of Policy The policy should begin with a clear statement of purpose. Consider a policy that covers the issue of fair and responsible use of the Internet. The introductory section of this policy should outline these topics: What is the scope of this policy? Who is responsible and accountable for policy implementation? What technologies and issues does it address?

Authorized Access and Usage of Equipment This section of the policy statement addresses *who* can use the technology governed by the policy, and *what* it can be used for. Remember that an organization's information systems are the exclusive property

Components of An ISSP
1. Statement of policy
a. Scope and applicability
b. Definition of technology addressed
c. Responsibilities
2. Authorized access and usage of equipment
a. User access
b. Fair and responsible use
c. Protection of privacy
3. Prohibited usage of equipment
a. Disruptive use or misuse
b. Criminal use
c. Offensive or harassing materials
d. Copyrighted, licensed, or other intellectual property
e. Other restrictions
4. Systems management
a. Management of stored materials
b. Employer monitoring
c. Virus protection
d. Physical security
e. Encryption
5. Violations of policy
a. Procedures for reporting violations
b. Penalties for violations
6. Policy review and modification
a. Scheduled review of policy procedures for modification
b. Legal disclaimers
7. Limitations of liability
a. Statements of liability
b. Other disclaimers as needed

Table 5-2 Components of an ISSP[9]

of the organization, and users have no particular rights of use. Each technology and process is provided for business operations. Use for any other purpose constitutes misuse of equipment. This section defines "fair and responsible use" of equipment and other organizational assets and should also address key legal issues, such as protection of personal information and privacy.

Prohibited Use of Equipment Unless a particular use is clearly prohibited, the organization cannot penalize its employees for misuse. The following can be prohibited: personal use, disruptive use or misuse, criminal use, offensive or harassing materials, and infringement of copyrighted, licensed, or other intellectual property. As an alternative approach, categories 2 and 3 of Table 5-2 can be collapsed into a single category—appropriate use. Many organizations use an ISSP section titled "Appropriate Use" to cover both categories.

Systems Management The systems management section of the ISSP policy statement focuses on the users' relationship to systems management. Specific rules from management include regulating the use of e-mail, the storage of materials, the authorized monitoring of employees, and the physical and electronic scrutiny of e-mail and other electronic documents. It is important that all such responsibilities are designated as belonging to either the systems administrator or the users; otherwise both parties may infer that the responsibility belongs to the other party.

Violations of Policy The people to whom the policy applies must understand the penalties and repercussions of violating the policy. Violations of policy should carry appropriate, not draconian, penalties. This section of the policy statement should contain not only the specifics of the penalties for each category of violation but also instructions on how individuals in the organization can report observed or suspected violations. Many people think that powerful individuals in the organization can discriminate, single out, or otherwise retaliate against someone who reports violations. Allowing anonymous submissions is often the only way to convince users to report the unauthorized activities of other, more influential employees.

Policy Review and Modification Because any document is only useful if it is up-to-date, each policy should contain procedures and a timetable for periodic review. As the organization's needs and technologies change, so must the policies that govern their use. This section should specify a methodology for the review and modification of the policy to ensure that users do not begin circumventing it as it grows obsolete.

Limitations of Liability If an employee is caught conducting illegal activities with organizational equipment or assets, management does not want the organization held liable. The policy should state that if employees violate a company policy or any law using company technologies, the company will not protect them, and the company is not liable for its actions. In fact, many organizations assist in the prosecution of employees who violate laws when their actions violate policies. It is inferred that such violations occur without knowledge or authorization by the organization.

Systems-Specific Policy (SysSP)

While issue-specific policies are formalized as written documents readily identifiable as policy, system-specific security policies (SysSPs) sometimes have a different look. SysSPs often function as standards or procedures to be used when configuring or maintaining systems. For example, a SysSP might describe the configuration and operation of a network firewall. This document could include a statement of managerial intent; guidance to network engineers on the selection, configuration, and operation of firewalls; and an access control list that defines levels of access for each authorized user. SysSPs can be separated into two general groups, **managerial guidance** and **technical specifications**, or they can be combined into a single policy document.

Managerial Guidance SysSPs A managerial guidance SysSP document is created by management to guide the implementation and configuration of technology as well as to address the behavior of people in the organization in ways that support the security of information.

For example, while the method for implementing a firewall belongs in the technical specifications SysSP, the firewall's configuration must follow guidelines established by management. An organization might not want its employees to access the Internet via the organization's network, for instance; in that case, the firewall should be implemented accordingly.

Firewalls are not the only technology that may require system-specific policies. Any system that affects the confidentiality, integrity, or availability of information must be assessed to evaluate the trade-off between improved security and restrictions.

System-specific policies can be developed at the same time as ISSPs, or they can be prepared in advance of their related ISSPs. Before management can craft a policy informing users what they can do with the technology and how they are supposed to do it, it might be necessary for system administrators to configure and operate the system. Some organizations may prefer to develop ISSPs and SysSPs in tandem, so that operational procedures and user guidelines are created simultaneously.

Technical Specifications SysSPs While a manager can work with a systems administrator to create managerial policy as described in the preceding section, the system administrator may in turn need to create a policy to implement the managerial policy. Each type of equipment requires its own set of policies, which are used to translate the management intent for the technical control into an enforceable technical approach. For example, an ISSP may require that user passwords be changed quarterly; a systems administrator can implement a technical control within a specific application to enforce this policy. There are two general methods of implementing such technical controls: access control lists and configuration rules.

Access Control Lists Access control lists (ACLs) consist of the user access lists, matrices, and capability tables that govern the rights and privileges of users. ACLs can control access to file storage systems, software components, or network communications devices. A **capabilities table** specifies which subjects and objects users or groups can access; in some systems, capabilities tables are called user profiles or user policies. These specifications frequently take the form of complex matrices, rather than simple lists or tables. The **access control matrix** includes a combination of tables and lists, such that organizational assets are listed along the column headers, while users are listed along the row headers. The resulting matrix contains ACLs in columns for a particular device or asset, and capability tables in rows for a particular user.

As illustrated in Figures 5-2 and 5-3, both Novell Netware 5.x/6.x and Microsoft Windows systems translate ACLs into sets of configurations that administrators use to control access to their systems. The level of detail may differ from system to system, but in general ACLs can restrict access for a particular user, computer, time, duration—even a particular file. This specificity provides powerful control to the administrator. In general, ACLs regulate the following:

- *Who* can use the system
- *What* authorized users can access
- *When* authorized users can access the system
- *Where* authorized users can access the system from

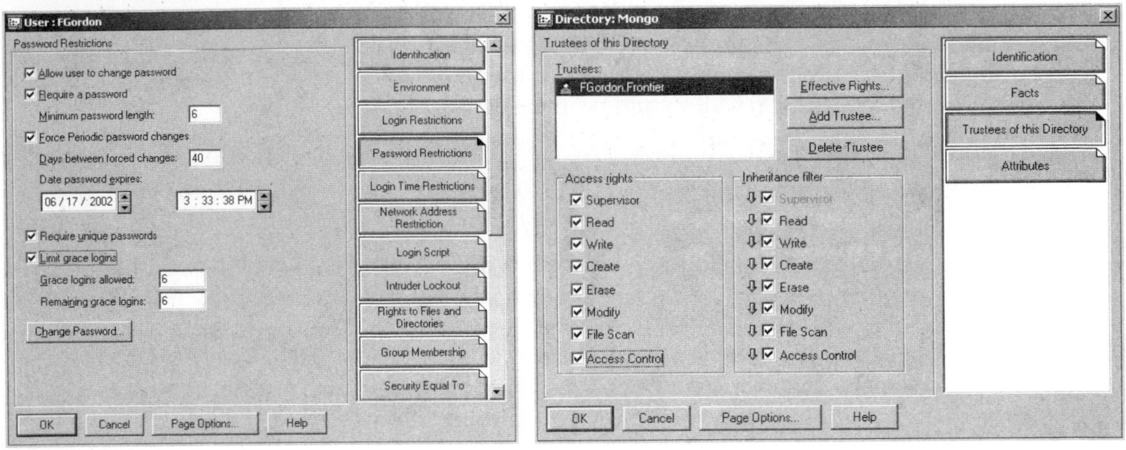

Figure 5-2 Novell's Use of ACLs

Source: Course Technology/Cengage Learning

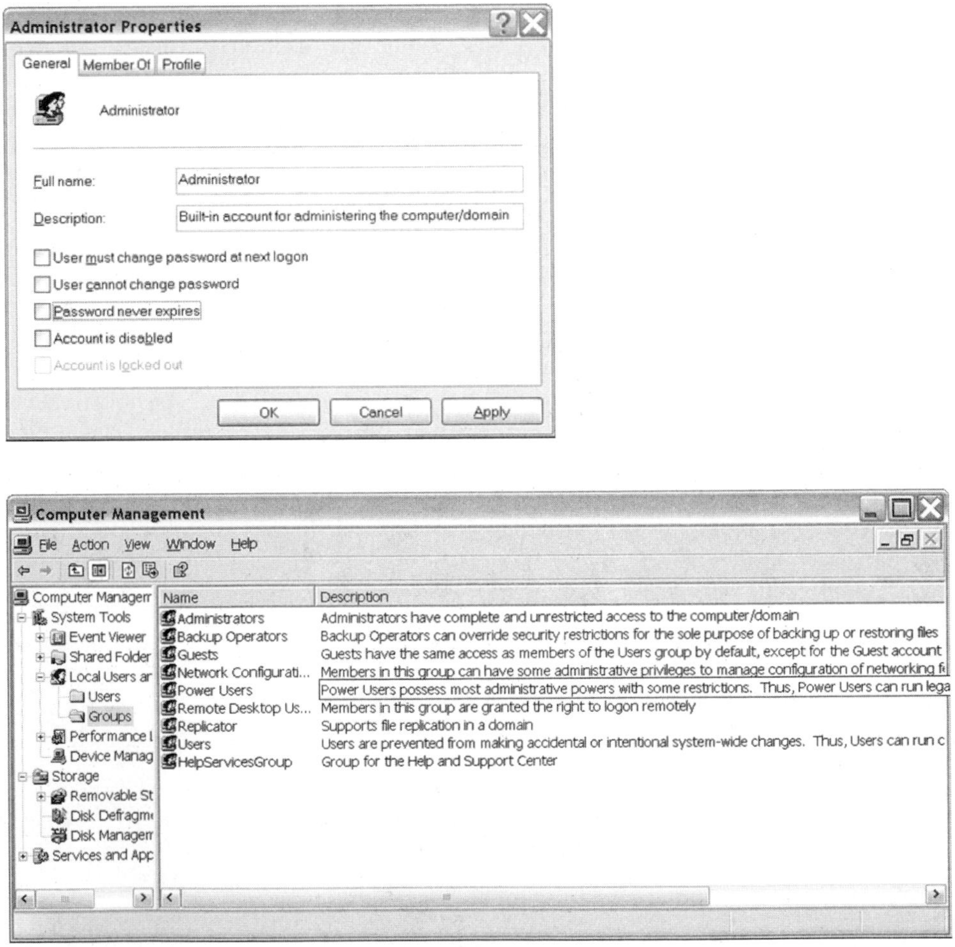

Figure 5-3 Microsoft Windows XP Use of ACLs

Source: Course Technology/Cengage Learning

The *who* of ACL access may be determined by a person's identity or by a person's membership in a group. Restricting *what* authorized users are permitted to access—whether by type (printers, files, communication devices, or applications), name, or location—is achieved by adjusting the resource privileges for a person or group to one of Read, Write, Create, Modify, Delete, Compare, or Copy. To control *when* access is allowed, some organizations implement time-of-day and/or day-of-week restrictions for some network or system resources. To control *where* resources can be accessed from, many network-connected assets block remote usage and also have some levels of access that are restricted to locally connected users. When these various ACL options are applied concurrently, the organization can govern how its resources can be used.

Figures 5-2 and 5-3 show how the ACL security model has been implemented by Novell and Microsoft operating systems.

Configuration Rule Policies Configuration rule policies are the specific instructions that govern how a security system reacts to the data it receives. Rule-based policies are more specific to the operation of a system than ACLs are, and they may or may not deal with users directly. Many security systems, for example firewalls, intrusion detection and prevention systems (IDPSs), and proxy servers, use specific configuration scripts that represent the configuration rule policy to determine how the system handles each data element they process. The examples in Figures 5-4 and 5-5 show how network security policy has been implemented by a Check Point firewall's rule set and by Inox Verisys (File Integrity Monitor) in a host-based IDPS rule set.

Combination SysSPs Many organizations create a single document that combines the management guidance SysSP and the technical specifications SysSP. While this document can be somewhat confusing to casual users, it is practical to have the guidance from both managerial and technical perspectives in a single place. If this approach is employed, care should be taken to clearly articulate the required actions. Some might consider this type of policy document a procedure, but it is actually a hybrid that combines policy with procedural guidance for the convenience of the implementers of the system being managed. This approach is best used by

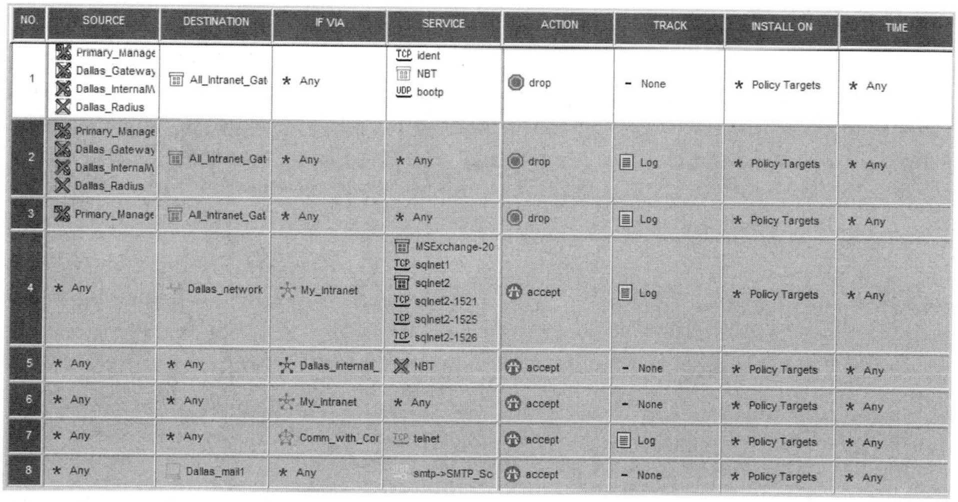

NO.	SOURCE	DESTINATION	IF VIA	SERVICE	ACTION	TRACK	INSTALL ON	TIME
1	Primary_Manage, Dallas_Gateway, Dallas_InternalM, Dallas_Radius	All_Intranet_Gat	Any	TCP ident, NBT, UDP bootp	drop	– None	Policy Targets	Any
2	Primary_Manage, Dallas_Gateway, Dallas_InternalM, Dallas_Radius	All_Intranet_Gat	Any	Any	drop	Log	Policy Targets	Any
3	Primary_Manage	All_Intranet_Gat	Any	Any	drop	Log	Policy Targets	Any
4	Any	Dallas_network	My_Intranet	MSExchange-20, TCP sqlnet1, sqlnet2, TCP sqlnet2-1521, TCP sqlnet2-1525, TCP sqlnet2-1526	accept	Log	Policy Targets	Any
5	Any	Any	Dallas_internall_	NBT	accept	– None	Policy Targets	Any
6	Any	Any	My_Intranet	Any	accept	– None	Policy Targets	Any
7	Any	Any	Comm_with_Cor	TCP telnet	accept	Log	Policy Targets	Any
8	Any	Dallas_mail1	Any	smtp->SMTP_Sc	accept	– None	Policy Targets	Any

Figure 5-4 Check Point VPN-1/Firewall-1 Policy Editor

Source: VPN-1/Firewall-1 Policy Editor courtesy of Check Point Software technologies Ltd.

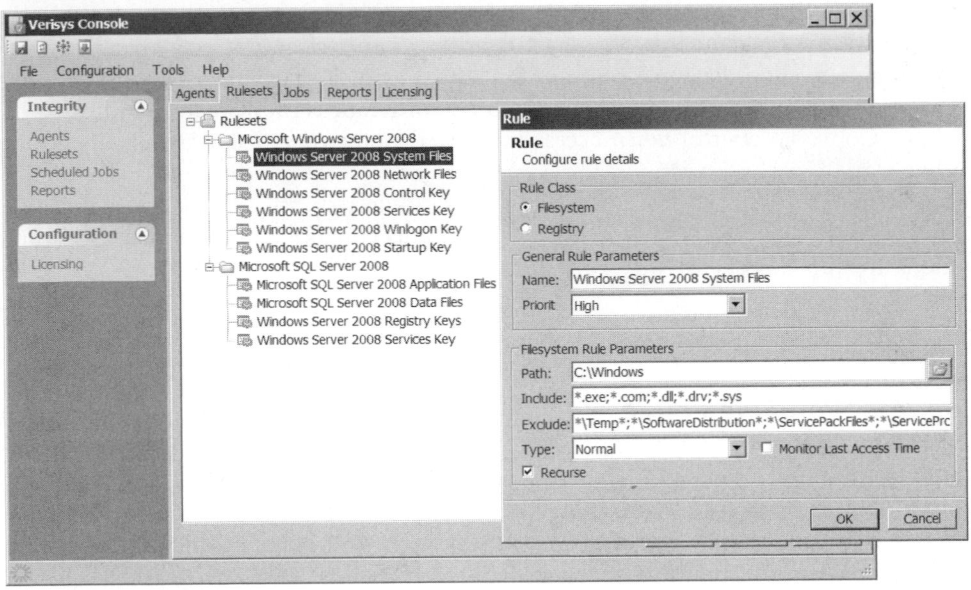

Figure 5-5 Inox Verisys (File Integrity Monitor) Use of Rules

Source: Course Technology/Cengage Learning

organizations that have multiple technical control systems of different types, and by smaller organizations that are seeking to document policy and procedure in a compact format.

Policy Management

Policies are living documents that must be managed. It is unacceptable to create such an important set of documents and then shelve it. These documents must be properly disseminated (distributed, read, understood, agreed to, and uniformly applied) and managed. How they are managed should be specified in the policy management section of the issue-specific policy described earlier. Good management practices for policy development and maintenance make for a more resilient organization. For example, all policies, including security policies, undergo tremendous stress when corporate mergers and divestitures occur; in such situations, employees are faced with uncertainty and many distractions. System vulnerabilities can arise if, for instance, incongruent security policies are implemented in different parts of a new, merged organization. When two companies merge but retain separate policies, the difficulty of implementing security controls increases. Likewise, when one company with unified policies splits in two, each new company may require different policies.

To remain viable, security policies must have a responsible individual, a schedule of reviews, a method for making recommendations for reviews, and a policy issuance and revision date.

Responsible Individual Just as information systems and information security projects must have champions and managers, so must policies. The policy champion and manager is called the **policy administrator**. Typically the policy administrator is a midlevel staff member and is responsible for the creation, revision, distribution, and storage of the policy. Note that the policy administrator does not necessarily have to be proficient in the relevant technology. While practicing information security professionals require extensive technical knowledge, policy management and policy administration requires only a moderate technical background.

It is good practice, however, for policy administrators to solicit input both from technically adept information security experts and from business-focused managers in each community of interest when making revisions to security policies. The administrator should also notify all affected members of the organization when the policy is modified.

It is disheartening when a policy that required hundreds of staff-hours to develop and document is ignored. Thus, someone must be responsible for placing the policy and all subsequent revisions into the hands of those who are accountable for its implementation. The policy administrator must be clearly identified on the policy document as the primary point of contact for additional information or for revision suggestions to the policy.

Schedule of Reviews Policies can only retain their effectiveness in a changing environment if they are periodically reviewed for currency and accuracy and modified accordingly. Policies that are not kept current can become liabilities, as outdated rules are enforced (or not) and new requirements are ignored. In order to demonstrate due diligence, an organization must actively seek to meet the requirements of the market in which it operates. This applies to both public (government, academic, and nonprofit) and private (commercial and for-profit) organizations. A properly organized schedule of reviews should be defined and published as part of the document. Typically a policy should be reviewed at least annually to ensure that it is still an effective control.

Review Procedures and Practices To facilitate policy reviews, the policy manager should implement a mechanism by which individuals can comfortably make recommendations for revisions, whether via e-mail, office mail, or an anonymous drop box. If the policy is controversial, anonymous submission of recommendations may be the best way to encourage staff opinions. Many employees are intimidated by management and hesitate to voice honest opinions about a policy unless they can do so anonymously. Once the policy has come up for review, all comments should be examined and management-approved improvements should be implemented. In reality, most policies are drafted by a single responsible individual and are then reviewed by a higher-level manager. But even this method does not preclude the collection and review of employee input.

Policy and Revision Date The simple action of dating the policy is often omitted. When policies are drafted and published without dates, confusion can arise. If policies are not reviewed and kept current, or if members of the organization are following undated versions, disastrous results and legal headaches can ensue. Such problems are particularly common in a high-turnover environment. It is, therefore, important that the policy contain the date of origin, along with the date(s) of any revisions. Some policies may also need a **sunset clause** indicating their expiration date, particularly those that govern information use in short-term business associations. Establishing a policy end date prevents a temporary policy from mistakenly becoming permanent, and it also enables an organization to gain experience with a given policy before adopting it permanently.

Automated Policy Management Recent years have seen the emergence of a new category of software for the management of information security policies. This type of software was developed in response to needs articulated by information security practitioners. While many software products can meet the need for a specific technical control, there is now software to meet the need for automating some of the busywork of policy management. Automation can streamline the repetitive steps of writing policy, tracking the workflow of policy approvals, publishing policy once it is written and approved, and tracking when individuals have read the policy. Using techniques from computer-based training and testing, organizations can train staff members and also improve the organization's awareness program. To quote the marketing literature from NetIQ Corporation:

> *SOFTWARE THAT PUTS YOU IN CONTROL OF SECURITY POLICY CREATION, DISTRIBUTION, EDUCATION, AND TRACKING FOR COMPLIANCE.*
>
> *VigilEnt Policy Center now makes it possible to manage security policy dynamically so that you can create, distribute, educate, and track understanding of your information security policies for all employees in your organization. It enables you to keep policies up-to-date, change them quickly as needed, and ensure that they are being understood properly, all through a new automated, interactive, Web-based software application.*[10]

The Information Security Blueprint

Once an organization has developed its information security policies and standards, the information security community can begin developing the blueprint for the information security program. If one or more components of policies, standards, or practices have not been completed, management must determine whether or not to nonetheless proceed with the development of the blueprint.

After the information security team has inventoried the organization's information assets and assessed and prioritized the threats to those assets, it must conduct a series of risk assessments using quantitative or qualitative analyses, as well as feasibility studies and cost benefit analyses. These assessments, which include determining each asset's current protection level, are used to decide whether or not to proceed with any given control. Armed with a general idea of the vulnerabilities in the information technology systems of the organization, the security team develops a design blueprint for security, which is used to implement the security program.

This **security blueprint** is the basis for the design, selection, and implementation of all security program elements including policy implementation, ongoing policy management, risk management programs, education and training programs, technological controls, and maintenance of the security program. The security blueprint, built on top of the organization's information security policies, is a scalable, upgradeable, comprehensive plan to meet the organization's current and future information security needs. It is a detailed version of the **security framework**, which is an outline of the overall information security strategy for the organization and a roadmap for planned changes to the information security environment of the organization. The blueprint specifies the tasks and the order in which they are to be accomplished.

To select a methodology in which to develop an information security blueprint, you can adapt or adopt a published information security model or framework. This framework can outline steps to take to design and implement information security in the organization. There are a number of published information security frameworks, including ones from government sources, which are presented later in this chapter. Because each information security environment is unique, the security team may need to modify or adapt pieces from several frameworks. Experience teaches you that what works well for one organization may not precisely fit another.

1.	Risk Assessment and Treatment
2.	Security Policy
3.	Organization of Information Security
4.	Asset Management
5.	Human Resource Security
6.	Physical and Environmental Security
7.	Communications and Operations
8.	Access Control
9.	Information Systems Acquisition, Development and Maintenance
10.	Information Security Incident Management
11.	Business Continuity Management
12.	Compliance

Table 5-3 The Sections of the ISO/IEC 27002[14]

The ISO 27000 Series

One of the most widely referenced security models is the *Information Technology—Code of Practice for Information Security Management*, which was originally published as British Standard BS7799. In 2000, this code of practice was adopted as an international standard framework for information security by the International Organization for Standardization (ISO) and the International Electrotechnical Commission (IEC) as ISO/IEC 17799. The document was revised in 2005 (becoming ISO 17799:2005), and it was then renamed to ISO 27002 in 2007, to align it with the document ISO 27001, discussed later in this chapter. While the details of ISO/IEC 27002 are available to those who purchase the standard, its structure and general organization are well known. For a summary description, see Table 5-3. For more details on ISO/IEC sections, see *wwsw.praxiom.com/iso-17799-2005.htm*.

The stated purpose of ISO/IEC 27002 is to "give recommendations for information security management for use by those who are responsible for initiating, implementing, or maintaining security in their organization. It is intended to provide a common basis for developing organizational security standards and effective security management practice and to provide confidence in inter-organizational dealings."[11] Where ISO/IEC 27002 is focused on a broad overview of the various areas of security, providing information on 127 controls over ten broad areas, ISO/IEC 27001 provides information on how to implement ISO/IEC 27002 and how to set up an information security management system (ISMS). The overall methodology for this process and its major steps are presented in Figure 5-6.

In the United Kingdom, correct implementation of these standards (both volumes), as determined by a BS7799 certified evaluator, allowed organizations to obtain information security management system (ISMS) certification and accreditation. When the standard first came out, several countries, including the United States, Germany, and Japan, refused to adopted it, claiming that there were fundamental problems, including:

- The global information security community had not defined any justification for a code of practice as identified in the ISO/IEC 17799.

- ISO/IEC 17799 lacked "the necessary measurement precision of a technical standard."[12]

- There was no reason to believe that ISO/IEC 17799 was more useful than any other approach.
- ISO/IEC 17799 was not as complete as other frameworks.
- ISO/IEC 17799 was hurriedly prepared given the tremendous impact its adoption could have on industry information security controls.[13]

ISO/IEC 27002 is an interesting framework for information security, but aside from those relatively few U.S. organizations that operate in the European Union (or are otherwise obliged to meet its terms), most U.S. organizations are not expected to comply with it.

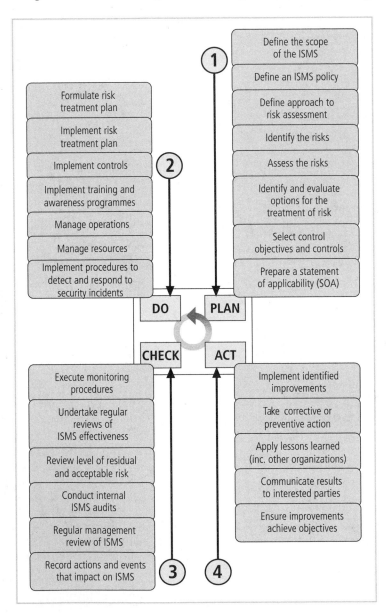

Figure 5-6 BS7799:2 Major Process Steps

Source: Course Technology/Cengage Learning

ISO/IEC 27001:2005: The Information Security Management System

ISO/IEC 27001 provides implementation details using a Plan-Do-Check-Act cycle, as described in Table 5-4 and shown in Figure 5-7 in abbreviated form:

Plan-Do-Check-Act Cycle	
Plan:	
1.	Define the scope of the ISMS.
2.	Define an ISMS policy.
3.	Define the approach to risk assessment.
4.	Identify the risks.
5.	Assess the risks.
6.	Identify and evaluate options for the treatment of risk.
7.	Select control objectives and controls.
8.	Prepare a statement of applicability (SOA).
Do:	
9.	Formulate a risk treatment plan.
10.	Implement the risk treatment plan.
11.	Implement controls.
12.	Implement training and awareness programs.
13.	Manage operations.
14.	Manage resources.
15.	Implement procedures to detect and respond to security incidents.
Check:	
16.	Execute monitoring procedures.
17.	Undertake regular reviews of ISMS effectiveness.
18.	Review the level of residual and acceptable risk.
19.	Conduct internal ISMS audits.
20.	Undertake regular management review of the ISMS.
21.	Record actions and events that impact an ISMS.
Act:	
22.	Implement identified improvements.
23.	Take corrective or preventive action.
24.	Apply lessons learned.
25.	Communicate results to interested parties.
26.	Ensure improvements achieve objectives.

Table 5-4 The ISO/IEC 27001: 2005 Plan-Do-Check-Act Cycle[15]

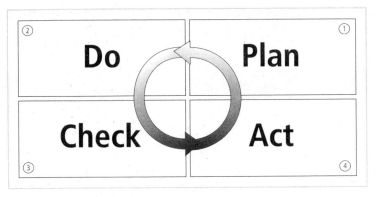

Figure 5-7 BS7799:2—Plan-Do-Check-Act

Source: Course Technology/Cengage Learning

Although ISO/IEC 27001 provides some implementation information, it simply specified *what* must be done—not *how* to do it. As noted by Gamma Secure Systems, "The standard has an appendix that gives guidance on the use of the standard, in particular to expand on the Plan-Do-Check-Act concept. It is important to realize that there will be many Plan-Do-Check-Act cycles within a single ISMS all operating asynchronously at different speeds."[16]

As stated earlier, ISO/IEC 27001's primary purpose is to enable organizations that adopt it to obtain certification, and thus it serves better as an assessment tool than as an implementation framework.

In 2007, the International Standards Organization announced plans for the numbering of current and impending standards related to information security issues and topics. It is expected that over the next few years the standards that are shown in Table 5-5 will be published in the areas shown.

NIST Security Models

Other approaches are described in the many documents available from the Computer Security Resource Center of the National Institute for Standards and Technology (*http://csrc.nist.gov*). Because the NIST documents are publicly available at no charge and have been available for some time, they have been broadly reviewed by government and industry professionals, and are among the references cited by the federal government when it decided not to select the ISO/IEC 17799 standards. The following NIST documents can assist in the design of a security framework:

- SP 800-12: *An Introduction to Computer Security: The NIST Handbook*
- SP 800-14: *Generally Accepted Security Principles and Practices for Securing Information Technology Systems*
- SP 800-18 Rev. 1: *Guide for Developing Security Plans for Federal Information Systems*
- SP 800-26: *Security Self-Assessment Guide for Information Technology Systems* (removed from active list but still available in archives)
- SP 800-30: *Risk Management Guide for Information Technology Systems*

ISO 27000 Series Standard	Pub Date	Title or Topic	Comment
27000	2009	Series Overview and Terminology	Defines terminology and vocabulary for the standard series
27001	2005	Information Security Management System Specification	Drawn from BS 7799:2
27002	2007	Code of Practice for Information Security Management	Renamed from ISO/IEC 17799; drawn from BS 7799:1
27004	2009	Information Security Measurements and Metrics	
27005	2008	ISMS Risk Management	Supports 27001, but doesn't recommend any specific risk method
27006	2007	Requirements for Bodies Providing Audit and Certification of an ISMS	Largely intended to support the accreditation of certification bodies providing ISMS certification
Planned 27000 Series Standards			
27003	Planned	Information Security Management Systems Implementation Guidelines	Expected in 2010
27007	Planned	Guideline for ISMS Auditing	Focuses on management systems
27008	Planned	Guideline for Information Security Auditing	Focuses on security controls
27013	Planned	Guideline on the Integrated Implementation of ISO/IEC 20000-1 and ISO/IEC 27001	
27014	Planned	Information Security Governance Framework	
27015	Planned	Information Security Management Guidelines for Finance and Insurance Sectors	

Table 5-5 ISO 27000 Series Current and Planned Standards

Note: There are additional 27000 series documents in preparation that are not included here.

(Source: http://en.wikipedia.org/wiki/ISO/IEC_27000-series)

Many of these documents have been referenced earlier in this book as sources of information for the management of security. The following sections examine these documents as they apply to the blueprint for information security.

NIST Special Publication SP 800-12

SP 800-12, *An Introduction to Computer Security: The NIST Handbook*, is an excellent reference and guide for the security manager or administrator in the routine management of information security. It provides little guidance, however, on design and implementation of new security systems, and therefore should be used only as a precursor to understanding an information security blueprint.

NIST Special Publication 800-14 *Generally Accepted Principles and Practices for Securing Information Technology Systems* provides best practices and security principles that can direct the security team in the development of a security blueprint. In addition to detailing security best practices across the spectrum of security areas, it provides philosophical principles that the security team should integrate into the entire information security process. Table 5-6 presents the table of contents of the NIST SP 800-14. The document can guide the development of the security framework and should be combined with other NIST publications providing the necessary structure to the entire security process.

The scope of NIST SP 800-14 is broad. It is important to consider each of the security principles it presents, and therefore the following sections examine some of the more significant points in more detail.

2.1 Security Supports the Mission of the Organization: Failure to develop an information security system based on the organization's mission, vision, and culture guarantees the failure of the information security program.

2.2 Security Is an Integral Element of Sound Management: Effective management includes planning, organizing, leading, and controlling. Security enhances management functions by providing input during the planning process for organizational initiatives. Information security controls support sound management via the enforcement of both managerial and security policies.

2.3 Security Should Be Cost-Effective: The costs of information security should be considered part of the cost of doing business, much like the cost of the computers, networks, and voice communications systems. These are not profit-generating areas of the organization and may not lead to competitive advantages. Information security should justify its own costs. The use of security measures that do not justify their cost must have a strong business justification (such as a legal requirement).

2.4 Systems Owners Have Security Responsibilities Outside Their Own Organizations: Whenever systems store and use information from customers, patients, clients, partners, or others, the security of this information becomes the responsibility of the owner of the systems. Each system's owners are expected to diligently work with those who have systems that are interconnected with their own to assure the confidentiality, integrity, and availability of the entire value chain of interconnected systems.

2.5 Security Responsibilities and Accountability Should Be Made Explicit: Policy documents should clearly identify the security responsibilities of users, administrators, and managers. To be legally binding, the policies must be documented, disseminated, read, understood, and agreed to by all involved members of the organization. As noted in Chapter 3, ignorance of the law is no excuse, but ignorance of policy is. Organizations should also provide information about relevant laws in issue-specific security policies.

2.6 Security Requires a Comprehensive and Integrated Approach: Security personnel alone cannot effectively implement security. As emphasized throughout this textbook, *security is everyone's responsibility*. The three communities of interest (information technology management and professionals, information security management and professionals, and users, managers, administrators, and other stakeholders) should participate in the process of developing a comprehensive information security program.

NIST SP800-15 Table of Contents
2.   Generally Accepted System Security Principles
2.1   Computer Security Supports the Mission of the Organization
2.2   Computer Security Is an Integral Element of Sound Management
2.3   Computer Security Should Be Cost-Effective
2.4   Systems Owners Have Security Responsibilities Outside Their Own Organizations
2.5   Computer Security Responsibilities and Accountability Should Be Made Explicit
2.6   Computer Security Requires a Comprehensive and Integrated Approach
2.7   Computer Security Should Be Periodically Reassessed
2.8   Computer Security Is Constrained by Societal Factors
3.   Common IT Security Practices
3.1   Policy
3.1.1   Program Policy
3.1.2   Issue Specific Policy
3.1.3   System-Specific Policy
3.1.4   All Policies
3.2   Program Management
3.2.1   Central Security Program
3.2.2   System-Level Program
3.3   Risk Management
3.3.1   Risk Assessment
3.3.2   Risk Mitigation
3.3.3   Uncertainty Analysis
3.4   Life Cycle Planning
3.4.1   Security Plan
3.4.2   Initiation Phase
3.4.3   Development/Acquisition Phase
3.4.4   Implementation Phase
3.4.5   Operation/Maintenance Phase
3.4.6   Disposal Phase
3.5   Personnel/User Issues
3.5.1   Staffing
3.5.2   User Administration

Table 5-6   NIST SP 800-14 Generally Accepted Principles and Practices for Securing Information Technology Systems[17]

Table 5-6 NIST SP 800-14 Generally Accepted Principles and Practices for Securing Information Technology Systems (continued)

2.7 Security Should Be Periodically Reassessed: Information security that is implemented and then ignored is considered negligent, the organization having not demonstrated due diligence. Security is an ongoing process. To be effective against a constantly shifting set of threats and a changing user base, the security process must be periodically repeated. Continuous analyses of threats, assets, and controls must be conducted and new blueprints developed. Only thorough preparation, design, implementation, eternal vigilance, and ongoing maintenance can secure the organization's information assets.

2.8 Security Is Constrained by Societal Factors: There are a number of factors that influence the implementation and maintenance of security. Legal demands, shareholder requirements, even business practices affect the implementation of security controls and safeguards. For example, security professionals generally prefer to isolate information assets from the Internet, which is the leading avenue of threats to the assets, but the business requirements of the organization may preclude this control measure.

Table 5-7 presents the "Principles for Securing Information Technology Systems," which is part of NIST SP 800-14. You can use this document to make sure the key elements needed for a successful effort are factored into the design of an information security program and to produce a blueprint for an effective security architecture.

NIST Special Publication 800-18 Rev. 1 *The Guide for Developing Security Plans for Federal Information Systems* can be used as the foundation for a comprehensive security blueprint and framework. This publication provides detailed methods for assessing, designing, and implementing controls and plans for applications of varying size. SP 800-18 Rev. 1 can serve as a useful guide to the activities described in this chapter and as an aid in the planning process. It also includes templates for major application security plans. As with any publication of this scope and magnitude, SP 800-18 Rev. 1 must be customized to fit the particular needs of an organization. The table of contents for Publication 800-18 Rev. 1 is presented in Table 5-8.

IETF Security Architecture

The Security Area Working Group acts as an advisory board for the protocols and areas developed and promoted by the Internet Society and the Internet Engineering Task Force (IETF), and while the group endorses no specific information security architecture, one of its requests for comment (RFC), RFC 2196: *Site Security Handbook*, provides a good functional discussion of important security issues. RFC 2196: *Site Security Handbook* covers five basic areas of security with detailed discussions on development and implementation. There are also chapters on such important topics as security policies, security technical architecture, security services, and security incident handling.

The chapter within the RFC that deals with architecture begins with a discussion of the importance of security policies and continues with an examination of services, access controls, and other relevant areas. The table of contents for the RFC 2196: *Site Security Handbook* is represented in Table 5-9.

Baselining and Best Business Practices

As you learned in Chapter 4, baselining and best practices are reliable methods used by some organizations to assess security practices. Baselining and best practices don't provide a complete methodology for the design and implementation of all the practices needed by an organization; however, it is possible to piece together the desired outcome of the security process, and therefore to work backwards toward an effective design. The Federal Agency Security Practices (FASP) site, *http://csrc.nist.gov/groups/SMA/fasp*, is a popular place to look up best practices. FASP is designed to provide best practices for public agencies, but these practices can be adapted

Principles and Practices for Securing IT Systems	
1.	Establish a sound security policy as the foundation for design.
2.	Treat security as an integral part of the overall system design.
3.	Clearly delineate the physical and logical security boundaries governed by associated security policies.
4.	Reduce risk to an acceptable level.
5.	Assume that external systems are insecure.
6.	Identify potential trade-offs between reducing risk and increased costs and decrease in other aspects of operational effectiveness.
7.	Implement layered security (ensure no single point of vulnerability).
8.	Implement tailored system security measures to meet organizational security goals.
9.	Strive for simplicity.
10.	Design and operate an IT system to limit vulnerability and to be resilient in response.
11.	Minimize the system elements to be trusted.
12.	Implement security through a combination of measures distributed physically and logically.
13.	Provide assurance that the system is, and continues to be, resilient in the face of expected threats.
14.	Limit or contain vulnerabilities.
15.	Formulate security measures to address multiple overlapping information domains.
16.	Isolate public access systems from mission critical resources (e.g., data, processes, etc.).
17.	Use boundary mechanisms to separate computing systems and network infrastructures.
18.	Where possible, base security on open standards for portability and interoperability.
19.	Use common language in developing security requirements.
20.	Design and implement audit mechanisms to detect unauthorized use and to support incident investigations.
21.	Design security to allow for regular adoption of new technology, including a secure and logical technology upgrade process.
22.	Authenticate users and processes to ensure appropriate access control decisions both within and across domains.
23.	Use unique identities to ensure accountability.
24.	Implement least privilege.
25.	Do not implement unnecessary security mechanisms.
26.	Protect information while being processed, in transit, and in storage.
27.	Strive for operational ease of use.
28.	Develop and exercise contingency or disaster recovery procedures to ensure appropriate availability.
29.	Consider custom products to achieve adequate security.
30.	Ensure proper security in the shutdown or disposal of a system.
31.	Protect against all likely classes of "attacks."
32.	Identify and prevent common errors and vulnerabilities.
33.	Ensure that developers are trained in how to develop secure software.

Table 5-7 Principles for Securing Information Technology Systems NIST SP 800-14 Generally Accepted Principles and Practices for Securing Information Technology Systems[18]

Partial Table of Contents
2. System Boundary Analysis and Security Controls
2.1 System Boundaries
2.2 Major Applications
2.3 General Support Systems
2.4 Minor Applications
2.5 Security Controls
2.5.1 Scoping Guidance
2.5.2 Compensating Controls
2.5.3 Common Security Controls
3. Plan Development
3.1 System Name and Identifier
3.2 System Categorization
3.3 System Owner
3.4 Authorizing Official
3.5 Other Designated Contacts
3.6 Assignment of Security Responsibility
3.7 System Operational Status
3.8 Information System Type
3.9 General Description/Purpose
3.10 System Environment
3.11 System Interconnection/Information Sharing
3.12 Laws, Regulations, and Policies Affecting The System
3.13 Security Control Selection
3.14 Minimum Security Controls
3.15 Completion and Approval Dates
3.16 Ongoing System Security Plan Maintenance
Appendix A: Sample Information System Security Plan Template

Table 5-8   Guide for Developing Security Plans for Federal Information Systems[19]

easily to private institutions. The documents found at this site include specific examples of key policies and planning documents, implementation strategies for key technologies, and position descriptions for key security personnel. Of particular value is the section on program management, which includes:

- A summary guide: public law, executive orders, and policy documents
- Position description for computer system security officer

RFC 2196: Site Security Handbook Table of Contents

1. Introduction

    1.1   Purpose of this Work

    1.2   Audience

    1.3   Definitions

    1.4   Related Work

    1.5   Basic Approach

    1.6   Risk Assessment

2. Security Policies

    2.1   What Is a Security Policy and Why Have One?

    2.2   What Makes a Good Security Policy?

    2.3   Keeping the Policy Flexible

3. Architecture

    3.1   Objectives

    3.2   Network and Service Configuration

    3.3   Firewalls

4. Security Services and Procedures

    4.1   Authentication

    4.2   Confidentiality

    4.3   Integrity

    4.4   Authorization

    4.5   Access

    4.6   Auditing

    4.7   Securing Backups

5. Security Incident Handling

    5.1   Preparing and Planning for Incident Handling

    5.2   Notification and Points of Contact

    5.3   Identifying an Incident

    5.4   Handling an Incident

    5.5   Aftermath of an Incident

    5.6   Responsibilities

6. Ongoing Activities

7. Tools and Locations

8. Mailing Lists and Other Resources

9. References

Table 5-9 RFC 2196: Site Security Handbook Table of Contents[20]

- Position description for information security officer
- Position description for computer specialist
- Sample of an information technology (IT) security staffing plan for a large service application (LSA)
- Sample of information technology (IT) security program policy
- Security handbook and standard operating procedures
- Telecommuting and mobile computer security policy

In the later stages of creating an information security blueprint, these policy documents are particularly useful.

A number of other public and semipublic institutions provide information on best practices—one of these groups is the Computer Emergency Response Team Coordination Center (CERT/CC) at Carnegie Mellon University (*www.cert.org*). CERT/CC provides detailed and specific assistance on how to implement a sound security methodology.

Professional societies often provide information on best practices for their members. The Technology Manager's Forum (*www.techforum.com*) has an annual best practice award in a number of areas, including information security. The Information Security Forum (*www.isfsecuritystandard.com*) has a free publication titled "Standard of Good Practice." This publication outlines information security best practices.

Many organizations hold seminars and classes on best practices for implementing security; in particular, the Information Systems Audit and Control Association (*www.isaca.org*) hosts regular seminars. The International Association of Professional Security Consultants (*www.iapsc.org*) has a listing of best practices, as does the Global Grid Forum (*www.ogf.org*). At a minimum, information security professionals can peruse Web portals for posted security best practices. There are several free portals dedicated to security that have collections of best practices, such as SearchSecurity.com and NIST's Computer Resources Center. These are but a few of the many public and private organizations that promote solid best security practices. Investing a few hours searching the Web reveals dozens of locations for additional information.

Design of Security Architecture

To inform the discussion of information security program architecture and to illustrate industry best practices, the following sections outline a few key security architectural components. Many of these components are examined in detail in later chapters of this book, but this overview can help you assess whether a framework and/or blueprint are on target to meet an organization's needs.

Spheres of Security The spheres of security, shown in Figure 5-8, are the foundation of the security framework. Generally speaking, the spheres of security illustrate how information is under attack from a variety of sources. The sphere of use, on the left-hand side of Figure 5-8, illustrates the ways in which people access information. For example, people read hard copies of documents and can also access information through systems. Information, as the most important asset in this model, is at the center of the sphere. Information is always at risk from attacks whenever it is accessible by people or computer systems. Networks and the Internet are indirect threats, as exemplified by the fact that a person attempting to access information from the Internet must traverse local networks. The sphere of protection, on the right-hand side of Figure 5-8, illustrates that between each layer of the sphere of use there must exist a layer of protection, represented in the figure by the shaded bands. For example, the items labeled "Policy and law" and

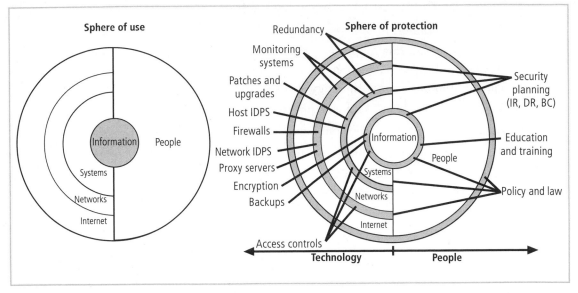

Figure 5-8 Spheres of Security

Source: Course Technology/Cengage Learning

"Education and training" are placed between people and the information. Controls are also implemented between systems and the information, between networks and the computer systems, and between the Internet and internal networks. This reinforces the concept of defense in depth. A variety of controls can be used to protect the information. The items of control shown in the figure are not intended to be comprehensive, but rather to illustrate some of the safeguards that can protect the systems that are located closer to the center of the sphere. Because people can directly access each ring as well as the information at the core of the model, the side of the sphere of protection that attempts to control access by relying on people requires a different approach to security than the side that uses technology. The members of the organization must become a safeguard that is effectively trained, implemented, and maintained, or else they too will present a threat to the information.

Information security is designed and implemented in three layers: policies, people (education, training, and awareness programs), and technology, commonly referred to as PPT. Each of the layers contains controls and safeguards that protect the information and information system assets that the organization values. The ordering of these controls follows the prioritization scheme developed in Chapter 4. But before any technical controls or other safeguards can be implemented, the policies defining the management philosophies that guide the security process must be in place.

Levels of Controls Information security safeguards provide three levels of control: managerial, operational, and technical. **Managerial controls** are security processes that are designed by strategic planners and implemented by the security administration of the organization. Management controls set the direction and scope of the security process and provide detailed instructions for its conduct, as well as addressing the design and implementation of the security planning process and security program management. They also address risk management and security control reviews (as described in Chapter 4), describe the necessity and scope of legal compliance, and set guidelines for the maintenance of the entire security life cycle.

Operational controls are management and lower-level planning functions that deal with the operational functionality of security in the organization, such as disaster recovery and incident response planning. Operational controls address personnel security, physical security, and the protection of production inputs and outputs. In addition, operational controls guide the development of education, training, and awareness programs for users, administrators, and management. Finally, they address hardware and software systems maintenance and the integrity of data.

Technical controls are the tactical and technical implementations of security in the organization. While operational controls address specific operational issues, such as developing and integrating controls into the business functions, technical controls are the components put in place to protect an organization's information assets. They include logical access controls, such as identification, authentication, authorization, accountability (including audit trails), cryptography, and the classification of assets and users.

Defense in Depth One of the basic tenets of security architectures is the layered implementation of security. This layered approach is called **defense in depth**. To achieve defense in depth, an organization must establish multiple layers of security controls and safeguards, which can be organized into policy, training and education, and technology, as per the CNSS model presented in Chapter 1. While policy itself may not prevent attacks, it certainly prepares the organization to handle them, and coupled with other layers, it can deter attacks. This is true of training and education, which can provide some defense against attacks enabled by employee ignorance and social engineering. Technology is also implemented in layers, with detection equipment working in tandem with reaction technology, all operating behind access control mechanisms. Implementing multiple types of technology and thereby precluding that the failure of one system will compromise the security of information is referred to as **redundancy**. Redundancy can be implemented at a number of points throughout the security architecture, such as in firewalls, proxy servers, and access controls. Figure 5-9 illustrates the concept of building controls in multiple, sometimes redundant layers. The figure shows the use of firewalls and prevention IDPS that use both packet-level rules (shown as the header in the diagram) and content analysis (shown as 0100101011 in the diagram). More information on firewalls and intrusion detection systems is presented in Chapters 6 and 7, respectively.

Security Perimeter A perimeter is boundary of an area. A **security perimeter** defines the boundary between the outer limit of an organization's security and the beginning of the outside world. A security perimeter is the level of security that protects all internal systems from outside threats, as pictured in Figure 5-10. Unfortunately, the perimeter does not protect against internal attacks from employee threats or onsite physical threats. There can be both an electronic security perimeter, usually at the organization's exterior network or Internet connection, and a physical security perimeter, usually at the entrance to the organization's offices. Both require perimeter security. Security perimeters can effectively be implemented as multiple technologies that segregate the protected information from potential attackers. Within security perimeters the organization can establish **security domains**, or areas of trust within which users can freely communicate. The assumption is that if individuals have access to one system within a security domain, they have authorized access to all systems within that particular domain. The security perimeter is an essential element of the overall security framework, and its implementation details are the

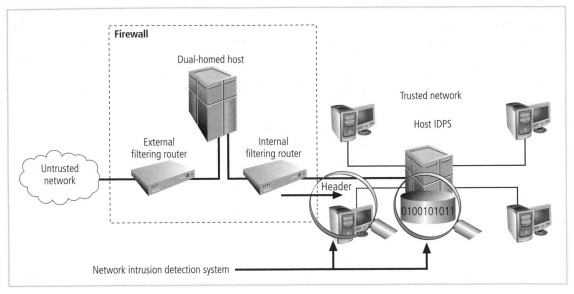

Figure 5-9 Defense in Depth

Source: Course Technology/Cengage Learning

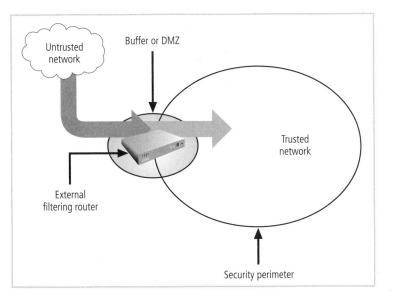

Figure 5-10 Security Perimeters

Source: Course Technology/Cengage Learning

core of the completed security blueprint. The key components of the security perimeter—firewalls, DMZs, proxy servers, and IDPSs—are presented in the following sections. You will learn more about information security technologies later in the book (in Chapters 6, 7, and 8).

Firewalls A **firewall** is a device that selectively discriminates against information flowing into or out of the organization. A firewall is usually a computing device or a specially configured computer that allows or prevents access to a defined area based on a set of rules. Firewalls are usually placed on the security perimeter, just behind or as part of a **gateway router**. While the gateway router's primary purpose is to connect the organization's systems to the outside world, it too can be used as the front-line defense against attacks, as it can be configured to allow only set types of protocols to enter. There are a number of types of firewalls—packet filtering, stateful packet filtering, proxy, and application level—and they are usually classified by the level of information they can filter. A firewall can be a single device or a **firewall subnet,** which consists of multiple firewalls creating a buffer between the outside and inside networks as shown in Figure 5-11.

DMZs A buffer against outside attacks is frequently referred to as a **demilitarized zone (DMZ).** The DMZ is a no-man's-land between the inside and outside networks; it is also where some organizations place Web servers. These servers provide access to organizational Web pages, without allowing Web requests to enter the interior networks.

Proxy Servers An alternative to firewall subnets or DMZs is a **proxy server,** or **proxy firewall**. A proxy server performs actions on behalf of another system. When deployed, a proxy server is configured to look like a Web server and is assigned the domain name that users would be expecting to find for the system and its services. When an outside client requests a particular Web page, the proxy server receives the request as if it were the subject of the request, then asks for the same information from the true Web server (acting as a proxy for the requestor), and then responds to the request. This gives requestors the response they need without allowing them to gain direct access to the internal and more sensitive server. The proxy server may be hardened and become a bastion host placed in the public area of the

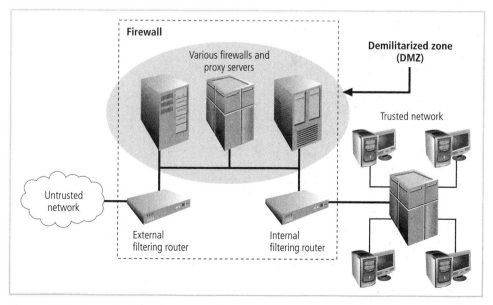

Figure 5-11 Firewalls, Proxy Servers, and DMZs

Source: Course Technology/Cengage Learning

network, or it might be placed within the firewall subnet or the DMZ for added protection. For more frequently accessed Web pages, proxy servers can cache or temporarily store the page, and thus are sometimes called **cache servers**. Figure 5-11 shows a representative example of a configuration using a proxy server.

Intrusion Detection and Prevention Systems (IDPSs) To detect unauthorized activity within the inner network or on individual machines, organizations can implement **intrusion detection and prevention systems (IDPSs)**. IDPSs come in two versions, with hybrids possible. **Host-based IDPSs** are usually installed on the machines they protect to monitor the status of various files stored on those machines. The IPDS learns the configuration of the system, assigns priorities to various files depending on their value, and can then alert the administrator of suspicious activity. **Network-based IDPSs** look at patterns of network traffic and attempt to detect unusual activity based on previous baselines. This could include packets coming into the organization's networks with addresses from machines that are within the organization (IP spoofing). It could also include high volumes of traffic going to outside addresses (as in cases of data theft) or coming into the network (as in a denial-of-service attack). The prevention component enables such devices to respond to intrusions by creating a new filtering rule that severs communications or other activity as configured by the administrator. Both host- and network-based IDPSs require a database of previous activity. In the case of host-based IDPSs, the system can create a database of file attributes, as well as a catalog of common attack signatures. Network-based IDPSs can use a similar catalog of common attack signatures and develop databases of "normal" activity for comparison with future activity. IDPSs can be used together for the maximum level of security for a particular network and set of systems. Figure 5-12 shows an example of an intrusion detection and prevention system.

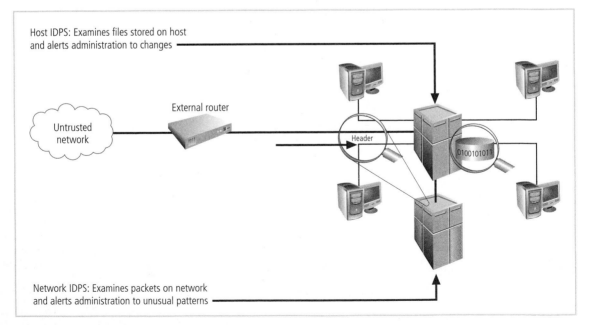

Host IDPS: Examines files stored on host and alerts administration to changes

External router

Untrusted network

Header

0100101011

Network IDPS: Examines packets on network and alerts administration to unusual patterns

Figure 5-12 Intrusion Detection and Prevention Systems

Source: Course Technology/Cengage Learning

Security Education, Training, and Awareness Program

Once your organization has defined the polces that will guide its security program and selected an overall security model by creating or adapting a security framework and a corresponding detailed implementation blueprint, it is time to implement a **security education, training, and awareness (SETA)** program. The SETA program is the responsibility of the CISO and is a control measure designed to reduce the incidences of accidental security breaches by employees. Employee errors are among the top threats to information assets, so it is well worth expending the organization's resources to develop programs to combat this threat. SETA programs are designed to supplement the general education and training programs that many organizations use to educate staff on information security. For example, if an organization detects that many employees are opening questionable e-mail attachments, those employees must be retrained. As a matter of good practice, systems development life cycles must include user training during the implementation phase.

The SETA program consists of three elements: security education, security training, and security awareness. An organization may not be capable of or willing to undertake all three of these elements, and may outsource elements to local educational institutions. The purpose of SETA is to enhance security by doing the following:

- Improving awareness of the need to protect system resources
- Developing skills and knowledge so computer users can perform their jobs more securely
- Building in-depth knowledge, as needed, to design, implement, or operate security programs for organizations and systems[21]

Table 5-10 compares the features of security education, training, and awareness within the organization.

	Education	Training	Awareness
Attribute	Why	How	What
Level	Insight	Knowledge	Information
Objective	Understanding	Skill	Exposure
Teaching	Theoretical instruction	Practical instruction	Media
method	• Discussion seminar	• Lecture	• Videos
	• Background reading	• Case study workshop	• Newsletters
	• Hands-on practice	• Posters	
Test measure	Essay (interpret learning)	Problem solving (apply learning)	• True or false • Multiple choice (identify learning)
Impact timeframe	Long term	Intermediate	Short term

Table 5-10   Comparative Framework of SETA (from NIST SP800-12[22])

Security Education

Everyone in an organization needs to be trained and made aware of information security, but not every member of the organization needs a formal degree or certificate in information security. When management agrees that formal education is appropriate, an employee can investigate available courses from local institutions of higher learning or continuing education. A number of universities have formal coursework in information security. For those interested in researching formal information security programs, there are resources available, such as the NSA-identified Centers of Excellence in Information Assurance Education *www. nsa.gov/ia/academic_outreach/nat_cae/index.shtml*. The Centers of Excellence program identifies outstanding universities with both coursework in information security and an integrated view of information security in the institution itself. Other local resources can also provide security education information, such as Kennesaw State's Center for Information Security Education (*http://infosec.kennesaw.edu*).

Security Training

Security training provides detailed information and hands-on instruction to employees to prepare them to perform their duties securely. Management of information security can develop customized in-house training or outsource the training program.

Alternatives to formal training programs are industry training conferences and programs offered through professional agencies such as SANS (*www.sans.org*), (ISC)^2 (*www.isc2.org*), ISSA (*www.issa.org*), and CSI (*www.gocsi.com*). Many of these programs are too technical for the average employee, but may be ideal for the continuing education requirements of information security professionals.

There are a number of available resources for conducting SETA programs that offer assistance in the form of sample topics and structures for security classes. For organizations, the Computer Security Resource Center at NIST provides several useful documents free of charge in their special publications area (*http://csrc.nist.gov*).

Security Awareness

One of the least frequently implemented, but most beneficial, programs is the security awareness program. A security awareness program is designed to keep information security at the forefront of users' minds. These programs don't have to be complicated or expensive. Good programs can include newsletters, security posters (see Figure 5-13 for an example), videos, bulletin boards, flyers, and trinkets. Trinkets can include security slogans printed on mouse pads, coffee cups, T-shirts, pens, or any object frequently used during the workday that reminds employees of security. In addition, a good security awareness program requires a dedicated individual willing to invest the time and effort into promoting the program, and a champion willing to provide the needed financial support.

The security newsletter is the most cost-effective method of disseminating security information and news to the employee. Newsletters can be distributed via hard copy, e-mail, or intranet. Newsletter topics can include new threats to the organization's information assets, the schedule for upcoming security classes, and the addition of new security personnel. The goal is to keep the idea of information security in users' minds and to stimulate users to care about security. If a security awareness program is not actively implemented, employees may begin to neglect security matters and the risk of employee accidents and failures is likely to increase.

Figure 5-13 Information Security Awareness at Kennesaw State University

Source: Course Technology/Cengage Learning

Continuity Strategies

A key role for all managers is contingency planning. Managers in the IT and information security communities are usually called on to provide strategic planning to assure the continuous availability of information systems.[23] Unfortunately for managers, however, the probability that some form of attack will occur—from inside or outside, intentional or accidental, human or nonhuman, annoying or catastrophic—is very high. Thus, managers from each community of interest must be ready to act when a successful attack occurs.

There are various types of contingency plans for events of this type: incident response plans, disaster recovery plans, and business continuity plans. In some organizations, these might be handled as a single integrated plan. In large, complex organizations, each of these plans may cover separate but related planning functions that differ in scope, applicability, and design. In a small organization, the security administrator (or systems administrator) may have one simple plan that consists of a straightforward set of media backup and recovery strategies and service agreements from the company's service providers. But the sad reality is that many organizations have a level of planning that is woefully deficient.

Incident response, disaster recovery, and business continuity planning are components of contingency planning, as shown in Figure 5-14. A **contingency plan** is prepared by the organization to anticipate, react to, and recover from events that threaten the security of information and information assets in the organization and, subsequently, to restore the organization to normal modes of business operations. The discussion of contingency planning begins with an

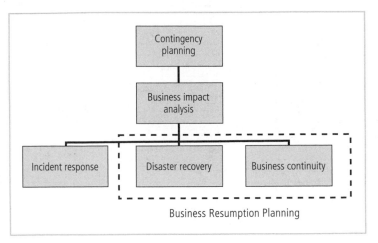

Figure 5-14 Components of Contingency Planning

Source: Course Technology/Cengage Learning

explanation of the differences among its various elements, and an examination of the points at which each element is brought into play.

An **incident** is any clearly identified attack on the organization's information assets that would threaten the assets' confidentiality, integrity, or availability. An **incident response (IR) plan** addresses the identification, classification, response, and recovery from an incident. A **disaster recovery (DR) plan** addresses the preparation for and recovery from a disaster, whether natural or man-made. A **business continuity (BC) plan** ensures that critical business functions continue if a catastrophic incident or disaster occurs. The primary functions of these three types of planning are as follows:

- The IR plan focuses on immediate response, but if the attack escalates or is disastrous (e.g., fire, flood, earthquake, or total blackout) the process moves on to disaster recovery and the BC plan.

- The DR plan typically focuses on restoring systems at the original site after disasters occur, and as such is closely associated with the BC plan.

- The BC plan occurs concurrently with the DR plan when the damage is major or ongoing, requiring more than simple restoration of information and information resources. The BC plan establishes critical business functions at an alternate site.

Some experts argue that the DR and BC plans are so closely linked that they are indistinguishable (they use the term business resumption planning). However, each has a distinct role and planning requirement. The following sections detail the tasks necessary for each of these three types of plans. You can also further distinguish among the three types of planning by examining when each comes into play during the life of an incident. Figure 5-15 shows a sample sequence of events and the overlap between when each plan comes into play. Disaster recovery activities typically continue even after the organization has resumed operations at the original site.

As you learn more about the individual components of contingency planning, you may notice that contingency planning is similar to the risk management process. The contingency plan is a microcosm of risk management activities, and it focuses on the specific steps required to return

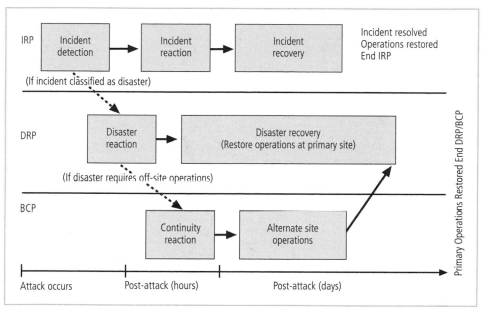

Figure 5-15 Contingency Planning Timeline

Source: Course Technology/Cengage Learning

all information assets to the level at which they were functioning before the incident or disaster. As a result, the planning process closely emulates the process of risk management.

Before any planning can begin, an assigned person or a planning team has to get the process started. In the usual case, a contingency planning management team (CPMT) is assembled for that purpose. A roster for this team may consist of the following members:

- Champion: As with any strategic function, the contingency planning project must have a high-level manager to support, promote, and endorse the findings of the project. This could be the CIO, or ideally the CEO.

- Project manager: A champion provides the strategic vision and the linkage to the power structure of the organization, but someone has to manage the project. A project manager, possibly a midlevel manager or even the CISO, must lead the project and make sure a sound project planning process is used, a complete and useful project plan is developed, and project resources are prudently managed to reach the goals of the project.

- Team members: The team members should be managers or their representatives from the various communities of interest: business, information technology, and information security. Representative business managers, familiar with the operations of their respective functional areas, should supply details on their activities and provide insight into the criticality of their functions to the overall sustainability of the business. Information technology managers on the project team should be familiar with the systems that could be at risk and with the IR, DR, and BC plans that are needed to provide technical content within the planning process. Information security managers must oversee the security planning of the project and provide information on the threats, vulnerabilities, attacks, and recovery requirements needed in the planning process.

The CPMT is responsible for a number of tasks, including the following:

- *Obtaining commitment and support from senior management*
- *Writing the contingency plan document*
- *Conducting the business impact analysis (BIA), which includes:*
  - *Assisting in identifying and prioritizing threats and attacks*
  - *Assisting in identifying and prioritizing business functions*
- *Organizing the subordinate teams, such as:*
  - *Incident response*
  - *Disaster recovery*
  - *Business continuity*
  - *Crisis management*

Obtaining senior management support is self-evident, and requires the assistance of the champion. The [CP] document expands the four elements noted earlier into a seven-step contingency process that an organization may apply to develop and maintain a viable contingency planning program for their IT systems. The CP document serves as the focus and collection point for the deliverables that come from the subsequent steps. These seven progressive steps are designed to be integrated into each stage of the system development life cycle:

1. *Develop the contingency planning policy statement: A formal department or agency policy provides the authority and guidance necessary to develop an effective contingency plan.*
2. *Conduct the BIA: The BIA helps to identify and prioritize critical IT systems and components. A template for developing the BIA is also provided to assist the user.*
3. *Identify preventive controls: Measures taken to reduce the effects of system disruptions can increase system availability and reduce contingency life cycle costs.*
4. *Develop recovery strategies: Thorough recovery strategies ensure that the system may be recovered quickly and effectively following a disruption.*
5. *Develop an IT contingency plan: The contingency plan should contain detailed guidance and procedures for restoring a damaged system.*
6. *Plan testing, training, and exercises: Testing the plan identifies planning gaps, whereas training prepares recovery personnel for plan activation; both activities improve plan effectiveness and overall agency preparedness.*
7. *Plan maintenance: The plan should be a living document that is updated regularly to remain current with system enhancements.*[24]

The remaining major project work modules performed by the contingency planning project team are shown in Figure 5-16. As you read the remainder of this chapter, it may help you to look back at this diagram, since many of the upcoming sections correspond to the steps depicted in the diagram. Note that each subordinate planning task actually begins with the creation (or update) of a corresponding policy document that specifies the purpose and scope of the plan and identifies the roles and responsibilities of those responsible for the plan's creation and implementation.

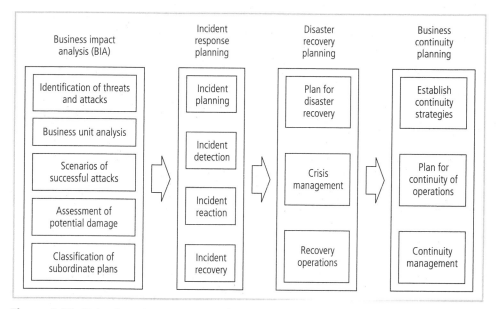

Figure 5-16 Major Steps in Contingency Planning

Source: Course Technology/Cengage Learning

Business Impact Analysis

The first phase in the development of the contingency planning process is the **business impact analysis (BIA)**. A BIA is an investigation and assessment of the impact that various attacks can have on the organization. BIA takes up where the risk assessment process leaves off. It begins with the prioritized list of threats and vulnerabilities identified in the risk management process from Chapter 4 and adds information about the criticality of the systems involved and a detailed assessment of the threats and vulnerabilities to which they are subjects. The BIA is a crucial component of the initial planning stages, as it provides detailed scenarios of the potential impact each attack could have on the organization. The BIA therefore helps to determine what the organization must do to respond to the attack, minimize the damage from the attack, recover from the effects, and return to normal operations. The fundamental distinction between a BIA and the risk management processes discussed in Chapter 4 is that the risk management approach identifies the threats, vulnerabilities, and attacks to determine what controls can protect the information, while the BIA assumes that an attack has succeeded despite these controls, and attempts to answer the question, what do you do now.

The contingency planning team conducts the BIA in the following stages, which are shown in Figure 5-16 and described in the sections that follow:

1. Threat attack identification and prioritization

2. Business unit analysis

3. Attack success scenario development

4. Potential damage assessment

5. Subordinate plan classification

Threat Attack Identification and Prioritization If this section sounds familiar, it's because you learned about identifying and prioritizing the threats facing the organization in the discussion of risk assessment earlier in this book. Organizations that have completed this process need only update the threat list with new developments and add one additional piece of information, the attack profile. An **attack profile** is a detailed description of the activities that occur during an attack. The items in an attack profile, shown in Table 5-11, include preliminary indications of an attack, as well as actions and outcomes. These profiles must be developed for every serious threat the organization faces, natural or man-made, deliberate or accidental. It is as important to know the typical hacker's profile as it is to know what kind of data entry mistakes employees make or the weather conditions that indicate a possible tornado or hurricane. The attack profile is useful in later planning stages to provide indicators of attacks. It is used here to determine the extent of damage that could result to a business unit if a given attack were successful.

Business Unit Analysis The second major task within the BIA is the analysis and prioritization of the business functions within the organization to determine which are most vital to continued operations. Each organizational unit must be evaluated to determine how important its functions are to the organization as a whole. For example, recovery operations would probably focus on the IT department and network operation before addressing the personnel department and hiring activities. Likewise, it is more urgent to reinstate a manufacturing company's assembly line than the maintenance tracking system for that assembly line. This is not to say that personnel functions and assembly line maintenance are not important to the business; but the reality is that if the organization's main revenue-producing operations cannot be restored quickly, there may cease to be a need for other functions.

Attack Success Scenario Development Once the threat attack profiles have been developed and the business functions prioritized, the business impact analysis team must create a series of scenarios depicting the impact of a successful attack from each threat on each

Date of analysis	June 21, 2011
Attack name and description	Mako worm
Threat and probable threat agent	Malicious code via automated attack
Known or possible vulnerabilities	All desktop systems not updated with all latest patches
Likely precursor activities or indicators	Attachments to e-mails
Likely attack activities or indicators of attack in progress	Systems sending e-mails to entries from address book; activity on port 80 without browser being used
Information assets at risk from this attack	All desktop and server systems
Damage or loss to information assets likely from this attack	Business partners and others connected to our networks
Other assets at risk from this attack	None identified at this time
Damage or loss to other assets likely from this attack	Will vary depending on severity; minimum disruption will be needed to repair worm infection

Table 5-11   Attack Profile

prioritized functional area. This can be a long and detailed process, as threats that succeed can affect many functions. Attack profiles should include scenarios depicting a typical attack with details on the method, the indicators, and the broad consequences of the attack. Once the attack profiles are completed, the business function details can be integrated with the attack profiles, after which more details are added to the attack profile, including alternate outcomes. These alternate outcomes should describe best, worst, and most likely outcomes for each type of attack on a particular business functional area. This level of detail allows planners to address each business function in turn.

Potential Damage Assessment Using the attack success scenarios, the BIA planning team must estimate the cost of the best, worst, and most likely cases. At this stage, you are *not* determining how much to spend on the protection of information assets, since this was analyzed during the risk management activities. Instead, you are identifying what must be done to recover from each possible case. These costs include the actions of the response team(s), which are described in subsequent sections, as they act to recover quickly and effectively from an incident or disaster. These cost estimates can also inform management representatives from all the organization's communities of interest of the importance of the planning and recovery efforts. The final result of the assessment is referred to as an **attack scenario end case**.

Subordinate Plan Classification Once the potential damage has been assessed, and each scenario and attack scenario end case has been evaluated, a subordinate plan must be developed or identified from among the plans already in place. These subordinate plans take into account the identification of, reaction to, and recovery from each attack scenario. An attack scenario end case is categorized as disastrous or not disastrous. Most attacks are not disastrous and therefore fall into the category of incident. Those scenarios that do qualify as disastrous are addressed in the disaster recovery plan. The qualifying difference is whether or not an organization is able to take effective action during the attack to combat its effects. Attack end cases that are disastrous find members of the organization waiting out the attack with hopes to recover effectively after it is over. In a typical disaster recovery operation, the lives and welfare of the employees are the most important priority *during* the attack, as most disasters are fires, floods, hurricanes, and tornadoes. Please note that there are attacks that are not natural disasters that fit this category as well, for example:

- Electrical blackouts
- Attacks on service providers that result in a loss of communications to the organization (either telephone or Internet)
- Massive malicious code attacks that sweep through an organization before they can be contained

The bottom line is that each scenario should be classified as a probable incident or disaster, and then the corresponding actions required to respond to the scenario should be built into either the IR or DR plan.

Incident Response Planning

Incident response planning includes the identification of, classification of, and response to an incident. The IR plan is made up of activities that are to be performed when an incident has been identified. Before developing such a plan, you should understand the philosophical approach to incident response planning.

What is an incident? What is incident response? As stated earlier, an incident is an attack against an information asset that poses a clear threat to the confidentiality, integrity, or availability of information resources. If an action that threatens information occurs and is completed, the action is classified as an incident. All of the threats identified in earlier chapters could result in attacks that would be classified as information security incidents. For purposes of this discussion, however, attacks are classified as incidents if they have the following characteristics:

- They are directed against information assets.
- They have a realistic chance of success.
- They could threaten the confidentiality, integrity, or availability of information resources.

Incident response (IR) is therefore the set of activities taken to plan for, detect, and correct the impact of an incident on information assets. Prevention is purposefully omitted, as this activity is more a function of information security in general than of incident response. In other words, IR is more reactive than proactive, with the exception of the planning that must occur to prepare the IR teams to be ready to react to an incident.

IR consists of the following four phases:

1. Planning
2. Detection
3. Reaction
4. Recovery

Before examining each of these phases, consider the following scenario from the not too distant past:

> The Second Armored Cavalry Regiment (2nd ACR) was the oldest cavalry regiment on continuous active duty until it was decommissioned in 1994. The 2nd ACR served as the vanguard of the first Armored Division in the sweep of Iraqi forces during the 1991 Gulf War. Before Desert Shield, the 2nd ACR was, for many years, responsible for the patrol and protection of the West German borders with East Germany and Czechoslovakia. This mission was carried out by placing one troop from each of the three front-line squadrons in various border patrol camps along the borders. Each of these border troops (a company-sized element) conducted constant surveillance of the border, ready to give early warning of potential border violations, political incidents, and even hostile invasions. Within the border camp, the border troop consisted of either a cavalry troop with twelve M3A1 Bradley Fighting Vehicles and nine M1A1 Abrams Main Battle Tanks, or a tank company, with fourteen M1A1s. Occasionally, units from outside the 2nd ACR took a shift on the border, but it was ultimately the 2nd ACR's responsibility to guard this stretch of territory.

> The unit occupying the border camp was required to organize a series of elements capable of deploying in reaction to an incident on the border—be it a border crossing by a political defector or an invasion by a military force. The smallest such element was the "reaction force" made up of eight to ten soldiers manning two battle vehicles (Bradleys or Abrams). It was required to be ready to deploy to an area outside the base within 15 minutes in order to combat a foe or report on an

incident. While routine patrols were conducted in HMMWVs (Hummers), the reaction elements had to deploy in battle vehicles. The next larger element was the "reaction platoon," the remainder of the reaction force's platoon (two additional Abrams, or four additional Bradleys, and eight to twenty additional soldiers) that had to be ready to deploy within 30 minutes. Had the incident warranted it, the entire troop had to be prepared to depart base within one hour. This deployment was rehearsed daily by the reaction force, weekly by the reaction platoon, and at least twice during border camp by the entire troop.

What does this scenario illustrate? An incident is an incident. The employees in an organization responding to a security incident are of course not expected to engage in armed combat against a physical threat. But the preparation and planning required to respond to an information security incident is not entirely different from that required to respond to a military incident; both situations require the same careful attention to detail, the examination of each potential threat scenario, and the development of a number of responses commensurate with the severity of the incident.

Incident Planning Planning for an incident requires a detailed understanding of the scenarios developed for the BIA. With this information in hand, the planning team can develop a series of predefined responses that guide the organization's incident response (IR) team and information security staff. The predefined responses enable the organization to react quickly and effectively to the detected incident. This assumes two things: first, the organization has an IR team, and second, the organization can detect the incident.

The IR team consists of those people who must be present to handle the systems and functional areas that can minimize the impact of an incident as it takes place. Picture a military movie in which U.S. forces have been attacked. If the movie is accurate in its portrayal of IR teams, you saw the military version of an IR team verifying the threat, determining the appropriate response, and coordinating the actions necessary to deal with the situation.

Incident Response Plan The process of planned military team responses can be used to guide incident response planners. The planners should develop a set of documents that direct the actions of each involved individual who reacts to and recovers from the incident. These plans must be properly organized and stored to be available when and where needed, and in a useful format. An example of such a document is presented later in this chapter in the section titled "Model for a Consolidated Contingency Plan."

Format and Content The IR plan must be organized to support quick and easy access to required information. This can be accomplished through a number of measures, the simplest of which is to create a directory of incidents with tabbed sections for each incident. To respond to an incident, the responder simply opens the binder, flips to the appropriate section, and follows the clearly outlined procedures for an assigned role. This means that the planners must develop the detailed procedures necessary to respond to each incident—procedures that must include both the actions to take *during* the incident, as well as the actions to take *after* the incident. In addition, the document should prepare the staff for the incident by providing procedures to perform *before* the incident.

Storage Information in the IR plan is sensitive and should be protected. If attackers gain knowledge of how a company responds to a particular incident, they can improve their chances of success. On the other hand, the organization needs to have this information readily available to those who must respond to the incident. This typically means storing the IR plan within arm's reach of the information assets that must be modified or manipulated during or immediately after the attack. The binder could be stored adjacent to the administrator's workstation, or in a bookcase in the server room. The bottom line is that the individuals responding to the incident should not have to search frantically for the needed information.

Testing   A plan untested is not a useful plan. Or in the military vernacular, "Train as you fight, and fight as you train." Even if an organization has what appears on paper to be an effective IR plan, the procedures may be ineffective unless the plan has been practiced or tested. Testing a plan can be done in many different ways, using one or more testing strategies. Five common testing strategies are presented here.[25]

1. Checklist: Copies of the IR plan are distributed to each individual with a role to play during an actual incident. These individuals each review the plan and create a checklist of correct and incorrect components. Although not a true test, the making of this checklist is an important step in reviewing the document before it is actually needed.

2. Structured walk-through: In a walk-through, each involved individual practices the steps he or she will take during an actual event. This can consist of an "on-the-ground" walk-through, in which everyone discusses his or her actions at each particular location and juncture, or it can be more of a "talk-through," in which all involved individuals sit around a conference table and discuss in turn how they would act as the incident unfolded.

3. Simulation: Here, each involved individual works individually, rather than in conference, simulating the performance of each task required to react to and recover from a simulated incident. The simulation stops short of the actual physical tasks required, such as installing the backup, or disconnecting a communications circuit. The major difference between a walk-through and a simulation is the independence of the individual performers in a simulation, as they work on their own tasks and assume responsibility for identifying the faults in their own procedures.

4. Parallel: In the parallel test, individuals act as if an actual incident occurred, performing their required tasks and executing the necessary procedures. The difference is that the normal operations of the business do not stop. The business continues to function, even though the IR team acts to contain the test incident. Great care must be taken to ensure that the procedures performed do not halt the operations of the business functions and thereby create an actual incident.

5. Full interruption: The final, most comprehensive and realistic test is to react to a mock incident as if it were real. In a full interruption test, the individuals follow each and every procedure, including the interruption of service, restoration of data from backups, and notification of appropriate individuals as discussed in subsequent sections. This is often performed after normal business hours in organizations that cannot afford to disrupt or simulate the disruption of business functions. This is the best practice the team can get, but is unfortunately too risky for most businesses.

At a minimum, organizations should conduct periodic walk-throughs (or talk-throughs) of the IR plan. As quickly as business and information resources change, a failure to update the IR plan can result in an inability to react effectively to an incident, or possibly cause greater damage than the incident itself. If this sounds like a major training effort, note the sayings below from the author Richard Marcinko, a former Navy SEAL—these remarks have been paraphrased (and somewhat sanitized) for your edification.[26]

- The more you sweat in training, the less you bleed in combat.
- Training and preparation hurt.
- Lead from the front, not the rear.
- You don't have to like it, just do it.
- Keep it simple.
- Never assume.
- You are paid for your results, not your methods.

Incident Detection Members of an organization sometimes notify systems administrators, security administrators, or their managers of an unusual occurrence. This is most often a complaint to the help desk from one or more users about a technology service. These complaints are often collected by the help desk and can include reports such as "the system is acting unusual," "programs are slow," "my computer is acting weird," or "data is not available." Incident detection relies on either a human or automated system, which is often the help desk staff, to identify an unusual occurrence and to classify it properly. The mechanisms that could potentially detect an incident include intrusion detection and prevention systems (both host-based and network-based), virus detection software, systems administrators, and even end users. Intrusion detection systems and virus detection software are examined in detail in later chapters. This chapter focuses on the human element.

Note that an incident, as previously defined, is any *clearly identified* attack on the organization's information assets. An ambiguously identified event could be an actual attack, a problem with heavy network traffic, or even a computer malfunction. Only by carefully training the user, the help desk, and all security personnel on the analysis and identification of attacks can the organization hope to identify and classify an incident quickly. Once an attack is properly identified, the organization can effectively execute the corresponding procedures from the IR plan. **Incident classification** is the process of examining a potential incident, or **incident candidate**, and determining whether or not the candidate constitutes an actual incident. Who does this? Anyone with the appropriate level of knowledge can classify an incident. Typically a help desk operator brings the issue forward to a help desk supervisor, the security manager, or a designated incident watch manager. Once a candidate has been classified as an actual incident, the responsible manager must decide whether to implement the incident response plan.

Incident Indicators There are a number of occurrences that signal the presence of an incident candidate. Unfortunately many of them are similar to the actions of an overloaded network, computer, or server, and some are similar to the normal operation of these information assets. Other incident candidates resemble a misbehaving computing system, software package, or other less serious threat. Donald Pipkin, an IT security expert, identifies three categories of incident indicators: possible, probable, and definite.[27]

The following four types of events are possible incident indicators:

1. Presence of unfamiliar files: If users discover files in their home directories or on their office computers, or administrators find files that do not seem to have been placed in a

logical location or that were not created by an authorized user, an incident may have occurred.

2. Presence or execution of unknown programs or processes: If users or administrators detect unfamiliar programs running or processes executing on office machines or network servers, an incident may have occurred.

3. Unusual consumption of computing resources: Many computer operating systems can monitor the consumption of resources. Windows 2000 and XP, as well as many UNIX variants, allow users and administrators to monitor CPU and memory consumption. Most computers can monitor hard drive space. Servers maintain logs of file creation and storage. The sudden consumption of resources, spikes, or drops can be indicators of candidate incidents.

4. Unusual system crashes: Some computer systems crash on a regular basis. Older operating systems running newer programs are notorious for locking up or rebooting whenever the OS is unable to execute a requested process or service. Many people are familiar with these system error messages, such as *Unrecoverable Application Error* and *General Protection Fault*, and many unfortunate users have seen the infamous NT Blue Screen of Death. But if a computer system seems to be crashing, hanging, rebooting, or freezing more than usual, it could be a candidate incident.

The following four types of events are probable indicators of incidents:

1. Activities at unexpected times: If traffic levels on the organization's network exceed the measured baseline values, it is probable that an incident is underway. If this surge in activity occurs when few members of the organization are at work, the probability that it is an incident is much higher. Similarly, if systems are accessing drives, such as floppies and CD-ROMs, when the operator is not using them, an incident may be in progress.

2. Presence of new accounts: Periodic review of user accounts can reveal an account (or accounts) that the administrator does not remember creating, or accounts that are not logged in the administrator's journal. Even one unlogged new account is a candidate incident. An unlogged new account with root or other special privileges has an even higher probability of being an actual incident.

3. Reported attacks: If users of the system report a suspected attack, there is a high probability that an incident is underway or has already occurred. When considering the probability of an attack, you should consider the technical sophistication of the person making the report.

4. Notification from IDPS: If the organization has installed host-based or network-based intrusion detection and prevention systems, and if they are correctly configured, the notification from the IDPS indicates a strong likelihood that an incident is in progress. The problem with most IDPSs is that they are seldom configured optimally, and even when they are, they tend to issue many false positives or false alarms. It is then up to the administrator to determine whether the notification is significant or the result of a routine operation by a user or other administrator.

The following five types of events are definite indicators of incidents. Definite indicators of incidents are those activities which clearly signal that an incident is in progress or has occurred:

1. Use of dormant accounts: Many network servers maintain default accounts that came with the system from the manufacturer. Although industry best practices dictate that

these accounts should be changed or removed, some organizations ignore these practices by making the default accounts inactive. In addition, systems may have any number of accounts that are not actively used, such as those of previous employees, employees on extended vacation or sabbatical, or dummy accounts set up to support system testing. If any of these dormant accounts suddenly becomes active without a change in status of the user, then an incident has almost certainly occurred.

2. Changes to logs: The smart administrator backs up systems logs as well as systems data. As part of a routine incident scan, these logs may be compared to the online version to determine if they have been modified. If they have been modified, and the systems administrator cannot determine explicitly that an authorized individual modified them, an incident has occurred.

3. Presence of hacker tools: The authors of this textbook have had a number of hacker tools installed or stored on their office computers. These are used periodically to scan internal computers and networks to determine what the hacker can see. They are also used to support research into attack profiles. Every time the authors' computers are booted, the antivirus program detects these tools as threats to the systems. If the authors did not positively know that they themselves had installed the tools, their presence would constitute an incident. Many organizations have policies that explicitly prohibit the installation of such tools without the written permission of the CISO. Installing these tools without the proper authorization is a policy violation and should result in disciplinary action. Most organizations that have sponsored and approved penetration-testing operations require that all tools in this category be confined to specific systems that are not used on the general network unless active penetration testing is underway.

4. Notifications by partner or peer: Many organizations have business partners, upstream and downstream value chain associations, and even hierarchical superior or subordinate organizations. If one of these organizations indicates that it is being attacked, and that the attackers are using your computing systems, an incident has occurred or is in progress.

5. Notification by hacker: Some hackers enjoy taunting their victims. If your Web page suddenly begins displaying a "gotcha" from a hacker, it's an incident. If you receive an e-mail from a hacker containing information from your "secured" corporate e-mail, it's an incident. If you receive an extortion request for money in exchange for your customers' credit card files, it's an incident.

There are also several other situations that are definite incident indicators. These include the following:

1. Loss of availability: Information or information systems become unavailable.

2. Loss of integrity: Users report corrupt data files, garbage where data should be, or data that just look wrong.

3. Loss of confidentiality: You are notified of sensitive information leaks, or that information you thought was protected has been disclosed.

4. Violation of policy: Organizational policies addressing information or information security have been violated.

5. Violation of law: The law has been broken, and the organization's information assets are involved.

Incident Reaction Incident reaction consists of actions outlined in the IR plan that guide the organization in attempting to stop the incident, mitigate the impact of the incident, and provide information for recovery from the incident. These actions take place as soon as the incident is over. There are a number of actions that must occur quickly, including notification of key personnel and documentation of the incident. These should be prioritized and documented in the IR plan for quick use in the heat of the moment.

Notification of Key Personnel As soon as the help desk, user, or systems administrator determines that an incident is in progress, he or she must immediately notify the right people in the right order. Most organizations, including the military, maintain an alert roster for just such an emergency. An **alert roster** is a document containing contact information for the people to be notified in the event of an incident; note that it should name only those who must respond to the incident. There are two types of alert rosters: sequential and hierarchical. A **sequential roster** is activated as a contact person calls each person on the roster. A **hierarchical roster** is activated as the first person calls a few other people on the roster, who in turn call a few other people. Each has its advantages and disadvantages. The hierarchical roster is quicker, with more people calling at the same time, but the message may get distorted as it is passed from person to person. The sequential roster is more accurate, as the contact person provides each person with the same message, but it takes longer.

The **alert message** is a scripted description of the incident, usually just enough information so that each individual knows what portion of the IR plan to implement, and not enough to slow down the notification process. The alert roster, as with any document, must be maintained and tested to ensure accuracy. The notification process must be periodically rehearsed to assure it is effective and efficient.

There are other personnel who must also be notified but may not be part of the scripted alert notification process, because they are not needed until preliminary information has been collected and analyzed. Management must be notified, of course, but not so early as to cause undue alarm (if the incident is minor, or a false alarm), and not so late that the media or other external sources learn of the incident before management. Some incidents are disclosed to the employees in general, as a lesson in security, and some are not, as a measure of security. If the incident spreads beyond the target organization's information resources, or if the incident is part of a larger-scale assault, it may be necessary to notify other organizations. An example of a larger-scale assault is Mafiaboy's DDoS attack on multiple Web-based vendors in late 1999. In such cases, it is up to the IR plan development team to determine whom to notify and when to offer guidance about additional notification steps to be taken.

Documenting an Incident As soon as an incident or disaster has been declared, key personnel must be notified and the documentation of the unfolding event begun. There are many reasons for documenting the event. First, documenting the event enables an organization to learn what happened, how it happened, and what actions were taken. The documentation records the who, what, when, where, why, and how of the event. Therefore, it can serve as a case study that the organization can use to determine if the right actions were taken and if these actions were actually effective. Second, documenting the event can prove, should there ever be a question, that the organization did everything possible to prevent the spread of the incident. From a legal standpoint, the standards of due care protect the organization in cases where an incident affects individuals inside and outside the organization or other organizations that use the targeted organization's systems. Lastly, the documentation of an incident can also be used to run a simulation in future training sessions.

Incident Containment Strategies The first priority of incident reaction is to stop the incident or contain its scope or impact. Unfortunately, the most direct means of containment, which is simply "cutting the wire," is often not an option for an organization. Incident containment strategies vary depending on the incident and on the amount of damage it causes or may cause. However, before an incident can be contained, you need to determine which information and information systems have been affected. This is not the time to conduct a detailed analysis of the affected areas; such an analysis is typically performed after the fact in the forensics process. You need, instead, to determine what kind of containment strategy is best and which systems or networks need to be contained. In general, incident containment strategies focus on two tasks: stopping the incident and recovering control of the systems.

The organization can stop the incident and attempt to recover control through a number of strategies:

- If the incident originates outside the organization, the simplest and most straightforward approach is to sever the affected communication circuits. However, if the organization's lifeblood runs through that circuit, it may not be feasible to take so drastic a measure. If the incident does not threaten the most critical functional areas, it may be more feasible to monitor the incident and contain it in another way. One approach used by some organizations is to apply filtering rules dynamically to limit certain types of network access. For example, if a threat agent is attacking a network by exploiting a vulnerability in the Simple Network Management Protocol (SNMP), applying a blocking filter for the commonly used IP ports stops the attack without compromising other network services. Depending on the nature of the attack and the technical capabilities of the organization, ad hoc controls such as these can sometimes be used to gain valuable time to devise a more permanent control strategy.

- If the incident is using compromised accounts, those accounts can be disabled.

- If the incident is bypassing a firewall, the firewall can be reconfigured to block that particular traffic.

- If the incident is using a particular service or process, that process or service can be disabled temporarily.

- If the incident is using the organization's e-mail system to propagate itself, the application or server that supports e-mail can be taken down.

The ultimate containment option, reserved for only the most drastic of scenarios, involves a full stop of all computers and network devices in the organization. Obviously, this step is taken only when all control of the infrastructure has been lost, and the only hope is to preserve the data stored on the computers with the idea that these data can be used in the future to restore operations.

The bottom line is that containment consists of isolating the affected channels, processes, services, or computers, and stopping the losses. Taking down the entire system, servers, and network may accomplish this. The incident response manager, with the guidance of the IR plan, determines the length of the interruption.

Incident Recovery Once the incident has been contained and control of the systems regained, the next stage of the IR plan, which must be immediately executed, is incident recovery. As with reaction to the incident, the first task is to identify the needed human resources and launch them into action. Almost simultaneously, the organization must assess the full extent of the damage in order to determine what must be done to restore the system to a fully functional state. Next, the process of computer forensics determines how the incident occurred and what happened. These facts emerge from a reconstruction of the data recorded before and during the incident. Next the organization repairs vulnerabilities, addresses any shortcomings in safeguards, and restores the data and services of the systems.

Prioritization of Efforts As the dust from the incident settles, a state of confusion and disbelief may follow. The fallout from stressful workplace activity is well-documented and the common view is that cyber attacks, like conflicts of all kinds, affect everyone involved. To recover from the incident, you must keep people focused on the task ahead and make sure that the necessary personnel begin recovery operations as per the IR plan.

Damage Assessment Incident damage assessment is the rapid determination of the scope of the breach of the confidentiality, integrity, and availability of information and information assets during or just following an incident. A damage assessment may take mere moments, or it may take days or weeks, depending on the extent of the damage. The damage caused by an incident can range from minor—a curious hacker snooped around—to extremely severe—a credit card number theft or the infection of hundreds of computer systems by a worm or virus.

Several sources of information can be used to determine the type, scope, and extent of damage, including system logs, intrusion detection logs, configuration logs and documents, the documentation from the incident response, and the results of a detailed assessment of systems and data storage. Using these logs and documentation as a basis for comparison, the IR team can evaluate the current state of the information and systems. Related to the task of incident damage assessment is the field of computer forensics. **Computer forensics** is the process of collecting, analyzing, and preserving computer-related evidence. **Evidence** is a physical object or documented information that proves an action occurred or identifies the intent of a perpetrator. Computer evidence must be carefully collected, documented, and maintained to be useable in formal or informal proceedings. Organizations may have informal proceedings when dealing with internal violations of policy or standards of conduct. They may also need to use evidence in formal administrative or legal proceedings. Sometimes the fallout from an incident lands in a courtroom for a civil trial. Each of these circumstances requires that individuals who examine the damage incurred receive special training, so that if an incident becomes part of a crime or results in a civil action, the individuals are adequately prepared to participate.

Recovery Once the extent of the damage has been determined, the recovery process can begin in earnest. Full recovery from an incident requires that you perform the following:

1. Identify the vulnerabilities that allowed the incident to occur and spread. Resolve them.

2. Address the safeguards that failed to stop or limit the incident, or were missing from the system in the first place. Install, replace, or upgrade them.

3. Evaluate monitoring capabilities (if present). Improve their detection and reporting methods, or simply install new monitoring capabilities.

4. Restore the data from backups. See the Technical Details boxes on the following topics for more information: (1) data storage and management, (2) system backups and recovery, and (3) redundant array of independent disks (RAID). Restoration requires the IR team to understand the backup strategy used by the organization, restore the data contained in backups, and then recreate the data that were created or modified since the last backup.

5. Restore the services and processes in use. Compromised services and processes must be examined, cleaned, and then restored. If services or processes were interrupted during the process of regaining control of the systems, they need to be brought back online.

6. Continuously monitor the system. If an incident happened once, it can easily happen again. Just because the incident is over doesn't mean the organization is in the clear. Hackers frequently boast of their abilities in chat rooms and dare their peers to match their efforts. If word gets out, others may be tempted to try their hands at the same or different attacks. It is therefore important to maintain vigilance during the entire IR process.

7. Restore the confidence of the organization's communities of interest. It may be advisable to issue a short memorandum that outlines the incident and assures everyone that it was handled and the damage controlled. If the incident was minor, say so. If the incident was major or severely damaged the systems or data, reassure the users that they can expect operations to return to normal shortly. The objective is not to placate or lie, but to prevent panic or confusion from causing additional disruptions to the operations of the organization.

Before returning to routine duties, the IR team must conduct an **after-action review** or AAR. The after-action review is a detailed examination of the events that occurred from first detection to final recovery. All key players review their notes and verify that the IR documentation is accurate and precise. All team members review their actions during the incident and identify areas in which the IR plan worked, didn't work, or should be improved. This allows the team to update the IR plan while the needed changes are fresh in their minds. The AAR is documented and can serve as a training case for future staff. It also brings to a close the actions of the IR team.

Backup Media   The brief overview of backup media and strategies in the Technical Details sections of this chapter provides additional insight into the backup management process. Most common types of backup media include digital audio tapes (DAT), quarter-inch cartridge drives (QIC), 8mm tape, and digital linear tape (DLT). Each type of tape has its restrictions and advantages. Backups can also be performed to CD-ROM and DVD options (CD-R, CD-RW, and DVD-RW), specialized drives (Zip, Jaz, and Bernouli), or tape arrays.

Automated Response
New technologies are emerging in the field of incident response, some of which build on existing technologies and extend their capabilities and functions. Although traditional systems were configured to detect incidents and then notify a human administrator, new systems can respond to the incident threat autonomously, based on preconfigured options. A more complete discussion of these technologies is presented in Chapter 7.

The downsides of current automated response systems may outweigh their benefits. Legal issues with tracking individuals via the systems of others have yet to be resolved. What if

Technical Details
Data Storage and Management

To better understand what goes on during incident response or disaster recovery data restoration, you should understand how system backups are created.

Data backup is a complex operation and involves selecting the backup type, establishing backup schedules, and even duplicating data automatically using a variety of redundant array of independent drives (RAID) structures (described in the Technical Details box on RAID).

There are three basic types of backups: full, differential, and incremental. A **full backup** is just that, a full and complete backup of the entire system, including all applications, operating systems components, and data. The advantage of a full backup is that it takes a comprehensive snapshot of the organization's system. The primary disadvantages are that it requires a lot of media to store such a large file, and the backup can be time consuming. A **differential backup** is the storage of all files that have changed or been added since the last full backup. The differential backup works faster and uses less storage space than the full backup, but each daily differential backup is larger and slower than that of the day before. For example, if you conduct a full backup on Sunday, then Monday's backup contains all the files that have changed since Sunday, and Tuesday's backup also contains all the files that have changed since Sunday. By Friday, the file size will have grown substantially. Also, if one backup is corrupt, the previous day's backup contains almost all of the same information. The third type of backup is the incremental backup. The **incremental backup** only archives the files that have been modified that day, and thus requires less space and time than the differential. The downside to incremental backups is that if an incident occurs, multiple backups would be needed to restore the full system.

The first component of a backup and recovery system is the scheduling of the backups, coupled with the storage of these backups. The most common schedule is a daily onsite incremental or differential backup, with a weekly offsite full backup. Most backups are conducted during twilight hours, when systems activity is lowest and the probability of user interruption is limited. There are also some other popular methods for selecting the files to back up. These include grandfather/father/son and Towers of Hanoi (see the Technical Details box on general backup and recovery strategies).

Regardless of the strategy employed, some fundamental principles remain the same. All onsite and offsite storage must be secured. It is common practice to use fireproof safes or filing cabinets to store tapes. The offsite storage in particular must be in a safe location, such as a safety deposit box in a bank or a professional backup and recovery service. The trunk of the administrator's car is not secure offsite storage. It is also important to provide a conditioned environment for the tapes, preferably an airtight, humidity-free, static-free storage container. Each tape must be clearly labeled and write-protected. Because tapes frequently wear out, it is important to retire them periodically and introduce new media.

Technical Details
System Backups and Recovery—General Strategies

Two of the more popular methods for selecting the files to back up are outlined below.

Grandfather, father, son: Assuming that backups are taken every night, with five tapes used every week, this method is based on a fifteen-tape strategy.

The first week uses the first five tapes (set A).

The second week uses the second five tapes (set B).

The third week uses a third set of five tapes (set C).

The fourth week, the set A tapes are reused.

The fifth week, the set B tapes are reused.

The sixth week, the set C tapes are reused.

Every second or third month, a set of tapes is taken out of the cycle for permanent storage and a new set is brought in. This method equalizes the wear and tear on the tapes and helps to prevent tape failure.

Towers of Hanoi: The Towers of Hanoi is more complex and is actually based on mathematical principles. With this method, different tapes are used with different frequencies. This strategy assumes a five-tape-per-week strategy, with a backup each night.

The first night, tape A is used.

The second night, tape B is used.

The third night, tape A is reused.

The fourth night, tape C is used.

The fifth night, tape A is reused.

The sixth night, tape B is reused.

The seventh night, tape A is reused.

The eighth night, tape D is used.

The ninth night, tape A is reused.

The tenth night, tape B is reused.

The eleventh night, tape A is reused.

The twelfth night, tape C is reused.

The thirteenth night, tape A is reused.

The fourteenth night, tape B is reused.

The fifteenth night, tape A is reused.

The sixteenth night, tape E is used.

Tape A is used for incremental backups after its first use and must be monitored closely as it tends to wear out faster than the other tapes.

Technical Details
System Backups and Recovery—RAID

One form of data backup for online usage is the **redundant array of independent drives (RAID)** system. Unlike tape backups, RAID uses a number of hard drives to store information across multiple drive units. This spreads out data and minimizes the impact of a single drive failure. There are nine established RAID configurations:

RAID Level 0. RAID 0 is not actually a form of redundant storage—it creates one larger logical volume across several available hard disk drives and stores the data in segments, called stripes, across all the disk drives in the array. This is also often called **disk striping** without parity, and is frequently used to combine smaller drive volumes into fewer, larger volumes. Unfortunately, failure of one drive may make all data inaccessible.

RAID Level 1. Commonly called **disk mirroring**, RAID Level 1 uses twin drives in a computer system. The computer records all data to both drives simultaneously, providing a backup if the primary drive fails. It's a rather expensive and inefficient use of media. A variation of mirroring is called **disk duplexing**. With mirroring, the same drive controller manages both drives, but with disk duplexing each drive has its own controller. Mirroring is often used to create duplicate copies of operating system volumes for high-availability systems.

RAID Level 2. This is a specialized form of disk striping with parity, and is not widely used. It uses a specialized parity coding mechanism, known as the Hamming Code, to store stripes of data on multiple data drives and corresponding redundant error correction on separate error correcting drives. This approach allows the reconstruction of data in the event some of the data or redundant parity information is lost. There are no commercial implementations of RAID Level 2.

RAID Levels 3 and 4. RAID 3 is byte-level and RAID 4 is block-level striping of data in which the data are stored in segments on dedicated data drives, and parity information is stored on a separate drive. As with RAID 0, one large volume is used for the data, but the parity drive operates independently to provide error recovery.

RAID Level 5. This form of RAID is most commonly used in organizations that balance safety and redundancy against the costs of acquiring and operating the systems. It is similar to RAID 3 and 4 in that it stripes the data across multiple drives, but there is no dedicated parity drive. Instead, segments of data are interleaved with parity data and are written across all of the drives in the set. RAID 5 drives can also be **hot swapped**, meaning they can be replaced without taking the entire system down.

RAID Level 6. This is a combination of RAID 1 and RAID 5.

(continued)

RAID Level 7. This is a variation on RAID 5 in which the array works as a single virtual drive. RAID Level 7 is sometimes performed by running special software over RAID 5 hardware.

RAID Level 10. This is a combination of RAID 1 and RAID 0.

Additional redundancy can be provided by mirroring entire servers called redundant servers or **server fault tolerance** (SFTIII in Novell).

the hacker that is backtracked is actually a compromised system running an automated attack? What are the legal liabilities of a counterattack? How can security administrators condemn a hacker when they themselves may have illegally hacked systems to track the hacker? These issues are complex but must be resolved to give the security professionals better tools to combat incidents.

Disaster Recovery Planning

An event can be categorized as a disaster when (1) the organization is unable to mitigate the impact of an incident during the incident, and (2) the level of damage or destruction is so severe that the organization is unable to recover quickly. The difference between an incident and a disaster may be subtle; the contingency planning team must make the distinction between disasters and incidents, and it may not be possible to make this distinction until an attack occurs. Often an event that is initially classified as an incident is later determined to be a disaster. When this happens, the organization must change how it is responding and take action to secure its most valuable assets to preserve value for the longer term even at the risk of more disruption in the short term.

Disaster recovery (DR) planning is the process of preparing an organization to handle and recover from a disaster, whether natural or man-made. The key emphasis of a DR plan is to reestablish operations at the primary site, the location at which the organization performs its business. The goal is to make things whole, or as they were before the disaster.

The Disaster Recovery Plan Similar in structure to the IR plan, the DR plan provides detailed guidance in the event of a disaster. It is organized by the type or nature of the disaster, and specifies recovery procedures during and after each type of disaster. It also provides details on the roles and responsibilities of the people involved in the disaster recovery effort, and identifies the personnel and agencies that must be notified. Just as the IR plan must be tested, so must the DR plan, using the same testing mechanisms. At a minimum, the DR plan must be reviewed during a walk-through or talk-through on a periodic basis.

Many of the same precepts of incident response apply to disaster recovery:

1. Priorities must be clearly established. The first priority is always the preservation of human life. The protection of data and systems immediately falls to the wayside if the disaster threatens the lives, health, or welfare of the employees of the organization or

members of the community in which the organization operates. Only after all employees and neighbors have been safeguarded can the disaster recovery team attend to nonhuman asset protection.

2. Roles and responsibilities must be clearly delineated. Everyone assigned to the DR team should be aware of his or her expected actions during a disaster. Some people are responsible for coordinating with local authorities, such as fire, police, and medical staff. Others are responsible for the evacuation of personnel, if required. Still others are tasked simply to pack up and leave.

3. Someone must initiate the alert roster and notify key personnel. Those to be notified may be the fire, police, or medical authorities mentioned earlier. They may also include insurance agencies, disaster teams like the Red Cross, and management teams.

4. Someone must be tasked with the documentation of the disaster. Just as in an IR reaction, someone must begin recording what happened to serve as a basis for later determination of why and how the event occurred.

5. If and only if it is possible, attempts must be made to mitigate the impact of the disaster on the operations of the organization. If everyone is safe, and all needed authorities have been notified, some individuals can be tasked with the evacuation of physical assets. Some can be responsible for making sure all systems are securely shut down to prevent further loss of data.

Recovery Operations Reactions to a disaster can vary so widely that it is impossible to describe the process with any accuracy. It is up to each organization to examine the scenarios developed at the start of contingency planning and determine how to respond.

Should the physical facilities be spared after the disaster, the disaster recovery team should begin the restoration of systems and data to reestablish full operational capability. If the organization's facilities do not survive, alternative actions must be taken until new facilities can be acquired. When a disaster threatens the viability of the organization at the primary site, the disaster recovery process transitions into the process of business continuity planning.

Business Continuity Planning

Business continuity planning prepares an organization to reestablish critical business operations during a disaster that affects operations at the primary site. If a disaster has rendered the current location unusable, there must be a plan to allow the business to continue to function. Not every business needs such a plan or such facilities. Small companies or fiscally sound organizations may have the latitude to cease operations until the physical facilities can be restored. Manufacturing and retail organizations may not have this option, because they depend on physical commerce and may not be able to relocate operations.

Developing Continuity Programs Once the incident response and disaster recovery plans are in place, the organization needs to consider finding temporary facilities to support the continued viability of the business in the event of a disaster. The development of the BC plan is somewhat simpler than that of the IR plan or DR plan, in that it consists primarily of selecting a continuity strategy and integrating the offsite data storage and recovery functions into this strategy. Some of the components of the BC plan could already be integral to the normal operations of the organization, such as an offsite backup service. Others require special consideration and negotiation. The first part of business continuity planning is performed when the joint DR/BC plan is developed. The identification of critical business functions and the resources needed to support them is the cornerstone of BC plan. When a disaster strikes, these functions are the first to be reestablished at the alternate site. The contingency planning team needs to appoint a group of individuals to evaluate and compare the various alternatives available and recommend which strategy should be selected and implemented. The strategy selected usually involves some form of offsite facility, which should be inspected, configured, secured, and tested on a periodic basis. The selection should be reviewed periodically to determine if a superior alternative has emerged or if the organization needs a different solution.

Continuity Strategies There are a number of strategies from which an organization can choose when planning for business continuity. The determining factor when selecting from among these options is usually cost. In general, there are three exclusive options: hot sites, warm sites, and cold sites; and three shared functions: time-share, service bureaus, and mutual agreements.

Hot Sites A hot site is a fully configured computer facility, with all services, communications links, and physical plant operations including heating and air conditioning. Hot sites duplicate computing resources, peripherals, phone systems, applications, and workstations. A hot site is the pinnacle of contingency planning, a duplicate facility that needs only the latest data backups and personnel to become a fully operational twin of the original. A hot site can be operational in a matter of minutes, and in some cases may be built to provide a process that is seamless to system users (sometimes called a seamless fail-over) by picking up the processing load from a failing site. The hot site is therefore the most expensive alternative available. Other disadvantages include the need to provide maintenance for all the systems and equipment in the hot site, as well as physical and information security. However, if the organization needs a 24/7 capability for near real-time recovery, a hot site is the way to go.

Warm Sites The next step down from the hot site is the warm site. A **warm site** provides many of the same services and options of the hot site. However, it typically does not include the actual applications the company needs, or the applications may not yet be installed and configured. A warm site frequently includes computing equipment and peripherals with servers but not client workstations. A warm site has many of the advantages of a hot site, but at a lower cost. The downside is that it requires hours, if not days, to make a warm site fully functional.

Cold Sites The final dedicated site option is the cold site. A **cold site** provides only rudimentary services and facilities. No computer hardware or peripherals are provided. All communications services must be installed after the site is occupied. Basically a cold site is an empty room with heating, air conditioning, and electricity. Everything else is an option. Although the obvious disadvantages may preclude its selection, a cold site is better than nothing. The main advantage of cold sites over hot and warm sites is the cost. Furthermore, if the warm or hot site is based on a shared capability, not having to contend with organizations sharing space and equipment should a widespread disaster occur may make the cold site a more controllable option, albeit slower. In spite of these advantages, some organizations feel it would be easier to lease a new space on short notice than pay maintenance fees on a cold site.

Time-shares A **time-share** is a hot, warm, or cold site that is leased in conjunction with a business partner or sister organization. The time-share allows the organization to maintain a disaster recovery and business continuity option, but at a reduced overall cost. The advantages are identical to the type of site selected (hot, warm, or cold). The primary disadvantage is the possibility that more than one organization involved in the time-share may need the facility simultaneously. Other disadvantages include the need to stock the facility with the equipment and data from all organizations involved, the negotiations for arranging the time-share, and associated agreements should one or more parties decide to cancel the agreement or to sublease its options. This option is much like agreeing to co-lease an apartment with a group of friends. One can only hope the organizations remain on amiable terms, as they would all have physical access to each other's data.

Service Bureaus A **service bureau** is an agency that provides a service for a fee. In the case of disaster recovery and continuity planning, the service is the agreement to provide physical facilities in the event of a disaster. These types of agencies also frequently provide offsite data storage for a fee. With service bureaus, contracts can be carefully created, specifying exactly what the organization needs, without the need to reserve dedicated facilities. A service agreement usually guarantees space when needed, even if the service bureau has to acquire additional space in the event of a widespread disaster. This option is much like the rental car clause in your car insurance policy. The disadvantage is that it is a service and must be renegotiated periodically. Also, using a service bureau can be quite expensive.

Mutual Agreements A **mutual agreement** is a contract between two or more organizations that specifies how each will assist the other in the event of a disaster. It stipulates that each organization is obligated to provide the necessary facilities, resources, and services until the receiving organization is able to recover from the disaster. This type of arrangement is much like moving in with relatives or even friends: it doesn't take long to outstay your welcome. While this may seem like a viable solution, many organizations balk at the idea of having to fund (even in the short term) duplicate services and resources should the other agreeing parties need them. The arrangement is ideal if you need the assistance, but not if you are the host. Still, mutual agreements between divisions of the same parent company, between subordinate and superior organizations, or between business partners may be a cost-effective solution.

Other Options There are some specialized alternatives available, such as a rolling mobile site configured in the payload area of a tractor or trailer, or externally stored resources. These can consist of a rental storage area containing duplicate or second-generation equipment to be extracted in the event of an emergency. An organization can also contract with a prefabricated building contractor for immediate, temporary facilities (mobile offices) to be placed onsite in the event of a disaster. These alternatives should be considered when evaluating strategy options.

Offsite Disaster Data Storage To get these types of sites up and running quickly, the organization must be able to move data into the new site's systems. There are a number of options for getting operations up and running quickly, and some of these options can be used for purposes other than restoration of continuity. The options include electronic vaulting, remote journaling, and database shadowing, methods that are, of course, in addition to the traditional backup methods mentioned earlier.

- Electronic vaulting: The transfer of large batches of data to an offsite facility is called **electronic vaulting**. This transfer is usually conducted through leased lines, or services provided for a fee. The receiving server archives the data until the next electronic vaulting process is received. Some disaster recovery companies specialize in electronic vaulting services.

- Remote journaling: The transfer of live transactions to an offsite facility is called **remote journaling**. It differs from electronic vaulting in that (1) only transactions are transferred, not archived data, and (2) the transfer is in real time. Electronic vaulting is much like a traditional backup, with a dump of data to the offsite storage, but remote journaling involves activities on a systems level, much like server fault tolerance, with the data written to two locations simultaneously.

- Database shadowing: An improvement to the process of remote journaling, **database shadowing** not only processes duplicate, real-time data storage, but also duplicates the databases at the remote site to multiple servers. It combines the server fault tolerance mentioned earlier with remote journaling, writing three or more copies of the database simultaneously.

Crisis Management

Disasters are, of course, larger in scale and less manageable than incidents, but the planning processes are the same and in many cases are conducted simultaneously. What may truly distinguish an incident from a disaster are the actions of the response teams. An incident response team typically rushes to duty stations or to the office from home. The first act is to reach for the IR plan. A disaster recovery team may not have the luxury of flipping through a binder to see what must be done. Disaster recovery personnel must know their roles without any supporting documentation. This is a function of preparation, training, and rehearsal. You probably all remember the frequent fire, tornado, or hurricane drills—and even the occasional nuclear blast drills—from your public school days. Just because you move from school to the business world doesn't lessen the threat of a fire or other disaster.

The actions taken during and after a disaster are referred to as **crisis management**. Crisis management differs dramatically from incident response, as it focuses first and foremost on the people involved. The disaster recovery team works closely with the crisis management team. According to Gartner Research, the crisis management team is:

> *"responsible for managing the event from an enterprise perspective and covers the following major activities:*
>
> - *Supporting personnel and their loved ones during the crisis*
> - *Determining the event's impact on normal business operations and, if necessary, making a disaster declaration*
> - *Keeping the public informed about the event and the actions being taken to ensure the recovery of personnel and the enterprise*
> - *Communicating with major customers, suppliers, partners, regulatory agencies, industry organizations, the media, and other interested parties."*[28]

The crisis management team should establish a base of operations or command center to support communications until the disaster has ended. The crisis management team includes individuals from all functional areas of the organization to facilitate communications and cooperation. Some key areas of crisis management include the following:

- Verifying personnel head count: Everyone must be accounted for, including those on vacations, leaves of absence, and business trips.
- Checking the alert roster: Alert rosters and general personnel phone lists are used to notify individuals whose assistance may be needed, or simply to tell employees not to report to work until the crisis or event is over.
- Checking emergency information cards: It is important that each employee has two types of emergency information cards. The first is personal emergency information that lists whom to notify in case of an emergency (next of kin), medical conditions, and a form of identification. The second is a set of instructions on what to do in the event of an emergency. This mini-snapshot of the disaster recovery plan should contain, at a minimum, a contact number or hot line, emergency services numbers (fire, police, medical), evacuation and assembly locations (storm shelters, for example), the name and number of the disaster recovery coordinator, and any other needed information.

Crisis management must balance the needs of the employees with the needs of the business in providing personnel with support for personal and family issues during disasters.

Model for a Consolidated Contingency Plan

To help you understand the structure and use of the incident response and disaster recovery plans, this section presents a comprehensive model that incorporates the basics of each type of planning in a single document. It is not uncommon for small- to medium-sized organizations to use such a document. The single document supports concise planning and encourages smaller organizations to develop, test, and use IR and DR plans. The model presented is based on analyses of disaster recovery and incident response plans of dozens of organizations.

The Planning Document The first document created for the IR and DR document set is the incident reaction document. The key players in an organization, typically the top computing executive, systems administrators, security administrator, and a few functional area managers, get together to develop the IR and DR plan. The first task is to establish the responsibility for managing the document, which typically falls to the security administrator. A secretary is appointed to document the activities and results of the planning session. First, independent incident response and disaster recovery teams are formed. For this model, the two groups include the same individuals as the planning committee, plus additional systems administrators. Next, the roles and responsibilities are outlined for each team member. At this point, general responsibilities are being addressed, not procedural activities. The alert roster is developed as are lists of critical agencies.

Next, the group identifies and prioritizes threats to the organization's information and information systems. Because of the integrated nature of the IR, DR, and BC plans, the overall contingency planning process addresses areas within each. These are the six steps in the consolidated contingency planning process:[29]

1. Identifying the mission- or business-critical functions: The organization identifies those areas of operation that must continue in a disaster to enable the organization to operate.

These must be prioritized from most critical to least critical to allow optimal allocation of resources (time, money, and personnel) in the event of a disaster.

2. Identifying the resources that support the critical functions: For each critical function, the organization identifies the required resources. These resources can include people, computing capability, applications, data, services, physical infrastructure, and documentation.

3. Anticipating potential contingencies or disasters: The organization brainstorms potential disasters and determines what functions they would affect.

4. Selecting contingency planning strategies: The organization identifies methods of dealing with each anticipated scenario and outlines a plan to prepare for and react to the disaster.

   - Armed with this information, the actual consolidated plan begins to take shape. For each incident scenario, three sets of procedures are created and documented:

   - The procedures that must be performed *during the incident*. These procedures are grouped and assigned to individuals. The planning committee begins to draft a set of these function-specific procedures.

   - The procedures that must be performed immediately *after the incident has ceased*. Again, separate functional areas may be assigned different procedures.

   - The procedures that must be performed to *prepare for the incident*. These are the details of the data backup schedules, the disaster recovery preparation, training schedules, testing plans, copies of service agreements, and business continuity plans.

   At this level, the business continuity plan can consist simply of additional material about a service bureau that can store offsite data via electronic vaulting with an agreement to provide office space and lease equipment as needed.

   Finally, the IR portion of the plan is assembled. Sections detailing the organization's DR planning and BC planning efforts are placed after the incident response sections. Critical information as outlined in these planning sections is recorded, including information on alternate sites. Figure 5-17 shows some specific formats for the contingency plan. Multiple copies for each functional area are created, catalogued, and signed out to responsible individuals.

5. Implementing the contingency strategies: The organization signs contracts, acquires services, and implements backup programs that integrate the new strategy into the organization's routine operations.

6. Testing and revising the strategy: The organization periodically tests and revises the plan.

These are the words that all contingency planners live by: *plan for the worst and hope for the best.*

Law Enforcement Involvement

There may come a time when an incident, whether an attack or a breach of policy, constitutes a violation of law. Perhaps what was originally believed to be an accident turns out to be an attempt at corporate espionage, sabotage, or theft. When an organization considers involving law enforcement, there are several questions that must be answered. When should the organization get law enforcement involved? What level of law enforcement agency should be involved—local, state, or federal? What happens when a law enforcement agency is

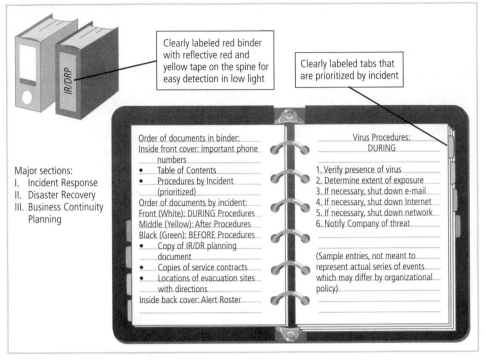

Major sections:
I. Incident Response
II. Disaster Recovery
III. Business Continuity
    Planning

Figure 5-17 Contingency Plan Format

Source: Course Technology/Cengage Learning

involved? Some of these questions are best answered by the organization's legal department. Organizations should be prepared to address these questions in the absence of their legal department. When these incidents occur, they are often underway at times and under circumstances that do not allow for leisurely decision making.

Federal Authorities Selecting which level of law enforcement to involve depends in part on the type of crime suspected. The Federal Bureau of Investigation (FBI) deals with many computer crimes that are categorized as felonies. There are other federal agencies available to deal with various criminal activity, including the U.S. Secret Service for crimes involving U.S. currency, counterfeiting, credit cards, and identity theft. The U.S. Treasury Department has a bank fraud investigation unit, and the Securities and Exchange Commission has investigation and fraud control units as well. However, because of the heavy caseload these agencies handle, they typically give priority to incidents that affect the national critical infrastructure or that have significant economic impact. The FBI Web site states that the FBI Computer Intrusion Squad pursues "the investigation of cyber-based attacks, primarily unauthorized access (intrusion) and denial-of-service, directed at the major components of this country's critical information, military, and economic infrastructures. Critical infrastructure includes the nation's power grids and power-supply systems, transportation control systems, money transfer and accounting systems, defense-related systems, and telecommunications networks. Additionally, the Squad investigates cyber attacks directed at private industry and public institutions that maintain information vital to national security and/or the economic success of the nation."[30] In other words, if the crime is not directed at or does not affect the national infrastructure, the FBI may not be able to assist as effectively as state or local agencies. However, as a rule of thumb, if the crime crosses state lines, it's a federal matter. The FBI may also become involved at the request of a state agency, if it has available personnel.

State Investigative Services Many states have their own version of the FBI. In Georgia, it's called the Georgia Bureau of Investigation (GBI), and in other states it may be a division of the state police. (FYI: in Texas, it is the legendary Texas Rangers.) The GBI arrests individuals, serves warrants, and enforces laws that regulate property owned by the state or any state agency. The GBI also assists local law enforcement officials in pursuing criminals and enforcing state laws. Some organizations may reside in states whose investigative offices do not have a special agency dedicated to computer crime. If, in these cases, there is a state law pertinent to computer crimes, the appropriate authority handles those cases. In those states where one agency is responsible, that agency also assists local law enforcement, and sometimes businesses or nonprofit agencies, by request.

Local Law Enforcement Each county and city has its own law enforcement agency. These agencies enforce all local and state laws and handle suspects and secure crime scenes for state and federal cases. Local law enforcement agencies seldom have a computer crimes task force, but the investigative (detective) units are quite capable of processing crime scenes, and handling most common criminal activities, such as physical theft or trespassing, damage to property, and the apprehension and processing of suspects of computer-related crimes.

Benefits and Drawbacks of Law Enforcement Involvement Involving law enforcement agencies has both advantages and disadvantages. The agencies may be much better able to process evidence than a particular organization. In fact, unless the security forces in the organization have been trained in processing evidence and computer forensics, they may do more harm than good when extracting the necessary information to legally convict a suspected criminal. Law enforcement agencies can also issue the warrants and subpoenas necessary to document a case. They are also adept at obtaining statements from witnesses, affidavits, and other required documents. Law enforcement personnel can be a security administrator's greatest ally in the war on computer crime. Therefore, it is important to get to know the local and state officials charged with enforcing information security laws, before you have to make a call announcing a suspected crime. Most state and federal agencies even offer awareness programs, including guest speakers at conferences, and programs like the InfraGard program of the FBI's National Information Protection Center (*www.infragard.net*). These agents appreciate the challenges facing security administrators, who often have a law enforcement background.

However, once a law enforcement agency takes over a case, the organization cannot entirely control the chain of events, the collection of information and evidence, and the prosecution of suspects. Someone the organization believes to deserve censure and dismissal may instead face criminal charges, and all the attendant publicity. The organization may not be informed about the progress of the case for weeks or even months. Equipment vital to the organization's business may be tagged as evidence, to be removed, stored, and preserved until it is no longer needed for the criminal case, or in fact may never be returned.

However, if an organization detects a criminal act, it is legally obligated to involve the appropriate law enforcement officials. Failure to do so can subject the organization and its officers to prosecution as accessories to the crimes, or as impeding the course of an investigation.

It is up to the security administrator to ask questions of their law enforcement counterparts to determine when each agency wishes to be involved, and specifically which crimes are to be addressed by each agency.

Selected Readings

There are many excellent sources of additional information in the area of information security. A few that are worthy of your attention that can add to your understanding of this chapter's content are listed as follows:

- *Information Security Policies Made Easy*, Version 10, by Charles Cresson Wood. 2005. Information Shield.
- *Management of Information Security*, by Michael E. Whitman and Herbert J. Mattord. 2007. Course Technology.
- *Principles of Incident Response and Disaster Recovery*, by Michael E. Whitman and Herbert J. Mattord. 2006. Course Technology.

Chapter Summary

- Information security governance is the application of the principles of corporate governance—that is, executive management's responsibility to provide strategic direction, ensure the accomplishment of objectives, oversee that risks are appropriately managed, and validate responsible resource utilization—to the information security function.

- The enterprise information security policy (EISP) should be a driving force in the planning and governance activities of the organization as a whole.

- There are a number of published information security frameworks, including ones from government organizations as well as private organizations and professional societies, that supply information on best practices for their members.

- One of the foundations of security architectures is the layered implementation of security. This layered approach is referred to as defense in depth.

- Management must use policies as the basis for all information security planning, design, and deployment. Policies direct how issues should be addressed and technologies used.

- Standards are more detailed than policies and describe the steps that must be taken to conform to policies.

- Management must define three types of security policies: general or security program policies, issue-specific security policies, and systems-specific security policies.

- Information security policy is best disseminated in a comprehensive security education, training, and awareness (SETA) program. One of the least frequently implemented but most beneficial programs is the security awareness program. A security awareness program is designed to keep information security at the forefront of the users' minds.

- Contingency planning (CP) comprises a set of plans designed to ensure the effective reaction to and recovery from an attack and the subsequent restoration to normal modes of business operations.

- Organizations must develop disaster recovery plans, incident response plans, and business continuity plans using the business impact analysis process, which consists of five stages: identification and prioritization of the threat attack, business unit analysis and prioritization, attack success scenario development, potential damage assessment, and subordinate plan classification.

- Incident response planning consists of four phases: incident planning, incident detection, incident reaction, and incident recovery.

- Disaster recovery planning outlines the response to and recovery from a disaster, whether natural or man-made.

- Business continuity planning includes the steps organizations take so that they can function when business cannot be resumed at the primary site.

- Crisis management refers to the actions an organization takes during and immediately after a disaster and focuses first and foremost on the people involved.

- It is important to understand when and if to involve law enforcement. Getting to know local and state law enforcement can assist in these decisions.

Review Questions

1. How can a security framework assist in the design and implementation of a security infrastructure? What is information security governance? Who in the organization should plan for it?

2. Where can a security administrator find information on established security frameworks?

3. What is the ISO 27000 series of standards? Which individual standards make up the series?

4. What are the inherent problems with ISO 17799, and why hasn't the United States adopted it? What are the recommended alternatives?

5. What documents are available from the NIST Computer Resource Center, and how can they support the development of a security framework?

6. What benefit can a private, for-profit agency derive from best practices designed for federal agencies?

7. What Web resources can aid an organization in developing best practices as part of a security framework?

8. Briefly describe management, operational, and technical controls, and explain when each would be applied as part of a security framework.

9. What are the differences between a policy, a standard, and a practice? What are the three types of security policies? Where would each be used? What type of policy would be needed to guide use of the Web? E-mail? Office equipment for personal use?

10. Who is ultimately responsible for managing a technology? Who is responsible for enforcing policy that affects the use of a technology?

11. What is contingency planning? How is it different from routine management planning? What are the components of contingency planning?

12. When is the IR plan used?

13. When is the DR plan used?

14. When is the BC plan used? How do you determine when to use the IR, DR, and BC plans?

15. What are the five elements of a business impact analysis?

16. What are Pipkin's three categories of incident indicators?

17. What is containment, and why is it part of the planning process?

18. What is computer forensics? When are the results of computer forensics used?

19. What is an after-action review? When is it performed? Why is it done?

20. List and describe the six continuity strategies identified in the text.

Exercises

1. Using a graphics program, design several security awareness posters on the following themes: updating antivirus signatures, protecting sensitive information, watching out for e-mail viruses, prohibiting the personal use of company equipment, changing and protecting passwords, avoiding social engineering, and protecting software copyrights. What other themes can you come up with?

2. Search the Web for security education and training programs in your area. Keep a list and see which category has the most examples. See if you can determine the costs associated with each example. Which do you think would be more cost-effective in terms of both time and money?

3. Search the Web for examples of issue-specific security policies. What types of policies can you find? Draft a simple issue-specific policy using the format provided in the text that outlines "Fair and Responsible Use of College Computers" and is based on the rules and regulations provided by your institution. Does your school have a similar policy? Does it contain all the elements listed in the text?

4. Use your library or the Web to find a reported natural disaster that occurred at least 180 days ago. From the news accounts, determine if local or national officials had prepared disaster plans and if these plans were used. See if you can determine how the plans helped the officials improve the response to the disaster. How do the plans help the recovery?

5. Classify each of the following occurrences as an incident or disaster. If an occurrence is a disaster, determine whether or not business continuity plans would be called into play.

   a. A hacker gets into the network and deletes files from a server.

   b. A fire breaks out in the storeroom and sets off sprinklers on that floor. Some computers are damaged, but the fire is contained.

   c. A tornado hits a local power company, and the company will be without power for three to five days.

d. Employees go on strike, and the company could be without critical workers for weeks.

e. A disgruntled employee takes a critical server home, sneaking it out after hours.

For each of the scenarios (a–e), describe the steps necessary to restore operations. Indicate whether or not law enforcement would be involved.

Case Exercises

Charlie sat at his desk the morning after his nightmare. He had answered the most pressing e-mail in his Inbox and had a piping hot cup of coffee at his elbow. He looked down at a blank legal pad ready to make notes about what to do in case his nightmare became reality.

Questions:

1. What would be the first note you would write down if you were Charlie?

2. What else should be on Charlie's list?

Endnotes

1. IT Governance Institute. *Board Briefing on IT Governance*, 2nd Edition. 2003. *www. itgi.org*. The Chartered Institute of Management Accountants (CIMA) and the International Federation of Accountants (IFAC) also adopted this definition in 2004.

2. ITGI. Information Security Governance: Guidance for Information Security Managers. Accessed 15 May, 2010 from www.isaca.org.

3. Wood, Charles Cresson. "Integrated Approach Includes Information Security." *Security* 37, no. 2 (February 2000): 43–44.

4. Johnson, Carrie. "Enron Auditor Admits Crime: Andersen's Duncan Ordered Shredding." May 14, 2004. Accessed 30 April, 2007 from *http://foi.missouri.edu/enronande tal/duncantest1.html*.

5. Beltran, Luisa. "Andersen Exec: Shredding Began after E-mail." January 21, 2002. Accessed 30 April, 2007 from *http://money.cnn.com/2002/01/21/companies/enron_odom/*.

6. National Institute of Standards and Technology. *An Introduction to Computer Security: The NIST Handbook.* SP 800-12.

7. Derived from a number of sources, the most notable of which is *www.wustl.edu/poli cies/infosecurity.html*.

8. Aalberts, Robert J., Townsend, Anthony M., and Whitman, Michael E. "Considerations for an Effective Telecommunications Use Policy." *Communications of the ACM* 42, no. 6 (June 1999): 101–109.

9. National Institute of Standards and Technology. *An Introduction to Computer Security: The NIST Handbook.* SP 800-12.

10. NetIQ Security Technologies, Inc. "Enterprise Security Infrastructure Solution." *NetIQ Online*. Accessed 25 March 2004 from *www.netiq.com/products/*.

11. National Institute of Standards and Technology. *Information Security Management, Code of Practice for Information Security Management*. ISO/IEC 17799. 6 December 2001.

12. Ibid.

13. Ibid.

14. Ibid.

15. Humphries, T. "The Newly Revised Part 2 of BS 7799." Accessed 27 May 2003 from *www.gammassl.co.uk/bs7799/The%20Newly%20Revised%20Part%202%20of%20BS%207799ver3a.pdf*.

16. "How 7799 Works." Accessed May 27 2003 from *www.gammassl.co.uk/bs7799/works.html*.

17. National Institute of Standards and Technology. *Generally Accepted Principles and Practices for Securing Information Technology Systems*. SP 800-14. September 1996.

18. Ibid.

19. Swanson, M., Hash, J., and Bowen, P. *National Institute of Standards and Technology SP 800-18 Rev. 1. Guide for Developing Security Plans for Federal Information Systems*. Accessed February 2006 from *csrc.nist.gov/publications/nistpubs/800-18-Rev1/sp800-18-Rev1-final.pdf*.

20. Fraser, B. *Site Security Handbook – RFC 2196*. September 1997. Accessed 26 March 2004 from *www.ietf.org/rfc/rfc2196.txt*.

21. National Institute of Standards and Technology. *An Introduction to Computer Security: The NIST Handbook*. SP 800-12.

22. Ibid.

23. King, William R., and Gray, Paul. *The Management of Information Systems*. Chicago: Dryden Press, 1989, 359.

24. Swanson, M., Wohl, A., Pope, L., Grance, T., Hash, J., and Thomas, R. *Contingency Planning Guide for Information Technology Systems*. NIST Special Publication 800-34. Accessed 25 April 2010 from *http://csrc.nist.gov/publications/nistpubs/800-34/sp800-34.pdf*.

25. Krutz, Ronald L., and Vines, Russell Dean. *The CISSP Prep Guide: Mastering the Ten Domains of Computer Security*. New York: John Wiley and Sons Inc., 2001, 288.

26. Marcinko, Richard, and Weisman, John. *Designation Gold*. New York: Pocket Books, 1998, preface.

27. Pipkin, D.L. *Information Security: Protecting the Global Enterprise*. Upper Saddle River, NJ: Prentice Hall, 2000, 256.

28. Witty, Roberta. "What is Crisis Management?" *Gartner Online*. 19 September 2001. Accessed 30 April 2007 from *www.gartner.com/DisplayDocument?id=340971*.

29. NIST. "Special Publication 800-12: An Introduction to Computer Security: The NIST Handbook." October 1995. Accessed 30 April 2007 from *csrc.nist.gov/publications/nistpubs/800-12/*.

30. Federal Bureau of Investigation. *Technology Crimes*. Accessed 5 March 2007 from *http://sanfrancisco.fbi.gov/sfcomputer.htm*.

chapter 6

Security Technology: Firewalls and VPNs

If you think technology can solve your security problems, then you don't understand the problems and you don't understand the technology.

BRUCE SCHNEIER, AMERICAN CRYPTOGRAPHER,
COMPUTER SECURITY SPECIALIST, AND WRITER

Kelvin Urich came into the meeting room a few minutes late. He took an empty chair at the conference table, flipped open his notepad, and went straight to the point. "Okay, folks, I'm scheduled to present a plan to Charlie Moody and the IT planning staff in two weeks. I saw in the last project status report that you still don't have a consensus for the Internet connection architecture. Without that, we can't select a technical approach, so we haven't even started costing the project and planning for deployment. We cannot make acquisition and operating budgets, and I will look very silly at the presentation. What seems to be the problem?"

Laverne Nguyen replied, "Well, we seem to have a difference of opinion among the members of the architecture team. Some of us want to set up a screened subnet with bastion hosts, and others want to use a screened subnet with proxy servers. That decision will affect the way we implement application and Web servers."

Miller Harrison, a contractor brought in to help with the project, picked up where Laverne had left off. "We can't seem to move beyond this impasse, but we have done all the planning up to that point."

"Laverne, what does the consultant's report say?"

Laverne said, "She proposed two alternative designs and noted that a decision will have to be made between them at a later date."

Miller looked sour.

Kelvin said, "Sounds like we need to make a decision, and soon. Get a conference room reserved for tomorrow, ask the consultant if she can come in for a few hours first thing, and let everyone on the architecture team know we will meet from 8 to 11 on this matter. Now, here is how I think we should prepare for the meeting."

LEARNING OBJECTIVES:

Upon completion of this material, you should be able to:

- Recognize the important role of access control in computerized information systems, and identify and discuss widely-used authentication factors
- Describe firewall technology and the various approaches to firewall implementation
- Identify the various approaches to control remote and dial-up access by means of the authentication and authorization of users
- Discuss content filtering technology
- Describe the technology that enables the use of virtual private networks

Introduction

Technical controls are essential to a well-planned information security program, particularly to enforce policy for the many IT functions that are not under direct human control. Networks and computer systems make millions of decisions every second and operate in ways and at speeds that people cannot control in real time. Technical control solutions, properly implemented, can improve an organization's ability to balance the often conflicting objectives of making information readily and widely available and of preserving the information's confidentiality and integrity. This chapter, along with Chapters 7 and 8, describes how many of the more common technical control solutions function, and also explains how they fit into the physical design of an information security program. Students who want to acquire expertise on the configuration and maintenance of technology-based control systems will require additional education and usually specialized training in these areas.

Access Control

Access control is the method by which systems determine whether and how to admit a user into a trusted area of the organization—that is, information systems, restricted areas such as computer rooms, and the entire physical location. Access control is achieved by means of a combination of policies, programs, and technologies. Access controls can be mandatory, nondiscretionary, or discretionary.

Mandatory access controls (MACs) use data classification schemes; they give users and data owners limited control over access to information resources. In a data classification scheme, each collection of information is rated, and each user is rated to specify the level of information that user may access. These ratings are often referred to as sensitivity levels, and they indicate the level of confidentiality the information requires. A variation of this form of access control is called **lattice-based access control**, in which users are assigned a matrix of authorizations for particular areas of access. The level of authorization may vary between levels, depending on the classification authorizations individuals possess for each group of information or resources. The lattice structure contains subjects and objects, and the boundaries associated with each pair are demarcated. Lattice-based control specifies the level of access each subject has to each object. With this type of control, the column of attributes associated with a particular object (such as a printer) is referred to as an **access control list** (ACL). The row of attributes associated with a particular subject (such as a user) is referred to as a **capabilities table**.

Nondiscretionary controls are a strictly-enforced version of MACs that are managed by a central authority in the organization and can be based on an individual's role—**role-based controls**—or a specified set of tasks (subject- or object-based)—**task-based controls**. Role-based controls are tied to the role a user performs in an organization, and task-based controls are tied to a particular assignment or responsibility. The role and task controls make it easier to maintain the controls and restrictions associated with a particular role or task, especially if the individual performing the role or task changes often. Instead of constantly assigning and revoking the privileges of individuals who come and go, the administrator simply assigns the associated access rights to the role or task, and then whenever individuals are associated with that role or task, they automatically receive the corresponding access. When their turns are over, they are removed from the role or task and the access is revoked.

Discretionary access controls (DACs) are implemented at the discretion or option of the data user. The ability to share resources in a peer-to-peer configuration allows users to control and possibly provide access to information or resources at their disposal. The users can allow general, unrestricted access, or they can allow specific individuals or sets of individuals to access these resources. For example, a user has a hard drive containing information to be shared with office coworkers. This user can elect to allow access to specific individuals by providing access, by name, in the share control function.

Figure 6-1 shows an example of a discretionary access control from a peer-to-peer network using Microsoft Windows.

In general, all access control approaches rely on as the following mechanisms:

- Identification
- Authentication
- Authorization
- Accountability

Identification

Identification is a mechanism whereby an unverified entity—called a supplicant—that seeks access to a resource proposes a label by which they are known to the system. The label applied to the supplicant (or supplied by the supplicant) is called an identifier (ID), and must be mapped to one and only one entity within the security domain. Some organizations use composite identifiers, concatenating elements—department codes, random numbers, or special characters—to make unique identifiers within the security domain. Other organizations

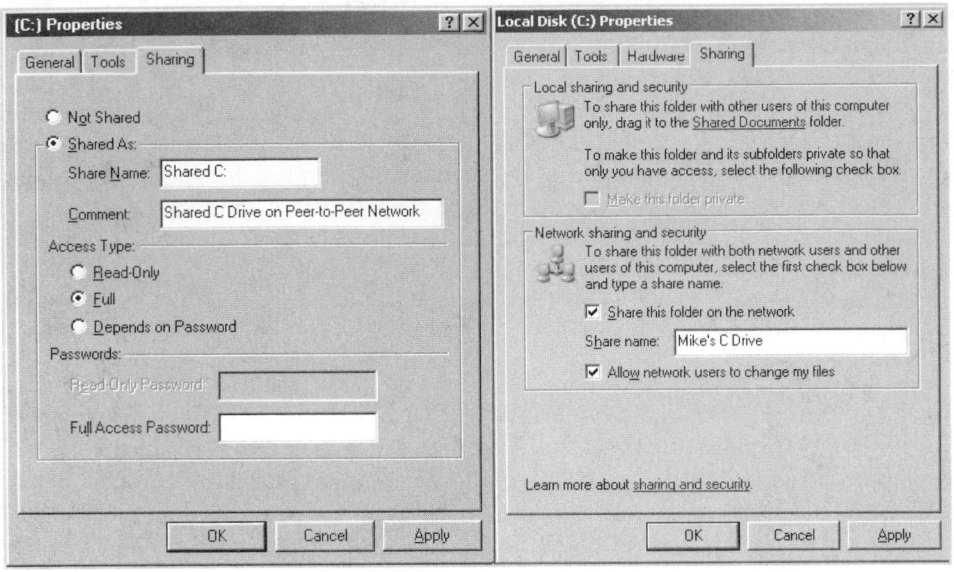

Figure 6-1 Example Discretionary Access Control

Source: Course Technology/Cengage Learning

generate random IDs to protect the resources from potential attackers. Most organizations use a single piece of unique information, such as a complete name or the user's first initial and surname.

Authentication

Authentication is the process of validating a supplicant's purported identity. There are three widely used authentication mechanisms, or **authentication factors**:

- Something a supplicant knows
- Something a supplicant has
- Something a supplicant is

Something a Supplicant Knows This factor of authentication relies upon what the supplicant knows and can recall—for example, a password, passphrase, or other unique authentication code, such as a personal identification number (PIN). A **password** is a private word or combination of characters that only the user should know. One of the biggest debates in the information security industry concerns the complexity of passwords. On the one hand, a password should be difficult to guess, which means it cannot be a series of letters or a word that is easily associated with the user, such as the name of the user's spouse, child, or pet. Nor should a password be a series of numbers easily associated with the user, such as a phone number, Social Security number, or birth date. On the other hand, the password must be something the user can easily remember, which means it should be short or easily associated with something the user can remember.

A **passphrase** is a series of characters, typically longer than a password, from which a **virtual password** is derived. For example, while a typical password might be "23skedoo," a typical passphrase might be "MayTheForceBeWithYouAlways," represented as "MTFBWYA."

Something a Supplicant Has This authentication factor relies upon something a supplicant has and can produce when necessary. One example is **dumb cards**, such as ID cards or ATM cards with magnetic stripes containing the digital (and often encrypted) user PIN, against which the number a user input is compared. The **smart card** contains a computer chip that can verify and validate a number of pieces of information instead of just a PIN. Another common device is the token, a card or key fob with a computer chip and a liquid crystal display that shows a computer-generated number used to support remote login authentication. Tokens are synchronous or asynchronous. Once **synchronous tokens** are synchronized with a server, both devices (server and token) use the same time or a time-based database to generate a number that must be entered during the user login phase. **Asynchronous tokens**, which don't require that the server and tokens all maintain the same time setting, use a challenge/response system, in which the server challenges the supplicant during login with a numerical sequence. The supplicant places this sequence into the token and receives a response. The prospective user then enters the response into the system to gain access.

Something a Supplicant Is or Can Produce This authentication factor relies upon individual characteristics, such as fingerprints, palm prints, hand topography, hand geometry, or retina and iris scans, or something a supplicant can produce on demand, such as voice patterns, signatures, or keyboard kinetic measurements. Some of these characteristics, known collectively as biometrics, are covered in more depth in Chapter 7.

Note: Certain critical logical or physical areas may require the use of **strong authentication**— at minimum two different authentication mechanisms drawn from two different factors of authentication, most often something you have and something you know. For example, access to a bank's ATM services requires a banking card plus a PIN. Such systems are called two-factor authentication, because two separate mechanisms are used. Strong authentication requires that at least one of the mechanisms be something other than what you know.

Authorization

Authorization is the matching of an authenticated entity to a list of information assets and corresponding access levels. This list is usually an ACL or access control matrix.

In general, authorization can be handled in one of three ways:

- Authorization for each authenticated user, in which the system performs an authentication process to verify each entity and then grants access to resources for only that entity. This quickly becomes a complex and resource-intensive process in a computer system.

- Authorization for members of a group, in which the system matches authenticated entities to a list of group memberships, and then grants access to resources based on the group's access rights. This is the most common authorization method.

- Authorization across multiple systems, in which a central authentication and authorization system verifies entity identity and grants it a set of credentials.

Authorization credentials (sometimes called authorization tickets) are issued by an authenticator and are honored by many or all systems within the authentication domain. Sometimes called single sign-on (SSO) or reduced sign-on, authorization credentials are becoming more common and are frequently enabled using a shared directory structure such as the Lightweight Directory Access Protocol (LDAP).

Accountability

Accountability, also known as **auditability**, ensures that all actions on a system—authorized or unauthorized—can be attributed to an authenticated identity. Accountability is most often accomplished by means of system logs and database journals, and the auditing of these records.

Systems logs record specific information, such as failed access attempts and systems modifications. Logs have many uses, such as intrusion detection, determining the root cause of a system failure, or simply tracking the use of a particular resource.

Firewalls

In commercial and residential construction, firewalls are concrete or masonry walls that run from the basement through the roof, to prevent a fire from spreading from one section of the building to another. In aircraft and automobiles, a firewall is an insulated metal barrier that keeps the hot and dangerous moving parts of the motor separate from the inflammable interior where the passengers sit. A **firewall** in an information security program is similar to a building's firewall in that it prevents specific types of information from moving between the outside world, known as the **untrusted network** (for example, the Internet), and the inside world, known as the **trusted network**. The firewall may be a separate computer system, a software service running on an existing router or server, or a separate network containing a number of supporting devices. Firewalls can be categorized by processing mode, development era, or structure.

Firewall Processing Modes

Firewalls fall into five major processing-mode categories: packet-filtering firewalls, application gateways, circuit gateways, MAC layer firewalls, and hybrids.[1] Hybrid firewalls use a combination of the other four modes, and in practice, most firewalls fall into this category, since most firewall implementations use multiple approaches.

The **packet-filtering firewall**, also simply called a filtering firewall, examines the header information of data packets that come into a network. A packet-filtering firewall installed on a TCP/IP- based network typically functions at the IP level and determines whether to drop a packet (deny) or forward it to the next network connection (allow) based on the rules programmed into the firewall. Packet-filtering firewalls examine every incoming packet header and can selectively filter packets based on header information such as destination address, source address, packet type, and other key information. Figure 6-2 shows the structure of an IPv4 packet.

Packet-filtering firewalls scan network data packets looking for compliance with or violation of the rules of the firewall's database. Filtering firewalls inspect packets at the network layer, or Layer 3, of the Open Systems Interconnect (OSI) model, which represents the seven layers of networking processes. (The OSI model is shown later in this chapter in Figure 6-6.) If the device finds a packet that matches a restriction, it stops the packet from traveling from one

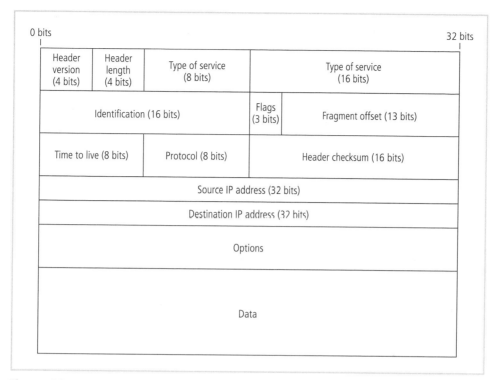

0 bits   32 bits

Header version (4 bits)	Header length (4 bits)	Type of service (8 bits)	Type of service (16 bits)	

Identification (16 bits)	Flags (3 bits)	Fragment offset (13 bits)

Time to live (8 bits)	Protocol (8 bits)	Header checksum (16 bits)

Source IP address (32 bits)

Destination IP address (32 bits)

Options

Data

Figure 6-2 IP Packet Structure

Source: Course Technology/Cengage Learning

network to another. The restrictions most commonly implemented in packet-filtering fire-walls are based on a combination of the following:

- IP source and destination address
- Direction (inbound or outbound)
- Protocol (for firewalls capable of examining the IP protocol layer)
- Transmission Control Protocol (TCP) or User Datagram Protocol (UDP) source and destination port requests (for firewalls capable of examining the TCP/UPD layer)

Packet structure varies depending on the nature of the packet. The two primary service types are TCP and UDP (as noted above). Figures 6-3 and 6-4 show the structures of these two major elements of the combined protocol known as TCP/IP.

Simple firewall models examine two aspects of the packet header: the destination and source address. They enforce **address restrictions**, rules designed to prohibit packets with certain addresses or partial addresses from passing through the device. They accomplish this through ACLs, which are created and modified by the firewall administrators. Figure 6-5 shows how a packet-filtering router can be used as a simple firewall to filter data packets from inbound connections and allow outbound connections unrestricted access to the public network.

To better understand an address restriction scheme, consider Table 6-1. If an administrator were to configure a simple rule based on the content of Table 6-1, any connection attempt

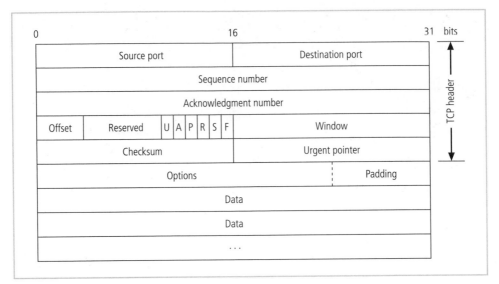

Figure 6-3 TCP Packet Structure

Source: Course Technology/Cengage Learning

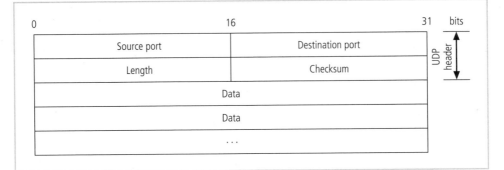

Figure 6-4 UDP Datagram Structure

Source: Course Technology/Cengage Learning

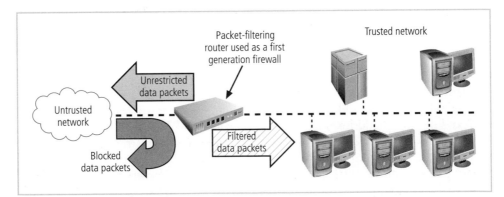

Figure 6-5 Packet-Filtering Router

Source: Course Technology/Cengage Learning

Source Address	Destination Address	Service (HTTP, SMTP, FTP, Telnet)	Action (Allow or Deny)
172.16.x.x	10.10.x.x	Any	Deny
192.168.x.x	10.10.10.25	HTTP	Allow
192.168.0.1	10.10.10.10	FTP	Allow

Table 6-1 Sample Firewall Rule and Format

made by an external computer or network device in the 192.168.x.x address range (192.168.0.0–192.168.255.255) is allowed. The ability to restrict a specific service, rather than just a range of IP addresses, is available in a more advanced version of this first generation firewall. Additional details on firewall rules and configuration are presented in a later section of this chapter.

The ability to restrict a specific service is now considered standard in most routers and is invisible to the user. Unfortunately, such systems are unable to detect whether packet headers have been modified, an advanced technique used in some attacks, including IP spoofing attacks.

There are three subsets of packet-filtering firewalls: static filtering, dynamic filtering, and stateful inspection. Static filtering requires that the filtering rules be developed and installed with the firewall. The rules are created and sequenced either by a person directly editing the rule set, or by a person using a programmable interface to specify the rules and the sequence. Any changes to the rules require human intervention. This type of filtering is common in network routers and gateways.

A dynamic filtering firewall can react to an emergent event and update or create rules to deal with that event. This reaction could be positive, as in allowing an internal user to engage in a specific activity upon request, or negative, as in dropping all packets from a particular address when an increase in the presence of a particular type of malformed packet is detected. While static filtering firewalls allow entire sets of one type of packet to enter in response to authorized requests, the **dynamic packet-filtering firewall** allows only a particular packet with a particular source, destination, and port address to enter. It does this by opening and closing "doors" in the firewall based on the information contained in the packet header, which makes dynamic packet filters an intermediate form between traditional static packet filters and application proxies (which are described later).

Stateful inspection firewalls, also called stateful firewalls, keep track of each network connection between internal and external systems using a **state table**. A state table tracks the state and context of each packet in the conversation by recording which station sent what packet and when. Like first generation firewalls, stateful inspection firewalls perform packet filtering, but they take it a step further. Whereas simple packet-filtering firewalls only allow or deny certain packets based on their address, a stateful firewall can expedite incoming packets that are responses to internal requests. If the stateful firewall receives an incoming packet that it cannot match in its state table, it refers to its ACL to determine whether to allow the packet to pass. The primary disadvantage of this type of firewall is the additional processing required to manage and verify packets against the state table. This can leave the system vulnerable to a DoS or DDoS attack. In such an attack, the system receives a large number of external packets, which slows the firewall because it attempts to compare all of the incoming

Source Address	Source Port	Destination Address	Destination Port	Time Remaining in Seconds	Total Time in Seconds	Protocol
192.168.2.5	1028	10.10.10.7	80	2725	3600	TCP

Table 6-2 State Table Entries

packets first to the state table and then to the ACL. On the positive side, these firewalls can track connectionless packet traffic, such as UDP and remote procedure calls (RPC) traffic. Dynamic stateful filtering firewalls keep a dynamic state table to make changes (within predefined limits) to the filtering rules based on events as they happen. A state table looks similar to a firewall rule set but has additional information, as shown in Table 6-2. The state table contains the familiar source IP and port, and destination IP and port, but adds information on the protocol used (i.e., UDP or TCP), total time in seconds, and time remaining in seconds. Many state table implementations allow a connection to remain in place for up to 60 minutes without any activity before the state entry is deleted. The example shown in Table 6-2 shows this in the column labeled *Total Time*. The time remaining column shows a countdown of the time that is left until the entry is deleted.

Application Gateways
The **application gateway**, also known as an **application-level firewall** or **application firewall**, is frequently installed on a dedicated computer, separate from the filtering router, but is commonly used in conjunction with a filtering router. The application firewall is also known as a **proxy server** since it runs special software that acts as a proxy for a service request. For example, an organization that runs a Web server can avoid exposing the server to direct user traffic by installing a proxy server configured with the registered domain's URL. This proxy server receives requests for Web pages, accesses the Web server on behalf of the external client, and returns the requested pages to the users. These servers can store the most recently accessed pages in their internal cache, and are thus also called *cache servers*. The benefits from this type of implementation are significant. For one, the proxy server is placed in an unsecured area of the network or in the demilitarized zone (DMZ)—an intermediate area between a trusted network and an untrusted network—so that it, rather than the Web server, is exposed to the higher levels of risk from the less trusted networks. Additional filtering routers can be implemented behind the proxy server, limiting access to the more secure internal system, and thereby further protecting internal systems.

One common example of an application-level firewall (or proxy server) is a firewall that blocks all requests for and responses to requests for Web pages and services from the internal computers of an organization, and instead makes all such requests and responses go to intermediate computers (or proxies) in the less protected areas of the organization's network. This technique is still widely used to implement electronic commerce functions, although most users of this technology have upgraded to take advantage of the DMZ approach discussed below.

The primary disadvantage of application-level firewalls is that they are designed for one or a few specific protocols and cannot easily be reconfigured to protect against attacks on other protocols. Since application firewalls work at the application layer (hence the name), they are typically restricted to a single application (e.g., FTP, Telnet, HTTP, SMTP, and SNMP).

The processing time and resources necessary to read each packet down to the application layer diminishes the ability of these firewalls to handle multiple types of applications.

Circuit Gateways The **circuit gateway firewall** operates at the transport layer. Again, connections are authorized based on addresses. Like filtering firewalls, circuit gateway firewalls do not usually look at traffic flowing between one network and another, but they do prevent direct connections between one network and another. They accomplish this by creating tunnels connecting specific processes or systems on each side of the firewall, and then allowing only authorized traffic, such as a specific type of TCP connection for authorized users, in these tunnels. A circuit gateway is a firewall component often included in the category of application gateway, but it is in fact a separate type of firewall. Writing for NIST in SP 800-10, John Wack describes the operation of a circuit gateway as follows: "A circuit-level gateway relays TCP connections but does no extra processing or filtering of the protocol. For example, the Telnet application gateway example provided here would be an example of a circuit-level gateway, since once the connection between the source and destination is established, the firewall simply passes bytes between the systems. Another example of a circuit-level gateway would be for NNTP, in which the NNTP server would connect to the firewall, and then internal systems' NNTP clients would connect to the firewall. The firewall would, again, simply pass bytes."[2]

MAC Layer Firewalls While not as well known or widely referenced as the firewall approaches above, MAC layer firewalls are designed to operate at the media access control sublayer of the data link layer (Layer 2) of the OSI network model. This enables these firewalls to consider the specific host computer's identity, as represented by its MAC or network interface card (NIC) address in its filtering decisions. Thus, MAC layer firewalls link the addresses of specific host computers to ACL entries that identify the specific types of packets that can be sent to each host, and block all other traffic.

Figure 6-6 shows where in the OSI model each of the firewall processing modes inspects data.

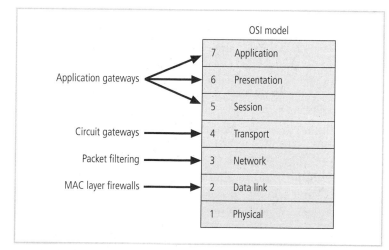

Figure 6-6 Firewall Types and the OSI Model

Source: Course Technology/Cengage Learning

Hybrid Firewalls Hybrid firewalls combine the elements of other types of firewalls—that is, the elements of packet filtering and proxy services, or of packet filtering and circuit gateways. A hybrid firewall system may actually consist of two separate firewall devices; each is a separate firewall system, but they are connected so that they work in tandem. For example, a hybrid firewall system might include a packet-filtering firewall that is set up to screen all acceptable requests, then pass the requests to a proxy server, which in turn requests services from a Web server deep inside the organization's networks. An added advantage to the hybrid firewall approach is that it enables an organization to make a security improvement without completely replacing its existing firewalls.

Firewalls Categorized by Generation

Firewalls are also frequently categorized by their position on a developmental continuum—that is, by generation. The first generation of firewall devices consists of routers that perform only simple packet-filtering operations. More recent generations of firewalls offer increasingly complex capabilities, including the increased security and convenience of a DMZ—"demilitarized zone." At present, there are five generally recognized generations of firewalls, and these generations can be implemented in a wide variety of architectures.

- **First generation firewalls** are static packet-filtering firewalls—that is, simple networking devices that filter packets according to their headers as the packets travel to and from the organization's networks.

- **Second generation firewalls** are application-level firewalls or proxy servers—that is, dedicated systems that are separate from the filtering router and that provide intermediate services for requestors.

- **Third generation firewalls** are stateful inspection firewalls, which, as described previously, monitor network connections between internal and external systems using state tables.

- **Fourth generation firewalls,** which are also known as dynamic packet-filtering firewalls, allow only a particular packet with a particular source, destination, and port address to enter.

- **Fifth generation firewalls** include the **kernel proxy**, a specialized form that works under Windows NT Executive, which is the kernel of Windows NT. This type of firewall evaluates packets at multiple layers of the protocol stack, by checking security in the kernel as data is passed up and down the stack. Cisco implements this technology in the security kernel of its Centri Firewall. The Cisco security kernel contains three component technologies:[3] The Interceptor/Packet Analyzer, the Security Verification ENgine (SVEN), and Kernel Proxies. The Interceptor captures packets arriving at the firewall server and passes them to the Packet Analyzer, which reads the header information, extracts signature data, and passes both the data and the packets to the SVEN. The SVEN receives this information and determines whether to drop the packet, map it to an existing session, or create a new session. If a current session exists, the SVEN passes the information through a custom-built protocol stack created specifically for that session. The temporary protocol stack uses a customized implementation of the approach widely known as Network Address Translation (NAT). The SVEN enforces the security policy that is configured into the Kernel Proxy as it inspects each packet.

Firewalls Categorized by Structure

Firewalls can also be categorized by the structures used to implement them. Most commercial-grade firewalls are dedicated *appliances*. Specifically, they are stand-alone units running on fully customized computing platforms that provide both the physical network connection and firmware programming necessary to perform their function, whatever that function (static packet filtering, application proxy, etc.) may be. Some firewall appliances use highly customized, sometimes proprietary hardware systems that are developed exclusively as firewall devices. Other commercial firewall systems are actually off-the-shelf general purpose computer systems that run custom application software on standard operating systems like Windows or Linux/Unix, or on specialized variants of these operating systems. Most small office or residential-grade firewalls are either simplified dedicated appliances running on computing devices or application software installed directly on the user's computer.

Commercial-Grade Firewall Appliances Firewall appliances are stand-alone, self-contained combinations of computing hardware and software. These devices frequently have many of the features of a general-purpose computer with the addition of firmware-based instructions that increase their reliability and performance and minimize the likelihood of their being compromised. The customized software operating system that drives the device can be periodically upgraded, but can only be modified via a direct physical connection or after running extensive authentication and authorization protocols. The firewall rule sets are stored in nonvolatile memory, and thus they can be changed by technical staff when necessary but are available each time the device is restarted.

These appliances can be manufactured from stripped-down general purpose computer systems, and/or designed to run a customized version of a general-purpose operating system. These variant operating systems are tuned to meet the type of firewall activity built into the application software that provides the firewall functionality.

Commercial-Grade Firewall Systems A commercial-grade firewall system consists of application software that is configured for the firewall application and run on a general-purpose computer. Organizations can install firewall software on an existing general purpose computer system, or they can purchase hardware that has been configured to specifications that yield optimum firewall performance. These systems exploit the fact that firewalls are essentially application software packages that use common general-purpose network connections to move data from one network to another.

Small Office/Home Office (SOHO) Firewall Appliances As more and more small businesses and residences obtain fast Internet connections with digital subscriber lines (DSL) or cable modem connections, they become more and more vulnerable to attacks. What many small business and work-from-home users don't realize is that, unlike dial-up connections, these high-speed services are always on; therefore, the computers connected to them are much more likely to be visible to the scans performed by attackers than those connected only for the duration of a dial-up session. Coupled with the typically lax security capabilities of legacy home computing operating systems like Windows 95, Windows 98, and even Windows Millennium Edition, most of these systems are wide open to outside intrusion. Even Windows XP Home Edition, a home computing operating system which can be securely configured, is rarely configured securely by its users. (Newer operating systems like Windows Vista offer the promise of improved security "out of the box.") Just as organizations must protect their information, residential users must also implement some form of firewall to prevent loss, damage, or disclosure of personal information.

One of the most effective methods of improving computing security in the SOHO setting is by means of a SOHO or residential-grade firewall. These devices, also known as broadband gateways or DSL/cable modem routers, connect the user's local area network or a specific computer system to the Internetworking device—in this case, the cable modem or DSL router provided by the Internet service provider (ISP). The SOHO firewall serves first as a stateful firewall to enable inside-to-outside access and can be configured to allow limited TCP/IP port forwarding and/or screened subnet capabilities (see later sections of this chapter for definitions of these terms).

In recent years, the broadband router devices that can function as packet-filtering firewalls have been enhanced to combine the features of wireless access points (WAPs) as well as small stackable LAN switches in a single device. These convenient combination devices give the residential/SOHO user the strong protection that comes from the use of Network Address Translation (NAT) services. NAT assigns nonrouting local addresses to the computer systems in the local area network and uses the single ISP-assigned address to communicate with the Internet. Since the internal computers are not visible to the public network, they are very much less likely to be scanned or compromised. Many users implement these devices primarily to allow multiple internal users to share a single external Internet connection. Figure 6-7 shows a few examples of the SOHO firewall devices currently available on the market.

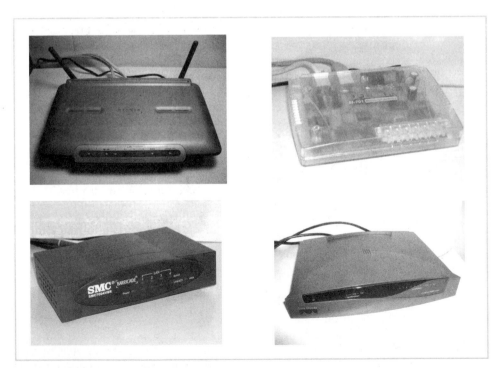

Figure 6-7 SOHO Firewall Devices

Source: Course Technology/Cengage Learning

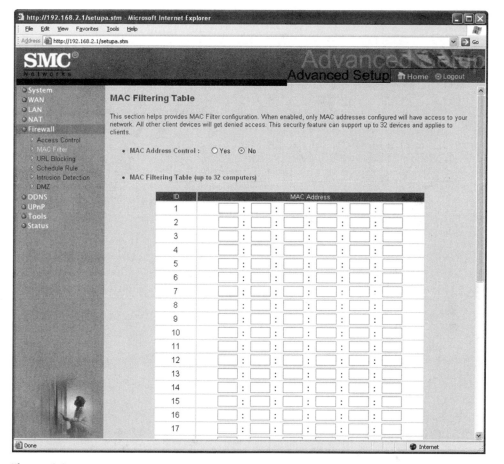

Figure 6-8 Barricade MAC Address Restriction Screen

Source: Course Technology/Cengage Learning

Many of these firewalls provide more than simple NAT services. As illustrated in Figures 6-8 through 6-11, some SOHO/residential firewalls include packet filtering, port filtering, and simple intrusion detection systems, and some can even restrict access to specific MAC addresses. Users may be able to configure port forwarding and enable outside users to access specific TCP or UDP ports on specific computers on the protected network.

Figure 6-8 shows an example of the setup screen from the SMC Barricade residential broadband router that can be used to designate which computers inside the trusted network may access the Internet.

Some firewall devices provide a limited intrusion detection capability. (Intrusion detection is covered in detail in Chapter 7.) Figure 6-9 shows the configuration screen from the SMC Barricade residential broadband router that enables the intrusion detection feature. When enabled, this feature detects specific intrusion attempts—that is, attempts to compromise the protected network that are known to the device manufacturer and that are detectable. In addition to recording intrusion attempts, the router can be configured to use the contact information provided on this screen to notify the firewall administrator of an intrusion attempt.

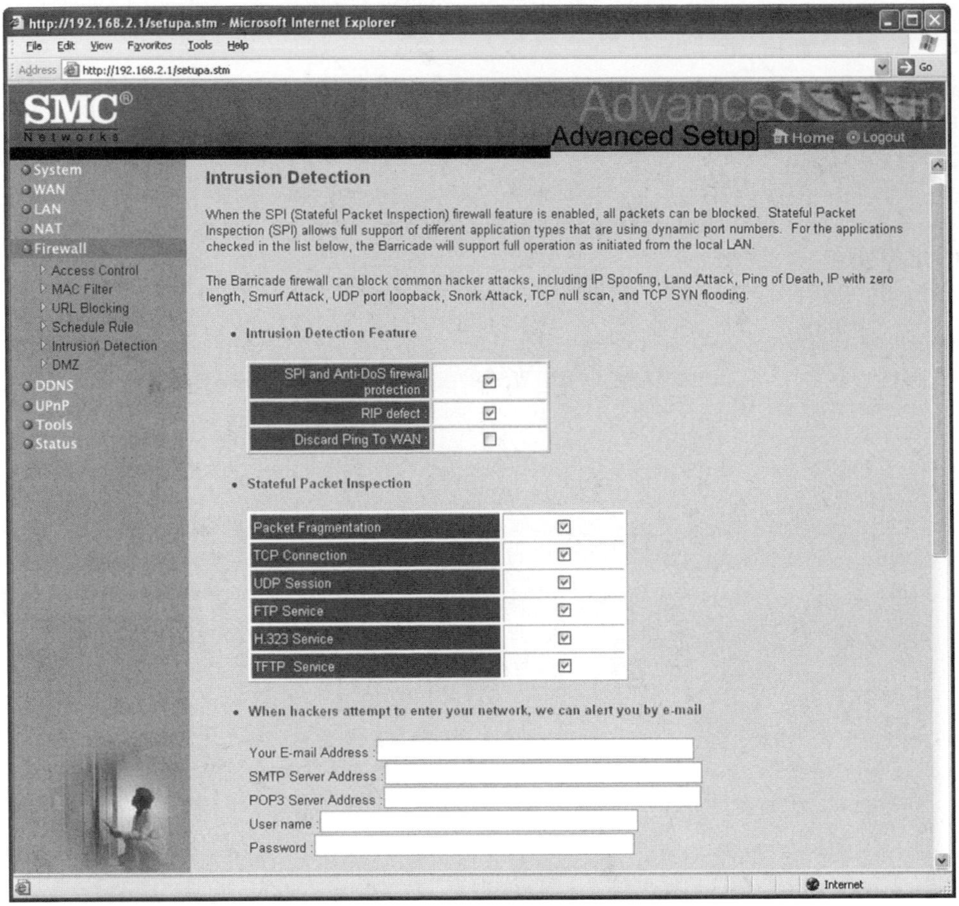

Figure 6-9 Barricade Firewall/Intrusion Detection Screen

Source: Course Technology/Cengage Learning

Figure 6-10 shows a continuation of the configuration screen for the intrusion detection feature. Note that the intrusion criteria are limited in number, but the actual threshold levels of the various activities detected can be customized by the administrator.

Figure 6-11 illustrates that even simple residential firewalls can be used to create a logical screened subnetwork (often called a demilitarized zone or DMZ) that can provide Web services. This screen shows how the Barricade can be configured to allow Internet clients access to servers inside the trusted network. The network administrator is expected to ensure that the servers are sufficiently secured for this type of exposure.

Residential-Grade Firewall Software Another method of protecting the residential user is to install a software firewall directly on the user's system. Many people have implemented these residential-grade software-based firewalls (some of which also provide antivirus or intrusion detection capabilities), but, unfortunately, they may not be as fully protected as they think. The most commonly used of residential-grade software-based firewalls are listed in Table 6-3. Note that in addition to the tools shown in Table 6-3, many commercial products have desktop endpoint security systems (IBM Proventia, Checkpoint, etc.) which

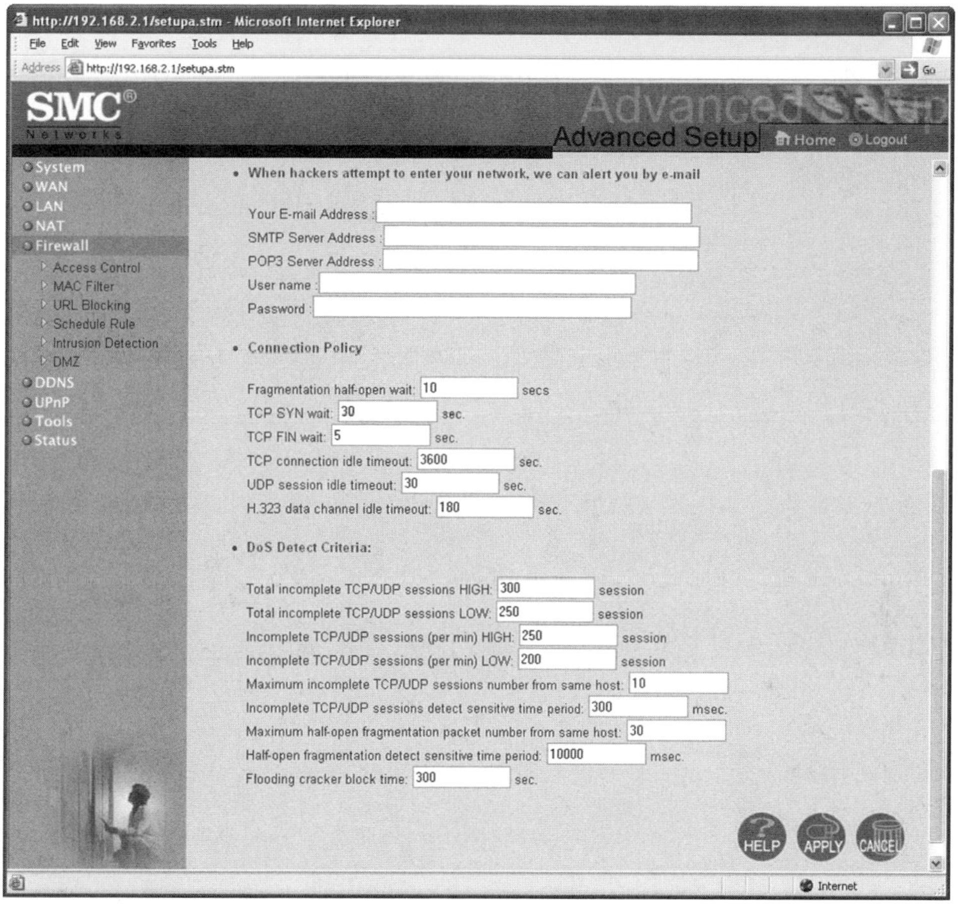

Figure 6-10 Barricade Firewall/Intrusion Detection Screen (Cont.)

Source: Course Technology/Cengage Learning

are not listed here. These applications claim to detect and prevent intrusion into the user's system without affecting usability. However, many of the applications in Table 6-3 provide free versions of their software that are not fully functional, and the old adage "you get what you pay for" certainly applies to software in this category. Users who implement this free, less-capable software often find that it delivers less than complete protection.

There are limits to the level of configurability and protection that software firewalls can provide. Many of the applications in Table 6-3 have very limited configuration options ranging from none to low to medium to high security. With only three or four levels of configuration, users may find that the application becomes increasingly difficult to use in everyday situations. They find themselves sacrificing security for usability, because at higher levels of security the application constantly asks for instruction on whether to allow a particular application, packet, or service to connect internally or externally. The Microsoft Windows 2000, XP, and Vista versions of Internet Explorer have a similar configuration settings that allow users to choose from a list of preconfigured options or to configure a custom setting with more detailed security options.

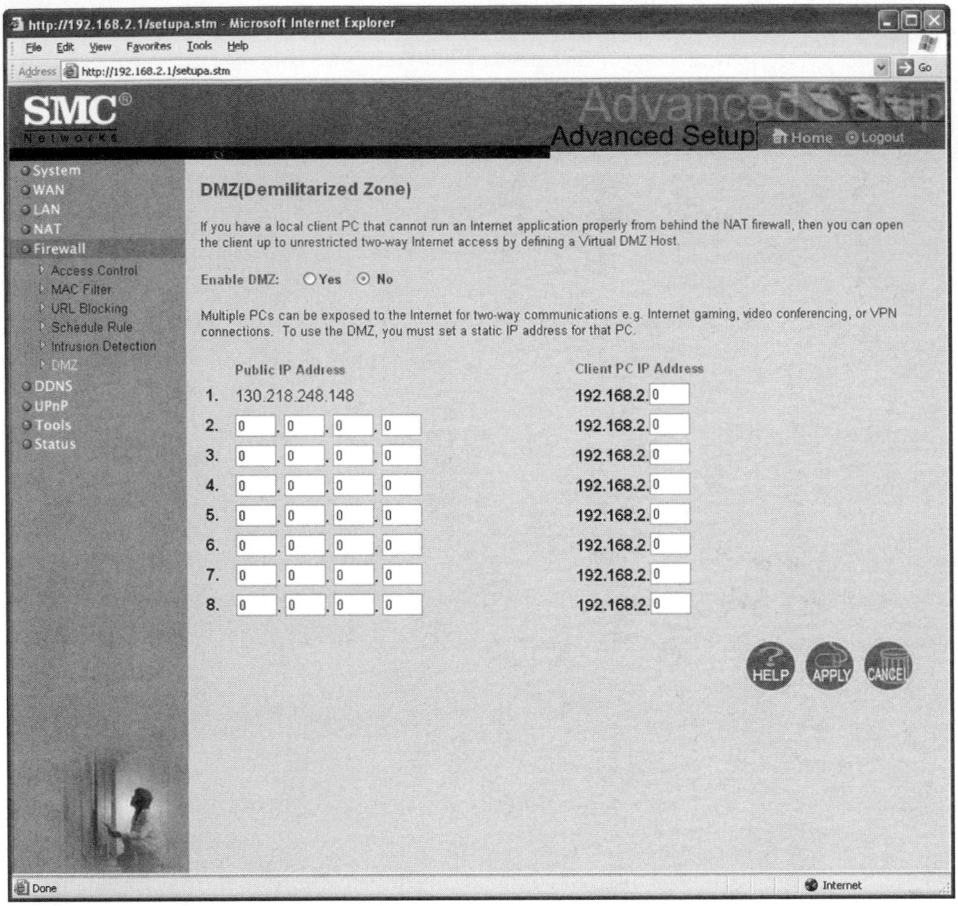

Figure 6-11 Barricade Demilitarized Zone

Source: Course Technology/Cengage Learning

Software Versus Hardware: The SOHO Firewall Debate So which type of firewall should the residential user implement? Many users swear by their software firewalls. Personal experience will produce a variety of opinionated perspectives. Ask yourself this question: *Where* would you rather defend against the attacker? The software option allows the hacker inside your computer to battle a piece of software (free software, in many cases) that may not be correctly installed, configured, patched, upgraded, or designed. If the software happens to have a known vulnerability, the attacker could bypass it and then have unrestricted access to your system. With a hardware firewall, even if the attacker manages to crash the firewall system, your computer and information are still safely behind the now disabled connection. The hardware firewall's use of nonroutable addresses further extends the protection, making it virtually impossible for the attacker to reach your information. A former student of one of the authors responded to this debate by installing a hardware firewall, and then visiting a hacker chat room. He challenged the group to penetrate his system. A few days later, he received an e-mail from a hacker claiming to have accessed his system. The hacker included a graphic of a screen showing a C:\ prompt, which he claimed was from the student's system. After doing a bit of research, the student found out that the

Firewall (date in parentheses is year posted on *download.cnet.com*)	CNET Editor's Rating (number of stars out of 5)
Norton 360	4
ZoneAlarm Extreme Security (2010)	3
Trend Micro Internet Security (2009)	3.5
Panda Internet Security (2009)	3.5
McAfee Internet Security (2009)	3.5
PC Tools Firewall Plus (2009)	4
Agnitum Outpost Firewall Pro (2009)	4
Sygate Personal Firewall 5.6.2808 (2007)	4
AVG Anti-virus plus Firewall 9.0.700 (2009)	unrated
Comodo Internet Security 3.12 (2009)	5
Ashampoo FireWall Free 1.2 (2007)	5
Webroot AV with AntiSpyware and Firewall 6.1 (2007)	unrated
VisNetic Firewall 3.0 (2007)	unrated
Kerio WinRoute Firewall 6.7 (2009)	unrated
Microsoft Windows Firewall (integral to Windows XP, Vista, 7 systems)	unrated
CA Internet Security Suite Plus (2009)	2.5

Table 6-3 **Common Software Firewalls**

Note: This list includes only those firewalls posted since 2007. Ratings shown here come from http://www.cnet.com/internet-security/

firewall had an image stored in firmware that was designed to distract attackers. It was an image of a command window with a DOS prompt. The hardware (NAT) solution had withstood the challenge.

Firewall Architectures

All firewall devices can be configured in a number of network connection architectures. These approaches are sometimes mutually exclusive and sometimes can be combined.

The configuration that works best for a particular organization depends on three factors: the objectives of the network, the organization's ability to develop and implement the architectures, and the budget available for the function. Although literally hundreds of variations exist, there are four common architectural implementations: Packet-filtering routers, screened host firewalls, dual-homed firewalls, and screened subnet firewalls.

Packet-Filtering Routers   Most organizations with an Internet connection have some form of a router at the boundary between the organization's internal networks and the external service provider. Many of these routers can be configured to reject packets that the organization does not want to allow into the network. This is a simple but effective way to lower the organization's risk from external attack. The drawbacks to this type of system include a lack of auditing and strong authentication. Also, the complexity of the ACLs used to filter the packets can degrade network performance. Figure 6-5 is an example of this type of architecture.

Screened Host Firewalls Screened host firewalls combine the packet-filtering router with a separate, dedicated firewall, such as an application proxy server. This approach allows the router to prescreen packets to minimize the network traffic and load on the internal proxy. The application proxy examines an application layer protocol, such as HTTP, and performs the proxy services. This separate host is often referred to as a **bastion host**; it can be a rich target for external attacks and should be very thoroughly secured. Even though the bastion host/application proxy actually contains only cached copies of the internal Web documents, it can still present a promising target, because compromise of the bastion host can disclose the configuration of internal networks and possibly provide attackers with internal information. Since the bastion host stands as a sole defender on the network perimeter, it is commonly referred to as the **sacrificial host**. To its advantage, this configuration requires the external attack to compromise two separate systems before the attack can access internal data. In this way, the bastion host protects the data more fully than the router alone. Figure 6-12 shows a typical configuration of a screened host architecture.

Dual-Homed Host Firewalls The next step up in firewall architectural complexity is the dual-homed host. When this architectural approach is used, the bastion host contains two NICs (network interface cards) rather than one, as in the bastion host configuration. One NIC is connected to the external network, and one is connected to the internal network, providing an additional layer of protection. With two NICs, all traffic *must* physically go through the firewall to move between the internal and external networks. Implementation of this architecture often makes use of NAT. As described earlier in this chapter, NAT is a method of mapping real, valid, external IP addresses to special ranges of nonroutable internal IP addresses, thereby creating yet another barrier to intrusion from external

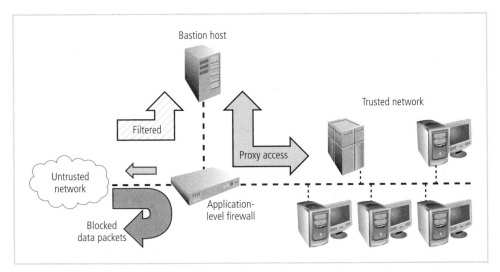

Figure 6-12 Screened Host Firewall

Source: Course Technology/Cengage Learning

attackers. The internal addresses used by NAT consist of three different ranges. Organizations that need a large group of addresses for internal use will use the Class A address range of 10.x.x.x, which has more than 16.5 million usable addresses. Organizations that need smaller groups of internally assigned addresses can select from the reserved group of sixteen Class B address blocks found in the 172.16.x.x to 172.31.x.x range (about 1.05 million total addresses). Finally, those with smaller needs can use Class C addresses, in the 192.168.x.x range, each of which has approximately 65,500 addresses. See Table 6-4 for a recap of the IP address ranges reserved for nonpublic networks. Messages sent with internal addresses within these three reserved ranges cannot be routed externally, so that if a computer with one of these internal-use addresses is directly connected to the external network, and avoids the NAT server, its traffic cannot be routed on the public network. Taking advantage of this, NAT prevents external attacks from reaching internal machines with addresses in specified ranges. If the NAT server is a multi-homed bastion host, it translates between the true, external IP addresses assigned to the organization by public network naming authorities and the internally assigned, nonroutable IP addresses. NAT translates by dynamically assigning addresses to internal communications and tracking the conversations with sessions to determine which incoming message is a response to which outgoing traffic. Figure 6-13 shows a typical configuration of a dual-homed host firewall that uses NAT and proxy access to protect the internal network.

Class	From	To	CIDR Mask	Decimal Mask
Class A or 24 Bit	10.0.0.0	10.255.255.255	/8	255.0.0.0
Class B or 20 Bit	172.16.0.0	172.31.255.255	/12 or /16	255.240.0.0 or 255.255.0.0
Class C or 16 Bit	192.168.0.0	192.168.255.255	/16 or /24	255.255.0.0 or 255.255.255.0

Table 6-4 **Reserved Nonroutable Address Ranges**

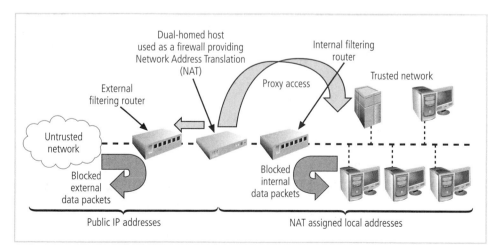

Figure 6-13 Dual-Homed Host Firewall

Source: Course Technology/Cengage Learning

Another benefit of a dual-homed host is its ability to translate between many different protocols at their respective data link layers, including Ethernet, token ring, Fiber Distributed Data Interface (FDDI), and asynchronous transfer mode (ATM). On the downside, if this dual-homed host is compromised, it can disable the connection to the external network, and as traffic volume increases it can become overloaded. However, compared to more complex solutions this architecture provides strong overall protection with minimal expense.

Screened Subnet Firewalls (with DMZ) The dominant architecture used today is the screened subnet firewall. The architecture of a screened subnet firewall provides a DMZ. The DMZ can be a dedicated port on the firewall device linking a single bastion host, or it can be connected to a screened subnet, as shown in Figure 6-14. Until recently, servers providing services through an untrusted network were commonly placed in the DMZ. Examples of these include Web servers, file transfer protocol (FTP) servers, and certain database servers. More recent strategies using proxy servers have provided much more secure solutions.

A common arrangement finds the subnet firewall consisting of two or more internal bastion hosts behind a packet-filtering router, with each host protecting the trusted network. There are many variants of the screened subnet architecture. The first general model consists of two filtering routers, with one or more dual-homed bastion hosts between them. In the second general model, as illustrated in Figure 6-14, the connections are routed as follows:

- Connections from the outside or untrusted network are routed through an external filtering router.

- Connections from the outside or untrusted network are routed into—and then out of—a routing firewall to the separate network segment known as the DMZ.

- Connections into the trusted internal network are allowed only from the DMZ bastion host servers.

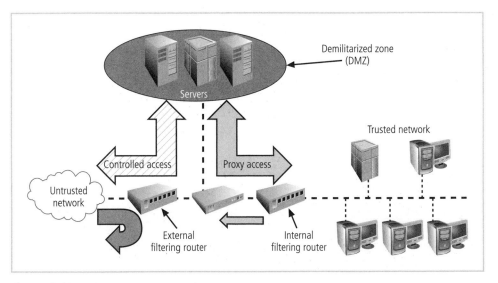

Figure 6-14 Screened Subnet (DMZ)

Source: Course Technology/Cengage Learning

The **screened subnet** is an entire network segment that performs two functions: it protects the DMZ systems and information from outside threats by providing a network of intermediate security (more secure than the general public networks but less secure than the internal network); and it protects the internal networks by limiting how external connections can gain access to them. Although extremely secure, the screened subnet can be expensive to implement and complex to configure and manage. The value of the information it protects must justify the cost.

Another facet of the DMZ is the creation of an area known as an extranet. An **extranet** is a segment of the DMZ where additional authentication and authorization controls are put into place to provide services that are not available to the general public. An example is an online retailer that allows anyone to browse the product catalog and place items into a shopping cart, but requires extra authentication and authorization when the customer is ready to check out and place an order.

SOCKS Servers Deserving of brief special attention is the SOCKS firewall implementation. SOCKS is the protocol for handling TCP traffic via a proxy server. The SOCKS system is a proprietary circuit-level proxy server that places special SOCKS client-side agents on each workstation. The general approach is to place the filtering requirements on the individual workstation rather than on a single point of defense (and thus point of failure). This frees the entry router from filtering responsibilities, but it requires that each workstation be managed as a firewall detection and protection device. A SOCKS system can require support and management resources beyond those of traditional firewalls since it entails the configuration and management of hundreds of individual clients, as opposed to a single device or small set of devices.

Selecting the Right Firewall

When trying to determine which is the best firewall for an organization, you should consider the following questions:[4]

1. Which type of firewall technology offers the right balance between protection and cost for the needs of the organization?

2. What features are included in the base price? What features are available at extra cost? Are all cost factors known?

3. How easy is it to set up and configure the firewall? How accessible are the staff technicians who can competently configure the firewall?

4. Can the candidate firewall adapt to the growing network in the target organization?

The most important factor is, of course, the extent to which the firewall design provides the required protection. The second most important factor is cost. Cost may keep a certain make, model, or type out of reach. As with all security decisions, certain compromises may be necessary in order to provide a viable solution under the budgetary constraints stipulated by management.

Configuring and Managing Firewalls

Once the firewall architecture and technology have been selected, the organization must provide for the initial configuration and ongoing management of the firewall(s). Good policy and practice dictates that each firewall device, whether a filtering router, bastion host, or other firewall implementation, must have its own set of configuration rules. In theory, packet filtering-firewalls examine each incoming packet using a rule set to determine whether to allow or deny the packet. That set of rules is made up of simple statements that identify source and destination addresses and the type of requests a packet contains based on the ports specified in the packet. In fact, the configuration of firewall policies can be complex and difficult. IT professionals familiar with application programming can appreciate the difficulty of debugging both syntax errors and logic errors. Syntax errors in firewall policies are usually easy to identify, as the systems alert the administrator to incorrectly configured policies. However, logic errors, such as allowing instead of denying, specifying the wrong port or service type, and using the wrong switch, are another story. A myriad of simple mistakes can take a device designed to protect users' communications and turn it into one giant choke point. A choke point that restricts all communications or an incorrectly configured rule can cause other unexpected results. For example, novice firewall administrators often improperly configure a virus-screening e-mail gateway (think of this as a type of e-mail firewall) so that, instead of screening e-mail for malicious code, it blocks all incoming e-mail and causes, understandably, a great deal of frustration among users.

Configuring firewall policies is as much an art as it is a science. Each configuration rule must be carefully crafted, debugged, tested, and placed into the ACL in the proper sequence—good, correctly sequenced firewall rules ensure that the actions taken comply with the organization's policy. In a well-designed, efficient firewall rule set, rules that can be evaluated quickly and govern broad access are performed before ones that may take longer to evaluate and affect fewer cases. The most important thing to remember when configuring firewalls is this: when security rules conflict with the performance of business, security often loses. If users can't work because of a security restriction, the security administration is usually told, in no uncertain terms, to remove the safeguard. In other words, organizations are much more willing to live with potential risk than certain failure.

Best Practices for Firewalls This section outlines some of the best practices for firewall use.[5] Note that these rules are not presented in any particular sequence. For sequencing of rules, refer to the next section.

- All traffic from the trusted network is allowed out. This allows members of the organization to access the services they need. Filtering and logging of outbound traffic can be implemented when required by specific organizational policies.

- The firewall device is never directly accessible from the public network for configuration or management purposes. Almost all administrative access to the firewall device is denied to internal users as well. Only authorized firewall administrators access the device through secure authentication mechanisms, preferably via a method that is based on cryptographically strong authentication and uses two-factor access control techniques.

- Simple Mail Transport Protocol (SMTP) data is allowed to enter through the firewall, but is routed to a well-configured SMTP gateway to filter and route messaging traffic securely.

- All Internet Control Message Protocol (ICMP) data should be denied. Known as the ping service, ICMP is a common method for hacker reconnaissance and should be turned off to prevent snooping.

- Telnet (terminal emulation) access to all internal servers from the public networks should be blocked. At the very least, Telnet access to the organization's Domain Name System (DNS) server should be blocked to prevent illegal zone transfers and to prevent attackers from taking down the organization's entire network. If internal users need to access an organization's network from outside the firewall, the organization should enable them to use a Virtual Private Network (VPN) client or other secure system that provides a reasonable level of authentication.

- When Web services are offered outside the firewall, HTTP traffic should be blocked from internal networks through the use of some form of proxy access or DMZ architecture. That way, if any employees are running Web servers for internal use on their desktops, the services are invisible to the outside Internet. If the Web server is behind the firewall, allow HTTP or HTTPS (also known as Secure Sockets Layer or SSL[6]) through for the Internet at large to view it. The best solution is to place the Web servers containing critical data inside the network and use proxy services from a DMZ (screened network segment), and also to restrict Web traffic bound for internal network addresses to allow only those requests that originated from internal addresses. This restriction can be accomplished using NAT or other stateful inspection or proxy server firewall approaches. All other incoming HTTP traffic should be blocked. If the Web servers only contain advertising, they should be placed in the DMZ and rebuilt on a timed schedule or when—not *if*, but *when*—they are compromised.

- All data that is not verifiably authentic should be denied. When attempting to convince packet-filtering firewalls to permit malicious traffic, attackers frequently put an internal address in the *source* field. To avoid this problem, set rules so that the external firewall blocks all inbound traffic with an organizational source address.

Firewall Rules As noted earlier in this chapter, firewalls operate by examining a data packet and performing a comparison with some predetermined logical rules. The logic is based on a set of guidelines programmed in by a firewall administrator or created dynamically and based on outgoing requests for information. This logical set is commonly referred to as firewall rules, rule base, or firewall logic. Most firewalls use packet header information to determine whether a specific packet should be allowed to pass through or should be dropped. Firewall rules operate on the principle of "that which is not permitted is prohibited," also known as expressly permitted rules. In other words, unless there is a rule explicitly permitting an action, it is denied.

In order to better understand more complex rules, you must be able to create simple rules and understand how they interact. In the exercise that follows, many of the rules are based on the best practices outlined earlier. For the purposes of this discussion, assume a network configuration as illustrated in Figure 6-15, with an internal and an external filtering firewall. In the exercise, the rules for both firewalls are discussed, and a recap at the end of the exercise shows the complete rule sets for each filtering firewall. It is important to note that separate rule lists (e.g., access control lists) are created for each interface on a firewall and *bound* to that interface. This creates a set of unidirectional flow checks for dual-homed hosts, for example, which means that some of the rules shown here are designed for *inbound* traffic, from the untrusted to the trusted side of the firewall, and some are designed for *outbound* traffic, from the trusted to the untrusted side. It is important to ensure that the appropriate rule is used, as permitting certain traffic on the wrong side of the device can have

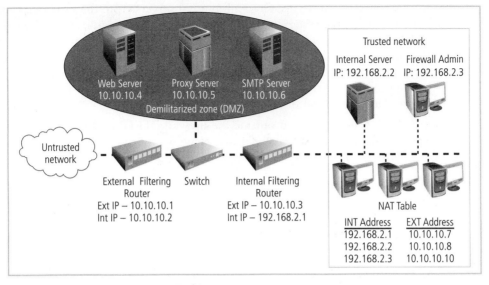

Figure 6-15 Example Network Configuration

Source: Course Technology/Cengage Learning

unintended consequences. These examples assume that the firewall can process information beyond the IP level (TCP/UDP) and thus can access source and destination port addresses. If it could not, you could substitute the IP "Protocol" field for the source/destination port fields.

Some firewalls can filter packets by protocol name as opposed to protocol port number. For instance, Telnet protocol packets usually go to TCP port 23, but can sometimes be redirected to another much higher port number in an attempt to conceal the activity. The system (or well-known) ports are those from 0 through 1023, user (or registered) ports are those from 1024 through 49151, and dynamic (or private) ports are those from 49152 through 65535 (see *www.iana.org/assignments/port-numbers* for more information).

The following example uses the port numbers associated with several well-known protocols to build a rule base (listed in Table 6-5).

Rule Set 1: Responses to internal requests are allowed. In most firewall implementations, it is desirable to allow a response to an internal request for information. In dynamic or stateful firewalls, this is most easily accomplished by matching the incoming traffic to an outgoing request in a state table. In simple packet filtering, this can be accomplished with the following rule for the external filtering router. (Note that the network address for the destination ends with .0; some firewalls use a notation of .x instead.) Extreme caution should be used in deploying this rule, as some attacks use port assignments above the 1023 level. Most modern firewalls use stateful inspection filtering and make this concern obsolete.

In Table 6-6, you can see that this rule states that *any* inbound packet (with any source address and from any source port) that is destined for the internal network (whose destination address is 10.10.10.0) and for a destination port greater than 1023 (that is, any port out of the number range for the well-known ports) is allowed to enter. Why allow all such

Port Number	Protocol
7	Echo
20	File Transfer [Default Data] (FTP)
21	File Transfer [Control] (FTP)
23	Telnet
25	Simple Mail Transfer Protocol (SMTP)
53	Domain Name Services (DNS)
80	Hypertext Transfer Protocol (HTTP)
110	Post Office Protocol version 3 (POP3)
161	Simple Network Management Protocol (SNMP)

Table 6-5   Select Well-Known Port Numbers

Source Address	Source Port	Destination Address	Destination Port	Action
Any	Any	10.10.10.0	>1023	Allow

Table 6-6   Rule Set 1

packets? While outbound communications request information from a specific port (i.e., a port 80 request for a Web page), the response is assigned a number outside the well-known port range. If multiple browser windows are open at the same time, each window can request a packet from a Web site, and the response is directed to a specific destination port, allowing the browser and Web server to keep each conversation separate. While this rule is sufficient for the external router (firewall), it is dangerous simply to allow any traffic in just because it is destined to a high port range. A better solution is to have the internal firewall router use state tables that track connections (as in stateful packet inspection) and thus prevent dangerous packets from entering this upper port range.

Rule Set 2: The firewall device is never accessible directly from the public network. If attackers can directly access the firewall, they may be able to modify or delete rules and allow unwanted traffic through. For the same reason, the firewall itself should never be allowed to access other network devices directly. If hackers compromise the firewall and then use its permissions to access other servers or clients, they may cause additional damage or mischief. The rules shown in Table 6-7 prohibit anyone from directly accessing the firewall, and prohibit the firewall from directly accessing any other devices. Note that this example is for the external filtering router/firewall only. Similar rules should be crafted for the internal router. Why are there separate rules for each IP address? The 10.10.10.*1* address regulates external access to and by the firewall, while the 10.10.10.*2* address regulates internal access. Not all attackers are outside the firewall!

Note that if the firewall administrator needs direct access to the firewall, from inside or outside the network, a permission rule allowing access from his or her IP address should preface this rule. Be aware that it is possible to access the interface on the opposite side of the device, as traffic would be routed through the box and "boomerang" back when it hits the

Source Address	Source Port	Destination Address	Destination Port	Action
Any	Any	10.10.10.1	Any	Deny
Any	Any	10.10.10.2	Any	Deny
10.10.10.1	Any	Any	Any	Deny
10.10.10.2	Any	Any	Any	Deny

Table 6-7 Rule Set 2

Source Address	Source Port	Destination Address	Destination Port	Action
10.10.10.0	Any	Any	Any	Allow

Table 6-8 Rule Set 3

first router on the far side. Thus it protects both interfaces in both the inbound and outbound rule set.

Rule Set 3: All traffic from the trusted network is allowed out. As a general rule it is wise not to restrict outbound traffic, unless separate routers and firewalls are configured to handle it, to avoid overloading the firewall. If an organization wants control over outbound traffic, it should use a separate filtering device. The rule shown in Table 6-8 allows internal communications out, and as such would be used on the outbound interface.

Why should rule set 3 come after rule set 1 and 2? It makes sense to allow the rules that unambiguously impact the most traffic to be earlier in the list. The more rules a firewall must process to find one that applies to the current packet, the slower the firewall will run. Therefore, most widely applicable rules should come first since the firewall employs the first rule that applies to any given packet.

Rule Set 4: The rule set for the Simple Mail Transport Protocol (SMTP) data is shown in Table 6-9. As shown, the packets governed by this rule are allowed to pass through the firewall, but are all routed to a well-configured SMTP gateway. It is important that e-mail traffic reach your e-mail server and *only* your e-mail server. Some attackers try to disguise dangerous packets as e-mail traffic to fool a firewall. If such packets can reach only the e-mail server, and the e-mail server has been properly configured, the rest of the network ought to be safe. Note that if the organization allows home access to an internal e-mail server, then it may wish to implement a second, separate server to handle the POP3 protocol that retrieves mail for e-mail clients like Outlook and Thunderbird. This is usually a low-risk operation, especially if e-mail encryption is in place. More challenging is the sending of e-mail using the SMTP protocol, a service attractive to spammers who may seek to hijack an outbound mail server.

Source Address	Source Port	Destination Address	Destination Port	Action
Any	Any	10.10.10.6	25	Allow

Table 6-9 Rule Set 4

Rule Set 5: All Internet Control Message Protocol (ICMP) data should be denied. Pings, formally known as ICMP Echo requests, are used by internal systems administrators to ensure that clients and servers can communicate. There is virtually no legitimate use for ICMP outside the network, except to test the perimeter routers. ICMP uses port 7 to request a response to a query (e.g., "Are you there?") and can be the first indicator of a malicious attack. It's best to make all directly connected networking devices "black holes" to external probes. Traceroute uses a variation on the ICMP Echo requests, so restricting this one port provides protection against two types of probes. Allowing internal users to use ICMP requires configuring two rules, as shown in Table 6-10.

The first of these two rules allows internal administrators (and users) to use ping. Note that this rule is unnecessary if internal permissions rules like those in rule set 2 is used. The second rule in Table 6-10 does not allow anyone else to use ping. Remember that rules are processed in order. If an internal user needs to ping an internal or external address, the firewall allows the packet and stops processing the rules. If the request does not come from an internal source, then it bypasses the first rule and moves to the second.

Rule Set 6: Telnet (terminal emulation) access to all internal servers from the public networks should be blocked. Though not used much in Windows environments, Telnet is still useful to systems administrators on Unix/Linux systems. But the presence of external requests for Telnet services can indicate an attack. Allowing internal use of Telnet requires the same type of initial permission rule you use with ping. See Table 6-11. Note that this rule is unnecessary if internal permissions rules like those in rule set 2 is used.

Rule Set 7: When Web services are offered outside the firewall, HTTP traffic (and HTTPS traffic) should be blocked from the internal networks via the use of some form of proxy access or DMZ architecture. With a Web server in the DMZ you simply allow HTTP to access the Web server, and use rule set 8, the cleanup rule (which will be described shortly), to prevent any other access. In order to keep the Web server inside the internal network, direct all HTTP requests to the proxy server and configure the internal filtering router/firewall only to allow the proxy server to access the internal Web server. The rule shown in Table 6-12 illustrates the first example.

This rule accomplishes two things: it allows HTTP traffic to reach the Web server, and it prevents non-HTTP traffic from reaching the Web server. It does the latter via the cleanup

Source Address	Source Port	Destination Address	Destination Port	Action
10.10.10.0	Any	Any	7	Allow
Any	Any	10.10.10.0	7	Deny

Table 6-10 Rule Set 5

Source Address	Source Port	Destination Address	Destination Port	Action
10.10.10.0	Any	10.10.10.0	23	Allow
Any	Any	10.10.10.0	23	Deny

Table 6-11 Rule Set 6

Source Address	Source Port	Destination Address	Destination Port	Action
Any	Any	10.10.10.4	80	Allow

Table 6-12 Rule Set 7a

rule (Rule 8). If someone tries to access the Web server with non-HTTP traffic (other than port 80), then the firewall skips this rule and goes to the next.

Proxy server rules allow an organization to restrict all access to a device. The external firewall would be configured as shown in Table 6-13.

The effective use of a proxy server of course requires that the DNS entries be configured as if the proxy server were the Web server. The proxy server is then configured to repackage any HTTP request packets into a new packet and retransmit to the Web server inside the firewall. The retransmission of the repackaged request requires that the rule shown in Table 6-14 enables the proxy server at 10.10.10.5 to send to the internal router, assuming the IP address for the internal Web server is 10.10.10.10. Note that in situations where an internal NAT server is used, the rule for the inbound interface uses the externally routable address, because the device performs rule filtering *before* it performs address translation. For the outbound interface, however, the address is in the native 192.168.x.x format.

The restriction on the source address then prevents anyone else from accessing the Web server from outside the internal filtering router/firewall.

Rule Set 8: The cleanup rule. As a general practice in firewall rule construction, if a request for a service is not explicitly allowed by policy, that request should be denied by a rule. The rule shown in Table 6-15 implements this practice and blocks any requests that aren't explicitly allowed by other rules.

Additional rules restricting access to specific servers or devices can be added, but they must be sequenced before the cleanup rule. Order is extremely important, as misplacement of a

Source Address	Source Port	Destination Address	Destination Port	Action
Any	Any	10.10.10.5	80	Allow

Table 6-13 Rule Set 7b

Source Address	Source Port	Destination Address	Destination Port	Action
10.10.10.5	any	10.10.10.8	80	Allow

Table 6-14 Rule Set 7c

Source Address	Source Port	Destination Address	Destination Port	Action
Any	Any	Any	Any	Deny

Table 6-15 Rule Set 8

particular rule can result in unforeseen results. One organization installed a new $50,000 firewall, only to discover that the security the firewall provided was too perfect—that is, nothing was allowed in, and nothing was allowed out! It wasn't until the firewall administrators realized that the rule base was out of sequence that the problem was resolved.

Tables 6-16 through 6-19 show the rule sets, in their proper sequences, for both the external and internal firewalls.

Note that the first rule prevents spoofing of internal IP addresses. The rule allowing responses to internal communications (appearing in Table 6-16 as rule 6), comes after the four rules prohibiting direct communications to or from the firewall (rules 2–5 in Table 6-16). In reality rules 4 and 5 are redundant—rule 1 covers their actions. They are listed here for illustrative purposes. Next comes the rules governing access to the SMTP server, denial of ping and Telnet access, and access to the HTTP server. If heavy traffic to the HTTP server is expected, move the HTTP server rule closer to the top (for example, into the position of rule 2), which would expedite rule processing for external communications. Rules 8 and 9 are actually unnecessary as the cleanup rule would take care of their tasks. The final rule in Table 6-16 denies any other types of communications. In the outbound rule set (Table 6-17) the first rule allows the firewall, system, or network administrator to access any device, including the firewall. Since this rule is on the outbound side, you do not need to worry about external attackers or spoofers. The next four rules prohibit access to and by the firewall itself, with the remaining rules allowing outbound communications and denying all else.

Note the similarities and differences in the two firewalls' rule sets. The internal filtering router/ firewall rule sets, shown in Tables 6-18 and 6-19, have to both protect against traffic to and allow traffic from the internal network (192.168.2.0). Most of the rules in Tables 6-18 and 6-19 are similar to those in Tables 6-16 and 6-17: allowing responses to internal communications; denying communications to and from the firewall itself; and allowing all outbound internal traffic.

Rule #	Source Address	Source Port	Destination Address	Destination Port	Action
1	10.10.10.0	Any	Any	Any	Deny
2	Any	Any	10.10.10.1	Any	Deny
3	Any	Any	10.10.10.2	Any	Deny
4	10.10.10.1	Any	Any	Any	Deny
5	10.10.10.2	Any	Any	Any	Deny
6	Any	Any	10.10.10.0	>1023	Allow
7	Any	Any	10.10.10.6	25	Allow
8	Any	Any	10.10.10.0	7	Deny
9	Any	Any	10.10.10.0	23	Deny
10	Any	Any	10.10.10.4	80	Allow
11	Any	Any	Any	Any	Deny

Table 6-16 External Filtering Firewall Inbound Interface Rule Set

Rule #	Source Address	Source Port	Destination Address	Destination Port	Action
1	10.10.10.12	Any	10.10.10.0	Any	Allow
2	Any	Any	10.10.10.1	Any	Deny
3	Any	Any	10.10.10.2	Any	Deny
4	10.10.10.1	Any	Any	Any	Deny
5	10.10.10.2	Any	Any	Any	Deny
6	10.10.10.0	Any	Any	Any	Allow
7	Any	Any	Any	Any	Deny

Table 6-17 External Filtering Firewall Outbound Interface Rule Set

Rule #	Source Address	Source Port	Destination Address	Destination Port	Action
1	Any	Any	10.10.10.3	Any	Deny
2	Any	Any	10.10.10.7	Any	Deny
3	10.10.10.3	Any	Any	Any	Deny
4	10.10.10.7	Any	Any	Any	Deny
5	Any	Any	10.10.10.0	>1023	Allow
7	10.10.10.5	Any	10.10.10.8	Any	Allow
8	Any	Any	Any	Any	Deny

Table 6-18 Internal Filtering Firewall Inbound Interface Rule Set

Rule #	Source Address	Source Port	Destination Address	Destination Port	Action
1	Any	Any	10.10.10.3	Any	Deny
2	Any	Any	192.168.2.1	Any	Deny
3	10.10.10.3	Any	Any	Any	Deny
4	192.168.2.1	Any	Any	Any	Deny
5	Any	Any	192.168.2.0	>1023	Allow
6	192.168.2.0	Any	Any	Any	Allow
8	Any	Any	Any	Any	Deny

Table 6-19 Internal Filtering Firewall Outbound Interface Rule Set

Because the 192.168.2.x network is an unrouteable network, external communications are handled by the NAT server, which maps internal (192.168.2.0) addresses to external (10.10.10.0) addresses. This prevents an attacker from compromising one of the internal boxes and accessing the internal network with it. The exception is the proxy server (rule 7 in

Table 6-19 on the internal router's inbound interface), which should be very carefully configured. If the organization does not need the proxy server, as in cases where all externally accessible services are provided from machines in the DMZ, then rule 7 is not needed. Note that there are no ping and Telnet rules in Tables 6-18 or 6-19. This is because the external firewall filters these external requests out. The last rule, rule 8, provides cleanup and may not be needed, depending on the firewall.

Content Filters

Another utility that can help protect an organization's systems from misuse and unintentional denial-of-service problems, and which is often closely associated with firewalls, is the **content filter**. A content filter is a software filter—technically not a firewall—that allows administrators to restrict access to content from within a network. It is essentially a set of scripts or programs that restricts user access to certain networking protocols and Internet locations, or restricts users from receiving general types or specific examples of Internet content. Some refer to content filters as **reverse firewalls**, as their primary purpose is to restrict internal access to external material. In most common implementation models, the content filter has two components: rating and filtering. The rating is like a set of firewall rules for Web sites and is common in residential content filters. The rating can be complex, with multiple access control settings for different levels of the organization, or it can be simple, with a basic allow/deny scheme like that of a firewall. The filtering is a method used to restrict specific access requests to the identified resources, which may be Web sites, servers, or whatever resources the content filter administrator configures. This is sort of a reverse ACL (technically speaking, a capability table), in that whereas an ACL normally records a set of users that have access to resources, this control list records resources which the user cannot access.

The first content filters were systems designed to restrict access to specific Web sites, and were stand-alone software applications. These could be configured in either an exclusive or inclusive manner. In an exclusive mode, certain sites are specifically excluded. The problem with this approach is that there may be thousands of Web sites that an organization wants to exclude, and more might be added every hour. The inclusive mode works from a list of sites that are specifically permitted. In order to have a site added to the list, the user must submit a request to the content filter manager, which could be time-consuming and restrict business operations. Newer models of content filters are protocol-based, examining content as it is dynamically displayed and restricting or permitting access based on a logical interpretation of content.

The most common content filters restrict users from accessing Web sites with obvious non-business related material, such as pornography, or deny incoming spam e-mail. Content filters can be small add-on software programs for the home or office, such as NetNanny or SurfControl, or corporate applications, such as the Novell Border Manager. The benefit of implementing content filters is the assurance that employees are not distracted by non-business material and cannot waste organizational time and resources. The downside is that these systems require extensive configuration and ongoing maintenance to keep the list of unacceptable destinations or the source addresses for incoming restricted e-mail up-to-date. Some newer content filtering applications (like newer antivirus programs) come with a service of downloadable files that update the database of restrictions. These applications work by matching either a list of disapproved or approved Web sites and by matching key content words, such as "nude" and "sex." Creators of restricted content have, of course, realized this and work to bypass the restrictions by suppressing these types of trip words, thus creating additional problems for networking and security professionals.

Protecting Remote Connections

The networks that organizations create are seldom used only by people at that location. When connections are made between one network and another, the connections are arranged and managed carefully. Installing such network connections requires using leased lines or other data channels provided by common carriers, and therefore these connections are usually permanent and secured under the requirements of a formal service agreement. But when individuals—whether they be employees in their homes, contract workers hired for specific assignments, or other workers who are traveling—seek to connect to an organization's network(s), a more flexible option must be provided. In the past, organizations provided these remote connections exclusively through dial-up services like Remote Authentication Service (RAS). Since the Internet has become more widespread in recent years, other options such as virtual private networks (VPNs) have become more popular.

Remote Access

Before the Internet emerged, organizations created private networks and allowed individuals and other organizations to connect to them using dial-up or leased line connections. (In the current networking environment, where Internet connections are quite common, dial-up access and leased lines from customer networks are used less frequently.) The connections between company networks and the Internet use firewalls to safeguard that interface. Although connections via dial-up and leased lines are becoming less popular, they are still quite common. And it is a widely held view that these unsecured, dial-up connection points represent a substantial exposure to attack. An attacker who suspects that an organization has dial-up lines can use a device called a war dialer to locate the connection points. A **war dialer** is an automatic phone-dialing program that dials every number in a configured range (e.g., 555-1000 to 555-2000), and checks to see if a person, answering machine, or modem picks up. If a modem answers, the war dialer program makes a note of the number and then moves to the next target number. The attacker then attempts to hack into the network via the identified modem connection using a variety of techniques. Dial-up network connectivity is usually less sophisticated than that deployed with Internet connections. For the most part, simple username and password schemes are the only means of authentication. However, some technologies, such as RADIUS systems, TACACS, and CHAP password systems, have improved the authentication process, and there are even systems now that use strong encryption.

RADIUS, TACACS, and Diameter RADIUS and TACACS are systems that authenticate the credentials of users who are trying to access an organization's network via a dial-up connection. Typical dial-up systems place the responsibility for the authentication of users on the system directly connected to the modems. If there are multiple points of entry into the dial-up system, this authentication system can become difficult to manage. The **Remote Authentication Dial-In User Service (RADIUS)** system centralizes the management of user authentication by placing the responsibility for authenticating each user in the central

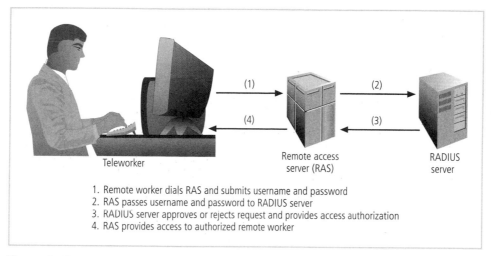

Figure 6-16 RADIUS Configuration

Source: Course Technology/Cengage Learning

RADIUS server. When a remote access server (RAS) receives a request for a network connection from a dial-up client, it passes the request, along with the user's credentials, to the RADIUS server. RADIUS then validates the credentials and passes the resulting decision (accept or deny) back to the accepting remote access server. Figure 6-16 shows the typical configuration of an RAS system.

An emerging alternative that is derived from RADIUS is the Diameter protocol. The **Diameter protocol** defines the minimum requirements for a system that provides authentication, authorization, and accounting (AAA) services and can go beyond these basics and add commands and/or object attributes. Diameter security uses existing encryption standards including Internet Protocol Security (IPSec) or Transport Layer Security (TLS), both well-regarded protocols, and its cryptographic capabilities are extensible and will be able to use future encryption protocols as they are implemented. Diameter capable devices are emerging into the marketplace and this protocol is expected to become the dominant form of AAA services.

The **Terminal Access Controller Access Control System (TACACS)** is another remote access authorization system that is based on a client/server configuration. Like RADIUS, it contains a centralized database, and it validates the user's credentials at this TACACS server. There are three versions of TACACS: TACACS, Extended TACACS, and TACACS+. The original version combines authentication and authorization services. The extended version separates the steps needed to authenticate the individual or system attempting access from the steps needed to verify that the authenticated individual or system is allowed to make a given type of connection. The extended version keeps records for accountability, and to ensure that the access attempt is linked to a specific individual or system. The plus version uses dynamic passwords and incorporates two-factor authentication.

Securing Authentication with Kerberos Two authentication systems can provide secure third-party authentication: Kerberos and SESAME. **Kerberos**—named after the three-headed dog of Greek mythology (spelled Cerberus in Latin) that guards the gates to the underworld—uses symmetric key encryption to validate an individual user to various network resources. Kerberos keeps a database containing the private keys of clients and servers—in the case of a client, this key is simply the client's encrypted password. Network services running on servers in the network register with Kerberos, as do the clients that use those services. The Kerberos system knows these private keys and can authenticate one network node (client or server) to another. For example, Kerberos can authenticate a user once—at the time the user logs in to a client computer—and then, at a later time during that session, it can authorize the user to have access to a printer without requiring the user to take any additional action. Kerberos also generates temporary session keys, which are private keys given to the two parties in a conversation. The session key is used to encrypt all communications between these two parties. Typically a user logs into the network, is authenticated to the Kerberos system, and is then authenticated to other resources on the network by the Kerberos system itself.

Kerberos consists of three interacting services, all of which use a database library:

1. *Authentication server (AS), which is a Kerberos server that authenticates clients and servers.*
2. *Key Distribution Center (KDC), which generates and issues session keys.*
3. *Kerberos ticket granting service (TGS), which provides tickets to clients who request services. In Kerberos a ticket is an identification card for a particular client that verifies to the server that the client is requesting services and that the client is a valid member of the Kerberos system and therefore authorized to receive services. The ticket consists of the client's name and network address, a ticket validation starting and ending time, and the session key, all encrypted in the private key of the server from which the client is requesting services.*

Kerberos is based on the following principles:

- *The KDC knows the secret keys of all clients and servers on the network.*
- *The KDC initially exchanges information with the client and server by using these secret keys.*
- *Kerberos authenticates a client to a requested service on a server through TGS and by issuing temporary session keys for communications between the client and KDC, the server and KDC, and the client and server.*
- *Communications then take place between the client and server using these temporary session keys.*[7]

Figures 6-17 and 6-18 illustrate this process.

Kerberos may be obtained free of charge from MIT at *http://web.mit.edu/Kerberos/*, but if you use it, be aware of some fundamental problems. If the Kerberos servers are subjected to denial-of-service attacks, no client can request services. If the Kerberos servers, service providers, or clients' machines are compromised, their private key information may also be compromised.

SESAME The Secure European System for Applications in a Multivendor Environment (SESAME) is the result of a European research and development project partly funded by the European Commission. SESAME is similar to Kerberos in that the user is first authenticated to an authentication server and receives a token. The token is then presented to a

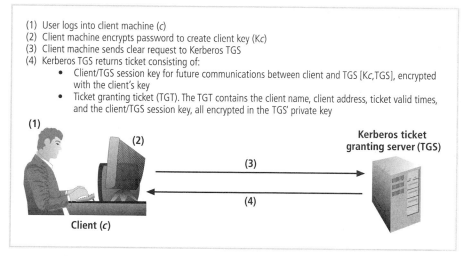

(1) User logs into client machine (*c*)
(2) Client machine encrypts password to create client key (K*c*)
(3) Client machine sends clear request to Kerberos TGS
(4) Kerberos TGS returns ticket consisting of:
  - Client/TGS session key for future communications between client and TGS [K*c*,TGS], encrypted with the client's key
  - Ticket granting ticket (TGT). The TGT contains the client name, client address, ticket valid times, and the client/TGS session key, all encrypted in the TGS' private key

(1)

(2)

Kerberos ticket granting server (TGS)

(3)

(4)

Client (*c*)

Figure 6-17 Kerberos Login

Source: Course Technology/Cengage Learning

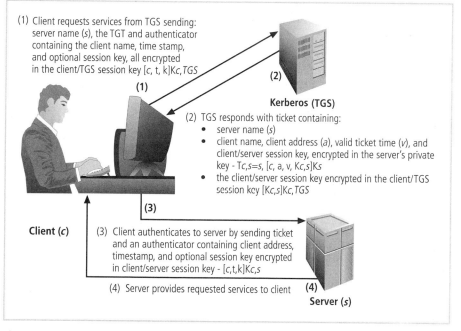

(1) Client requests services from TGS sending: server name (*s*), the TGT and authenticator containing the client name, time stamp, and optional session key, all encrypted in the client/TGS session key [*c*, t, k]K*c*,TGS

(1)

(2)

Kerberos (TGS)

(2) TGS responds with ticket containing:
  - server name (*s*)
  - client name, client address (*a*), valid ticket time (*v*), and client/server session key, encrypted in the server's private key - T*c*,*s*=*s*, [*c*, a, v, K*c*,*s*]K*s*
  - the client/server session key encrypted in the client/TGS session key [K*c*,*s*]K*c*,TGS

(3)

Client (*c*)

(3) Client authenticates to server by sending ticket and an authenticator containing client address, timestamp, and optional session key encrypted in client/server session key - [*c*,t,k]K*c*,*s*

(4) Server provides requested services to client

(4)

Server (*s*)

Figure 6-18 Kerberos Request for Services

Source: Course Technology/Cengage Learning

privilege attribute server (instead of a ticket granting service as in Kerberos) as proof of identity to gain a privilege attribute certificate (PAC). The PAC is like the ticket in Kerberos; however, a PAC conforms to the standards of the European Computer Manufacturers Association (ECMA) and the International Organization for Standardization/International Telecommunications Union (ISO/ITU-T). The remaining differences lie in the security protocols and distribution methods. SESAME uses public key encryption to distribute secret keys. SESAME also builds on the Kerberos model by adding additional and more sophisticated access control features, more scalable encryption systems, improved manageability, auditing features, and the option to delegate responsibility for allowing access.

Virtual Private Networks (VPNs)

Virtual private networks are implementations of cryptographic technology (which you learn about in Chapter 8 of this book). A **virtual private network** (VPN) is a private and secure network connection between systems that uses the data communication capability of an unsecured and public network. The Virtual Private Network Consortium (VPNC) (*www.vpnc. org*) defines a VPN as "a private data network that makes use of the public telecommunication infrastructure, maintaining privacy through the use of a tunneling protocol and security procedures."[8] VPNs are commonly used to securely extend an organization's internal network connections to remote locations. The VPNC defines three VPN technologies: trusted VPNs, secure VPNs, and hybrid VPNs. A **trusted VPN**, also known as a legacy VPN, uses leased circuits from a service provider and conducts packet switching over these leased circuits. The organization must trust the service provider, who provides contractual assurance that no one else is allowed to use these circuits and that the circuits are properly maintained and protected—hence the name *trusted* VPN.[9] **Secure VPNs** use security protocols and encrypt traffic transmitted across unsecured public networks like the Internet. A **hybrid VPN** combines the two, providing encrypted transmissions (as in secure VPN) over some or all of a trusted VPN network.

A VPN that proposes to offer a secure and reliable capability while relying on public networks must accomplish the following, regardless of the specific technologies and protocols being used:

- *Encapsulation* of incoming and outgoing data, wherein the native protocol of the client is embedded within the frames of a protocol that can be routed over the public network and be usable by the server network environment.

- *Encryption* of incoming and outgoing data to keep the data contents private while in transit over the public network, but usable by the client and server computers and/or the local networks on both ends of the VPN connection.

- *Authentication* of the remote computer and, perhaps, the remote user as well. Authentication and the subsequent authorization of the user to perform specific actions are predicated on accurate and reliable identification of the remote system and/or user.

In the most common implementation, a VPN allows a user to turn the Internet into a private network. As you know, the Internet is anything but private. However, an individual or organization can set up tunneling points across the Internet and send encrypted data back and forth, using the IP-packet-within-an-IP-packet method to transmit data safely and securely. VPNs are simple to set up and maintain and usually require only that the tunneling points be dual-homed—that is, connecting a private network to the Internet or to another outside connection point. There is VPN support built into most Microsoft server software, including NT and 2000, as well as client support for VPN services built into XP. While true private network services connections can cost hundreds of thousands of dollars to lease, configure, and maintain, a VPN can cost only a modest amount. There are a number of ways to implement a VPN. IPSec, the dominant protocol used in VPNs, uses either transport mode or tunnel mode. IPSec can be used as a stand-alone protocol, or coupled with the Layer Two Tunneling Protocol (L2TP).

Transport Mode In transport mode, the data within an IP packet is encrypted, but the header information is not. This allows the user to establish a secure link directly with the remote host, encrypting only the data contents of the packet. The downside to this implementation is that packet eavesdroppers can still identify the destination system. Once an attacker knows the destination, he or she may be able to compromise one of the end nodes and acquire the packet information from it. On the other hand, transport mode eliminates the need for special servers and tunneling software, and allows the end users to transmit traffic from anywhere. This is especially useful for traveling or telecommuting employees. Figure 6-19 illustrates the transport mode methods of implementing VPNs.

There are two popular uses for transport mode VPNs. The first is the end to end transport of encrypted data. In this model, two end users can communicate directly, encrypting and decrypting their communications as needed. Each machine acts as the end node VPN server and client. In the second, a remote access worker or teleworker connects to an office network over the Internet by connecting to a VPN server on the perimeter. This allows the teleworker's system to work as if it were part of the local area network. The VPN server in this example acts as an intermediate node, encrypting traffic from the secure intranet and transmitting it to the remote client, and decrypting traffic from the remote client and transmitting it to its final destination. This model frequently allows the remote system to act as its own VPN server, which is a weakness, since most work-at-home employees do not have the same level of physical and logical security they would have if they worked in the office.

Tunnel Mode Tunnel mode establishes two perimeter tunnel servers that encrypt all traffic that will traverse an unsecured network. In tunnel mode, the entire client packet is encrypted and added as the data portion of a packet addressed from one tunneling server

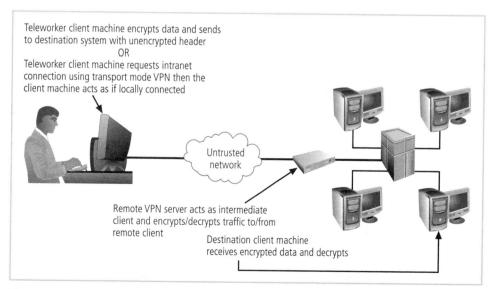

Figure 6-19 Transport Mode VPN

Source: Course Technology/Cengage Learning

Offline
VPN v. Dial-up[10]

Modern organizations can no longer afford to have their knowledge workers "chained" to hardwired local networks and resources. The increase in broadband home services and public Wi-Fi networks has increased use of VPN technologies, enabling remote connections to the organization's network to be established from remote locations, as when, for example, employees work from home or are traveling on business trips. Road warriors can now access their corporate e-mail and local network resources from wherever they happen to be.

Remote access falls into three broad categories: (1) connections with full network access, where the remote computer acts as if it were a node on the organization's network; (2) feature-based connections, where users need access to specific, discrete network features like e-mail or file transfers; and (3) connections that allow remote control of a personal computer, usually in the worker's permanent office. It is the first category of connections that use VPN technologies instead of the traditional dial-up access based on dedicated inbound phone lines.

In the past, mobile workers used remote access servers (RAS) over dial-up or ISDN leased lines to connect to company networks from remote locations (that is, when they were working from home or traveling). All things considered, RAS was probably more secure than a solution that uses VPN technology, as the connection was made on a truly private network. However, RAS is expensive because it depends on dedicated phone circuits, specialized equipment, and aging infrastructure.

VPN networking solutions make use of the public Internet. It is a solution that offers industrial-grade security. VPN today uses two different approaches to the technology—IPSec and Secure Sockets Layer (SSL). IPSec is more secure, but is more expensive and requires more effort to administer. SSL is already available on most common Internet browsers and offers broader compatibility without requiring special software on the client computer. While SSL-based VPNs have a certain attractiveness on account of their wide applicability and lower cost, they are not a perfect solution. The fact that they can be used nearly anywhere makes losses from user lapses and purposeful abuse more likely.

to another. The receiving server decrypts the packet and sends it to the final address. The primary benefit to this model is that an intercepted packet reveals nothing about the true destination system.

One example of a tunnel mode VPN is provided with Microsoft's Internet Security and Acceleration (ISA) Server. With ISA Server, an organization can establish a gateway-to-gateway tunnel, encapsulating data within the tunnel. ISA can use the Point-to-Point Tunneling Protocol (PPTP), L2TP, or IPSec technologies. Additional detail on these protocols is provided in Chapter 8. Figure 6-20 shows an example of tunnel mode VPN implementation. On the

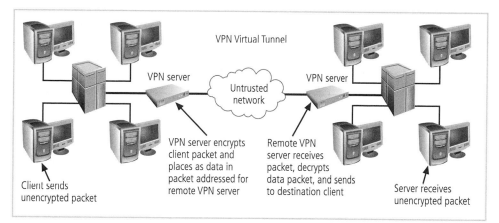

Figure 6-20 Tunnel Mode VPN

Source: Course Technology/Cengage Learning

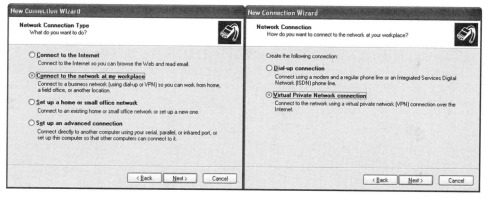

Figure 6-21 VPN Client in Windows XP

Source: Course Technology/Cengage Learning

client end, a user with Windows 2000 or XP can establish a VPN by configuring his or her system to connect to a VPN server. The process is straightforward. First, connect to the Internet through an ISP or direct network connection. Second, establish the link with the remote VPN server. Figure 6-21 shows the connection screens used to configure the VPN link.

Selected Readings

There are many excellent sources of additional information in the area of information security. A few that can add to your understanding of this chapter's content are listed here:

- *Building Internet Firewalls*, 2nd Edition by Elizabeth D. Zwicky, Simon Cooper, and D. Brent Chapman. 2000. O'Reilly Media.

- *Firewall Policies and VPN Configurations* by Syngress Publishing. 2006.

- *Firewall Fundamentals* by Wes Noonan and Ido Dubrawsky. 2006. Cisco Press.

Chapter Summary

- Access control is a process that describes how systems determine if and how to admit a user into a trusted area of the organization.

- Mandatory access controls offer users and data owners little or no control over access to information resources. MACs are often associated with a data classification scheme where each collection of information is rated with a sensitivity level. This is sometimes called lattice-based access control.

- Nondiscretionary controls are strictly-enforced versions of MACs that are managed by a central authority, whereas discretionary access controls are implemented at the discretion or option of the data user.

- All access control approaches rely on identification, authentication, authorization, and accountability.

- Authentication ensures that the entity requesting access is the entity claimed. There are three widely used types of authentication factors: something a person knows; something a person has; and something a person is or can produce.

- Strong authentication requires a minimum of two different authentication mechanisms drawn from two different authentication factors.

- A firewall is any device that prevents a specific type of information from moving between the outside network, known as the untrusted network, and the inside network, known as the trusted network.

- Firewalls can be categorized into five groupings: packet filtering, circuit gateways, MAC layers, application gateways, and hybrid firewalls.

- Packet-filtering firewalls can be implemented as static filtering, dynamic filtering, and stateful inspection firewalls.

- Firewalls are often categorized by the generation of the technology with which they are implemented, which ranges from the first to the fifth generations.

- Firewalls can be categorized by the structural approach used for the implementation, including commercial appliances, commercial systems, residential/SOHO appliances, and residential software firewalls.

- There are four common architectural implementations of firewalls: packet-filtering routers, screened host firewalls, dual-homed firewalls, and screened subnet firewalls.

- Content filtering can improve security and assist organizations in improving the manageability of the use of technology.

- Firewalls operate by evaluating data packet contents against logical rules. This logical set is most commonly referred to as firewall rules, rule base, or firewall logic.

- Dial-up protection mechanisms help secure those organizations that use modems for remote connectivity. Kerberos and SESAME are authentication technologies that add security to this technology.

- Virtual private network technology can be used to enable remote offices and users to connect to private networks securely over public networks.

Review Questions

1. What is the typical relationship among the untrusted network, the firewall, and the trusted network?

2. What is the relationship between a TCP and UDP packet? Will any specific transaction usually involve both types of packets?

3. How is an application layer firewall different from a packet-filtering firewall? Why is an application layer firewall sometimes called a proxy server?

4. How is static filtering different from dynamic filtering of packets? Which is perceived to offer improved security?

5. What is stateful inspection? How is state information maintained during a network connection or transaction?

6. What is a circuit gateway, and how does it differ from the other forms of firewalls?

7. What special function does a cache server perform? Why is this useful for larger organizations?

8. Describe how the various types of firewalls interact with the network traffic at various levels of the OSI model.

9. What is a hybrid firewall?

10. List the five generations of firewall technology. Which generations are still in common use?

11. How does a commercial-grade firewall appliance differ from a commercial-grade firewall system? Why is this difference significant?

12. Explain the basic technology that makes residential/SOHO firewall appliances effective in protecting a local network. Why is this usually adequate for protection?

13. What key features point up the superiority of residential/SOHO firewall appliances over personal computer-based firewall software?

14. How do screened host architectures for firewalls differ from screened subnet firewall architectures? Which of these offers more security for the information assets that remain on the trusted network?

15. What a sacrificial host? What is a bastion host?

16. What is a DMZ? Is this really an appropriate name for the technology, considering the function this type of subnet performs?

17. What are the three questions that must be addressed when selecting a firewall for a specific organization?

18. What is RADIUS? What advantage does it have over TACACS?

19. What is a content filter? Where is it placed in the network to gain the best result for the organization?

20. What is a VPN? Why is it becoming more widely used?

Exercises

1. Using the Web, search for "software firewalls." Examine the various alternatives available and compare their functionality, cost, features, and type of protection. Create a weighted ranking according to your own evaluation of the features and specifications of each software package.

2. Using Figure 6-15, create rule(s) necessary for both the internal and external firewalls to allow a remote user to access an internal machine from the Internet using the software Timbuktu. This requires researching the ports used by this software packet.

3. Using Figure 6-15, suppose management wants to create a "server farm" that is configured to allow a proxy firewall in the DMZ to access an internal Web server (rather than a Web server in the DMZ). Do you foresee any technical difficulties in deploying this architecture? What advantages and disadvantages are there to this implementation?

4. Using the Internet, determine what applications are commercially available to enable secure remote access to a PC.

5. Using a Microsoft Windows XP, Vista, or 7 system, open Internet Explorer. Click Internet Options on the Tools menu. Examine the contents of the Security and Privacy tabs. How can these tabs be configured to provide: (a) content filtering and (b) protection from unwanted items like cookies?

Case Exercises

The next morning at 8 o'clock, Kelvin called the meeting to order.

The first person to address the group was the network design consultant, Susan Hamir. She reviewed the critical points from her earlier design report, going over the options it had presented and outlining the tradeoffs in those design choices.

When she finished, she sat down and Kelvin addressed the group again: "We need to break the logjam on this design issue. We have all the right people in this room to make the right choice for the company. Now here are the questions I want us to consider over the next three hours." Kelvin pressed the key on his PC to show a slide with a list of discussion questions on the projector screen.

Questions:

1. What questions do you think Kelvin should have included on his slide to start the discussion?

2. If the questions to be answered were broken down into two categories, they would be cost versus maintaining high security while keeping flexibility. Which is most important for SLS?

Endnotes

1. Avolio, Frederic. "Firewalls and Internet Security, the Second Hundred (Internet) Years." Accessed 6 May 2007 from *www.cisco.com/web/about/ac123/ac147/ac174/ac200/about_cisco_ipj_archive_article09186a00800c85ae.html*.

2. Wack, John. "Keeping Your Site Comfortably Secure: An Introduction to Internet Firewalls." 16 October 2002. Accessed 7 March 2007 from *www.windowsecurity.com/whitepaper/Keeping_Your_Site_Comfortably_Secure__Introduction_ to_Firewalls.html*.

3. Cisco Systems, Inc. "Inside the Cisco Centri Firewall." *Cisco Online*. Accessed 14 May 2007 from *www.cisco.com/univercd/cc/td/doc/product/iaabu/centri4/user/scf4ch5.htm#xtocid157876*.

4. Elron Software, Inc. "Choosing the Best Firewall for Your Growing Network." *ZDNet.co.uk*. 22 April 2002. Accessed 7 March 2007 from *http://whitepapers.zdnet.co.uk/0,1000000651,260001940p-39000460q,00.htm*.

5. Laura Taylor. "Guidelines for Configuring your Firewall Rule-Set." *Tech Update Online*. 12 April 2001. Accessed 14 May 2007 from *http://techupdate.zdnet.com/techupdate/stories/main/0,14179,2707159,00.html*.

6. Webopedia.com. "SSL." Accessed 14 May 2007 from *www.webopedia.com/TERM/S/SSL.html*.

7. Krutz, Ronald L., and Vines, Russell Dean. *The CISSP Prep Guide: Mastering the Ten Domains of Computer Security*. New York: John Wiley and Sons Inc., 2001, 40.

8. VPN Consortium. "VPN Technologies: Definitions and Requirements." March 2006. Accessed 14 May 2007 from *www.vpnc.org/vpn-technologies.html*.

9. Ibid.

10. Lee, Oo Gin. "Reach for the Remote." *Asia Computer Weekly*. 3 December 2003, 1.

6

Security Technology: Intrusion Detection and Prevention Systems, and Other Security Tools

Do not wait; the time will never be just right. Start where you stand, and work with whatever tools you may have at your command, and better tools will be found as you go along.

NAPOLEON HILL (1883–1970)
FOUNDER OF *THE SCIENCE OF SUCCESS*

Miller Harrison was going to make them sorry and make them pay. Earlier today, his contract with SLS had been terminated, and he'd been sent home. Oh sure, the big shot manager, Charlie Moody, had said Miller would still get paid for the two weeks remaining in his contract, and that the decision was based on "changes in the project and evolving needs as project work continued," but Miller knew better. He knew he'd been let go because of that know-nothing Kelvin and his simpering lapdog Laverne Nguyen. And now he was going to show them and everyone else at SLS who knew more about security.

Miller knew that the secret to hacking into a network successfully was to apply the same patience, attention to detail, and dogged determination that defending a network required. He also knew that the first step in a typical hacking protocol was footprinting—that is, getting a fully annotated diagram of the network. Miller already had one of these—in a violation of company policy, he had brought a copy home last week when Laverne first started trying to tell him how to do his job.

When they terminated his contract today, Miller's supervisors made him turn in his company laptop and then actually had the nerve to search his briefcase. By then, however, Miller had already stashed all the files and access codes he needed to wage an attack.

To begin, he activated his VPN client to connect to the SLS network from his rented connection at an Internet cafe. He realized almost immediately that Charlie Moody had also confiscated the crypto-token that enabled him to use the VPN for remote access. No problem, Miller thought. If the front door was locked, he would try the back door. He cabled his laptop to the analog phone line, opened up a modem dialing program and typed in the dial-up number for SLS he had gotten from the network administrator last week. After the dialer established the connection, Miller positioned his hands on the keyboard, and then he read the prompt on his monitor:

> *SLS Inc. Company Use Only. Unauthorized use is prohibited and subject to prosecution.*
>
> *Enter Passphrase:*

Apparently the SLS security team had rerouted all dial-up requests to the same RADIUS authentication server that the VPN used. So, he was locked out of the back door too. But Miller moved on to his next option, which was to use another back door of his very own. The back door consisted of a zombie program he'd installed on the company's extranet quality assurance server. No one at SLS worried about securing the QA server since it did not store any production data. In fact, the server wasn't even subject to all the change control procedures that were applied to other systems on the extranet. Miller activated the program he used to remotely control the zombie program and typed in the IP address of the computer running the zombie. No response. He opened up a command window and pinged the zombie. The computer at that address answered each ping promptly, which meant that it was alive and well. Miller checked the zombie's UDP port number and ran an Nmap scan against that single computer for that port. It was closed tight. He cursed the firewall, the policy that controlled it, and the technicians that kept it up to date.

With all of his pre-planned payback cut off at the edge of SLS's network, he decided to continue his hack by going back to the first step—specifically, to perform a detailed fingerprinting of all SLS Internet addresses. Since the front and both back doors were locked, it was time to get a new floor plan. He launched a simple network port scanner on his Linux laptop. He restarted Nmap and configured it to scan the entire IP address range for SLS's extranet. With a single keystroke, he unleashed the port scanner on the SLS network.

LEARNING OBJECTIVES:

Upon completion of this material, you should be able to:

- Identify and describe the categories and operating models of intrusion detection and prevention systems
- Define and describe honeypots, honeynets, and padded cell systems
- List and define the major categories of scanning and analysis tools, and describe the specific tools used within each of these categories
- Explain the various methods of access control, including the use of biometric access mechanisms

Introduction

The protection of an organization's information assets relies at least as much on people as on technical controls, but technical solutions, guided by policy and properly implemented, are an essential component of an information security program. Chapter 6 introduced the subject of security technology and covered some specific technologies, including firewalls, dial-up protection mechanisms, content filtering, and VPNs. This chapter builds on that discussion by describing additional and more advanced technologies—intrusion detection and prevention systems, honeypots, honeynets, padded cell systems, scanning and analysis tools, and access controls—that organizations can use to enhance the security of their information assets.

Intrusion Detection and Prevention Systems

An **intrusion** occurs when an attacker attempts to gain entry into or disrupt the normal operations of an information system, almost always with the intent to do harm. Even when such attacks are self-propagating, as in the case of viruses and distributed denial-of-service attacks, they are almost always instigated by someone whose purpose is to harm an organization. Often, the differences among intrusion types lie with the attacker—some intruders don't care which organizations they harm and prefer to remain anonymous, while others crave notoriety.

Intrusion *prevention* consists of activities that deter an intrusion. Some important intrusion prevention activities are writing and implementing good enterprise information security policy, planning and executing effective information security programs, installing and testing technology-based information security countermeasures (such as firewalls and intrusion detection systems), and conducting and measuring the effectiveness of employee training and awareness activities. Intrusion *detection* consists of procedures and systems that identify system intrusions. Intrusion *reaction* encompasses the actions an organization takes when an intrusion is detected. These actions seek to limit the loss from an intrusion and return operations to a normal state as rapidly as possible. Intrusion *correction* activities finalize the restoration of operations to a normal state and seek to identify the source and method of the intrusion in order to ensure that the same type of attack cannot occur again—thus reinitiating intrusion prevention.

Information security **intrusion detection systems (IDSs)** became commercially available in the late 1990s. An IDS works like a burglar alarm in that it detects a violation (some system activity analogous to an opened or broken window) and activates an alarm. This alarm can be audible and/or visual (producing noise and lights, respectively), or it can be silent (an e-mail message or pager alert). With almost all IDSs, system administrators can choose the configuration of the various alerts and the alarm levels associated with each type of alert. Many IDSs enable administrators to configure the systems to notify them directly of trouble via e-mail or pagers. The systems can also be configured—again like a burglar alarm—to notify an external security service organization of a "break-in." The configurations that enable IDSs to provide customized levels of detection and response are quite complex. A current extension of IDS technology is the **intrusion prevention system (IPS)**, which can detect an intrusion and also prevent that intrusion from successfully attacking the organization by means of an active response. Because the two systems often coexist, the combined term **intrusion detection and prevention system (IDPS)** is generally used to describe current anti-intrusion technologies.

IDPS Terminology

In order to understand IDPS operational behavior, you must first become familiar with some IDPS terminology. The following list of IDPS industry standard terms and definitions is taken from a well-known information security company, TruSecure:

- **Alert** or **alarm:** An indication that a system has just been attacked or is under attack. IDPS alerts and alarms take the form of audible signals, e-mail messages, pager notifications, or pop-up windows.

- **Evasion:** The process by which attackers change the format and/or timing of their activities to avoid being detected by the IDPS.

- **False attack stimulus:** An event that triggers an alarm when no actual attack is in progress. Scenarios that test the configuration of IDPSs may use false attack stimuli to determine if the IDPSs can distinguish between these stimuli and real attacks.

- **False negative:** The failure of an IDPS to react to an actual attack event. This is the most grievous failure, since the purpose of an IDPS is to detect and respond to attacks.

- **False positive:** An alert or alarm that occurs in the absence of an actual attack. A false positive can sometimes be produced when an IDPS mistakes normal system activity for an attack. False positives tend to make users insensitive to alarms and thus reduce their reactivity to actual intrusion events.

- **Noise:** Alarm events that are accurate and noteworthy but that do not pose significant threats to information security. Unsuccessful attacks are the most common source of IDPS noise, and some of these may in fact be triggered by scanning and enumeration tools deployed by network users without intent to do harm.

- **Site policy:** The rules and configuration guidelines governing the implementation and operation of IDPSs within the organization.

- **Site policy awareness:** An IDPS's ability to dynamically modify its configuration in response to environmental activity. A so-called smart IDPS can adapt its reactions in response to administrator guidance over time and circumstances of the current local environment. A smart IDPS logs events that fit a specific profile instead of minor events, such as file modification or failed user logins. The smart IDPS knows when it does *not* need to alert the administrator—for example, when an attack is using a known and documented exploit that the system is protected from.

- **True attack stimulus:** An event that triggers alarms and causes an IDPS to react as if a real attack is in progress. The event may be an actual attack, in which an attacker is at work on a system compromise attempt, or it may be a drill, in which security personnel are using hacker tools to conduct tests of a network segment.

- **Tuning:** The process of adjusting an IDPS to maximize its efficiency in detecting true positives, while minimizing both false positives and false negatives.

- **Confidence value:** The measure of an IDPS's ability to correctly detect and identify certain types of attacks. The confidence value an organization places in the IDPS is based on experience and past performance measurements. The confidence value, which is based upon *fuzzy logic*, helps an administrator determine how likely it is that an IDPS alert or alarm indicates an actual attack in progress. For example, if a system deemed 90 percent capable of accurately reporting a denial-of-service attack sends a denial-of-service alert, there is a high probability that an actual attack is occurring.

- **Alarm filtering:** The process of classifying IDPS alerts so that they can be more effectively managed. An IDPS administrator can set up alarm filtering by running the system for a while to track what types of false positives it generates and then adjusting the alarm classifications. For example, the administrator may set the IDPS to discard alarms produced by false attack stimuli or normal network operations. Alarm filters are similar to packet filters in that they can filter items by their source or destination IP addresses, but they can also filter by operating systems, confidence values, alarm type, or alarm severity.

- **Alarm clustering and compaction:** A process of grouping almost identical alarms that happen at close to the same time into a single higher-level alarm. This consolidation reduces the number of alarms generated, thereby reducing administrative overhead, and also identifies a relationship among multiple alarms. This clustering may be based on combinations of frequency, similarity in attack signature, similarity in attack target, or other criteria that are defined by the system administrators.

Why Use an IDPS?

According to the NIST documentation on industry best practices, there are several compelling reasons to acquire and use an IDPS:

1. To prevent problem behaviors by increasing the perceived risk of discovery and punishment for those who would attack or otherwise abuse the system

2. To detect attacks and other security violations that are not prevented by other security measures

3. To detect and deal with the preambles to attacks (commonly experienced as network probes and other "doorknob rattling" activities)

4. To document the existing threat to an organization

5. To act as quality control for security design and administration, especially in large and complex enterprises

6. To provide useful information about intrusions that do take place, allowing improved diagnosis, recovery, and correction of causative factors[1]

One of the best reasons to install an IDPS is that they serve as deterrents by increasing the fear of detection among would-be attackers. If internal and external users know that an organization has an intrusion detection and prevention system, they are less likely to probe or attempt to compromise it, just as criminals are much less likely to break into a house that has an apparent burglar alarm.

Another reason to install an IDPS is to cover the organization when its network cannot protect itself against known vulnerabilities or is unable to respond to a rapidly changing threat environment. There are many factors that can delay or undermine an organization's ability to secure its systems from attack and subsequent loss. For example, even though popular information security technologies such as scanning tools (discussed later in this chapter) allow security administrators to evaluate the readiness of their systems, they may still fail to detect or correct a known deficiency or may perform the vulnerability-detection process too infrequently. In addition, even when a vulnerability is detected in a timely manner, it cannot always be corrected quickly. Also, because such corrective measures usually require that the administrator install patches and upgrades, they are subject to fluctuations in the administrator's workload. To further complicate the matter, sometimes services known to be vulnerable cannot be disabled or otherwise protected because they are essential to ongoing operations. At such times—namely, when there is a known vulnerability or deficiency in the system—an IDPS can be set up to detect attacks or attempts to exploit existing weaknesses, and thus it becomes an important part of the strategy of defense in depth.

IDPSs can also help administrators detect the preambles to attacks. Most attacks begin with an organized and thorough probing of the organization's network environment and its defenses. This initial estimation of the defensive state of an organization's networks and systems is called *doorknob rattling* and is accomplished by means of *footprinting* (activities that gather information about the organization and its network activities and assets) and *fingerprinting* (activities that scan network locales for active systems and then identify the network services offered by the host systems). A system capable of detecting the early warning signs of footprinting and fingerprinting functions like a neighborhood watch that spots would-be burglars testing doors and windows, enabling administrators to prepare for a potential attack or to take actions to minimize potential losses from an attack.

A fourth reason for acquiring an IDPS is threat documentation. The implementation of security technology usually requires that project proponents document the threat from which the organization must be protected. IDPSs are one means of collecting such data. (To collect attack information in support of an IDPS implementation, you can begin with a freeware IDPS tool such as Snort).

Data collected by an IDPS can also help management with quality assurance and continuous improvement; IDPSs consistently pick up information about attacks that have successfully compromised the outer layers of information security controls such as a firewall. This information can be used to identify and repair emergent or residual flaws in the security and network architectures and thus help the organization expedite its incident response process and make other continuous improvements.

Finally, even if an IDPS fails to prevent an intrusion, it can still assist in the after-attack review by providing information on how the attack occurred, what the intruder accomplished, and which methods the attacker employed. This information can be used to remedy deficiencies and to prepare the organization's network environment for future attacks. The IDPS can also provide forensic information that may be useful should the attacker be caught and prosecuted or sued.[2]

> *According to the NIST 800-94 guide,*
>
> *IPS technologies are differentiated from IDS technologies by one characteristic: IPS technologies can respond to a detected threat by attempting to prevent it from succeeding. They use several response techniques, which can be divided into the following groups:*
>
> - *The IPS stops the attack itself. Examples of how this could be done are as follows:*
>   - *Terminate the network connection or user session that is being used for the attack*
>   - *Block access to the target (or possibly other likely targets) from the offending user account, IP address, or other attacker attribute*
>   - *Block all access to the targeted host, service, application, or other resource.*

- *The IPS changes the security environment. The IPS could change the configuration of other security controls to disrupt an attack. Common examples are reconfiguring a network device (e.g., firewall, router, switch) to block access from the attacker or to the target and altering a host-based firewall on a target to block incoming attacks. Some IPSs can even cause patches to be applied to a host if the IPS detects that the host has vulnerabilities.*

- *The IPS changes the attack's content. Some IPS technologies can remove or replace malicious portions of an attack to make it benign. A simple example is an IPS removing an infected file attachment from an e-mail and then permitting the cleaned e-mail to reach its recipient. A more complex example is an IPS that acts as a proxy and normalizes incoming requests, which means that the proxy repackages the payloads of the requests, discarding header information. This might cause certain attacks to be discarded as part of the normalization process.*[3]

Types of IDPS

IDPSs operate as network- or host-based systems. A network-based IDPS is focused on protecting network information assets. Two specialized subtypes of network-based IDPS are the wireless IDPS and the network behavior analysis (NBA) IDPS. The wireless IDPS focuses on wireless networks, as the name indicates, while the NBA IDPS examines traffic flow on a network in an attempt to recognize abnormal patterns like DDoS, malware, and policy violations.

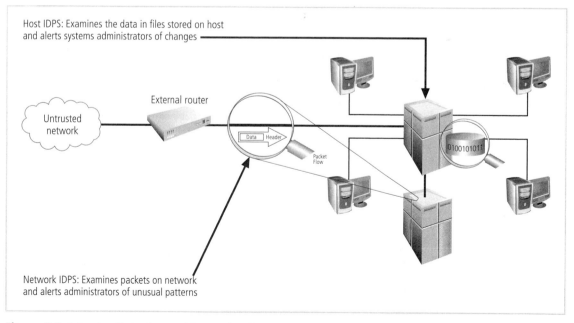

Figure 7-1 Intrusion Detection and Prevention Systems

Source: Course Technology/Cengage Learning

A host-based IDPS protects the server or host's information assets; the example shown in Figure 7-1 monitors both network connection activity and current information states on host servers. The application-based model works on one or more host systems that support a single application and defends that specific application from special forms of attack.

Network-Based IDPS A **network-based IDPS** (**NIDPS**) resides on a computer or appliance connected to a segment of an organization's network and monitors network traffic on that network segment, looking for indications of ongoing or successful attacks. When the NIDPS identifies activity that it is programmed to recognize as an attack, it responds by sending notifications to administrators. When examining incoming packets, an NIDPS looks for patterns within network traffic such as large collections of related items of a certain type—which could indicate that a denial-of-service attack is underway—or the exchange of a series of related packets in a certain pattern—which could indicate that a port scan is in progress. An NIDPS can detect many more types of attacks than a host-based IDPS, but it requires a much more complex configuration and maintenance program.

A NIDPS is installed at a specific place in the network (such as on the inside of an edge router) from where it is possible to monitor the traffic going into and out of a particular network segment. The NIDPS can be deployed to monitor a specific grouping of host computers on a specific network segment, or it may be installed to monitor all traffic between the systems that make up an entire network. When placed next to a hub, switch, or other key networking device, the NIDPS may use that device's monitoring port. The **monitoring port** also known as a switched port analysis (SPAN) port or mirror port, is a specially configured connection on a network device that is capable of viewing all of the traffic that moves through the entire device. In the early 1990s, before switches became standard for connecting networks in a shared-collision domain, hubs were used. Hubs receive traffic from one node and retransmit it to all other nodes. This configuration allows any device connected to the hub to monitor all traffic passing through the hub. Unfortunately, it also represents a security risk, since anyone connected to the hub can monitor all the traffic that moves through that network segment. Switches, on the other hand, create dedicated point-to-point links between their ports. These links create a higher level of transmission security and privacy and effectively prevent anyone from capturing, and thus eavesdropping on, the traffic passing through the switch. Unfortunately, the ability to capture the traffic is necessary for the use of an IDPS. Thus, monitoring ports are required. These connections enable network administrators to collect traffic from across the network for analysis by the IDPS as well as for occasional use in diagnosing network faults and measuring network performance.

Figure 7-2 shows data from the Snort Network IDPS Engine (see *www.snort.org*). In this case, the display is a sample screen from Snorby (see *snorby.org*), a client that can manage Snort as well as display the alerts generated.

To determine whether an attack has occurred or is underway, NIDPSs compare measured activity to known signatures in their knowledge base. This is accomplished by means of a special implementation of the TCP/IP stack that reassembles the packets and applies protocol stack verification, application protocol verification, or other verification and comparison techniques.

In the process of **protocol stack verification**, the NIDPSs look for invalid data packets—that is, packets that are malformed under the rules of the TCP/IP protocol. A data packet is

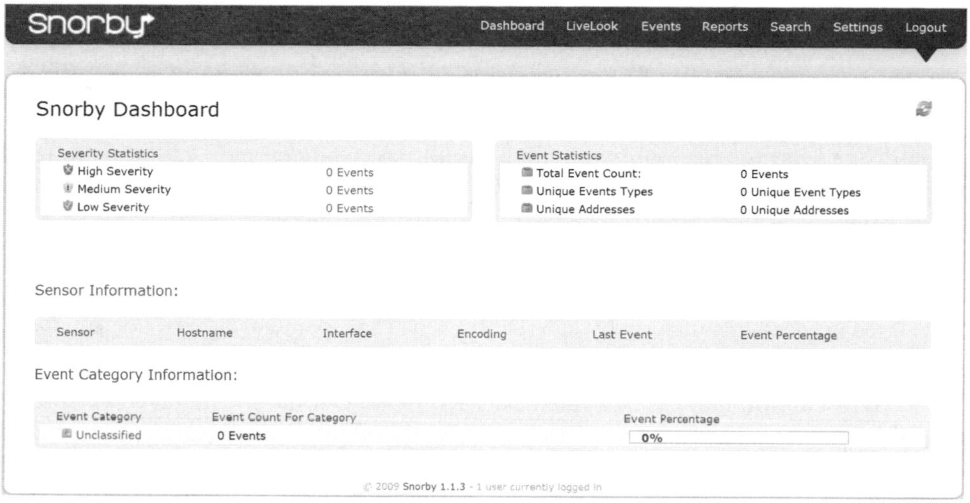

Figure 7-2 Snorby Manages Snort and Displays Alerts
Source: Course Technology/Cengage Learning

verified when its configuration matches one that is defined by the various Internet protocols. The elements of these protocols (IP, TCP, UDP, and application layers such as HTTP) are combined in a complete set called the *protocol stack* when the software is implemented in an operating system or application. Many types of intrusions, especially DoS and DDoS attacks, rely on the creation of improperly formed packets to take advantage of weaknesses in the protocol stack in certain operating systems or applications.

In **application protocol verification**, the higher-order protocols (HTTP, FTP, and Telnet) are examined for unexpected packet behavior or improper use. Sometimes an attack uses valid protocol packets but in excessive quantities (in the case of the tiny fragment attack, the packets are also excessively fragmented). While the protocol stack verification looks for violations in the protocol packet *structure*, the application protocol verification looks for violations in the protocol packet's *use*. One example of this kind of attack is DNS cache poisoning, in which valid packets exploit poorly configured DNS servers to inject false information to corrupt the servers' answers to routine DNS queries from other systems on the network. Unfortunately, this higher-order examination of traffic can have the same effect on an IDPS as it can on a firewall—that is, it slows the throughput of the system. It may be necessary to have more than one NIDPS installed, with one of them performing protocol stack verification and one performing application protocol verification.

The advantages of NIDPSs include the following:

1. Good network design and placement of NIDPS devices can enable an organization to use a few devices to monitor a large network.

2. NIDPSs are usually passive devices and can be deployed into existing networks with little or no disruption to normal network operations.

3. NIDPSs are not usually susceptible to direct attack and, in fact, may not be detectable by attackers.[4]

The disadvantages of NIDPSs include the following:

1. A NIDPS can become overwhelmed by network volume and fail to recognize attacks it might otherwise have detected. Some IDPS vendors are accommodating the need for ever faster network performance by improving the processing of detection algorithms in dedicated hardware circuits to gain a performance advantage. Additional efforts to optimize rule set processing may also reduce overall effectiveness in detecting attacks.

2. NIDPSs require access to all traffic to be monitored. The broad use of switched Ethernet networks has replaced the ubiquity of shared collision domain hubs. Since many switches have limited or no monitoring port capability, some networks are not capable of providing aggregate data for analysis by a NIDPS. Even when switches do provide monitoring ports, they may not be able to mirror all activity with a consistent and reliable time sequence.

3. NIDPSs cannot analyze encrypted packets, making some of the network traffic invisible to the process. The increasing use of encryption that hides the contents of some or all of the packet by some network services (such as SSL, SSH, and VPN) limits the effectiveness of NIDPSs.

4. NIDPSs cannot reliably ascertain if an attack was successful or not. This requires the network administrator to be engaged in an ongoing effort to evaluate the results of the logs of suspicious network activity.

5. Some forms of attack are not easily discerned by NIDPSs, specifically those involving fragmented packets. In fact, some NIDPSs are particularly vulnerable to malformed packets and may become unstable and stop functioning.[5]

Wireless NIDPS. A wireless IDPS monitors and analyzes wireless network traffic, looking for potential problems with the wireless protocols (Layers 2 and 3 of the OSI model). Unfortunately, wireless IDPSs cannot evaluate and diagnose issues with higher-layer protocols like TCP and UDP. Wireless IDPS capability can be built into a device that provides a wireless access point.

Sensor locations for wireless networks can be located at the access points, on specialized sensor components, or incorporated into selected mobile stations. Centralized management stations collect information from these sensors, much as other network-based IDPSs do, and aggregate information into a comprehensive assessment of wireless network intrusions. Some issues associated with the implementation of wireless IDPSs include:

- **Physical security:** Unlike wired network sensors, which can be physically secured, many wireless sensors are located in public areas like conference rooms, assembly areas, and hallways in order to obtain the widest possible network range. Some of these locations may even be outdoors, as more and more organization are deploying networks in external locations. Thus the physical security of these devices is an issue, which may likely require additional security configuration and monitoring.

- **Sensor range:** A wireless device's range can be affected by atmospheric conditions, building construction, and the quality of both the wireless network card and access point. Some IDPS tools allow an organization to identify the optimal location for sensors by modeling the wireless footprint based on signal strength. Sensors are most effective when their footprints overlap.

- **Access point and wireless switch locations:** Wireless components with bundled IDPS capabilities must be carefully deployed to optimize the IDPS sensor detection grid. The minimum range is just that; you must guard against the possibility of an attacker connecting to a wireless access point from a range far beyond the minimum.

- **Wired network connections:** Wireless network components work independently of the wired network when sending and receiving between stations and access points. However, a network connection eventually integrates wireless traffic with the organization's wired network. Where there is no available wired network connection, it may be impossible to deploy a sensor.

- **Cost:** The more sensors deployed, the more expensive the configuration. Wireless components typically cost more than their wired counterparts, and thus the total cost of ownership of IDPS of both wired and wireless varieties should be carefully considered.[6]

In addition to the traditional types of intrusions detected by other IDPSs, the wireless IDPS can also detect:

- Unauthorized WLANs and WLAN devices
- Poorly secured WLAN devices
- Unusual usage patterns
- The use of wireless network scanners
- Denial of service (DoS) attacks and conditions
- Impersonation and man-in-the-middle attacks[7]

Wireless IDPSs are unable to detect certain passive wireless protocol attacks, in which the attacker monitors network traffic without active scanning and probing. They are also susceptible to evasion techniques, which are described earlier in this chapter. By simply looking at wireless devices, which are often visible in public areas, attackers can custom-design evasion methods to exploit the system's channel scanning scheme. Wireless IDPSs can protect the WLAN with which they are associated, but may be susceptible to logical and physical attacks on the wireless access point or the wireless IDPS devices themselves. The best-configured IDPS in the world cannot withstand an attack from a well-placed brick.[8]

Network Behavior Analysis System NBA systems examine network traffic in order to identify problems related to the flow of traffic. They use a version of the anomaly detection method described later in this section to identify excessive packet flows such as might occur in the case of equipment malfunction, DoS attacks, virus and worm attacks, and some forms of network policy violations. NBA IDPSs typically monitor internal networks but occasionally monitor connections between internal and external networks. Typical flow data particularly relevant to intrusion detection and prevention includes:

- Source and destination IP addresses
- Source and destination TCP or UDP ports or ICMP types and codes
- Number of packets and bytes transmitted in the session
- Starting and ending timestamps for the session[9]

  Most NBA sensors can be deployed in **passive mode** *only, using the same connection methods (e.g., network tap, switch spanning port) as network-based IDPSs.*

Passive sensors that are performing direct network monitoring should be placed so that they can monitor key network locations, such as the divisions between networks, and key network segments, such as demilitarized zone (DMZ) subnets. **Inline sensors** *are typically intended for network perimeter use, so they would be deployed in close proximity to the perimeter firewalls, often between the firewall and the Internet border router to limit incoming attacks that could overwhelm the firewall. The types of events most commonly detected by NBA sensors include the following:*

- *DoS attacks (including DDoS attacks)*
- *Scanning*
- *Worms*
- *Unexpected application services (e.g., tunneled protocols, back doors, use of forbidden application protocols)*
- *Policy violations*

NBA sensors offer various intrusion prevention capabilities, including the following (grouped by sensor type):

- *Passive only*
- *Ending the current TCP session. A passive NBA sensor can attempt to end an existing TCP session by sending TCP reset packets to both endpoints.*
- *Inline only*
  - *Performing inline firewalling. Most inline NBA sensors offer firewall capabilities that can be used to drop or reject suspicious network activity.*
- *Both passive and inline*
  - *Reconfiguring other network security devices. Many NBA sensors can instruct network security devices such as firewalls and routers to reconfigure themselves to block certain types of activity or route it elsewhere, such as a quarantine virtual local area network (VLAN).*
  - *Running a third-party program or script. Some NBA sensors can run an administrator-specified script or program when certain malicious activity is detected.*[10]

Host-Based IDPS   While a network-based IDPS resides on a network segment and monitors activities across that segment, a **host-based IDPS (HIDPS)** resides on a particular computer or server, known as the host, and monitors activity only on that system. HIDPSs are also known as **system integrity verifiers**[11] because they benchmark and monitor the status of key system files and detect when an intruder creates, modifies, or deletes monitored files. An HIDPS has an advantage over an NIDPS in that it can access encrypted information traveling over the network and use it to make decisions about potential or actual attacks. Also, since the HIDPS works on only one computer system, all the traffic it examines traverses that system. The packet delivery mode, whether switched or in a shared-collision domain, is not a factor.

An HIDPS is also capable of monitoring system configuration databases, such as Windows registries, in addition to stored configuration files like .ini, .cfg, and .dat files. Most HIDPSs work on the principle of configuration or change management, which means that they record the sizes, locations, and other attributes of system files. The HIDPS triggers an alert when one of the following occurs: file attributes change, new files are created, or existing files are deleted. An HIDPS can also monitor systems logs for predefined events. The HIDPS examines these files and logs to determine if an attack is underway or has occurred and if the attack is succeeding or was successful. The HIDPS maintains its own log file so that an audit trail is available even when hackers modify files on the target system to cover their tracks. Once properly configured, an HIDPS is very reliable. The only time an HIDPS produces a false positive alert is when an authorized change occurs for a monitored file. This action can be quickly reviewed by an administrator, who may choose to disregard subsequent changes to the same set of files. If properly configured, an HIDPS can also detect when users attempt to modify or exceed their access authorization level.

An HIDPS classifies files into various categories and then sends notifications when changes occur. Most HIDPSs provide only a few general levels of alert notification. For example, an administrator can configure an HIDPS to report changes in a system folder (e.g., in C:\Windows or C:\WINNT) and changes to a security-related application (such as C:\TripWire). The configuration rules may classify changes to a specific application folder (e.g., C:\Program Files\Office) as normal and hence unreportable. Administrators can configure the system to log all activity but to page them or e-mail them only if a reportable security event occurs. Since internal application files, such as dictionaries and configuration files, and data files are frequently modified, a poorly configured HIDPS can generate a large volume of false alarms.

Managed HIDPSs can monitor multiple computers simultaneously by creating a configuration file on each monitored host and by making each HIDPS report back to a master console system, which is usually located on the system administrator's computer. This master console monitors the information provided by the managed hosts and notifies the administrator when it senses recognizable attack conditions. Figure 7-3 shows a sample screen from Inox Verisys (File Integrity Monitor), a popular HIDPS (see *www.ionx.co.uk*).

One of the most common methods of categorizing folders and files is by color coding. Critical systems components are coded red and usually include the system registry, any folders containing the OS kernel, and application software. Critically important data should also be included in the red category. Support components, such as device drivers and other relatively important files, are generally coded yellow; user data is usually coded green, not because it is unimportant, but because monitoring changes to user data is practically difficult and strategically less urgent. User data files are frequently modified, but systems kernel files, for example, should only be modified during upgrades or installations. If the three-tier system is too simplistic, an organization can use a scale of 0–100, with 100 being most mission-critical and 0 being unimportant. It is not unusual, however, for such systems to result in confusion over issues such as how to respond to level 67 and 68 intrusions. Sometimes simpler is better.

The advantages of HIDPSs include:

1. An HIDPS can detect local events on host systems and also detect attacks that may elude a network-based IDPS.

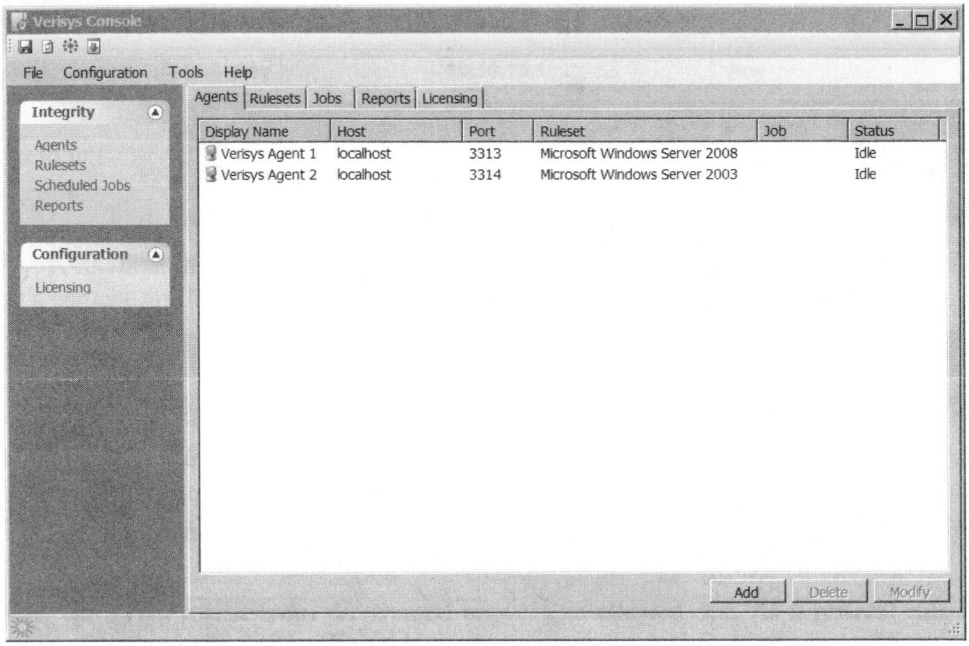

Figure 7-3 Inox Verisys (File Integrity Monitor) HIDPS
Source: Course Technology/Cengage Learning

2. An HIDPS functions on the host system, where encrypted traffic will have been decrypted and is available for processing.

3. The use of switched network protocols does not affect an HIDPS.

4. An HIDPS can detect inconsistencies in how applications and systems programs were used by examining the records stored in audit logs. This can enable it to detect some types of attacks, including Trojan horse programs.[12]

The disadvantages of HIDPSs include:

1. HIDPSs pose more management issues because they are configured and managed on each monitored host. Operating an HIDPS requires more management effort to install, configure, and operate than does a comparably sized NIDPS solution.

2. An HIDPS is vulnerable both to direct attacks and to attacks against the host operating system. Either circumstance can result in the compromise and/or loss of HIDPS functionality.

3. An HIDPS is not optimized to detect multihost scanning, nor is it able to detect the scanning of non-host network devices, such as routers or switches. Unless complex correlation analysis is provided, the HIDPS will not be aware of attacks that span multiple devices in the network.

4. An HIDPS is susceptible to some denial-of-service attacks.

5. An HIDPS can use large amounts of disk space to retain the host OS audit logs; to function properly, it may be necessary to add disk capacity to the system.

6. An HIDPS can inflict a performance overhead on its host systems, and in some cases may reduce system performance below acceptable levels.[13]

IDPS Detection Methods

IDPSs use a variety of detection methods to monitor and evaluate network traffic. Three methods dominate: the signature-based approach, the statistical-anomaly approach, and the stateful packet inspection approach.

Signature-Based IDPS

A **signature-based IDPS** (sometimes called a **knowledge-based IDPS** or a **misuse-detection IDPS**) examines network traffic in search of patterns that match known **signatures**—that is, preconfigured, predetermined attack patterns. Signature-based IDPS technology is widely used because many attacks have clear and distinct signatures, for example: (1) footprinting and fingerprinting activities use ICMP, DNS querying, and e-mail routing analysis; (2) exploits use a specific attack sequence designed to take advantage of a vulnerability to gain access to a system; (3) DoS and DDoS attacks, during which the attacker tries to prevent the normal usage of a system, overload the system with requests so that the system's ability to process them efficiently is compromised or disrupted.[14]

A potential problem with the signature-based approach is that new attack strategies must continually be added into the IDPS's database of signatures; otherwise, attacks that use new strategies will not be recognized and might succeed. Another weakness of the signature-based method is that a slow, methodical attack might escape detection if the relevant IDPS attack signature has a shorter time frame. The only way a signature-based IDPS can resolve this vulnerability is to collect and analyze data over longer periods of time, a process that requires substantially larger data storage capability and additional processing capacity.

Statistical Anomaly-Based IDPS

The **statistical anomaly-based IDPS (stat IDPS)** or **behavior-based IDPS** collects statistical summaries by observing traffic that is known to be normal. This normal period of evaluation establishes a performance baseline. Once the baseline is established, the stat IDPS periodically samples network activity and, using statistical methods, compares the sampled network activity to this baseline. When the measured activity is outside the baseline parameters—exceeding what is called the **clipping level**—the IDPS sends an alert to the administrator. The baseline data can include variables such as host memory or CPU usage, network packet types, and packet quantities.

The advantage of the statistical anomaly-based approach is that the IDPS can detect new types of attacks, since it looks for abnormal activity of any type. Unfortunately, these systems require much more overhead and processing capacity than signature-based IDPSs, because they must constantly compare patterns of activity against the baseline. Another drawback is that these systems may not detect minor changes to system variables and may generate many false positives. If the actions of the users or systems on a network vary widely, with periods of low activity interspersed with periods of heavy packet traffic, this type of IDPS may not be suitable, because the dramatic swings from one level to another will almost certainly generate false alarms. Because of its complexity and impact on the overhead computing load of the host computer as well as the number of false positives it can generate, this type of IDPS is less commonly used than the signature-based type.

Stateful Protocol Analysis IDPS As you learned in Chapter 6, stateful inspection firewalls track each network connection between internal and external systems using a state table to record which station sent which packet and when, essentially pairing communicating parties. An IDPS extension of this concept is stateful protocol analysis. According to SP 800-94, "**Stateful protocol analysis (SPA)** is a process of comparing predetermined profiles of generally accepted definitions of benign activity for each protocol state against observed events to identify deviations. Stateful protocol analysis relies on vendor-developed universal profiles that specify how particular protocols should and should not be used."[15] Essentially, the IDPS knows how a protocol, such as FTP, is supposed to work, and therefore can detect anomalous behavior. By storing relevant data detected in a session and then using that data to identify intrusions that involve multiple requests and responses, the IDPS can better detect specialized, multisession attacks. This process is sometimes called *deep packet inspection* because SPA closely examines packets at the application layer for information that indicates a possible intrusion.

Stateful protocol analysis can also examine authentication sessions for suspicious activity as well as for attacks that incorporate "unexpected sequences of commands, such as issuing the same command repeatedly or issuing a command without first issuing a command upon which it is dependent, as well as 'reasonableness' for commands such as minimum and maximum lengths for arguments."[16]

The models used for SPA are similar to signatures in that they are provided by vendors. These models are based on industry protocol standards established by such entities as the Internet Engineering Task Force, but they vary along with the protocol implementations in such documents. Also, proprietary protocols are not published in sufficient detail to enable the IDPS to provide accurate and comprehensive assessments.

Unfortunately, the analytical complexity of session-based assessments is the principal drawback to this type of IDPS method, which also requires heavy processing overhead to track multiple simultaneous connections. Additionally, unless a protocol violates its fundamental behavior, this IDPS method may completely fail to detect an intrusion. One final issue is that the IDPS may in fact interfere with the normal operations of the protocol it's examining, especially with client- and server-differentiated operations.[17]

Log File Monitors A **log file monitor (LFM)** IDPS is similar to a NIDPS. Using LFM, the system reviews the log files generated by servers, network devices, and even other IDPSs, looking for patterns and signatures that may indicate that an attack or intrusion is in process or has already occurred. While an individual host IDPS can only examine the activity in one system, the LFM is able to look at multiple log files from a number of different systems. The patterns that signify an attack can be subtle and difficult to distinguish when one system is examined in isolation, but they may be more identifiable when the events recorded for the entire network and each of the systems in it can be viewed as a whole. Of course this holistic approach requires considerable resources since it involves the collection, movement, storage, and analysis of very large quantities of log data.

IDPS Response Behavior

Each IDPS responds to external stimulation in a different way, depending on its configuration and function. Some respond in active ways, collecting additional information about the intrusion, modifying the network environment, or even taking action against the intrusion.

Others respond in passive ways, for example by setting off alarms or notifications or collecting passive data through SNMP traps.

IDPS Response Options When an IDPS detects a possible intrusion, it has a number of response options, depending on the implementing organization's policy, objectives, and system capabilities. When configuring an IDPS's responses, the system administrator must exercise care to ensure that a response to an attack (or potential attack) does not inadvertently exacerbate the situation. For example, if an NIDPS reacts to suspected DoS attacks by severing the network connection, the attack is a success, and such attacks repeated at intervals will thoroughly disrupt an organization's business operations.

An analogy to this approach is a car thief who approaches a desirable target in the early a.m., strikes the car with a rolled-up newspaper to trigger the alarm, and then ducks into the bushes. The car owner wakes up, checks the car, determines there is no danger, resets the alarm, and goes back to bed. The thief repeats the triggering action every half hour or so until the owner disables the alarm. The thief is now free to steal the car without worrying about triggering the alarm.

IDPS responses can be classified as active or passive. An active response is a definitive action automatically initiated when certain types of alerts are triggered and can include collecting additional information, changing or modifying the environment, and taking action against the intruders. Passive response IDPSs simply report the information they have collected and wait for the administrator to act. Generally, the administrator chooses a course of action after analyzing the collected data. The passive IDPS is the most common implementation, although most systems include some active options that are disabled by default.

The following list describes some of the responses an IDPS can be configured to produce. Note that some of these apply only to a network-based or a host-based IDPS, while others are applicable to both.[18]

- Audible/visual alarm: The IDPS can trigger a .wav file, beep, whistle, siren, or other audible or visual notification to alert the administrator of an attack. The most common type of such notifications is the computer pop-up, which can be configured with color indicators and specific messages, and can also contain specifics about the suspected attack, the tools used in the attack, the level of confidence the system has in its own determination, and the addresses and/or locations of the systems involved.

- SNMP traps and plug-ins: The Simple Network Management Protocol contains trap functions, which allow a device to send a message to the SNMP management console indicating that a certain threshold has been crossed, either positively or negatively. The IDPS can execute this trap, telling the SNMP console an event has occurred. Some of the advantages of this operation include the relatively standard implementation of SNMP in networking devices, the ability to configure the network system to use SNMP traps in this manner, the ability to use systems specifically to handle SNMP traffic, including IDPS traps, and the ability to use standard communications networks.

- E-mail message: The IDPS can send e-mail to notify network administrators of an event. Many administrators use smartphones and other e-mail enabled devices to check for alerts and other notifications frequently. Organizations should use caution in relying on e-mail systems as the primary means of communication between the IDPS and security personnel—e-mail is inherently unreliable, and an attacker could compromise the e-mail system and block such messages.

- Page or phone message: The IDPS can be configured to dial a phone number and produce an alphanumeric page or a modem noise.

- Log entry: The IDPS can enter information about the event (e.g., addresses, time, systems involved, protocol information) into an IDPS system log file or operating system log file. These files can be stored on separate servers to prevent skilled attackers from deleting entries about their intrusions.

- Evidentiary packet dump: Organizations that require an audit trail of the IDPS data may choose to record all log data in a special way. This method allows the organization to perform further analysis on the data and also to submit the data as evidence in a civil or criminal case. Once the data has been written using a cryptographic hashing algorithm (discussed in detail in Chapter 8), it becomes evidentiary documentation— that is, suitable for criminal or civil court use. This packet logging can, however, be resource-intensive, especially in denial-of-service attacks.

- Take action against the intruder: It has become possible, although not advisable, to take action against an intruder. Known as trap-and-trace, back-hacking, or traceback, this response option involves configuring intrusion detection systems to trace the data from the target system to the attacking system in order to initiate a counterattack. While this may sound tempting, it is ill-advised and may not be legal. An organization only owns a network to its perimeter, and conducting traces or back-hacking to systems outside that perimeter may make the organization just as criminally liable as the individual(s) who began the attack. Also, in some cases the "attacking system" is in fact a compromised intermediary system, and in other cases attackers use address spoofing; either way, any counterattack would actually only harm an innocent third party. Any organization planning to configure any sort of retaliation effort into an automated intrusion detection system is strongly encouraged to seek legal counsel.

- Launch program: An IDPS can be configured to execute a specific program when it detects specific types of attacks. A number of vendors have specialized tracking, tracing, and response software that can be part of an organization's intrusion response strategy.

- Reconfigure firewall: An IDPS can send a command to the firewall to filter out suspected packets by IP address, port, or protocol. (It is, unfortunately, still possible for a skilled attacker to break in by simply spoofing a different address, shifting to a different port, or changing the protocols used in the attack.) While it may not be easy, an IDPS can block or deter intrusions via one of the following methods:

  - Establishing a block for all traffic from the suspected attacker's IP address, or even from the entire source network from which the attacker appears to be operating. This blocking can be set for a specific period of time and reset to normal rules after that period has expired.

  - Establishing a block for specific TCP or UDP port traffic from the suspected attacker's address or source network, blocking only the services that seem to be under attack.

  - Blocking all traffic to or from a network interface (such as the organization's Internet connection) if the severity of the suspected attack warrants that level of response.[19]

- Terminate session: Terminating the session by using the TCP/IP protocol specified packet *TCP close* is a simple process. Some attacks would be deterred or blocked by session termination, but others would simply continue when the attacker issues a new session request.

- Terminate connection: The last resort for an IDPS under attack is to terminate the organization's internal or external connections. Smart switches can cut traffic to or from a specific port, should that connection be linked to a system that is malfunctioning or otherwise interfering with efficient network operations. As indicated earlier, this response should be the last resort to protect information, as it may be the very goal of the attacker.

[*The following sections have been adapted from NIST SP 800-94 "Guide to Intrusion Detection and Prevention Systems" and its predecessor, SP 800-31 "Intrusion Detection Systems".*]

Reporting and Archiving Capabilities Many, if not all, commercial IDPSs can generate routine reports and other detailed information documents, such as reports of system events and intrusions detected over a particular reporting period (for example, a week or a month). Some provide statistics or logs in formats suitable for inclusion in database systems or for use in report generating packages.

Failsafe Considerations for IDPS Responses Failsafe features protect an IDPS from being circumvented or defeated by an attacker. There are several functions that require failsafe measures. For instance, IDPSs need to provide silent, reliable monitoring of attackers. Should the response function of an IDPS break this silence by broadcasting alarms and alerts in plaintext over the monitored network, attackers can detect the IDPS and might then directly target it in the attack. Encrypted tunnels or other cryptographic measures that hide and authenticate communications are excellent ways to secure and ensure the reliability of the IDPS.

Selecting IDPS Approaches and Products

The wide array of available intrusion detection products addresses a broad range of organizational security goals and considerations; the process of selecting products that represent the best fit for any particular organization is challenging. The following considerations and questions may help you prepare a specification for acquiring and deploying an intrusion detection product.

Technical and Policy Considerations In order to determine which IDPS best meets an organization's needs, first consider the organizational environment in technical, physical, and political terms.

What Is Your Systems Environment? The first requirement for a potential IDPS is that it function in your systems environment. This is important; if an IDPS is not designed to accommodate the information sources that are available on your systems, it will not be able to see anything—neither normal activity nor an attack—on your systems.

- What are the technical specifications of your systems environment?

  First, specify the technical attributes of your systems environment—network diagrams and maps specifying the number and locations of hosts; operating systems for each host; the number and types of network devices such as routers, bridges, and switches; the number and types of terminal servers and dial-up connections; and descriptions of any network servers, including types, configurations, and application software and versions running on each. If you run an enterprise network management system, specify it here.

- What are the technical specifications of your current security protections?

  Describe the security protections you already have in place. Specify numbers, types, and locations of network firewalls, identification and authentication servers, data and link encryptors, antivirus packages, access control products, specialized security hardware (such as crypto accelerator hardware for Web servers), virtual private networks, and any other security mechanisms on your systems.

- What are the goals of your enterprise?

  Some IDPSs are designed to accommodate the special needs of certain industries or market niches such as electronic commerce, health care, or financial services. Define the functional goals of your enterprise (there can be several goals associated with a single organization) that are supported by your systems.

- How formal is the system environment and management culture in your organization?

  Organizational styles vary, depending on the function of the organization and its traditional culture. For instance, the military and other organizations that deal with national security issues tend to operate with a high degree of formality, especially when contrasted with university or other academic environments. Some IDPSs support enforcement of formal use policies, with built-in configuration options that can enforce common issue-specific or system-specific security policies, as well as provide a library of reports for typical policy violations as well as routine matters.

What Are Your Security Goals and Objectives? The next step is to articulate the goals and objectives you wish to attain by using an IDPS.

- Is the primary concern of your organization protecting from threats originating outside your organization?

  Perhaps the easiest way to identify security goals is by categorizing your organization's threat concerns. Identify the concerns that your organization has regarding external threats.

- Is your organization concerned about insider attack?

  Address concerns about threats that originate from within your organization, encompassing not only a user who attacks the system from within (such as a shipping clerk who attempts to access and alter the payroll system) but also the authorized user who exceeds his privileges, thereby violating organizational security policy or laws (such as a customer service agent who, driven by curiosity, accesses earnings and payroll records for public figures).

- Does your organization want to use the output of your IDPS to determine new needs?

  System usage monitoring is sometimes provided as a generic system management tool to determine when system assets require upgrading or replacement.

- Does your organization want to use an IDPS to maintain managerial control (non-security related) over network usage?

  Some organizations, implement system use policies that may be classified as personnel management rather than system security, such as prohibiting access to certain kinds of Web sites (such as ones containing pornography) or the use of organizational systems to send e-mail or other messages for the purpose of harassing individuals. Some IDPSs provide features that detect such violations of management controls.

What Is Your Existing Security Policy?

You should review your existing organization security policy, which will serve as the template against which your IDPS will be configured. You may find you need to augment the policy, or else derive the following items from it.

- How is it structured?

  It is helpful to articulate the goals outlined in the security policy in terms of the standard security goals (integrity, confidentiality, and availability) as well as more generic management goals (privacy, protection from liability, and manageability).

- What are the general job descriptions of your system users?

  List the general job functions of system users (there are often several functions assigned to a single user) as well as the data and network accesses that each function requires.

- Does the policy include reasonable use policies or other management provisions?

  As mentioned above, the security policies of many organizations include system use policies.

- Has your organization defined processes for dealing with specific policy violations?

  It is helpful to have a clear idea of what the organization wishes to do when the IDPS detects that a policy has been violated. If the organization doesn't intend to react to such violations, it may not make sense to configure the IDPS to detect them. If, on the other hand, the organization wishes to actively respond to such violations, the IDPS's operational staff should be informed of the response policy so that it can deal with alarms in an appropriate manner.

Organizational Requirements and Constraints

Your organization's operational goals, constraints, and culture will affect the selection of the IDPS and other security tools and technologies to protect your systems. Consider the following organizational requirements and limitations.

What Requirements Are Levied from Outside the Organization?

- Is your organization subject to oversight or review by another organization?

  If so, does that oversight authority require IDPSs or other specific system security resources?

- Are there requirements for public access to information on your organization's systems?

  Do regulations or statutes require that information on your system be accessible by the public during certain hours of the day, or during certain date or time intervals?

- Are there other security-specific requirements levied by law? Are there legal requirements for protection of personal information (such as earnings information or medical records) stored on your systems?

  Are there legal requirements for investigation of security violations that divulge or endanger that information?

- Are there internal audit requirements for security best practices or due diligence?

  Do any of these audit requirements specify functions that the IDPSs must provide or support?

- Is the system subject to accreditation?

  If so, what is the accreditation authority's requirement for IDPSs or other security protection?

- Are there requirements for law enforcement investigation and resolution of security incidents?

  Do they require any IDPS functions, especially having to do with collection and protection of IDPS logs as evidence?

What Are Your Organization's Resource Constraints? IDPSs can protect the systems of an organization, but at a price. It makes little sense to incur additional expense for IDPS features if your organization does not have sufficient systems or personnel to handle the alerts they will generate.

- What is the budget for acquisition and life cycle support of intrusion detection hardware, software, and infrastructure?

  Remember that the IDPS software is not the only element of the total cost of ownership; you may also have to acquire a system on which to run the software, obtain specialized assistance to install and configure the system, and train your personnel. Ongoing operations may also require additional staff or outside contractors.

- Is there sufficient existing staff to monitor an intrusion detection system full time?

  Some IDPSs require around-the-clock attendance by systems personnel. If you do not anticipate having such personnel available, you may wish to explore those systems that accommodate less than full-time attendance or unattended use.

- Does your organization have authority to instigate changes based on the findings of an intrusion detection system?

  It is critical that you and your organization be clear about what you plan to do about the problems uncovered by an IDPS. If you are not empowered to handle the incidents that arise as a result of the monitoring, you should consider coordinating your selection and configuration of the IDPS with the party who is empowered.

IDPSs Product Features and Quality It's important to carefully evaluate any IDPS product by considering the following questions:

Is the Product Sufficiently Scalable for Your Environment? Many IDPSs cannot function within large or widely distributed enterprise network environments.

How Has the Product Been Tested? Simply asserting that an IDPS has certain capabilities is not sufficient demonstration that those capabilities are real. You should request demonstrations of a particular IDPS to evaluate its suitability for your environment and goals.

- Has the product been tested against functional requirements?

  Ask the vendor about the assumptions made regarding the goals and constraints of customer environments.

- Has the product been tested against attack?

  Ask vendors for details of the security testing to which its products have been subjected. If the product includes network-based vulnerability assessment features, ask also whether test routines that produce system crashes or other denials of service have been identified and flagged in system documentation and interfaces.

What Is the User Level of Expertise Targeted by the Product? Different IDPS vendors target users with different levels of technical and security expertise. Ask the vendor what their assumptions are regarding the users of their products.

Is the Product Designed to Evolve as the Organization Grows? One important product design goal is the ability to adapt to your needs over time.

- Can the product adapt to growth in user expertise?

  Ask here whether the IDPS's interface can be configured (with shortcut keys, customizable alarm features, and custom signatures) on the fly. Ask also whether these features are documented and supported.

- Can the product adapt to growth and change of the organization's systems infrastructure?

  This question has to do with the ability of the IDPS to scale to an expanding and increasingly diverse network. Most vendors have experience in adapting their products as target networks grow. Ask also about commitments to support new protocol standards and platform types.

- Can the product adapt to growth and change in the security threat environment?

  This question is especially critical given the current Internet threat environment, in which thirty to forty new attacks are posted to the Web every month.

What Are the Support Provisions for the Product? Like other systems, IDPSs require maintenance and support over time. These needs should be identified in a written report.

- What are the commitments for product installation and configuration support?

  Many vendors provide expert assistance to customers installing and configuring IDPSs; others expect that your own staff will handle these functions and provide only telephone or e-mail help desk functions.

- What are the commitments for ongoing product support?

  Ask about the vendor's commitment to supporting your use of their IDPS product.

- Are subscriptions to signature updates included?

  Most IDPSs are misuse-detectors, so the value of the product is only as good as the signature database against which events are analyzed. Most vendors provide subscriptions to signature updates for some period of time (a year is typical).

- How often are subscriptions updated?

  In today's threat environment, in which thirty to forty new attacks are published every month, this is a critical question.

- How quickly after a new attack is made public will the vendor ship a new signature?

  If you are using IDPSs to protect highly visible or heavily traveled Internet sites, it is especially critical that you receive the signatures for new attacks as soon as possible.

- Are software updates included?

  Most IDPSs are software products and therefore subject to bugs and revisions. Ask the vendor about software update and bug patch support, and determine to what extent they are included in the product you purchase.

- How quickly will software updates and patches be issued after a problem is reported to the vendor?

  As software bugs in IDPSs can allow attackers to nullify their protective effect, it is extremely important that problems be fixed, reliably and quickly.

- Are technical support services included? What is the cost?

  In this category, technical support services mean vendor assistance in tuning or adapting your IDPS to accommodate special needs, be they monitoring a custom or legacy system within your enterprise or reporting IDPS results in a custom protocol or format.

- What are the provisions for contacting technical support (e-mail, telephone, online chat, Web-based reporting)?

  The contact provisions will likely tell you whether these technical support services are accessible enough to support incident handling or other time-sensitive needs.

- Are there any guarantees associated with the IDPS?

  As with other software products, IDPSs traditionally have few guarantees associated with them; however, in an attempt to gain market share, some vendors are initiating guarantee programs.

- What training resources does the vendor provide?

  Once an IDPS is selected, installed, and configured, it must still be operated by your personnel. In order for these people to make optimal use of the IDPS, they should be trained in its use. Some vendors provide this training as part of the product package.

- What additional training resources are available from the vendor and at what cost?

  If the vendor does not provide training as part of the IDPS package, you should budget appropriately to train your operational personnel.

Strengths and Limitations of IDPSs

Although intrusion detection systems are a valuable addition to an organization's security infrastructure, there are things they do well and things they do not do well. As you plan the security strategy for your organization's systems, it is important for you to understand what IDPSs should be trusted to do and what goals might be better served by other security mechanisms.

Strengths of Intrusion Detection and Prevention Systems

Intrusion detection and prevention systems perform the following functions well:

- Monitoring and analysis of system events and user behaviors
- Testing the security states of system configurations
- Baselining the security state of a system, then tracking any changes to that baseline
- Recognizing patterns of system events that correspond to known attacks
- Recognizing patterns of activity that statistically vary from normal activity
- Managing operating system audit and logging mechanisms and the data they generate
- Alerting appropriate staff by appropriate means when attacks are detected
- Measuring enforcement of security policies encoded in the analysis engine
- Providing default information security policies
- Allowing non-security experts to perform important security monitoring functions

Limitations of Intrusion Detection and Prevention Systems

Intrusion detection systems cannot perform the following functions:

- Compensating for weak or missing security mechanisms in the protection infrastructure, such as firewalls, identification and authentication systems, link encryption systems, access control mechanisms, and virus detection and eradication software
- Instantaneously detecting, reporting, and responding to an attack when there is a heavy network or processing load
- Detecting newly published attacks or variants of existing attacks
- Effectively responding to attacks launched by sophisticated attackers
- Automatically investigating attacks without human intervention
- Resisting all attacks that are intended to defeat or circumvent them
- Compensating for problems with the fidelity of information sources
- Dealing effectively with switched networks

There is also the considerable challenge of configuring an IDPS to respond accurately to a perceived threat. Once a device is empowered to react to an intrusion by filtering or even severing an communication session or by severing a communication circuit, the impact from a false positive becomes significant. It's one thing to fill an administrator's e-mail box or compile a large log file with suspected attacks; it's quite another to shut down critical communications. Some forms of attacks, conducted by attackers called **IDPS terrorists**, are designed to trip the organization's IDPS, essentially causing the organization to conduct its own DoS attack by overreacting to an actual, but insignificant, attack.

[*The preceding sections were drawn and adapted from NIST SP 800-94* "Guide to Intrusion Detection and Prevention Systems" *and its predecessor, NIST SP 800-31* "Intrusion Detection Systems"]

Deployment and Implementation of an IDPS

Deploying and implementing an IDPS is not always a straightforward task. The strategy for deploying an IDPS should take into account a number of factors, the foremost being how the IDPS will be managed and where it should be placed. These factors determine the number of administrators needed to install, configure, and monitor the IDPS, as well as the number of management workstations, the size of the storage needed for retention of the data generated by the systems, and the ability of the organization to detect and respond to remote threats.

IDPS Control Strategies
An IDPS can be implemented via one of three basic control strategies. A control strategy determines how an organization supervises and maintains the configuration of an IDPS. It also determines how the input and output of the IDPS is managed. The three commonly utilized control strategies are centralized, partially distributed, and fully distributed. The IT industry has been exploring technologies and practices to enable the distribution of computer processing cycles and data storage for many years. These explorations have long considered the advantages and disadvantages of the centralized strategy versus strategies with varying degrees of distribution. In the early days of computing, all systems were fully centralized, resulting in a control strategy that provided high levels of security and control, as well as efficiencies in resource allocation and management. During the 1980s and 1990s, with the rapid growth in networking and computing capabilities, the trend was to implement a fully distributed strategy. In the mid-1990s, however, the high costs of a fully distributed architecture became apparent, and the IT industry shifted toward a mixed strategy of partially distributed control. A strategy of partial distribution, where some features and components are distributed and others are centrally controlled, has now emerged as the recommended practice for IT systems in general and for IDPS control systems in particular.

Centralized Control Strategy
As illustrated in Figure 7-4, in a **centralized IDPS control strategy** all IDPS control functions are implemented and managed in a central location, represented in the figure with the large square symbol labeled "IDPS Console." The IDPS console includes the management software, which collects information from the remote sensors (triangular symbols in the figure), analyzes the systems or networks, and determines whether the current situation has deviated from the preconfigured baseline. All reporting features are implemented and managed from this central location. The primary advantages of this strategy are cost and control. With one central implementation, there is one management system, one place to go to monitor the status of the systems or networks, one location for reports, and one set of administrative management. This centralization of IDPS management supports task specialization, since all managers are either located near the IDPS management console

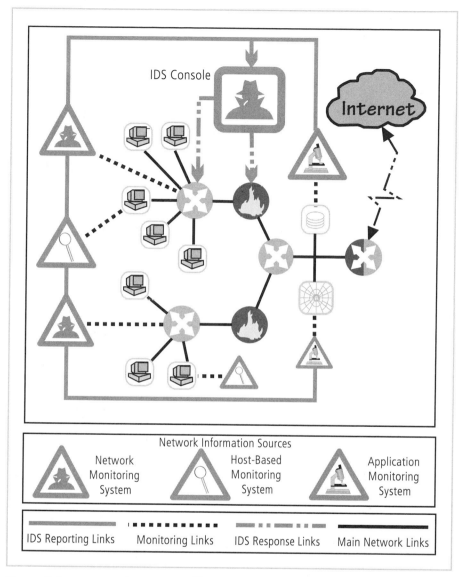

Figure 7-4 Centralized IDPS Control[13]

Source: This figure adapted from Scarfone and Mell, NIST SP800-94.

or can acquire an authenticated remote connection to it, and technicians are located near the remote sensors. This means that each person can focus specifically on an assigned task. In addition, the central control group can evaluate the systems and networks as a whole, and since it can compare pieces of information from all sensors, the group is better positioned to recognize a large-scale attack.

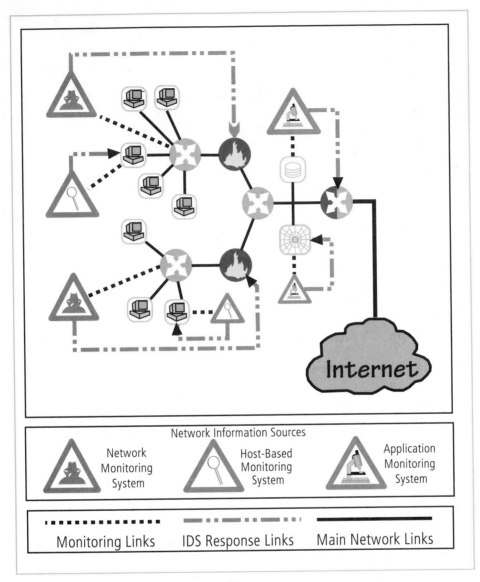

Figure 7-5 Fully Distributed IDPS Control[14]

Source: This figure adapted from Scarfone and Mell, NIST SP800-94.

Fully Distributed Control Strategy A fully distributed IDPS control strategy, illustrated in Figure 7-5, is the opposite of the centralized strategy. All control functions (which appear in the figure as small square symbols enclosing a computer icon) are applied at the physical location of each IDPS component. Each monitoring site uses its own paired sensors to perform its own control functions to achieve the necessary detection, reaction, and response functions. Thus, each sensor/agent is best configured to deal with its own environment. Since the IDPSs do not have to wait for a response from a centralized control facility, their response time to individual attacks is greatly enhanced.

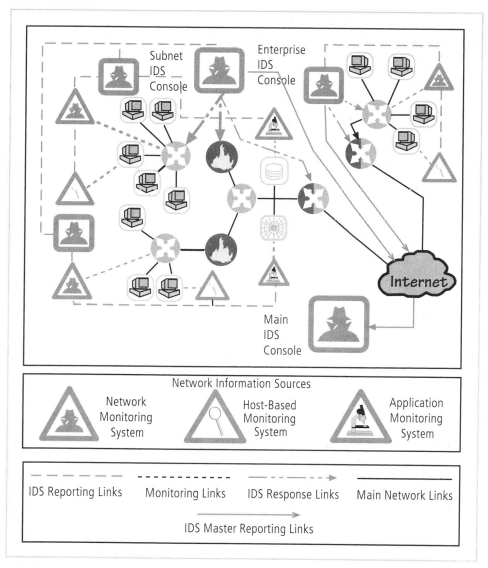

Figure 7-6 Partially Distributed IDPS Control[15]

Source: This figure adapted from Scarfone and Mell, NIST SP800-94.

Partially Distributed Control Strategy A **partially distributed IDPS control strategy,** depicted in Figure 7-6, combines the best of the other two strategies. While the individual agents can still analyze and respond to local threats, their reporting to a hierarchical central facility enables the organization to detect widespread attacks. This blended approach to reporting is one of the more effective methods of detecting intelligent attackers, especially those who probe an organization at multiple points of entry, trying to identify the systems' configurations and weaknesses, before they launch a concerted attack. The partially distributed control strategy also allows the organization to optimize for economy of scale in the implementation of key management software and personnel, especially in the reporting areas. When the organization can create a pool of security managers to evaluate reports from multiple distributed IDPS systems, it becomes better able to detect these distributed attacks before they become unmanageable.

IDPS Deployment Given the highly technical skills required to implement and configure IDPSs and the imperfection of the technology, great care must be taken when deciding where to locate the components, both in their physical connection to the network and host devices and in how they are logically connected to each other and the IDPS administration team. Since IDPSs are designed to detect, report, and even react to anomalous stimuli, placing IDPSs in an area where such traffic is common can result in excessive reporting. Moreover, the administrators monitoring systems located in such areas can become desensitized to the information flow and may fail to detect actual attacks in progress.

As an organization selects an IDPS and prepares for implementation, planners must select a deployment strategy that is based on a careful analysis of the organization's information security requirements and that integrates with the organization's existing IT infrastructure but, at the same time, causes minimal impact. After all, the purpose of the IDPS is to detect anomalous situations—not create them. One consideration is the skill level of the personnel who install, configure, and maintain the systems. An IDPS is a complex system in that it involves numerous remote monitoring agents (on both individual systems and networks) that require proper configuration to gain the proper authentication and authorization. As the IDPS is deployed, each component should be installed, configured, fine-tuned, tested, and monitored. A mistake in any step of the deployment process may produce a range of problems—from a minor inconvenience to a network-wide disaster. Thus, both the individuals installing the IDPS and the individuals using and managing the system require proper training.

NIDPS and HIDPS can be used in tandem to cover both the individual systems that connect to an organization's networks and the networks themselves. To do this, it is important for an organization to use a phased implementation strategy so as not to affect the entire organization all at once. A phased implementation strategy also allows security technicians to resolve the problems that do arise without compromising the very information security the IDPS is installed to protect. When sequencing the implementation, the organization should first implement the NIDPSs, as they are less problematic and easier to configure than their host-based counterparts. After the NIDPSs are configured and running without issue, the HIDPSs can be installed to protect the critical systems on the host server. Once the NIDPSs and HIDPSs are both operational, administrators should scan the network with a vulnerability scanner like Nmap or Nessus to determine if (a) the scanners pick up anything new or unusual, and (b) if the IDPS can detect the scans.

Deploying Network-Based IDPSs The placement of the sensor agents is critical to the operation of all IDPSs, and is especially critical in the case of NIDPSs. NIST recommends the following four locations for NIDPS sensors:

Location 1: Behind each external firewall, in the network DMZ (See Figure 7-7, location 1)

Advantages:

- IDPS sees attacks that originate from the outside that may penetrate the network's perimeter defenses.

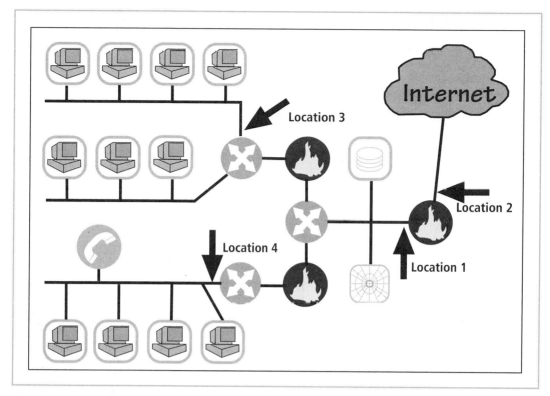

Figure 7-7 Network IDPS Sensor Locations[17]

Source: This figure adapted from Scarfone and Mell, NIST SP800-94.

- IDPS can identify problems with the network firewall policy or performance.
- IDPS sees attacks that might target the Web server or FTP server, both of which commonly reside in this DMZ.
- Even if the incoming attack is not detected, the IDPS can sometimes recognize, in the outgoing traffic, patterns that suggest that the server has been compromised.

Location 2: Outside an external firewall (See Figure 7-7, location 2)

Advantages:

- IDPS documents the number of attacks originating on the Internet that target the network.
- IDPS documents the types of attacks originating on the Internet that target the network.

Location 3: On major network backbones (See Figure 7-7, location 3)

Advantages:

- IDPS monitors a large amount of a network's traffic, thus increasing its chances of spotting attacks.

- IDPS detects unauthorized activity by authorized users within the organization's security perimeter.

Location 4: On critical subnets (See Figure 7-7, location 4)

Advantages:

- IDPS detects attacks targeting critical systems and resources.
- This location allows organizations with limited resources to focus these resources on the most valuable network assets.[20]

Deploying Host-Based IDPSs The proper implementation of HIDPSs can be a painstaking and time-consuming task, as each HIDPS must be custom configured to its host systems. Deployment begins with implementing the most critical systems first. This poses a dilemma for the deployment team, since the first systems to be implemented are mission-critical, and any problems in the installation could be catastrophic to the organization. Thus it may be beneficial to practice an implementation on one or more test servers configured on a network segment that resembles the mission-critical systems. Practice helps the installation team gain experience and also helps determine if the installation might trigger any unusual events. Gaining an edge on the learning curve by training on nonproduction systems benefits the overall deployment process by reducing the risk of unforeseen complications.

Installation continues until all systems are installed or the organization reaches the planned degree of coverage it is willing to live with, in terms of the number of systems or percentage of network traffic. To provide ease of management, control, and reporting, each HIDPS should, as discussed earlier, be configured to interact with a central management console.

Just as technicians can install the HIDPS in offline systems to develop expertise and identify potential problems, users and managers can gain expertise and understanding of the operation of the HIDPS by using a test facility. This test facility could use the offline systems configured by the technicians but also be connected to the organization's backbone to allow the HIDPS to process actual network traffic. This setup will also enable technicians to create a baseline of normal traffic for the organization. During the system testing process, training scenarios can be developed that will enable users to recognize and respond to common attack situations. To ensure effective and efficient operation, the management team can establish policy for the operation and monitoring of the HIDPS.

Measuring the Effectiveness of IDPSs

When selecting an IDPS one typically looks at the following four measures of comparative effectiveness:

- *Thresholds: A threshold is a value that sets the limit between normal and abnormal behavior. Thresholds usually specify a maximum acceptable level, such as x failed connection attempts in 60 seconds, or x characters for a filename length. Thresholds are most often used for anomaly-based detection and stateful protocol analysis.*
- *Blacklists and whitelists: A blacklist is a list of discrete entities, such as hosts, TCP or UDP port numbers, ICMP types and codes,*

applications, usernames, URLs, filenames, or file extensions, that have been associated with malicious activity. Blacklists, also known as hot lists, typically allow IDPSs to block activity that is highly likely to be malicious, and may also be used to assign a higher priority to alerts that match blacklist entries. Some IDPSs generate dynamic blacklists that are used to temporarily block recently detected threats (e.g., activity from an attacker's IP address). A whitelist is a list of discrete entities that are known to be benign. Whitelists are typically used on a granular basis, such as protocol-by-protocol, to reduce or ignore false positives involving known benign activity from trusted hosts. Whitelists and blacklists are most commonly used in signature-based detection and stateful protocol analysis.

- *Alert settings: Most IDPS technologies allow administrators to customize each alert type. Examples of actions that can be performed on an alert type include:*

  - *Toggling it on or off*

  - *Setting a default priority or severity level*

  - *Specifying what information should be recorded and what notification methods (e.g., e-mail, pager) should be used*

  - *Specifying which prevention capabilities should be used*

  Some products also suppress alerts if an attacker generates many alerts in a short period of time and may also temporarily ignore all future traffic from the attacker. This is to prevent the IDPS from being overwhelmed by alerts.

- *Code viewing and editing: Some IDPS technologies permit administrators to see some or all of the detection-related code. This is usually limited to signatures, but some technologies allow administrators to see additional code, such as programs used to perform stateful protocol analysis.*[18]

Once implemented, IDPSs are evaluated using two dominant metrics: first, administrators evaluate the number of attacks detected in a known collection of probes; second, the administrators examine the level of use, commonly measured in megabits per second of network traffic, at which the IDPSs fail. An evaluation of an IDPS might read something like this: *at 100 Mb/s, the IDPS was able to detect 97 percent of directed attacks.* This is a dramatic change from the previous method used for assessing IDPS effectiveness, which was based on the total number of signatures the system was currently running—a sort of "more is better" approach. This evaluation method of assessment was flawed for several reasons. Not all IDPSs use simple signature-based detection. Some systems, as discussed earlier, use the almost infinite combination of network performance characteristics of statistical-anomaly-based detection to detect a potential attack. Also, some more sophisticated signature-based systems actually use *fewer* signatures or rules than older, simpler versions—which, in direct contrast to the signature-based assessment method, suggests that less may actually be more. The recognition that the size of the signature base is an insufficient measure of an IDPS's effectiveness led to the development of stress test measurements for evaluating IDPS performance. These only work, however, if the administrator has a collection of known negative and positive actions that can be proven to elicit a desired response. Since developing this collection can be tedious, most IDPS vendors provide testing mechanisms that verify that their systems are performing as expected. Some of these testing processes will enable the administrator to do the following:

- Record and retransmit packets from a real virus or worm scan
- Record and retransmit packets from a real virus or worm scan with incomplete TCP/IP session connections (missing SYN packets)
- Conduct a real virus or worm attack against a hardened or sacrificial system

This last measure is important, since future IDPSs will probably include much more detailed information about the overall site configuration. According to experts in the field, "it may be necessary for the IDPSs to be able to actively probe a potentially vulnerable machine, in order to either pre-load its configuration with correct information, or perform a retroactive assessment. An IDPS that performed some kind of actual system assessment would be a complete failure in today's generic testing labs, which focus on replaying attacks and scans against nonexistent machines."[19]

With the rapid growth in technology, each new generation of IDPSs will require new testing methodologies. However, the measured values that will continue to be of interest to IDPS administrators and managers will most certainly include some assessment of how much traffic the IDPS can handle, the numbers of false positives and false negatives it generates, and a measure of the IDPS's ability to detect actual attacks. Vendors of IDPS systems could also include a report of the alarms sent and the relative accuracy of the system in correctly matching the alarm level to the true seriousness of the threat. Some planned metrics for IDPSs include the flexibility of signatures and detection policy customization.

IDPS administrators may soon be able to purchase tools that test IDPS effectiveness. Until these tools are available from a neutral third party, the diagnostics from the IDPS vendors will always be suspect. No vendor, no matter how reliable, would provide a test that their system would fail.

One note of caution: There is a strong tendency among IDPS administrators to use common vulnerability assessment tools, like Nmap or Nessus, to evaluate the capabilities of an IDPS. While this may seem like a good idea, it will not work as expected, because most IDPS systems are equipped to recognize the differences between a locally implemented vulnerability assessment tool and a true attack.

In order to perform a true assessment of the effectiveness of IDPS systems, the test process should be as realistic as possible in its simulation of an actual event. This means coupling realistic traffic loads with realistic levels of attacks. You cannot expect an IDPS to respond to a few packet probes as if they represent a denial-of-service attack. In one reported example, a program was used to create a synthetic load of network traffic made up of many TCP sessions, with each session consisting of a SYN (or synchronization) packet, a series of data, and ACK (or acknowledgement) packets, but no FIN or connection termination packets. Of the several IDPS systems tested, one of them crashed due to lack of resources while it waited for the sessions to be closed. Another IDPS passed the test with flying colors because it did not perform state tracking on the connections. Neither of the tested IDPS systems worked as expected, but the one that didn't perform state tracking was able to stay operational and was, therefore, given a better score on the test.[20]

Honeypots, Honeynets, and Padded Cell Systems

A class of powerful security tools that go beyond routine intrusion detection is known variously as honeypots, honeynets, or padded cell systems. To understand why these tools are not yet widely used, you must first understand how they differ from a traditional IDPS. **Honeypots** are decoy systems designed to lure potential attackers away from critical systems. In the industry, they are also known as decoys, lures, and fly-traps. When a collection of honeypots connects several honeypot systems on a subnet, it may be called a **honeynet**. A honeypot system (or in the case of a honeynet, an entire subnetwork) contains pseudo-services that emulate well-known services, but is configured in ways that make it look vulnerable to attacks. This combination is meant to lure potential attackers into committing an attack, thereby revealing themselves—the idea being that once organizations have detected these attackers, they can better defend their networks against future attacks targeting real assets. In sum, honeypots are designed to do the following:

- Divert an attacker from critical systems
- Collect information about the attacker's activity
- Encourage the attacker to stay on the system long enough for administrators to document the event and, perhaps, respond

Because the information in a honeypot appears to be valuable, any unauthorized access to it constitutes suspicious activity. Honeypots are instrumented with sensitive monitors and event loggers that detect attempts to access the system and collect information about the potential attacker's activities. A screenshot from a simple IDPS that specializes in honeypot techniques, called Deception Toolkit, is shown in Figure 7-8. This screenshot shows the configuration of the honeypot as it is waiting for an attack.

A **padded cell** is a honeypot that has been protected so that that it cannot be easily compromised—in other words, a hardened honeypot. In addition to attracting attackers with tempting data, a padded cell operates in tandem with a traditional IDPS. When the IDPS detects attackers, it seamlessly transfers them to a special simulated environment where they can cause no harm—the nature of this host environment is what gives the approach the name "padded cell." As in honeypots, this environment can be filled with interesting data, which can convince an attacker that the attack is going according to plan. Like honeypots, padded cells are well-instrumented and offer unique opportunities for a target organization to monitor the actions of an attacker.

IDPS researchers have used padded cell and honeypot systems since the late 1980s, but until recently no commercial versions of these products were available. It is important to seek guidance from legal counsel before deciding to use either of these systems in your operational environment, since using an attractant and then launching a back hack or counterstrike might be illegal, and could make the organization vulnerable to a lawsuit or criminal complaint.

The advantages and disadvantages of using the honeypot or padded cell approach are summarized below:

Advantages:

- Attackers can be diverted to targets that they cannot damage.
- Administrators have time to decide how to respond to an attacker.

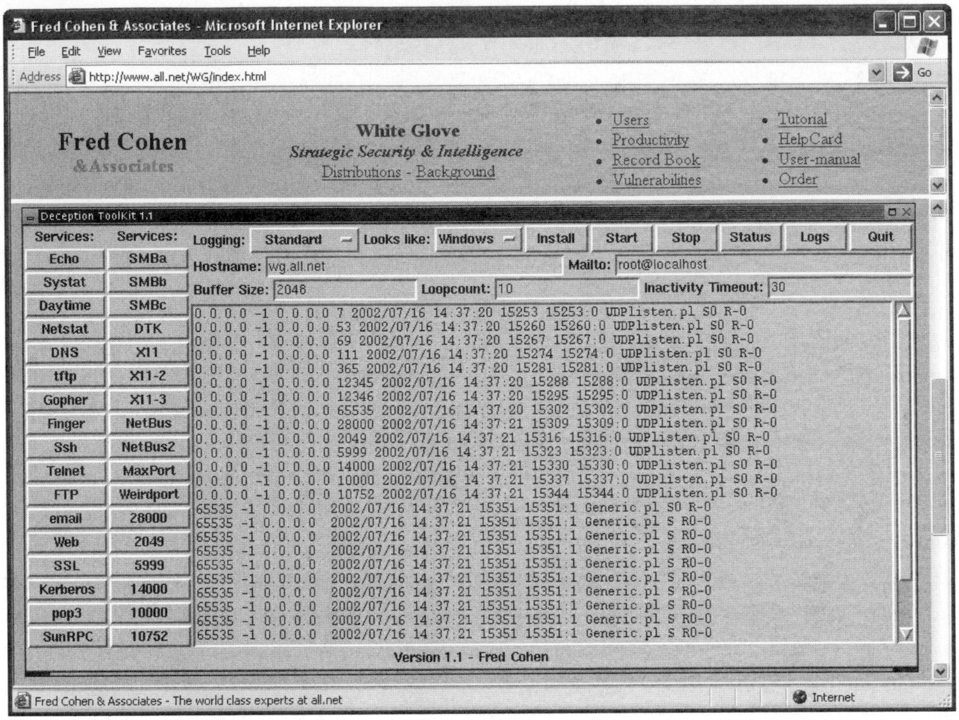

Figure 7-8 Deception Toolkit

Source: Course Technology/Cengage Learning

- Attackers' actions can be easily and more extensively monitored, and the records can be used to refine threat models and improve system protections.

- Honeypots may be effective at catching insiders who are snooping around a network.

Disadvantages:

- The legal implications of using such devices are not well understood.

- Honeypots and padded cells have not yet been shown to be generally useful security technologies.

- An expert attacker, once diverted into a decoy system, may become angry and launch a more aggressive attack against an organization's systems.

- Administrators and security managers need a high level of expertise to use these systems.[21]

Trap-and-Trace Systems

Trap-and-trace applications, which are an extension of the attractant technologies discussed in the previous section, are growing in popularity. These systems use a combination of techniques to detect an intrusion and then trace it back to its source. The trap usually consists of a honeypot or padded cell and an alarm. While the intruders are distracted, or trapped, by what they perceive to be successful intrusions, the system notifies the administrator of their presence. The trace feature is an extension to the honeypot or padded cell approach. The trace—which is similar to caller ID—is a process by which the organization attempts to identify an entity discovered in unauthorized areas of the network or systems. If the intruder is someone inside the organization, the administrators are completely within their power to track the individual and turn him or her over to internal or external authorities. If the intruder is outside the security perimeter of the organization, then numerous legal issues arise. One popular professional trap-and-trace software suite, ManHunt, and its companion honeypot application, ManTrap, was discontinued in 2006. No similar products have arisen to take their place, due to the drawbacks and complications of using these technologies.

On the surface, trap-and-trace systems seem like an ideal solution. Security is no longer limited to defense. Now security administrators can go on the offense. They can track down the perpetrators and turn them over to the appropriate authorities. Under the guise of justice, some less scrupulous administrators may even be tempted to **back hack**, or hack into a hacker's system to find out as much as possible about the hacker. Vigilante justice would be a more appropriate term for these activities, which are in fact deemed unethical by most codes of professional conduct. In tracking the hacker, administrators may end up wandering through other organizations' systems, especially when the wily hacker has used IP spoofing, compromised systems, or a myriad of other techniques to throw trackers off the trail. The backhacking administrator becomes the hacker.

There are more legal drawbacks to trap-and-trace. The trap portion frequently involves the use of honeypots or honeynets. When using honeypots and honeynets, administrators should be careful not to cross the line between enticement and entrapment. **Enticement** is the act of attracting attention to a system by placing tantalizing information in key locations. **Entrapment** is the act of luring an individual into committing a crime to get a conviction. Enticement is legal and ethical, whereas entrapment is not. It is difficult to gauge the effect such a system can have on the average user, especially if the individual has been nudged into looking at the information. Administrators should also be wary of the *wasp trap syndrome*. In this syndrome, a concerned homeowner installs a wasp trap in his back yard to trap the few insects he sees flying about. Because these traps use scented bait, however, they wind up attracting far more wasps than were originally present. Security administrators should keep the wasp trap syndrome in mind before implementing honeypots, honeynets, padded cells, or trap-and-trace systems.

Active Intrusion Prevention

Some organizations would like to do more than simply wait for the next attack and implement active countermeasures to stop attacks. One tool that provides active intrusion prevention is known as LaBrea (http://*labrea.sourceforge.net/labrea-info.html*). LaBrea is a "sticky" honeypot and IDPS and works by taking up the unused IP address space within a network. When LaBrea notes an ARP request, it checks to see if the IP address requested is actually valid on the network. If the address is not currently being used by a real computer or network device, LaBrea pretends to be a computer at that IP address and allows the attacker to complete the TCP/IP connection request, known as the three-way handshake. Once the handshake is complete, LaBrea changes the TCP sliding window size to a low number to hold open the TCP connection from the attacker for many hours, days, or even months. Holding the connection open but inactive greatly slows down network-based worms and other attacks. It allows the LaBrea system time to notify the system and network administrators about the anomalous behavior on the network.

Scanning and Analysis Tools

In order to secure a network, it is imperative that someone in the organization knows exactly where the network needs securing. This may sound simple and obvious; however, many companies skip this step. They install a simple perimeter firewall, and then, lulled into a sense of security by this single layer of defense, they relax. To truly assess the risk within a computing environment, you must deploy technical controls using a strategy of defense in depth, which is likely to include intrusion detection systems (IDSs), active vulnerability scanners, passive vulnerability scanners, automated log analyzers, and protocol analyzers (commonly referred to as sniffers). As you've learned, the first item in this list, the IDPS, helps to secure networks by detecting intrusions; the remaining items in the list also help secure networks, but they do this by helping administrators identify where the network needs securing. More specifically, scanner and analysis tools can find vulnerabilities in systems, holes in security components, and unsecured aspects of the network.

Although some information security experts may not perceive them as defensive tools, scanners, sniffers, and other such vulnerability analysis tools can be invaluable because they enable administrators to see what the attacker sees. Some of these tools are extremely complex and others are rather simple. The tools also range from expensive commercial products to free. Many of the best scanning and analysis tools are those developed by the hacker community and are available free on the Web. Good administrators should have several hacking Web sites bookmarked and should try to keep up with chat room discussions on new vulnerabilities, recent conquests, and favorite assault techniques. There is nothing wrong with a security administrator using the tools that potential attackers use in order to examine network defenses and find areas that require additional attention. In the military, there is a long and distinguished history of generals inspecting the troops under their command before battle, walking down the line checking out the equipment and mental preparedness of each soldier. In a similar way, the security administrator can use vulnerability analysis tools to inspect the units (host computers and network devices) under his or her command. A word of caution, though: many of these scanning and analysis tools have distinct signatures, and some Internet service providers (ISPs) scan for these signatures. If the ISP discovers someone using hacker tools, it can pull that person's access privileges. It is probably best for administrators to establish a working relationship with their ISPs and notify the ISP of their plans.

Scanning tools are, as mentioned earlier, typically used as part of an attack protocol to collect information that an attacker would need to launch a successful attack. The **attack protocol** is a series of steps or processes used by an attacker, in a logical sequence, to launch an attack against a target system or network. One of the preparatory parts of the attack protocol is the collection of publicly available information about a potential target, a process known as footprinting. **Footprinting** is the organized research of the Internet addresses owned or controlled by a target organization. The attacker uses public Internet data sources to perform keyword searches to identify the network addresses of the organization. This research is augmented by browsing the organization's Web pages. Web pages usually contain quantities of information about internal systems, individuals developing Web pages, and other tidbits, which can be used for social engineering attacks. The *view source* option on most popular Web browsers allows the user to see the source code behind the graphics. A number of details in the source code of the Web page can provide clues to potential attackers and give them insight into the configuration of an internal network, such as the locations and directories for Common Gateway Interface (CGI) script bins and the names or possibly addresses of computers and servers.

In addition, public business Web sites (such as Forbes or Yahoo Business) often reveal information about company structure, commonly used company names, and other information that attackers find useful. Furthermore, common search engines allow attackers to query for any site that links to their proposed target. By doing a little bit of initial Internet research into a company, an attacker can often find additional Internet locations that are not commonly associated with the company—that is, business-to-business (B2B) partners and subsidiaries. Armed with this information, the attacker can find the "weakest link" into the target network.

For example, consider Company X, which has a large datacenter in Atlanta. The datacenter has been secured, and thus it will be very hard for an attacker to break into it via the Internet. However, the attacker has run a "link:" query on the search engine *www.altavista.com* and found a small Web server that links to Company X's main Web server. After further investigation, the attacker learns that the small Web server was set up by an administrator at a remote facility and that the remote facility has, via its own leased lines, an unrestricted internal link into Company X's corporate datacenter. The attacker can now attack the weaker site at the remote facility and use this compromised network—which is an internal network—to attack the true target. While it may seem trite or clichéd, the phrase "a chain is only as strong as its weakest link" is very relevant to network and computer security. If a company has a trusted network connection with fifteen business partners, one weak business partner can compromise all sixteen networks.

To assist in the footprint intelligence collection process, you can use an enhanced Web scanner that, among other things, can scan entire Web sites for valuable pieces of information, such as server names and e-mail addresses. One such scanner is called Sam Spade, the details of which can be found in the program's help file. Since the original site no longer offers the software, to obtain it you must search the Web for a copy of the last version (1.14). A sample screenshot from Sam Spade is shown in Figure 7-9. Sam Spade can also do a host of other scans and probes, such as sending multiple ICMP information requests (pings), attempting to retrieve multiple and cross-zoned DNS queries, and performing network analysis queries (known, from the commonly used UNIX command for performing the analysis, as traceroutes). All of these are powerful diagnostic and hacking activities. Sam Spade is not, however, considered to be hackerware (or hacker-oriented software), but rather it is a utility that happens to be useful to network administrators and miscreants alike.

For Linux or BSD systems, there is a tool called "wget" that allows a remote individual to "mirror" entire Web sites. With this tool, attackers can copy an entire Web site and then go through the source HTML, JavaScript, and Web-based forms at their leisure, collecting and collating all of the data from the source code that will be useful to them for their attack.

The next phase of the attack protocol is a data-gathering process called **fingerprinting**. This is a systematic survey of all of the target organization's Internet addresses (which were collected during the footprinting phase described above); the survey is conducted to identify the network services offered by the hosts in that range. Fingerprinting, which deploys various tools as described in the following sections, reveals useful information about the internal structure and operational nature of the target system or network for the anticipated attack. Since these tools were created to find vulnerabilities in systems and networks quickly and with a minimum of effort, they are valuable to the network defender since they can quickly pinpoint the parts of the systems or network that need a prompt repair to close the vulnerability.

Figure 7-9 Sam Spade

Source: Course Technology/Cengage Learning

Port Scanners

Port scanning utilities, or **port scanners**, are tools used by both attackers and defenders to identify (or fingerprint) the computers that are active on a network, as well as the ports and services active on those computers, the functions and roles the machines are fulfilling, and other useful information. These tools can scan for specific types of computers, protocols, or resources, or their scans can be generic. It is helpful to understand the network environment so that you can use the tool most suited to the data collection task at hand. For instance, if you are trying to identify a Windows computer in a typical network, a built-in feature of the operating system, nbtstat, may be able to get the answer you need very quickly without the use of a scanner. This tool will not work on other types of networks, however, so you must know your tools in order to make the best use of the features of each.

The more specific the scanner is, the more useful the information it provides to attackers and defenders. However, you should keep a generic, broad-based scanner in your toolbox to help locate and identify rogue nodes on the network that administrators may be unaware of. Probably the most popular port scanner is Nmap, which runs on both Unix and Windows systems. You can find out more about Nmap at *www.insecure.org*.

A port is a network channel or connection point in a data communications system. Within the TCP/IP networking protocol, TCP and User Datagram Protocol (UDP) port numbers differentiate the multiple communication channels that are used to connect to the network services being offered on the same network device. Each application within TCP/IP has a unique port number. Some have default ports but can also use other ports. Some of the well-known port numbers are presented in Table 7-1. In all, there are 65,536 port numbers in use for TCP and another 65,536 port numbers for UDP. Services using the TCP/IP protocol can run

TCP Port Numbers	TCP Service
20 and 21	File Transfer Protocol (FTP)
22	Secure Shell (SSH)
23	Telnet
25	Simple Mail Transfer Protocol (SMTP)
53	Domain Name Services (DNS)
67 and 68	Dynamic Host Configuration Protocol (DHCP)
80	Hypertext Transfer Protocol (HTTP)
110	Post Office Protocol (POP3)
161	Simple Network Management Protocol (SNMP)
194	IRC chat port (used for device sharing)
443	HTTP over SSL
8080	Used for proxy services

Table 7-1 Select Commonly Used Port Numbers

on any port; however, services with reserved ports generally run on ports 1–1023. Port 0 is not used. Ports greater than 1023 are typically referred to as ephemeral ports and may be randomly allocated to server and client processes.

Why secure open ports? Simply put, an open port can be used by an attacker to send commands to a computer, potentially gain access to a server, and possibly exert control over a networking device. The general rule of thumb is to remove from service or secure any port not absolutely necessary to conducting business. For example, if a business doesn't host Web services, there is no need for port 80 to be available on its servers.

Firewall Analysis Tools

Understanding exactly where an organization's firewall is located and what the existing rule sets on the firewall do are very important steps for any security administrator. There are several tools that automate the remote discovery of firewall rules and assist the administrator (or attacker) in analyzing the rules to determine exactly what they allow and what they reject.

The Nmap tool mentioned earlier has some advanced options that are useful for firewall analysis. The Nmap option called *idle scanning* (which is run with the -I switch) will allow the Nmap user to bounce your scan across a firewall by using one of the idle DMZ hosts as the initiator of the scan. More specifically, since most operating systems do not use truly random IP packet identification numbers (IP IDs), if there is more than one host in the DMZ and one host uses nonrandom IP IDs, then the attacker can query the server (server X) and obtain the currently used IP ID as well as the known algorithm for incrementing the IP IDs. The attacker can then spoof a packet that is allegedly from server X and destined for an internal IP address behind the firewall. If the port is open on the internal machine, the internal machine replies to server X with a SYN-ACK packet, which forces server X to respond with a TCP RESET packet. In responding with the TCP RESET, server X increments its IP ID number. The attacker can now query server X a second time to see if the IP ID has incremented. If it has, the attacker knows that the internal machine is alive and that the internal machine has the queried service port open. In a nutshell, running the Nmap idle scan allows an attacker to scan an internal network as if he or she were physically located on a trusted machine inside the DMZ.

Another tool that can be used to analyze firewalls is Firewalk. Written by noted author and network security expert Mike Schiffman, Firewalk uses incrementing Time-To-Live (TTL) packets to determine the path into a network as well as the default firewall policy. Running Firewalk against a target machine reveals where routers and firewalls are filtering traffic to the target host. More information on Firewalk can be obtained from *www. packetstormsecurity.org/UNIX/audit/firewalk*.

A final firewall analysis tool worth mentioning is HPING, which is a modified ping client. It supports multiple protocols and has a command-line method of specifying nearly any of the ping parameters. For instance, you can use HPING with modified TTL values to determine the infrastructure of a DMZ. You can use HPING with specific ICMP flags in order to bypass poorly configured firewalls (i.e., firewalls that allow all ICMP traffic to pass through) and find internal systems. HPING can be found at *www.hping.org*.

Incidentally, administrators who are wary of using the same tools that attackers use should remember two important points: regardless of the tool that is used to validate or analyze a firewall's configuration, it is user intent that dictates how the information gathered is used; in order to defend a computer or network well, it is necessary to understand the ways it can be attacked. Thus, a tool that can help close up an open or poorly configured firewall will help the network defender minimize the risk from attack.

Operating System Detection Tools

Detecting a target computer's operating system is very valuable to an attacker, because once the OS is known, all of the vulnerabilities to which it is susceptible can easily be determined. There are many tools that use networking protocols to determine a remote computer's OS. One specific tool worth mentioning is XProbe, which uses ICMP to determine the remote OS. This tool can be found at *www.sourceforge.net/projects/xprobe*. When run, XProbe sends many different ICMP queries to the target host. As reply packets are received, XProbe matches these responses from the target's TCP/IP stack with its own internal database of known responses. Because most OSs have a unique way of responding to ICMP requests, Xprobe is very reliable in finding matches and thus detecting the operating systems of remote computers. System and network administrators should take note of this and restrict the use of ICMP through their organization's firewalls and, when possible, within its internal networks.

Vulnerability Scanners

Active vulnerability scanners scan networks for highly detailed information. An active scanner is one that initiates traffic on the network in order to determine security holes. As a class, this type of scanner identifies exposed usernames and groups, shows open network shares, and exposes configuration problems and other vulnerabilities in servers. An example of a vulnerability scanner is GFI LANguard Network Security Scanner (NSS), which is available as freeware for noncommercial use. Another example of a vulnerability scanner is Nessus, which is a professional freeware utility that uses IP packets to identify the hosts available on the network, the services (ports) they are offering, the operating system and OS version they are running, the type of packet filters and firewalls in use, and dozens of other characteristics of the network. Figures 7-10 and 7-11 show sample LANguard and Nessus result screens.

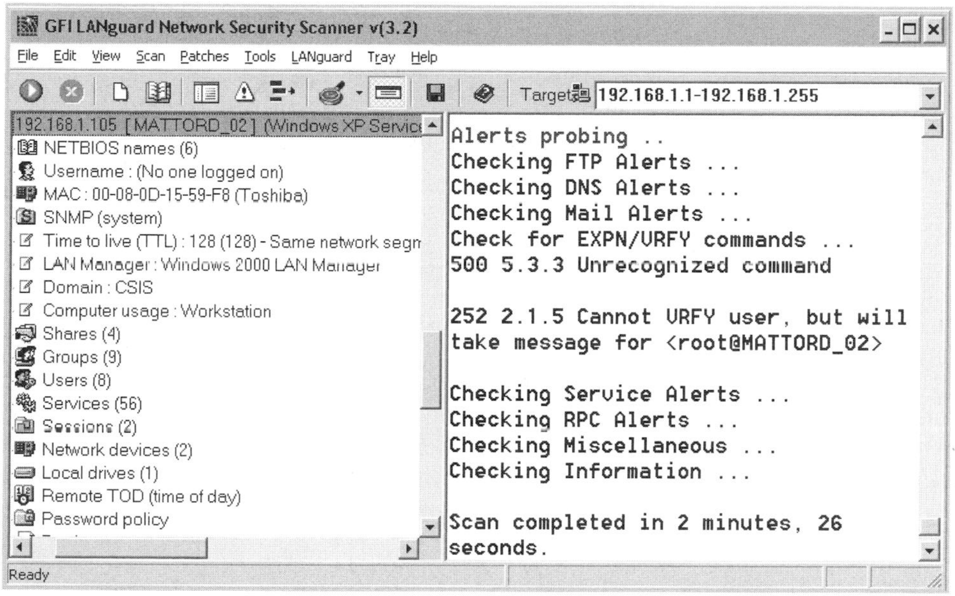

Figure 7-10 LANguard

Source: Course Technology/Cengage Learning

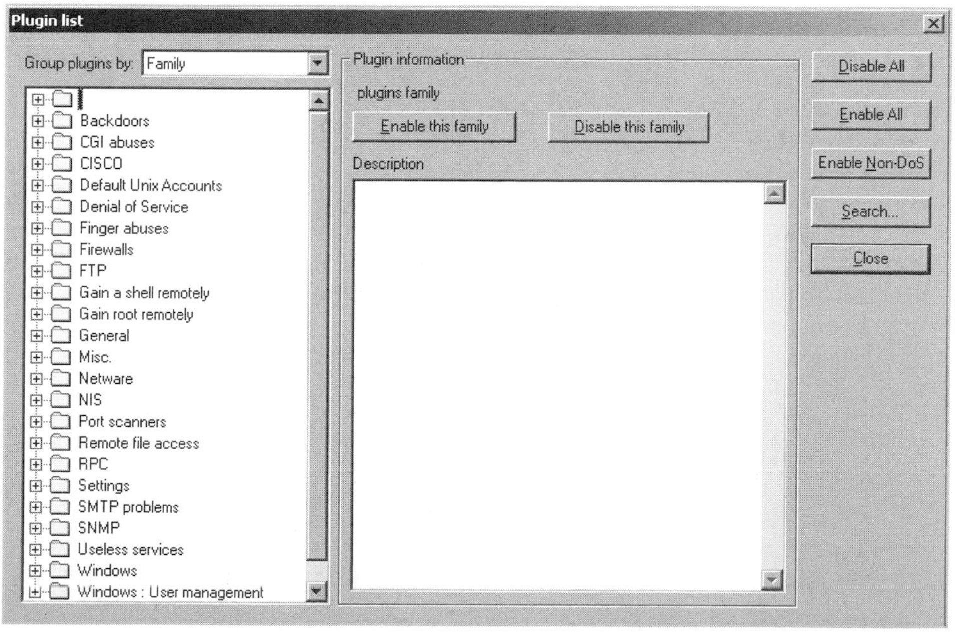

Figure 7-11 Nessus

Source: Course Technology/Cengage Learning

Vulnerability scanners should be proficient at finding known, documented holes. But what happens if the Web server is from a new vendor or the application was developed by an internal development team? There is a class of vulnerability scanners called blackbox scanners, or fuzzers. Fuzz testing is a straightforward testing technique that looks for vulnerabilities in a program or protocol by feeding random input to the program or a network running the protocol. Vulnerabilities can be detected by measuring the outcome of the random inputs. One example of a fuzz scanner is SPIKE, which has two primary components. The first is the SPIKE Proxy, which is a full-blown proxy server. As Web site visitors utilize the proxy, SPIKE builds a database of each of the traversed pages, forms, and other Web-specific information. When the Web site owner determines that enough history has been collected to fully characterize the Web sites, SPIKE can be used to check the Web site for bugs—that is, administrators can use the usage history collected by SPIKE to traverse all known pages, forms, active programs (e.g., asp, cgi-bin), and so forth, and can test the system by attempting overflows, SQL injection, cross-site scripting, and many other classes of Web attacks.

SPIKE also has a core functionality to fuzz any protocol that utilizes TCP/IP. By sniffing a session and building a SPIKE script, or building a full-blown C program using the SPIKE API, a user can simulate and "fuzz" nearly any protocol. Figure 7-12 shows the SPIKE Proxy configuration screen. Figure 7-13 shows a sample SPIKE script being prepared to fuzz the ISAKAMP protocol (which is used by VPNs). Figure 7-14 shows the SPIKE program, generic_send_udp, fuzzing an IKE server using the SPIKE script. As you can see, SPIKE can be used to quickly fuzz and find weaknesses in nearly any protocol.

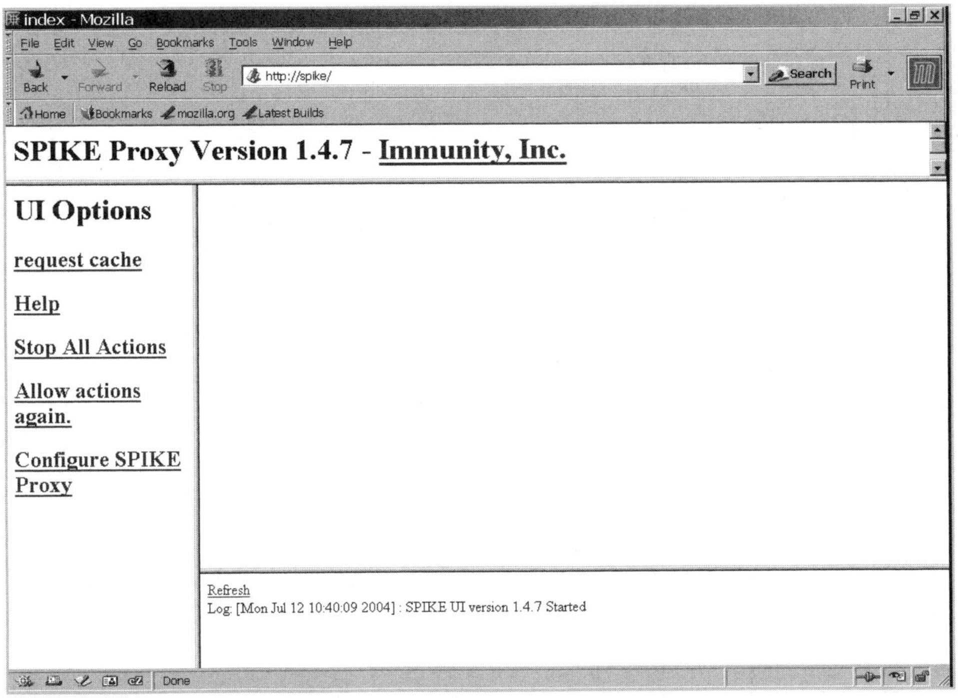

Figure 7-12 SPIKE Proxy

Source: Course Technology/Cengage Learning

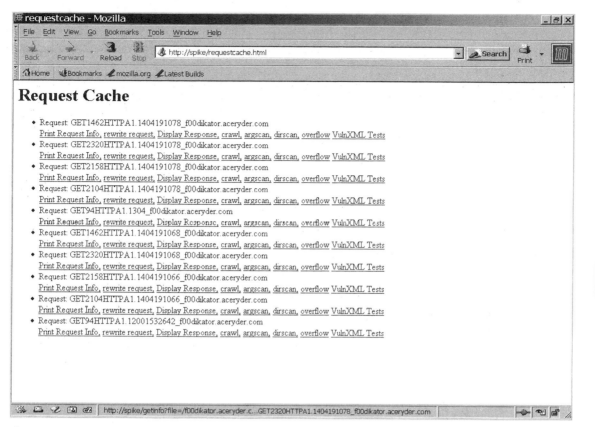

Figure 7-13 SPIKE in Action

Source: Course Technology/Cengage Learning

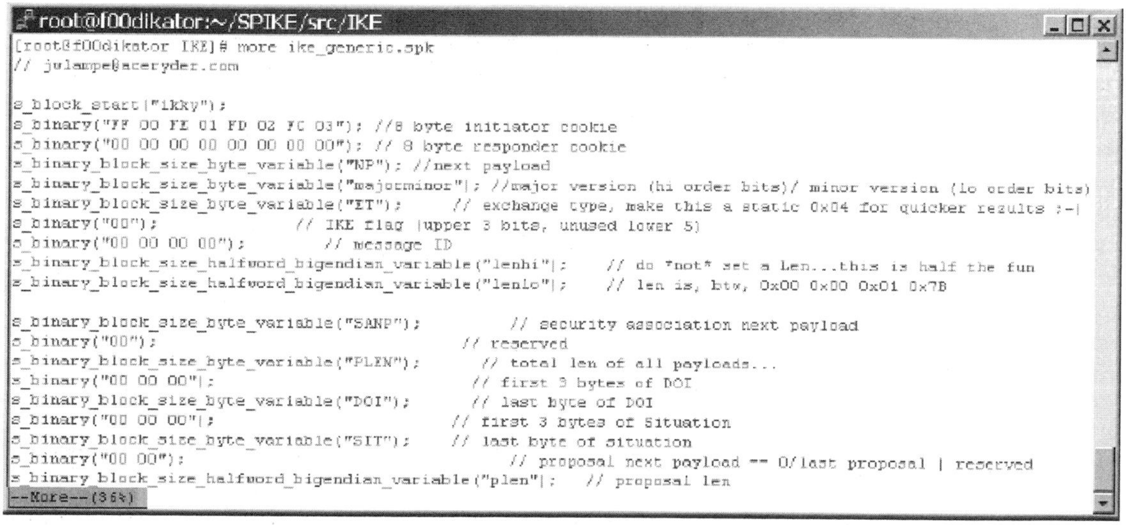

Figure 7-14 SPIKE Versus IKE

Source: Course Technology/Cengage Learning

Similar in function, the Nessus scanner has a class of attacks called *destructive*. If enabled, Nessus attempts common overflow techniques against a target host. Fuzzers or blackbox scanners and Nessus in destructive mode can be very dangerous tools and should only be used in a lab environment. In fact, these tools are so powerful that even system defenders who use them are not likely to use them in the most aggressive modes on their production networks. At the time of this writing, the most popular scanners seem to be Nessus (a commercial version of Nessus for Windows is available), Retina, and Internet Scanner. The Nessus scanner is available at no cost; the other two require a license fee.

Often times, some members of an organization require proof that a system is actually vulnerable to a certain attack. They may require such proof in order to avoid having system administrators attempt to repair systems that are not in fact broken, or because they have not yet built a satisfactory relationship with the vulnerability assessment team. In these instances, there exists a class of scanners that actually exploit the remote machine and allow the vulnerability analyst (sometimes called a penetration tester) to create an account, modify a Web page, or view data. These tools can be very dangerous and should only be used when absolutely necessary. Three tools that can perform this action are Core Impact, Immunity's CANVAS, and the Metasploit Framework.

Of these three tools, only the Metasploit Framework is available without a license fee (see *www.metasploit.com*). The Metasploit Framework is a collection of exploits coupled with an interface that allows the penetration tester to automate the custom exploitation of vulnerable systems. For instance, if you wished to exploit a Microsoft Exchange server and run a single command (perhaps add the user "security" into the administrators group), the tool allows you to customize the overflow in this manner. See Figure 7-15 for a screenshot of the Metasploit Framework in action.

A **passive vulnerability scanner** is one that listens in on the network and determines vulnerable versions of both server and client software. At the time of this writing, there are two primary vendors offering this type of scanning solution: Tenable Network Security with its Passive Vulnerability Scanner (PVS) and Sourcefire with its RNA product. Passive scanners are advantageous in that they do not require vulnerability analysts to get approval prior to testing. These tools simply monitor the network connections to and from a server to obtain a list of vulnerable applications. Furthermore, passive vulnerability scanners have the ability to find client-side vulnerabilities that are typically not found by active scanners. For instance, an active scanner operating without DOMAIN Admin rights would be unable to determine the version of Internet Explorer running on a desktop machine, whereas a passive scanner can make that determination by observing the traffic to and from the client. See Figure 7-16 for a screenshot of the Tenable PVS passive vulnerability scanner running on Windows XP.

Table 7-2 provides Web addresses for the products mentioned in the vulnerability scanners section.

Packet Sniffers

Another tool worth mentioning is the packet sniffer. A **packet sniffer** (sometimes called a network protocol analyzer) is a network tool that collects copies of packets from the network and analyzes them. It can provide a network administrator with valuable information for diagnosing and resolving networking issues. In the wrong hands, however, a sniffer can be used to eavesdrop on network traffic. There are both commercial and open-source sniffers—more

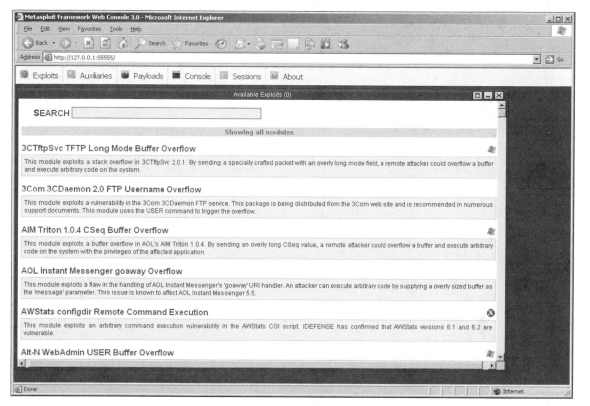

Figure 7-15 Metasploit

Source: Course Technology/Cengage Learning

specifically, Sniffer is a commercial product, and Snort is open-source software. An excellent free, client-based network protocol analyzer is Wireshark (*www.wireshark.org*), formerly known as Ethereal. Wireshark allows the administrator to examine data from both live network traffic and captured traffic. Wireshark has several features, including a language filter and TCP session reconstruction utility. Figure 7-17 shows a sample screen from Wireshark. To use these types of programs most effectively, the user must be connected to a network from a central location. Simply tapping into an Internet connection floods you with more data than can be readily processed and technically constitutes a violation of the wiretapping act. To use a packet sniffer legally, the administrator must (1) be on a network that the organization owns, (2) be under direct authorization of the owners of the network, and (3) have knowledge and consent of the content creators. If all three conditions are met, the administrator can selectively collect and analyze packets to identify and diagnose problems on the network. Conditions one and two are self-explanatory. The third, consent, is usually handled by having all system users sign a release when they are issued a user ID and passwords. Incidentally, these three items are the same requirements for employee monitoring in general, and packet sniffing should be construed as a form of employee monitoring.

Many administrators feel that they are safe from sniffer attacks when their computing environment is primarily a switched network environment. This couldn't be farther from the truth. There are a number of open-source sniffers that support alternate networking

Figure 7-16 Tenable PVS

Source: Course Technology/Cengage Learning

Product	Web Page
Nessus	*www.nessus.org*
Nessus for Windows	*www.tenablesecurity.com*
GFI LANguard Network Security Scanner	*www.gfi.com/languard*
SPIKE – SPIKE Proxy	*www.immunitysec.com*
Retina	*www.eeye.com*
Internet Scanner	*www.iss.net*
Core Impact	*www.coresecurity.com*
Metasploit Framework	*www.metasploit.com*

Table 7-2 Vulnerability Scanner Products and Web Pages

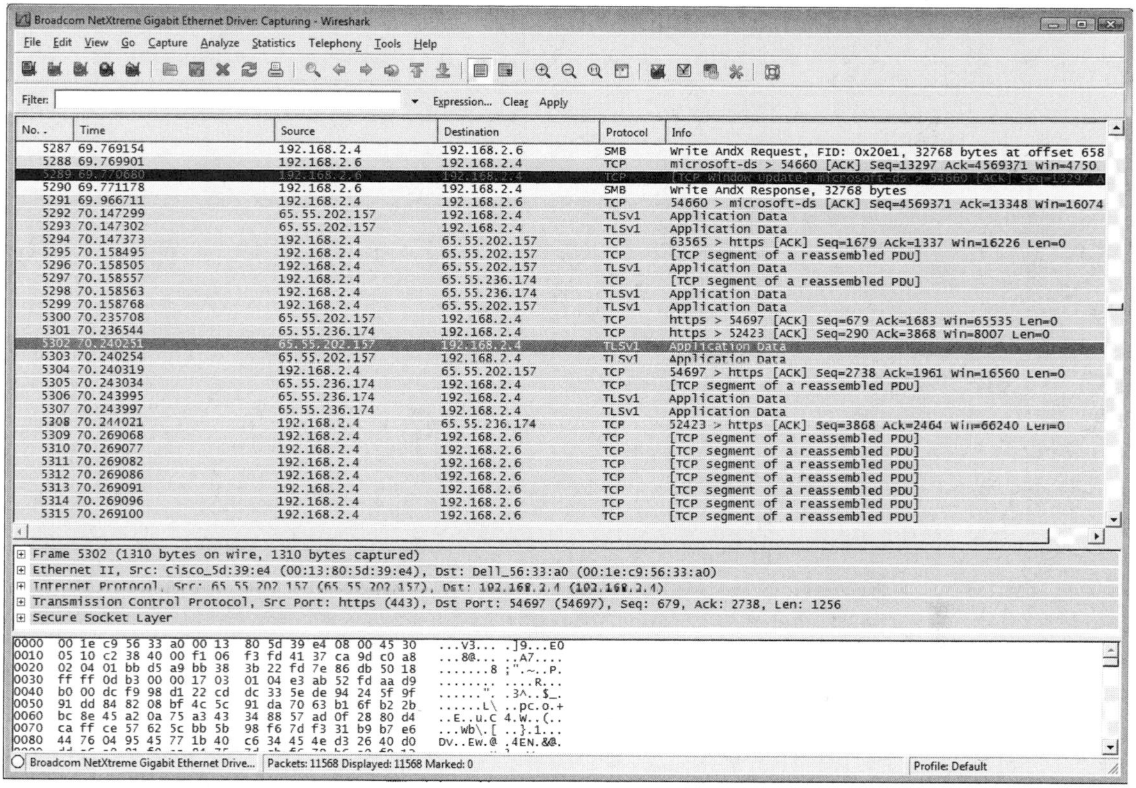

Figure 7-17 Wireshark

Source: Course Technology/Cengage Learning

approaches that can, in turn, enable packet sniffing in a switched network environment. Two of these alternate networking approaches are ARP-spoofing and session hijacking (which uses tools like ettercap). To secure data in transit across any network, organizations must use encryption to be assured of content privacy.

Wireless Security Tools

802.11 wireless networks have sprung up as subnets on nearly all large networks. A wireless connection, while convenient, has many potential security holes. An organization that spends all of its time securing the wired network and leaves wireless networks to operate in any manner is opening itself up for a security breach. As a security professional, you must assess the risk of wireless networks. A wireless security toolkit should include the ability to sniff wireless traffic, scan wireless hosts, and assess the level of privacy or confidentiality afforded on the wireless network. In 2006, Insecure.org conducted a survey to identify the top five wireless tools. (See http://sectools.org/wireless.html) The winners were:

- Kismet, a powerful wireless sniffer, network detector, and IDPS, which works by passively sniffing the networks

- Netstumbler, a freeware Windows destumbler available at *www.netstumbler.org*

- Aircrack, a WEP/WPA cracking tool

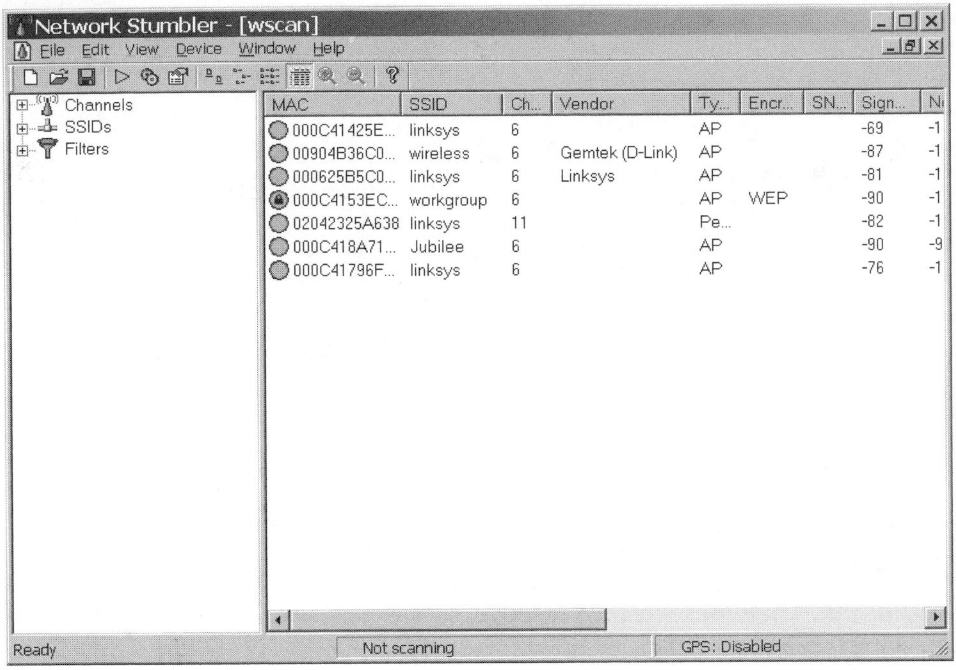

Figure 7-18 NetStumbler

Source: Course Technology/Cengage Learning

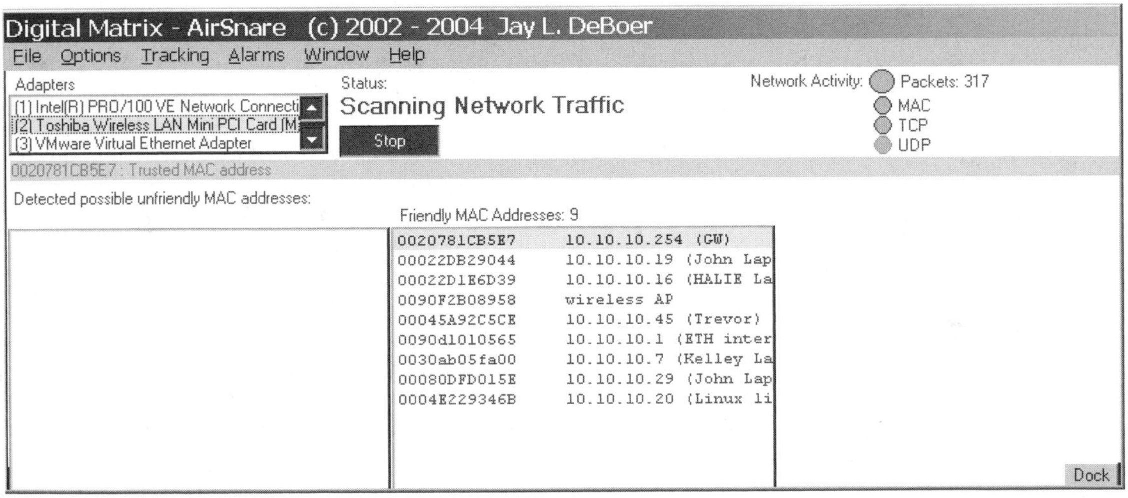

Figure 7-19 AirSnare

Source: Course Technology/Cengage Learning

- Airsnort, an 802.11 WEP encryption cracking tool

- KisMac, a GUI passive wireless stumbler for Mac OS X (variation of Kismet)

NetStumbler is offered as freeware and can be found at *www.netstumbler.org*. Figure 7-18 shows NetStumbler being run from a Windows XP machine. Another wireless tool worth mentioning is AirSnare. AirSnare is a free tool that can be run on a low-end wireless work-station. AirSnare monitors the airwaves for any new devices or access points. When it finds one, AirSnare sounds an alarm alerting the administrators that a new, potentially dangerous, wireless apparatus is attempting access on a closed wireless network. Figure 7-19 shows Air-Snare in action.

The tools discussed so far help the attacker and the defender prepare themselves to complete the next steps in the attack protocol: attack, compromise, and exploit. These steps are beyond the scope of this text, and are usually covered in more advanced classes on computer and network attack and defense.

Biometric Access Controls

You learned the basics of access control and authentication in Chapter 6. In this section you will build on that foundation and learn about the technology associated with biometric access control.

Biometric access control is based on the use of some measurable human characteristic or trait to authenticate the identity of a proposed systems user (a supplicant). It relies upon rec-ognition—the same thing you rely upon to identify friends, family, and other people you know. The use of biometric-based authentication is expected to have a significant impact in the future as technical and ethical issues with the technology are resolved.

Biometric authentication technologies include the following:

- Fingerprint comparison of the supplicant's actual fingerprint to a stored fingerprint
- Palm print comparison of the supplicant's actual palm print to a stored palm print
- Hand geometry comparison of the supplicant's actual hand to a stored measurement
- Facial recognition using a photographic ID card, in which a human security guard compares the supplicant's face to a photo
- Facial recognition using a digital camera, in which a supplicant's face is compared to a stored image
- Retinal print comparison of the supplicant's actual retina to a stored image
- Iris pattern comparison of the supplicant's actual iris to a stored image

Among all possible biometrics, only three human characteristics are usually considered truly unique. They are as follows:

- Fingerprints
- Retina of the eye (blood vessel pattern)
- Iris of the eye (random pattern of features found in the iris, including freckles, pits, striations, vasculature, coronas, and crypts)

Figure 7-20 depicts some of these human recognition characteristics.

Most of the technologies that scan human characteristics convert these images to some form of minutiae. **Minutiae** are unique points of reference that are digitized and stored in an encrypted format when the user's system access credentials are created. Each subsequent

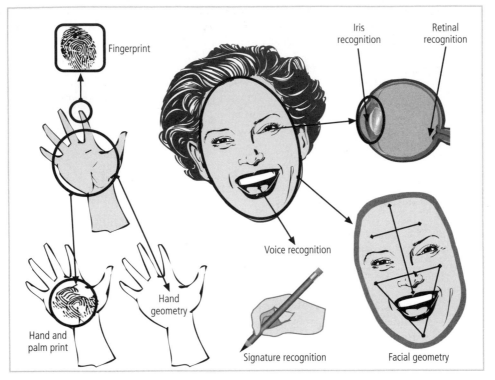

Figure 7-20 Biometric Recognition Characteristics

Source: Course Technology/Cengage Learning

access attempt results in a measurement that is compared with the encoded value to determine if the user is who he or she claims to be. A problem with this method is that some human characteristics can change over time, due to normal development, injury, or illness, which means that system designers must create fallback or failsafe authentication mechanisms.

Signature and voice recognition technologies are also considered to be biometric access controls measures. Signature recognition has become commonplace. Retail stores use signature recognition, or at least signature capture, for authentication during a purchase. The customer signs a digital pad with a special stylus that captures the signature. The signature is digitized and either saved for future reference, or compared with a signature on a database for validation. Currently, the technology for signature capturing is much more widely accepted than that for signature comparison, because signatures change due to a number of factors, including age, fatigue, and the speed with which the signature is written.

Voice recognition works in a similar fashion in that an initial voiceprint of the user reciting a phrase is captured and stored. Later, when the user attempts to access the system, the authentication process requires the user to speak this same phrase so that the technology can compare the current voiceprint against the stored value.

Effectiveness of Biometrics

Biometric technologies are evaluated on three basic criteria: first, the false reject rate, which is the percentage of supplicants who are in fact authorized users but are denied access; second, the false accept rate, which is the percentage of supplicants who are unauthorized users but are granted access; and third, the crossover error rate, which is the level at which the number of false rejections equals the false acceptances.

False Reject Rate The false reject rate is the percentage of identification instances in which authorized users are denied access as a result of a failure in the biometric device. This failure is known as a Type I error. While a nuisance to supplicants who are authorized users, this error rate is probably of least concern to security professionals since rejection of an authorized user represents no threat to security. The false reject rate is often ignored unless it reaches a level high enough to generate complaints from irritated supplicants. Most people have experienced the frustration of having a credit card or ATM card fail to perform because of problems with the magnetic strip. In the field of biometrics, similar problems can occur when a system fails to pick up the various information points it uses to authenticate a prospective user properly.

False Accept Rate The false accept rate is the percentage of identification instances in which unauthorized users are allowed access to systems or areas as a result of a failure in the biometric device. This failure is known as a Type II error, and is unacceptable to security professionals.

Crossover Error Rate (CER) The crossover error rate (CER) is the level at which the number of false rejections equals the false acceptances, and is also known as the equal error rate. This is possibly the most common and important overall measure of the accuracy of a biometric system. Most biometric systems can be adjusted to compensate for both false positive and false negative errors. Adjustment to one extreme creates a system that requires perfect matches and results in high false rejects, but almost no false accepts. Adjustment to the other extreme produces low false rejects, but high false accepts. The trick is to find the balance between providing the requisite level of security and minimizing the frustration level of authentic users. Thus, the optimal setting is found to be somewhere near the point at which these two error rates are equal; that is, at the crossover error rate or CER. CERs are used to compare various biometrics and may vary by manufacturer. A biometric device that provides a CER of 1 percent is a device for which the failure rate for false rejection and the failure rate for false acceptance are both 1 percent. A device with a CER of 1 percent is considered superior to a device with a CER of 5 percent.

Acceptability of Biometrics

As you've learned, a balance must be struck between how acceptable a security system is to its users and how effective it is in maintaining security. Many biometric systems that are highly reliable and effective are considered somewhat intrusive to users. As a result, many information security professionals, in an effort to avoid confrontation and possible user boycott of the biometric controls, don't implement them. Table 7-3 shows how certain biometrics rank in terms of effectiveness and acceptance. Interestingly, the order of effectiveness is nearly exactly opposite the order of acceptance.

Biometrics	Universality	Uniqueness	Permanence	Collectability	Performance	Acceptability	Circumvention
Face	H	L	M	H	L	H	L
Fingerprint	M	H	H	M	H	M	H
Hand Geometry	M	M	M	H	M	M	M
Keystroke Dynamics	L	L	L	M	L	M	M
Hand Vein	M	M	M	M	M	M	H
Iris	H	H	H	M	H	L	H
Retina	H	H	M	L	H	L	H
Signature	L	L	L	H	L	H	L
Voice	M	L	L	M	L	H	L
Facial Thermogram	H	H	L	H	M	H	H
DNA	H	H	H	L	H	L	L

Table 7-3 **Ranking of Biometric Effectiveness and Acceptance**

H=High, M=Medium, L=Low

Reproduced from The '123' of Biometric Technology, *2003, by Yun, Yau Wei*[22]

Selected Readings

- *Intrusion Detection and Prevention* by Carl Endorf, Gene Schultz, and Jim Mellander. 2003, McGraw-Hill Osborne Media.

- *Guide to Biometrics* by Ruud Bolle, Jonathan Connell, Sharanthchandra Pankanti, Nalini Ratha, and Andrew Senior. 2003, Springer Professional Computing.

- National Institute of Standards and Technology (NIST) Special Publication 800-31, "Intrusion Detection Systems" by Rebecca Bace and Peter Mell. Available from the archive section of the NIST Computer Security Resource Center at *http://csrc.nist.gov.*

- National Institute of Standards and Technology (NIST) Special Publication 800-94, "Guide to Intrusion Detection and Prevention Systems" by Karen Scarfone and Peter Mell. Available from the NIST Computer Security Resource Center at *http://csrc.nist.gov.*

Chapter Summary

- Intrusion detection systems (IDSs) detect potential intrusions and sound an alarm. The more recently developed intrusion prevention systems (IPSs) also detect intrusions and can also take action to defend the network.

- An intrusion detection and prevention system (IDPS) works like a burglar alarm by detecting network traffic that is a violation of the rules with which it is configured (corresponding to an opened or broken window) and activates an alarm.

- A network-based IDPS (NIDPS) monitors network traffic, and when a predefined event occurs, it responds and notifies the appropriate administrator. A host-based IDPS (HIDPS) resides on a particular computer or server and monitors activity on that system.

- Signature-based IDPSs, also known as knowledge-based IDPSs, examine data traffic for patterns that match signatures, which are preconfigured, predetermined attack patterns. Statistical anomaly-based IDPSs, also known as behavior-based IDPSs, collect data from normal traffic and establish a baseline. When an activity is found to be outside the baseline parameters (or clipping level), these IDPSs activate an alarm to notify the administrator.

- Selecting IDPS products that best fit an organization's specific needs is a challenging and complex process since there are a wide array of products and vendors, each with its own approach and capabilities.

- Deploying and implementing IDPS technology is a complex undertaking that requires knowledge of the system and experience with the technology. After deployment, each organization should measure the effectiveness of its IDPS and then continue to assess its effectiveness periodically after the initial deployment.

- Honeypots are decoy systems designed to lure potential attackers away from critical systems. In the security industry, these systems are also known as decoys, lures, or flytraps. Two variations on this technology are known as honeynets and padded cell systems.

- Trap-and-trace applications are designed to react to an intrusion event by tracing it back to its source. This process is fraught with professional and ethical issues—some in the field believe that the back hack in the trace process is as significant a violation as the initial attack.

- Active intrusion prevention seeks to limit the damage that attackers can perpetrate by making the local network resistant to inappropriate use.

- Scanning and analysis tools are used to pinpoint vulnerabilities in systems, holes in security components, and unsecured aspects of the network. Although these tools are used by attackers, they can also be used by an administrator not only to learn more about his or her own system but also to identify and repair system weaknesses before they result in losses.

- Biometric authentication encompasses a set of technical means that measure one or more physical characteristics in order to verify a person's identity.

- Biometric technologies are evaluated on three basic criteria: the false reject rate, the false accept rate, and the crossover error rate.

Review Questions

1. What common security system is an IDPS most like? In what ways are these systems similar?

2. How does a false positive alarm differ from a false negative one? From a security perspective, which is least desirable?

3. How does a network-based IDPS differ from a host-based IDPS?

4. How does a signature-based IDPS differ from a behavior-based IDPS?

5. What is a monitoring (or SPAN) port? What is it used for?

6. List and describe the three control strategies proposed for IDPS control.

7. What is a honeypot? How is it different from a honeynet?

8. How does a padded cell system differ from a honeypot?

9. What is network footprinting? What is network fingerprinting? How are they related?

10. Why do many organizations ban port scanning activities on their internal networks? Why would ISPs ban outbound port scanning by their customers?

11. What is an open port? Why is it important to limit the number of open ports to only those that are absolutely essential?

12. What is a vulnerability scanner? How is it used to improve security?

13. What is the difference between active and passive vulnerability scanners?

14. What kind of data and information can be found using a packet sniffer?

15. What capabilities should a wireless security toolkit include?

16. What is biometric authentication? What does the term *biometric* mean?

17. Are any biometric recognition characteristics considered more reliable than others? Which are the most reliable?

18. What is a false reject rate? What is a false accept rate? What is their relationship to the crossover error rate?

19. What is the most widely accepted biometric authorization technology? Why do you think this technology is acceptable to users?

20. What is the most effective biometric authorization technology? Why do you think this technology is deemed to be most effective by security professionals?

Exercises

1. A key feature of hybrid IDPS systems is event correlation. After researching event correlation online, define the following terms as they are used in this process: compression, suppression, and generalization.

2. ZoneAlarm is a PC-based firewall and IDPS tool. Visit the product manufacturer at *www.zonelabs.com*, and find the product specification for the IDPS features of Zone-Alarm. Which of the ZoneAlarm products offer these features?

3. Using the Internet, search for commercial IDPS systems. What classification systems and descriptions are used, and how can these be used to compare the features and components of each IDPS? Create a comparison spreadsheet identifying the classification systems you find.

4. Use the Internet to find vendors of thumbprint and iris scanning tools. Which of these tools is more economical? Which of these is least intrusive?

5. There are several online passphrase generators available. Locate at least two of them on the Internet, and try them out. What did you observe?

Case Exercises

Miller Harrison was still working his way down his attack protocol.

Nmap started out as it usually did: giving the program identification and version number. Then it started reporting back on the first host in the SLS network. It reported all of the open ports on this server. Then the program moved on to a second host and began reporting back the open ports on that system, too. Once it reached the third host, however, it suddenly stopped.

Miller restarted Nmap, using the last host IP as the starting point for the next scan. No response. He opened up another command window and tried to ping the first host he had just port-scanned. No luck. He tried to ping the SLS firewall. Nothing. He happened to know the IP address for the SLS edge router. He pinged that and got the same result. He had been blackholed—meaning his IP address had been put on a list of addresses from which the SLS edge router would no longer accept packets. This was, ironically, his own doing. The IDPS he had been helping SLS configure seemed to be working just fine at the moment. His attempt to hack the SLS network was shut down cold.

Questions:

1. Do you think Miller is out of options as he pursues his vendetta? If you think there are additional actions he could take in his effort to damage the SLS network, what are they?

2. Suppose a system administrator at SLS happened to read the details of this case. What steps should he or she take to improve the company's information security program?

Endnotes

1. Scarfone, K., and Mell, P. "Guide to Intrusion Detection and Prevention Systems (IDPS)." NIST Special Publication 800-94. 2007 Accessed 21 June 2007 from http://csrc.nist.gov/publications/nistpubs/800-94/SP800-94.pdf.

2. ibid.

3. ibid.

4. ibid.

5. ibid.

6. ibid.

7. ibid.

8. ibid.

9. ibid.

10. ibid.

11. Graham, R. "FAQ: Intrusion Detection Systems." March 2000. Accessed 21 June 2007 from www.linuxsecurity.com/resource_files/intrusion_detection/network-intrusion-detection.html.

12. Scarfone and Mell.

13. ibid.

14. ibid.

15. ibid.

16. ibid.

17. ibid.

18. ibid.

19. Ranum, Marcus J. "False Positives: A User's Guide to Making Sense of IDS Alarms," ICSA Labs IDSC. February 2003. Accessed 15 March 2004 from *www.icsalabs.com/html/communities/ids/whitepaper/FalsePositives.pdf*.

20. Scarfone and Mell.

21. ibid.

22. Yun, W. "The '123' of Biometric Technology." 2003. Accessed 21 November 2005 from *www.itsc.org.sg/synthesis/2002/biometric.pdf*.

chapter 8

Cryptography

Yet it may roundly be asserted that human ingenuity cannot concoct a cipher which human ingenuity cannot resolve.

EDGAR ALLAN POE, *THE GOLD BUG*

Peter Hayes, CFO of Sequential Label and Supply, was working late. He opened an e-mail from the manager of the accounting department. The e-mail had an attachment—probably a spreadsheet or a report of some kind—and from the file icon he could tell it was encrypted. He saved the file to his computer's hard drive and then double-clicked the icon to open it.

His computer operating system recognized that the file was encrypted and started the decryption program, which prompted Peter for his passphrase. Peter's mind went blank. He couldn't remember the passphrase. "Oh, good grief!" he said to himself aloud, reaching for his phone.

"Charlie, good, you're still here. I'm having trouble with a file in my e-mail program. My computer is prompting me for my passphrase, and I think I forgot it."

"Uh-oh," said Charlie.

"What do you mean 'Uh-oh'?"

"I mean you're S.O.L." Charlie replied. "Simply outta luck."

"Out of luck?" said Peter. "Why? Can't you do something? I have quite a few files that are encrypted with this PGP program. I need my files."

Charlie let him finish, then said, "Peter, remember how I told you it was important to remember your passphrase?" Charlie heard a sigh on the other end of the line, but decided to ignore it. "And do you remember I said that PGP is only free for individuals and that you weren't to use it for company files since we didn't buy a license for the company? We only set that program up on your PC for your personal mail—for when your sister wanted to send you some financial records. When did you start using it for company business?"

"Well," Peter answered, "one of my staff had some financials that were going to be ready a few weeks ago while I was traveling. I swapped public keys with him before I left, and then he sent the files to me securely by e-mail while I was in Dubai. It worked out great. So the next week I encrypted quite a few files. Now I can't get to any of them because I can't seem to remember my passphrase." There was a long pause, when he said, "Can you hack it for me?"

Charlie chuckled a bit and then said, "Sure, Peter, no problem. Send me the files and I'll put the biggest server we have to work on it. Since we set you up in PGP with 128-bit 3DES, I should be able to apply a little brute force and crack the key to get the plaintext in two or three hundred million years or so."

LEARNING OBJECTIVES:

Upon completion of this material, you should be able to:

- Chronicle the most significant events and discoveries in the history of cryptology
- Explain the basic principles of cryptography
- Describe the operating principles of the most popular cryptographic tools
- List and explicate the major protocols used for secure communications
- Discuss the nature and execution of the dominant methods of attack used against cryptosystems

Introduction

The science of cryptography is not as enigmatic as you might think. A variety of cryptographic techniques are used regularly in everyday life. For example, open your newspaper to the entertainment section and you'll find the *Daily Cryptogram*, which is a word puzzle that involves unscrambling letters to find a hidden message. Also, although it is a dying art, many secretaries still use shorthand, or stenography, an abbreviated, symbolic writing method, to take rapid dictation. A form of cryptography is used even in knitting patterns, where directions are written in a coded form, in such patterns as K1P1 (knit 1, purl 1) that only an initiate can understand. These examples illustrate one important application of cryptography—the efficient and rapid transmittal of information—but cryptography also protects and verifies data transmitted via information systems.

The science of encryption, known as **cryptology**, encompasses *cryptography* and *cryptanalysis*. **Cryptography**, which comes from the Greek words *kryptos*, meaning "hidden," and *graphein*, meaning "to write," is the process of making and using codes to secure the transmission of information. Cryptanalysis is the process of obtaining the original message (called the **plaintext**) from an encrypted message (called the **ciphertext**) without knowing the algorithms and keys used to perform the encryption. **Encryption** is the process of converting an original message into a form that is unreadable to unauthorized individuals—that is, to anyone without the tools to convert the encrypted message back to its original format. **Decryption** is the process of converting the ciphertext message back into plaintext so that it can be readily understood.

The field of cryptology is so complex it can fill many volumes. This textbook provides only a general overview of cryptology and some specific information about cryptographic tools. In the early sections of this chapter you learn the background of cryptology as well as key concepts in cryptography and common cryptographic tools. In later sections you will learn about common cryptographic protocols and some of the attack methods used against cryptosystems.

Foundations of Cryptology

Cryptology has a long and multicultural history. Table 8-1 provides an overview of the history of cryptosystems.

Date	Event
1900 B.C.	Egyptian scribes used nonstandard hieroglyphs while inscribing clay tablets; this is the first documented use of written cryptography.
1500 B.C.	Mesopotamian cryptography surpassed that of the Egyptians. This is demonstrated by a tablet that was discovered to contain an encrypted formula for pottery glazes; the tablet used symbols that have different meanings than when used in other contexts.
500 B.C.	Hebrew scribes writing the book of Jeremiah used a reversed alphabet substitution cipher known as ATBASH.
487 B.C.	The Spartans of Greece developed the *skytale*, a system consisting of a strip of papyrus wrapped around a wooden staff. Messages were written down the length of the staff, and the papyrus was unwrapped. The decryption process involved wrapping the papyrus around a shaft of similar diameter.
50 B.C.	Julius Caesar used a simple substitution cipher to secure military and government communications. To form an encrypted text, Caesar shifted the letter of the alphabet three places. In addition to this monoalphabetic substitution cipher, Caesar strengthened his encryption by substituting Greek letters for Latin letters.
Fourth to sixth centuries	The *Kama Sutra of Vatsayana* listed cryptography as the 44th and 45th of the 64 arts (yogas) that men and women should practice:*(44) The art of understanding writing in cipher, and the writing of words in a peculiar way; (45) The art of speaking by changing the forms of the word.*
725	Abu 'Abd al-Rahman al-Khalil ibn Ahman ibn 'Amr ibn Tammam al Farahidi al-Zadi al Yahmadi wrote a book (now lost) on cryptography; he also solved a Greek cryptogram by guessing the plaintext introduction.
855	Abu Wahshiyyaan-Nabati, a scholar, published several cipher alphabets that were used to encrypt magic formulas.
1250	Roger Bacon, an English monk, wrote *Epistle of Roger Bacon on the Secret Works of Art and of Nature and Also on the Nullity of Magic*, in which he described several simple ciphers.

Table 8-1 History of Cryptology

Date	Event
1392	*The Equatorie of the Planetis*, an early text possibly written by Geoffrey Chaucer, contained a passage in a simple substitution cipher.
1412	*Subhalasha*, a 14-volume Arabic encyclopedia, contained a section on cryptography, including both substitution and transposition ciphers, as well as ciphers with multiple substitutions, a technique that had never been used before.
1466	Leon Battista Alberti, the Father of Western cryptography, worked with polyalphabetic substitution and also designed a cipher disk.
1518	Johannes Trithemius wrote the first printed book on cryptography and invented a steganographic cipher, in which each letter was represented as a word taken from a succession of columns. He also described a polyalphabetic encryption method using a rectangular substitution format that is now commonly used. He is credited with introducing the method of changing substitution alphabets with each letter as it is deciphered.
1553	Giovan Batista Belaso introduced the idea of the passphrase (password) as a key for encryption; this polyalphabetic encryption method is misnamed for another person who later used the technique and is called "The Vigenère Cipher" today.
1563	Giovanni Battista Porta wrote a classification text on encryption methods, categorizing them as transposition, substitution, and symbol substitution.
1623	Sir Francis Bacon described an encryption method employing one of the first uses of steganography; he encrypted his messages by slightly changing the type-face of a random text so that each letter of the cipher was hidden within the text.
1790s	Thomas Jefferson created a 26-letter wheel cipher, which he used for official communications while ambassador to France; the concept of the wheel cipher would be reinvented in 1854 and again in 1913.
1854	Charles Babbage reinvented Thomas Jefferson's wheel cipher.
1861–5	During the U.S. Civil War, Union forces used a substitution encryption method based on specific words, and the Confederacy used a polyalphabetic cipher whose solution had been published before the start of the Civil War.
1914–17	During World War I, the Germans, British, and French used a series of transposition and substitution ciphers in radio communications throughout the war. All sides expended considerable effort to try to intercept and decode communications, and thereby created the science of cryptanalysis. British cryptographers broke the Zimmerman Telegram, in which the Germans offered Mexico U.S. territory in return for Mexico's support. This decryption helped to bring the United States into the war.
1917	William Frederick Friedman, the father of U.S. cryptanalysis, and his wife, Elizabeth, were employed as civilian cryptanalysts by the U.S. government. Friedman later founded a school for cryptanalysis in Riverbank, Illinois.
1917	Gilbert S. Vernam, an AT&T employee, invented a polyalphabetic cipher machine that used a nonrepeating random key.
1919	Hugo Alexander Koch filed a patent in the Netherlands for a rotor-based cipher machine; in 1927, Koch assigned the patent rights to Arthur Scherbius, the inventor of the Enigma machine, which was a mechanical substitution cipher.
1927–33	During Prohibition, criminals in the U.S. began using cryptography to protect the privacy of messages used in criminal activities.

Table 8-1 History of Cryptology (*Continued*)

Date	Event
1937	The Japanese developed the Purple machine, which was based on principles similar to those of Enigma and used mechanical relays from telephone systems to encrypt diplomatic messages. By late 1940, a team headed by William Friedman had broken the code generated by this machine and constructed a machine that could quickly decode Purple's ciphers.
1939–42	The Allies secretly broke the Enigma cipher, undoubtedly shortening World War II.
1942	Navajo code talkers entered World War II; in addition to speaking a language that was unknown outside a relatively small group within the United States, the Navajos developed code words for subjects and ideas that did not exist in their native tongue.
1948	Claude Shannon suggested using frequency and statistical analysis in the solution of substitution ciphers.
1970	Dr. Horst Feistel led an IBM research team in the development of the Lucifer cipher.
1976	A design based upon Lucifer was chosen by the U.S. National Security Agency as the Data Encryption Standard and found worldwide acceptance.
1976	Whitefield Diffie and Martin Hellman introduced the idea of public-key cryptography.
1977	Ronald Rivest, Adi Shamir, and Leonard Adleman developed a practical public-key cipher for both confidentiality and digital signatures; the RSA family of computer encryption algorithms was born.
1978	The initial RSA algorithm was published in the Communication of ACM.
1991	Phil Zimmermann released the first version of PGP (Pretty Good Privacy); PGP was released as freeware and became the worldwide standard for public cryptosystems.
2000	Rijndael's cipher was selected as the Advanced Encryption Standard.

Table 8-1 History of Cryptology (*Continued*)

Today, many common IT tools use embedded encryption technologies to protect sensitive information within applications. For example, all the popular Web browsers use built-in encryption features to enable secure e-commerce, such as online banking and Web shopping.

Terminology

To understand the fundamentals of cryptography, you must know the meanings of the following terms:

- **Algorithm:** The programmatic steps used to convert an unencrypted message into an encrypted sequence of bits that represent the message; sometimes refers to the programs that enable the cryptographic processes

- **Cipher** or **cryptosystem:** An encryption method or process encompassing the algorithm, key(s) or cryptovariable(s), and procedures used to perform encryption and decryption

- **Ciphertext** or **cryptogram:** The encoded message resulting from an encryption

- **Code:** The process of converting components (words or phrases) of an unencrypted message into encrypted components

- **Decipher:** To decrypt, decode, or convert, ciphertext into the equivalent plaintext

- **Encipher:** To encrypt, encode, or convert, plaintext into the equivalent ciphertext

- **Key** or **cryptovariable:** The information used in conjunction with an algorithm to create the ciphertext from the plaintext or derive the plaintext from the ciphertext; the key can be a series of bits used by a computer program, or it can be a passphrase used by humans that is then converted into a series of bits used by a computer program

- **Keyspace:** The entire range of values that can be used to construct an individual key

- **Link encryption:** A series of encryptions and decryptions between a number of systems, wherein each system in a network decrypts the message sent to it and then reencrypts it using different keys and sends it to the next neighbor, and this process continues until the message reaches the final destination

- **Plaintext** or **cleartext:** The original unencrypted message, or a message that has been successfully decrypted

- **Steganography:** The hiding of messages—for example, within the digital encoding of a picture or graphic

- **Work factor:** The amount of effort (usually in hours) required to perform cryptanalysis to decode an encrypted message when the key or algorithm (or both) are unknown

Cipher Methods

There are two methods of encrypting plaintext: the bit stream method or the block cipher method. In the bit stream method, each bit in the plaintext is transformed into a cipher bit one bit at a time. In the block cipher method, the message is divided into blocks, for example, sets of 8-, 16-, 32-, or 64-bit blocks, and then each block of plaintext bits is transformed into an encrypted block of cipher bits using an algorithm and a key. Bit stream methods commonly use algorithm functions like the exclusive OR operation (XOR), whereas block methods can use substitution, transposition, XOR, or some combination of these operations, as described in the following sections. Note that most computer-based encryption methods operate on data at the level of its binary digits (bits), but some operate at the byte or character level.

Substitution Cipher

To use a **substitution cipher,** you substitute one value for another, for example a letter in the alphabet with the letter three values to the right. Or you can substitute one bit for another bit that is four places to its left. A three-character substitution to the right results in the following transformation of the standard English alphabet:

Initial alphabet yields   ABCDEFGHIJKLMNOPQRSTUVWXYZ
Encryption alphabet   DEFGHIJKLMNOPQRSTUVWXYZABC

Within this substitution scheme, the plaintext MOM would be encrypted into the ciphertext PRP.

This is a simple enough method by itself but very powerful if combined with other operations. This type of substitution is based on a **monoalphabetic substitution,** because it only uses one alphabet. More advanced substitution ciphers use two or more alphabets, and are referred to as **polyalphabetic substitutions.**

To extend the previous example, consider the following block of text:

Plaintext =   ABCDEFGHIJKLMNOPQRSTUVWXYZ
Substitution cipher 1 =   DEFGHIJKLMNOPQRSTUVWXYZABC
Substitution cipher 2 =   GHIJKLMNOPQRSTUVWXYZABCDEF
Substitution cipher 3 =   JKLMNOPQRSTUVWXYZABCDEFGHI
Substitution cipher 4 =   MNOPQRSTUVWXYZABCDEFGHIJKL

The first row here is the plaintext, and the next four rows are four sets of substitution ciphers, which taken together constitute a single polyalphabetic substitution cipher. To encode the word TEXT with this cipher, you substitute a letter from the second row for the first letter in TEXT, a letter from the third row for the second letter, and so on—a process that yields the ciphertext WKGF. Note how the plaintext letter T is transformed into a W or a F, depending on its order of appearance in the plaintext. Complexities like these make this type of encryption substantially more difficult to decipher when one doesn't have the algorithm (in this case, the rows of ciphers) and the key, which is the method used (in this case the use of the second row for first letter, third for second, and so on). A logical extension to this process is to randomize the cipher rows completely in order to create a more complex operation.

One example of a substitution cipher is the cryptogram in the daily newspaper (see Figure 8-1); another is the once famous *Radio Orphan Annie Decoder Pin* (shown in Figure 8-2), which consisted of two alphabetic rings that could be rotated to a predetermined pairing to form a simple substitution cipher. The device was made to be worn as a pin so one could always be at the ready. As mentioned in Table 8-1, Julius Caesar reportedly used a three-position shift to the right to encrypt his messages (so A became D, B became E, and so on), and thus this particular substitution cipher was given his name—the *Caesar Cipher*.

An advanced type of substitution cipher that uses a **simple polyalphabetic** code is the **Vigenère cipher**. The cipher is implemented using the Vigenère square (or table), which is made up of twenty-six distinct cipher alphabets. Table 8-2 illustrates the setup of the Vigenère square. In the header row, the alphabet is written in its normal order. In each subsequent row, the alphabet is shifted one letter to the right until a 26 × 26 block of letters is formed. There are a number of ways to use the Vigenère square. You could perform an encryption by simply starting in the first row and finding a substitute for the first letter of plaintext, and

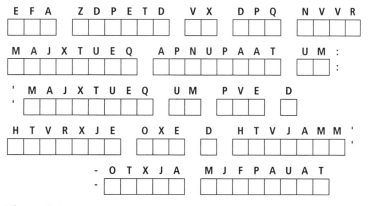

Figure 8-1 Daily Cryptogram

Source: Course Technology/Cengage Learning

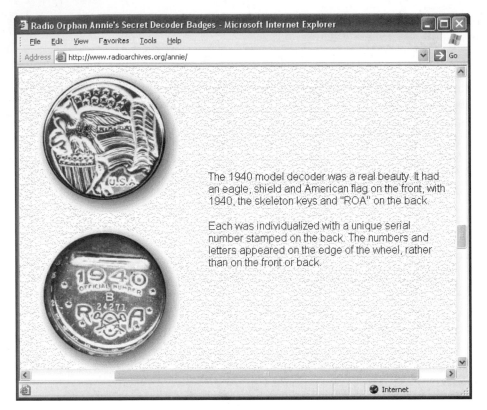

The 1940 model decoder was a real beauty. It had an eagle, shield and American flag on the front, with 1940, the skeleton keys and "ROA" on the back.

Each was individualized with a unique serial number stamped on the back. The numbers and letters appeared on the edge of the wheel, rather than on the front or back.

Figure 8-2 Radio Orphan Annie's Decoder Pin

Source: Course Technology/Cengage Learning

then moving down the rows for each subsequent letter of plaintext. With this method, the word SECURITY in plaintext becomes TGFYWOAG in ciphertext.

A much more sophisticated way to use the Vigenère square is to use a keyword to represent the shift. To accomplish this, you begin by writing a keyword above the plaintext message. For example, suppose the plaintext message was "SACK GAUL SPARE NO ONE" and the keyword was ITALY. We thus end up with the following:

```
ITALYITALYITALYITA
SACKGAULSPARENOONE
```

Now you use the keyword letter and the message (plaintext) letter below it in combination. Returning to the Vigenère square, notice how the first column of text, like the first row, forms the normal alphabet. To perform the substitution, start with the first combination of keyword and message letters, IS. Use the keyword letter to locate the column, and the message letter to find the row, and then look for the letter at their intersection. Thus, for column "I" and row "S," you will find the ciphertext letter "A." After you follow this procedure for each of the letters in the message, you will produce the encrypted ciphertext ATCVEINLDNI-KEYMWGE. One weakness of this method is that any keyword-message letter combination containing an "A." row or column reproduces the plaintext message letter. For example, the third letter in the plaintext message, the C (of SACK), has a combination of AC, and thus is

	A	B	C	D	E	F	G	H	I	J	K	L	M	N	O	P	Q	R	S	T	U	V	W	X	Y	Z
1	B	C	D	E	F	G	H	I	J	K	L	M	N	O	P	Q	R	S	T	U	V	W	X	Y	Z	A
2	C	D	E	F	G	H	I	J	K	L	M	N	O	P	Q	R	S	T	U	V	W	X	Y	Z	A	B
3	D	E	F	G	H	I	J	K	L	M	N	O	P	Q	R	S	T	U	V	W	X	Y	Z	A	B	C
4	E	F	G	H	I	J	K	L	M	N	O	P	Q	R	S	T	U	V	W	X	Y	Z	A	B	C	D
5	F	G	H	I	J	K	L	M	N	O	P	Q	R	S	T	U	V	W	X	Y	Z	A	B	C	D	E
6	G	H	I	J	K	L	M	N	O	P	Q	R	S	T	U	V	W	X	Y	Z	A	B	C	D	E	F
7	H	I	J	K	L	M	N	O	P	Q	R	S	T	U	V	W	X	Y	Z	A	B	C	D	E	F	G
8	I	J	K	L	M	N	O	P	Q	R	S	T	U	V	W	X	Y	Z	A	B	C	D	E	F	G	H
9	J	K	L	M	N	O	P	Q	R	S	T	U	V	W	X	Y	Z	A	B	C	D	E	F	G	H	I
10	K	L	M	N	O	P	Q	R	S	T	U	V	W	X	Y	Z	A	B	C	D	E	F	G	H	I	J
11	L	M	N	O	P	Q	R	S	T	U	V	W	X	Y	Z	A	B	C	D	E	F	G	H	I	J	K
12	M	N	O	P	Q	R	S	T	U	V	W	X	Y	Z	A	B	C	D	E	F	G	H	I	J	K	L
13	N	O	P	Q	R	S	T	U	V	W	X	Y	Z	A	B	C	D	E	F	G	H	I	J	K	L	M
14	O	P	Q	R	S	T	U	V	W	X	Y	Z	A	B	C	D	E	F	G	H	I	J	K	L	M	N
15	P	Q	R	S	T	U	V	W	X	Y	Z	A	B	C	D	E	F	G	H	I	J	K	L	M	N	O
16	Q	R	S	T	U	V	W	X	Y	Z	A	B	C	D	E	F	G	H	I	J	K	L	M	N	O	P
17	R	S	T	U	V	W	X	Y	Z	A	B	C	D	E	F	G	H	I	J	K	L	M	N	O	P	Q
18	S	T	U	V	W	X	Y	Z	A	B	C	D	E	F	G	H	I	J	K	L	M	N	O	P	Q	R
19	T	U	V	W	X	Y	Z	A	B	C	D	E	F	G	H	I	J	K	L	M	N	O	P	Q	R	S
20	U	V	W	X	Y	Z	A	B	C	D	E	F	G	H	I	J	K	L	M	N	O	P	Q	R	S	T
21	V	W	X	Y	Z	A	B	C	D	E	F	G	H	I	J	K	L	M	N	O	P	Q	R	S	T	U
22	W	X	Y	Z	A	B	C	D	E	F	G	H	I	J	K	L	M	N	O	P	Q	R	S	T	U	V
23	X	Y	Z	A	B	C	D	E	F	G	H	I	J	K	L	M	N	O	P	Q	R	S	T	U	V	W
24	Y	Z	A	B	C	D	E	F	G	H	I	J	K	L	M	N	O	P	Q	R	S	T	U	V	W	X
25	Z	A	B	C	D	E	F	G	H	I	J	K	L	M	N	O	P	Q	R	S	T	U	V	W	X	Y
26	A	B	C	D	E	F	G	H	I	J	K	L	M	N	O	P	Q	R	S	T	U	V	W	X	Y	Z

Table 8-2 The Vigenère Square

unchanged in the ciphertext. To minimize the effects of this weakness, you should avoid choosing a keyword that contains the letter "A."

Transposition Cipher

Like the substitution operation, the transposition cipher is simple to understand, but it can, if properly used, produce ciphertext that is difficult to decipher. In contrast to the substitution cipher, however, the **transposition cipher** (or **permutation cipher**) simply rearranges the values within a block to create the ciphertext. This can be done at the bit level or at the byte (character) level. For an example, consider the following transposition key pattern.

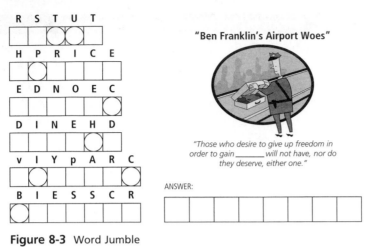

Figure 8-3 Word Jumble

Source: Course Technology/Cengage Learning

Key pattern: 1→4, 2→8, 3→1, 4→5, 5→7, 6→2, 7→6, 8→3

In this key, the bit or byte (character) in position 1 (with position 1 being at the far right) moves to position 4 (counting from the right), and the bit or byte in position 2 moves to position 8, and so on. This is similar to another newspaper puzzle favorite: the Word Jumble, as illustrated in Figure 8-3.

The following rows show the numbering of bit locations for this key; the plaintext message 00100101011010111001010101010100, which is broken into 8-bit blocks for clarity; and the ciphertext that is produced when the transposition key depicted above is applied to the plaintext:

Bit locations:	87654321 87654321 87654321 87654321
Plaintext 8-bit blocks:	00100101|01101011|10010101|01010100
Ciphertext:	00001011|10111010|01001101|01100001

Reading from right to left in the example above, the first bit of plaintext (position 1 of the first byte) becomes the fourth bit (in position 4) of the first byte of the ciphertext. Similarly, the second bit of the plaintext (position 2) becomes the eighth bit (position 8) of the ciphertext, and so on.

To examine further how this transposition key works, look at its effects on a plaintext message comprised of letters instead of bits. Replacing the 8-bit block of plaintext with the example plaintext message presented earlier, "SACK GAUL SPARE NO ONE," yields the following:

Letter locations:	87654321|87654321|87654321|87654321|
Plaintext:	SACKGAUL|SPARENOO|NE | |
Key: Same key as above, but characters transposed, not bits.	
Ciphertext:	UKAGLSCA|ORPEOSAN| E N | |

Here, reading from right to left, the letter in position 1 of the first block of plaintext, "L," becomes the letter at position 4 in the ciphertext. In other words, the "L" that is the eighth letter of the plaintext is the "L" at the fifth letter of the ciphertext. The letter in position 2 of the first block of plaintext, "U," becomes the letter at position 8 in the ciphertext. In other words, the "U" that is the seventh letter of the plaintext is the "U" that is the first letter of the ciphertext. This process continues using the specified pattern.

In addition to being credited with inventing a substitution cipher, Julius Caesar was associated with an early version of the transposition cipher. In the Caesar block cipher, the recipient of the coded message knows to fit the text to a prime number square (in practice, this means that if there are fewer than twenty-five characters, the recipient uses a 5 x 5 square). For example, if you are the recipient of the Caesar ciphertext shown below you would make a square of five columns and five rows, and then write the letters of the message into the square, filling the slots from left to right, top to bottom. Then you read the message from the opposite direction—that is, from top to bottom, left to right.

```
Ciphertext:      SGS_NAAPNECUAO_KLR _ _ _ _ EO
                 S   G   S   _   N
                 A   A   P   N   E
                 C   U   A   O
                 K   L   R   _   _
                 _   _   E   O   _
```

Reading from top to bottom, left to right reveals the plaintext "SACK GAUL SPARE NO ONE."

When mechanical and electronic cryptosystems became more widely used, transposition ciphers and substitution ciphers were combined to produce highly secure encryption processes. To make the encryption even stronger (more difficult to cryptanalyze) the keys and block sizes can be made much larger (up to 64 or 128 bits in size), which produces substantially more complex substitutions or transpositions.

Exclusive OR

The **exclusive OR operation (XOR)** is a function of Boolean algebra in which two bits are compared, and if the two bits are identical, the result is a binary 0. If the two bits are not the same, the result is a binary 1. XOR encryption is a very simple symmetric cipher that is used in many applications where security is not a defined requirement. Table 8-3 shows an XOR truth table with the results of all the possible combinations of two bits.

To see how XOR works, consider an example in which the plaintext is the word "CAT." The ASCII binary representation of the plaintext is "01000011 01000001 01010100". In order to encrypt the plaintext, a key value should be selected. In this case, the bit pattern for the letter "V" (01010110) is used, and is repeated for each character to be encrypted, written

First Bit	Second Bit	Result
0	0	0
0	1	1
1	0	1
1	1	0

Table 8-3 XOR Truth Table

Text Value	Binary Value
CAT as bits	0 1 0 0 0 0 1 1 0 1 0 0 0 0 0 1 0 1 0 1 0 1 0 0
VVV as key	0 1 0 1 0 1 1 0 0 1 0 1 0 1 1 0 0 1 0 1 0 1 1 0
Cipher	0 0 0 1 0 1 0 1 0 0 0 1 0 1 1 1 0 0 0 0 0 0 1 0

Table 8-4 Example XOR Encryption

left to right. Performing the XOR operation on the two bit streams (the plaintext and the key) produces the result shown in Table 8-4.

The row of Table 8-4 labeled "Cipher" contains the bit stream that will be transmitted; when this cipher is received, it can be decrypted using the key value "V." Note that the XOR encryption method is very simple to implement and equally simple to break. The XOR encryption method should not be used by itself when an organization is transmitting or storing sensitive data. Actual encryption algorithms used to protect data typically use the XOR operator as part of a more complex encryption process.

You can combine the XOR operation with a block cipher operation to produce a simple but powerful operation. In the example that follows, the first row shows a character message "5E5+•" requiring encryption. The second row shows this message in binary notation. In order to apply an 8-bit block cipher method, the binary message is broken into 8-bit blocks in the row labeled "Message blocks." The fourth row shows the 8-bit key (01010101) chosen for the encryption. To encrypt the message, you must perform the XOR operation on each 8-bit block by using the XOR function on the message bit and the key bit to determine the bits of the ciphertext until the entire message is enciphered. The result is shown in the row labeled "Ciphertext." This ciphertext can now be sent to a receiver, who will be able to decipher the message by simply knowing the algorithm (XOR) and the key (01010101).

Message (text):	"5E5+•"				
Message (binary):	00110101	01000101	00110101	00101011	10010101
Message blocks:	00110101	01000101	00110101	00101011	10010101
Key:	01010101	01010101	01010101	01010101	01010101
Ciphertext:	01100000	00010000	01100000	01111110	11000000

If the receiver cannot apply the key to the ciphertext and derive the original message, either the cipher was applied with an incorrect key or the cryptosystem was not used correctly.

Vernam Cipher

Also known as the one-time pad, the **Vernam cipher**, which was developed by AT&T, uses a set of characters only one time for each encryption process (hence the name *one-time pad*). The pad in the name comes from the days of manual encryption and decryption when the key values for each ciphering session were prepared by hand and bound into an easy-to-use form—that is, a pad of paper. To perform the Vernam cipher encryption operation, the pad values are added to numeric values that represent the plaintext that needs to be encrypted. Each character of the plaintext is turned into a number and a pad value for that position is added to it. The resulting sum for that character is then converted back to a ciphertext letter for transmission. If the sum of the two values exceeds 26, then 26 is subtracted from the total. (The process of keeping a computed number within a specific range is called a modulo; thus, requiring that all numbers be in the range 1–26 is referred to as modulo 26. In modulo 26, if a number is larger than 26, then 26 is sequentially subtracted from it until the number is in the proper range.)

To examine the Vernam cipher and its use of modulo, consider the following example, which uses "SACK GAUL SPARE NO ONE" as plaintext. In the first step of this encryption process, the letter "S" is converted into the number 19 (because it is the nineteenth letter of the alphabet), and the same conversion is applied to the rest of the letters of the plaintext message, as shown below.

Plaintext:	S	A	C	K	G	A	U	L	S	P	A	R	E	N	O	O	N	E
Plaintext value:	19	01	03	11	07	01	21	12	19	16	01	18	05	14	15	15	14	05
One-time pad text:	F	P	Q	R	N	S	B	I	E	H	T	Z	L	A	C	D	G	J
One time pad value:	06	16	17	18	14	19	02	09	05	08	20	26	12	01	03	04	07	10
Sum of plaintext and pad:	25	17	20	29	21	20	23	21	24	24	21	44	17	15	18	19	21	15
After modulo Subtraction:				03								18						
Ciphertext:	Y	Q	T	C	U	T	W	U	X	X	U	R	Q	O	R	S	U	O

Rows three and four in this example show, respectively, the one-time pad text that was chosen for this encryption and the one-time pad value. As you can see, the pad value, like the plaintext value, is derived from the position of each pad text letter in the alphabet; thus the pad text letter "F" is assigned the position number 06. This conversion process is repeated for the entire one-time pad text. Next, the plaintext value and the one-time pad value are added together—the first such sum is 25. Since 25 is in the range of 1 to 26, no modulo 26 subtraction is required. The sum remains 25, and yields the ciphertext "Y," as shown above. Skipping ahead to the fourth character of the plaintext, "K," we find that the plaintext value for it is 11. The pad text is "R" and the pad value is 18. The sum of 11 and 18 is 29. Since 29 is larger than 26, 26 is subtracted from it, which yields the value 3. The ciphertext for this plaintext character is then the third letter of the alphabet, "C."

Decryption of any ciphertext generated from a one-time pad requires either knowledge of the pad values or the use of elaborate and (the encrypting party hopes) very difficult cryptanalysis. Using the pad values and the ciphertext, the decryption process works as follows: "Y" becomes the number 25, from which we subtract the pad value for the first letter of the message, 06. This yields a value of 19, or the letter "S." This pattern continues until the fourth letter of the ciphertext where the ciphertext letter is "C" and the pad value is 18. Subtracting 18 from 3 yields negative 15. Since modulo 26 is employed, which requires that all numbers are in the range of 1–26, you must *add* 26 to the negative 15. This operations gives a sum of 11, which means that fourth letter of the message is "K."

Book or Running Key Cipher

One encryption method made popular by spy movies involves using the text in a book as the key to decrypt a message. The ciphertext consists of a list of codes representing the page number, line number, and word number of the plaintext word. The algorithm is the mechanical process of looking up the references from the ciphertext and converting each reference to a word by using the ciphertext's value and the key (the book). For example, from a copy of a particular popular novel, one may send the message: 259,19,8; 22,3,8; 375,7,4; 394,17,2. Although almost any book can be used, dictionaries and thesauruses are typically the most popular sources as they are likely to contain almost any word that might be needed. The recipient of a running key cipher must first know which book is used—in this case, suppose it is the science fiction novel *A Fire Upon the Deep*, the 1992 TOR edition. To decrypt the ciphertext, the receiver acquires the book and turns to page 259, finds line 19, and selects the eighth word in that line (which is "sack"). Then the receiver turns to page 22, line 3, and selects the eighth word again, and so forth. In this example, the resulting message is "SACK ISLAND SHARP PATH." If dictionaries are used, the message consists of only the page number and the number of the word on the page. An even more sophisticated version might use multiple books, perhaps even in a particular sequence for each word or phrase.

Hash Functions

In addition to ciphers, another important encryption technique that is often incorporated into cryptosystems is the hash function. **Hash functions** are mathematical algorithms that generate a message summary or digest (sometimes called a fingerprint) to confirm the identity of a specific message and to confirm that there have not been any changes to the content. While they do not create a ciphertext, hash functions confirm message identity and integrity, both of which are critical functions in e-commerce.

Hash algorithms are public functions that create a hash value, also known as a message digest, by converting variable-length messages into a single fixed-length value. The **message digest** is a fingerprint of the author's message that is compared with the recipient's locally calculated hash of the same message. If both hashes are identical after transmission, the message has arrived without modification. Hash functions are considered one-way operations in that the same message always provides the same hash value, but the hash value itself cannot be used to determine the contents of the message.

Hashing functions do not require the use of keys, but it is possible to attach a **message authentication code (MAC)**—a key-dependent, one-way hash function—that allows only specific recipients (symmetric key holders) to access the message digest. Because hash functions are one-way, they are used in password verification systems to confirm the identity of the user. In such systems, the hash value, or message digest, is calculated based upon the originally issued password, and this message digest is stored for later comparison. When the user logs on for the next session, the system calculates a hash value based on the user's password input, and this value is compared against the stored value to confirm identity.

The **Secure Hash Standard (SHS)** is a standard issued by the National Institute of Standards and Technology (NIST). Standard document FIPS 180-1 specifies SHA-1 (Secure Hash Algorithm 1) as a secure algorithm for computing a condensed representation of a message or data file. SHA-1 produces a 160-bit message digest, which can be used as an input to a digital signature algorithm. SHA-1 is based on principles modeled after MD4 (which is part of the MDx family of hash algorithms created by Ronald Rivest). New hash algorithms (SHA-256, SHA-384, and SHA-512) have been proposed by NIST as standards for 128, 192, and 256 bits, respectively. The number of bits used in the hash algorithm is a measurement of the strength of the algorithm against collision attacks. SHA-256 is essentially a 256-bit block cipher algorithm that creates a key by encrypting the intermediate hash value, with the message block functioning as the key. The compression function operates on each 512-bit message block and a 256-bit intermediate message digest.[1] As shown in Figure 8-4, there are free tools that can calculate hash values using a number of popular algorithms.

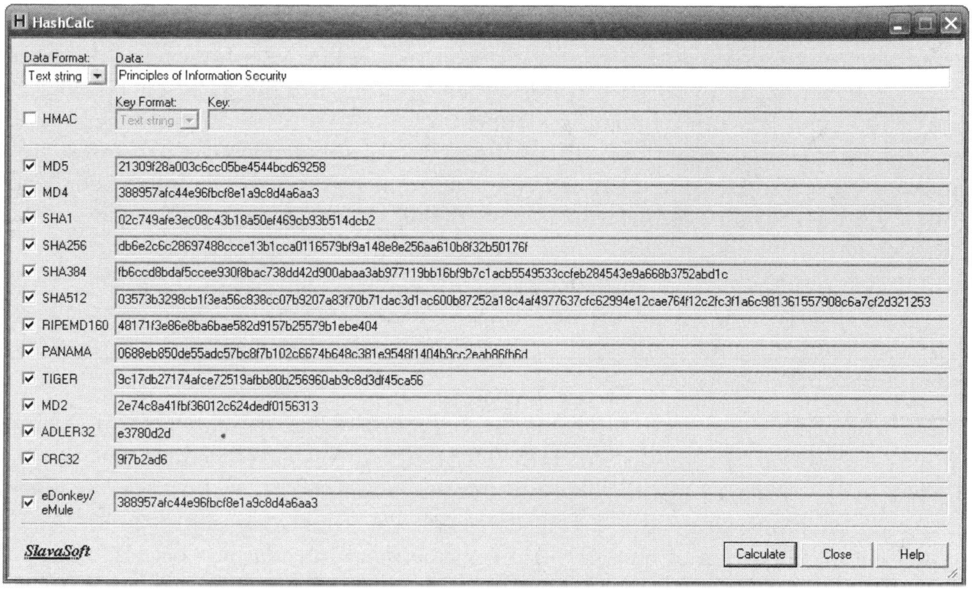

Figure 8-4 Various Hash Values

Source: Course Technology/Cengage Learning

A recent attack method called rainbow cracking has generated concern about the strength of the processes used for password hashing. In general, if attackers gain access to a file of hashed passwords, they can use a combination of brute force and dictionary attacks to reveal user passwords. Passwords that are dictionary words or poorly constructed can be easily cracked. Well-constructed passwords take a long time to crack even using the fastest computers, but by using a rainbow table—a database of precomputed hashes from sequentially calculated passwords—the rainbow cracker simply looks up the hashed password and reads out the text version, no brute force required. This type of attack is more properly classified as a **time–memory tradeoff attack**.

To defend against this type of attack, you must first protect the file of hashed passwords and implement strict limits to the number of attempts allowed per login session. You can also use an approach called password hash salting. Salting is the process of providing a non-secret, random piece of data to the hashing function when the hash is first calculated. The use of the salt value creates a different hash and when a large set of salt values are used, rainbow cracking fails since the time-memory tradeoff is no longer in the attacker's favor. The salt value is not kept a secret: it is stored along with the account identifier so that the hash value can be recreated during authentication.[2]

Cryptographic Algorithms

In general, cryptographic algorithms are often grouped into two broad categories—symmetric and asymmetric—but in practice, today's popular cryptosystems use a hybrid combination of symmetric and asymmetric algorithms. Symmetric and asymmetric algorithms are distinguished by the types of keys they use for encryption and decryption operations.

Symmetric Encryption

Encryption methodologies that require the same **secret key** to encipher and decipher the message are using what is called **private key encryption** or **symmetric encryption**. Symmetric encryption methods use mathematical operations that can be programmed into extremely fast computing algorithms so that the encryption and decryption processes are executed quickly by even small computers. As you can see in Figure 8-5, one of the challenges is that both the sender and the recipient must have the secret key. Also, if either copy of the key falls into the wrong hands, messages can be decrypted by others and the sender and intended receiver may not know the message was intercepted. The primary challenge of symmetric key encryption is getting the key to the receiver, a process that must be conducted out of band (meaning through a channel or band other than the one carrying the ciphertext) to avoid interception.

There are a number of popular symmetric encryption cryptosystems. One of the most widely known is the **Data Encryption Standard (DES)**, which was developed by IBM and is based on the company's Lucifer algorithm, which uses a key length of 128 bits. As implemented, DES uses a 64-bit block size and a 56-bit key. DES was adopted by NIST in 1976 as a federal standard for encryption of non-classified information, after which it became widely employed in commercial applications. DES enjoyed increasing popularity for almost twenty years, until 1997, when users realized that a 56-bit key size did not provide acceptable levels of security. In 1998, a group called the Electronic Frontier Foundation (*www.eff.org*), using a specially designed computer, broke a DES key in less than three days (just over 56 hours, to be precise). Since then, it has been theorized that a dedicated attack supported by the proper hardware (not necessarily a specialized computer) can break a DES key in less than four hours.

Triple DES (3DES) was created to provide a level of security far beyond that of DES. 3DES was an advanced application of DES, and while it did deliver on its promise of encryption strength beyond DES, it too soon proved too weak to survive indefinitely—especially as

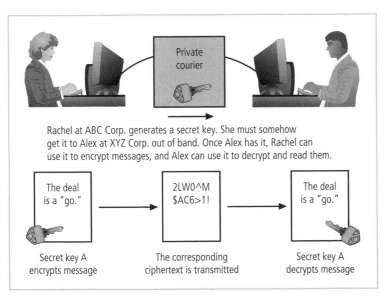

Rachel at ABC Corp. generates a secret key. She must somehow get it to Alex at XYZ Corp. out of band. Once Alex has it, Rachel can use it to encrypt messages, and Alex can use it to decrypt and read them.

| The deal is a "go." | 2LW0^M $AC6>1! | The deal is a "go." |
| Secret key A encrypts message | The corresponding ciphertext is transmitted | Secret key A decrypts message |

Figure 8-5 Example of Symmetric Encryption

Source: Course Technology/Cengage Learning

Technical Details
Cryptographic Notation

The notation used to represent the encryption process varies, depending on its source. The notation in this text uses the letter M to represent the original message, C to represent the ending ciphertext, and E to represent the encryption process: thus, $E(M) = C$,[3] in which encryption (E) is applied to a message (M) to create ciphertext (C). In this notation scheme, the letter D represents the decryption or deciphering process, thus the formula $D[E(M)] = M$ states that if you decipher (D) an enciphered message [E(M)], you get the original message (M). This can also be stated as $D[C] = M$, or the deciphering of the ciphertext (remember that $C = E(M)$) results in the original message M. Finally, the letter K is used to represent the key, therefore $E(M,K) = C$ states that encrypting (E) the message (M) with the key (K) results in the ciphertext (C). Similarly, $D(C,K) = D[E(M,K),K] = M$, that is, deciphering the ciphertext with key K results in the original plaintext message—or, to translate this formula even more precisely, deciphering with key K the message encrypted with key K results in the original message.

To encrypt a plaintext set of data, you can use one of two methods: bit stream and block cipher. In the bit stream method, each bit is transformed into a cipher bit, one after the other. In the block cipher method, the message is divided into blocks, e.g., 8-, 16-, 32-, or 64-bit blocks, and then each block is transformed using the algorithm and key. Bit stream methods most commonly use algorithm functions like XOR, whereas block methods can use XOR, transposition, or substitution.

computing power continued to double every 18 months. Within just a few years, 3DES needed to be replaced.

The successor to 3DES is the **Advanced Encryption Standard (AES)**. AES is a federal information processing standard (FIPS) that specifies a cryptographic algorithm used within the U.S. government to protect information in federal agencies that are not a part of the national defense infrastructure. (Agencies that are considered a part of national defense use other, more secure methods of encryption, which are provided by the National Security Agency.) The requirements for AES stipulate that the algorithm should be unclassified, publicly disclosed, and available royalty-free worldwide. AES has been developed to replace both DES and 3DES. While 3DES remains an approved algorithm for some uses, its expected useful life is limited. Historically, cryptographic standards approved by FIPS have been adopted on a voluntary basis by organizations outside government entities. The AES selection process involved cooperation between the U.S. government, private industry, and academia from around the world. AES was approved by the Secretary of Commerce as the official federal governmental standard on May 26, 2002.

AES implements a block cipher called the Rijndael Block Cipher with a variable block length and a key length of 128, 192, or 256 bits. Experts estimate that the special computer used by the Electronic Frontier Foundation to crack DES within a couple of days would require approximately 4,698,864 quintillion years (4,698,864,000,000,000,000,000) to crack AES. To learn more about the AES, see the Technical Details box titled "Advanced Encryption Standard (AES)."

Asymmetric Encryption

While symmetric encryption systems use a single key to both encrypt and decrypt a message, **asymmetric encryption** uses two different but related keys, and either key can be used to encrypt or decrypt the message. If, however, key A is used to encrypt the message, only key B can decrypt it, and if key B is used to encrypt a message, only key A can decrypt it. Asymmetric encryption can be used to provide elegant solutions to problems of secrecy and verification. This technique has its highest value when one key is used as a private key, which means that it is kept secret (much like the key in symmetric encryption), known only to the owner of the key pair, and the other key serves as a public key, which means that it is stored in a public location where anyone can use it. This is why the more common name for asymmetric encryption is **public-key encryption**.

Technical Details
Triple DES (3DES)

3DES was created to provide a level of security far beyond that of standard DES. (In between, there was a 2DES; however, it was statistically shown that the double DES did not provide significantly stronger security than DES.) 3DES uses three 64-bit keys for an overall key length of 192 bits. 3DES encryption is the same as that of standard DES, repeated three times. 3DES can be employed using two or three keys and a combination of encryption or decryption for additional security. The most common implementations involve encrypting and/or decrypting with two or three different keys, a process that is described shortly. 3DES employs forty-eight rounds in its encryption computation, generating ciphers that are approximately 256 times stronger than standard DES ciphers but require only three times longer to process. One example of 3DES encryption is as follows:

1. In the first operation, 3DES encrypts the message with key 1, then decrypts it with key 2, and then it encrypts it again with key 1. In cryptographic notation, this is [E{D[E(M,K1)],K2},K1]. Decrypting with a different key is essentially another encryption, but it reverses the application of the traditional encryption operations.

2. In the second operation, 3DES encrypts the message with key 1, then it encrypts it again with key 2, and then it encrypts it a third time with key 1 again, or [E{E[E(M,K1)],K2},K1].

3. In the third operation, 3DES encrypts the message three times with three different keys; [E{E[E(M,K1)],K2},K3]. This is the most secure level of encryption possible with 3DES.

Technical Details
Advanced Encryption Standard (AES)

Of the many ciphers that were submitted from around the world for consideration in the AES selection process, five finalists were chosen: MARS, RC6, Rijndael, Serpent, and Twofish. On October 2, 2000, NIST announced the selection of Rijndael, and this block cipher was approved by the Secretary of Commerce as the official federal governmental standard as of May 26, 2002.

The AES version of Rijndael can use a multiple round based system. Depending on the key size, the number of rounds varies from nine to thirteen: for a 128-bit key, nine rounds plus one end round are used; for a 192-bit key, eleven rounds plus one end round are used; and for a 256-bit key, thirteen rounds plus one end round are used. Once Rijndael was adopted as the AES, the ability to use variable-sized blocks was standardized to a single 128 bit block for simplicity.

There are four steps within each Rijndael round, and these are described in "The Advanced Encryption Standard (Rijndael)," by John Savard, as follows:

1. "The Byte Sub step. Each byte of the block is replaced by its substitute in an S-box (substitution box). [*Author's Note: The S-box consists of a table of computed values, the calculation of which is beyond the scope of this text.*]

2. The Shift Row step. Considering the block to be made up of bytes 1 to 16, these bytes are arranged in a rectangle, and shifted as follows:

	from					to		
1	5	9	13		1	5	9	13
2	6	10	14		6	10	14	2
3	7	11	15		11	15	3	7
4	8	12	16		16	4	8	12

   Other shift tables are used for larger blocks.

3. The Mix Column step. Matrix multiplication is performed; each column is multiplied by the matrix:

2	3	1	1
1	2	3	1
1	1	2	3
3	1	1	2

4. The Add Round Key step. This simply XORs in the subkey for the current round.

   The extra final round omits the Mix Column step, but is otherwise the same as a regular round."[4]

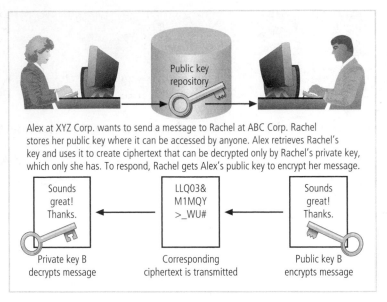

Figure 8-6 Example of Asymmetric Encryption

Source: Course Technology/Cengage Learning

Consider the following example, illustrated in Figure 8-6. Alex at XYZ Corporation wants to send an encrypted message to Rachel at ABC Corporation. Alex goes to a public key registry and obtains Rachel's public key. Remember that the foundation of asymmetric encryption is that the same key cannot be used to both encrypt and decrypt the same message. So when Rachel's public key is used to encrypt the message, only Rachel's private key can be used to decrypt the message, and that private key is held by Rachel alone. Similarly, if Rachel wants to respond to Alex's message, she goes to the registry where Alex's public key is held and uses it to encrypt her message, which of course can only be read by Alex's private key. This approach, which keeps private keys secret and encourages the sharing of public keys in reliable directories, is an elegant solution to the key management problems of symmetric key applications.

Asymmetric algorithms are one-way functions. A one-way function is simple to compute in one direction, but complex to compute in the opposite direction. This is the foundation of public-key encryption. Public-key encryption is based on a hash value, which, as you learned earlier in this chapter, is calculated from an input number using a hashing algorithm. This hash value is essentially a summary of the original input values. It is virtually impossible to derive the original values without knowing how those values were used to create the hash value. For example, if you multiply 45 by 235 you get 10,575. This is simple enough. But if you are simply given the number 10,575, can you determine which two numbers were multiplied to determine this number? Now assume that each multiplier is 200 digits long and prime. The resulting multiplicative product would be up to 400 digits long. Imagine the time you'd need to factor that out. There is a shortcut, however. In mathematics, it is known as a trapdoor (which is different from the software trapdoor). A mathematical **trapdoor** is a "secret mechanism that enables you to easily accomplish the reverse function in a one-way function."[5] With a trapdoor, you can use a key to encrypt or decrypt the ciphertext, but not both, thus requiring two keys. The public key becomes the true key, and the private key is derived from the public key using the trapdoor.

If you understand modulo mathematics, you can appreciate the complexities of the RSA algorithm. The RSA algorithm is based on the computational difficulty of factoring large composite numbers and computing the eth *roots modulo*, a composite number for a specified odd integer e. Encryption in RSA is accomplished by raising the message *M* to a nonnegative integer power e. The product is then divided by the nonnegative modulus *n* (n should have a bit length of at least 1024 bits), and the remainder is the ciphertext *C*. This process results in a one-way operation (shown below) when n is a very large number.

$$C = Me / mod\ n$$

In the decryption process, the ciphertext C is raised to the power *d*, a nonnegative integer, as follows:

$$d = e-1\ mod\ ((p - 1)(q - 1))$$

C is then reduced by modulo n. In order for the recipient to calculate the decryption key, the *p* and *q* factors must be known. The modulus n, which is a composite number, is determined by multiplying two large nonnegative prime numbers, p and q:

$$n = p \infty q$$

In RSA's asymmetric algorithm, which is the basis of most modern public-key infrastructure (PKI) systems (a topic covered later in this chapter), the public and private keys are generated using the following procedure, which is from the RSA Corporation:

- "Choose two large prime numbers, p and q, of equal length, and compute $p \times q = n$, which is the public modulus.

- Choose a random public key, e, so that e and $(p - 1)(q - 1)$ are relatively prime.

- Compute $e \times d = 1\ mod\ (p - 1)(q - 1)$, where d is the private key.

- Thus $d = e - 1\ mod\ [(p - 1)(q - 1)]$, where "(d, n) is the private key; (e, n) is the public key. P is encrypted to generate ciphertext C as $C = P^e\ mod\ n$, and is decrypted to recover the plaintext, P as $P = C^d\ mod\ n$."[6]

Essentially, the RSA algorithm can be divided into the following three steps:

1. *Key generation:* Prime factors p and q are selected by a statistical technique known as probabilistic primality testing and then multiplied together to form n. The encryption exponent e is selected, and the decryption exponent d is calculated.

2. *Encryption:* M is raised to the power of e, reduced by modulo n, and remainder C is the ciphertext.

3. *Decryption:* C is raised to the power of d and reduced by modulo n.

The sender publishes the public key, which consists of modulus n and exponent e. The remaining variables d, p, and q are kept secret.

A message can then be encrypted by: $C = M^e$ (recipient) mod n(recipient)

Digitally signed by: $C' = M'^d$ (sender) mod n(sender)

Verified by: $M' = C'^e$ (sender) mod n(sender)

Decrypted by: $M = C^d$ (recipient) mod n(recipient)

Examples

The following sections contain practice examples to help you better understand the machinations of the RSA algorithms.

RSA Algorithm Example:[7] Work through the following steps to better understand how the RSA algorithm functions:

1. Choose two large, random prime numbers: P, Q (usually P, Q > 10^100) → This means 10 to the power 100.

2. Compute:
    $N = P \times Q$
    $Z = (P - 1Q - 1)$

3. Choose a relatively prime number with Z and call it D.
    D < N; relatively prime means that D and Z have no common factors except 1.

4. Find number E, such that → $E \times D = 1$ mod Z.

5. The public key is (N, E); the private key is (N, D).

6. Create cipher (encrypted text):
    C = | TEXT |E (MOD N)
    C → Encrypted text → this is the text that is transmitted
    | TEXT | → Plaintext to be encrypted (its numerical correspondent)

7. Decrypt the message:
    D = Plaintext = CD (MOD N), C = Ciphertext from part 6.

   Note that it is almost impossible to obtain the private key, knowing the public key, and it's almost impossible to factor N into P and Q.

RSA Numerical Example: Work through the following steps to better understand RSA numericals:

1. Choose P = 3, Q = 11 (two prime numbers). Note that small numbers have been chosen for the example so that you can easily work with them. In real-life encryption, they are larger than 10^{100}.

2. $N = P \infty Q = 3 \infty 11 = 33$; $Z = (P-1)(Q-1) = 2 \infty 10 = 20$

3. Choose a number for D that is relatively prime with Z, for example, D = 7 → (20 and 7 have no common divisors, except 1).

4. E = ? such as E ∞ D = 1 MOD Z (1 MOD Z means that the remainder of E/D division is 1).
    E ∞ D / Z → E ∞ 7 / 20 → E = 3
    Check E ∞ D / Z → 3 ∞ 7 / 20 → 21/20 → Remainder = 1

5. So, the public key is (N,E) = (33,3) → This key will be used to encrypt the message. The private key is (N,D) = (33,7) → This key will be used to decrypt the message.

English Alphabet and Corresponding Numbers for Each Letter:[8] In real-life applications, the ASCII code is used to represent each of the characters of a message. For this example, the position of the letter in the alphabet is used instead to simplify the calculations: A = 01, B = 02, ... Z = 26.

Encrypt the Word "Technology" as Illustrated in Table 8-5:[9] Now you can use the corresponding numerical and the previous calculations to calculate values for the public key (N,E) = (33,3) and the private key (N,D) = (33,7).

The cipher (encrypted message) is 14262717050912091316. This is what is transmitted over unreliable lines. Note that there are two digits per letter. To decrypt the transmitted message we apply the private key (^{D}) and re-MOD the product, the result of which is the numerical equivalent of the original plaintext.

As you can see in Table 8-6, although very small P and Q numbers were used, the numbers required for decrypting the message are relatively large. Now you have a good idea of what kind of numbers are needed when P and Q are large (that is, in the 10^{100} range).

If P and Q are not big enough to make the cipher secure, they must be made bigger. The strength of this encryption algorithm relies on how difficult it is to factor P and Q from N if N is known. If N is not known, of course the algorithm is even harder to break.

Plaintext	Text Value	(Text)^E	(Text)^E MOD N = Ciphertext
T	20	8000	8000 MOD 33 = 14
E	05	125	125 MOD 33 = 26
C	03	27	27 MOD 33 = 27
H	08	512	512 MOD 33 = 17
N	14	2744	2744 MOD 33 = 05
O	15	3375	3375 MOD 33 = 09
L	12	1728	1728 MOD 33 = 12
O	15	3375	3375 MOD 33 = 09
G	07	343	343 MOD 33 = 13
Y	25	15625	15625 MOD 33 = 16

Table 8-5 Encryption

Ciphertext	(Cipher)^D	(Cipher)^D MOD N = |Text|	Plaintext
14	105413504	105413504 MOD 33 = 20	T
26	8031810176	8031810176 MOD 33 = 05	E
27	10460353203	10460353203 MOD 33 = 03	C
17	410338673	410338673 MOD 33 = 08	H
05	78125	78125 MOD 33 = 14	N
09	4782969	4782969 MOD 33 = 15	O
12	35831808	35831808 MOD 33 = 12	L
09	4782969	4782969 MOD 33 = 15	O
13	62748517	62748517 MOD 33 = 07	G
16	268435456	268435456 MOD 33 = 25	Y

Table 8-6   Encryption

One of the most popular public key cryptosystems is RSA, whose name is derived from Rivest-Shamir-Adleman, the algorithm's developers. The **RSA algorithm** was the first public key encryption algorithm developed (in 1977) and published for commercial use. It is very popular and has been embedded in both Microsoft and Netscape Web browsers to enable them to provide security for e-commerce applications. The patented RSA algorithm has in fact become the de facto standard for public-use encryption applications. To learn how this algorithm works, see the Technical Details box entitled "RSA Algorithm."

The problem with asymmetric encryption, as shown earlier in the example in Figure 8-6, is that holding a single conversation between two parties requires four keys. Moreover, if four organizations want to exchange communications, each party must manage its private key and four public keys. In such scenarios, determining which public key is needed to encrypt a particular message can become a rather confusing problem, and with more organizations in the loop, the problem expands. This is why asymmetric encryption is sometimes regarded by experts as inefficient. Compared to symmetric encryption, asymmetric encryption is also not as efficient in terms of CPU computations. Consequently, hybrid systems, such as those described in the section of this chapter titled "Public-Key Infrastructure (PKI)," are more commonly used than pure asymmetric systems.

Encryption Key Size

When deploying ciphers, users have to decide on the size of the cryptovariable or key. This is very important, because the strength of many encryption applications and cryptosystems is measured by key size. How exactly does key size affect the strength of an algorithm? Typically, the length of the key increases the number of random guesses that have to be made in order to break the code. Creating a larger universe of possibilities increases the time required to make guesses, and thus a longer key directly influences the strength of the encryption.

It may surprise you to learn that when it comes to cryptosystems, the security of encrypted data is *not* dependent on keeping the encrypting algorithm secret; in fact, algorithms should be (and often are) published, to enable research to uncover their weaknesses. In fact, the security of any cryptosystem depends on keeping some or all of the elements of the cryptovariable(s) or key(s) secret, and effective security is maintained by manipulating the size (bit length) of the keys and by following proper procedures and policies for key management.

For a simple example of how key size is related to encryption strength, suppose you have an algorithm that uses a three-bit key. You may recall from earlier in the chapter that keyspace is the range from which the key can be drawn. Also, you may recall that in binary notation, three bits can be used to represent values from 000 to 111, which correspond to the numbers 0 to 7 in decimal notation, and thus provide a keyspace of eight keys. This means that an algorithm that uses a three-bit key has eight possible keys (the numbers 0 to 7 in binary are 000, 001, 010, 011, 100, 101, 110, 111). If you know how many keys you have to choose from, you can program a computer to try all the keys to attempt to crack the encrypted message.

The preceding statement presumes a few things: (1) you know the algorithm, (2) you have the encrypted message, and (3) you have time on your hands. It is easy to satisfy the first criterion. The encryption tools that use the Data Encryption Standard (DES) can be purchased over the counter. Many of these tools are based on encryption algorithms that are standards, as is DES itself, and therefore it is relatively easy to get a cryptosystem based on DES that enables you to decrypt an encrypted message if you possess the key. The second criterion requires the interception of an encrypted message, which is illegal but not impossible. As for the third criterion, the task required is a brute force attack, in which a computer randomly (or sequentially) selects possible keys of the known size and applies them to the encrypted text or a piece of the encrypted text. If the result is plaintext—bingo! But as indicated earlier in this chapter, it can take quite a long time to exert brute force on the more advanced cryptosystems. In fact, the strength of an algorithm is determined by how long it takes to guess the key.

But when it comes to keys, how big is big? At the beginning of this section, you learned that a three-bit system has eight possible keys. An eight-bit system has 256 possible keys. Note, however, that if you use a 32-bit key, puny by modern standards, you have almost 16.8 million possible keys. Even so, a modern PC, such as the one described in Table 8-7, could discover this key in mere seconds. But, as Table 8-7 shows, the amount of time needed to crack a cipher by guessing its key grows very quickly—that is, exponentially with each additional bit.

One thing to keep in mind is that even though the estimated time to crack grows rapidly with respect to the number of bits in the encryption key and the odds of cracking seem at first glance to be insurmountable, Table 8-7 doesn't account for the fact that computing power has increased and continues to increase. Therefore, these days even the once-standard 56-bit encryption can't stand up to brute force attacks by personal computers, especially if multiple computers are used together to crack these keys. Each additional computer reduces the amount of time needed. Two computers can divide the keyspace (the entire set of possible combinations of bits that can be the cryptovariable or key) and crack the key in approximately half the time, and so on. Thus, 285 computers can crack a 56-bit key in one year; ten times as many would do it in a little over a month.

Why do encryption systems such as DES incorporate multiple elements or operations? Consider this: if you use the same operation (XOR, substitution, or transposition) multiple times, you gain no additional benefit. For example, if you use a substitution cipher, and substitute B for A, and then R for B, and then Q for R, it has the same effect as substituting Q for A. Similarly, if you transpose a character in position 1, then position 4, then position 3, you could more easily have transposed the character from position 1 to position 3. There is no net advantage for sequential operations unless each subsequent operation is different.

It is estimated that to crack an encryption key using a brute force attack, a computer needs to perform a maximum of 2^k operations (2^k guesses), where k is the number of bits in the key. In reality, the average estimated time to crack is half that time.

Using an average modern 2008-era dual-core PC performing 30,000 MIPS (million instructions per second):

Key Length (bits)	Maximum Number of Operations (guesses)	Maximum Time to Crack	Estimated Average Time to Crack
8	256	0.0000000085 seconds	0.0000000043 seconds
16	65,636	0.0000022 seconds	0.00000109 seconds
24	16,777,216	0.00056 seconds	0.00028 seconds
32	4,294,967,296	0.143 seconds	0.072 seconds
56	72,057,594,037,927,900	27.800 days	13.9 days
64	18,446,744,073,709,600,000	19.498 years	9.7 years
128	3.40282E+38	359,676,102,360,201,000,000 years	179,838,051,180,100,000,000 years
256	1.15792E+77	122,391,435,436,027,000,000,000,000,000,000,000,000,000,000,000,000,000,000 years	61,195,717,718,013,400,000,000,000,000,000,000,000,000,000,000,000,000 years
512	1.3408E+154	14,171,960,013,891,600,000,000,000,000,000,000,000,000,000,000,000,000,000,000,000,000,000,000,000,000,000,000,000,000,000,000,000,000,000,000,000 years	7,085,980,006,945,820,000,000,000,000,000,000,000,000,000,000,000,000,000,000,000,000,000,000,000,000,000,000,000,000,000,000,000,000,000,000 years

Table 8-7 Encryption Key Power

Note: Arguably, it takes one operation to calculate each password value and then at least one operation to test the password; however, this example simply assumes each guess only requires one operation. Realistically, doubled, tripled, or even quadrupled, the relative values of the times don't vary much—56 bit or less is insufficient for sensitive data, 64 bits are marginal, and 128-bit and larger key lengths are more than sufficient. The modern standards are 128- and 256-bit (AES), with 512- and 1024-bit encryption available.

Therefore, if you substitute, then transpose, then XOR, then substitute again, you have dramatically scrambled, substituted, and recoded the original plaintext with ciphertext that is untraceable without the key.

Cryptographic Tools

The ability to conceal the contents of sensitive messages and to verify the contents of messages and the identities of their senders have the potential to be useful in all areas of business. To be actually useful, these cryptographic capabilities must be embodied in tools that allow IT and information security practitioners to apply the elements of cryptography in the everyday world of computing. This section covers a number of the more widely used tools that bring the functions of cryptography to the world of information systems.

Public-Key Infrastructure (PKI)

Public-key Infrastructure (PKI) is an integrated system of software, encryption methodologies, protocols, legal agreements, and third-party services that enables users to communicate securely. PKI systems are based on public-key cryptosystems and include digital certificates and certificate authorities (CAs).

Digital certificates are public-key container files that allow computer programs to validate the key and identify to whom it belongs. (More information about digital certificates appears in later sections of this chapter.) PKI and the digital certificate registries they contain enable the protection of information assets by making verifiable digital certificates readily available to business applications. This, in turn, allows the applications to implement several of the key characteristics of information security and to integrate these characteristics into business processes across an organization. These processes include the following:

- Authentication: Individuals, organizations, and Web servers can validate the identity of each of the parties in an Internet transaction.

- Integrity: Content signed by the certificate is known to not have been altered while in transit from host to host or server to client.

- Privacy: Information is protected from being intercepted during transmission.

- Authorization: The validated identity of users and programs can enable authorization rules that remain in place for the duration of a transaction; this reduces some of the overhead and allows for more control of access privileges for specific transactions.

- Nonrepudiation: Customers or partners can be held accountable for transactions, such as online purchases, which they cannot later dispute.

A typical PKI solution protects the transmission and reception of secure information by integrating the following components:

- A **certificate authority (CA)**, which issues, manages, authenticates, signs, and revokes users' digital certificates, which typically contain the user name, public key, and other identifying information.

- A **registration authority (RA)**, which operates under the trusted collaboration of the certificate authority and can handle day-to-day certification functions, such as verifying registration information, generating end-user keys, revoking certificates, and validating user certificates.

- Certificate directories, which are central locations for certificate storage that provide a single access point for administration and distribution.

- Management protocols, which organize and manage the communications among CAs, RAs, and end users. This includes the functions and procedures for setting up new users, issuing keys, recovering keys, updating keys, revoking keys, and enabling the transfer of certificates and status information among the parties involved in the PKI's area of authority.

- Policies and procedures, which assist an organization in the application and management of certificates, in the formalization of legal liabilities and limitations, and in actual business use.

Common implementations of PKI include systems that issue digital certificates to users and servers; directory enrollment; key issuing systems; tools for managing the key issuance; and verification and return of certificates. These systems enable organizations to apply an enterprise-wide solution that provides users within the PKI's area of authority the means to engage in authenticated and secure communications and transactions.

The CA performs many housekeeping activities regarding the use of keys and certificates that are issues and used in its zone of authority. Each user authenticates himself or herself with the CA, and the CA can issue new or replacement keys, track issued keys, provide a directory of public key values for all known users, and perform other management activities. When a private key is compromised, or when the user loses the privilege of using keys in the area of authority, the CA can revoke the user's keys. The CA periodically distributes a **certificate revocation list (CRL)** to all users. When important events occur, specific applications can make a real-time request to the CA to verify any user against the current CRL.

The issuance of certificates (and the keys inside of them) by the CA enables secure, encrypted, nonrepudiable e-business transactions. Some applications allow users to generate their own certificates (and the keys inside of them), but a key pair generated by the end user can only provide nonrepudiation and not reliable encryption. A central system operated by a CA or RA can generate cryptographically strong keys that are considered by all users to be independently trustworthy, and can provide services for users such as private key backup, key recovery, and key revocation.

The strength of a cryptosystem relies on both the raw strength of its key's complexity and the overall quality of its key management security processes. PKI solutions can provide several mechanisms for limiting access and possible exposure of the private keys. These mechanisms include password protection, smart cards, hardware tokens, and other hardware-based key storage devices that are memory-capable (like flash memory or PC memory cards). PKI users should select the key security mechanisms that provide a level of key protection appropriate to their needs. Managing the security and integrity of the private keys used for nonrepudiation or the encryption of data files is critical to the successful use of encryption and nonrepudiation services within the PKI's area of trust.[10]

Digital Signatures

Digital signatures were created in response to the rising need to verify information transferred via electronic systems. Asymmetric encryption processes are used to create digital signatures. When an asymmetric cryptographic process uses the sender's private key to encrypt a message, the sender's public key must be used to decrypt the message. When the decryption is successful, the process verifies that the message was sent by the sender and thus cannot be refuted. This process is known as **nonrepudiation** and is the principle of cryptography that underpins the authentication mechanism collectively known as a digital signature. **Digital signatures** are, therefore, encrypted messages that can be mathematically proven authentic.

The management of digital signatures is built into most Web browsers. The Internet Explorer digital signature management screen is shown in Figure 8-7. In general, digital signatures should be created using processes and products that are based on the **Digital Signature Standard** (DSS). When processes and products are certified as DSS compliant, they have been approved and endorsed by U.S. federal and state governments, as well as by many foreign governments, as a means of authenticating the author of an electronic document. NIST has approved a number of algorithms that can be used to generate and verify digital signatures.

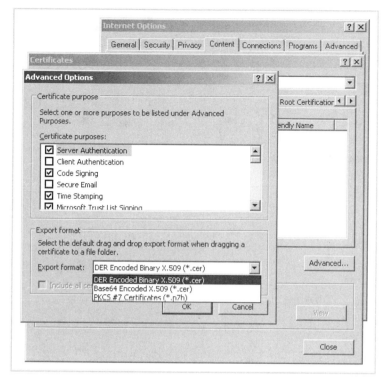

Figure 8-7 Managing Digital Signature

Source: Course Technology/Cengage Learning

These algorithms can be used in conjunction with the sender's public and private keys, the receiver's public key, and the Secure Hash Standard (described earlier in this chapter) to quickly create messages that are both encrypted and nonrepudiable. This process first creates a message digest using the hash algorithm, which is then input into the digital signature algorithm along with a random number to generate the digital signature. The digital signature function also depends upon the sender's private key and other information provided by the CA. The resulting encrypted message contains the digital signature, which can be verified by the recipient using the sender's public key.

Digital Certificates

As you learned earlier in this chapter, a digital certificate is an electronic document or container file that contains a key value and identifying information about the entity that controls the key. The certificate is often issued and certified by a third party, usually a certificate authority. A digital signature attached to the certificate's container file certifies the file's origin and integrity. This verification process often occurs when you download or update software via the Internet. The window in Figure 8-8 shows, for example, that the downloaded files do in fact come from the purported originating agency, Amazon.com, and thus can be trusted.

Unlike digital signatures, which help authenticate the origin of a message, digital certificates authenticate the cryptographic key that is embedded in the certificate. When used properly these

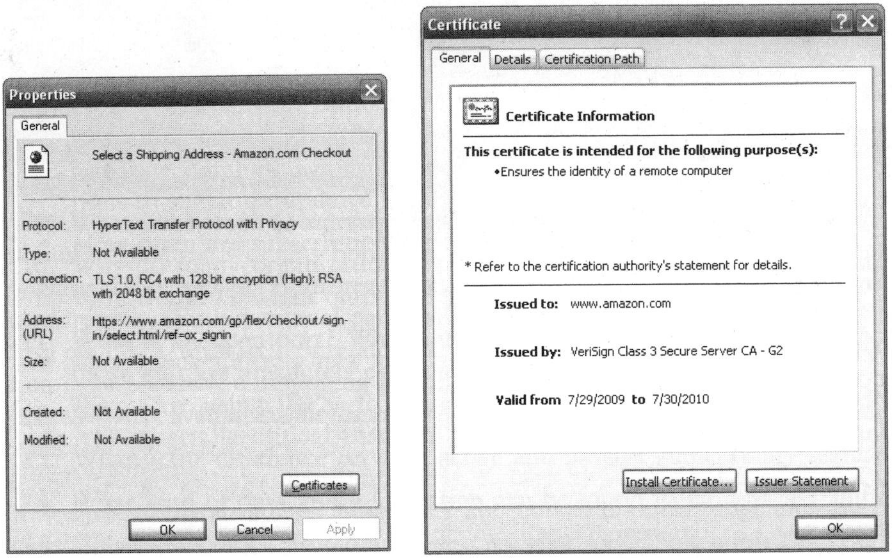

Figure 8-8 Digital Certificate

Source: Course Technology/Cengage Learning

certificates enable diligent users to verify the authenticity of any organization's certificates. This is much like what happens when the Federal Deposit Insurance Corporation issues its FDIC logo to banks to assure customers that their bank is authentic. Different client-server applications use different types of digital certificates to accomplish their assigned functions, as follows:

- The CA application suite issues and uses certificates (keys) that identify and establish a trust relationship with a CA to determine what additional certificates (keys) can be authenticated.

- Mail applications use Secure/Multipurpose Internet Mail Extension (S/MIME) certificates for signing and encrypting e-mail as well as for signing forms.

- Development applications use object-signing certificates to identify signers of object-oriented code and scripts.

- Web servers and Web application servers use Secure Sockets Layer (SSL) certificates to authenticate servers via the SSL protocol (which is described shortly) in order to establish an encrypted SSL session.

- Web clients use client SSL certificates to authenticate users, sign forms, and participate in single sign-on solutions via SSL.

Two popular certificate types are those created using Pretty Good Privacy (PGP) and those created using applications that conform to International Telecommunication Union's (ITU-T) X.509 version 3. The X.509 v3 certificate, whose structure is outlined in Table 8-8, is an ITU-T recommendation that essentially defines a directory service that maintains a database (also known as a repository) of information about a group of users holding X.509 v3 certificates. An X.509 v3 certificate binds a **distinguished name (DN)**, which uniquely identifies a certificate entity, to a user's public key. The certificate is signed and placed in the directory by the CA for retrieval and verification by the user's associated public key. The X.509 v3

X.509 v3 Certificate Structure
Version
Certificate Serial Number
Algorithm ID • Algorithm ID • Parameters
Issuer Name
Validity • Not Before • Not After
Subject Name
Subject Public Key Info • Public Key Algorithm • Parameters • Subject Public Key
Issuer Unique Identifier (Optional)
Subject Unique Identifier (Optional)
Extensions (Optional) • Type • Criticality • Value
Certificate Signature Algorithm
Certificate Signature

Table 8-8 X.509 v3 Certificate Structure[11]

standard's recommendation does not specify an encryption algorithm, though RSA, with its hashed digital signature, is typically used.

Hybrid Cryptography Systems

Except in digital certificates, asymmetric key encryption in its pure form is not widely used, but it is often used in conjunction with symmetric key encryption—thus, as part of a hybrid encryption system. The most common hybrid system is based on the **Diffie-Hellman key exchange**, which is a method for exchanging private keys using public key encryption. Diffie-Hellman key exchange uses asymmetric encryption to exchange **session keys**. These are limited-use symmetric keys for temporary communications; they allow two entities to conduct quick, efficient, secure communications based on symmetric encryption, which is more efficient than asymmetric encryption for sending messages. Diffie-Hellman provides the foundation for subsequent developments in public key encryption. It protects data from exposure to third parties, which is sometimes a problem when keys are exchanged out-of-band.

A hybrid encryption approach is illustrated in Figure 8-9, and it works as follows: Alex at XYZ Corp. wants to communicate with Rachel at ABC Corp., so Alex first creates a session key. Alex encrypts a message with this session key, and then gets Rachel's public key. Alex uses

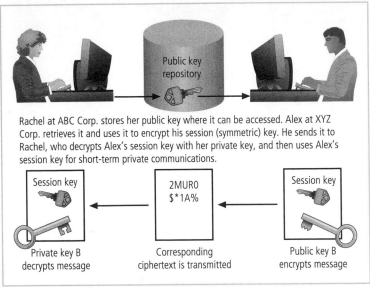

Rachel at ABC Corp. stores her public key where it can be accessed. Alex at XYZ Corp. retrieves it and uses it to encrypt his session (symmetric) key. He sends it to Rachel, who decrypts Alex's session key with her private key, and then uses Alex's session key for short-term private communications.

Session key

2MUR0 $*1A%

Session key

Private key B decrypts message

Corresponding ciphertext is transmitted

Public key B encrypts message

Figure 8-9 Example of Hybrid Encryption

Source: Course Technology/Cengage Learning

Rachel's public key to encrypt both the session key and the message, which is already encrypted. Alex transmits the entire package to Rachel, who uses her private key to decrypt the package containing the session key and the encrypted message, and then uses the session key to decrypt the message. Rachel can then continue to use only this session key for electronic communications until the session key expires. The asymmetric session key is used in the much more efficient symmetric encryption and decryption processes. After the session key expires (usually in just a few minutes), a new session key is chosen and shared using the same process.

Steganography

The word **steganography**—the art of secret writing—is derived from the Greek words *steganos*, meaning "covered" and *graphein*, meaning "to write." The Greek historian Herodotus described one of the first steganographers, a fellow Greek who sent a message to warn of an imminent invasion by writing it on the wood beneath a wax writing tablet.[12] While steganography is technically not a form of cryptography, it is another way of protecting the confidentiality of information in transit. The most popular modern version of steganography involves hiding information within files that contain digital pictures or other images.

To understand how this form of steganography works, you must first know a little about how images are stored. Most computer graphics standards use a combination of three color values—red, blue, and green (RGB)—to represent a picture element, or pixel. Each of the three color values usually requires an 8-bit code for that color's intensity (e.g., 00000000 for no red and 11111111 for maximum red). Each color image pixel requires 3 colors × 8 bits = 24 bits to represent the color mix and intensity. (Some image encoding standards use more or fewer bits per pixel.) When a picture is created (by a digital camera or a computer program), the number of horizontal and vertical pixels captured and recorded is known as the image's *resolution*. Thus, for example, if 1024 horizontal pixels are recorded and 768 vertical pixels are captured, the image has a 1024 × 768 resolution and is said to have 786,432 pixels or three-quarters of a megapixel. Thus, an image that is 1024 × 768 pixels contains 786,432 groups of 24 bits to represent the red, green, and blue data. The raw image size can be calculated as 1024 × 768 × 24, or 5.66 megabytes. There are plenty of bits in this picture data file in which to hide a secret message.

To the naked eye, there is no discernable difference between a pixel with a red intensity of 00101001 and another slightly different pixel with a red intensity level of 00101000. This provides the steganographer with one bit per color (or three bits per pixel) to use for encoding data into an image file. If a steganographic process uses three bits per pixel for all 786,432 pixels, it will be able to store 236 kilobytes of hidden data within the uncompressed image.

Some steganographic tools can calculate the maximum size image that can be stored before being detectable. Messages can also be hidden in non-image computer files that do not utilize all of their available bits by placing the data in places where software ignores it and humans almost never look. Some applications can hide messages in .bmp, .wav, .mp3, and .au files, as well as in otherwise unused storage space on CDs and DVDs. One program can take a text or document file and hide a message in the unused whitespace.

Even before the attacks of September 11, 2001, U.S. federal agencies came to believe that terrorist organizations were "hiding maps and photographs of terrorist targets and posting instructions for terrorist activities in sports chat rooms, pornographic bulletin boards, and other Web sites" by means of steganographic methods. No documented proof of this activity has been made public.[13] However, the Electronic Frontier Foundation (www.eff.org) established that the U.S. Secret Service worked with several color laser printer manufacturers to use steganography to encode printer serial numbers in printed documents.

Protocols for Secure Communications

Much of the software currently used to protect the confidentiality of information are not true cryptosystems. Instead, they are applications to which cryptographic protocols have been added. This is perhaps particularly true of Internet protocols; some experts claim that the Internet and its corresponding protocols were designed without any consideration for security, which was added later as an afterthought. Whether or not this is true, the lack of threats in the environment in which it was launched allowed the Internet to grow rapidly. But as the number of threats grew, so did the need for additional security measures.

Securing Internet Communication with S-HTTP and SSL

S-HTTP (Secure Hypertext Transfer Protocol) and SSL (Secure Sockets Layer) are two protocols designed to enable secure network communications across the Internet. S-HTTP and SSL ensure Internet security via different mechanisms and can be used independently or together.

Netscape developed the **Secure Sockets Layer (SSL)** protocol to use public key encryption to secure a channel over the Internet, thus enabling secure communications. Most popular browsers, including Internet Explorer, use SSL. In addition to providing data encryption, integrity, and server authentication, SSL can, when properly configured, provide client authentication.

The SSL protocol works as follows: during a normal client/server HTTP session, the client requests access to a portion of the Web site that requires secure communications, and the server sends a message to the client indicating that a secure connection must be established. The client sends its public key and security parameters. This handshaking phase is complete when the server finds a public key match and sends a digital certificate to the client in order to authenticate itself. Once the client verifies that the certificate is valid and trustworthy, the SSL session is established. Until the client or the server terminates the session, any amount of data can be transmitted securely.

SSL provides two protocol layers within the TCP framework: SSL Record Protocol and Standard HTTP. The **SSL Record Protocol** is responsible for the fragmentation, compression, encryption, and attachment of an SSL header to the plaintext prior to transmission. Received encrypted messages are decrypted and reassembled for presentation to the higher levels of the protocol. The SSL Record Protocol provides basic security and communication services to the top levels of the SSL protocol stack. **Standard HTTP** provides the Internet communication services between client and host without consideration for encryption of the data that is transmitted between client and server.

Secure HTTP (S-HTTP) is an extended version of Hypertext Transfer Protocol that provides for the encryption of individual messages transmitted via the Internet between a client and server. S-HTTP is the application of SSL over HTTP, which allows the encryption of all information passing between two computers through a protected and secure virtual connection. Unlike SSL, in which a secure channel is established for the duration of a session, S-HTTP is designed for sending individual messages over the Internet and therefore a session for each individual exchange of data must be established. To establish a session, the client and server must have compatible cryptosystems and agree on the configuration. The S-HTTP client then must send the server its public key so that the server can generate a session key. The session key from the server is then encrypted with the client's public key and returned to the client. The client decrypts the key using its private key, and the client and server now possess identical session keys, which they can use to encrypt the messages sent between them.

S-HTTP can provide confidentiality, authentication, and data integrity through a variety of trust models and cryptographic algorithms. In addition, this protocol is designed for easy integration with existing HTTP applications and for implementation in conjunction with HTTP.

Securing E-mail with S/MIME, PEM, and PGP

A number of cryptosystems have been adapted to work with the dominant e-mail protocols in an attempt to incorporate some degree of security into this notoriously insecure communication medium. Some of the more popular adaptations included Secure Multipurpose Internet Mail Extensions, Privacy Enhanced Mail (PEM), and Pretty Good Privacy (PGP).

Secure Multipurpose Internet Mail Extensions (S/MIME) builds on the encoding format of the Multipurpose Internet Mail Extensions (MIME) protocol and uses digital signatures based on public key cryptosystems to secure e-mail. **Privacy Enhanced Mail (PEM)** was proposed by the Internet Engineering Task Force (IETF) and is a standard that uses 3DES symmetric key encryption and RSA for key exchanges and digital signatures. **Pretty Good Privacy (PGP)** was developed by Phil Zimmermann and uses the IDEA cipher for message encoding. PGP also uses RSA for symmetric key exchange and digital signatures. PGP is discussed in more detail in a later section in this chapter.

Header Field	Function
MIME-version	States conformity to RFCs 2045 and 2046
Content-ID	Identifies MIME entities
Content-type	Describes data in body of message
Content-description	Describes body object
Content-transfer-encoding	Identifies type of conversion used in message body

Table 8-9 MIME Message Header Fields[14]

Function	Algorithm
Hash code for digital signatures	Secure Hash Algorithm 1 (SHA-1)
Digital signatures	DSS
Encryption session keys	ElGamal (variant of Diffie-Hellman)
Digital signatures and session keys	RSA
Message encryption	3DES, RC2

Table 8-10 S/MIME Functions and Algorithms

The first commonly used Internet e-mail standard was SMTP/RFC 822, also called SMTP, but this standard has problems and limitations, such as an inability to transmit executable files or binary objects and an inability to handle character sets other than 7-bit ASCII. These limitations make SMTP unwieldy for organizations that need greater security and support for international character sets. MIME, the Multipurpose Internet Mail Extension, whose message header fields are shown in Table 8-9, was developed to address the problems associated with SMTP. In Table 8-9, you can see that MIME's message header fields were designed to identify and describe the e-mail message and to handle a variety of e-mail content. In addition to the message header fields, the MIME specification includes predefined content types and conversion transfer encodings, such as 7-bit, 8-bit, binary, and radix-64, which it uses to deliver e-mail messages reliably across a wide range of systems.

S/MIME, an extension to MIME, is the second generation of enhancements to the SMTP standard. MIME and S/MIME have the same message header fields, except for those added to support new functionality. Like MIME, S/MIME uses a canonical form format, which allows it to standardize message content type among systems, but it has the additional ability to sign, encrypt, and decrypt messages. Table 8-10 summarizes the functions and algorithms used by S/MIME. It should be mentioned that PGP is functionally similar to S/MIME, incorporates some of the same algorithms, and can, to some degree, interoperate with S/MIME.

Securing Web Transactions with SET, SSL, and S-HTTP

Just as PGP, PEM, and S/MIME work to secure e-mail operations, a number of related protocols work to secure Web browsers, especially at electronic commerce sites. Among these are Secure Electronic Transactions (SET), Secure Sockets Layer (SSL), Secure Hypertext Transfer Protocol (S-HTTP), Secure Shell (SSH-2), and IP Security (IPSec). You learned about SSL and S-HTTP earlier in this chapter.

Secure Electronic Transactions (SET) was developed by MasterCard and VISA in 1997 to protect against electronic payment fraud. SET uses DES to encrypt credit card information transfers and RSA for key exchange. SET provides security for both Internet-based credit card transactions and credit card swipe systems in retail stores. Secure Sockets Layer, as you learned earlier in this chapter, also provides secure online electronic commerce transactions. SSL uses a number of algorithms, but mainly relies on RSA for key transfer and IDEA, DES, or 3DES for encrypted symmetric key-based data transfer. Figure 8-8, shown earlier, illustrates the kind of certificate and SSL information that is displayed when you are checking out of an e-commerce site. If your Web connection does not automatically display such certificates, you can right-click in your browser's window and select *Properties* to view the connection encryption and certificate properties.

Securing Wireless Networks with WEP and WPA

Wireless local area networks (also known by the brand name Wi-Fi, or wireless fidelity networks) are thought by many in the IT industry to be inherently insecure. The communication channel between the wireless network interface of any computing device and the access point that provides its services uses radio transmissions. Without some form of protection, these signals can be intercepted by anyone with a wireless packet sniffer. In order to prevent interception of these communications, these networks must use some form of cryptographic security control. Two sets of protocols are currently widely used to help secure wireless transmissions: Wired Equivalent Privacy and Wi-Fi Protected Access. Both are designed for use with the IEEE 802.11 wireless networks.

Wired Equivalent Privacy (WEP) WEP was an early attempt to provide security with the 802.11 network protocol. It is now considered too cryptographically weak to provide any meaningful protection from eavesdropping, but for a time it did provide some measure of security for low-sensitivity networks. WEP uses the RC4 cipher stream to encrypt each packet using a 64-bit key. This key is created using a 24-bit initialization vector and a 40-bit key value. The packets are formed using an XOR function to use the RC4 key value stream to encrypt the data packet. A 4-byte integrity check value (ICV) is calculated for each packet and then appended.[15] According to many experts, WEP is too weak for use in most network settings because:[16]

- Key management is not effective since most networks use a single shared secret key value for each node. Synchronizing key changes is a tedious process, and no key management is defined in the protocol, so keys are seldom changed.

- The initialization vector (IV) is too small, resulting in the recycling of IVs. An attacker can reverse engineer the RC4 cipher stream and decrypt subsequent packets, or can forge future packets. In 2007, this was accomplished in less than one minute.[17]

In summary, an intruder who collects enough data can threaten a WEP network in just a few minutes by decrypting or altering the data being transmitted, or by forging the WEP key to gain unauthorized access to the network. WEP also lacks a means of validating user credentials to ensure that only those who should be on the network are allowed to access it.[18]

Wi-Fi Protected Access (WPA and WPA2)
WPA was created to resolve the issues with WEP. WPA has a key size of 128 bits, and instead of static, seldom-changed keys it uses dynamic keys created and shared by an authentication server. WPA accomplishes this through the use of the Temporal Key Integrity Protocol (TKIP).

TKIP is a suite of algorithms that attempts to deliver the best security that can be obtained given the constraints of the wireless network environment. The algorithms are designed to work with legacy networking devices. TKIP adds four new algorithms in addition to those that were used in WEP:

- A cryptographic message integrity code, or MIC, called Michael, to defeat forgeries
- A new IV sequencing discipline, to remove replay attacks from the attacker's arsenal
- A per-packet key mixing function, to de-correlate the public IVs from weak keys
- A rekeying mechanism, to provide fresh encryption and integrity keys, undoing the threat of attacks stemming from key reuse.[19]

While it offered dramatically improved security over WEP, WPA was not the most secure wireless protocol design. Some compromises were made in the security design to allow compatibility with existing wireless network components. Protocols to replace TKIP are currently under development. Table 8-11 provides a summary of the differences between WEP and WPA.

In 2004, WPA2 was made available as a replacement for WPA. WPA2 provided many of the elements missing from WPA, most notably AES-based encryption. Beginning in 2006, WPA2 became mandatory for all new Wi-Fi devices. WPA2 is backwardly compatible with WPA, although some older network cards have difficulty using it.

Next Generation Wireless Protocols
Robust Secure Networks (RSN), a protocol planned for deployment as a replacement for TKIP in WPA, uses the Advanced Encryption Standard (AES), along with 802.1x and EAP. RSN extends AES with the Counter Mode CBC MAC Protocol (CCMP). AES supports key lengths up to 256 bits, but is not compatible with older hardware. However, a specification called Transitional Security Network (TSN) allows RSN and WEP to coexist on the same wireless local area network (WLAN). Note, however, that a WLAN on which devices are still using WEP is not optimally secured.

	WEP	WPA
Encryption	Broken by scientists and hackers	Overcomes all WEP shortcomings
	40-bit key	128-bit key
	Static key—the same value is used by everyone on the network	Dynamic keys. Each user is assigned a key per session with additional keys calculated for each packet
	Manual key distribution—each key is typed by hand into each device	Automatic key distribution
Authentication	Broken, used WEP key itself for authentication	Improved user authentication, utilizing stronger 802.1X and EAP

Table 8-11 WEP Versus WPA

Source: www.wi-fi.org/files/wp_8_WPA%20Security_4-29-03.pdf

The RSN protocol functions as follows:

1. The wireless NIC sends a probe request.
2. The wireless access point sends a probe response with an RSN Information Exchange (IE) frame.
3. The wireless NIC requests authentication via one of the approved methods.
4. The wireless access point provides authentication for the wireless NIC.
5. The wireless NIC sends an association request with an RSN Information Exchange (IE) frame.
6. The wireless access point sends an association response.[20]

Bluetooth Bluetooth is a de facto industry standard for short-range wireless communications between devices. It is used to establish communications links between wireless telephones and headsets, between PDAs and desktop computers, and between laptops. It was established by Ericsson scientists, and soon involved Intel, Nokia, IBM, and Toshiba. Microsoft, Lucent Technologies, and 3Com joined the industry group shortly after its inception.

The Bluetooth wireless communications link can be exploited by anyone within the approximately 30 foot range, unless suitable security controls are implemented. It has been estimated that there will be almost a billion Bluetooth-enabled devices by the end of the decade. In discoverable mode—which allows other Bluetooth systems to detect and connect— devices can easily be accessed, much as a shared folder can on a networked computer. Even in nondiscoverable mode, the device is susceptible to access by other devices that have connected with it in the past.[21] By default Bluetooth does not authenticate connections; however, Bluetooth does implement some degree of security when devices access certain services such as dial-up accounts and local-area file transfers. Paired devices, usually a computer or a phone and a peripheral that a user plans to connect to it, require that the same passkey be entered on both devices. This key is used to generate a session key, which is used for all future communications. Unfortunately some attacks can get around this. If an attacker uses a device to simulate a Bluetooth access point, they can trick the device into connecting with it. The fake access point can capture and store all communications, including the passkey submission.

In August 2005, one of the first attacks on Bluetooth-enabled smartphones occurred. At the Athletics World Championships in Helsinki, a virus called Cabir infected dozens of phones. It spread quickly, via a prompt requesting a question that many users accepted without thinking, thus downloading the virus, which only drained the phones' batteries but demonstrated such devices are not immune to this type of attack. A Finnish security firm, F-Secure, deployed staff to the event to assist in removing the virus.[22]

The only way to secure Bluetooth-enabled devices is to incorporate a twofold approach: (1) turn off Bluetooth when you do not intend to use it and (2) do not accept an incoming communications pairing request unless you know who the requestor is.

Securing TCP/IP with IPSec and PGP

Internet Protocol Security (IPSec) is an open-source protocol framework for security development within the TCP/IP family of protocol standards. It is used to secure communications across IP-based networks such as LANs, WANs, and the Internet. The protocol is designed to protect data integrity, user confidentiality, and authenticity at the IP packet level. IPSec is the cryptographic authentication and encryption product of the IETF's IP Protocol Security Working Group. It is often described as the security system from IP version 6 (the future version of the TCP/IP protocol), retrofitted for use with IP version 4 (the current version). IPSec is defined in Request for Comments (RFC) 1825, 1826, and 1827 and is widely used to create virtual private networks (VPNs), which are described in Chapter 6. IPSec itself is actually an open framework.

IPSec includes the IP Security protocol itself, which specifies the information to be added to an IP packet as well as how to encrypt packet data; and the Internet Key Exchange, which uses an asymmetric-based key exchange and negotiates the security associations. IPSec operates in two modes: transport and tunnel. In **transport mode** only the IP data are encrypted, not the IP headers. This allows intermediate nodes to read the source and destination addresses. In **tunnel mode** the entire IP packet is encrypted and is then placed into the content portion of another IP packet. This requires other systems at the beginning and end of the tunnel to act as proxies and to send and receive the encrypted packets. These systems then transmit the decrypted packets to their true destinations.

IPSec uses several different cryptosystems:

- Diffie-Hellman key exchange for deriving key material between peers on a public network
- Public key cryptography for signing the Diffie-Hellman exchanges to guarantee the identity of the two parties
- Bulk encryption algorithms, such as DES, for encrypting the data
- Digital certificates signed by a certificate authority to act as digital ID cards[23]

Within IPSec, IP layer security is achieved by means of an application header protocol or an encapsulating security payload protocol. The **application header (AH) protocol** provides system-to-system authentication and data integrity verification, but does not provide secrecy for the content of a network communication. The **encapsulating security payload (ESP) protocol** provides secrecy for the contents of network communications as well as system-to-system authentication and data integrity verification. When two networked systems form an association that uses encryption and authentication keys, algorithms, and key lifetimes, they can implement either the AH or the ESP protocol, but not both. If the security functions of both the AH and ESP are required, multiple security associations must be bundled to provide the correct sequence through which the IP traffic must be processed to deliver the desired security features.

The AH protocol is designed to provide data integrity and IP packet authentication. Although AH does not provide confidentiality protection, IP packets are protected from replay attacks and address spoofing as well as other types of cyberattacks against open networks. Figure 8-10 shows the packet format of the IPSec authentication header protocol. As shown in this diagram, the security parameter index (SPI) references the session key and algorithm used to protect the data being transported. Sequence numbers allow packets to arrive out of sequence for reassembly. The integrity check value (ICV) of the authentication data serves as a checksum to verify that the packet itself is unaltered. Whether used in IPv4 or IPv6, authentication secures the entire packet, excluding mutable fields in the new IP header. In tunnel mode, however, the entire inner IP packet is secured by the authentication header protocol.

The encapsulating security payload protocol provides confidentiality services for IP packets across insecure networks. ESP can also provide the authentication services of AH. Figure 8-10 shows information on the ESP packet header. ESP in tunnel mode can be

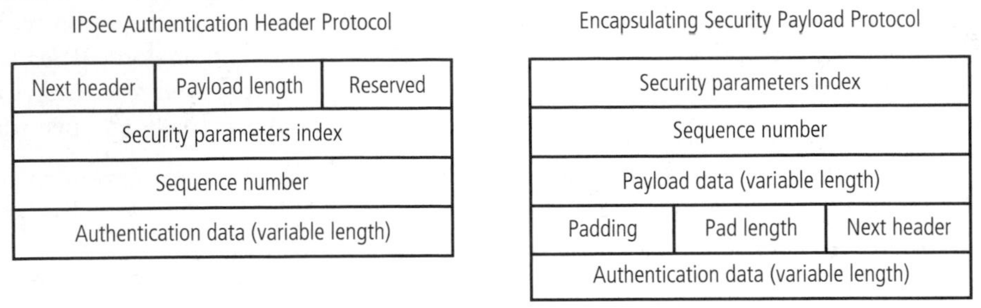

IPSec Authentication Header Protocol

Next header	Payload length	Reserved
Security parameters index		
Sequence number		
Authentication data (variable length)		

Encapsulating Security Payload Protocol

Security parameters index		
Sequence number		
Payload data (variable length)		
Padding	Pad length	Next header
Authentication data (variable length)		

Next header: Identifies the next higher level
protocol, such as TCP or ESP.
Payload length: Specifies the AH contents length.
Reserved: For future use.
Security parameters index: Identifies the
security association for this IP packet.
Sequence number: Provides a monotonically
increasing counter number for each packets
sent. Allows the recipient to order the packets
and provides protection against replay attacks.
Authentication data: A variable-length (multiple
of 32 bits) containing the ICV (integrity
check value) for this packet.

Security parameters index: Identifies the
security association for this IP packet.
Sequence number: Provides a monotonically
increasing counter number for each packet
sent. Allows the recipient to order the packets
and provides protection against replay attacks.
Payload data: Contains the encrypted data
of the IP packet.
Padding: Space for adding bytes if required by
encryption algorithm; also helps conceal
the actual payload size.
Pad length: Specifies how much of the payload
is padding.
Next header: Identifies the next higher level
protocol, such as TCP.
Authentication data: A variable-length (multiple
of 32 bits) containing the ICV (integrity check
value) for this packet.

Figure 8-10 IPSec Headers

Source: Course Technology/Cengage Learning

used to establish a virtual private network, assuring encryption and authentication between networks communicating via the Internet. In tunnel mode, the entire IP packet is encrypted with the attached ESP header. A new IP header is attached to the encrypted payload, providing the required routing information.

An ESP header is inserted into the IP packet prior to the TCP header, and an ESP trailer is placed after the IPv4 packet. If authentication is desired, an ESP authentication data field is appended after the ESP trailer. The complete transport segment, in addition to the ESP trailer, is encrypted. In an IPv6 transmission, the ESP header is placed after the hop-by-hop and routing headers. Encryption under IPv6 covers the transport segment and the ESP trailer. Authentication in both IPv4 and IPv6 covers the ciphertext data plus the ESP header. IPSec ESP-compliant systems must support the implementation of the DES algorithm utilizing the CBC (cipher block chaining) mode, which incorporates the following encryption algorithms: Triple DES, IDEA, RC5, CAST, and Blowfish.

Pretty Good Privacy (PGP) is a hybrid cryptosystem that combines some of the best available cryptographic algorithms and has become the open-source de facto standard for encryption and authentication of e-mail and file storage applications. Both freeware and low-cost commercial versions of PGP are available for a wide variety of platforms. Table 8-12 lists the PGP functions.

PGP Suite of Security Solutions
The PGP security solution provides six services: authentication by digital signatures, message encryption, compression, e-mail compatibility, segmentation, and key management.

As shown in Table 8-12, one of the algorithms used in the PGP public-key encryption is Secure Hash Algorithm 1 (SHA-1), which is used to compute hash values for calculating a 160-bit hash code based on the plaintext message. The hash code is then encrypted with DSS or RSA and appended to the original message. The recipient uses the sender's public key to decrypt and recover the hash code. Using the same encryption algorithm, the recipient then generates a new hash code from the same message. If the two hash codes are identical, then the message and the sender are authentic.

A sender may also want the entire contents of the message protected from unauthorized view. 3DES, IDEA, or CAST, which are all standard algorithms, may be used to encrypt the message contents with a unique, randomly generated 128-bit session key. The session key is encrypted by RSA, using the recipient's public key, and then appended to the message. The recipient uses his private key with RSA to decrypt and recover the session key. The recovered session key is used to decrypt the message. Authentication and message encryption can be used together by first digitally signing the message with a private key, encrypting the message with a unique session key, and then encrypting the session key with the intended recipient's public key.

PGP uses the freeware ZIP algorithm to compress the message after it has been digitally signed but before it is encrypted. This saves space and generates a more secure encrypted document since a smaller file offers an attacker fewer chances to look for patterns in the data and fewer characters with which to perform frequency analysis. PGP also uses a process known as Radix-64, which encodes non-textual data and assures that encrypted data can be transferred using e-mail systems by maintaining the required 8-bit blocks of ASCII text. The format maps three octets of binary data into four ASCII characters and appends a cyclic redundancy check (CRC) to detect transmission errors.

Because many Internet facilities impose restrictions on message size, PGP can automatically subdivide messages into a manageable stream size. This segmentation is performed after all other encryption and conversion functions have been processed. At the recipient end, PGP reassembles the segment's message blocks prior to decompression and decryption.

PGP does not impose a rigid structure for public key management, but it can assign a level of trust within the confines of PGP, though it does not specify the actual degree of trust the user should place in any specific key. Trust can be addressed and assured by using the public

Function	Algorithm	Application
Public key encryption	RSA/SHA-1 or DSS/SHA-1	Digital signatures
Conventional encryption	3DES, RSA, IDEA or CAST	Message encryption
File management	ZIP	Compression

Table 8-12 PGP Functions[24]

key ring structure. In a public key ring structure, each specific set of public key credentials is associated with a key legitimacy field, a signature trust field, and an owner trust field. These fields contain a trust-flag byte that identifies whether the credential is trusted in each of these three fields. In the event that the trust of a given credential has been broken, as when a key is compromised, the owner can issue a digitally signed key revocation certificate that updates the credential trust bytes when the credential is next verified.

Attacks on Cryptosystems

Historically, attempts to gain unauthorized access to secure communications have used brute force attacks, in which the ciphertext is repeatedly searched for clues that can lead to the algorithm's structure. These ciphertext attacks involve a hacker searching for a common text structure, wording, or syntax in the encrypted message that can enable him or her to calculate the number of each type of letter used in the message. This process, known as frequency analysis, is used along with published frequency of occurrence patterns of various languages and can allow an experienced attacker to crack almost any code quickly with a large enough sample of the encoded text. To protect against this, modern algorithms attempt to remove the repetitive and predictable sequences of characters from the ciphertext.

Occasionally, an attacker may obtain duplicate texts, one in ciphertext and one in plaintext, and thus reverse-engineer the encryption algorithm in a **known-plaintext attack** scheme. Alternatively, attackers may conduct a **selected-plaintext attack** by sending potential victims a specific text that they are sure the victims will forward on to others. When the victim does encrypt and forward the message, it can be used in the attack if the attacker can acquire the outgoing encrypted version. At the very least, reverse engineering can usually lead the attacker to discover which cryptosystem is being employed.

Most publicly available encryption methods are generally released to the information and computer security communities to test the encryption algorithm's resistance to cracking. In addition, attackers are kept informed of which methods of attack have failed. Although the purpose of sharing this information is to develop a more secure algorithm, it does prevent attackers from wasting their time, freeing them up to find new weaknesses in the cryptosystem or new, more challenging means of obtaining encryption keys.

In general, attacks on cryptosystems fall into four general categories: man-in-the-middle, correlation, dictionary, and timing. Although you learned about several of these attacks in Chapter 2, they are discussed here to evaluate their impact on cryptosystems.

Man-in-the-Middle Attack

A **man-in-the-middle attack**, as you learned in Chapter 2, attempts to intercept a public key or even to insert a known key structure in place of the requested public key. Thus, attackers attempt to place themselves between the sender and receiver, and once they've intercepted the request for key exchanges, they send each participant a valid public key, which is known only to them. To the victims of such attacks, encrypted communication appears to be occurring normally, but in fact the attacker is receiving each encrypted message and decoding it (with the key given to the sending party), and then encrypting and sending it to the intended recipient. Establishing public keys with digital signatures can prevent the traditional man-in-the-middle attack, as the attacker cannot duplicate the signatures.

Correlation Attacks

As the complexities of encryption methods have increased, so too have the tools and methods of cryptanalysts. **Correlation attacks** are a collection of brute-force methods that attempt to deduce statistical relationships between the structure of the unknown key and the ciphertext generated by the cryptosystem. Differential and linear cryptanalysis, which are advanced methods of code breaking that are beyond the scope of this text, have been used to mount successful attacks on block cipher encryptions such as DES. If these advanced approaches can calculate the value of the public key in a reasonable time, all messages written with that key can be decrypted. The only defense against this attack is the selection of strong cryptosystems that have stood the test of time, thorough key management, and strict adherence to the best practices of cryptography in the frequency of key changes.

Dictionary Attacks

In a **dictionary attack**, the attacker encrypts every word in a dictionary using the same cryptosystem as used by the target in an attempt to locate a match between the target ciphertext and the list of encrypted words. Dictionary attacks can be successful when the ciphertext consists of relatively few characters, as for example files which contain encrypted usernames and passwords. An attacker who acquires a system password file can run hundreds of thousands of potential passwords from the dictionary he or she has prepared against the stolen list. Most computer systems use a well-known one-way hash function to store passwords in such files, but an attacker can almost always find at least a few matches in any stolen password file. After a match is found, the attacker has essentially identified a potential valid password for the system.

Timing Attacks

In a **timing attack**, the attacker eavesdrops on the victim's session and uses statistical analysis of patterns and inter-keystroke timings to discern sensitive session information. While timing analysis may not directly result in the decryption of sensitive data, it can be used to gain information about the encryption key and perhaps the cryptosystem. It may also eliminate some algorithms, thus narrowing the attacker's search and increasing the odds of eventual success. Having broken an encryption, the attacker may launch a **replay attack**, which is an attempt to resubmit a recording of the deciphered authentication to gain entry into a secure source.

Defending Against Attacks

Encryption is a very useful tool in protecting the confidentiality of information that is in storage or transmission. However, it is just that—another tool in the information security administrator's arsenal against threats to information security. Frequently, the uninformed describe information security exclusively in terms of encryption (and possibly firewalls and antivirus software). But encryption is simply the process of hiding the true meaning of information. Over millennia, mankind has developed dramatically more sophisticated means of hiding information from those who should not see it, but no matter how sophisticated encryption and cryptosystems have become, they retain the flaw that was present in the very first such system: If you discover the key, that is, the method used to perform the encryption, you can read the message. Thus, key management is not so much the management of technology but rather the management of people.

Encryption can, however, protect information when it is most vulnerable—that is, when it is outside the organization's systems. Information in transit through public or leased networks is outside the organization's control, and with loss of control can come loss of security. Encryption helps organizations secure information that must travel through public and leased networks by guarding the information against the efforts of those who sniff, spoof, and otherwise skulk around. As such, encryption is a vital piece of the security puzzle.

Selected Readings

- *Applied Cryptography, Second Edition* by Bruce Schneier. John Wiley & Sons, 1996.
- *Public Key Infrastructure: Building Trusted Applications and Web Services* by John R. Vacca. Auerbach, 2004.

Chapter Summary

- Encryption is the process of converting a message into a form that is unreadable to unauthorized individuals.

- The science of encryption, known as cryptology, encompasses cryptography (making and using encryption codes) and cryptanalysis (breaking encryption codes).

- Cryptology has a long history and continues to change and improve.

- Two basic processing methods are used to convert plaintext data into encrypted data—bit stream and block ciphering. The other major methods used for scrambling data include substitution ciphers, transposition ciphers, XOR function, Vigenère cipher, and the Vernam cipher.

- The strength of many encryption applications and cryptosystems is determined by key size. All other things being equal, the length of the key directly affects the strength of the encryption.

- Hash functions are mathematical algorithms that generate a message summary, or digest, that can be used to confirm the identity of a specific message and to confirm that the message has not been altered.

- Most cryptographic algorithms can be grouped into two broad categories, symmetric and asymmetric. In practice, most popular cryptosystems are hybrids that combine symmetric and asymmetric algorithms.

- Public-Key Infrastructure (PKI) is an integrated system of software, encryption methodologies, protocols, legal agreements, and third-party services that enables users to communicate securely. PKI includes digital certificates and certificate authorities.

- Digital signatures are encrypted messages that are independently verified by a central facility, and which provide nonrepudiation. A digital certificate is an electronic document, similar to a digital signature, that is attached to a file to certify that the file is from the organization it claims to be from and has not been modified from its original format.

- Steganography is the hiding of information, and while it is not properly a form of cryptography, like cryptography it is used to protect confidential information while in transit.

- S-HTTP (Secure Hypertext Transfer Protocol), Secure Electronic Transactions (SET), and SSL (Secure Sockets Layer) are protocols designed to enable secure communications across the Internet. IPSec is the protocol used to secure communications across any IP-based network such as LANs, WANs, and the Internet. Secure Multipurpose Internet Mail Extensions (S/MIME), Privacy Enhanced Mail (PEM), and Pretty Good Privacy (PGP) are protocols that are used to secure electronic mail. PGP is a hybrid cryptosystem that combines some of the best available cryptographic algorithms and has become the open source de facto standard for encryption and authentication of e-mail and file storage applications.

- Wireless networks require their own cryptographic protection. Originally protected with WEP and WPA, most modern Wi-Fi networks are now protected with WPA2. Bluetooth—a short-range wireless protocol used predominantly for wireless phones and PDAs—can be exploited by anyone within its 30-foot range.

- Unauthorized attempts to access to secure communications often use brute force or ciphertext attacks that perform frequency analysis on the encoded text. Therefore, modern algorithms attempt to remove the repetitive and predictable statistical bias from the ciphertext. If attackers obtain duplicate texts, one in ciphertext and one in plaintext, they can reverse-engineer the encryption algorithm. This is referred to as a known-plaintext attack or a selected-plaintext attack. Attacks against cryptosystems include the man-in-the-middle attack, correlation attacks, dictionary attacks, and timing attacks.

- Most well-known encryption methods are released to the information and computer security communities for testing, which leads to the development of more secure algorithms.

Review Questions

1. What are cryptography and cryptanalysis?
2. What were some of the first uses of cryptography?
3. What is a key, and what is it used for?
4. What are the three basic operations in cryptography?
5. What is a hash function, and what can it be used for?
6. Why is it important to exchange keys out of band in symmetric encryption?
7. What is the fundamental difference between symmetric and asymmetric encryption?
8. How does Public-Key Infrastructure protect information assets?
9. What are the six components of PKI?
10. What is the difference between digital signatures and digital certificates?
11. What drawbacks to symmetric and asymmetric encryption are resolved by using a hybrid method like Diffie-Hellman?
12. What is steganography, and what can it be used for?
13. Which security protocols are predominantly used in Web-based electronic commerce?

14. Which security protocols are used to protect e-mail?

15. IPSec can be used in two modes. What are they?

16. Which kind of attack on cryptosystems involves using a collection of pre-identified terms? Which kind of attack involves sequential guessing of all possible key combinations?

17. If you were setting up an encryption-based network, what size key would you choose and why?

18. What is the average key size of a strong encryption system in use today?

19. What is the standard for encryption currently recommended by NIST?

20. What is the most popular symmetric encryption system used over the Web? The most popular asymmetric system? Hybrid system?

Exercises

1. Go to a popular online electronic commerce site like Amazon.com. Place several items in your shopping cart, and then go to check out. When you reach the screen that asks for your credit card number, right-click on the Web browser and select "Properties." What can you find out about the cryptosystems and protocols in use to protect this transaction?

2. Repeat Exercise 1 on a different Web site. Does this site use the same or different protocols? Describe them.

3. Go to the Web site for PGP, *www.pgp.com/downloads/desktoptrial/index.html*. Download and install the trial version of PGP Desktop. Using PGP and your favorite e-mail program, send a PGP-signed e-mail to your instructor. What looks different in this e-mail compared to your other e-mails?

4. Visit the NIST Web site and view the document "Announcing the Advanced Encryption Standard (AES)" which can be found at *http://csrc.nist.gov/publications/fips/fips197/fips-197.pdf*. Review the FIPS-197 standard. Examine the document to determine an overview of the development and implementation of this cryptosystem.

5. Search the Web for steganographic tools. What do you find? Download and install a trial version of one of the tools. Embed a text file within an image. In a side-by-side comparison of the two images, can you tell the difference between the original image and the image with the embedded file?

Case Exercises

Charlie was just getting ready to head home when the phone rang. Caller ID showed it was Peter.

"Hi, Peter," he said into the receiver. "Want me to start the file cracker on your spreadsheet?"

"No, thanks," Peter answered, taking the joke well. "I remembered my passphrase. But I want to get your advice on what we need to do to make the use of encryption more effective and to get it properly licensed for the whole company. I see the value in using it for certain kinds of information, but I'm worried about forgetting a passphrase again or even worse, that someone else forgets a passphrase or leaves the company. How would we get their files back?"

"We need to use a feature called key recovery, which is usually part of PKI software," said Charlie. "Actually, if we invest in PKI software, we could solve that problem as well as several others."

"OK," said Peter. "Can you see me tomorrow at 10 o'clock to talk about this PKI solution and how we can make better use of encryption?"

Questions:

1. Was Charlie exaggerating when he gave Peter an estimate for the time that would be required to crack the encryption key using a brute force attack?

2. Are there any tools that someone like Peter can use safely, other than key recovery, to avoid losing his or her passphrase?

Endnotes

1. Anderson, T. "Polyalphabetic Substitution." *Le Canard Volant Non Identifie Online.* 30 January 1999. Accessed 21 June 2007 from *http://cvni.net/radio/nsnl/nsnl010/nsnl10poly.html.*

2. Varughese, S. "Rainbow Cracking and Password Security", Palisade Application Security Online. 2006. Accessed 21 June 2007 from *http://palisade.plynt.com/issues/2006Feb/rainbow-tables/.*

3. Krutz, Ronald L., and Vines, Russell Dean. *The CISSP Prep Guide: Mastering the Ten Domains of Computer Security.* New York: John Wiley and Sons Inc., 2001, 131.

4. Savard, John. "The Advanced Encryption Standard (Rijndael)." Accessed 31 March 2004 from *http://home.ecn.ab.ca/~jsavard/crypto/co040401.htm.*

5. National Institute of Standards and Technology. *Data Encryption Standards (DES).* FIPS PUB 46-3. 25 October 1999.

6. Burnett, Steve, and Paine, Stephen. *RSA Security's Official Guide to Cryptography.* New York: Osborne/McGraw-Hill, 2001.

7. Special thanks to a reviewer of a prior edition of this text for this example: Robert Statica, Associate Director, Cryptography and Telecommunications Laboratory, New Jersey Institute of Technology.

8. Burnett, Steve, and Paine, Stephen. *RSA Security's Official Guide to Cryptography.* New York: Osborne/McGraw-Hill, 2001.

9. Ibid.

10. Kelm, S. "The PKI Page." *Secorvo Security Consulting Online.* 2007. Accessed 21 June 2007 from *www.pki-page.org/.*

11. Stallings, W. *Cryptography and Network Security, Principles and Practice.* New Jersey: Prentice Hall, 1999.

12. Conway, M. "Code Wars: Steganography, Signals Intelligence, and Terrorism." Accessed 21 June 2007 from *www.transactionpub.metapress.com/app/home/contribution.asp?referrer=parent&backto=issue,6,9;journal,14,30;linkingpublicationresults,1:105285,1.*

13. McCullagh, D. "Bin Laden: Steganography Master?" Accessed 21 June 2007 from *www.wired.com/news/politics/0,1283,41658,00.html.*

14. William Stallings. *Cryptography and Network Security, Principles and Practice.* New Jersey: Prentice Hall, 1999.

15. "WEP (Wired Equivalent Privacy)." Accessed 10 April 2007 from *www.networkworld.com/details/715.html.*

16. iLabs Wireless Security Team. "What's Wrong with WEP?" 9 September 2002. Accessed 9 April 2007 from *www.networkworld.com/research/2002/0909wepprimer.html.*

17. Leyden, J. "WEP Key Wireless Cracking Made Easy." *The Register.* 4 April 2007. Accessed 30 June 2007 from *www.theregister.co.uk/2007/04/04/wireless_code_cracking.*

18. Wi-Fi Alliance. "Wi-Fi Protected Access: Strong, Standards-Based, Interoperable Security for Today's Wi-Fi Networks." 2003. Accessed 9 April 2007 from *www.wi-fi.org/files/wp_8_WPA%20Security_4-29-03.pdf.*

19. Walker, J. "802.11 Security Series Part II: The Temporal Key Integrity Protocol (TKIP)." Accessed 10 April 2007 from *http://cache-www.intel.com/cd/00/00/01/77/17769_80211_part2.pdf.*

20. "What Is RSN (Robust Secure Network)?" *Tech FAQ Online.* Accessed 21 June 2007 from *www.tech-faq.com/rsn-robust-secure-network.shtml.*

21. Bialoglowy, M. "Bluetooth Security Review, Part I: Introduction to Bluetooth." Accessed 15 April 2007 from *www.securityfocus.com/infocus/1830.*

22. Leyden, J. "Cabir Mobile Worm Gives Track Fans the Run Around" 12 August 2005. Accessed 15 April 2007 from *www.theregister.co.uk/2005/08/12/cabir_stadium_outbreak/.*

23. Cisco Systems, Inc. "White Paper: IPSec." *Cisco Online.* 21 November 2000. Accessed 1 July 2002 from *www.cisco.com/warp/public/cc/so/neso/sqso/eqso/ipsec_wp.htm.*

24. The International PGP Home Page. *PGPI Online.* Accessed 21 June 2007 from *www.pgpi.org/.*

chapter 9

Physical Security

*If someone really wants to get at the information, it is not difficult if
they can gain physical access to the computer or hard drive.*

MICROSOFT WHITE PAPER, JULY 1999

Amy Windahl was back early from lunch. As she was walking toward the SLS building
from the parking lot, she saw one of the accounting clerks go through the building's
double glass doors. Behind him followed someone she didn't recognize, a tall, blond man
in nondescript business casual clothes. The two of them walked past the lobby security
guard and headed for the elevators. Amy got on the next elevator and pressed the button
for her floor.

When the elevator doors opened, she saw the blond man in the second floor elevator lobby
looking at the company's phone list. She walked over to the secure doors that led to the
offices and cocked her right hip, where her badge was clipped, toward the sensor for the
locks. When she heard the electric lock release, Amy went through. As the door began to
shut, the stranger grabbed it and came through behind her.

Amy knew now that he was a *tailgater*, a person who follows authorized people after they
have used their badges to open locked doors. Just last week a security bulletin had emphasized that tailgaters should be reported. Everyone in the staff meeting joked about turning
each other in the next time any two of them came through the door together. But now she
was beginning to understand the seriousness of the bulletin.

Amy went back to the second floor lobby and used the phone there to call building security and report the tailgater.

"Do you guys want to check it out?"

"Yes, ma'am. We have someone nearby. I'll have him meet you in the lobby," said the security dispatcher.

When the security officer arrived, Amy described the man, and said, "He went down the hall, toward the programming offices."

The guard said, "Wait here. If he comes through here again, call dispatch at extension 3333. I'll be right back."

A few minutes later, Amy saw the blond man walking briskly toward the doors; the guard was right behind him. As the stranger opened the door, the guard called out, "Sir, please stop. I need to speak with you. What's your name?" Before the blond man could answer, the elevator opened, and two more guards came into the lobby.

The stranger said, "Alan Gaskin."

The guard asked, "What's your business here?"

"Just visiting a friend," said the man.

"And who would that be?" the guard asked.

The stranger looked a bit surprised, and then said, "Uh, William Walters, in the accounting department, I think."

The guard reached for his PDA and punched a few buttons. Then he said, "Mr. Gaskin, there are no employees with that name working here, in accounting or any other department. Do you want to try another answer?"

The intruder took a few steps toward the stairwell, but the other two guards moved up and cut him off. As they held the man's arms to keep him from escaping, a brown paper bag dropped out from under his jacket, its contents spilling out on the carpet. Amy saw several office badges, a watch, two small tablet computers and several cell phones.

The first guard radioed dispatch. "Contact the local police and advise them we have a thief and we plan to press charges." The other guards led the man toward the elevators, while the first guard told Amy: "Call your supervisor and tell her you'll be delayed. We need a statement from you."

LEARNING OBJECTIVES:

Upon completion of this material, you should be able to:

- Discuss the relationship between information security and physical security
- Describe key physical security considerations, including fire control and surveillance systems
- Identify critical physical environment considerations for computing facilities, including uninterruptible power supplies

Introduction

As you learned in Chapter 1, information security requires the protection of both data and physical assets. You have already learned about many of the mechanisms used to protect data, including firewalls, intrusion detection systems, and monitoring software.

Physical security encompasses the design, implementation, and maintenance of countermeasures that protect the physical resources of an organization, including the people, hardware, and supporting system elements and resources that control information in all its states (transmission, storage, and processing). Most technology-based controls can be circumvented if an attacker gains physical access to the devices being controlled. In other words, if it is easy to steal the hard drives from a computer system, then the information on those hard drives is not secure. Therefore, physical security is just as important as logical security to an information security program.

In earlier chapters, you encountered a number of threats to information security that could be classified as threats to physical security. For example, an employee accidentally spilling coffee on a laptop threatens the physical security of the information in the computer—in this case, the threat is an act of human error or failure. A compromise to intellectual property can include an employee without an appropriate security clearance copying a classified marketing plan. A deliberate act of espionage or trespass could be a competitor sneaking into a facility with a camera. Deliberate acts of sabotage or vandalism can be physical attacks on individuals or property. Deliberate acts of theft include employees stealing computer equipment, credentials, passwords, and laptops. Quality of service deviations from service providers, especially power and water, also represent physical security threats, as do various environmental anomalies. In his book, *Fighting Computer Crime*, Donn B. Parker lists the following "Seven Major Sources of Physical Loss":

1. Extreme temperature: heat, cold

2. Gases: war gases, commercial vapors, humid or dry air, suspended particles

3. Liquids: water, chemicals

4. Living organisms: viruses, bacteria, people, animals, insects

5. Projectiles: tangible objects in motion, powered objects

6. Movement: collapse, shearing, shaking, vibration, liquefaction, flow waves, separation, slide

7. Energy anomalies: electrical surge or failure, magnetism, static electricity, aging circuitry; radiation: sound, light, radio, microwave, electromagnetic, atomic[1]

As with all other areas of security, the implementation of physical security measures requires sound organizational policy. Physical security policies guide users on the appropriate use of computing resources and information assets, as well as on the protection of their own personal safety in day-to-day operations. Physical security is designed and implemented in several layers. Each of the organization's communities of interest is responsible for components within these layers, as follows:

- General management is responsible for the security of the facility in which the organization is housed and the policies and standards for secure operation. This includes exterior security, fire protection, and building access, as well as other controls such as guard dogs and door locks.

- IT management and professionals are responsible for environmental and access security in technology equipment locations, and for the policies and standards that govern secure equipment operation. This includes access to server rooms, and power conditioning and server room temperature and humidity controls, and more specialized controls like static and dust contamination equipment.

- Information security management and professionals are responsible for risk assessments and for reviewing the physical security controls implemented by the other two groups.

Physical Access Controls

A number of physical access controls are uniquely suited to governing the movement of people within an organization's facilities—specifically, controlling their physical access to company resources. While logical access to systems, in this age of the Internet, is a very important subject, the control of physical access to the assets of the organization is also of critical importance. Some of the technology used to control physical access is also used to control logical access, including biometrics, smart cards, and wireless enabled keycards.

Before learning more about physical access controls, you need to understand what makes a facility secure. An organization's general management oversees its physical security. Commonly, a building's access controls are operated by a group called **facilities management**. Larger organizations may have an entire staff dedicated to facilities management, while smaller organizations often outsource these duties.

In facilities management, a **secure facility** is a physical location that has in place controls to minimize the risk of attacks from physical threats. The term *secure facility* might bring to mind military bases, maximum-security prisons, and nuclear power plants, but while securing a facility requires some adherence to rules and procedures, the environment does not necessarily have to be that constrained. It is also not necessary that a facility resemble a fortress to minimize risk from physical attacks. In fact, a secure facility can sometimes use its natural terrain, local traffic flow, and surrounding development to enhance its physical security, along with protection mechanisms such as fences, gates, walls, guards, and alarms.

Physical Security Controls

There are a number of physical security controls that an organization's communities of interest should consider when implementing physical security inside and outside the facility. Some of the major controls are:

- Walls, fencing, and gates
- Guards
- Dogs
- ID cards and badges
- Locks and keys

- Mantraps
- Electronic monitoring
- Alarms and alarm systems
- Computer rooms and wiring closets
- Interior walls and doors

Walls, Fencing, and Gates Some of the oldest and most reliable elements of physical security are walls, fencing, and gates. While not every organization needs to implement external perimeter controls, walls and fences with suitable gates are an essential starting point for organizations whose employees require access to physical locations the organization owns or controls. These types of controls vary widely in appearance and function, ranging from chain link or privacy fences that control where people should park or walk, to imposing concrete or masonry barriers designed to withstand the blast of a car bomb. Each exterior perimeter control requires expert planning to ensure that it fulfills the security goals and that it presents an image appropriate to the organization.

Guards Controls like fences and walls with gates are static, and are therefore unresponsive to actions, unless they are programmed to respond with specific actions to specific stimuli, such as opening for someone who has the correct key. Guards, on the other hand, can evaluate each situation as it arises and make reasoned responses. Most guards have clear **standard operating procedures (SOPs)** that help them to act decisively in unfamiliar situations. In the military, for example, guards are given general orders (see the Offline on guard duty), as well as special orders that are particular to their posts.

Dogs If an organization is protecting valuable resources, dogs can be a valuable part of physical security if they are integrated into the plan and managed properly. Guard dogs are useful because their keen sense of smell and hearing can detect intrusions that human guards cannot, and they can be placed in harm's way when necessary to avoid risking the life of a person.

ID Cards and Badges An **identification (ID) card** is typically concealed, whereas a **name badge** is visible. Both devices can serve a number of purposes. First, they serve as simple forms of biometrics in that they use the cardholder's picture to authenticate his or her access to the facility. The cards may be visibly coded to specify which buildings or areas may be accessed. Second, ID cards that have a magnetic strip or radio chip that can be read by automated control devices allow an organization to restrict access to sensitive areas within the facility. ID cards and name badges are not foolproof, however; and even the cards designed to communicate with locks can be easily duplicated, stolen, or modified. Because of this inherent weakness, such devices should not be an organization's only means of controlling access to restricted areas.

Another inherent weakness of this type of physical access control technology is the human factor. As depicted in this chapter's opening vignette, **tailgating** occurs when an authorized person presents a key to open a door, and other people, who may or may not be authorized, also enter. Launching a campaign to make employees aware of tailgating is one way to combat this problem. There are also technological means of discouraging tailgating, such as

"General Orders:

I will guard everything within the limits of my post and quit my post only when properly relieved.

I will obey my special orders and perform all of my duties in a military manner.

I will report violations of my special orders, emergencies, and anything not covered in my instructions to the commander of the relief."[2]

How do guards meet these responsibilities? They apply the force necessary to accomplish their missions, including deadly force in approved situations. Deadly force is the application of coercive control that may result in death or severe bodily harm. It is applied only to the extent necessary to make an apprehension.

"Deadly force can only be used for [the following situations]:

1. Self-defense in the event of imminent danger of death or serious bodily harm;

2. To prevent the actual theft or destruction of property designated for protection; and

3. As directed by the Standard Operating Procedures of his individual guard post."[3]

Adapted from "Guard Duty," www.armystudyguide.com/content/army_board_study_guide_topics/guard_ duty/guard-duty-study-guide.shtml. In the military, guard duty is a serious responsibility. A guard must memorize, understand, and comply with his or her general orders, and the orders particular to his or her assignment.

mantraps (which are discussed in a following section) or turnstiles. These extra levels of control are usually expensive, in that they require floor space and/or construction, and are inconvenient for those required to use them. Consequently, anti-tailgating controls are only used where there is significant security risk from unauthorized entry.

Locks and Keys There are two types of lock mechanisms: mechanical and electromechanical. The **mechanical lock** may rely on a key that is a carefully shaped piece of metal, which is rotated to turn tumblers that release secured loops of steel, aluminum, or brass (as in, for example, brass padlocks). Alternatively, a mechanical lock may have a dial that rotates slotted discs until the slots on multiple disks are aligned, and then retracts a securing bolt (as in combination and safe locks). Although mechanical locks are conceptually simple, some of the technologies that go into their development are quite complex. Some of these modern enhancements have led to the creation of the electromechanical lock. **Electromechanical locks** can accept a variety of inputs as keys, including magnetic strips on ID cards, radio signals from name badges, personal identification numbers (**PINs**) typed into a keypad, or some combination of these to activate an electrically powered locking mechanism.

Locks can also be divided into four categories based on the triggering process: manual, programmable, electronic, and biometric. **Manual locks** such as padlocks and combination locks, are commonplace and well understood. If you have the key (or combination) you can open the lock. These locks are often preset by the manufacturer and therefore unchangeable. In other words, once manual locks are installed into doors, they can only be changed by highly trained locksmiths. Programmable locks can be changed after they are put in service, allowing for combination or key changes without a locksmith and even allowing the owner to change to another access method (key or combination) to upgrade security. Many examples of these types of locks are shown in Figure 9-1. Mechanical push button locks, shown in the left-most photo in Figure 9-1, are popular for securing computer rooms and wiring closets, as they have a code that can be reset and don't require electricity to operate.

Electronic locks can be integrated into alarm systems and combined with other building management systems. Also, these locks can be integrated with sensors to create various combinations of locking behavior. One such combination is a system that coordinates the use of fire alarms and locks to improve safety during alarm conditions (i.e., fires). Such a system changes a location's required level of access authorization when that location is in an alarm condition. Another example is a combination system in which a lock is fitted with a sensor that notifies guard stations when that lock has been activated. Another common form of electronic locks are electric strike locks, which usually require people to announce themselves before being "buzzed" through a locked door. In general, electronic locks lend themselves to uses where they can be activated or deactivated by a switch controlled by an agent, usually a secretary or guard. Electronic push button locks, like their mechanical cousins, have a numerical keypad over the knob, requiring the individual user to enter a personal code and open the door. These locks usually use battery backups to power the keypad in case of a power failure.

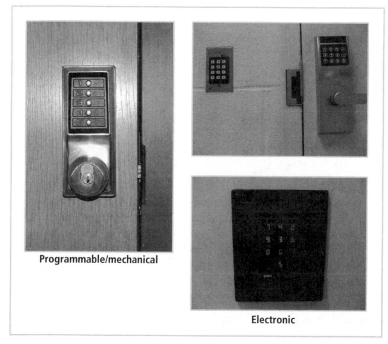

Programmable/mechanical

Electronic

Figure 9-1 Locks

Source: Course Technology/Cengage Learning

Some locks use smart cards, as described previously—keys that contain computer chips. These smart cards can carry critical information, provide strong authentication, and offer a number of other features. Keycard readers based on smart cards are often used to secure computer rooms, communications closets, and other restricted areas. The card reader can track entry and provide accountability. In a locking system that uses smart cards, the access level of individuals can be adjusted according to their current status (i.e., current employee, recently resigned) and thus personnel changes do not require replacement of the lock. A specialized type of keycard reader is the **proximity reader**, which, instead of requiring individuals to insert their cards, allows them simply to place their cards within the reader's range. Some of these readers can recognize the card even when it is inside a pocket.

The most sophisticated locks are **biometric locks**. Finger, palm, and hand readers, iris and retina scanners, and voice and signature readers fall into this category. The technology that underlies biometric devices is discussed in Chapter 7.

The management of keys and locks is fundamental to the fulfillment of general management's responsibility to secure an organization's physical environment. As you will learn in Chapter 11, when people are hired, fired, laid off, or transferred, their access controls, whether physical or logical, must be appropriately adjusted. Failure to do so can result in employees cleaning out their offices and taking more than their personal effects. Also, when locksmiths are hired, they should be carefully screened and monitored, as there is a chance that they could have complete access to the facility.

Sometimes locks fail, and thus facilities need to have alternative procedures in place for controlling access. These procedures must take into account that locks fail in one of two ways: the door lock fails and the door becomes unlocked—a **fail-safe lock**; or the door lock fails and the door remains locked—a **fail-secure lock**. In practice, the most common reason why technically sophisticated locks fail is loss of power and activation through fire control systems. A fail-safe lock is usually used to secure an exit, where it is essential that in the event of, for instance, a fire, the door is unlocked. A fail-secure lock is used when human safety in the area being controlled is not the dominant factor. One example of this is a situation in which the security of nuclear or biological weapons needs to be controlled; here, preventing a loss of control of these weapons is more critical to security (meaning it is a security issue of greater magnitude) than protecting the lives of the personnel guarding the weapons.

Understanding lock mechanisms is important, because locks can be exploited by an intruder to gain access to the secured location. If an electronic lock is short circuited, it may become fail-safe and allow the intruder to bypass the control and enter the room.

Mantraps A common enhancement for locks in high security areas is the mantrap. A **mantrap** is a small enclosure that has separate entry and exit points. To gain access to the facility, area, or room, a person enters the mantrap, requests access via some form of electronic or biometric lock and key, and if confirmed, exits the mantrap into the facility. Otherwise the person cannot leave the mantrap until a security official overrides the enclosure's automatic locks. Figure 9-2 provides an example of a typical mantrap layout.

Electronic Monitoring Monitoring equipment can be used to record events within a specific area that guards and dogs might miss, or in areas where other types of physical controls are not practical. Although you may not know it, many of you are, thanks to the silver globes attached to the ceilings of many retail stores, already subject to cameras viewing you

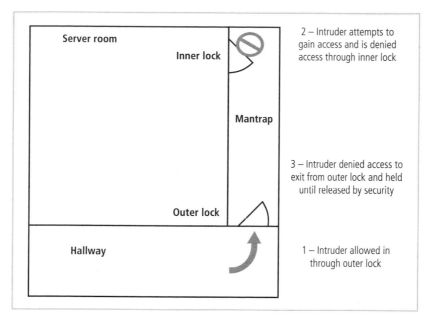

Figure 9-2 Mantraps

Source: Course Technology/Cengage Learning

from odd corners—that is, video monitoring. Attached to these cameras are video cassette recorders (VCRs) and related machinery that capture the video feed. Electronic monitoring includes **closed-circuit television (CCT)** systems. Some CCT systems collect constant video feeds, while others rotate input from a number of cameras, sampling each area in turn.

These video monitoring systems have drawbacks: for the most part they are passive and do not prevent access or prohibited activity. Another drawback to these systems is that people must view the video output, because there are no intelligent systems capable of reliably evaluating a video feed. To determine if unauthorized activities have occurred, a security staff member must constantly review the information in real time or review the information collected in video recordings. For this reason, CCT is most often used as an evidence collection device after an area has been broken into than as a detection instrument. In high-security areas (such as banks, casinos, and shopping centers), however, security personnel monitor CCT systems constantly, looking for suspicious activity.

Alarms and Alarm Systems Closely related to monitoring are the alarm systems that notify people or systems when a predetermined event or activity occurs. Alarms, which are similar to the IDPSs you learned about in Chapter 7, can detect a *physical* intrusion or other untoward event. This could be a fire, a break-in, an environmental disturbance such as flooding, or an interruption in services such as a loss of power. One example of an alarm system is the burglar alarm commonly found in residential and commercial environments. Burglar alarms detect intrusions into unauthorized areas and notify either a local or remote security agency to react. To detect intrusions, these systems rely on a number of different types of sensors: motion detectors, thermal detectors, glass breakage detectors, weight sensors, and contact sensors. **Motion detectors** detect movement within a confined space and are either active or passive. Some motion sensors emit energy beams, usually in the form of infrared or laser light, ultrasonic sound or sound waves, or some form of electromagnetic radiation. If the energy from the beam projected into the area being monitored is disrupted, the alarm is activated. Other types of motion sensors are passive in that they constantly measure the energy (infrared or ultrasonic) from the monitored space and detect rapid changes in this energy. The passive measurement of these energies can be blocked or disguised and is therefore fallible. **Thermal detectors** measure rates of change in the ambient temperature in the room. They can, for example, detect when a person with a body temperature of 98.6 degrees Fahrenheit enters a room with a temperature of 65 degrees Fahrenheit, because the person's presence changes the room's ambient temperature. Thermal detectors are also used in fire detection (as is described in later sections). **Contact and weight sensors** work when two contacts are connected as, for example, when a foot steps on a pressure-sensitive pad under a rug, or a window is opened, triggering a pin-and-spring sensor. **Vibration sensors** also fall into this category, except that they detect movement of the sensor rather than movement in the environment.

Computer Rooms and Wiring Closets
Computer rooms and wiring and communications closets require special attention to ensure the confidentiality, integrity, and availability of information. For an outline of the physical and environmental controls needed for computer rooms, read the Technical Details box entitled "Physical and Environmental Controls for Computer Rooms."

Logical access controls are easily defeated if an attacker gains physical access to the computing equipment. Custodial staff members are often the least scrutinized employees (or nonemployees) who have access to an organization's offices. Yet custodians are given the greatest degree of unsupervised access. They are often handed the master keys to the entire building and then ignored, even though they collect paper from every office, dust many desks, and move large containers from every area. It is, therefore, not difficult for this type of worker to gather critical information and computer media or copy proprietary and classified information. All this is not to say that an organization's custodial staff should be under constant suspicion of espionage, but to note that the wide-reaching access that custodians have can be a vulnerability that attackers exploit to gain unauthorized information. Factual accounts exist of technically trained agents working as custodians in the offices of their competition. Thus, custodial staffs should be carefully managed not only by the organization's general management, but also by IT management.

Interior Walls and Doors
The security of information assets can sometimes be compromised by the nature of the construction of the walls and doors of the facility. The walls in a facility are typically of two types: standard interior and firewall. Building codes require that each floor have a number of **firewalls**, or walls that limit the spread of damage should a fire break out in an office. While the network firewalls discussed in an earlier chapter isolate the logical subnetworks of the organization, physical firewalls isolate the physical spaces of the organization's offices. Between the firewalls, standard interior walls compartmentalize the individual offices. Unlike firewalls, these interior walls reach only part way to the next floor, which leaves a space above the ceiling but below the floor of the next level up. This space is called a **plenum**, and is usually one to three feet to allow for ventilation systems that can inexpensively collect return air from all the offices on the floor. For security, however, this design is not ideal, because it means that an individual can climb over the wall

from one office to the other. As a result, all high-security areas, such as computer rooms and wiring closets, must have firewall-grade walls surrounding them. This provides physical security not only from potential intruders, but also from fires.

The doors that allow access into high-security rooms should also be evaluated. Standard office-grade doors provide little or no security. For example, one of the authors of this textbook once locked himself out of his office by accidentally breaking the key off in the lock. When the locksmith arrived, he carried a curious contraption. Instead of disassembling the lock or deploying other locksmith secrets, he carried a long piece of heavy-duty wire, bent into the shape of a bow, with a string tied to each end. He slid one end of this bow through the one-inch gap under the door, stood it on one end and yanked the string. The wire bow slid over the door handle and the string looped over it. When the locksmith yanked the string, the door swung open. (Note: to see this device in action visit *http://gizmodo.com/5477600/hotel-locks-defeated-by-piece-of-wire-secured-by-towel*, or search on the term "hotel locks defeated by piece of wire.") This information is not meant to teach you how to access interior offices but to warn you that no office is completely secure. How can you avoid this problem? In most interior offices, you can't. Instead, IT security professionals must educate the organization's employees about how to secure the information and systems within their offices.

To secure doors, install push or crash bars on computer rooms and closets. These bars are much more difficult to open from the outside than the standard door pull handles and thus provide much higher levels of security, but they also allow for safe egress in the event of an emergency.

Fire Security and Safety

The most important security concern is the safety of the people present in an organization's physical space—workers, customers, clients, and others. The most serious threat to that safety is fire. Fires account for more property damage, personal injury, and death than any other threat to physical security. As a result, it is imperative that physical security plans examine and implement strong measures to detect and respond to fires and fire hazards.

Fire Detection and Response

Fire suppression systems are devices that are installed and maintained to detect and respond to a fire, potential fire, or combustion danger situation. These systems typically work by denying an environment one of the three requirements for a fire to burn: temperature (ignition source), fuel, and oxygen.

While the temperature of ignition, or **flame point**, depends upon the material, it can be as low as a few hundred degrees. Paper, the most common combustible in the office, has a flame point of 451 degrees Fahrenheit (a fact that is used to dramatic effect in Ray Bradbury's novel *Fahrenheit 451*). Paper can reach that temperature when it is exposed to a carelessly dropped cigarette, malfunctioning electrical equipment, or other accidental or purposeful misadventures.

Water and water mist systems, which are described in detail in subsequent paragraphs, work both to reduce the temperature of the flame in order to extinguish it and to saturate some types of fuels (such as paper) to prevent ignition. Carbon dioxide systems (CO_2) rob fire of

Technical Details
Physical and Environmental Controls for Computer Rooms

The following list of physical and environmental controls for computer rooms is intended to be representative, not comprehensive.

- Card keys for building and entrances to work area
- Twenty-four-hour guards at all entrances and exits
- Cipher lock on computer room door
- Raised floor in computer room
- Dedicated cooling system
- Humidifier in tape library
- Emergency lighting in computer room
- Four fire extinguishers rated for electrical fires
- One fire extinguisher with a combination of a class B and class C fire control rating (note that fire control ratings are discussed below)
- Smoke, water, and heat detectors
- Emergency power shutoff switch by exit door
- Surge suppressor
- Emergency replacement server
- Zoned dry-pipe sprinkler system
- Uninterruptible power supply for LAN servers
- Power strips and suppressors for peripherals
- Power strips and suppressors for computers
- Controlled access to file server room
- Plastic sheets for water protection
- Closed-circuit television monitors

Adapted from "Guide for Developing Security Plans for Information Technology Systems"[4] by M. Swanson, NIST Special Publication 800-18, February 2006.

its oxygen. Soda acid systems deny fire its fuel, preventing the fire from spreading. Gas-based systems, such as Halon and its Environmental Protection Agency-approved replacements, disrupt the fire's chemical reaction but leave enough oxygen for people to survive for a short time. Before a fire can be suppressed, however, it must be detected.

Fire Detection Fire detection systems fall into two general categories: manual and automatic. **Manual fire detection systems** include human responses, such as calling the fire department, as well as manually activated alarms, such as sprinklers and gaseous systems. Organizations must use care when manually triggered alarms are tied directly to suppression systems, since false alarms are not uncommon. Organizations should also ensure that proper security remains in place until all employees and visitors have been cleared from the building and their evacuation has been verified. During the chaos of a fire evacuation, an attacker can easily slip into offices and obtain sensitive information. To help prevent such intrusions, fire safety programs often designate an individual from each office area to serve as a floor monitor.

There are three basic types of fire detection systems: thermal detection, smoke detection, and flame detection. **Thermal detection systems** contain a sophisticated heat sensor that operates in one of two ways. **Fixed temperature** sensors detect when the ambient temperature in an area reaches a predetermined level, usually between 135 degrees Fahrenheit and 165 degrees Fahrenheit, or 57 degrees Centigrade to 74 degrees Centigrade.[5] **Rate-of-rise** sensors detect an unusually rapid increase in the area temperature within a relatively short period of time. In either case, if the criteria are met, the alarm and suppression systems are activated. Thermal detection systems are inexpensive and easy to maintain. Unfortunately, thermal detectors usually don't catch a problem until it is already in progress, as in a full-blown fire. As a result, thermal detection systems are not a sufficient means of fire protection in areas where human safety could be at risk. They are also not recommended for areas with high-value items or items that could be easily damaged by high temperatures.

Smoke detection systems are perhaps the most common means of detecting a potentially dangerous fire, and they are required by building codes in most residential dwellings and commercial buildings. Smoke detectors operate in one of three ways. **Photoelectric sensors** project and detect an infrared beam across an area. If the beam is interrupted (presumably by smoke), the alarm or suppression system is activated. **Ionization sensors** contain a small amount of a harmless radioactive material within a detection chamber. When certain by-products of combustion enter the chamber, they change the level of electrical conductivity within the chamber and activate the detector. Ionization sensor systems are much more sophisticated than photoelectric sensors and can detect fires much earlier, since invisible by-products can be detected long before enough visible material enters a photoelectric sensor to trigger a reaction. **Air-aspirating detectors** are sophisticated systems and are used in high-sensitivity areas. They work by taking in air, filtering it, and moving it through a chamber containing a laser beam. If the laser beam is diverted or refracted by smoke particles, the system is activated. These types of systems are typically much more expensive than systems that use photoelectric or ionization sensors; however, they are much better at early detection and are commonly used in areas where extremely valuable materials are stored.

The third major category of fire detection systems is the **flame detector**. The flame detector is a sensor that detects the infrared or ultraviolet light produced by an open flame. These systems compare a scanned area's light signature to a database of known flame light signatures to determine whether or not to activate the alarm and suppression systems. While highly sensitive, flame detection systems are expensive and must be installed where they can scan all areas of the protected space. They are not typically used in areas with human lives at stake; however, they are quite suitable for chemical storage areas where normal chemical emissions might activate smoke detectors.

Fire Suppression Fire suppression systems can consist of portable, manual, or automatic apparatus. Portable extinguishers are used in a variety of situations where direct application of suppression is preferred, or fixed apparatus is impractical. Portable extinguishers are much more efficient for smaller fires, because triggering an entire building's sprinkler systems can do a lot of damage. Portable extinguishers are rated by the type of fire they can combat, as follows:

- Class A fires: Those fires that involve ordinary combustible fuels such as wood, paper, textiles, rubber, cloth, and trash. **Class A fires** are extinguished by agents that interrupt the ability of the fuel to be ignited. Water and multipurpose dry chemical fire extinguishers are ideal for these types of fires.

- Class B fires: Those fires fueled by combustible liquids or gases, such as solvents, gasoline, paint, lacquer, and oil. **Class B fires** are extinguished by agents that remove oxygen from the fire. Carbon dioxide, multipurpose dry chemical, and Halon fire extinguishers are ideal for these types of fires.

- Class C fires: Those fires with energized electrical equipment or appliances. **Class C fires** are extinguished with non-conducting agents only. Carbon dioxide, multipurpose dry chemical, and Halon fire extinguishers are ideal for these types of fires. Never use a water fire extinguisher on a Class C fire.

- Class D fires: Those fires fueled by combustible metals, such as magnesium, lithium, and sodium. **Class D fires** require special extinguishing agents and techniques.

The Technical Details box on Halon and the EPA describes the ban on new installations of Halon-based systems and lists the approved replacements.

Technical Details
Halon Q & A

Halon Substitutes Under SNAP as of 21 August 2003[6]

When was the production of Halons banned?
Under the Clean Air Act (CAA), the United States banned the production and import of virgin Halons 1211, 1301, and 2402 beginning January 1, 1994, in compliance with the Montreal Protocol on Substances that Deplete the Ozone Layer. Recycled Halon and inventories produced before January 1, 1994 are now the only sources of supply. EPA's final rule published March 5, 1998 (63 FR 11084) bans the formulation of any blend of two or more of these Halons with one exception. An exemption is provided for Halon blends formulated using recycled Halon solely for the purpose of aviation fire protection, provided that blends produced under this exemption are recycled to meet the relevant purity standards for each individual Halon. A fact sheet summarizing this rule is also available from the Stratospheric Ozone Protection Hotline.

Must I now dismantle my Halon fire protection system?

No. It is legal to continue to use your existing Halon system. It is even legal to purchase recycled Halon and Halon produced before the phase-out to recharge your system.

However, because Halons deplete the ozone layer, users are encouraged to consider replacing their system and making their Halon stock available for users with more critical needs.

Are there any federal laws on emissions of Halons?

EPA's final rule published March 5, 1998 (63 FR 11084) prohibits the intentional release of Halon 1211, Halon 1301, and Halon 2402 during the testing, repairing, maintaining, servicing, or disposal of Halon-containing equipment or during the use of such equipment for technician training. The rule also requires appropriate training of technicians regarding emissions reduction and proper disposal of Halon and Halon-containing equipment. The rule became effective April 6, 1998.

What are the acceptable substitutes for Halon?

There are a number of acceptable substitutes for Halon 1211 and 1301 (the two most common types of Halon-based systems).

The various options are summarized in Table 9-1.

Acceptable Substitutes for Halon 1211 Streaming Agents Under the Significant New Alternatives Policy (SNAP) Program as of 5 July 2007[7]		
Substitute	**Trade Name**	**Comments**
HCFC-123	FE-232	Nonresidential uses only
HCFC-124	FE-241	Nonresidential uses only
[HCFC Blend] B	Halotron 1	Nonresidential uses only
[HCFC Blend] C	NAF P-III	Nonresidential uses only
[HCFC Blend] D	Blitz III	Nonresidential uses only
Gelled Halocarbon / Dry chemical suspension	Envirogel	Allowable in the residential use market
[Surfactant Blend] A	Cold Fire, Flameout	
Water mist systems using potable or natural sea water		
Carbon dioxide		
Dry chemical		
Foam		

Table 9-1 Acceptable Substitutes

Acceptable Substitutes for Halon 1211 Streaming Agents Under the Significant New Alternatives Policy (SNAP) Program as of 5 July 2007		
Substitute	**Trade Name**	**Comments**
Powdered Aerosol C	PyroGen, Dynameco	For use in unoccupied areas only
Powdered Aerosol A	SFE	For use in unoccupied areas only
Carbon dioxide system		Design must adhere to OSHA 1910.162(b)(5) and NFPA Standard 12
Water		Water mist systems using potable or natural sea water
Foam A	Phirex+	This agent is not a clean agent, but is a low-density, short duration foam
HCFC-22		Use of this agent and all following agents must be in accordance with safety guidelines in NFPA 2001 standard for clean agent fire extinguishing systems
HCFC-124 HCFC Blend A (NAF S-III)	FE-241	
HFC-23 (FE-13)		
HFC-125 (FE 25)		
HFC-227ea (FM-200, FE-227)		
HFC-134a		
IG-100 (NM 100)		
IG-01 (Argotec; formally Inert Gas Blend C)		
IG-55 (Argonite; formally Inert Gas Blend B)		
IG-541 (Inergen)		
C6-perfluoroketone [1,1,1,2,2,4,5,5,5-nonafluoro-4-(trifluoromethyl)-3-pentanone] (Novec 1230)		
Gelled Halocarbon/Dry Chemical Suspension (Envirogel) with ammonium polyphosphate additive		
HFC-125 with 0.1% d-limonene (NAF S-125) HFC-227ea with 0.1% d-limonene (NAF S 227)		

Table 9-1 Acceptable Substitutes (*continued*)

From The Environmental Protection Agency, Online, 7 July 2007.

Manual and automatic fire response systems include those designed to apply suppressive agents. These are usually either sprinkler or gaseous systems. All **sprinkler systems** are designed to apply liquid, usually water, to all areas in which a fire has been detected, but an organization can choose from one of three implementations: wet-pipe, dry-pipe, or pre-action systems. A **wet-pipe** system has pressurized water in all pipes and has some form of valve in each protected area. When the system is activated, the valves open, sprinkling the area. This is best for areas where the fire represents a serious risk to people, but where damage to property is not a major concern. The most obvious drawback to this type of system is water damage to office equipment and materials. A wet-pipe system is not usually appropriate in computer rooms, wiring closets, or anywhere electrical equipment is used or stored. There is also the risk of accidental or unauthorized activation. Figure 9-3 shows a wet-pipe water sprinkler system that is activated when the ambient temperature reaches 140 degrees Fahrenheit to 150 degrees Fahrenheit, bringing the special liquid in the glass tube to a boil, which causes the tube to shatter and open the valve. Once the valve is open, water flows through the diffuser, which disperses the water over the area.

A **dry-pipe system** is designed to work in areas where electrical equipment is used. Instead of water, the system contains pressurized air. The air holds valves closed, keeping the water away from the target areas. When a fire is detected, the sprinkler heads are activated, the pressurized air escapes, and water fills the pipes and exits through the sprinkler heads. This reduces the risk of accidental leakage from the system. Some sprinkler system, called **deluge systems**, keep open all of the individual sprinkler heads, and as soon as the system is activated, water is immediately applied to all areas. This is not, however, the optimal solution

9

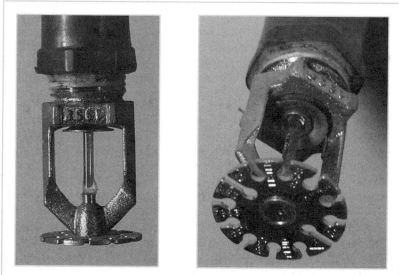

When the ambient temperature reaches 140-150° F,
the liquid-filled glass tube trigger breaks, releasing the stopper and
allowing water to hit the diffuser, spraying water throughout the area

Figure 9-3 Water Sprinkler System

Source: Course Technology/Cengage Learning

for computing environments, since there are other more sophisticated systems that can suppress the fire without damage to computer equipment.

A variation of the dry-pipe system is the **pre-action system**. This approach has a two-phase response to a fire. Under normal conditions, the system has nothing in the delivery pipes. When a fire is detected, the first phase is initiated, and valves allow water to enter the system. At that point, the system resembles a wet-pipe system. The pre-action system does not deliver water into the protected space until the individual sprinkler heads are triggered, at which time water flows only into the area of the activated sprinkler head.

Water mist sprinklers are the newest form of sprinkler systems and rely on ultra-fine mists instead of traditional shower-type systems. The water mist systems work like traditional water system by reducing the ambient temperature around the flame, therefore minimizing its ability to sustain the necessary temperature needed to maintain combustion. Unlike traditional water sprinkler systems, however, these systems produce a fog-like mist that, because the droplets are much less susceptible to gravity, stays buoyant (airborne) much longer. As a result, a much smaller quantity of water is required; also the fire is extinguished more quickly, which causes less collateral damage. Relative to gaseous systems (which are discussed shortly), water-based systems are low cost, nontoxic, and can often be created by using an existing sprinkler system that may have been present in earlier construction.

Gaseous Emission Systems Gaseous (or chemical gas) emission systems can be used in the suppression of fires. They are often used to protect chemical and electrical processing areas, as well as facilities that house computing systems. A typical configuration of such systems is shown in Figure 9-4.

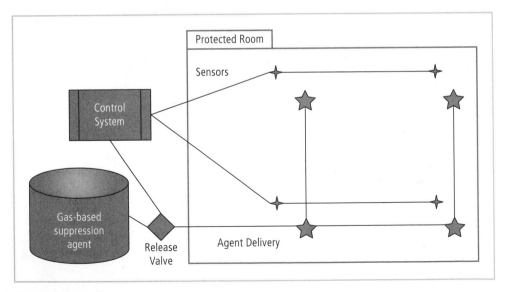

Figure 9-4 Gaseous Fire Suppression System

Source: Course Technology/Cengage Learning

Gaseous fire suppression systems are either self-pressurizing or must be pressurized with an additional agent. Until recently there were only two major types of gaseous systems: carbon dioxide and Halon. Carbon dioxide extinguishes a fire by removing its supply of oxygen. Unfortunately, any living organisms that also rely on oxygen are similarly extinguished. As a result, carbon dioxide systems are not commonly used in residential or office environments where people or animals are likely to be present. The alternative is Halon. Halon is one of a few chemicals designated as a **clean agent**, which means that it does not leave any residue after use, nor does it interfere with the operation of electrical or electronic equipment. As a result, Halon gas-based systems are the preferred solution for computer rooms and communications closets. Unlike carbon dioxide, Halon does not rob the fire of its oxygen but instead relies on a chemical reaction with the flame to extinguish it. As a result, Halon is much safer than carbon dioxide when people or animals are present. Although Halon can cause suffocation like a carbon dioxide system, the dosage levels required are much higher, and therefore Halon-based systems provide additional time for people to exit areas. Because the EPA has classified Halon as an ozone-depleting substance, new installations of the controlled types of Halon are prohibited in commercial and residential locations. There are a number of alternatives, as presented in Table 9-1 in the Technical Details box called Halon Q & A although, as is often the case, the alternatives are reported to be less effective than Halon.

A physical security plan requires that every building have clearly marked fire exits and maps posted throughout the facility. It is important to have drills to rehearse fire alarm responses and designate individuals to be in charge of escorting everyone from the location and ensuring that no one is left behind. It is also important to have fire suppression systems that are both manual and automatic, and that are inspected and tested regularly.

Failure of Supporting Utilities and Structural Collapse

Supporting utilities, such as heating, ventilation and air conditioning, power, water, and other utilities, have a significant impact on the safe operation of a facility. Extreme temperatures and humidity levels, electrical fluctuations and the interruption of water, sewage, and garbage services can create conditions that inject vulnerabilities in systems designed to protect information. Thus, each of these utilities must be properly managed in order to prevent damage to information and information systems.

Heating, Ventilation, and Air Conditioning

Although traditionally a facilities management responsibility, the operation of the heating, ventilation, and air-conditioning (HVAC) system can have dramatic impact on information and information systems operations and protection. Specifically, the temperature, filtration, humidity, and static electricity controls must be monitored and adjusted to reduce risks to information systems.

Temperature and Filtration Computer systems are electronic, and as such are subject to damage from extreme temperature and particulate contamination. Temperatures as low as 100 degrees Fahrenheit can damage computer media, and at 175 degrees Fahrenheit, computer hardware can be damaged or destroyed. When the temperature approaches

32 degrees Fahrenheit, media are susceptible to cracking and computer components can actually freeze together. Rapid changes in temperature, from hot to cold or from cold to hot, can produce condensation, which can create short circuits or otherwise damage systems and components. The optimal temperature for a computing environment (and for people) is between 70 and 74 degrees Fahrenheit. Properly installed and maintained systems keep the environment within the manufacturer-recommended temperature range. In the past it was thought necessary to fully filter all particles from the air flow from the HVAC system. Modern computing equipment is designed to work better in typical office environments, and thus the need to provide extensive filtration for air-conditioning is now limited to particularly sensitive environments such as chip fabrication and component assembly areas. In other words, filtration is no longer as significant a factor as it once was for most commercial data processing facilities.

Humidity and Static Electricity Humidity is the amount of moisture in the air. High humidity levels create condensation problems, and low humidity levels can increase the amount of static electricity in the environment. With condensation comes the short-circuiting of electrical equipment and the potential for mold and rot in paper-based information storage. **Static electricity** is caused by a process called **triboelectrification**, which occurs when two materials make contact and exchange electrons, and results in one object becoming more positively charged and the other more negatively charged. When a third object with an opposite charge or ground is encountered, electrons flow again, and a spark is produced. One of the leading causes of damage to sensitive circuitry is **electrostatic discharge (ESD)**. Integrated circuits in a computer are designed to use between two and five volts of electricity; any voltage level above this range introduces a risk of microchip damage. Static electricity is not even noticeable to humans until levels approach 1,500 volts, and the spark can't be seen until the level approaches 4,000 volts. Moreover, a person can generate up to 12,000 volts of static current by merely walking across a carpet. Table 9-2 shows some static charge voltages and the damage they can cause to systems.

In general, ESD damage to chips produces two types of failures. Immediate failures, also known as catastrophic failures, occur right away, are usually totally destructive, and require chip replacement. Latent failures or delayed failures can occur weeks or even months after the damage occurs. The damage may not be noticeable, but the chip may suffer intermittent problems. (It has been observed, however, that with the overall poor quality of some of the current popular operating systems, this type of damage may be hard to notice.) As a result, it is imperative to maintain the optimal level of humidity, which is between 40 percent and

Volts	Results
40	High probability of damage to sensitive circuits and transistors
1,000	Scrambles monitor display
1,500	Can cause disk drive data loss
2,000	High probability of system shutdown
4,000	May jam printers
17,000	Causes certain and permanent damage to almost all microcircuitry

Table 9-2 Static Charge Damage in Computers[8]

60 percent, in the computing environment. Humidity levels below this range create static, and levels above create condensation. Humidification or dehumidification systems can regulate humidity levels.

Ventilation Shafts While the ductwork in residential buildings is quite small, in large commercial buildings, it may be large enough for a person to climb through. This is one of Hollywood's favorite methods for villains or heroes to enter buildings, but these ventilation shafts aren't quite as negotiable as the movies would have you believe. In fact, with moderate security precautions, these shafts can be completely eliminated as a security vulnerability. In most new buildings, the ducts to the individual rooms are no larger than 12 inches in diameter and are flexible, insulated tubes. The size and nature of the ducts precludes most people from using them, but access may be possible via the plenum. If the ducts are much larger, the security team can install wire mesh grids at various points to compartmentalize the runs.

Power Management and Conditioning

Electrical power is another aspect of the organization's physical environment that is usually considered within the realm of physical security. It is critical that power systems used by information-processing equipment be properly installed and correctly grounded. Interference with the normal pattern of the electrical current is referred to as **noise**. Because computers sometimes use the normal 60 Hertz cycle of the electricity in alternating current to synchronize their clocks, noise that interferes with this cycle can result in inaccurate time clocks or, even worse, unreliable internal clocks inside the CPU.

Grounding and Amperage Grounding ensures that the returning flow of current is properly discharged to the ground. If the grounding elements of the electrical system are not properly installed, anyone touching a computer or other electrical device could become a ground source, which would cause damage to equipment and injury or death to the person. Computing and other electrical equipment in areas where water can accumulate must be uniquely grounded, using **ground fault circuit interruption** (GFCI) equipment. GFCI is capable of quickly identifying and interrupting a ground fault—that is, a situation in which a person has come into contact with water and becomes a better ground than the electrical circuit's current source.

Power should also be provided in sufficient amperage to support needed operations. Nothing is more frustrating than plugging in a series of computers, only to have the circuit breaker trip. Consult a qualified electrician when designing or remodeling computer rooms to make sure sufficiently high amperage circuits are available to provide the needed power. Overloading a circuit not only trips circuit breakers, but can also create a load on an electrical cable that is in excess of what the cable is rated to handle, and thus increase the risk of its overheating and starting a fire.

Uninterruptible Power Supply (UPS) The primary power source for an organization's computing equipment is most often the electric utility that serves the area where the organization's buildings are located. This source of power can experience interruptions. Therefore, organizations should identify the computing systems that are critical to their operations (in other words, the systems that must continue to operate during interruptions) and make sure those systems are connected to a device that assures the delivery of electric power without interruption—that is, an uninterruptible power supply (UPS).

The capacity of UPS devices is measured using the volt-ampere (or VA) power output rating. UPS devices typically run up to 1,000 VA and can be engineered to exceed 10,000 VA. A typical PC might use 200 VA, and a server in a computer room may need 2,000 to 5,000 VA, depending on how much running time is needed. Figure 9-5 shows a number of types of UPS. This section describes the following basic configurations: the standby, line-interactive, standby on-line hybrid, standby-ferro, double conversion online (also known as true online), and delta conversion online.

A **standby** or **offline UPS** is an offline battery backup that detects the interruption of power to the equipment and activates a transfer switch that provides power from batteries, through a DC to AC converter, until the power is restored or the computer is shut down. Because this type of UPS is not truly uninterruptible, it is often referred to as a standby power supply (SPS). The advantage of an SPS is that it is the most cost-effective type of UPS. However, the significant drawbacks, such as the limited run time and the amount of time it takes to switch from standby to active, may outweigh the cost savings. Switching time may also become an issue because very sensitive computing equipment may not be able to handle the transfer delay, and may reset and suffer data loss or damage. Also, SPS systems do not provide power conditioning, a feature of more sophisticated UPSs (discussed below). As a result, an SPS is seldom used in critical computing applications and is best suited for home and light office use.

A **ferroresonant standby UPS** improves upon the standby UPS design. It is still an offline UPS, with the electrical service providing the primary source of power and the UPS serving as a battery backup. The primary difference is that a ferroresonant transformer replaces the UPS transfer switch. The transformer provides line filtering to the primary power source, reducing the effect of some power problems and reducing noise that may be present in the power as it is delivered. This transformer also stores energy in its coils, thereby providing a buffer to fill in the gap between the interruption of service and the activation of an alternate source of power (usually a battery backup). This greatly reduces the probability of system reset and data loss. Ferroresonant standby UPS systems are better suited to settings that require a large capacity of conditioned and reliable power, since they are available for uses up to 14,000 VA. With the improvement in other UPS designs, however, many manufacturers have abandoned this design in favor of other configurations.

The **line-interactive UPS** has a substantially different design than the previously mentioned UPS models. In line-interactive UPSs, the internal components of the standby models are replaced with a pair of inverters and converters. The primary power source, as in both the SPS and the ferroresonant UPS, remains the power utility company, with a battery serving as backup. However, the inverters and converters both charge the battery and provide power when needed. When utility power is interrupted, the converter begins supplying power to the systems. Because this device is always connected to the output as opposed to relying on a switch, this model has a much faster response time and also incorporates power conditioning and line filtering.

In a **true online UPS**, the primary power source is the battery, and the power feed from the utility is constantly recharging this battery. This model allows constant use of the system, while completely eliminating power fluctuation. True online UPS can deliver a constant, smooth, conditioned power stream to the computing systems. If the utility-provided power fails, the computer systems are unaffected as long as the batteries hold out. The online UPS is considered the top-of-the-line option and is the most expensive. The only major

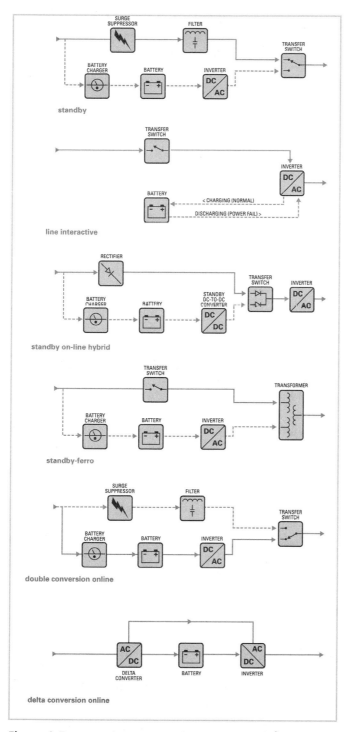

Figure 9-5 Types of Uninterruptible Power Supplies[9]

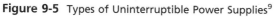

Source: Courtesy of American Power Conversion Corporation

drawback, other than cost, is that the process of constantly converting from the AC feed from the utility to the DC used by the battery storage and then converting back to AC for use by the systems generates a lot of heat. An improved model resolves this issue by incorporating a device known as a delta-conversion unit, which allows some of the incoming power to be fed directly to the destination computers, thus reducing the amount of energy wasted and heat generated. Should the power fail, the delta unit shuts off, and the batteries automatically compensate for the increased power draw.

Selecting the best UPS can be a lesson in electrical engineering, because you must calculate the load that the protected systems require from the UPS. This can be quite complex and proves challenging in practice. Fortunately, many UPS vendors provide sample scenarios that can help you select the optimal device. Because a high-quality UPS may cost several thousand dollars, it is advisable to select the smallest UPS necessary to provide the desired effect. To calculate manually the rating needed in a UPS, you should begin by reviewing the computer systems and all connected support equipment to be protected. For example, the back panel of a monitor may indicate that the monitor is rated at 110 volts and 2 amps. Since volts times amps yields the power needs of a device, to calculate the power you need to run this device, you multiply 110 by 2; the production of this equation is the rating of the monitor, 220 VA. Now suppose the computer draws 3 amps at 110 volts, and therefore has a rating of 330 VA. Together the total is 550 VA. Once you have this information, you can select a UPS capable of supporting this power level. Generally, UPS systems provide information on how long they would run at specific VA levels. Some smaller-scale UPSs can run for approximately six minutes at 600 VA at full voltage. You should look for a UPS that provides enough time for the computing equipment to ride out minor power fluctuations, and for the user to shut down the computer safely if necessary.

Emergency Shutoff One important aspect of power management in any environment is the ability to stop power immediately should the current represent a risk to human or machine safety. Most computer rooms and wiring closets are equipped with an emergency power shutoff, which is usually a large red button that is prominently placed to facilitate access, and has a cover to prevent unintentional use. These devices are the last line of defense against personal injury and machine damage in the event of flooding or sprinkler activation. The last person out of the computer room hits the switch to stop the flow of electricity to the room, preventing the water that might be used to extinguish the fire from short-circuiting the computers. While it is never advisable to allow water to come into contact with a computer, there is a much higher probability of recovering the systems if they were not powered up when they got wet. At a minimum, hard drives and other sealed devices may be recoverable. Some disaster recovery companies specialize in water damage recovery.

Water Problems

Another critical utility infrastructure element is water service. On the one hand, lack of water poses problems to systems, including fire suppression and air-conditioning systems. On the other hand, a surplus of water, or water pressure, poses a real threat. Flooding, leaks, and the presence of water in areas where it should not be is catastrophic to paper and electronic storage of information. Water damage can result in complete failure of computer systems and the structures that house them. It is therefore important to integrate water detection systems into the alarm systems that regulate overall facilities operations.

Structural Collapse

Unavoidable environmental factors or forces of nature can cause failures in the structures that house the organization. Structures are designed and constructed with specific load limits, and overloading these design limits inevitably results in structural failure. Personal injury and potential for loss of life are also likely. Scheduling periodic inspections by qualified civil engineers will enable managers to identify potentially dangerous structural conditions before the structure fails.

Maintenance of Facility Systems

Just as with any phase of the security process, the implementation of the physical security phase must be constantly documented, evaluated, and tested; once the physical security of a facility is established, it must be diligently maintained. Ongoing maintenance of systems is required as part of the systems' operations. Documentation of the facility's configuration, operation, and function should be integrated into disaster recovery plans and standard operating procedures. Testing provides information necessary to improve the physical security in the facility and identifies weak points.

Interception of Data

There are three methods of data interception: direct observation, interception of data transmission, and electromagnetic interception. The first method, *direct observation*, requires that an individual be close enough to the information to breach confidentiality. The physical security mechanisms described in the previous sections limit the possibility of an individual accessing unauthorized areas and directly observing information. There is, however, a risk when the information is removed from a protected facility. If an employee is browsing documents over lunch in a restaurant or takes work home, the risk of direct observation rises substantially. A competitor can more easily intercept vital information at a typical employee's home than at a secure office. Incidences of interception, such as shoulder surfing, can be avoided if employees are prohibited from removing sensitive information from the office or required to implement strong security at their homes.

The second method, *interception of data transmissions*, has become easier in the age of the Internet. If attackers can access the media transmitting the data, they needn't be anywhere near the source of the information. In some cases, the attacker can use sniffer software, which was described in previous chapters, to collect data. Other means of interception, such as tapping into a LAN, require some proximity to the organization's computers or networks. It is important for network administrators to conduct periodic physical inspections of all data ports to ensure that no unauthorized taps have occurred. If direct wiretaps are a concern, the organization should consider using fiber-optic cable, as the difficulty of splicing into this type of cable makes it much more resistant to tapping. If wireless LANs are used, the organization should be concerned about eavesdropping, since an attacker can snoop from a location that can be—depending on the strength of the wireless access points (WAPs)—hundreds of feet outside the organization's building. Since wireless LANs are uniquely susceptible to eavesdropping, and current generation wireless sniffers are very potent tools, all wireless communications should be secured via encryption. Incidentally, it may interest you to know that the U.S. federal laws that deal with wiretapping do not cover wireless communications, except for commercial cellular phone calls; courts have ruled that users have no expectation of privacy with radio-based communications media.

The third method of data interception, *electromagnetic interception*, sounds like it could be from a *Star Trek* episode. For decades, scientists have known that electricity moving through cables emits electromagnetic signals (EM). It is possible to eavesdrop on these signals and therefore determine the data carried on the cables without actually tapping into them. In 1985, scientists proved that computer monitors also emitted radio waves, and that the image on the screens could be reconstructed from these signals.[10] More recently, scientists have determined that certain devices with LED displays actually emit information encoded in the light that pulses in these LEDs.[11]

Whether devices that emit **electromagnetic radiation** (EMR) can actually be monitored such that the data being processed or displayed can be reconstructed has been a subject of debate (and rumor) for many years. James Atkinson, an electronics engineer certified by the National Security Agency (NSA), says that there is no such thing as practical monitoring of electronic emanations and claims that stories about such monitoring are just urban legends. He goes on to say that most modern computers are shielded to prevent interference with other household and office equipment—not to prevent eavesdropping. Atkinson does concede that receiving emanations from a computer monitor is theoretically possible, but notes that it would be an extremely difficult, expensive, and impractical undertaking.[12]

Legend or not, a good deal of money is being spent by the government and military to protect computers from electronic remote eavesdropping. In fact, the U.S. government has developed a program, named **TEMPEST**, to reduce the risk of EMR monitoring. (In keeping with the speculative fancy surrounding this topic, some believe that the acronym TEMPEST was originally a code word created by the U.S. government in the 1960s, but was later defined as Transient Electromagnetic Pulse Emanation Surveillance Technology or Telecommunications Electronics Material Protected from Emanating Spurious Transmissions.) In general, TEMPEST involves the following procedures: ensuring that computers are placed as far as possible from outside perimeters, installing special shielding inside the CPU case, and implementing a host of other restrictions, including maintaining distances from plumbing and other infrastructure components that carry radio waves. Additional information about this subject and the controls that have been developed can be found at *www.fas.org/irp/program/security/tempest.htm* or *www.cnss.gov/Assets/pdf/nstissam_tempest_1-00.pdf*. Regardless of whether the threat from eavesdropping on electromagnetic emanations is real, many procedures that protect against emanations also protect against threats to physical security.

Mobile and Portable Systems

Mobile computing requires even more security than the average in-house system. Most mobile computing systems—laptops, handhelds, and PDAs—have valuable corporate information stored within them, and some are configured to facilitate user access into the organization's secure computing facilities. Forms of access include VPN connections, dial-up configurations, and databases of passwords. In addition, many users keep the locations of files and clues about the storage of information in their portable computers. Many users like the convenience of allowing the underlying operating systems to remember their usernames and passwords because it provides easier access and because they frequently have multiple accounts, with different usernames and passwords, to manage. While it is tempting to allow operating systems to enable easier access to frequently used accounts, the downside of setting up these arrangements on a portable system is obvious: loss of the system means loss of the access control mechanisms.

A relatively new technology to help locate lost or stolen laptops can provide additional security. For example, Absolute Software's CompuTrace Laptop Security is computer software that is installed on a laptop, as illustrated in Figure 9-6. Periodically, when the computer is on the Internet, the software reports itself and the electronic serial number of the computer on which it is installed to a central monitoring center. If the laptop is reported stolen, this software can trace the computer to its current location for possible recovery. The software is undetectable on the system, even if the thief knows the software is installed. Moreover, CompuTrace remains installed even if the laptop's hard drive is formatted and the operating system is reinstalled.

Also available for laptops are burglar alarms made up of a PC card or other device that contains a motion detector. If the device is armed, and the laptop is moved more than expected, the alarm triggers a very loud buzzer or horn. The security system may also disable the computer or use an encryption option to render the information stored in the system unusable.

For maximum security, laptops should be secured at all times. If you are traveling with a laptop, you should have it in your possession at all times. Special care should be exercised when flying, as laptop thefts are common in airports. The following list comes from the Metropolitan Police of the District of Columbia and outlines steps you can take to prevent your laptop from being stolen or carelessly damaged:

- Don't leave a laptop in an unlocked vehicle, even if the vehicle is in your driveway or garage, and never leave it in plain sight, even if the vehicle is locked—that's just inviting trouble. If you must leave your laptop in a vehicle, the best place is in a locked trunk. If you don't have a trunk, cover it up and lock the doors.

- Parking garages are likely areas for thefts from vehicles, as they provide numerous choices and cover for thieves. Again, never leave your laptop in plain sight; cover it or put it in the trunk.

- Do be aware of the damage extreme temperatures can cause to computers.

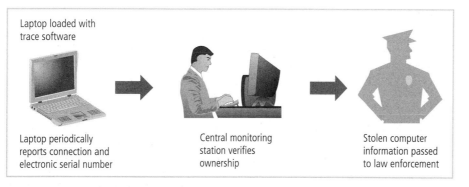

Laptop loaded with trace software

Laptop periodically reports connection and electronic serial number

Central monitoring station verifies ownership

Stolen computer information passed to law enforcement

Figure 9-6 Laptop Theft Deterrence

Source: Course Technology/Cengage Learning

- Carry your laptop in a nondescript carrying case, briefcase, or bag when moving about. Placing it in a case designed for computers is an immediate alert to thieves that you have a laptop.

- Going to lunch or taking a break? Don't leave a meeting or conference room without your laptop. Take it with you, or you run the risk that it won't be there when you return.

- Lock the laptop in your office during off-hours. Don't have your own office? Use a cable lock that wraps around a desk or chair leg, or put the laptop in a locked closet or cabinet.

- Don't let unaccompanied strangers wander around in your workplace. Offer assistance and deliver the visitors to their destinations.

- Apply distinctive paint markings to make your laptop unique and easily identifiable. Liquid white-out is a good substance to apply.

- Consider purchasing one of the new theft alarm systems specially made for laptops.

- Be aware that if your computer is stolen, automatic logins can make it easy for a thief to send inappropriate messages with your account.

- Back up your information on disks today, and store the disks at home or the office.[13]

Remote Computing Security

Remote site computing, which is becoming increasingly popular, involves a wide variety of computing sites that are distant from the base organizational facility and includes all forms of telecommuting. **Telecommuting** is off site computing that uses Internet connections, dial-up connections, connections over leased point-to-point links between offices, and other connection mechanisms.

Telecommuting from users' homes deserves special attention. One of the appeals of telecommuting for both the employee and employer is that by avoiding physical commuting, telecommuting employees have more time to focus on the work they do. But as more people become telecommuters, the risk to information traveling via the often unsecured connections that telecommuters use is substantial. The problem is that not enough organizations provide secure connections to their office networks, and even fewer provide secure systems, should the employee's home computer be compromised. To secure the entire network, the organization must dedicate security resources to protecting these home connections. Although the installation of a VPN may go a long way toward protecting the data in transmission, telecommuters frequently store office data on their home systems, in home filing cabinets, and on off-site media. To ensure a secure process, the computers that telecommuters use must be made *more* secure than the organization's systems, as they are outside the security perimeter. An attacker breaking into someone's home would probably find a much lower level of security than at an office. Most office systems require users to log in, but the telecommuter's home computer is probably the employee's personal machine, and thus is likely to have a much less secure operating system and may not use a password. Telecommuters must use a securable operating system that requires password authentication, such as Windows XP/Vista/7 or Server 2003/2008. They must store all loose data in locking filing cabinets and loose media in locking fire safes. They must handle data at home more carefully than they would at the office, since the general level of security for the average home is lower than that of a commercial building.

The same applies to workers using mobile computers on the road. Employees using notebooks in hotel rooms should presume that their unencrypted transmissions are being monitored, and that any unsecured notebook computer can be stolen. The off-site worker using leased facilities does not know who else is physically attached to the network and therefore who might be listening to his or her data conversations. VPNs are a must in all off-site-to-on-site communications, and the use of associated advanced authentication systems is strongly recommended.

Although it is possible to secure remote sites, organizations cannot assume that employees will invest their own funds for security. Many organizations barely tolerate telecommuting for a number of reasons, including that telecommuting employees generally require two sets of computing equipment, one for the office and one for the home. This extra expense is difficult to justify, especially when the employee is the only one gaining the benefit from telecommuting. In those rare cases in which allowing an employee or consultant to telecommute is the only way to gain extremely valuable skills, the organization is usually willing to do what is necessary to secure its systems. Only when additional research into telecommuting clearly displays a bottom-line advantage do organizations begin to invest sufficient resources into securing the equipment of their telecommuters. However, there are some organizations that support telecommuting, and these organizations typically fall into one of three groups. The first is the mature and therefore fiscally sound organization with a sufficient budget to support telecommuting and thus enhance its standing with employees and its organizational image. In recent years, the option to telecommute has become a factor in the organizational rankings undertaken by various magazines. Some organizations seek to improve employee work conditions and also improve their position in the best-places-to-work ranking by adding telecommuting as an option for employees. The second group is the new high-technology company, with a large number of geographically diverse employees who telecommute almost exclusively. These companies use technology extensively and are determined to make the adoption of technology and its use the cornerstone of their organizations. The third group overlaps with the second and is called a virtual organization. A **virtual organization** is a group of individuals brought together for a specific task, usually from different organizations, divisions, or departments. These individuals form a virtual company, either in leased facilities or through 100-percent telecommuting arrangements. When the job is done, the organization is either redirected or dissolved. These organizations rely almost exclusively on remote computing and telecommuting, but they are extremely rare and therefore not well documented or studied.

Special Considerations for Physical Security

There are a number of special considerations to take into account when developing a physical security program. The first of these is the question of whether to handle physical security in-house or to outsource it. As with any aspect of information security, the make-or-buy decision should not be made lightly. There are a number of qualified and professional agencies that provide physical security consulting and services. The benefits of outsourcing physical security include gaining the experience and knowledge of these agencies, many of which have been in the field for decades. Outsourcing unfamiliar operations always frees an organization to focus on its primary objectives, rather than support operations. The downside includes the expense, the loss of control over the individual components of the physical security solution, and the need to trust another company to perform an essential business function. An organization must not only trust the processes used by the contracted company, but also its ability to hire and retain trustworthy employees who respect the security of the contracting company even though they have no allegiance to it. This level of trust is often the most difficult aspect of the decision to outsource, because the reality of outsourcing physical security is that nonemployees will be providing a safeguard that the organization administers only marginally.

Another physical security consideration is social engineering. As you learned in previous chapters, social engineering involves using people skills to obtain confidential information from employees. While most social engineers prefer to use the telephone or computer to solicit information, some attempt to access the information more directly. As in the previously mentioned cases in which technically proficient agents are placed into janitorial positions at a competitor's office, there are a number of ways an outsider can gain access to an organization's resources. Most organizations do not, for example, have very thorough procedures for authenticating and controlling nonemployees who access their facility. When there is no procedure in place, no one gives the wandering repairman, service worker, or city official a second look. It is not difficult to dress like a telephone repairman, construction worker, or building inspector and move freely throughout a building. Some might even say that to go almost anywhere in any building, all one really needs is a clipboard and an attitude. If you look as if you have a mission and appear competent, most people will leave you alone. How can organizations combat this type of attack? By requiring that all individuals entering the facility display appropriate visitor badges and be escorted when they are in restricted areas.

Inventory Management

Like other organizational resources, computing equipment should be inventoried and inspected on a regular basis. The management of computer inventory is an important part of physical security. How else can corporate security know if an employee has been pilfering computer supplies or a former employee has taken organizational equipment home? Similarly, classified information should also be inventoried and managed. In the military, whenever a classified document needs is reproduced, a stamp is placed on the original before it is copied. This stamp states the document's classification level and the text imprint "of " so that the person making the copies can mark the sequence number for each copy as well as the total number of copies being made. If, for example, twenty-five copies are to be made, the person responsible for copying the document writes "26" in the right blank, makes copies, and then numbers them. Why 26 and not 25? The original is always document number one. After the numbering, each classified copy is issued to the assigned person, who signs for it. While this procedure may be overkill for most organizations, it does ensure that the inventory management of classified documents is secure at all times. Also, the formality of having to sign for a document cements its worth in the mind of the recipient.

Selected Readings

- *Effective Physical Security, Third Edition* by Lawrence Fennelly. Butterworth-Heinemann.
- *Build the Best Data Center Facility for Your Business* by Douglas Alger. Cisco Press.
- *Guard Force Management, Updated Edition* by Lucien Canton. Butterworth-Heinemann.

Chapter Summary

- Physical security requires the design, implementation, and maintenance of counter-measures that protect the physical resources of an organization.

- Many threats to information security can also be classified as threats to physical security. An organization's policy should guide the planning for physical security throughout the development life cycle.

- In facilities management, a secure facility is a physical location that has controls to minimize the risk of attacks from physical threats. A secure facility can use natural terrain, traffic flow, and urban development, and can complement these environmental elements with protection mechanisms, such as fences, gates, walls, guards, and alarms.

- The management of keys and locks is a fundamental part of general management's responsibility for the organization's physical environment.

- A fail-safe lock is usually used on an exit door where human safety in the event of a fire or other emergency is the essential consideration. A fail-secure lock is used when human safety is not a factor.

- Monitoring equipment can record events that guards and dogs might miss and can be used in areas where other types of physical controls are not practical.

- Just as with any phase of the security process, the implementation of physical security must be constantly documented, evaluated, and tested; also once the physical security of a facility is established, it must be diligently maintained.

- Fire detection systems are devices that detect and respond to a fire or potential fire. Fire suppression systems stop the progress of a fire once activated.

- There are three basic types of fire detection systems: thermal detection, smoke detection, and flame detection.

- There are four environmental variables controlled by HVAC systems that can cause damage to information-carrying systems: temperature, filtration, humidity, and static electricity.

- Computer systems depend on stable power supplies to function; when power levels are too high, too low, or too erratic, computer circuitry can be damaged or destroyed. The power provided to computing and networking equipment should contain no unwanted fluctuations, and should have no embedded signaling.

- Water problems and the weakening and subsequent failure of a building's physical structure represent potential threats to the safety of people and to the integrity and availability of information assets.

- Data can be intercepted electronically and manually. There are three routes of data interception: direct observation, interception of data transmission, and interception of electromagnetic radiation.

- TEMPEST is a technology that prevents the loss of data that may result from the emission of electromagnetic radiation (EMR).

- With the increased use of laptops, handhelds, and PDAs, organizations should be aware that mobile computing requires even more security than the average in-house system.

- Remote site computing requires a secure extension of the organization's internal networks and special attention to security for any connected home or off-site computing technology.

- Like computing equipment, classified information should also be inventoried and managed. If multiple copies of a classified document are made, they should be numbered and tracked.

Review Questions

1. What is physical security? What are the primary threats to physical security? How are they made manifest in attacks against the organization?

2. What are the roles of IT, security, and general management with regard to physical security?

3. How does physical access control differ from the logical access control described in earlier chapters? How is it similar?

4. Define a secure facility. What is the primary objective of the design of such a facility? What are some of the secondary objectives of the design of a secure facility?

5. Why are guards considered the most effective form of control for situations that require decisive action in the face of unfamiliar stimuli? Why are they usually the most expensive controls to deploy? When should dogs be used for physical security?

6. List and describe the four categories of locks. In which situation is each type of lock preferred?

7. What are the two possible modes that locks use when they fail? What implications do these modes have for human safety? In which situation is each mode preferred?

8. What is a mantrap? When should it be used?

9. What is the most common form of alarm? What does it detect? What types of sensors are commonly used in this type of alarm system?

10. Describe a physical firewall that is used in buildings. List the reasons why an organization might need firewalls for physical security controls.

11. What is considered the most serious threat within the realm of physical security? Why is it valid to consider this threat the most serious?

12. What three elements must be present for a fire to ignite and continue to burn? How do fire suppression systems manipulate the three elements to quell fires?

13. List and describe the three fire detection technologies covered in the chapter. Which is currently the most commonly used?

14. List and describe the four classes of fire described in the text. Does the class of a fire dictate how to control the fire?

15. What is Halon, and why is its use restricted?

16. What is the relationship between HVAC and physical security? What four physical characteristics of the indoor environment are controlled by a properly designed HVAC system? What are the optimal temperature and humidity ranges for computing systems?

17. List and describe the four primary types of UPS systems. Which is the most effective and the most expensive, and why?

18. What two critical functions are impaired when water is not available in a facility? Why are these functions important to the operation of the organization's information assets?

19. List and describe the three fundamental ways that data can be intercepted. How does a physcial security program protect against each of these data interception methods?

20. What can you do to reduce the risk of laptop theft?

Exercises

1. Assume that your organization is planning to have a server room that functions without human beings—in other words, the functions are automated (such a room is often called a lights-out server room). Describe the fire control system(s) you would install in that room.

2. Assume that you have converted part of an area of general office space into a server room. Describe the factors you would consider when planning for each of the following:

   a. Walls and doors

   b. Physical access control

   c. Fire detection

   d. Fire suppression

   e. Heating, ventilating, and air-conditioning

   f. Power quality and distribution

3. Assume that you have been asked to review the power needs for a standalone computer system which processes important but noncritical data and does not have to be online at all times, and which stores valuable data that could be corrupted if the power to the system were suddenly interrupted. Which UPS features are most important to such a system ? Which type of UPS do you recommend for this system?

4. Using the floor plan of a building you are familiar with, design an electronic monitoring plan that includes closed-circuit television, burglar alarms with appropriate sensors, fire detectors, and fire suppression and physical access controls for key entrances.

5. Define the required wattage for a UPS for the following systems:

   a. Monitor: 2 amps; CPU: 3 amps; printer: 3 amps

   b. Monitor: 3 amps; CPU: 4 amps; printer: 3 amps

   c. Monitor: 3 amps; CPU: 4 amps; printer: 4 amps

   Search the Web for a UPS that provides the wattage necessary to run the systems listed above for at least 15 minutes during a power outage.

9

Case Exercises

Amy walked into her office cubicle and sat down. The entire episode with the blond man had taken well over two hours of her day. Plus, the police officers had told her the district attorney would also be calling to make an appointment to speak to her, which meant she would have to spend even more time dealing with this incident. She hoped her manager would understand.

Questions:

1. Based on this case study, what security awareness and training documents and posters had an impact in this event?

2. Do you think that Amy should have done anything differently? What would you have done in the situation in which she found herself?

Endnotes

1. Parker, Donn B. *Fighting Computer Crime.* New York: John Wiley and Sons Inc., 1998, 250–251.

2. Military-net.com. "General Military Knowledge." *Military-net.com Online.* Accessed 5 July 2007 from *www.military-net.com/education/mpdgeneral.html.*

3. Army Study Guide.com. Online. Accessed 5 July 2007 from *www.armystudyguide. com/content/army_board_study_guide_topics/guard_duty/guard-duty-study-guide. shtml.*

4. Swanson, Marianne. *Guide for Developing Security Plans for Information Technology Systems.* December 1998. National Institute of Standards and Technology SP 800-18, 30. Accessed 5 July 2007 from *http://csrc.nist.gov/publications/nistpubs/800-18-Rev1/ sp800-18-Rev1-final.pdf.*

5. Artim, Nick. *An Introduction to Fire Detection, Alarm, and Automatic Fire Sprinklers.* Emergency Management, Technical Leaflet 2, sec. 3. Middlebury: Fire Safety Network.

6. Environmental Protection Agency. "Halon Substitutes Under SNAP as of 21 August 2003." *EPA Online.* Accessed 5 July 2007 from *www.epa.gov/ozone/snap/fire/halo. pdf.*

7. Ibid.

8. Webopedia. "Static Electricity and Computers." *Webopedia Online.* May 2003. Accessed 7 July 2007 from *www.webopedia.com/DidYouKnow/Computer_Science/ 2002/static.asp.*

9. Kozierok, Charles M. "Uninterruptible Power Supply Types." *PC Guide Online.* 17 April 2001. Accessed 5 July 2007 from *www.pcguide.com/ref/power/ext/ups/types.htm.*

10. Van Eck, Wim. "Electromagnetic Radiation from Video Display Units: An Eavesdropping Risk?" *Computers & Security* 4 (1985): 269–286.

11. Loughry, Joe, and Umphress, David A. "Information Leakage from Optical Emanations." *ACM* *Transactions on Information and System Security* 7, no. 7, accepted March 2002.

12. PC Privacy. "Is Tempest a Threat or Hoax?" *PC Privacy* 8, no. 4 (April 2000).

13. Metropolitan Police of the District of Columbia. "Tips for Preventing Laptop Computer Theft." *Government of The District of Columbia Online.* Accessed 7 July 2007 from *http://mpdc.dc.gov/mpdc/cwp/view,a,1237,q,543203,mpdcNav_GID,1548.asp.*

chapter 10

Implementing Information Security

Change is good. You go first!

DILBERT (BY SCOTT ADAMS)

Kelvin Urich arrived early for the change control meeting. In the large, empty conference room, he reviewed his notes and then flipped through the handouts one final time. During the meeting last week, the technical review committee members had approved his ideas, and now he was confident that the project plan he'd come up with was complete, tight, and well-ordered.

The series of change requests resulting from this project would keep the company's technical analysts busy for months to come, but he hoped the scope and scale of the project, and the vast improvements it was sure to bring to the SLS information security program, would inspire his colleagues. To help the project proceed smoothly, he had loaded his handouts with columns of tasks, subtasks, and action items, and had assigned dates to every action step and personnel to each required task. He checked that the handouts were stapled properly and that he had plenty of copies. Everything was under control.

Naomi Jackson, the change control supervisor, also arrived a few minutes early. She nodded to Kelvin as she placed a stack of revised agendas in the middle of the conference table. Everyone attending had received the detailed report of planned changes the previous day. Charlie Moody came in, also nodding to Kelvin, and took his usual seat.

Once the room filled, Naomi said, "Time to get started." She picked up her copy of the planned change report and announced the first change control item for discussion, Item 742.

One of the members of the UNIX support team responded, "As planned," meaning that the item, a routine maintenance check, would occur as scheduled.

Naomi continued down the list in numeric order. Most items received the response, "As planned," from the sponsoring team member. Occasionally, someone answered, "Cancelled," or, "Will be rescheduled," but for the most part, the review of the change items proceeded as usual until they came to Kelvin's information security change requests.

Naomi said, "Items 761 through 767. Kelvin Urich from the security team is here to discuss these items with the change control group."

Kelvin distributed his handouts around the table. He waited, a little nervously, until everyone had a copy, and then began speaking: "I'm sure most of you are already aware of the information security upgrades we've been working on for the past few months. We've created an overall strategy based on the revised policies that were published last month and a detailed analysis of the threats to our systems. As the project manager, I've created what I think is a very workable plan. The seven change requests on the list today are all network changes and are all top priority. In the coming weeks, I'll be sending each department head a complete list of all planned changes and the expected dates. Of course, detailed change requests will be filed in advance for these change control meetings, but each department can find out when it is coming up by checking the master list. As I said, there are more changes coming, and I hope we can all work together to make this a success."

"Comments or questions?" asked Naomi.

Instantly six hands shot into the air. All of them belonged to senior technical analysts. Kelvin realized belatedly that none of these analysts were on the technical review committee that had approved his plan. He also noticed that half the people in the room, like Amy Windahl from the user group and training committee, were busy pulling calendars and PDAs out of briefcases and bags, and that Davey Martinez from accounting was engaged in a private but heated discussion with Charlie Moody, Kelvin's boss—and that Charlie did not look pleased.

Above the noise, Kelvin heard someone ask, "I should have been warned if we are going to have all this work dumped on us all at once." Someone else said, "We can't make this happen on this schedule."

In the midst of the sudden chaos that had broken out during an otherwise orderly meeting, it occurred to Kelvin that his plan might not be as simple as he'd thought. He braced himself—it was going to be a very long afternoon.

LEARNING OBJECTIVES:

Upon completion of this material, you should be able to:

- Explain how an organization's information security blueprint becomes a project plan
- Enumerate the many organizational considerations that a project plan must address

- Explain the significance of the project manager's role in the success of an information security project
- Establish the need for professional project management for complex projects
- Describe technical strategies and models for implementing a project plan
- Anticipate and mitigate the nontechnical problems that organizations face in times of rapid change

Introduction

First and foremost, an information security project manager must realize that implementing an information security project takes time, effort, and a great deal of communication and coordination. This chapter and the next discuss the two stages of the **security systems development life cycle** (SecSDLC) implementation phase and describe how to successfully execute the information security blueprint. In general, the implementation phase is accomplished by changing the configuration and operation of the organization's information systems to make them more secure. It includes changes to the following:

- Procedures (for example, through policy)
- People (for example, through training)
- Hardware (for example, through firewalls)
- Software (for example, through encryption)
- Data (for example, through classification)

As you may recall from earlier chapters, the SecSDLC involves collecting information about an organization's objectives, its technical architecture, and its information security environment. These elements are used to form the information security blueprint, which is the foundation for the protection of the confidentiality, integrity, and availability of the organization's information.

During the implementation phase, the organization translates its blueprint for information security into a **project plan**. The project plan instructs the individuals who are executing the implementation phase. These instructions focus on the security control changes that are needed to improve the security of the hardware, software, procedures, data, and people that make up the organization's information systems. The project plan as a whole must describe how to acquire and implement the needed security controls and create a setting in which those controls achieve the desired outcomes.

Before developing a project plan, however, management should coordinate the organization's information security vision and objectives with the communities of interest involved in the execution of the plan. This type of coordination ensures that only controls that add value to the organization's information security program are incorporated into the project plan. If a statement of the vision and objectives for the organization's security program does not exist, one must be developed and incorporated into the project plan. The vision statement should be concise. It should state the mission of the information security program and its objectives. In other words, the project plan is built upon the vision statement, which serves as a compass for guiding the changes necessary for the implementation phase. The components of the project plan should never conflict with the organization's vision and objectives.

Information Security Project Management

As the opening vignette of this chapter illustrates, organizational change is not easily accomplished. The following sections discuss the issues a project plan must address, including project leadership; managerial, technical, and budgetary considerations; and organizational resistance to the change.

The major steps in executing the project plan are as follows:

- Planning the project
- Supervising tasks and action steps
- Wrapping up

The project plan can be developed in any number of ways. Each organization has to determine its own project management methodology for IT and information security projects. Whenever possible, information security projects should follow the organization's project management practices.

Developing the Project Plan

Planning for the implementation phase requires the creation of a detailed project plan. The task of creating such a project plan is often assigned to either a project manager or the project champion. This individual manages the project and delegates parts of it to other decision makers. Often the project manager is from the IT community of interest, because most other employees lack the requisite information security background and the appropriate management authority and/or technical knowledge.

The project plan can be created using a simple planning tool such as the **work breakdown structure (WBS)**, an example of which is shown later in Tables 10-1 and 10-2. To use the WBS approach, you first break down the project plan into its major tasks. The major project tasks are placed into the WBS, along with the following attributes for each:

- Work to be accomplished (activities and deliverables)
- Individuals (or skill set) assigned to perform the task
- Start and end dates for the task (when known)
- Amount of effort required for completion in hours or work days
- Estimated capital expenses for the task
- Estimated noncapital expenses for the task
- Identification of dependencies between and among tasks

Each major task on the WBS is then further divided into either smaller tasks (subtasks) or specific action steps. For the sake of simplicity, the sample project plan described later in this chapter (and summarized in Tables 10-1 and 10-2) divides each major task into action steps. Be aware that in an actual project plan, major tasks are often much more complex and must be divided into subtasks before action steps can be identified and assigned to the individual or skill set. Given the variety of possible projects, there are few formal guidelines for deciding what level of detail—that is, at which level a task or subtask should become an action step—is appropriate. There is, however, one hard-and-fast rule you can use to make this determination: a task or subtask becomes an action step when it can be completed by one individual or skill set and has a single deliverable.

The WBS can be prepared with a simple desktop PC spreadsheet program. The use of more complex project management software tools often leads to **projectitis**, wherein the project manager spends more time documenting project tasks, collecting performance measurements, recording project task information, and updating project completion forecasts than in accomplishing meaningful project work. Recall Kelvin's handouts from the opening vignette, which were loaded with dates and details. Kelvin's case of projectitis led him to develop an elegant, detailed plan before gaining consensus for the required changes; new to project management, he did not realize that simpler software tools would help him focus on organizing and coordinating with the project team.

Work to Be Accomplished The work to be accomplished encompasses both activities and deliverables. A **deliverable** is a completed document or program module that can either serve as the beginning point for a later task or become an element in the finished project. Ideally, the project planner provides a label and thorough description for the task. The description should be complete enough to avoid ambiguity during the later tracking process, yet not so detailed as to make the WBS unwieldy. For instance, if the task is to write firewall specifications for the preparation of a **request for proposal** (RFP), the planner should note that the deliverable is a specification document suitable for distribution to vendors.

Assignees The project planner should describe the skill set or person, often called a **resource**, needed to accomplish the task. The naming of individuals should be avoided in the early planning efforts, a rule Kelvin ignored when he named individuals for every task in the first draft of his project plan. Instead of assigning individuals, the project plan should focus on organizational roles or known skill sets. For example, if any of the engineers in the networks group can write the specifications for a router, the assigned resource would be noted as "network engineer" on the WBS. As planning progresses, however, the specific tasks and action steps can and should be assigned to individuals. For example, when *only* the manager of the networks group can evaluate the responses to the RFP and make an award for a contract, the project planner should identify the network manager as the resource assigned to this task.

Start and End Dates In the early stages of planning, the project planner should attempt to specify completion dates only for major project milestones. A **milestone** is a specific point in the project plan when a task that has a noticeable impact on the progress of the project plan is complete. For example, the date for sending the final RFP to vendors is a milestone, because it signals that all RFP preparation work is complete. Assigning too many dates to too many tasks early in the planning process exacerbates projectitis. This is another mistake Kelvin made, and was a significant cause of the resistance he faced from his coworkers. Planners can avoid this pitfall by assigning only key or milestone start and end dates early in the process. Later in the planning process, planners may add start and end dates as needed.

Amount of Effort Planners need to estimate the effort required to complete each task, subtask, or action step. Estimating effort hours for technical work is a complex process. Even when an organization has formal governance, technical review processes, and change control procedures, it is always good practice to ask the people who are most familiar with the tasks or with similar tasks to make these estimates. After these estimates are made, all those assigned to action steps should review the estimated effort hours, understand the tasks, and agree with the estimates. Had Kelvin collaborated with his peers more effectively and adopted a more flexible planning approach, much of the resistance he encountered in the meeting would not have emerged.

Estimated Capital Expenses Planners need to estimate the capital expenses required for the completion of each task, subtask, or action item. While each organization budgets and expends capital according to its own established procedures, most differentiate between capital outlays for durable assets and expenses for other purposes. For example, a firewall device costing $5,000 may be a capital outlay for an organization, but the same organization might not consider a $5,000 software package to be a capital outlay because its accounting rules classify all software as expense items, regardless of cost.

Estimated Noncapital Expenses Planners need to estimate the noncapital expenses for the completion of each task, subtask, or action item. Some organizations require that this cost include a recovery charge for staff time, while others exclude employee time and only project contract or consulting time as a noncapital expense. As mentioned earlier, it is important to determine the practices of the organization for which the plan is to be used. For example, at some companies a project to implement a firewall may charge only the costs of the firewall hardware as capital and consider all costs for labor and software as expense, regarding the hardware element as a durable good that has a lifespan of many years. Another organization might use the aggregate of all cash outflows associated with the implementation as the capital charge and make no charges to the expense category. The justification behind using this aggregate, which might include charges for items similar to hardware, labor, and freight, is that the newly implemented capability is expected to last for many years and is an improvement to the organization's infrastructure. A third company may charge the whole project as expense if the aggregate amount falls below a certain threshold, under the theory that small projects are a cost of ongoing operations.

Task Dependencies Planners should note wherever possible the dependencies of other tasks or action steps on the task or action step at hand. Tasks or action steps that come before the specific task at hand are called **predecessors**, and those that come after the task at hand are called **successors**. There can be more than one type of dependency, but such details are typically covered in courses on project management and are beyond the scope of this text.

A sample project plan is provided below to help you better understand the process of creating one. In this example, a small information security project has been assigned to Jane Smith for planning. The project is to design and implement a firewall for a single small office. The hardware is a standard organizational product and will be installed at a location that already has a network connection.

Jane's first step is to list the major tasks:

1. Contact field office and confirm network assumptions.
2. Purchase standard firewall hardware.

Task or Subtask	Resources	Start and End Dates	Estimated Effort in Hours	Estimated Capital Expense	Estimated Noncapital Expense	Dependencies
1 Contact field office and confirm network assumptions	Network architect	S: 9/22 E:	2	0	200	
2 Purchase standard firewall hardware	Network architect and purchasing group	S: E:	4	4,500	250	1
3 Configure firewall	Network architect	S: E:	8	0	800	2
4 Package and ship to field office	Student intern	S: E: 10/15	2	0	85	3
5 Work with local technical resource to install and test firewall	Network architect	S: E:	6	0	600	4
6 Complete vulnerability assessment by penetration test team	Network architect and penetration test team	S: E:	12	0	1,200	5
7 Get remote office sign-off and update all network drawings and documentation	Network architect	S: E: 11/30	8	0	800	6

Table 10-1 Example Project Plan Work Breakdown Structure–Early Draft

3. Configure firewall.
4. Package and ship firewall to field office.
5. Work with local technical resource to install and test firewall.
6. Coordinate vulnerability assessment by penetration test team.
7. Get remote office sign-off and update all network drawings and documentation.

The first draft of Jane's WBS-based project plan is shown in Table 10-1.

After all the people involved review and refine Jane's plan, she revises it to add more dates to the tasks listed. This more detailed version is shown in Table 10-2. Note that this version of the project plan has been further developed and illustrates the breakdown of tasks 2 and 6 into action steps.

Task or Subtask	Resources	Start and End Dates	Estimated Effort in Hours	Estimated Capital Expense	Estimated Noncapital Expense	Depend-encies
1 Contact field office and confirm network assumptions	Network architect	S: 9/22 E: 9/22	2	0	200	
2 Purchase standard firewall hardware						
2.1 Order firewall through purchasing group	Network architect	S: 9/23 E: 9/23	1		100	1
2.2 Order firewall from manufacturer	Purchasing group	S: 9/24 E: 9/24	2	4,500	100	2.1
2.3 Firewall delivered	Purchasing group	E: 10/3	1		50	2.2
3 Configure firewall	Network architect	S: 10/3 E: 10/5	8	0	800	2.3
4 Package and ship to field office	Student intern	S: 10/6 E: 10/15	2	0	85	3
5 Work with local technical resource to install and test	Network architect	S: 10/22 E: 10/31	6	0	600	4
6 Penetration test						
6.1 Request Penetration test	Network architect	S: 11/1 E: 11/1	1	0	100	5
6.2 Perform Penetration test	Penetration test team	S: 11/2 E: 11/12	9	0	900	6.1
6.3 Verify that results of penetration test were passing	Network architect	S: 11/13 E: 11/15	2	0	200	6.2
7 Get remote office sign-off and update all network drawings and documentation	Network architect	S: 11/16 E: 11/30	8	0	800	6.2

Table 10-2 Example Project Plan Work Breakdown Structure–Later Draft

Project Planning Considerations

As the project plan is developed, adding detail is not always straightforward. The following sections discuss factors that project planners must consider as they decide what to include in the work plan, how to break tasks into subtasks and action steps, and how to accomplish the objectives of the project.

Financial Considerations

Financial Considerations Regardless of an organization's information security needs, the amount of effort that can be expended depends on the available funds. A **cost benefit analysis (CBA)**, typically prepared in the analysis phase of the SecSDLC, must be reviewed and verified prior to the development of the project plan. The CBA determines the impact that a specific technology or approach can have on the organization's information assets and what it may cost.

Each organization has its own approach to the creation and management of budgets and expenses. In many organizations, the information security budget is a subsection of the overall IT budget. In others, information security is a separate budget category that may have the same degree of visibility and priority as the IT budget. Regardless of where in the budget information security items are located, monetary constraints determine what can (and can not) be accomplished.

Public organizations tend to be more predictable in their budget processes than private organizations, because the budgets of public organizations are usually the product of legislation or public meetings. This makes it difficult to obtain additional funds once the budget is determined. Also, some public organizations rely on temporary or renewable grants for their budgets and must stipulate their planned expenditures when the grant applications are written. If new expenses arise, funds must be requested via new grant applications. Also, grant expenditures are usually audited and cannot be misspent. However, many public organizations must spend all budgeted funds within the fiscal year—otherwise, the subsequent year's budget is reduced by the unspent amount. As a result, these organizations often conduct end-of-fiscal-year spend-a-thons. This is often the best time to acquire, for example, that remaining piece of technology needed to complete the information security architecture.

Private (for-profit) organizations have budgetary constraints that are determined by the marketplace. When a for-profit organization initiates a project to improve security, the funding comes from the company's capital and expense budgets. Each for-profit organization determines its capital budget and the rules for managing capital spending and expenses differently. In almost all cases, however, budgetary constraints affect the planning and actual expenditures for information security. For example, a preferred technology or solution may be sacrificed for a less desirable but more affordable solution. The budget ultimately guides the information security implementation.

To justify the amount budgeted for a security project at either a public or for-profit organization, it may be useful to benchmark expenses of similar organizations. Most for-profit organizations publish the components of their expense reports. Similarly, public organizations must document how funds are spent. A savvy information security project manager might find a number of similarly sized organizations with larger expenditures for security to justify planned expenditures. While such tactics may not improve this year's budget, they could improve future budgets. Ironically, attackers can also help information security project planners justify the information security budget. If attacks successfully compromise secured information systems, management may be more willing to support the information security budget.

Priority Considerations In general, the most important information security controls in the project plan should be scheduled first. Budgetary constraints may have an effect on the assignment of a project's priorities. As you learned in Chapter 4, the implementation of controls is guided by the prioritization of threats and the value of the threatened information assets. A less-important control may be prioritized if it addresses a group of specific vulnerabilities and improves the organization's security posture to a greater degree than other individual higher-priority controls.

Time and Scheduling Considerations Time and scheduling can affect a project plan at dozens of points—consider the time between ordering and receiving a security control, which may not be immediately available; the time it takes to install and configure the control; the time it takes to train the users; and the time it takes to realize the return on the investment in the control. For example, if a control must be in place before an organization can implement its electronic commerce product, the selection process is likely to be influenced by the speed of acquisition and implementation of the various alternatives.

Staffing Considerations The need for qualified, trained, and available personnel also constrains the project plan. An experienced staff is often needed to implement technologies and to develop and implement policies and training programs. If no staff members are trained to configure a new firewall, the appropriate personnel must be trained or hired.

Procurement Considerations There are often constraints on the equipment and services selection processes—for example, some organizations require the use of particular service vendors or manufacturers and suppliers. These constraints may limit which technologies can be acquired. For example, in a recent budget cycle, the authors' lab administrator was considering selecting an automated risk analysis software package. The leading candidate promised to integrate everything, including vulnerability scanning, risk weighting, and control selection. Upon receipt of the RFP, the vendor issued a bid to accomplish the desired requirements for a heart-stopping $75,000, plus a 10 percent annual maintenance fee. If an organization has an annual information security capital budget of $30,000, it must eliminate a package like this from consideration—despite how promising the software's features are. Also, consider the chilling effect on innovation when an organization requires elaborate supporting documentation and/or complex bidding for even small-scale purchases. Such procurement constraints, designed to control losses from occasional abuses, may actually increase costs when the lack of operating agility is taken into consideration.

Organizational Feasibility Considerations Whenever possible, security-related technological changes should be transparent to system users, but sometimes such changes require new procedures, for example additional authentication or validation. A successful project requires that an organization be able to assimilate the proposed changes. New technologies sometimes require new policies, and both require employee training and education. Scheduling training after the new processes are in place (that is, after the users have had to deal with the changes without preparation) can create tension and resistance, and might undermine security operations. Untrained users may develop ways to work around unfamiliar security procedures, and their bypassing of controls may create additional vulnerabilities. Conversely, users should not be prepared so far in advance that they forget the new training techniques and requirements. The optimal time frame for training is usually one to three weeks before the new policies and technologies come online.

Training and Indoctrination Considerations The size of the organization and the normal conduct of business may preclude a single large training program on new security procedures or technologies. If so, the organization should conduct a phased-in or pilot implementation, such as roll-out training for one department at a time (see the section titled "Conversion Strategies" later in the chapter for details about various implementation approaches). When a project involves a change in policies, it may be sufficient to brief supervisors on the new policy and assign them the task of updating end users in regularly scheduled meetings. Project planners must ensure that compliance documents are also distributed and that all employees are required to read, understand, and agree to the new policies.

Scope Considerations

Project scope describes the amount of time and effort-hours needed to deliver the planned features and quality level of the project deliverables. The scope of any given project plan should be carefully reviewed and kept as small as possible given the project's objectives. To control project scope, organizations should implement large information security projects in stages, as in the bull's-eye approach discussed later in this chapter.

There are several reasons why the scope of information security projects must be evaluated and adjusted with care. First, in addition to the challenge of handling many complex tasks at one time, the installation of information security controls can disrupt the ongoing operations of an organization, and may also conflict with existing controls in unpredictable ways. For example, if you install a new packet filtering router and a new application proxy firewall at the same time and, as a result, users are blocked from accessing the Web, which technology caused the conflict? Was it the router, the firewall, or an interaction between the two? Limiting the project scope to a set of manageable tasks does not mean that the project should only allow change to one component at a time, but a good plan carefully considers the number of tasks that are planned for the same time in a single department.

Recall from the opening vignette that all of Kelvin's change requests are in the area of networking, where the dependencies are particularly complex. If the changes in Kelvin's project plan are not deployed exactly as planned, or if unanticipated complexities arise, there could be extensive disruption to Sequential Label and Supply's daily operations. For instance, an error in the deployment of the primary firewall rules could interrupt all Internet connectivity, which might, in turn, make the early detection of (and recovery from) the original error more difficult.

The Need for Project Management

Project management requires a unique set of skills and a thorough understanding of a broad body of specialized knowledge. In the opening vignette, Kelvin's inexperience as a project manager makes this all too clear. Realistically, most information security projects require a trained project manager—a CISO or a skilled IT manager who is trained in project management techniques. Even experienced project managers are advised to seek expert assistance when engaging in a formal bidding process to select advanced or integrated technologies or outsourced services.

Supervised Implementation Although it is not an optimal solution, some organizations designate a champion from the general management community of interest to supervise the implementation of an information security project plan. In this case, groups of tasks are delegated to individuals or teams from the IT and information security communities of interest. An alternative is to designate a senior IT manager or the CIO of the organization to lead the implementation. In this case, the detailed work is delegated to cross-functional teams. The optimal solution is to designate a suitable person from the information security community of interest. In the final analysis, each organization must find the project leadership that best suits its specific needs and the personalities and politics of the organizational culture.

Executing the Plan Once a project is underway, it is managed using a process known as a **negative feedback loop** or cybernetic loop, which ensures that progress is measured periodically. In the negative feedback loop, measured results are compared to expected results. When significant deviation occurs, corrective action is taken to bring the deviating task back into compliance with the project plan, or else the projection is revised in light of new information. See Figure 10-1 for an overview of this process.

Corrective action is taken in two basic situations: either the estimate was flawed, or performance has lagged. When an estimate is flawed, as when the number of effort-hours required is underestimated, the plan should be corrected and downstream tasks updated to reflect the change. When performance has lagged, due, for example, to high turnover of skilled employees, corrective action may take the form of adding resources, making longer schedules, or reducing the quality or quantity of the deliverable. Corrective action decisions are usually expressed in terms of trade-offs. Often a project manager can adjust one of the three following planning parameters for the task being corrected:

- Effort and money allocated
- Elapsed time or scheduling impact
- Quality or quantity of the deliverable

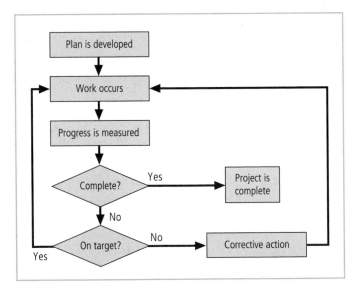

Figure 10-1 Negative Feedback Loop

Source: Course Technology/Cengage Learning

When too much effort and money is being spent, you may decide to take more time to complete the project tasks or to lower the deliverable quality or quantity. If the task is taking too long to complete, you should probably add more resources in staff time or money or else lower deliverable quality or quantity. If the quality of the deliverable is too low, you must usually add more resources in staff time or money or take longer to complete the task. Of course, there are complex dynamics among these variables, and these simplistic solutions do not serve in all cases, but this simple trade-off model can help the project manager to analyze available options.

Project Wrap-up Project wrap-up is usually handled as a procedural task and assigned to a mid-level IT or information security manager. These managers collect documentation, finalize status reports, and deliver a final report and a presentation at a wrap-up meeting. The goal of the wrap-up is to resolve any pending issues, critique the overall project effort, and draw conclusions about how to improve the process for the future.

Technical Aspects of Implementation

Some aspects of the implementation process are technical in nature and deal with the application of technology, while others deal instead with the human interface to technical systems. In the following sections, conversion strategies, prioritization among multiple components, outsourcing, and technology governance are discussed.

Conversion Strategies

As the components of the new security system are planned, provisions must be made for the changeover from the previous method of performing a task to the new method. Just like IT systems, information security projects require careful conversion planning. In both cases, four basic approaches used for changing from an old system or process to a new one are:

- Direct changeover: Also known as going "cold turkey," a **direct changeover** involves stopping the old method and beginning the new. This could be as simple as having employees follow the existing procedure one week and then use a new procedure the next. Some cases of direct changeover are simple, such as requiring employees to use a new password (which uses a stronger degree of authentication) beginning on an announced date; some may be more complex, such as requiring the entire company to change procedures when the network team disables an old firewall and activates a new one. The primary drawback to the direct changeover approach is that if the new system fails or needs modification, users may be without services while the system's bugs are worked out. Complete testing of the new system in advance of the direct changeover reduces the probability of such problems.

- Phased implementation: A **phased implementation** is the most common conversion strategy and involves a measured rollout of the planned system, with a part of the whole being brought out and disseminated across an organization before the next piece is implemented. This could mean that the security group implements only a small portion of the new security profile, giving users a chance to get used to it and resolving issues as they arise. This is usually the best approach to security project implementation. For example, if an organization seeks to update both its VPN and IDPS systems, it may first introduce the new VPN solution that employees can use to connect to the organization's network while they're traveling. Each week another department will be allowed to use the new VPN, with this process continuing until all departments are using the new approach. Once the new VPN has been phased into operation, revisions to the organization's IDPS can begin.

- Pilot implementation: In a pilot implementation, the entire security system is put in place in a single office, department, or division, and issues that arise are dealt with before expanding to the rest of the organization. The pilot implementation works well when an isolated group can serve as the "guinea pig," which prevents any problems with the new system from dramatically interfering with the performance of the organization as a whole. The operation of a research and development group, for example, may not affect the real-time operations of the organization and could assist security in resolving issues that emerge.

- Parallel operations: The **parallel operations** strategy involves running the new methods alongside the old methods. In general, this means running two systems concurrently; in terms of information systems, it might involve, for example, running two firewalls concurrently. Although this approach is complex, it can reinforce an organization's information security by allowing the old system(s) to serve as backup for the new systems if they fail or are compromised. Drawbacks usually include the need to deal with both systems and maintain both sets of procedures.

The Bull's-Eye Model

A proven method for prioritizing a program of complex change is the **bull's-eye method**. This methodology, which goes by many different names and has been used by many organizations, requires that issues be addressed from the general to the specific, and that the focus be on systematic solutions instead of individual problems. The increased capabilities—that is, increased expenditures—are used to improve the information security program in a systematic and measured way. As presented here and illustrated in Figure 10-2, the approach relies on a process of project plan evaluation in four layers:

1. Policies: This is the outer, or first, ring in the bull's-eye diagram. The critical importance of policies has been emphasized throughout this textbook, and particularly in Chapter 5.

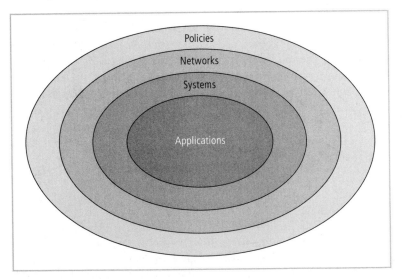

Figure 10-2 The Bull's-Eye Model

Source: Course Technology/Cengage Learning

The foundation of all effective information security programs is sound information security and information technology policy. Since policy establishes the ground rules for the use of all systems and describes what is appropriate and what is inappropriate, it enables all other information security components to function correctly. When deciding how to implement complex changes and choose from conflicting options, you can use policy to clarify what the organization is trying to accomplish with its efforts.

2. Networks: In the past, most information security efforts focused on this layer, and so until recently information security was often considered synonymous with network security. In today's computing environment, implementing information security is more complex because networking infrastructure often comes into contact with threats from the public network. Those organizations new to the Internet find (as soon as their policy environment defines how their networks should be defended) that designing and implementing an effective DMZ is the primary way to secure an organization's networks. Secondary efforts in this layer include providing the necessary authentication and authorization when allowing users to connect over public networks to the organization's systems.

3. Systems: Many organizations find that the problems of configuring and operating information systems in a secure fashion become more difficult as the number and complexity of these systems grow. This layer includes computers used as servers, desktop computers, and systems used for process control and manufacturing systems.

4. Applications: The layer that receives attention last is the one that deals with the application software systems used by the organization to accomplish its work. This includes packaged applications, such as office automation and e-mail programs, as well as high-end enterprise resource planning (ERP) packages than span the organization. Custom application software developed by the organization for its own needs is also included.

By reviewing the information security blueprint and the current state of the organization's information security efforts in terms of these four layers, project planners can determine which areas require expanded information security capabilities. The bull's-eye model can also be used to evaluate the sequence of steps taken to integrate parts of the information security blueprint into a project plan. As suggested by its bull's-eye shape, this model dictates the following:

- Until sound and useable IT and information security policies are developed, communicated, and enforced, no additional resources should be spent on other controls.

- Until effective network controls are designed and deployed, all resources should go toward achieving this goal (unless resources are needed to revisit the policy needs of the organization).

- After policies and network controls are implemented, implementation should focus on the information, process, and manufacturing systems of the organization. Until there is well-informed assurance that all critical systems are being configured and operated in a secure fashion, all resources should be spent on reaching that goal.

- Once there is assurance that policies are in place, networks are secure, and systems are safe, attention should move to the assessment and remediation of the security of the organization's applications. This is a complicated and vast area of concern for many organizations. Most organizations neglect to analyze the impact of information security on existing purchased and their own proprietary systems. As in all planning efforts, attention should be paid to the most critical applications first.

To Outsource or Not

Not every organization needs to develop an information security department or program of its own. Just as some organizations outsource part of or all of their IT operations, so too can organizations outsource part of or all of their information security programs. The expense and time required to develop an effective information security program may be beyond the means of some organizations, and therefore it may be in their best interest to hire professional services to help their IT departments implement such a program.

When an organization outsources most or all IT services, information security should be part of the contract arrangement with the supplier. Organizations that handle most of their own IT functions may choose to outsource the more specialized information security functions. Small- and medium-sized organizations often hire outside consultants for penetration testing and information security program audits. Organizations of all sizes frequently outsource network monitoring functions to make certain that their systems are adequately secured and to gain assistance in watching for attempted or successful attacks.

Technology Governance and Change Control

Other factors that determine the success of an organization's IT and information security programs are technology governance and change control processes.

Technology governance, a complex process that organizations use to manage the effects and costs of technology implementation, innovation, and obsolescence, guides how frequently technical systems are updated and how technical updates are approved and funded. Technology governance also facilitates communication about technical advances and issues across the organization.

Medium- and large-sized organizations deal with the impact of technical change on the operation of the organization through a **change control** process. By managing the process of change, the organization can do the following:

- Improve communication about change across the organization
- Enhance coordination between groups within the organization as change is scheduled and completed
- Reduce unintended consequences by having a process to resolve conflict and disruption that change can introduce
- Improve quality of service as potential failures are eliminated and groups work together
- Assure management that all groups are complying with the organization's policies regarding technology governance, procurement, accounting, and information security

Effective change control is an essential part of the IT operation in all but the smallest organizations. The information security group can also use the change control process to ensure that the essential process steps that assure confidentiality, integrity, and availability are followed when systems are upgraded across the organization.

Nontechnical Aspects of Implementation

Some aspects of the information security implementation process are not technical in nature, and deal instead with the human interface to technical systems. In the sections that follow, the topic of creating a culture of change management and the considerations for organizations facing change are discussed.

The Culture of Change Management

The prospect of change, the familiar shifting to the unfamiliar, can cause employees to build up, either unconsciously or consciously, a resistance to that change. Regardless of whether the changes are perceived as good (as in the case of information security implementations) or bad (such as downsizing or massive restructuring), employees tend to prefer the old way of doing things. Even when employees embrace changes, the stress of actually making the changes and adjusting to the new procedures can increase the probability of mistakes or create vulnerabilities in systems. By understanding and applying some of the basic tenets of change management, project managers can lower employee resistance to change and can even build resilience to change, thereby making ongoing change more palatable to the entire organization.

The basic foundation of change management requires that those making the changes understand that organizations typically have cultures that represent their mood and philosophy. Disruptions to this culture must be properly addressed and their effects minimized. One of the oldest models of change is the Lewin change model,[1] which consists of:

- Unfreezing
- Moving
- Refreezing

Unfreezing involves thawing hard-and-fast habits and established procedures. Moving is the transition between the old way and the new. Refreezing is the integration of the new methods into the organizational culture, which is accomplished by creating an atmosphere in which the changes are accepted as the preferred way of accomplishing the necessary tasks.

Considerations for Organizational Change

Steps can be taken to make an organization more amenable to change. These steps reduce resistance to change at the beginning of the planning process and encourage members of the organization to be more flexible as changes occur.

Reducing Resistance to Change from the Start
The level of resistance to change affects the ease with which an organization is able to implement procedural and managerial changes. The more ingrained the existing methods and behaviors are, the more difficult making the change is likely to be. It's best, therefore, to improve the interaction between the affected members of the organization and the project planners in the early phases of an information security improvement project. The interaction between these groups can be improved through a three-step process in which project managers communicate, educate, and involve.

Communication is the first and most critical step. Project managers must communicate with the employees, so that they know that a new security process is being considered and that their feedback is essential to making it work. You must also constantly update employees on the progress of the SecSDLC and provide information on the expected completion dates. This ongoing series of updates keeps the process from being a last-minute surprise and primes people to accept the change more readily when it finally arrives.

At the same time, you must update and educate employees about exactly how the proposed changes will affect them individually and within the organization. While detailed information may not be available in earlier stages of a project plan, details that can be shared with employees may emerge as the SecSDLC progresses. Education also involves teaching employees to use the new systems once they are in place. This, as discussed earlier, means delivering high-quality training programs at the appropriate times.

Finally, project managers can reduce resistance to change by involving employees in the project plan. This means getting key representatives from user groups to serve as members of the SecSDLC development process. In systems development, this is referred to as **joint application development,** or JAD. Identifying a liaison between IT and information security implementers and the general population of the organization can serve the project team well in early planning stages, when unforeseen problems with acceptance of the project may need to be addressed.

Developing a Culture that Supports Change An ideal organization fosters resilience to change. This means the organization understands that change is a necessary part of the culture, and that embracing change is more productive than fighting it. To develop such a culture, the organization must successfully accomplish many projects that require change. A resilient culture can be either cultivated or undermined by management's approach. Strong management support for change, with a clear executive-level champion, enables the organization to recognize the necessity for and strategic importance of the change. Weak management support, with overly delegated responsibility and no champion, sentences the project to almost-certain failure. In this case, employees sense the low priority that has been given to the project and do not communicate with representatives from the development team because the effort seems useless.

Information Systems Security Certification and Accreditation

At first glance it may seem that only systems handling secret government data require security certification or accreditation. However, organizations are increasingly finding that, in order to comply with the myriad of new federal regulation protecting personal privacy, their systems need to have some formal mechanism for verification and validation.

Certification versus Accreditation

In security management, **accreditation** is what authorizes an IT system to process, store, or transmit information. It is issued by a management official and serves as a means of assuring that systems are of adequate quality. It also challenges managers and technical staff to find the best methods to assure security, given technical constraints, operational constraints, and mission requirements. In the same vein, **certification** is "the comprehensive evaluation of the technical and nontechnical security controls of an IT system to support the accreditation process that establishes the extent to which a particular design and implementation meets a set of specified security requirements."[2] Organizations pursue accreditation or certification to gain a competitive advantage or to provide assurance to their customers. Federal systems require accreditation under OMB Circular A-130 and the Computer Security Act of 1987. Accreditation demonstrates that management has identified an acceptable risk level and provided resources to control unacceptable risk levels.

Accreditation and certification are not permanent. Just as standards of due diligence and due care require an ongoing maintenance effort, most accreditation and certification processes require reaccreditation or recertification every few years (typically every three to five years).

NIST SP 800-37, Rev. 1: Guide for Applying the Risk Management Framework to Federal Information Systems: A Security Life Cycle Approach

Two documents provide guidance for the certification and accreditation of federal information systems: SP 800-37, Rev. 1: Guide for Applying the Risk Management Framework to Federal Information Systems: A Security Life Cycle Approach, and CNSS Instruction-1000: National Information Assurance Certification and Accreditation Process (NIACAP).

Information processed by the federal government is grouped into one of three categories: national security information (NSI), non-NSI, and intelligence community (IC). National security information is processed on national security systems (NSSs). NSSs are managed and operated by the Committee for National Systems Security (CNSS), and non-NSSs are managed and operated by the National Institute of Standards and Technology (NIST). Intelligence community (IC) information is a separate category and is handled according to guidance from the office of the Director of National Intelligence (DNI).

An NSS is defined as any information system (including any telecommunications system) used or operated by an agency or by a contractor of any agency, or other organization on behalf of an agency, the function, operation, or use of which:

- Involves intelligence activities
- Involves cryptologic activities related to national security
- Involves command and control of military forces
- Involves equipment that is an integral part of a weapon or weapon system
- Is subject to subparagraph (B), is critical to the direct fulfillment of military or intelligence missions, or is protected at all times by procedures for information that have been specifically authorized under criteria established by an executive order or an act of Congress to be kept classified in the interest of national defense or foreign policy

Subparagraph (B) states that this criterion "does not include a system that is to be used for routine administration and business applications (including payroll, finance, logistics, and personnel management applications.)" (Title 44 US Code Section 3542, Federal Information Security Management Act of 2002)

National security information must be processed on NSSs, which have more stringent requirements. NSSs (which process a mix of NSI and non-NSI) are accredited using CNSS guidance. Non-NSS systems follow NIST guidance. More than a score of major government agencies store, process, or transmit NSI, and many of them have both NSSs and systems that are not rated as NSSs. You can learn more about the CNSS community and how NSSs are managed and operated at *www.cnss.gov*.

In recent years, the Joint Task Force Transformation Initiative Working Group of the U.S. government and NIST have worked to overhaul the formal certification and accreditation (C&A) program for non-NSI systems from a separate C&A process into an integrated risk management framework (RMF), which can be used for normal operations and yet still provide assurance that the systems are capable of reliably housing confidential information. Revision 1 to NIST SP 800-37 provides a detailed description of the new RMF process. The following section is adapted from this document.

> *The revised process emphasizes: (i) building information security capabilities into federal information systems through the application of state-of-the-practice management, operational, and technical security controls; (ii) maintaining awareness of the security state of information systems on an ongoing basis though enhanced monitoring processes; and (iii) providing essential information to senior leaders to facilitate decisions regarding the acceptance of risk to organizational operations and assets, individuals, other organizations, and the Nation arising from the operation and use of information systems.*

> *... The risk management process described in this publication changes the traditional focus of C&A as a static, procedural activity to a more dynamic approach that provides the capability to more effectively manage information system-related security risks in highly diverse environments of complex and sophisticated cyber threats, ever-increasing system vulnerabilities, and rapidly changing missions.*

> *... The guidelines in SP 800-37 Rev. 1 are applicable to all federal information systems other than those systems designated as national security systems as defined in 44 U.S.C., Section 3542.[3]*

Risk management is the subject of Chapter 4, but because the U.S. federal government is replacing the old C&A process with a formal RMF, that framework is briefly described here. SP 800-37 Rev. 1 specifically refers to NIST SP 800-39, a new publication titled Integrated Enterprise-Wide Risk Management: Organization, Mission and Information Systems View as the reference for its RMF. The NIST RMF builds on a three-tiered approach to risk management that addresses risk-related concerns at the organization level, the mission and business process level, and the information system level, as illustrated in Figure 10-3.

> *Tier 1 addresses risk from an organizational perspective with the development of a comprehensive governance structure and organization-wide risk management strategy ...*

> *Tier 2 addresses risk from a mission and business process perspective and is guided by the risk decisions at Tier 1. Tier 2 activities are closely associated with enterprise architecture ...*

> *Tier 3 addresses risk from an information system perspective and is guided by the risk decisions at Tiers 1 and 2. Risk decisions at Tiers 1 and 2 impact the ultimate selection and deployment of needed safeguards and countermeasures (i.e., security controls) at the information system level. Information security requirements are satisfied by the selection of appropriate management, operational, and technical security controls from NIST Special Publication 800-53.*

> *The Risk Management Framework (RMF) [illustrated in Figure 10-4] provides a disciplined and structured process that integrates information security and*

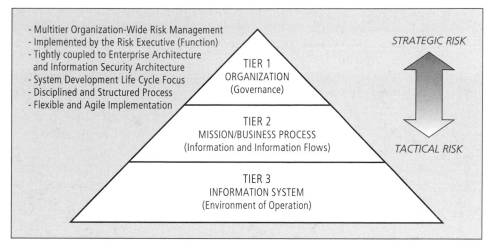

- Multitier Organization-Wide Risk Management
- Implemented by the Risk Executive (Function)
- Tightly coupled to Enterprise Architecture and Information Security Architecture
- System Development Life Cycle Focus
- Disciplined and Structured Process
- Flexible and Agile Implementation

TIER 1
ORGANIZATION
(Governance)

TIER 2
MISSION/BUSINESS PROCESS
(Information and Information Flows)

TIER 3
INFORMATION SYSTEM
(Environment of Operation)

STRATEGIC RISK

TACTICAL RISK

Figure 10-3 Tiered Risk Management Framework

Source: Course Technology/Cengage Learning

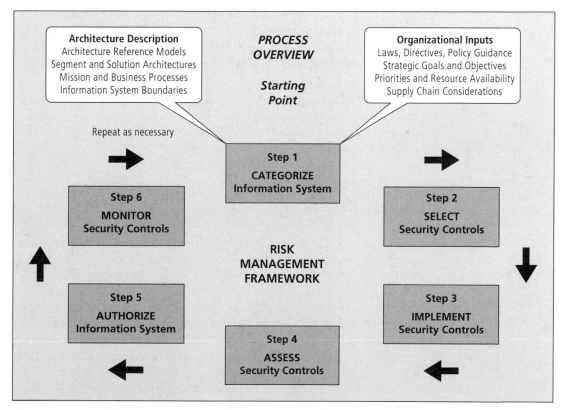

Architecture Description
Architecture Reference Models
Segment and Solution Architectures
Mission and Business Processes
Information System Boundaries

PROCESS OVERVIEW

Starting Point

Organizational Inputs
Laws, Directives, Policy Guidance
Strategic Goals and Objectives
Priorities and Resource Availability
Supply Chain Considerations

Repeat as necessary

Step 1
CATEGORIZE
Information System

Step 6
MONITOR
Security Controls

Step 2
SELECT
Security Controls

RISK MANAGEMENT FRAMEWORK

Step 5
AUTHORIZE
Information System

Step 3
IMPLEMENT
Security Controls

Step 4
ASSESS
Security Controls

Figure 10-4 Risk Management Framework

Source: Course Technology/Cengage Learning

risk management activities into the system development life cycle. The RMF operates primarily at Tier 3 in the risk management hierarchy but can also have interactions at Tiers 1 and 2 (e.g., providing feedback from ongoing authorization decisions to the risk executive [function], dissemination of updated threat and risk information to authorizing officials and information system owners). The RMF steps include:

- *Categorize the information system and the information processed, stored, and transmitted by that system based on an impact analysis.*

- *Select an initial set of baseline security controls for the information system based on the security categorization; tailoring and supplementing the security control baseline as needed based on an organizational assessment of risk and local conditions.*

- *Implement the security controls and describe how the controls are employed within the information system and its environment of operation.*

- *Assess the security controls using appropriate assessment procedures to determine the extent to which the controls are implemented correctly, operating as intended, and producing the desired outcome with respect to meeting the security requirements for the system.*

- *Authorize information system operation based on a determination of the risk to organizational operations and assets, individuals, other organizations, and the Nation resulting from the operation of the information system and the decision that this risk is acceptable.*

- *Monitor the security controls in the information system on an ongoing basis including assessing control effectiveness, documenting changes to the system or its environment of operation, conducting security impact analyses of the associated changes, and reporting the security state of the system to designated organizational officials.[4]*

With regard to using the RMF,

The organization has significant flexibility in deciding which families of security controls or specific controls from selected families in NIST Special Publication 800-53 are appropriate for the different types of allocations. Since the security control allocation process involves the assignment and provision of security capabilities derived from security controls, the organization ensures that there is effective communication among all entities either receiving or providing such capabilities. This communication includes, for example, ensuring that common control authorization results and continuous monitoring information are readily available to those organizational entities inheriting common controls, and that any changes to common controls are effectively communicated to those affected by such changes. [Figure 10-5] illustrates security control allocation within an organization and using the RMF to produce information for senior leaders (including authorizing officials) on the ongoing security state of organizational

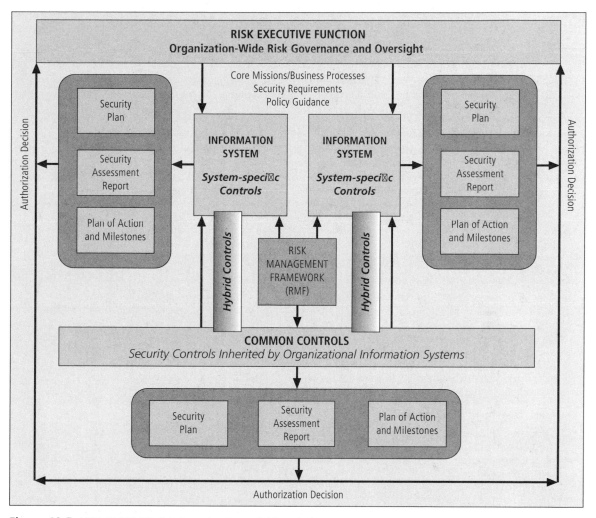

Figure 10-5 NIST SP 800-37, R.1: Security Control Allocation

Source: Course Technology/Cengage Learning

information systems and the missions and business processes supported by those systems."[5]

Chapter 3 of SP 800-37, Rev. 1 provides detailed guidance for implementing the RMF, including information on primary responsibility, supporting roles, system development life cycle phase, supplemental guidance, and references. An overview of the tasks involved is shown in Table 10-3.

Why is it important that you know this information? Your organization may someday wish to become (or may already be) a government contractor, and these guidelines apply to all systems that connect to U.S. government systems not identified as national security systems or as containing national security information.

RMF Step 1—Categorize Information System

1-1 (Security Categorization): Categorize the information system and document the results of the security categorization in the security plan.

1-2 (Information System Description): Describe the information system (including system boundary) and document the description in the security plan.

1-3 (Information System Registration): Register the information system with appropriate organizational program/management offices.

Milestone Checkpoint for RMF Step 1:

- Has the organization completed a security categorization of the information system including the information to be processed, stored, and transmitted by the system?
- Are the results of the security categorization process for the information system consistent with the organization's enterprise architecture and commitment to protecting organizational mission/business processes?
- Do the results of the security categorization process reflect the organization's risk management strategy?
- Has the organization adequately described the characteristics of the information system?
- Has the organization registered the information system for purposes of management, accountability, coordination, and oversight?

RMF Step 2—Select Security Controls

2-1 (Common Control Identification): Identify the security controls that are provided by the organization as common controls for organizational information systems and document the controls in a security plan (or equivalent document).

2-2 (Security Control Selection): Select the security controls for the information system and document the controls in the security plan.

2-3 (Monitoring Strategy): Develop a strategy for the continuous monitoring of security control effectiveness and any proposed or actual changes to the information system and its environment of operation.

2-4 (Security Plan Approval): Review and approve the security plan.

Milestone Checkpoint for RMF Step 2:

- Has the organization allocated all security controls to the information system as system-specific, hybrid, or common controls?
- Has the organization used its risk assessment (either formal or informal) to inform and guide the security control selection process?
- Has the organization identified authorizing officials for the information system and all common controls inherited by the system?
- Has the organization tailored and supplemented the baseline security controls to ensure that the controls, if implemented, adequately mitigate risks to organizational operations and assets, individuals, other organizations, and the nation?
- Has the organization addressed minimum assurance requirements for the security controls employed within and inherited by the information system?
- Has the organization consulted information system owners when identifying common controls to ensure that the security capability provided by the inherited controls is sufficient to deliver adequate protection?
- Has the organization supplemented the common controls with system-specific or hybrid controls when the security control baselines of the common controls are less than those of the information system inheriting the controls?
- Has the organization documented the common controls inherited from external providers?
- Has the organization developed a continuous monitoring strategy for the information system (including monitoring of security control effectiveness for system-specific, hybrid, and common controls) that reflects the organizational risk management strategy and organizational commitment to protecting critical missions and business functions?
- Have appropriate organizational officials approved security plans containing system-specific, hybrid, and common controls?

Table 10-3 **Executing the Risk Management Framework Tasks**[7]

RMF Step 3—Implement Security Controls

3-1 (Security Control Implementation): Implement the security controls specified in the security plan.

3-2 (Security Control Documentation): Document the security control implementation, as appropriate, in the security plan, providing a functional description of the control implementation (including planned inputs, expected behavior, and expected outputs).

Milestone Checkpoint for RMF Step 3:

- Has the organization allocated security controls as system-specific, hybrid, or common controls consistent with the enterprise architecture and information security architecture?
- Has the organization demonstrated the use of sound information system and security engineering methodologies in integrating information technology products into the information system and in implementing the security controls contained in the security plan?
- Has the organization documented how common controls inherited by organizational information systems have been implemented?
- Has the organization documented how system-specific and hybrid security controls have been implemented within the information system taking into account specific technologies and platform dependencies?
- Has the organization taken into account the minimum assurance requirements when implementing security controls?

RMF Step 4—Assess Security Controls

4-1 (Assessment Preparation): Develop, review, and approve a plan to assess the security controls.

4-2 (Security Control Assessment): Assess the security controls in accordance with the assessment procedures defined in the security assessment plan.

4-3 (Security Assessment Report): Prepare the security assessment report documenting the issues, findings, and recommendations from the security control assessment.

4-4 (Remediation Actions): Conduct initial remediation actions on security controls based on the findings and recommendations of the security assessment report and reassess remediated control(s), as appropriate.

Milestone Checkpoint for RMF Step 4:

- Has the organization developed a comprehensive plan to assess the security controls employed within or inherited by the information system?
- Was the assessment plan reviewed and approved by appropriate organizational officials?
- Has the organization considered the appropriate level of assessor independence for the security control assessment?
- Has the organization provided all of the essential supporting assessment-related materials needed by the assessor(s) to conduct an effective security control assessment?
- Has the organization examined opportunities for reusing assessment results from previous assessments or from other sources?
- Did the assessor(s) complete the security control assessment in accordance with the stated assessment plan?
- Did the organization receive the completed security assessment report with appropriate findings and recommendations from the assessor(s)?
- Did the organization take the necessary remediation actions to address the most important weaknesses and deficiencies in the information system and its environment of operation based on the findings and recommendations in the security assessment report?
- Did the organization update appropriate security plans based on the findings and recommendations in the security assessment report and any subsequent changes to the information system and its environment of operation?

RMF Step 5—Authorize Information System

5-1 (Plan of Action and Milestones): Prepare the plan of action and milestones based on the findings and recommendations of the security assessment report excluding any remediation actions taken.

5-2 (Security Authorization Package): Assemble the security authorization package and submit the package to the authorizing official for adjudication.

5-3 (Risk Determination): Determine the risk to organizational operations (including mission, functions, image, or reputation), organizational assets, individuals, other organizations, or the nation.

5-4 (Risk Acceptance): Determine if the risk to organizational operations, organizational assets, individuals, other organizations, or the nation is acceptable.

10

Table 10-3 Executing the Risk Management Framework Tasks[7] (continued)

Milestone Checkpoint for RMF Step 5:
- Did the organization develop a plan of action and milestones reflecting organizational priorities for addressing the remaining weaknesses and deficiencies in the information system and its environment of operation?
- Did the organization develop an appropriate authorization package with all key documents including the security plan, security assessment report, and plan of action and milestones (if applicable)?
- Did the final risk determination and risk acceptance by the authorizing official reflect the risk management strategy developed by the organization and conveyed by the risk executive (function)?
- Was the authorization decision conveyed to appropriate organizational personnel including information system owners and common control providers?

RMF Step 6—Monitor Security Controls

6-1 (Information System and Environment Changes): Determine the security impact of proposed or actual changes to the information system and its environment of operation.

6-2 (Ongoing Security Control Assessments): Assess a selected subset of the technical, management, and operational security controls employed within and inherited by the information system in accordance with the organization-defined monitoring strategy.

6-3 (Ongoing Remediation Actions): Conduct remediation actions based on the results of ongoing monitoring activities, assessment of risk, and outstanding items in the plan of action and milestones.

6-4 (Key Updates): Update the security plan, security assessment report, and plan of action and milestones based on the results of the continuous monitoring process.

6-5 (Security Status Reporting): Report the security status of the information system (including the effectiveness of security controls employed within and inherited by the system) to the authorizing official and other appropriate organizational officials on an ongoing basis in accordance with the monitoring strategy.

6-6 (Ongoing Risk Determination and Acceptance): Review the reported security status of the information system (including the effectiveness of security controls employed within and inherited by the system) on an ongoing basis in accordance with the monitoring strategy to determine whether the risk to organizational operations, organizational assets, individuals, other organizations, or the nation remains acceptable.

6-7 (Information System Removal and Decommissioning): Implement an information system decommissioning strategy, when needed, which executes required actions when a system is removed from service.

Milestone Checkpoint for RMF Step 6:
- Is the organization effectively monitoring changes to the information system and its environment of operation including the effectiveness of deployed security controls in accordance with the continuous monitoring strategy?
- Is the organization effectively analyzing the security impacts of identified changes to the information system and its environment of operation?
- Is the organization conducting ongoing assessments of security controls in accordance with the monitoring strategy?
- Is the organization taking the necessary remediation actions on an ongoing basis to address identified weaknesses and deficiencies in the information system and its environment of operation?
- Does the organization have an effective process in place to report the security status of the information system and its environment of operation to the authorizing officials and other designated senior leaders within the organization on an ongoing basis?
- Is the organization updating critical risk management documents based on ongoing monitoring activities?
- Are authorizing officials conducting ongoing security authorizations by employing effective continuous monitoring activities and communicating updated risk determination and acceptance decisions to information system owners and common control providers?

Table 10-3 **Executing the Risk Management Framework Tasks[7] (continued)**

Source: R. Ross and M. Swanson. Guidelines for the Security Certification and Accreditation of Federal Information Technology Systems. NIST SP 800-53. October 2002.

NSTISS Instruction-1000: National Information Assurance Certification and Accreditation Process (NIACAP)

National security interest systems have their own security C&A standards, which also follow the guidance of OMB Circular A-130. The Committee on National Systems Security (CNSS) (formerly known as the National Security Telecommunications and Information Systems Security Committee or, NSTISSC) document is titled "NSTISS Instruction 1000: National Information Assurance Certification and Accreditation Process (NIACAP)"; see *www.cnss.gov/Assets/pdf/nstissi_1000.pdf*. The following section contains excerpts from this document and provides an overview of the purpose and process of this certification and accreditation program.

1. National Security Telecommunications and Information Systems Security Instruction (NSTISSI) No. 1000, National Information Assurance Certification and Accreditation Process (NIACAP), establishes the minimum national standards for certifying and accrediting national security systems. This process provides a standard set of activities, general tasks, and a management structure to certify and accredit systems that will maintain the information assurance (IA) and security posture of a system or site. This process focuses on an enterprise-wide view of the information system (IS) in relation to the organization's mission and the IS business case.

2. The NIACAP is designed to certify that the IS meets documented accreditation requirements and will continue to maintain the accredited security posture throughout the system life cycle.

The key to the NIACAP is the agreement between the IS program manager, designated approving authority (DAA), certification agent (certifier), and user representative. (The DAA is also referred to as the accreditor in this book.) These individuals resolve critical schedule, budget, security, functionality, and performance issues.

The NIACAP agreements are documented in the system security authorization agreement (SSAA). The SSAA is used to guide and document the results of the C&A process. The objective is to use the SSAA to establish an evolving yet binding agreement on the level of security required before the system development begins or changes to a system are made. After accreditation, the SSAA becomes the baseline security configuration document.

The minimum NIACAP roles include the program manager, DAA, certifier, and user representative. Additional roles may be added to increase the integrity and objectivity of C&A decisions. For example, the information systems security officer (ISSO) usually performs a key role in the maintenance of the security posture after accreditation and may also play a key role in the C&A of the system.

The SSAA:

- Describes the operating environment and threat
- Describes the system security architecture
- Establishes the C&A boundary of the system to be accredited
- Documents the formal agreement among the DAA(s), certifier, program manager, and user representative

- Documents all requirements necessary for accreditation
- Minimizes documentation requirements by consolidating applicable information into the SSAA (security policy, concept of operations, architecture description, test procedures, etc)
- Documents the NIACAP plan
- Documents test plans and procedures, certification results, and residual risk
- Forms the baseline security configuration document

The NIACAP is composed of four phases as shown from several perspectives in Figures 10-6 to 10-10. These phases are definition, verification, validation, and post accreditation.

Phase 1, definition, determines the necessary security measures and effort level to achieve certification and accreditation. The objective of Phase 1 is to agree on the security requirements, C&A boundary, schedule, level of effort, and resources required.

Phase 2, verification, verifies the evolving or modified system's compliance with the information in the SSAA. The objective of Phase 2 is to ensure the fully integrated system is ready for certification testing.

Phase 3, validation, validates compliance of the fully integrated system with the security policy and requirements stated in the SSAA. The objective of Phase 3 is to produce the required evidence to support the DAA in making an informed decision to grant approval to operate the system (accreditation or interim approval to operate [IATO]).

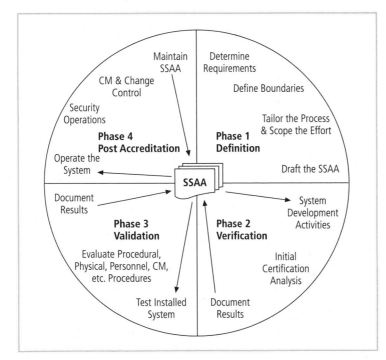

Figure 10-6 Overview of the NIACAP Process

Source: NSTISSI-1000

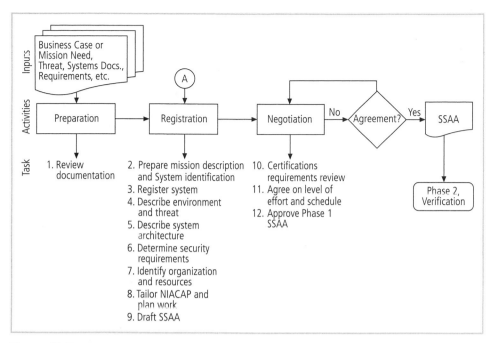

Figure 10-7 NIACAP Phase 1, Definition

Source: NSTISSI-1000

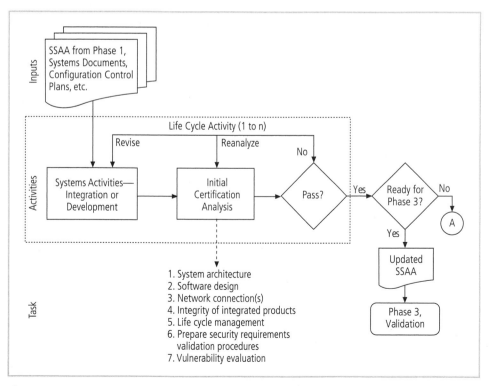

Figure 10-8 NIACAP Phase 2, Verification

Source: NSTISSI-1000

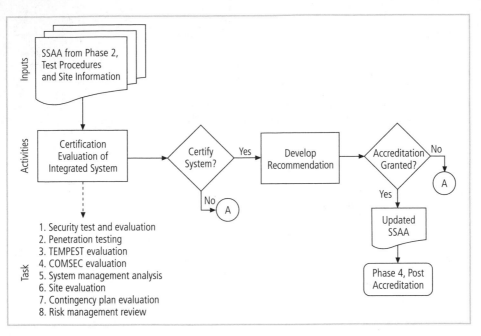

Figure 10-9 NIACAP Phase 3, Validation

Source: NSTISSI-1000

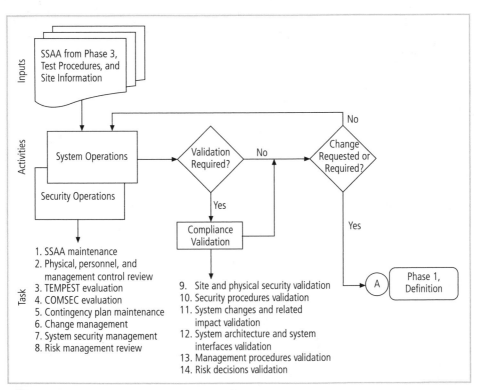

Figure 10-10 NIACAP Phase 4, Post Accrediation

Source: NSTISSI-1000

Phase 4, post accreditation, starts after the system has been certified and accredited for operations. Phase 4 includes those activities necessary for the continuing operation of the accredited IS and manages the changing threats and small-scale changes a system faces through its life cycle. The objective of Phase 4 is to ensure secure system management, operation, and maintenance sustain an acceptable level of residual risk.

The accreditation process itself is so complex that professional certifiers must be trained. The CNSS has a set of training standards for federal information technology workers who deal with information security. One of these documents, NSTISSI 4015, provides a national training standard for systems certifiers (see *www.cnss.gov/Assets/pdf/nstissi_4015.pdf*).

A qualified systems certifier must be formally trained in the fundamentals of INFOSEC and have field experience. It is recommended that system certifiers have system administrator and/or basic information system security officer (ISSO) experience, and be familiar with the knowledge, skills, and abilities required of the DAA, as illustrated in NSTISSI 4015. Once this professional completes training based on NSTISSI-4015, which includes material from NSTISSI-1000, they are eligible to be a federal agency systems certifier. Note: NSTISSI-1000 is currently under revision, and a revised version could be available within the next few years.

ISO 27001/27002 Systems Certification and Accreditation

Entities outside the United States apply the standards provided under the International Standards Organization standard ISO 27001 and 27002, discussed in Chapter 5. Recall that the standards were originally created to provide a foundation for British certification of information security management systems (ISMS). Organizations wishing to demonstrate their systems have met this international standard must follow the certification process, which includes the following phases:

> The first phase of the process involves your company preparing and getting ready for the certification of your ISMS: developing and implementing your ISMS, using and integrating your ISMS into your day to day business processes, training your staff and establishing an on-going program of ISMS maintenance.
>
> The second phase involves employing one of the accredited certification bodies to carry out an audit of your ISMS.
>
> The certificate that is awarded will last for three years after which the ISMS needs to be recertified. Therefore there is a third phase of the process (assuming the certification has been successful and a certificate has been issued), which involves the certification body visiting your ISMS site on a regular basis (e.g. every 6–9 months) to carry out a surveillance audit.[7]

Figure 10-11 shows the process flow of ISMS certification and accreditation in Japan.

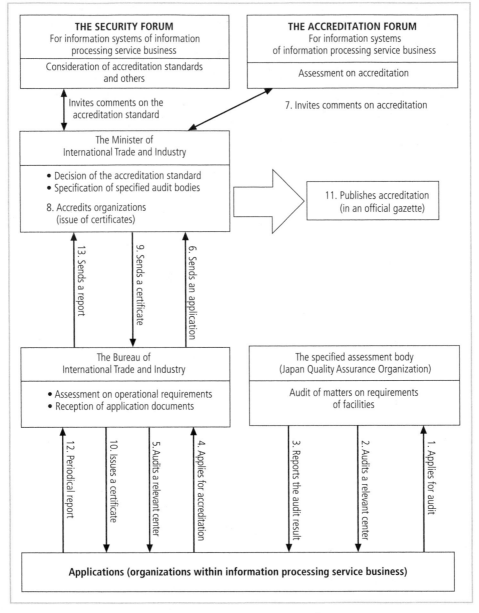

Figure 10-11 Japanese ISMS Certification and Accreditation[9]

Selected Readings

- *Information Technology Project Management, Fifth Edition*, by Kathy Schwalbe. Course Technology.

- *The PMI Project Management Fact Book, Second Edition*, by the Project Management Institute.

- NIST SP 800-37, Rev. 1: Guide for Applying the Risk Management Framework to Federal Information Systems: A Security Life Cycle Approach.
- NIST DRAFT SP 800-39, Managing Risk from Information Systems: An Organizational Perspective.

Chapter Summary

- The implementation phase of the security systems development life cycle involves making changes to the configuration and operation of the organization's information systems in order to make them more secure. These changes include changes to procedures, people, hardware, software, and data.

- During the implementation phase, the organization translates its blueprint for information security into a concrete project plan.

- Before developing a project plan, management should articulate and coordinate the organization's information security vision and objectives with the involved communities of interest.

- The major steps in executing the project plan are planning the project, supervising tasks and action steps within the project plan, and wrapping up the project plan.

- Each organization determines its own project management methodology for IT and information security projects. Whenever possible, an organization's information security projects should be in line with the organization's project management practices.

- Planning for the implementation phase involves the creation of a detailed project plan.

- The project plan can be created by using a simple planning tool such as the approach known as the work breakdown structure (WBS). The plan can be prepared with a simple desktop PC spreadsheet program or with more complex project management software tools. The WBS involves addressing major project tasks (and their related attributes) such as the following:
  - Work to be accomplished (activities and deliverables)
  - Individuals (or skills set) assigned to perform the task
  - Start and end dates for the task (when known)
  - Amount of effort required for completion (in hours or days)
  - Estimated capital expenses for the task
  - Estimated noncapital expenses for the task
  - Identification of task interdependencies

- Constraints and considerations should be addressed when developing the project plan, including financial, procurement, priority, time and scheduling, staffing, scope, organizational feasibility, training and indoctrination, change control, and technology governance considerations.

- Organizations usually designate a professional project manager to lead a security information project. Alternatively, some organizations designate a champion from a senior level of general management or a senior IT manager such as the CIO of the organization.

■ Once a project is underway, it can be managed to completion using a process known as a negative feedback loop or cybernetic loop. This process involves measuring variances from the project plan and then taking corrective action when needed.

■ As the components of the new security system are planned, provisions must be made for the changeover from the previous method of performing a task (or, in some cases, not performing the task) to the new method(s). The four common conversion strategies for performing this changeover are:

- Direct changeover
- Phased implementation
- Pilot implementation
- Parallel operations

■ The bull's-eye model is a proven method for prioritizing a program of complex change. Using this method, the project manager can address issues from the general to the specific and focus on systematic solutions instead of individual problems.

■ When the expense and time required to develop an effective information security program is beyond the reach of an organization, it is best for the organization to outsource to competent professional services.

■ Technology governance is a complex process that an organization uses to manage the impacts and costs resulting from technology implementation, innovation, and obsolescence.

■ The change control process is a method that medium- and large-sized organizations use to deal with the impact of technical change on their operations.

■ As with any project, there are certain aspects of change that must be addressed. In any major project, the prospect of moving from the familiar to the unfamiliar can cause employees to resist change, consciously or unconsciously.

■ Implementing and securing information systems often requires external certification or accreditation.

■ Accreditation is the authorization of an IT system to process, store, or transmit information issued by a management official assuring that systems are of adequate quality.

■ Certification is a comprehensive evaluation of the technical and nontechnical security controls of an IT system to validate an accreditation process.

■ A variety of accreditation and certification processes are in use globally including the U.S. Federal Agency system and the ISO 27001 and 27002 standards.

Review Questions

1. What is a project plan? List what a project plan can accomplish.

2. What is the value of a statement of vision and objectives? Why is it needed before a project plan is developed?

3. What categories of constraints to project plan implementation are noted in the chapter? Explain each of them.

4. List and describe the three major steps in executing the project plan.

5. What is a work breakdown structure (WBS)? Is it the only way to organize a project plan?

6. What is projectitis? How is it cured or its impact minimized?

7. List and define the common attributes of the tasks of a WBS.

8. How does a planner know when a task has been subdivided to an adequate degree and can be classified as an action step?

9. What is a deliverable? Name two uses for deliverables.

10. What is a resource? What are the two types?

11. Why is it a good practice to delay naming specific individuals as resources early in the planning process?

12. What is a milestone, and why is it significant to project planning?

13. Why is it good practice to assign start and end dates sparingly in the early stages of project planning?

14. Who is the best judge of effort estimates for project tasks and action steps? Why?

15. Within project management, what is a dependency? What is a predecessor? What is a successor?

16. What is a negative feedback loop? How is it used to keep a project in control?

17. When a task is not being completed according to the plan, what two circumstances are likely to be involved?

18. List and describe the four basic conversion strategies (as described in the chapter) that are used when converting to a new system. Under which circumstances is each of these the best approach?

19. What is technology governance? What is change control? How are they related?

20. What are certification and accreditation when applied to information systems security management? List and describe at least two certification or accreditation processes.

10

Exercises

1. Create a first draft of a WBS from the scenario below. Make assumptions as needed based on the section about project planning considerations and constraints in the chapter. In your WBS, describe the skill sets required for the tasks you have planned.

Scenario

Sequential Label and Supply is having a problem with employees surfing the Web to access material the company has deemed inappropriate for a professional environment. The technology exists to insert a filtering device in the company Internet connection that blocks certain Web locations and certain Web content. The vendor has provided the company with some initial information about the filter. The filter is a hardware appliance that costs $18,000 and requires a total of 150 effort-hours to install and configure. Technical support on the filter costs

18 percent of the purchase price and includes a training allowance for the year. A software component that runs on the administrator's desktop computer is needed for administering the filter, and it costs $550. A monthly subscription provides the list of sites to be blocked and costs $250 per month. The administrator must spend an estimated four hours per week for ongoing administrative functions.

Items you should consider:

- Your plan requires two parts, one for deployment and another for ongoing operation after implementation.

- The vendor offers a contracting service for installation at $140 per hour.

- Your change control process requires a seventeen-day lead time for change requests.

- The manufacturer has a fourteen-day order time and a seven-day delivery time for this device.

2. If you have access to a commercial project management software package (Microsoft Project, for example), use it to complete a project plan based on the data shown in Table 10-2. Prepare a simple WBS report (or Gantt chart) showing your work.

3. Write a job description for Kelvin Urich, the project manager described in the opening vignette of this chapter. Be sure to identify key characteristics of the ideal candidate, as well as his or her work experience and educational background. Also, justify why your job description is suitable for potential candidates of this position.

4. Search the World Wide Web for job descriptions of project managers. You can use any number of Web sites, including *www.monster.com* or *www.dice.com*, to find at least ten IT-related job descriptions. What common elements do you find among the job descriptions? What is the most unusual characteristic among them?

Case Exercise

Charlie looked across his desk at Kelvin, who was absorbed in the sheaf of handwritten notes from the meeting. Charlie had asked Kelvin to come his office to discuss the change control meeting that had occurred earlier that day.

"So what do you think?" he asked.

"I think I was blindsided by a bus!" Kelvin replied. "I thought I had considered all the possible effects of the change in my project plan. I tried to explain this, but everyone acted as if I had threatened their jobs."

"In a way you did," Charlie stated. "Some people believe that change is the enemy."

"But these changes are important."

"I agree," Charlie said. "But successful change usually occurs in small steps. What's your top priority?"

"All the items on this list are top priorities," Kelvin said. "I haven't even gotten to the second tier."

"So what should you do to accomplish these top priorities?" Charlie asked.

"I guess I should reprioritize within my top tier, but what then?"

"The next step is to build support before the meeting, not during it." Charlie smiled. "Never go into a meeting where you haven't done your homework, especially when other people in the meeting can reduce your chance of success."

Questions:

1. What project management tasks should Kelvin perform before his next meeting?

2. What change management tasks should Kelvin perform before his next meeting, and how do these tasks fit within the project management process?

3. Had you been in Kelvin's place, what would you have done differently to prepare for this meeting?

Endnotes

1. Schein, Edgar H. "Kurt Lewin's Change Theory in the Field and in the Classroom: Notes Toward a Model of Managed Learning." Working paper, MIT Sloan School of Management. Accessed 7 July 2007 from *www.solonline.org/res/wp/10006.html#one*.

2. National Institute of Standards and Technology. *Background.* Accessed 27 May 2003 from *http://csrc.nist.gov/sec-cert/ca-background.html*.

3. Joint Task Force Transformation Initiative. NIST Special Publication 800-37, Rev. 1: Guide for Applying the Risk Management Framework to Federal Information Systems: A Security Life Cycle Approach. February 2010. Accessed 27 March 2010 from *http://csrc.nist.gov/publications/PubsSPs.html*.

4. Joint Task Force Transformation Initiative. NIST Special Publication 800-37, Rev. 1: Guide for Applying the Risk Management Framework to Federal Information Systems: A Security Life Cycle Approach. February 2010. Accessed 27 March 2010 from *http://csrc.nist.gov/publications/PubsSPs.html*.

5. Joint Task Force Transformation Initiative. NIST Special Publication 800-37, Rev. 1: Guide for Applying the Risk Management Framework to Federal Information Systems: A Security Life Cycle Approach. February 2010. Accessed 27 March 2010 from *http://csrc.nist.gov/publications/PubsSPs.html*.

6. Adapted from Joint Task Force Transformation Initiative. NIST Special Publication 800-37, Rev. 1: Guide for Applying the Risk Management Framework to Federal Information Systems: A Security Life Cycle Approach. February 2010. Accessed 27 March 2010 from *http://csrc.nist.gov/publications/PubsSPs.html*.

7. Joint Task Force Transformation Initiative. NIST Special Publication 800-37, Rev. 1: Guide for Applying the Risk Management Framework to Federal Information Systems: A Security Life Cycle Approach. February 2010. Accessed 27 March 2010 from *http://csrc.nist.gov/publications/PubsSPs.html*.

8. ISMS Certification Process. ISMS International User Group Ltd. Accessed 22 April 2007 from *www.iso27001certificates.com/certification_directory.htm*.

9. ISMS Certification Process. ISMS International User Group Ltd. Accessed 22 April 2007 from *www.iso27001certificates.com/certification_directory.htm*.

10

chapter 11

Security and Personnel

I think we need to be paranoid optimists.

ROBERT J. EATON, CHAIRMAN OF THE BOARD OF
MANAGEMENT, DAIMLERCHRYSLER AG (RETIRED)

Among Iris Majwubu's morning e-mail was a message from Charlie Moody, with the subject line "I need to see you." As she opened the message, Iris wondered why on earth the senior manager of IT needed to see her. The e-mail read:

From: Charles Moody [cmoody@slsco.com]

To: Iris Majwubu [imajwubu@slsco.com]

Subject: I need to see you

Iris,

Since you were a material witness in the investigation, I wanted to advise you of the status of the Magruder case. We completed all of the personnel actions on this matter yesterday, and it is now behind us.

You might like to know that the Corporate Security Department believes that you helped us resolve this security matter in its early stages, so no company assets were compromised.

Please set up an appointment with me in the next few days to discuss a few things.

—Charlie

Two days later, Iris entered Charlie Moody's office. He was sitting behind his desk and stood as she entered.

"Come in, Iris," Charlie said. "Have a seat."

Nervously, she choose a chair closest to the door, not anticipating that Charlie would come around his desk and sit down next to her. As he took his seat, Iris noticed that the folder in his hand looked like her personnel file, and she took a deep breath.

"I'm sure you're wondering why I asked you to meet with me," said Charlie. "The company really appreciates your efforts in the Magruder case. Because you followed policy and acted so quickly, we avoided a significant loss. You were right to bring that issue to your manager's attention rather than confronting Magruder directly. You not only made the right choice, but you acted quickly and showed a positive attitude throughout the whole situation—basically, I think you demonstrated an information security mindset. And that's why I'd like to offer you a transfer to Kelvin Urich's information security group. I think Urich's team would really benefit from having someone like you on board."

"I'm glad I was able to help," Iris said, "but I'm not sure what to say. I've been a DBA for three years here. I really don't know much about information security other than what I learned from the company training and awareness sessions."

"That's not a problem," Charlie said. "What you don't know you can learn." He smiled. "So how about it, are you interested in the job?"

Iris said, "It does sound interesting, but to be honest I hadn't been considering a career change." She paused for a moment, then added, "I am willing to think about it, though. But I have a few questions...."

LEARNING OBJECTIVES:

Upon completion of this material, you should be able to:

- Describe where and how the information security function should be positioned within organizations
- Explain the issues and concerns related to staffing the information security function
- Enumerate the credentials that information security professionals can earn to gain recognition in the field
- Illustrate how an organization's employment policies and practices can support the information security effort
- Identify the special security precautions that must be taken when using contract workers
- Explain the need for the separation of duties
- Describe the special requirements needed to ensure the privacy of personnel data

Introduction

When implementing information security, an organization must address various issues. First, it must decide how to position and name the security function. Second, the information security community of interest must plan for the proper staffing (or adjustments to the staffing plan) for the information security function. Third, the IT community of interest must assess the impact of information security on every IT function and adjust job descriptions and documented practices accordingly. Finally, the general management community of interest must work with information security professionals to integrate solid information security concepts into the personnel management practices of the organization.

In order to assess the effect that the changes will have on the organization's personnel management practices, the organization should conduct a behavioral feasibility study *before* the implementation phase—that is, in the analysis phase. The study should include an investigation of the levels of employee acceptance of—and resistance to—change. Employees often feel threatened when an organization is creating or enhancing an information security program. Employees may perceive the program to be a manifestation of a Big Brother attitude, and might have questions such as:

- Why is management monitoring my work or my e-mail?
- Will information security staff go through my hard drive looking for evidence to fire me?
- How can I do my job well now that I have to deal with the added delays of the information security technology?

As you learned in Chapter 10, resolving these sorts of doubts and reassuring employees about the role of information security programs are fundamental objectives of the implementation process. Thus, it is important to gather employee feedback early and respond to it quickly. This chapter explores the issues involved in positioning the information security unit within the organization as well as in staffing the information security function. It also discusses how to manage the many personnel challenges that arise across the organization and demonstrates why these challenges can (and should) be considered part of the organization's overall information security program.

Positioning and Staffing the Security Function

There are several valid choices for positioning the information security department within an organization. The model commonly used by large organizations places the information security department within the information technology department and usually designates as its head the CISO (or CSO, Chief Security Officer), who reports directly to the company's top computing executive, or CIO. Such a structure implies that the goals and objectives of the CISO and CIO are aligned. This is not always the case, however. By its very nature, an information security program can, at times, be at odds with the goals and objectives of the information technology department as a whole. The CIO, as the executive in charge of the organization's technology, strives to create *efficiency* in the processing and accessing of the organization's information, and thus, anything that limits access or slows information processing can impede the CIO's mission for the entire organization. The CISO's function is more like that of an internal auditor in that the CISO must direct the information security department to examine existing systems in order to discover information security faults and flaws in technology, software, and employees' activities and processes. These examinations can disrupt the processing and accessing of an organization's information. Because the addition of multiple layers of security inevitably slows the data users' access to information, information security may be viewed as a hindrance to the organization's operations. A good information security program maintains a careful balance between access and security.

Because the goals and objectives of CIOs and CISOs tend to contradict each other (in other words, the mission statements of the two functions conflict), the trend among many organizations has been to separate their information security function from their IT division. An article titled "Where the Chief Security Officer Belongs" published by the IT-industry magazine *InformationWeek* summarizes the reasoning behind this trend, perhaps as succinctly as possible: "the people who do and the people who watch shouldn't report to a common manager."[1] A survey conducted by the consulting firm Meta Group found that while only 3 percent of its clients actually position the information security department outside IT, these clients regarded this positioning as the mark of a forward-thinking organization. Another group, Forrester Research, concludes that the traditional structure of the CISO/CSO reporting to the CIO structure will be prevalent for years to come, but that this structure will begin to involve numerous variations in which various IT sections report information to the CSO and thereby provide IS departments the critical input and control they need to protect the organization's IT assets.[2] In general, the data seems to suggest that while many organizations believe that the CISO/CSO should function as an independent, executive-level decision maker, information security and IT are currently too closely aligned to separate into two departments.

Actually, there are many ways to position the information security program within an organization. In his book *Information Security Roles and Responsibilities Made Easy*, Charles Cresson Wood compiles many of the best practices regarding the positioning of information security programs from many industry groups. According to Wood, the information security function can be placed within any of the following organizational functions:

- IT function, as a peer of other subfunctions such as networks, applications development, and the help desk
- Physical security function, as a peer of physical security or protective services
- Administrative services function, as a peer of human resources or purchasing
- Insurance and risk management function
- Legal department

Once an information security function's organizational position has been determined, the challenge is to design a reporting structure that balances the competing needs of each of the communities of interest. The placement of the information security unit in the reporting structure often reflects the fact that no one actually wants to manage it, and thus the unit is moved from place to place within the organization without regard to the impact on its effectiveness. Organizations should find a rational compromise by placing the information security function where it can best balance its duty to enforce organizational policy (that is, monitor compliance) with its ability to provide the education, training, awareness, and customer service needed to make information security an integral part of the organizational culture.

Staffing the Information Security Function

The selection of information security personnel is based on a number of criteria, some of which are within the control of the organization and some of which are not. Consider the fundamental concept of supply and demand. When the demand for any commodity—for example, a critical technical skill—increases too quickly, supply initially fails to meet demand. Many future IS professionals seek to enter the security market by gaining the skills, experience, and credentials they need to meet this demand. In other words, they enter high-demand markets by changing jobs, going to school, or becoming trained. Until the new supply reaches the demand level, organizations must pay the higher costs associated with limited supply. Once the supply meets or exceeds the demand, the organizations that are hiring people with these skills become selective, and the amount they are willing to pay drops. Hiring trends swing back and forth like a clock pendulum, from one end (high demand, low supply) to the other (low demand, high supply), because the real economy, unlike an econometric model, is seldom in a state of equilibrium. In 2002 the information security industry was in the midst of a period of high demand, with few qualified and experienced individuals available for organizations seeking their services. The economic realities of 2003 through 2006—namely, a climate of lower demand for all IT professionals—have led to more limited job growth for information security practitioners. But the latest forecasts for hiring in IT in general and information security in particular project more openings than in many previous years. According to the Bureau of Labor Statistics, information security positions and IT positions in general are predicted to continue to grow must faster than average for all occupations, with almost 300,000 new jobs expected over the 2008–2018 decade.[3] According to a 2010 study, about 9 percent of CIOs are predicting being able to hire new IT (and InfoSec) professionals in the coming year, with information security being among the most difficult areas to hire for.[4]

Qualifications and Requirements
A number of factors influence an organization's hiring decisions. Because information security has only recently emerged as a separate discipline, the hiring decisions in this field are further complicated by a lack of understanding among organizations about what qualifications a potential information security hire should exhibit. Currently in many organizations, information security teams lack established roles and responsibilities. Establishing better hiring practices in an organization requires the following:

- The general management community of interest should learn more about the skills and qualifications for both information security positions and those IT positions that impact information security.

- Upper management should learn more about the budgetary needs of the information security function and the positions within it. This will enable management to make sound fiscal decisions for both the information security function and the IT functions that carry out many of the information security initiatives.

- The IT and general management communities should grant appropriate levels of influence and prestige to the information security function, and especially to the role of chief information security officer.

In most cases, organizations look for a technically qualified information security generalist who has a solid understanding of how an organization operates. In many other fields, the more specialized professionals become, the more marketable they are. In the information security discipline, however, overspecialization can be risky. It is important, therefore, to balance technical skills with general information security knowledge.

When hiring information security professionals, organizations frequently look for individuals who understand the following:

- How an organization operates at all levels

- That information security is usually a management problem and is seldom an exclusively technical problem

- How to work with people and collaborate with end users, and the importance of strong communications and writing skills

- The role of policy in guiding security efforts, and the role of education and training in making employees and other authorized users part of the solution, rather than part of the problem

- Most mainstream IT technologies (not necessarily as experts, but as generalists)

- The terminology of IT and information security

- The threats facing an organization and how these threats can become attacks

- How to protect an organization's assets from information security attacks

- How business solutions (including technology-based solutions) can be applied to solve specific information security problems

Entry into the Information Security Profession Many information security professionals enter the field through one of two career paths: ex-law enforcement and military personnel involved in national security and cyber-security tasks, who move from those environments into business-oriented information security; and technical professionals—networking experts, programmers, database administrators, and systems administrators—who find themselves working on information security applications and processes more often than on traditional IT assignments. In recent years, a third (perhaps in some sense more traditional) career path has developed: college students who select and tailor their degree programs to prepare for work in the field of information security. Figure 11-1 illustrates these career paths.

Many hiring managers in the information security field prefer to recruit security professionals who have proven IT skills and professional experience in another IT field. IT professionals who move into information security, however, tend to focus on technology—sometimes in place of general information security issues. Organizations can foster greater

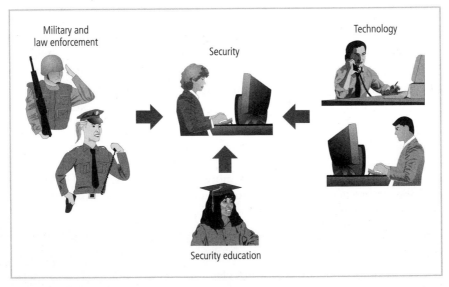

Figure 11-1 Career Paths to Information Security Positions

Source: Course Technology/Cengage Learning

professionalism in the information security discipline by expanding beyond the hiring of proven IT professionals and instead filling positions by matching qualified candidates to clearly defined information security roles and positions.

Information Security Positions The use of standard job descriptions can increase the degree of professionalism in the information security field as well as improve the consistency of roles and responsibilities among organizations. Organizations anticipating a revision of these roles and responsibilities can consult Charles Cresson Wood's book *Information Security Roles and Responsibilities Made Easy*, which offers a set of model job descriptions for information security positions. The book also identifies the responsibilities and duties of the members of the IT staff whose work involves information security.[5] Figure 11-2 illustrates a standard reporting structure for information security positions.

A study of information security positions conducted by Schwartz, Erwin, Weafer, and Briney found that the following positions can be classified into one of three areas: Those that *define* information security programs, those that *build* the systems and create the programs to implement the information security controls within the defined programs, and those that *administer* the information security control systems and programs that have been created.

> *Definers provide the policies, guidelines and standards ... They're the people who do the consulting and the risk assessment, who develop the product and technical architectures. These are senior people with a lot of broad knowledge, but often not a lot of depth ... [Builders are] the real techies, who create and install security solutions ... [Administrators] operate and administrate the security tools [and] the security monitoring function and ... continuously improve the processes, performing all the day-to-day ... work.... We often try to use the same people for all of these roles. We use builders all the time.... If you break your InfoSec professionals into these three groups, you can recruit them more efficiently, with the policy people being the more senior people, the builders being more technical and the operating people being those you can train to do a specific task.[6]*

Examples of some of the job titles that appear in Figure 11-2 are discussed in the following sections.

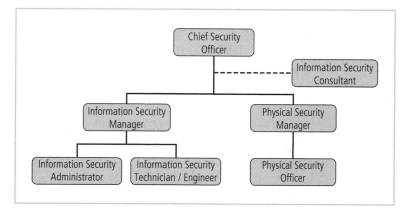

Figure 11-2 Positions in Information Securtiy

Source: Course Technology/Cengage Learning

Chief Information Security Officer (CISO or CSO) This is typically the top information security officer in the organization. As indicated earlier in the chapter, the CISO is usually not an executive-level position, and frequently the person in this role reports to the chief information officer. Though CISOs are business managers first and technologists second, they must be conversant in all areas of information security, including the technical, planning, and policy areas. In many cases, the CISO is the major definer or architect of the information security program. The CISO performs the following functions:

- Manages the overall information security program for the organization
- Drafts or approves information security policies
- Works with the CIO on strategic plans, develops tactical plans, and works with security managers on operational plans
- Develops information security budgets based on available funding
- Sets priorities for the purchase and implementation of information security projects and technology
- Makes decisions or recommendations on the recruiting, hiring, and firing of security staff
- Acts as the spokesperson for the information security team

The most common qualification for this type of position is the Certified Information Systems Security Professional (CISSP) accreditation, which is described later in this chapter. A graduate degree is also often required, although it may be from a number of possible disciplines, including information systems, computer science, another information technology field, criminal justice, military science, business, or other fields related to the broader topic of security. To qualify for this position, the candidate must demonstrate experience as a security manager (see the description of this position in the next section), and present experience with planning, policy, and budgets. As mentioned earlier, some organizations prefer to hire individuals with law enforcement experience. The following is an example of a typical job description for a CISO:

Position: *Director of Security*

Responsibilities: *Reporting to the Senior Vice President of Administration, the Director of Corporate Security will be responsible for all issues related to the security and protection of the company's employees, executives, facilities, proprietary data and information. Accountable for the planning and design of the company's security programs and procedures, this individual will facilitate protection from and resolution of theft, threats, and other situations that may endanger the well-being of the organization. Working through a small staff, the Director will be responsible for executive protection, travel advisories, employee background checks, and a myriad of other activities throughout the corporation on a case-by-case basis. The Director will serve as the company's chief liaison with law enforcement agencies and, most importantly, will serve as a security consultant to all of the company's autonomously run divisions. Travel requirements will be extensive.*

Qualifications: *The ideal candidate will have a successful background with a federal law enforcement agency, or other applicable experience, that will afford this individual an established network of contacts throughout the country. Additional private industry experience with a sizeable corporation—or as a consultant to same—is preferable. A proactive attitude with regard to security and protection is a must. The successful candidate must be capable of strategically assessing … client security needs and have a track record in areas such as crisis management, investigation, facility security, and executive protection. Finally, the candidate should have a basic understanding of the access and use of electronic information services as they apply to security issues. We seek candidates who are flexible enough to deal with varied business cultures and who possess the superior interpersonal skills to perform well in a consulting role where recommendations and advice are sought and valued, but perhaps not always acted upon. A college degree is required.*[7]

Security Manager Security managers are accountable for the day-to-day operation of the information security program. They accomplish objectives identified by the CISO and resolve issues identified by technicians. Management of technology requires an understanding of the technology administered, but does not necessarily require proficiency in the technology's configuration, operation, and fault resolution. (Note that there are a number of positions with titles that contain the word *manager* or other language that suggests management responsibilities, but only those people responsible for management functions, such as scheduling, setting relative priorities, or administering budgetary control, should be considered true managers.)

It is not uncommon for a candidate for this position to have a CISSP. Traditionally, managers earn the CISSP or CISM, and technical professionals earn the Global Information Assurance Certification (GIAC). (A number of certifications that are common in the information security field, such as CISSP, CISM, and GIAC, are discussed later in the chapter.) Security managers must have the ability to draft middle- and lower-level policies as well as standards and guidelines. They must have experience in traditional business matters: budgeting, project management, hiring, and firing. They must also be able to manage technicians, both in the assignment of tasks and the monitoring of activities. Experience with business continuity planning is usually a plus. The following is an example of a typical security manager job description. Note that there are several different types of security managers, as the security manager position is much more specialized than that of CISO. Thus, when applying for a particular job, you should read that job's description carefully, as this is the best way to determine exactly what the employer is looking for.

Position: *Information Security Manager*

Job description: *This management position reports to the Chef Information Security Officer. The successful candidate will manage the development of the information security programs and control systems in conformance with organizational policy and standards across the organization. This is a high-visibility role that involves the day-to-day management of IT Security staff and their career development. The principal accountabilities for this role are as follows:*

- *Develop and manage information security programs and control systems under the supervision of the CISO in conjunction with the evolving information security architecture of the organization.*

- *Monitor performance of information security programs and control systems to maintain alignment with organizational policy and common industry practices for emerging threats and technologies.*

- *Prepare and communicate risk assessments for business risk in software developments as well as ongoing systems events (to include merger, acquisition, and divestiture) and ensure effective risk management across the organization's IT Systems.*

- *Represent the information security organization in the organization's change management process.*

- *Perform assigned duties in the area of incident response management and disaster recovery response.*

- *Supervise assigned staff and perform other general management tasks as assigned including budgeting, staffing, and employee performance reviews.*

Compare the general job description above with this more specific job description found in a recent advertisement:

Position: *IT Security Compliance Manager*

Job description: *A job has arisen for an IT Security Compliance Manager reporting to the IT Security Manager. In this role you will manage the development of the client's IT Security standards and operate a compliance program to ensure conformance at all stages of the systems life cycle. This is a key, hands-on role with the job holder taking an active part in the delivery of the compliance program. The role will also involve the day-to-day management of IT Security staff and their career development. The principal accountabilities for this role are as follows:*

- *Develop and manage an IT security compliance program.*

- *Develop the client's security standards in line with industry standards and emerging threats and technologies.*

- *Identify IT-related business risk in new software and game developments and ensure that effective risk management solutions are identified and complied with.*

- *Manage and conduct IT security compliance reviews in conjunction with Operational and IT Audit staff.*

- *Conduct investigations into security breaches or vulnerabilities.*

Candidate profile: *The ideal candidate should have five years experience of managing the implementation of technical security controls and related operational procedures and must have sound business risk management skills. You must have a flexible approach to working and must be able and willing to work unsociable hours to meet the demands of the role.*[8]

The second example illustrates the confusion in the information security field regarding job titles and reporting relationships among information security professionals. Where the first job description identifies responsibilities for the position and describes points where information security interacts with other business functions, the second commingles responsibilities among several business functions and does not seem to reflect a clearly defined role for the position or the information security unit within the organization. Until some similarity in job titles and expected roles and responsibilities emerges, information security job candidates should carefully research roles and responsibilities for each position they apply to instead of relying solely on the job title.

Security Technician Security technicians are the technically qualified individuals tasked to configure firewalls, deploy IDPSs, implement security software, diagnose and troubleshoot problems, and coordinate with systems and network administrators to ensure that an organization's security technology is properly implemented. The position of security technician is often entry level, but to be hired in this role, candidates must possess some technical skills. This often poses a dilemma for applicants as many seeking to enter a new field find it is difficult to get a job without experience—which they can only attain by getting a job. Just as in the networking arena, security technicians tend to be specialized, focusing on one major security technology group (firewalls, IDPSs, servers, routers, or software) and further specializing in one particular software or hardware package, such as Check Point firewalls, Nokia firewalls, or Tripwire IDPSs. These areas are sufficiently complex to warrant a high level of specialization, but to move up in the corporate hierarchy, security technicians must expand their knowledge horizontally—that is, gain an understanding of the general organizational issues related to information security as well as its technical areas.

The technical qualifications and position requirements for a security technician vary. Organizations prefer the expert, certified, proficient technician. Regardless of the area, the particular job description covers some level of experience with a particular hardware and software package. Sometimes familiarity with a technology secures an applicant an interview; however, actual experience in using the technology is usually required. The following is a typical job announcement for a security technician:

Position: *Firewall Engineering Consultant*

Job Description: *Working for an exciting customer-focused security group within one of the largest managed network providers in Europe. You will have the opportunity to expand your experience and gain all the technical and professional support to achieve within the group. Must have experience to third line technical support of firewall technologies. Check Point certified. Experienced in Nokia systems.*

Package: *Possible company car, discretionary bonus, private health care, on-call pay, and overtime pay.*[9]

Because overtime and on-call pay are listed, this is probably an hourly position rather than a salaried one, which is commonly the case for security technician positions.

Credentials for Information Security Professionals

As mentioned earlier, many organizations seek industry-recognized certifications to screen candidates for the required level of technical proficiency. Unfortunately, however, most of the existing certifications are relatively new and not fully understood by hiring organizations. The certifying bodies are working hard to educate employers and potential professionals on the value and qualifications of their certificate programs. In the meantime, employers are trying to understand the match between certifications and position requirements, and hopeful professionals are trying to gain meaningful employment based on their newly received certifications.

(ISC)² Certifications

The International Information Systems Security Certification Consortium (ISC)² (see *www .isc2.org*) is considered one the foremost organizations offering information security certifications today. Currently (ISC)² offers three primary certifications and three specializations for its flagship certification. (ISC)² also offers an intermediate, or in-progress, certification to allow candidates who have not completed the experiential requirements of a certification to provide evidence of progress toward completing the certification.

Certified Information Systems Security Professional (CISSP) In order to sit
for the CISSP exam, the candidate must possess at least three years of direct full-time security professional work experience in one or more of the ten domains of information security knowledge listed below. The CISSP exam itself, which covers all ten domains, consists of 250 multiple-choice questions and must be completed within six hours.

- Access Control
- Application Security
- Business Continuity and Disaster Recovery Planning
- Cryptography
- Information Security and Risk Management
- Legal, Regulations, Compliance, and Investigations
- Operations Security
- Physical (Environmental) Security
- Security Architecture and Design
- Telecommunications and Network Security

The CISSP certification requires both the successful completion of the examination and an endorsement by a qualified third party, typically another CISSP-certified professional, the candidate's employer, or a licensed, certified, or commissioned professional. This is to ensure that the candidate meets the qualifications and requirements of the overall process. The breadth and depth covered in each of the ten domains makes the CISSP one of the most difficult-to-attain certifications on the market. Once a candidate receives the CISSP, he or she must earn a specific number of continuing education credits every three years to retain it.

CISSP Concentrations In recent years, the CISSP certification program has added a set of
concentration exams: the ISSEP (Information Systems Security Engineering Professional), the ISSAP (Information Systems Security Architecture Professional), and the ISSMP (Information Systems Security Management Professional). These certification extensions are designed to work in tandem with the CISSP credential; to sit for any of these concentration examinations, one must be a CISSP professional in good standing. A CISSP may demonstrate more in-depth knowledge in information security architecture by obtaining the ISSAP credential, much like

an English major at a university might demonstrate knowledge in Shakespeare by concentrating in British Literature.[10]

The development of the ISSEP concentration exam and its topical content are described by (ISC)² as follows:

> *ISSEP stands for Information Systems Security Engineering Professional. ISSEP was developed under a joint agreement between (ISC)² and the United States National Security Agency, Information Assurance Directorate (NSA/IAD). The motivation and justification for NSA's involvement in this project is found in NSD 42 and the Federal Technology Transfer Act of 1986 (15 U.S.C. Section 3710A).... The ISSEP provides the means for (ISC)² to offer CISSPs a mechanism to demonstrate specific competence in the concentrated area of information security engineering.... The major domains of the ISSEP examination are: Systems Security Engineering, Certification and Accreditation, Technical Management, and U.S. Government Information Assurance Regulations.[11]*

The development of the ISSAP concentration exam and its topical content are described by (ISC)² as follows:

> *ISSAP stands for Information Systems Security Architecture Professional. The development of concentration examinations is a direct response to (ISC)² research indicating that these needs of information security professionals were not being met. This examination is designed to provide CISSPs with a mechanism to demonstrate competence in the more in-depth and concentrated requirements of information security architecture, within the broader scope of information security knowledge identified in the CBK and required for CISSP certification. The major domains for this examination are: Access Control, Systems and Methodologies, Telecommunications and Network Security, Cryptography, Requirements Analysis & Security Standards, Guidelines, Criteria, and Technology Related BCP and DRP.[12]*

The development of the ISSMP concentration exam and its topical content are described by (ISC)² as follows:

> *ISSMP stands for Information Systems Security Management Professional. The development of concentration examinations is a direct response to (ISC)² research indicating that these needs of information security professionals were not being met. This examination is designed to provide CISSPs with a mechanism to demonstrate competence in the more in-depth and concentrated requirements of information security management.... The major domains for this examination are: Enterprise Security Management Practices, Enterprise-Wide System Development Security, Overseeing Compliance of Operations Security, Understanding BCP, DRP, and COOP, and Law, Investigations, Forensics, and Ethics.[13]*

Each CISSP concentration exam consists of 125 to 150 questions, depending on the subject matter, and has an allowed testing time of three hours. When a candidate passes the concentration exam, the credential obtained runs concurrently with the underlying CISSP credential. During subsequent certification periods, twenty of the 120 continuing professional education (CPE) hours required for the underlying CISSP certificate must be in the area of concentration. For example, if a CISSP-certified professional took the ISSMP concentration exam and passed, he or she would be required to document that at least twenty of the total 120 CPE hours required for the CISSP certificate were in the area of information security management.[14]

Systems Security Certified Practitioner (SSCP) Given the difficulty involved in mastering all ten domains, many information security professionals seek other, less rigorous certifications. In response, (ISC)² developed the Systems Security Certified Practitioner, or SSCP. SSCP was designed to recognize mastery of an international standard for information security and a common body of knowledge (sometimes called the CBK). The SSCP certification is oriented toward the security administrator. Like the CISSP, the SSCP certification is more applicable to the information security manager than the technician, because most questions focus on the operational nature of information security. In other words, the SSCP focuses "on practices, roles, and responsibilities as defined by experts from major IS industries."[15] Even so, an information security technician seeking advancement can benefit from acquiring this certification.

The SSCP exam consists of 125 multiple-choice questions and must be completed within three hours. Instead of the ten domains of the CISSP, the SSCP covers seven domains:

- Access Controls
- Cryptography
- Malicious Code and Activity
- Monitoring and Analysis
- Networks and Communications
- Risk, Response, and Recovery
- Security Operations and Administration

The SSCP is considered by many to be the little brother of the CISSP. It is a widely recognized certification and is easier to obtain than the CISSP. The seven domains are not a subset of the CISSP domains, but are an independent organization of similar content. The CBK defined for the SSCP contains slightly more technical content than the CBK for the CISSP. Just as with the CISSP, an SSCP recipient must earn continuing education credits to retain the certification, or else retake the exam.

Associate of (ISC)² The Associate of (ISC)² program is geared toward those who want to take the CISSP or SSCP exams before obtaining the requisite experience for certification. "The Associate of (ISC)² program is a mechanism for information security professionals, who are still in the process of acquiring the necessary experience to become CISSPs or SSCPs, to become associated with (ISC)² and obtain career-related support during this early period in his or her information security career."[16] Once candidates pass the examination and subscribe to the (ISC)² Code of Ethics, they receive the Associate Certification indicating satisfactory progress toward a certification. Once the experiential requirements have been met, they receive their CISSP or SSCP.

Certification and Accreditation Professional (CAP) The newest certification from (ISC)² is the Certification and Accreditation Professional (CAP), developed in cooperation with the U.S. Department of State's Office of Information Assurance. Certification and accreditation (C&A) was discussed in detail in Chapter 10. In order to qualify for the CAP certification, applicants must have a minimum of two years experience in one or more of the CAP common body of knowledge domains and thus be prepared to:

- Initiate the preparation phase (formerly known as the certification and accreditation process and certification phase)
- Perform the execution phase (formerly known as the accreditation process)
- Perform the maintenance phase (formerly known as continuous monitoring)
- Understand the purpose of security authorization (formerly known as certification and accreditation, or C&A)

The applicant must also pass the CAP examination, which consists of 125 questions. The recommended reading for this certification includes many documents from the NIST SP-800 series, including SP 800-18, -30, -37, -53, -60, and FIPS 199. The CAP candidate must also agree to the $(ISC)^2$ Code of Ethics and provide background and criminal history information.

ISACA Certifications

The Information Systems Audit and Control Association (ISACA) was founded by a group of individuals with similar jobs in computer auditing who sought to provide a centralized source of information and guidance. Today ISACA offers two well-recognized and respected certifications: the CISA certification for auditing, networking, and security professionals, and the CISM certification for information security management professionals. All ISACA certifications have the following common requirements:

- Successful completion of the requisite examination
- Experience as an information systems auditor, with a minimum of five years' professional experience in an area of direct interest to the certification
- Agreement to the ISACA Code of Professional Ethics
- Continuing education policy that requires maintenance fees and a minimum of twenty contact hours of continuing education each year and a minimum of 120 contact hours over the three-year certification period

Certified Information Systems Auditor (CISA) Although it does not primarily focus on information security certification, the Certified Information Systems Auditor or CISA certification covers many information security components. The CISA certification is open to those who have passed the CISA exam. The exam is offered once a year, contains 200 multiple-choice questions, and covers the following areas of information systems auditing:

- IS audit process (10 percent)—Provide IS audit services in accordance with IS audit standards, guidelines, and best practices to assist the organization in ensuring that its information technology and business systems are protected and controlled.
- IT governance (15 percent)—Provide assurance that the organization has the structure, policies, accountability, mechanisms, and monitoring practices in place to achieve the requirements of corporate governance of IT.

- Systems and infrastructure life cycle (16 percent)—Provide assurance that the management practices for the development/acquisition, testing, implementation, maintenance, and disposal of systems and infrastructure will meet the organization's objectives.

- IT service delivery and support (14 percent)—Provide assurance that the IT service management practices will ensure delivery of the level of services required to meet the organization's objectives.

- Protection of information assets (31 percent)—Provide assurance that the security architecture (policies, standards, procedures, and controls) ensures the confidentiality, integrity, and availability of information assets.

- Business continuity and disaster recovery (14 percent)—Provide assurance that, in the event of a disruption, the business continuity and disaster recovery processes will ensure the timely resumption of IT services while minimizing the business impact.[17]

The CISA applicant must provide evidence of a minimum of five years of professional IS audit, control, assurance or security work experience, with a waiver or substitution for up to two years based on education or previous certification. (Note: In 2011, the CISA exam will be revised to reflect the results of ISACA's new job practice study, undertaken every five years.)

Certified Information Security Manager (CISM) The second ISACA certificate program is the CISM. This certificate is open to those who have passed the CISM requirements, which are similar to the CISA. The applicant must pass the 200-question multiple-choice exam, which covers the following areas of information security practices:

- Information security governance (23 percent)

- Information risk management (22 percent)

- Information security program development (17 percent)

- Information security program management (24 percent)

- Incident management and response (14 percent)

The applicant must also provide evidence of five years of professional work experience in the field of information security, with a waiver or substitution of up to two years for education or previous certification. Many industry professionals consider the CISM to be the top managerial certification in information security, or at least as desirable as the CISSP.

SANS Global Information Assurance Certification (GIAC)

The System Administration, Networking, and Security Organization, better known as SANS (*www.sans.org*), developed a series of technical security certifications in 1999 that are known as the Global Information Assurance Certification (GIAC) family of certifications (see *www.giac.org*). When the GIAC was established, no technical certifications were available elsewhere—anyone who wished to be certified to work in the technical security field could obtain only vendor-specific networking or computing certifications, such as the MCSE (Microsoft Certified Systems Engineer) or CNE (Certified Novell Engineer). Now, individuals can choose to attain the various GIAC certifications separately or to pursue a comprehensive certification known as the GIAC Security Expert (GSE).

Unlike other certifications, the GIAC certifications require the applicant to complete a written practical assignment that tests the applicant's ability to apply skills and knowledge. These assignments are submitted to the SANS Information Security Reading Room for review by security practitioners, potential certificate applicants, and others with an interest in information security. Only when the practical assignment is complete is the candidate allowed to take the online exam. Once an individual has earned a particular GIAC certification, he or she can opt to earn an advanced recognition in that area by pursuing GIAC Gold Status for that certification by "completing a technical report covering an important area of security related to the certification."[18]

GIAC certifications are organized into five areas: audit, legal, management, security administration, and software security. Additional concentrations in malware and compliance can be pursued once the GSE certification has been earned. Individual certifications include:

- Audit
  - GIAC Certified ISO-17799 Specialist (G7799)
  - GIAC Systems and Network Auditor (GSNA)
- Legal
  - GIAC Legal Issues (GLEG)
- Management
  - GIAC Information Security Professional (GISP)
  - GIAC Security Leadership Certification (GSLC)
  - GIAC Certified Project Manager Certification (GCPM)
- Security Administration
  - GIAC Information Security Fundamentals (GISF)
  - GIAC Security Essentials Certification (GSEC)
  - GIAC Web Application Penetration Tester (GWAPT)
  - GIAC Certified Forensic Analyst (GCFA)
  - GIAC Certified Enterprise Defender (GCED)
  - GIAC Certified Firewall Analyst (GCFW)
  - GIAC Certified Intrusion Analyst (GCIA)
  - GIAC Certified Incident Handler (GCIH)
  - GIAC Certified Windows Security Administrator (GCWN)
  - GIAC Certified UNIX Security Administrator (GCUX)
  - GIAC Certified Penetration Tester (GPEN)
  - GIAC Reverse Engineering Malware (GREM)
  - GIAC Assessing Wireless Networks (GAWN)
- Software Security
  - GIAC Secure Software Programmer—.NET (GSSP-NET)
  - GIAC Secure Software Programmer—Java (GSSP-JAVA)[19]

GIAC distinguishes between a certificate (indicating completion of the requirements of a one- to two-day course) and a certification (indicating completion of a five- to six-day course).

11

Certificate applicants typically have ten weeks to compete the certificate requirements, where as certification applications have up to four months.

For more information see *www.giac.org/certifications/roadmap.php*, from which this information is drawn.

Security Certified Program (SCP)

One of the newer certifications in the information security discipline is the Security Certified Program's hands-on IT security certifications (see *www.securitycertified.net*). The SCP certifications provide three tracks: the SCNS (Security Certified Network Specialist), the SCNP (Security Certified Network Professional), and the SCNA (Security Certified Network Architect). All three tracks are designed for the security technician and have dominant technical components, although the SCNA also emphasizes authentication principles. Also, even though the SCNS, SCNP, and SCNA each have a networking focus, they concentrate on network security rather than on true networking (which, for example, is covered by MSCE and CNE).

The SCNS track focuses on tactical perimeter defense with only one exam focused on its specialization:

- Tactical Perimeter Defense (TPD) covers seven domains:

Examination Domain[20]	Percentage of Exam
1.0 – Network Defense Fundamentals	5%
2.0 – Hardening Routers and Access Control Lists	10%
3.0 – Implementing IPSec and Virtual Private Networks	10%
4.0 – Advanced TCP/IP	15%
5.0 – Securing Wireless Networks	15%
6.0 – Designing and Configuring Intrusion Detection Systems	20%
7.0 – Designing and Configuring Firewall Systems	25%

The SCNP track follows the SCNS exam and focuses on firewalls and intrusion detection. It requires one exam covering the following domains:

- Strategic Infrastructure Security (SIS) covers eight domains:

Examination Domain[21]	Percentage of Exam
1.0 – Analyzing Packet Structures	5%
2.0 – Creating Security Policies	5%
3.0 – Performing Risk Analysis	5%
4.0 – Ethical Hacking Techniques	10%
5.0 – Internet and WWW Security	15%
6.0 – Cryptography	20%
7.0 – Hardening Linux Computers	20%
8.0 – Hardening Windows Server 2003	20%

The SCNA program follows the SCNP and focuses more on building trusted networks, including biometrics and PKI. The two exams in the SCNA certification are:

- Enterprise Security Implementation (ESI) covers nine domains:

Examination Domain[20]	Percentage of Exam
1.0 – Law and Legislation	5%
2.0 – Forensics	15%
3.0 – Wireless Security	15%
4.0 – Secure E-mail	20%
5.0 – Biometrics	20%
6.0 – PKI Policy and Architecture	20%
7.0 – Digital Certificates and Digital Signatures	25%
8.0 – Cryptography	20%
9.0 – Strong Authentication	25%

- The Solution Exam – covers all four of the SCP courses and is solely based on security scenarios.

Although not as detailed as the GIAC certifications, SCP programs provide those new to the career field of information security a useful mechanism to getting started and are a vendor-neutral means by which a practitioner can document professional and technical skills.

CompTIA's Security+

CompTIA (*www.comptia.org*) has introduced the first truly vendor-neutral technical professional IT certifications—the A+ series. Offered as part of the A+ program, the Security+ certification focuses on the key skills that are necessary to perform security but is not tied to a particular software or hardware vendor package. According to the CompTIA Web site, "the CompTIA Security+ certification tests for security knowledge mastery of an individual with two years on-the-job networking experience, with emphasis on security. The exam covers industry-wide topics, including communication security, infrastructure security, cryptography, access control, authentication, external attack and operational and organization security."[21] In order to obtain the Security+ certification, applicants only have to take a single 100-question exam within 90 minutes, offered through most online testing centers. Successful applicants score at least 750 on a scale of 100–900. The exam objectives focus on:

- Systems security (21 percent)
- Network infrastructure (20 percent)
- Access control (17 percent)
- Assessments and audits (15 percent)
- Cryptography (15 percent)
- Organizational security (12 percent)[22]

11

Certified Computer Examiner (CCE)®

The Certified Computer Examiner (CCE)® certification is a computer forensics certification provided by the International Society of Forensic Computer Examiners (*www.isfce.com*). To complete the CCE certification process, the applicant must:

- Have no criminal record
- Meet minimum experience, training, or self-training requirements
- Abide by the certification's code of ethical standards
- Pass an online examination
- Successfully perform actual forensic examinations on three test media

The CCE certification process covers the following areas:

- Acquisition, marking, handling, and storage of evidence procedures
- Chain of custody
- Essential core forensic computer examination procedures
- The rules of evidence as they relate to computer examinations
- Basic PC hardware construction and theory
- Very basic networking theory
- Basic data recovery techniques
- Authenticating MS Word documents and accessing and interpreting metadata
- Basic CDR recording processes and accessing data on CDR media
- Basic password recovery techniques
- Basic Internet issues

This certification also has concentrations and endorsements corresponding to the various operating systems present in the current business environments. A CCE who earns three or more of these endorsements qualifies as Master Certified Computer Examiner (MCCE).[23]

Related Certifications

There are a number of certifications that are related to the field of information security or contain information security components. Such certifications have been developed by the following companies and associations:[24]

- Prosoft
  - CIW—Security Professional, requires Master CIW Administrator Certification which includes four exams; approximate cost $500 ($125 per exam)
- RSA Security
  - RSA/CSE—RSA Certified Systems Engineer, requires one exam
  - RSA/CA—RSA Certified Administrator, requires one exam
  - RSA/CI—RSA Certified Instructors, requires CSE or CA Cert + workshop
- CheckPoint
  - Check Point Certified Security Principles Associate (CCSPA)
  - Check Point Certified Security Administrator (CCSA)

- Check Point Certified Security Expert (CCSE)
- Check Point Certified Security Expert Plus (CCSE Plus)
- Check Point Certified Managed Security Expert (CCMSE)
- Check Point Certified Managed Security Expert Plus VSX (CCMSE Plus VSX)
- Check Point Certified Master Architect (CCMA)

- Cisco

  Cisco offers five levels of certification: entry, associate, professional, expert, and architect, along seven different paths:
  - Routing and Switching
  - Design
  - Network Security
  - Service Provider
  - Storage Networking
  - Voice
  - Wireless

The details of these certifications are too varied to cover here. Additional information on these and other certifications can be found on these companies' Web sites.

Certification Costs

Certifications cost money, and the better certifications can be quite expensive to attain. Some certification exams can run as much as $650 per examination, and their entire educational track can cost several thousand dollars. The cost of the formal training required to prepare for the certification can also be significant. While these courses should not serve as a candidate's only means of preparation, they can help round out knowledge and fill in gaps. As mentioned earlier, some of the exams, such as the CISSP, are very broad and others very technical. Even an experienced professional would find it difficult to sit for one of these exams without some preparation. Many candidates teach themselves using trade books. Others prefer the structure of classroom training, because it includes practicing the technical components on equipment the candidate may not be able to access on his or her own. Certifications are designed to recognize experts in their respective fields, and the cost of certification is meant to limit the number of candidates who take exams just to see if they can pass. Most examinations admit only candidates with two or three years of expertise in the skills being tested. Before attempting a certification exam, the successful candidate does all the required homework. Candidates for certification should look into the exam criteria, purpose, and requirements in order to ensure that the time and energy devoted to pursuing the certification are well spent. Figure 11-3 shows several approaches to preparing for security certification.

Advice for Information Security Professionals

As a future information security professional, you may benefit from the following suggestions:

- Always remember: business before technology. Technology solutions are tools for solving business problems. Information security professionals are sometimes guilty of looking for ways to apply the newest technology to problems that do not require technology-based solutions.

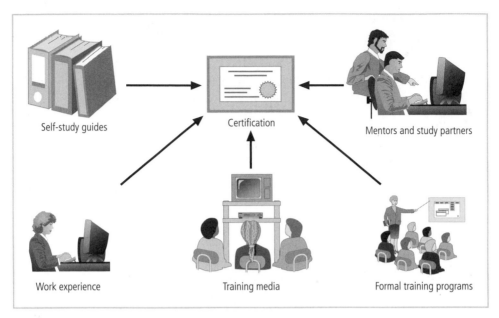

Figure 11-3 Preparing for Security Certification

Source: Course Technology/Cengage Learning

- When evaluating a problem, look at the source of the problem first, determine what factors impact the problem, and see where organizational policy can lead you in the design of a solution that is independent of technology; then use technology to deploy the controls necessary for the implementation of the solution. Technology can provide elegant solutions to some problems, but others it only exacerbates.

- Your job is to protect the organization's information and information systems resources. Never lose sight of the goal: protection.

- Be heard and not seen. Information security should be transparent to the users. With minor exceptions, the actions taken to protect the information should not interfere with the users' actions. Information security supports the work of end users, not the other way around. The only routine communications that should be conducted from the security team to the users should be the periodic awareness messages, training announcements, newsletters, and e-mails.

- Know more than you say, and be more skillful than you let on. Don't try to impress users, managers, and other nontechnical people with your level of knowledge and experience. One day you just might run into a Jedi master of information security who puts you in your place.

- Speak *to* users, not *at* them. While you are talking to users, use their language, not yours. Users aren't impressed with techno-babble and jargon. They may not comprehend the TLAs (three-letter acronyms), technical components, software, and hardware necessary to protect their systems, but they do know how to short-circuit your next budget request or pick out the flaws in your business report.

- Your education is never complete. As sensitive as you are to the fact that information technology is ever evolving, you must be equally sensitive to the fact that information security education is never complete. Just when you think you have mastered the latest skills, you will encounter changes in threats, protection technology, your business environment, or the regulatory environment. As a security professional, you must expect to continue with the learning process throughout your entire career. This is best accomplished by seeking out periodic seminars, training programs, and formal education. Even if the organization (or your pocketbook) cannot afford the more extensive and expensive training programs and conferences, you can keep abreast of the market by reading trade literature (magazines), textbooks, and news articles on security. You can also subscribe to the many mailing lists for information security professionals. Several are listed in the Offline entitled "What's in a Name?" Join at least one professional information security association, such as the Information Systems Security Association (*www.issa.org*). Whatever approach you take, keep on top of the reading, never stop learning, and make yourself the best-informed security professional possible. It can only enhance your worth to the organization and your career.

Offline
What's in a Name?

Here are some of the job titles listed in the job search databases that were reviewed to prepare this section. See if you can guess the position level based on the title.

- Senior security analyst
- SAP security analyst
- Security supervisor
- Direct loss prevention manager
- Security officer (not a guard job)
- Loss prevention consultant
- Site supervisor—security
- Safeguards and security specialist

To perform your own job title search or to search for an actual job in the field of information security, you can begin by reviewing the job search databases at the following Web sites:

- Commercial job listing sites such as *www.justsecurityjobs.com*, *www.itsecurity jobs.com*, and *securityjobs.net*
- U.S. Federal agency position listings such as *www.usajobs.gov*
- Job listing sites associated with periodicals such as *www.csoonline.com/security/ jobs/1* and *http://online.wsj.com/public/page/news-career-jobs.html*
- Job listing by professional organization such as *www.isc2.org/careers/* and *www. isaca.org* (click on Career Center)

Employment Policies and Practices

To create an environment in which information security is taken seriously, an organization should make information security a documented part of every employee's job description. In other words, the general management community of interest should integrate solid information security concepts into the organization's employment policies and practices. The section that follows examines the important information security-related issues associated with recruiting, hiring, firing, and managing human resources in an organization.

From an information security perspective, the hiring of employees is a responsibility laden with potential security pitfalls. Therefore, the CISO and information security manager should establish a dialogue with the human resources department to provide information security input to the guidelines used for hiring all personnel. Figure 11-4 highlights some of the hiring issues.

Job Descriptions

The process of integrating information security perspectives into the hiring process begins with reviewing and updating all job descriptions. To prevent people from applying for positions based solely on access to sensitive information, the organization should avoid revealing access privileges to prospective employees when it advertises open positions.

Interviews

Some interviews with job candidates are conducted with members of the human resources staff, and others include members of the department for which the new position is being offered. An opening within the information security department creates a unique opportunity for the security manager to educate HR on the various certifications and the specific experience each certification requires, as well as the qualifications of a good candidate. In all other areas of the organization, information security should, for the same reason mentioned during

Figure 11-4 Hiring Issues

Source: Course Technology/Cengage Learning

the discussion of job descriptions, advise HR to limit the information provided to the candidate about the responsibilities and access rights that the new hire would have. For those organizations that include onsite visits as part of their initial or follow-up interviews, it is important to exercise caution when showing a candidate around the facility. Avoid tours through secure and restricted sites. Candidates who are shown around may be able to retain enough information about the operations or information security functions to become a threat.

Background Checks

A background check should be conducted before an organization extends an offer to a candidate. A background check is an investigation into the candidate's past that specifically looks for criminal or other types of behavior that could indicate potential for future misconduct. There are a number of government regulations that govern what the organization can investigate and how much of the information uncovered can be allowed to influence the hiring decision. The security manager and HR manager should discuss these matters with legal counsel to determine what state and federal (and perhaps international) regulations impact the hiring process.

Background checks differ in the level of detail and depth with which they examine a candidate. In the military, background checks determine the individual's level of security classification, a requirement for many positions. In the business world, a background check can determine the level of trust the business places in the candidate. People being considered for security positions should expect to be subjected to a moderately high-level background check. Those considering careers in law enforcement or high-security positions may even be required to submit to polygraph tests. The following is a list of various types of background checks with the type of information each looks into:

- Identity checks: Validation of identity and Social Security number
- Education and credential checks: Validation of institutions attended, degrees and certifications earned, and certification status
- Previous employment verification: Validation of where candidates worked, why they left, what they did, and for how long
- Reference checks: Validation of references and integrity of reference sources
- Worker's compensation history: Investigation of claims from worker's compensation
- Motor vehicle records: Investigation of driving records, suspensions, and DUIs
- Drug history: Screening for drugs and drug usage, past and present
- Credit history: Investigation of credit problems, financial problems, and bankruptcy
- Civil court history: Investigation of involvement as the plaintiff or defendant in civil suits
- Criminal court history: Investigation of criminal background, arrests, convictions, and time served

As mentioned, there are federal regulations regarding the use of personal information in employment practices, including the Fair Credit Reporting Act (FCRA), which governs the activities of consumer credit reporting agencies and the uses of the information procured from these agencies.[25] These credit reports generally contain information on a job candidate's credit history, employment history, and other personal data.

Among other things, the FCRA prohibits employers from obtaining these reports unless the candidate is informed in writing that such a report will be requested as part of the employment process. FCRA also allows the candidate to request information on the nature and type of reporting used in making the employment decision and subsequently enables the candidate to learn the content of these reports. The FCRA also restricts the periods of time these reports can address. If the candidate earns less than $75,000 per year, the report can contain only seven years' worth of negative credit information. If the candidate earns $75,000 or more per year, there is no time limitation. Note that "any person who knowingly and willfully obtains information on a consumer from a consumer reporting agency under false pretenses shall be fined under title 18, United States Code, imprisoned for not more than two years, or both."[26]

Employment Contracts

Once a candidate has accepted a job offer, the employment contract becomes an important security instrument. Many of the policies discussed in Chapter 5, specifically the fair and responsible use policies, require an employee to agree in writing to monitoring and nondisclosure agreements. If an existing employee refuses to sign these contracts, the security personnel are placed in a difficult situation. They may not be able to force the employee to sign nor to deny the employee access to the systems necessary to perform his or her duties. With new employees, however, security personnel are in a different situation since the procedural step of policy acknowledgment can be made a requirement of employment. Policies that govern employee behavior and are applied to all employees may be classified as "employment contingent upon agreement." This classification means the employee is not actually employed until he or she agrees in a written affidavit to conform with these binding organizational policies. Some organizations choose to execute the remainder of the employment contract *after* the candidate has signed the security agreements. Although this may seem harsh, it is a necessary component of the security process. Employment contracts may also contain restrictive clauses regarding the creation and ownership of intellectual property while the candidate is employed by the organization. These provisions may require the employee to protect the information assets of the organization actively—especially those assets that are critical to security.

New Hire Orientation

When new employees are introduced into the organization's culture and workflow, they should receive as part of their employee orientation an extensive information security briefing. All major policies should be explained, along with the procedures for performing necessary security operations and the new position's other information security requirements. In addition, the levels of authorized access should be outlined for the new employees, and training should be provided to them regarding the secure use of information systems. By the time new employees are ready to report to their positions, they should be thoroughly briefed on the security component of their particular jobs, as well as the rights and responsibilities of all personnel in the organization.

On-the-Job Security Training

The organization should integrate the security awareness education described in Chapter 5 into a new hire's ongoing job orientation and make it a part of every employee's on-the-job security training. Keeping security at the forefront of employees' minds helps minimize employee mistakes and is, therefore, an important part of the information security team's mission. Formal external and informal internal seminars should also be used to increase the security awareness level of employees, especially that of security employees. An example of the importance of proper and ongoing security training awareness of employees can be found in *The 9/11 Commission Report*, which is a congressional examination (published in 2004) of the terrorist attacks of September 11, 2001. As the following excerpt shows, upon reviewing the videotapes made at the security checkpoints in airports when the terrorists were passing through, security investigators found the security process inadequate, not from a technological standpoint, but from a human one:

> *When the local civil aviation security office of the Federal Aviation Administration (FAA) later investigated these security screening operations, the screeners recalled nothing out of the ordinary. They could not recall that any of the passengers they screened were CAPPS selectees. We asked a screening expert to review the videotape of the hand-wanding, and he found the quality of the screener's work to have been "marginal at best." The screener should have "resolved" what set off the alarm; and in the case of both Moqed and Hazmi, it was clear that he did not.*[27]

This excerpt illustrates how physical security is dependent on the human element. The maintenance of information security also depends heavily on the consistent vigilance of people. In many information security breaches, the hardware and software usually accomplished what they were designed to do, but people failed to make the correct decisions and follow-up choices. Education and regular training of employees and authorized users are important elements of information security—and therefore cannot be ignored.

Evaluating Performance

To heighten information security awareness and minimize workplace behavior that poses risks to information security, organizations should incorporate information security components into employee performance evaluations. For example, if employees have been observed writing system passwords on notes stuck to their monitor, they should be warned, and if such behavior continues, they should be reminded of their failure to comply with the organization's information security regulations during their annual performance review. In general, employees pay close attention to job performance evaluations and are more likely to be motivated to take information security seriously if their performance with respect to information security tasks and responsibilities is documented in these evaluations.

Termination

Leaving the organization may or may not be a decision made by the employee. Organizations may downsize, be bought out or taken over, shut down, run out of business, or simply be forced to lay off, fire, or relocate their work force. In any event, when an employee leaves an organization, there are a number of security-related issues that arise. Key among these is the continuity of protection of all information to which the employee had access. Therefore, when an employee prepares to leave an organization, the following tasks must be performed:

- Access to the organization's systems must be disabled.
- Removable media must be returned.

- Hard drives must be secured.
- File cabinet locks must be changed.
- Office door locks must be changed.
- Keycard access must be revoked.
- Personal effects must be removed from the organization's premises.

After the employee has delivered keys, keycards, and other business property, he or she should be escorted from the premises.

In addition to the tasks listed above, many organizations use an **exit interview** to remind the employee of contractual obligations, such as nondisclosure agreements, and to obtain feedback on the employee's tenure in the organization. At this time, the employee should be reminded that should he or she fail to comply with contractual obligations, civil or criminal action may be initiated.

In reality, most employees are allowed to clean out their own offices and collect their personal belongings, and simply asked to return their keys. From a security standpoint, these procedures are risky and lax, for they expose the organization's information to disclosure and theft. To minimize such risks, an organization should ideally have security-minded termination procedures that are followed consistently—in other words, that are followed regardless of what level of trust the organization had placed in the employee and what the level of cordiality is generally maintained in the office environment. But this kind of universally consistent approach is a difficult and awkward practice to implement, which is why it's not often applied. Given the realities of workplaces, the simplest and best method for handling the out-processing of an employee may be to select, based on the employee's reasons for leaving, one of the scenarios that follows.

Hostile departures include termination for cause, permanent downsizing, temporary lay-off, or some instances of quitting. Before the employee knows that he or she is leaving, or as soon as the hostile resignation is tendered, the security staff should terminate all logical and keycard access. In the case of involuntary terminations, the employee should be escorted into the supervisor's office for the bad news. Upon receiving the termination notice or tendering a hostile resignation the employee should be escorted to his or her office, cubicle, or personal area and allowed to collect personal effects. No organizational property should be allowed to be taken from the premises, including diskettes, pens, papers, and books. Regardless of the claim the employee has on organizational property, he or she should not be allowed to take it from the premises. If there is property that the employee strongly wishes to retain, the employee should be informed that he or she can submit, in writing, a list of the particular items and the reasons why he or she should be allowed to retain them. After the employee's personal property has been gathered, the employee should be asked to surrender all company property such as (but not limited to) keys, keycards, organizational identification, physical access devices, PDAs, pagers, cell phones, and portable computers. The employee should then be escorted out of the building.

Friendly departures include resignation, retirement, promotion, or relocation. In this case, the employee may have tendered notice well in advance of the actual departure date. This scenario actually makes it much more difficult for the security team to maintain positive control over the employee's access and information usage. Employee accounts are usually allowed to continue to exist, though an expiration date can be set for the employee's declared date of

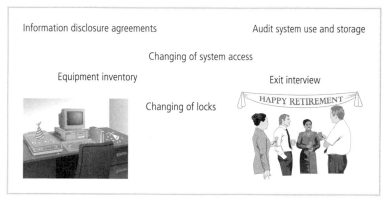

Figure 11-5 Termination Activities

Source: Course Technology/Cengage Learning

departure. Another complication associated with friendly departures is that until their departure date employees can come and go at will, which means they are usually collecting their own belongings and leaving under their own cognizance. As with hostile departures, employees should be asked to drop off all organizational property on their final way out.

In either circumstance (hostile or friendly), the offices and information used by the employee must be inventoried, files must be stored or destroyed, and all property must be returned to organizational stores. It is possible in either situation that the employees foresee their departure well in advance and, perhaps thinking that such items may be valuable in their future employment, start taking home organizational information such as files, reports, and data from databases. This may be impossible to prevent. Only by scrutinizing systems logs after the employee has departed and sorting out authorized actions from systems misuse or information theft can the organization determine if there has been a breach of policy or a loss of information. In the event that information is illegally copied or stolen, the action should be declared an incident and the appropriate policy followed. Figure 11-5 overviews some termination activities.

Security Considerations for Nonemployees

People who are not subject to rigorous screening, contractual obligations, and eventual secured termination often have access to sensitive organizational information. As outlined in the sections that follow, relationships with individuals in this category should be carefully managed to prevent a possible information leak or theft.

Temporary Employees

Temporary employees are hired by the organization to serve in a temporary position or to supplement the existing workforce. These employees do not work for the organization where they are performing their duties, but instead are usually the paid employees of a temp agency or organization that provides qualified individuals at the paid request of another company. Temps typically provide secretarial or administrative support, and thus may be exposed to a wide range of information. As they are not employed by the host organization, they are often not subject to the contractual obligations or general policies that govern other employees. If temps violate a policy or cause a problem, the strongest action the host organization can take is to terminate the relationships and request that they be censured. The employing agency is under no contractual obligation to do this, however, though it may censure the employee to appease an important client.

From a security standpoint, temporary employees' access to information should be limited to that which is necessary for them to perform their duties. The organization can attempt to have temporary employees sign nondisclosure agreements and fair use policies, but the temp agency may refuse, forcing the host organization to choose between arranging for a new temp agency, going without the assistance of a temp worker, or allowing the temp to work without the agreement. This can create a potentially awkward and dangerous situation, as temporary workers may inadvertently gain access to information that does not directly relate to their responsibilities. The only way to combat this threat is to ensure that the temp's supervisor restricts the information to which the temp has access and makes sure all employees follow good security practices, especially clean desk policies and the security of classified data. Temps can provide great benefits to the host organization, but should not be employed at the cost of sacrificing information security.

Contract Employees

Contract employees are typically hired to perform specific services for the organization. In such cases, the host company often makes a contract with a parent organization rather than with an individual for a particular task. Typical contract employees include groundskeepers, maintenance service people, electrical contractors, mechanical service contractors, and other service and repair people. Although some individuals may require access to virtually all areas of the organization to do their jobs, they seldom need access to information or information resources, except in the case where the organization has leased computing equipment or has contracted with a disaster recovery service. Contract employees may also need access to various facilities, but this does not mean they should be allowed to wander freely in and out of buildings. To maintain a secure facility, all contract employees should be escorted from room to room, as well as into and out of the facility. When these employees report for maintenance or repair services, the first step security personnel should take is to verify that these services are actually scheduled or called for. As indicated in earlier chapters, it is not unheard of for an attacker to dress up as a telephone repairman, maintenance technician, or janitor to gain physical access to a building, and therefore, direct supervision of contract employees is a necessity.

Another necessary aspect of hiring contract employees is making certain that restrictions or requirements are negotiated into the contract agreements when they are activated. The following regulations should be negotiated well in advance: the facility requires 24 to 48 hours notice of a maintenance visit; the facility requires all onsite personnel to undergo background checks; and the facility requires advance notice for cancellation or rescheduling of a maintenance visit.

Consultants

Sometimes onsite contracted employees are self-employed or are employees of an organization hired for a specific, one-time purpose. These people are typically referred to as consultants, and they have their own security requirements and contractual obligations. Consultants should have all specific requirements for information or facility access integrated into their contracts before these individuals are allowed into the workplace. Security and technology consultants especially must be prescreened, escorted, and subjected to nondisclosure agreements to protect the organization from possible intentional or accidental breaches of confidentiality. It is human nature (and a trait often found among consultants) to brag about the complexity of a particular job or an outstanding service provided to another client. If the organization does not want the consultant to mention its relationship with the consultant, or to disclose the least detail about its particular system configuration, the organization must write these restrictions into the contractual agreement. It should be noted that consultants typically request permission to present their work to other companies as part of their resumes, but a client organization is not obligated to grant this permission and can even explicitly deny permission in writing. Organizations should also remember that just because they are paying an information security consultant, this doesn't mean the protection of their information is the consultant's number one priority.

Business Partners

On occasion, businesses find themselves in strategic alliances with other organizations wishing to exchange information, integrate systems, or simply discuss operations for mutual advantage. In these situations, there must be a prior business agreement that specifies the level of exposure both organizations are willing to endure. Sometimes, one division of a company enters a strategic partnership with an organization that directly competes with another one of the company's own divisions. If the strategic partnership evolves into an integration of the systems of both companies, there is a chance that competing groups may exchange information that neither parent organization expected to share. As a result, there must be a meticulous, deliberate process of determining what information is to be exchanged, in what format, and with whom. Nondisclosure agreements must be in place. And as discussed in Chapter 2, the level of security of both systems must be examined before any physical integration takes place, because when systems are connected, the vulnerability of any one system becomes the vulnerability of all.

11

Internal Control Strategies

Among several internal control strategies, separation of duties is a cornerstone in the protection of information assets and in the prevention of financial loss. **Separation of duties** is used to reduce the chance of an individual violating information security and breaching the confidentiality, integrity, or availability of information. The control stipulates that the completion of a significant task that involves sensitive information should require at least two people. The idea behind this separation is that if only one person had the authorization to access a particular set of information, there may be nothing the organization can do to prevent this individual from copying the information and removing it from the premises. Separation of duties is especially important, and thus commonly implemented, when the information in question is financial. Consider, for example, how in a bank two people are required to issue a cashier's check. The first is authorized to prepare the check, acquire the numbered financial document, and ready the check for signature. The process then requires a second person, usually a supervisor, to sign the check. Only then can the check be issued. If one person had the authority to perform both functions, that person could write a number of checks, sign them, and steal large sums from the bank. The same level of control should be applied to critical data. One programmer updates the system, and a supervisor or coworker accesses the file location in which the updates are stored. Or, one employee can be authorized to run backups to the system, and another to install and remove the physical media. Related to the concept of separation of duties is that of **two-person control**, the requirement that two individuals review and approve each other's work before the task is categorized as finished. This is distinct from separation of duties, in which the two people work in sequence. In two-person control, each person completely finishes the necessary work and then submits it to the other coworker. Each coworker then examines the work performed, double-checking the actions performed and making sure no errors or inconsistencies exist. Figure 11-6 illustrates these operations.

Another control used to prevent personnel from misusing information assets is job rotation. **Job rotation** or **task rotation** is the requirement that every employee be able to perform the work of another employee. If it is not feasible that one employee learn the entire job of another, then the organization should at least try to ensure that for each critical task it has multiple individuals on staff who are capable of performing it. Job or task rotations such as these can greatly increase the chance that an employee's misuse of the system or abuse of the information will be detected by another. They also ensure that no one employee is performing actions that cannot be physically audited by another employee. In general, this method makes good business sense. One threat to information is the inability of an organization to perform the tasks of one employee in the event that the employee is unable or unwilling to perform his or her duties. If everyone knows at least part of the job of another person (thus serves, in effect, as part of a human RAID system), the organization can survive the loss of any one employee.

This leads to a control measure that may seem surprising: mandatory vacations. Why should a company *require* its employees to take vacations? A mandatory vacation, of at least one week, provides the organization with the ability to audit the work of an individual. Individuals who are stealing from the organization or otherwise misusing information or systems are, in general, reluctant to take vacations, for fear that their actions will be detected. Therefore, all employees should be required to take at least one one-week vacation so that their jobs can be audited. All this is not meant to imply that employees are untrustworthy, but

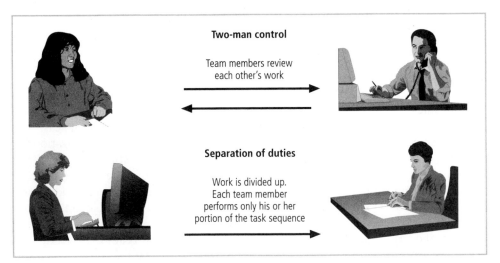

Figure 11-6 Internal Control Strategies

Source: Course Technology/Cengage Learning

rather to show how organizations must be creative—even consider the security situation as a potential attacker would—with the control measures they apply. The mandatory vacation policy is effective because it ensures that employees who want to abuse the system know that there is a strong probability of being caught. Information security professionals who think this practice impugns the character of their coworkers should note that in some industries bonding authorities, auditing agencies, or oversight boards not only require mandatory vacations, but apply this requirement universally (i.e., to all employees).

One final control measure: employees should be provided access to the minimal amount of information for the minimal amount of time necessary for them to perform their duties. In other words, there is no need for everyone in the organization to have access to all information. This principle is called **least privilege**. Similar to the concept of need-to-know, least privilege ensures that no unnecessary access to data exists and that only those individuals who must access the data do so. The whole purpose of information security is to allow those people with a need to use the information contained in a given system to do so without being concerned about the system's ability to maintain the confidentiality, integrity, and availability of the information. Organizations should keep in mind that everyone who can access data probably will, and that such a situation can have devastating consequences for the organization's information security.

Privacy and the Security of Personnel Data

Organizations are required by law to protect employee information that is sensitive or personal, as you learned in Chapter 3. This includes employee addresses, phone numbers, Social Security numbers, medical conditions, and even names and addresses of family members. While personnel data is, in principle, no different from other data that an organization's information security group must protect, there is a great deal more regulation covering its protection. As a result, information security groups should ensure that this data receives at least the same level of protection as does the other important data in the organization—such as intellectual property, strategic planning, and other business-critical information.

Selected Readings

There are many excellent sources of additional information in the area of information security. A few that can add to your understanding of this chapter's content are listed here:

- *Information Security Roles and Responsibilities Made Easy, Version 2* by Charles Cresson Wood. 2005. Information Shield.
- *Management Of Information Security, Third Edition* by Michael E. Whitman and Herbert J. Mattord. 2009. Course Technology.

Chapter Summary

- The placement of the information security function within the organization is a key decision facing the organization. The most popular options involve placing the information security function within the IT function or within the physical security function. Organizations searching for a rational compromise should place the information security function where it can balance its need to enforce organizational policy with its need to deliver service to the entire organization.

■ The selection of information security personnel is based on a number of criteria. Some of these factors are within the control of the organization and others are not.

■ In most cases, organizations look for a technically qualified information security generalist with a solid understanding of how an organization operates in addition to the following attributes:

- An attitude that information security is usually a management problem, not an exclusively technical problem

- Good people skills, communications skills, and writing skills and a tolerance for users

- An understanding of the role of policy in guiding security efforts

- An understanding of the role of education and training in making the users part of the solution

- An understanding of the threats facing an organization and how these threats can become attacks, as well as an understanding of how to protect the organization from information security attacks

- A working knowledge of many of the most common technologies and a general familiarity with most mainstream IT technologies

■ Many information security professionals enter the field through one of two career paths: via law enforcement or military personnel, or from other technical information systems professions. In recent years, college students have been able to take courses that prepare them to enter the information security workforce directly.

■ During the hiring process for an information security position, an organization should use standard job descriptions to increase the degree of professionalism among applicants and also to make sure the position's roles and responsibilities are consistent with those of similar information security positions in other organizations. Studies of information security positions have found that they can be classified into one of three areas: those that define, those that build, and those that administer.

■ When filling various information security positions, many organizations indicate the level of proficiency required for the job by specifying that the candidate have recognizable certifications. Some of the more popular certifications are:

- (ISC)^2 family of certifications: Certified Information Systems Security Professional (CISSP), Systems Security Certified Practitioner (SSCP), Associate of (ISC)^2, and Certification and Accreditation Professional (CAP)

- ISACA family of certifications: Certified Information Systems Auditor (CISA) and Certified Information Security Manager (CISM)

- Global Information Assurance Certification (GIAC) family of certifications

- Security Certified Professional (SCP)

- Security+

- Certified Computer Examiner

- The general management community of interest should integrate solid concepts regarding information security into the organization's employment policies and practices. Areas where information security should be a consideration include:
  - Hiring: job descriptions, interviews, and background checks
  - Employment contracts
  - New hire orientation
  - Performance evaluation
  - Termination
- Organizations may need the special services of nonemployees, but the resulting relationships should be carefully managed to prevent information leaks or theft. The categories of nonemployees are:
  - Temporary employees
  - Contract employees
  - Consultants
  - Business partners
- Separation of duties is a control used to reduce the chance of any one individual violating information security and breaching the confidentiality, integrity, or availability of information. The principle behind this control is that any major task that involves sensitive information should require two people to complete.
- Privacy and security of personnel and personal data have government-mandated requirements for special security considerations and must be covered in the organization's information security program.

11

Review Questions

1. Who in an organization should decide where in the organizational structure the information security function is located? Why?

2. List and describe the options available for the location of the information security functions within the organization. Discuss the advantages and disadvantages of each option.

3. For each of the major types of information security job titles covered in the chapter, list and describe the criteria used for selection.

4. What are some of the factors that influence an organization's information security hiring decisions?

5. What general attributes do organizations seek in candidates when hiring information security professionals across all positions? Prioritize the list and justify your ranking.

6. What are the critical considerations when dismissing an employee? Do these change according to whether the departure is friendly or hostile, or according to which position the employee is departing from?

7. How do the security considerations for temporary or contract employees differ from those for regular full-time employees?

8. What two career paths do most experienced professionals take when moving into the information security discipline? Are there other pathways available? If so, describe them.

9. Why is it important to use specific and clearly defined job descriptions for hiring information security professionals?

10. What functions does the CISO perform, and what are the key qualifications and requirements for the position?

11. What functions does the security manager perform, and what are the key qualifications and requirements for the position?

12. What functions does the security technician perform, and what are the key qualifications and requirements for the position?

13. What rationale should an aspiring information security professional use in acquiring professional credentials?

14. List and describe the credentials of the various information security certifications listed in this chapter.

15. Who should pay for the expenses of certification? Why?

16. List and describe the standard personnel practices that are part of the information security function. What happens to these practices when they are integrated with information security concepts?

17. Why shouldn't an organization give an employee candidate a tour of secure areas during the candidate's interview?

18. List and describe the typical relationships that organizations have with nonemployees. What are the special security precautions that an organization must consider for workers involved in these associations, and why are they significant?

19. What is separation of duties? How can it be used to improve an organization's information security practices?

20. What is job rotation, and what benefits does it offer an organization?

Exercises

1. Search your library's database and the Web for an article related to individuals violating their organization's policy and being terminated. Did you find many? Why or why not?

2. Go to the (ISC)² Web site at *www.isc2.org*. Research the knowledge areas included in the tests for both the CISSP and the SSCP. What areas must you study that are *not* included in this text?

3. Using the Web, identify some certifications with an information security component that were not discussed in this chapter.

4. Search the Web for at least five job postings for a security administrator. What qualifications do the listings have in common?

5. Search the Web for three different employee hiring and termination policies. Review each and look carefully for inconsistencies. Do each of the policies have sections addressing information security requirements? What clauses should a termination policy contain to prevent disclosure of an organization's information? Create your own version of either a hiring or termination policy.

Case Exercises

After her meeting with Charlie, Iris returned to her office. When she had completed her daily assignments, she pulled out a notepad and began to make some notes about the information security position Charlie had offered her.

Questions:

1. What questions should Iris ask Charlie about the new job, about Kelvin's team, and about the future of the company?

2. What questions should Iris ask Kelvin about the new job?

Endnotes

1. Hayes, M. "Where the Chief Security Officer Belongs." InformationWeek. 25 February 2002. Accessed 14 October 2010 from *www.informationweek.com/news/software/showArticle.jhtml?articleID=6500913&queryText=Where%20the%20Chief%20Security%20Officer%20Belongs*.

2. Hunt, Steve. "The CISO in 2010 Still Touches Technology." CSO Magazine. July 2004.

3. *BLS Occupational Outlook Handbook, 2010–2011 Edition*. Accessed 14 October 2010 from *www.bls.gov/oco/ocos305.htm*

4. Robert Half Technology. "CIOs Forecast Increase in Second-Quarter IT Hiring." Accessed 27 February 2010 from *http://rht.mediaroom.com/Q2ITHiring*.

5. Charles Cresson Wood. *Information Security Roles and Responsibilities Made Easy*. (Houston, TX: PentaSafe Corporation, 2002), 55–94.

6. Schwartz, Eddie, Erwin, Dan, Weafer, Vincent, and Briney, Andy "Roundtable: Info-Sec Staffing Help Wanted!" *Information Security Magazine Online*. April 2001. Accessed 5 July 2007 from *infosecuritymag.techtarget.com/articles/april01/features_roundtable.shtml*.

7. Security Jobs Network, Inc. "Sample Job Descriptions: Director of Security." *Security Jobs Network, Inc. Online*. Accessed 5 July 2007 from *securityjobs.net/documents/Director%20of%20Security%20Position,%20Cox.html*.

8. IT Security Jobs. "IT Security Vacancies." *SSR Personnel Online*. 22 July 2002. Accessed 5 July 2007 from *www.ssr-personnel.com/ucs/vacancies/IT%20Security.htm*.

9. IT Security Jobs. "623873—Firewall Engineering Consultant." *SSR Personnel Online*. 16 July 2002. Accessed 5 July 2007 from *www.itsecurityjobs.com/vacancies.htm*.

11

10. International Information Systems Security Certification Consortium. Accessed 14 October 2010 from *www.isc2.org/*.

11. *Ibid.*

12. *Ibid.*

13. *Ibid.*

14. *Ibid.*

15. International Information Systems Security Certification Consortium, Inc. "About SSCP Certification." *ISC² Online*. Accessed 14 October 2010 from *www.isc2.org/cgi-bin/content.cgi?page=815*.

16. International Information Systems Security Certification Consortium, Inc. "Associate of (ISC)? Designation." *ISC² Online*. Accessed 14 October 2010 from *www.isc2.org/cgi-bin/content.cgi?page=824*.

17. ISACA. "CISA Exam Bulletin of Information."Accessed 10 October 2010 from *www.isaca.org/Certification/CISA-Certified-Information-Systems-Auditor/Register-for-the-Exam/Documents/Dec%20CISA%20BOI.pdf*.

18. GIAC Gold Overview. Accessed 27 March 2010 from *www.giac.org/gold/*.

19. The SANS Institute. "GIAC Information Security Certifications." The SANS Institute Online. Accessed 26 October, 2010 from *www.giac.org/certifications*.

20. Global Information Assurance Certification. "Steps to ..." *SANS Institute Online*. Accessed 5 July 2007 from *www.giac.org/certifications/steps.php*.

21. Security_Objectives-08. Accessed 27 March 2010 from *www.comptia.org/certifications/testprep/examobjectives.aspx*.

22. CompTIA. "CompTIA Security+; Certification." Accessed 25 April 2007 from *certification.comptia.org/security/default.aspx*.

23. CompTIA. "Security+ Exam Objectives, v. 1.0." Accessed 25 April 2007 from *certification.comptia.org/resources/objectives/Security_Objectives.pdf*.

24. ISFCE. "The Certified Computer Examiner Content Areas." Accessed 14 October 2010 from *www.certified-computer-examiner.com*.

25. Reuscher, D. "Security Certification Essentials." Accessed 25 April 2007 from *certification.about.com/od/securitycerts/a/seccertessentls.htm*.

26. Background Check International, LLC. "BCI." *BCI Online*. Accessed 10 October 2010 from *www.bcint.com*.

27. Federal Trade Commission. *Fair Credit Reporting Act*. 2002. 15 U.S.C., S. 1681 et seq.

28. September 11th Commission Final Report, July 2004.

chapter 12

Information Security Maintenance

The only thing we can predict with certainty is change.
JAYNE SPAIN, DEPARTMENT OF CHILDREN AND
FAMILY LEARNING, STATE OF MINNESOTA

Charlie Moody leaned back in his chair. It was Monday morning, the first workday after the biggest conversion weekend in the implementation of Sequential Label and Supply's information security project. Charlie had just reviewed the results. So far, everything had gone according to plan. The initial penetration tests run on Sunday afternoon were clean, and every change request processed in the past three months had gone through without any issues. Charlie was eager for the routine to return to normal, that is, to the way things had been before the attack on the company's network had triggered the changes of the past few months.

Kelvin Urich tapped on the open door of Charlie's office. "Hey, Charlie," he said, "have you seen the e-mail I just sent? There's an urgent vulnerability report on BUGTRAQ about the version of UNIX we use. The vendor just released a critical patch to be applied right away. Should I get the system programming team started on it?"

"Absolutely! Get them to pull the download from the vendor's FTP site as soon as they can," said Charlie. "But before they install it on the production systems, be sure they try it out on the test lab servers. If that goes okay, have them patch the servers for the HQ development team. Oh, and could you get these change orders into change control ASAP, and add the production server change request to the paperwork for the overnight change window?"

"I'll get right on it," Kelvin said.

After Kelvin left, Charlie pulled up BUGTRAQ on his PC. He was reading about the new vulnerability when there was another knock on his door. It was Iris Majwubu.

"Hi, Charlie," Iris said. "Got a second?"

"Sure, Iris. How have you been? Settling in with Kelvin's team okay?"

She smiled and nodded. "Yeah, they're a good group. They have me studying the documentation trail from the time before the security program was implemented. I came to see you about the reassessment of the information asset inventory and the threat-vulnerability update that you asked for."

Charlie was confused for a second, but then he remembered what Iris was referring to. "Oh, right," he said, with a slight grimace. "Sorry—I had put the quarterly asset and threat review out of my mind while we were busy implementing the blueprint. I suppose it's time to start planning for the regular reviews, isn't it?"

Iris handed him a folder and said, "Here's the first draft of the plan for the review project. Kelvin has already seen it, and he suggested I review it with you. Could you take a look and let me know when you would like to go over it?"

LEARNING OBJECTIVES:

Upon completion of this material, you should be able to:

- Discuss the need for ongoing maintenance of the information security program
- List the recommended security management models
- Define a model for a full maintenance program
- Identify the key factors involved in monitoring the external and internal environment
- Describe how planning, risk assessment, vulnerability assessment, and remediation tie into information security maintenance
- Explain how to build readiness and review procedures into information security maintenance
- Define digital forensics, and describe the management of the digital forensics function
- Describe the process of acquiring, analyzing, and maintaining potential evidentiary material

Introduction

After successfully implementing and testing a new and improved information security profile, an organization may begin feeling more confident about the level of protection it is providing for its information assets. But it shouldn't, really. In all likelihood, a good deal of time has passed since the organization began implementing the changes to the information security program. In that time, the dynamic aspects of the organization's environment have, by definition, changed. Which aspects of a company's environment are dynamic? Virtually all of them. The threats that were originally assessed in the early stages of the project's SecSDLC have probably changed, and new priorities have emerged. New types of attacks, such as new viruses, worms, and denial-of-service attacks, along with new variants of existing attacks, have also probably emerged; in addition, a host of other variables outside and inside the organization have most likely changed.

Developing a comprehensive list of all the possible dynamic factors in an organization's environment is beyond the scope of this text. However, some changes that may affect an organization's information security environment are the following:

- The acquisition of new assets and the divestiture of old assets
- The emergence of vulnerabilities associated with the new or existing assets
- Shifting business priorities
- The formation of new partnerships
- The dissolution of old partnerships
- The departure of personnel who are trained, educated, and aware of policies, procedures, and technologies
- The hiring of personnel

As this list shows, by the time a cycle of the SecSDLC is completed, there's a high probability that the environment of an organization will have changed considerably. An information security team needs to be able to assure management periodically that the information security program is accommodating these changes. If the program is not adjusting adequately to change, it may be necessary to begin the cycle again. If an organization deals successfully with change and has created procedures and systems that can be adjusted to the environment, the existing security improvement program can continue to work well. The decision on whether to continue with the current information security improvement program or to renew the investigation, analysis, and design phases depends on how much change has occurred and how well the organization and its program for information security maintenance is adapting to its evolving environment.

Before learning about the maintenance model recommended by the text, you need some background on the management and operation of an information security program. In this chapter, you will learn about the various methods organizations use to monitor the three primary aspects of information security risk management (sometimes called the security triple): threats, assets, and vulnerabilities. You will also learn about digital forensics, a specialized area in information security. It is inevitable that at some point in the ongoing operations of the organization, someone within or outside the organization will do something wrong. In Chapter 5, you learned how incident response planning helps organizations anticipate, detect, react to, and recover from external and internal incidents. Digital forensics helps the organization understand what happened and how.

Security Management Maintenance Models

To manage and operate the ongoing security program, the information security community must adopt a management maintenance model. In general, management models are frameworks that structure the tasks of managing a particular set of activities or business functions.

NIST SP 800-100 Information Security Handbook: A Guide for Managers

NIST SP 800-100 *Information Security Handbook: A Guide for Managers* provides managerial guidance for the establishment and implementation of an information security program, in particular regarding the ongoing tasks expected of an information security manager once the program is operational and day-to-day operations are established.

For each of the thirteen areas of information security management presented in SP 800-100 there are specific monitoring activities—tasks security managers should do on an ongoing basis to monitor the function of the security program and take corrective actions when issues arise. Not all issues are negative, as is the incident described in the opening scenario. Some are normal changes in the business environment, while others are changes in the technology environment—for example, the emergence of new technologies that could improve organizational security or new security standards and regulations to which the organization should or could subscribe.

The following sections describe the monitoring actions for each of the thirteen information security areas. This information is adapted from SP 800-100.

1. Information Security Governance An effective information security governance program requires constant review. Agencies should monitor the status of their programs to ensure that:

- Ongoing information security activities are providing appropriate support to the agency mission
- Policies and procedures are current and aligned with evolving technologies, if appropriate
- Controls are accomplishing their intended purpose

Over time, policies and procedures may become inadequate because of changes in agency mission and operational requirements, threats, or the environment; deterioration in the degree of compliance; or changes in technology, infrastructure, or business processes. Periodic assessments and reports on activities can identify areas of noncompliance, remind users of their responsibilities, and demonstrate management's commitment to the security program. While an organization's mission does not frequently change, the agency may expand its mission to secure agency programs and assets and, by extension, require modification to its information security requirements and practices.

To facilitate ongoing monitoring, the CISO and other officials can compare and correlate a variety of real-time and static information available from a number of ongoing activities within and outside of their programs. Organizations should perform an annual assessment of their information security programs and report information security performance measures quarterly and annually. The intent of these reporting requirements is to facilitate close to real-time assessment and monitoring of information security program activities. Ongoing monitoring combines the use of existing data to oversee a security program and typically occurs throughout all phases of the program life cycle. Table 12-1 provides a broad overview of key ongoing activities that can assist in monitoring and improving an agency's information governance activities.

2. System Development Life Cycle As you learned in Chapter 1, the system development life cycle (SDLC) is the overall process of developing, implementing, and retiring information systems through a multistep process—initiation, analysis, design, implementation, and maintenance to disposal. Each phase of the SDLC includes a minimum set of information security–related activities required to effectively incorporate security into a system.

Activities	Description of Activities
Plans of Action and Milestones (POA&M)	POA&Ms assist in identifying, assessing, prioritizing, and monitoring the progress of corrective efforts for security weaknesses found in programs and systems. The POA&M tracks the measures implemented to correct deficiencies and to reduce or eliminate known vulnerabilities. POA&Ms can also assist in identifying performance gaps, evaluating an agency's security performance and efficiency, and conducting oversight.
Measurement and Metrics	Metrics are tools designed to improve performance and accountability through the collection, analysis, and reporting of relevant performance-related data. Information security metrics monitor the accomplishment of goals and objectives by quantifying the implementation level of security controls and the efficiency and effectiveness of the controls, by analyzing the adequacy of security activities, and by identifying possible improvement actions.
Continuous Assessment	The continuous assessment process monitors the initial security accreditation of an information system to track the changes to the information system, analyzes the security impact of those changes, makes appropriate adjustments to the security controls and to the system's security plan, and reports the security status of the system to appropriate agency officials.
Configuration Management	Configuration management (CM) is an essential component of monitoring the status of security controls and identifying potential security-related problems in information systems. This information can help security managers understand and monitor the evolving nature of vulnerabilities as they appear in a system under their responsibility, thus enabling managers to direct appropriate changes as required.
Network Monitoring	Information about network performance and user behavior on the network helps security program managers identify areas in need of improvement as well as pointing out potential performance improvements. This information can be correlated with other sources of information, such as the POA&M and CM, to create a comprehensive picture of security program status.
Incident and Event Statistics	Incident statistics are valuable in determining the effectiveness of security policies and procedures implementation. Incident statistics provide security program managers with further insights into the status of security programs under their purview, help them observe program activities performance trends, and inform them about the needs to change policies and procedures.

Table 12-1   Ongoing Information Security Governance Monitoring Activities

Special Publication (SP) 800-64 Rev. 1, *Security Considerations in the Information System Development Life Cycle*, presents a framework for incorporating security into all phases of the SDLC to ensure the selection, acquisition, and use of appropriate and cost-effective security controls. These considerations are summarized in Table 12-2.

An effective security program demands comprehensive and continuous understanding of program and system weaknesses. In the operation and maintenance phase of a SDLC, systems and products are in place and operating, enhancements and/or modifications to the system are developed and tested, and hardware and/or software is added or replaced. During this phase, the organization should continuously monitor performance of the system to ensure that it is consistent with preestablished user and security requirements and needed system modifications are incorporated.

For configuration management (CM) and control, it is important to document the proposed or actual changes in the security plan of the system. Information systems are typically in a constant state of evolution with upgrades to hardware, software, and firmware and possible modifications to the surrounding environment where the system resides. Documenting information system changes and assessing the potential impact of these changes on the security of a system is an essential part of continuous monitoring and key to avoiding a lapse in the system security accreditation.

A. Initiation Phase	
Needs Determination	• Define a problem that might be solved through product acquisition. • Establish and document need and purpose of the system.
Security Categorization	• Identify information that will be transmitted, processed, or stored by the system and define applicable levels of information categorization, especially the handling and safeguarding of personally identifiable information.
Preliminary Risk Assessment	• Establish an initial description of the basic security needs of the system. A preliminary risk assessment should define the threat environment in which the system or product will operate.
B. Development/Acquisition Phase	
Requirements Analysis/ Development	• Conduct a more in-depth study of the need that draws on and further develops the work performed during the initiation phase. • Develop and incorporate security requirements into specifications. • Analyze functional requirements that may include system security environment (e.g., enterprise information security policy and enterprise security architecture) and security functional requirements. • Analyze assurance requirements that address the acquisition and product integration activities required and assurance evidence needed to produce the desired level of confidence that the product will provide required information security features correctly and effectively.
Risk Assessment	• Conduct formal risk assessment to identify system protection requirements. This analysis builds on the initial risk assessment performed during the initiation phase, but is more in-depth and specific.
Cost Considerations and Reporting	• Determine how much of the product acquisition and integration cost can be attributed to information security over the life cycle of the system. These costs include hardware, software, personnel, and training.
Security Planning	• Fully document agreed-upon security controls, planned or in place. • Develop the system security plan. • Develop documents supporting the agency's information security program (e.g., CM plan, contingency plan, incident response plan, security awareness and training plan, rules of behavior, risk assessment, security test and evaluation results, system interconnection agreements, security authorizations/ accreditations, and plans of action and milestones). • Develop awareness and training requirements, including user manuals and operations/administrative manuals.
Security Control Development 27	• Develop, design, and implement security controls described in the respective security plans. For information systems currently in operation, the security plans for those systems may call for developing additional security controls to supplement the controls already in place or may call for modifying selected controls that are deemed to be less than effective.
Developmental Security Test and Evaluation	• Test security controls developed for a new information system or product for proper and effective operation. • Develop test plan, script, and scenarios.

Table 12-2 Information Security Ongoing Activities in the SDLC

Other Planning Components	• Ensure that all necessary components of the product acquisition and integration process are considered when incorporating security into the life cycle.

C. Implementation Phase

Security Test and Evaluation	• Develop test data. • Test unit, subsystem, and entire system. • Ensure system undergoes technical evaluation (e.g., according to applicable laws, regulations, policies, guidelines, and standards).
Inspection and Acceptance	• Verify and validate that the functionality described in the specification is included in the deliverables.
System Integration/ Installation	• Integrate the system at the operational site where it is to be deployed for operation. Enable security control settings and switches in accordance with vendor instructions and proper security implementation guidance.
Security Certification	• Ensure that the controls are effectively implemented through established verification techniques and procedures and give organization officials confidence that the appropriate safeguards and countermeasures are in place to protect the organization's information.
Security Accreditation	• Provide the necessary security authorization of an information system to process, store, or transmit information that is required.

D. Operations/Maintenance Phase

Configuration Management and Control	• Ensure adequate consideration of the potential security impacts due to specific changes to an information system or its surrounding environment.
	• Develop CM plan
	  – Establish baselines
	  – Identify configuration
	  – Describe configuration control process
	  – Identify schedule for configuration audits

Continuous Monitoring	• Monitor security controls to ensure that controls continue to be effective in their application through periodic testing and evaluation. • Perform self-administered or independent security audits or other assessments periodically. Types: using automated tools, internal control audits, security checklists, and penetration testing. • Monitor system and/or users. Methods: review system logs and reports, use automated tools, review change management, monitor external sources (trade literature, publications, electronic news, etc.), and perform periodic reaccreditation.

E. Disposal Phase:

Information Preservation	• Retain information, as necessary, to conform to current legal requirements and to accommodate future technology changes that may render the retrieval method obsolete. • Consult with agency office on retaining and archiving federal records. • Ensure long-term storage of cryptographic keys for encrypted data. • Determine archive, discard, or destroy information.
Media Sanitization	• Determine sanitization level (overwrite, degauss, or destroy). • Delete, erase, and overwrite data as necessary.
Hardware and Software Disposal	• Dispose of hardware and software as directed by governing agency policy.

12

Table 12-2 **Information Security Ongoing Activities in the SDLC (*continued*)**

Monitoring security controls helps to identify potential security-related problems in the information system that are not identified during the security impact analysis, which is conducted as part of the CM and control process.

3. Awareness and Training

As you learned in Chapter 5, once the program has been implemented, processes must be put in place to monitor compliance and effectiveness. An automated tracking system should be designed to capture key information on program activity (e.g., courses, dates, audience, costs, sources). The tracking system should capture this data at an agency level, so it can be used to provide enterprise-wide analysis and reporting regarding awareness, training, and education initiatives.

Tracking compliance involves assessing the status of the program as indicated by the database information and mapping it to standards established by the agency. Reports can be generated and used to identify gaps or problems. Corrective action and necessary follow-up can then be taken. This follow-up may take the form of formal reminders to management; additional awareness, training, or education offerings; and/or the establishment of a corrective plan with scheduled completion dates.

It is necessary to ensure that the program, as structured, continues to evolve as new technology and associated security issues emerge. Training needs shift as new skills and capabilities become necessary to respond to new architectural and technology changes. A change in the organizational mission and/or objectives can also influence ideas on how best to design training solutions and content. Emerging issues, such as homeland defense, also impact the nature and extent of security awareness and training activities necessary to keep users informed and/or trained about the latest threats, vulnerabilities, and countermeasures. New laws and court decisions may also impact agency policy that, in turn, may affect the development and/or implementation of awareness and training material. Finally, as security policies evolve, awareness and training material should reflect these changes.

4. Capital Planning and Investment Control

Increased competition for limited resources requires that departments allocate available funding toward their highest-priority information security investments to afford the organization, and its systems and data, the appropriate degree of security for their needs. This goal can be achieved through a formal enterprise capital planning and investment control (CPIC) process designed to facilitate and control the expenditure of agency funds.

To facilitate effective implementation of OMB capital planning and NIST security requirements, the Government Accountability Office (GAO) offers a Select-Control-Evaluate investment life cycle model as a best practices approach to investment management. While not compulsory, the framework articulates key activities for managing IT investments throughout the life cycle. The three phases ensure that investment management practices, including security, are disciplined and thorough throughout each phase of the investment life cycle. Figure 12-1 illustrates the three phases.

NIST Special Publication (SP) 800-65, *Integrating IT Security into the Capital Planning and Investment Control Process,* provides a seven-step process, illustrated in Figure 12-2, for prioritizing security activities and corrective actions for funding purposes.

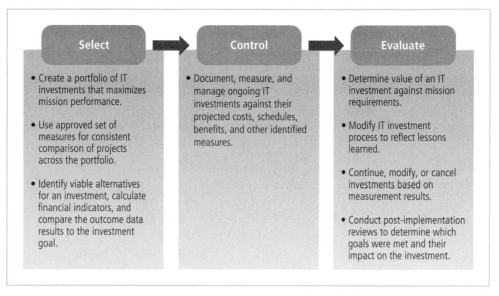

Figure 12-1 Select-Control-Evaluate Investment Life Cycle

Source: Course Technology/Cengage Learning

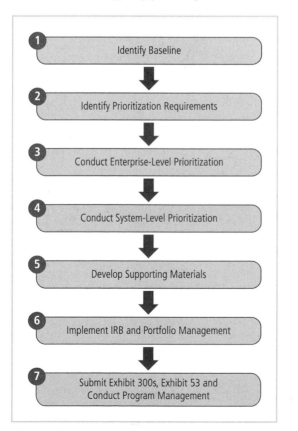

12

Figure 12-2 Integrating Information Security into the CPIC Process

Source: Course Technology/Cengage Learning

The major steps are:

1. Identify the baseline: Use information security metrics or other available data to baseline the current security posture.

2. Identify prioritization requirements: Evaluate security posture against legislative and chief information officer (CIO)-articulated requirements and agency mission.

3. Conduct enterprise-level prioritization: Prioritize potential enterprise-level information security investments against the mission and the financial impact of implementing appropriate security controls.

4. Conduct system-level prioritization: Prioritize potential system-level corrective actions against system category and corrective action impact.

5. Develop supporting materials: For enterprise-level investments, develop concept paper, business case analysis, and Exhibit 300. For system-level investments, adjust Exhibit 300 to request additional funding to mitigate prioritized weaknesses.

6. Implement investment review board (IRB) and portfolio management: Prioritize agency-wide business cases against requirements and CIO priorities and determine investment portfolio.

7. Submit Exhibit 300s and Exhibit 53, and conduct program management: Ensure approved 300s become part of the agency's Exhibit 53; ensure investments are managed through their life cycle.

(Note: Exhibit 300s and Exhibit 53 are part of a federal agency's budget submission to the U.S. Office of Management and Budget and provide an overview of an agency's IT portfolio, and thus do not apply to non-federal government organizations).

5. Interconnecting Systems

A system interconnection is defined as the direct connection of two or more information systems for sharing data and other information resources. Organizations choose to interconnect their information systems for a variety of reasons based on their organizational needs. For example, they may interconnect information systems to exchange data, collaborate on joint projects, or securely store data and backup files.

Interconnecting information systems can expose the participating organizations to risk. If the interconnection is not properly designed, security failures could compromise the connected systems and their data. Similarly, if one of the connected systems is compromised, the interconnection could be used as a conduit to compromise the other system and its data.

When organizations are properly managing interconnected systems, the added benefits include greater efficiency, centralized access to data, and greater functionality. The security controls of each of the interconnected systems should be evaluated and meet each other's requirements for implementing security controls that are appropriate for the particular interconnection.

NIST SP 800-47 details a four-phase life cycle management approach for interconnecting information systems that emphasizes proper attention to information security:

- Phase 1: planning the interconnection
- Phase 2: establishing the interconnection
- Phase 3: maintaining the interconnection
- Phase 4: disconnecting the interconnection

Table 12-3 provides a checklist organizations considering interconnecting multiple systems can follow when developing an interconnection security agreement (ISA). While many parts of this agreement are specified for a federal government agency, referring to the associated Special Publications and Federal Information Processing Standards (FIPS) can assist the organization in identifying issues to be resolved.

		YES	NO
1	**ISA Requirements:**		
A	Is there a formal requirement and justification for connecting two systems?		
B	Are there two systems being interconnected? If YES, have the systems been specified? If NO, the two systems need to be specified.		
C	Is there a list of benefits of required interconnection(s)?		
D	Is the agency name or organization that initiated the requirement listed?		
2	**System Security Considerations:**		
A	Has a security certification and accreditation of the system been completed?		
B	Has the security certification and accreditation status been verified?		
C	Are there security features in place to protect the confidentiality, integrity, and availability of the data and the systems being interconnected?		
D	Has each system's security categorization been identified per FIPS 199?		
E	Have minimum controls been identified for each system in accordance with NIST SP 800-53?		
F	Have both parties answered each subject item regardless of whether the subjected item only affects one party? If NO, both parties must go back and answer each item.		
G	Is there a general description of the information/data being made available, exchanged, or passed?		
H	Is there a description of the information services (e.g., e-mail, file transfer protocol, database query, file query, general computational services) offered over the interconnected system by each participating organization?		
I	Have system users been identified and has an approval been put in place?		
J	Is there a description of all system security technical services pertinent to the secure exchange of information/data among and between the systems in question?		
K	Are there documented rules of behavior for users of each system in the interconnection?		
L	Are there titles of the formal security policy(ies) that govern each system?		
M	Are there procedures for incidents related to the interconnection?		
N	Are there audit requirements?		
3	**Topological Drawing:**		
A	Is there a descriptive technical specification for the connections?		
4	**Signatory Authority:** ISA is valid for one year after the last date on either signature below. At that time, it will be reviewed, updated if necessary, and revalidated. This agreement may be terminated upon 30 days advanced notice by either party or in the event of a security exception that would necessitate an immediate response.		

Table 12-3 ISA Checklist for Interconnecting Systems

6. Performance Measures As mentioned in Chapter 4, a performance measures program provides numerous organizational and financial benefits to organizations. Organizations can develop information security metrics that measure the effectiveness of their security program, and provide data to be analyzed and used by program managers and system owners to isolate problems, justify investment requests, and target funds to the areas in need of improvement. By using metrics to target security investments, agencies can get the best value from available resources. The typical information performance management program consists of four interdependent components: senior management support, security policies and procedures, quantifiable performance metrics, and analyses.

Metrics are tools that support decision making. Like experience, external mandates, and strategies, metrics are one element of a manager's toolkit for making and substantiating decisions. Metrics are used to answer three basic questions:

- "Am I implementing the tasks for which I am responsible?"
- "How efficiently or effectively am I accomplishing those tasks?"
- "What impact are those tasks having on the mission?"

Figure 12-3 illustrates the place of information security metrics within a larger organizational context and demonstrates that information security metrics can be used to progressively measure implementation, efficiency, effectiveness, and the business impact of information security activities within organizations or for specific systems.

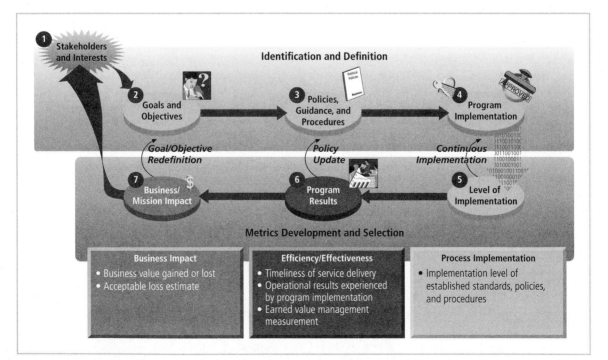

Figure 12-3 Information Security Metrics Development Process

Source: Course Technology/Cengage Learning

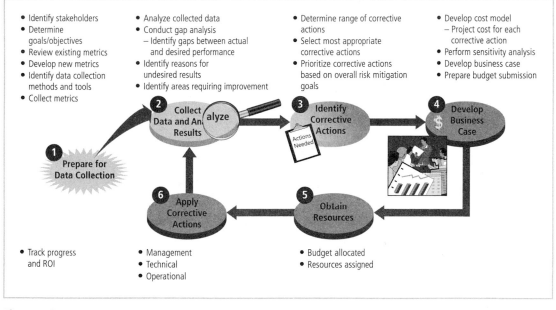

Figure 12-4 Information Security Metrics Program Implementation Process

Source: Course Technology/Cengage Learning

The information security metrics development process consists of two major activities:

1. Identifying and defining the current information security program
2. Developing and selecting specific metrics to measure implementation, efficiency, effectiveness, and the impact of the security controls.

Information security metrics should be used for monitoring information security control performance and initiating performance improvement actions. This iterative process consists of six phases, depicted in Figure 12-4.

Controls Performance Baselines and Metrics Because many information security technical controls are implemented on common IT processors, they are affected by the same factors as most computer-based technologies. It is therefore important to monitor the performance of security systems and their underlying IT infrastructure to determine if they are working effectively. This type of performance monitoring is especially important for network appliances such as firewalls and content filters that look for inappropriate use of Internet resources and operate as pass-by devices. When these types of appliances are not sized correctly or are not properly tuned for sufficient performance, the actions they are designed to block are not stopped. Some common system and network metrics used in performance management are also applicable in security, especially when the components being managed involve the ebb and flow of network traffic. The following list offers a few rules of thumb that security personnel can use when exploring the issues of system and network performance.

- When the memory usage associated with a particular CPU-based system averages or exceeds 60 percent over prolonged periods, consider adding more memory.

- When the CPU usage associated with a particular CPU-based system averages or exceeds 60 percent over prolonged periods, consider an upgrade for the CPU.

- When the network traffic on a particular link averages exceeds 60 percent over prolonged periods, consider an upgrade to the link, which can be accomplished by either increasing the bandwidth available or segmenting the traffic.

- When the amount of data stored on a particular hard drive exceeds 60 percent of available capacity over a prolonged period, consider an upgrade for the hard drive, which can be accomplished by either replacing the hard drive with a larger drive or adding additional drives.

To evaluate the performance of a security system, administrators must establish system performance baselines. Previous chapters of this text covered the procedures for establishing baselines across industries (see Chapter 4) and within organizations (also known as benchmarking, which is also discussed in Chapter 4). In this context, a performance baseline is an expected level of performance against which all subsequent levels of performance are compared. For example, network traffic levels are deemed to be high when traffic reaches or surpasses the level of the performance baseline. To put it another way, the planning of capacity upgrades should begin before users complain about slow-loading Web pages.

Organizations must establish baselines for a number of different criteria and for various periods of time, such as days of the week, weeks of the year, months of the year, and times of day (A.M. and P.M.), among others. To accomplish this, the organization must monitor all variables, collecting and archiving performance baseline data and then analyzing it. After the performance baseline matrix is established, continued monitoring and data collection allows administrators to compare current performance against the performance baseline to determine if an abnormal level of activity is occurring. Performance baselines are established for network traffic and also for firewall performance and IDPS performance. In fact, many security-related technologies rely on some form of performance baseline to interpret various levels of computer activity. Also, for many systems, such as behavior-based (statistical anomaly) IDPSs, establishing their own baselines is already integral to their mode of operation. These systems compare activity against their baselines to determine if an attack or intrusion is occurring.

While the details of the development and implementation of security performance measures (metrics) is beyond the scope of this text, SP 800-55 Rev. 1: *Performance Measurement Guide for Information Security* provides specific guidance on security performance measurement.

7. Security Planning Planning for information security was discussed in detail in Chapter 5. Planning is one of the most crucial ongoing responsibilities in security management. Strategic, tactical, and operational plans must be developed that align with and support organizational and IT plans, goals, and objectives.

This section of SP 800-100 focuses on the various controls available to address shortfalls identified in the planning process. Federal Information Processing Standard (FIPS) 200: Minimum Security Requirements for Federal Information and Information Systems specifies the minimum security requirements for federal information and information systems in seventeen security-related areas. For a review of the minimum security requirements that federal agencies must meet, and that private organizations would benefit from, review FIPS 200 and considering the use the security controls in Special Publication 800-53, Recommended Security Controls for Federal Information Systems. NIST SP 800-18 Rev. 1: *Guide for*

Developing Security Plans for Federal Information Systems provides a systems security plan template in Appendix A of the document.

8. Information Technology Contingency Planning Contingency planning, covered in Chapter 5, consists of a process for recovery and documentation of procedures for conducting recovery. Special Publication SP 800-34, *Contingency Planning for Information Technology Systems,* details a seven-step methodology for developing an IT contingency process and plan. Planning, implementing, and testing the contingency strategy are addressed by six of the seven steps; documenting the plan and establishing procedures and personnel organization to implement the strategy is the final step. SP 800-34 also includes technical considerations for developing recovery strategies.

Figure 12-5 highlights contingency planning activities involved in each step that should be addressed during all phases of the SDLC. The material in Chapter 5 was derived from this source, among others.

The ongoing responsibilities of security management involve the maintenance of the contingency plan. The contingency plan must always be in a ready state for use immediately upon notification. Periodic reviews of the plan must be conducted for currency of key personnel and vendor information, system components and dependencies, the recovery strategy, vital records, and operational requirements. While some changes may be obvious (e.g., personnel turnover or vendor changes), others require analysis. The BIA should be reviewed periodically and updated with new information to identify new contingency requirements and priorities. Changes made to the plan are noted in a record of changes, dated, and signed or initialed by the person making the change. The revised plan, or plan sections, is circulated to those with plan responsibilities. Because of the impact that plan changes may have on

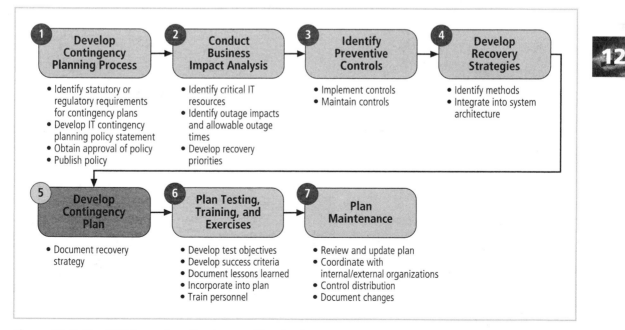

Figure 12-5 The NIST Seven-Step Contingency Planning Process

Source: Course Technology/Cengage Learning

interdependent business processes or information systems, the changes must be clearly communicated and properly annotated in the beginning of the document.

9. Risk Management Risk management, covered in Chapter 4, is an ongoing effort as well. The tasks of performing risk identification, analysis, and management are a cyclic and fundamental part of continuous improvement in information security. The principal goal of an organization's risk management process is to protect the organization and its ability to perform its mission, not just its information assets. The risk management process is an essential management function of the organization that is tightly woven into the SDLC, as depicted in Figure 12-6. Because risk cannot be eliminated entirely, the risk management process allows information security program managers to balance the operational and economic costs of protective measures and achieve gains in mission capability. By employing practices and procedures designed to foster informed decision making, agencies help protect their information systems and the data that support their own mission.

Many of the risk management activities are conducted during a snapshot in time—a static representation of a dynamic environment. All the changes that occur to systems during

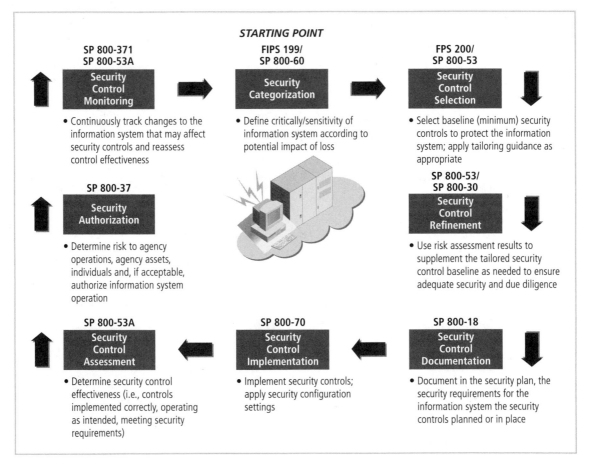

Figure 12-6 Risk Management in the System Security Life Cycle

Source: Course Technology/Cengage Learning

normal, daily operations have the potential to adversely affect the security of the system in some fashion, and it is the goal of the risk management evaluation and assessment process to ensure that the system continues to operate in a safe and secure manner. This goal can be partially reached by implementing a strong configuration management program. In addition to monitoring the security of an information system on a continuous basis, agencies must track findings from the security control assessment to ensure they are addressed appropriately and do not continue to pose or introduce new risks to the system.

The process of managing risk permeates the SDLC, beginning with the early stages of project inception through the retirement of the system and its data. From inception forward, agencies should consider the possible threats, vulnerabilities, and risks to the system so that they can better prepare it to operate in its intended environment securely, effectively, and within a select risk threshold as deemed acceptable by an agency senior official during the security certification and accreditation process.

10. Certification, Accreditation, and Security Assessments As described in Chapter 10, certification and accreditation for federal systems is radically changing for those systems designated as non-national security information systems. However, some organizations need to review their own systems for a certification and/or accreditation to be in compliance with banking, health care, international, or other regulations. Others may want the recognition that certifications like the ISO 27000 series offers. The security certification and accreditation process is designed to ensure that an information system will operate with the appropriate management review, that there is ongoing monitoring of security controls, and that reaccreditation occurs periodically.

The continuous monitoring of a security assessment program, as a function of certification and accreditation, is an essential component in any security program. During this phase, the status of the security controls in the information system is checked on an ongoing basis. An effective continuous monitoring program can be used to support the annual FISMA requirement for assessing the security controls in information systems. At a minimum, an effective monitoring program requires:

- Configuration management and configuration control processes for the information system
- Security impact analyses on changes to the information system
- Assessment of selected security controls in the information system and reporting of information system security status to appropriate agency officials

To determine which security controls to select for review, agencies should first prioritize testing on POA&M items that become closed. These newly implemented controls should be validated. Organizations should test against system-related security control changes that did not constitute a major change necessitating a new C&A. Organizations should identify all security controls that are continuously monitored as annual testing and evaluation activities. Once this is complete, organizations should look at the remaining controls that have not been tested for that year and make a decision on further annual testing based on risk, importance of control, and date of last test. The results of continuous monitoring should be reviewed by senior management on a regular basis and any necessary updates made to the system security plan. A continuous monitoring reporting form is provided in NIST SP 800-53A.

Part of ongoing security assessment is auditing. **Auditing** is the process of reviewing the use of a system to determine if misuse or malfeasance has occurred. Most of the computer-based systems used in information security can create logs of their activity. These logs are a vital part of the detective functions associated with determining what happened, when it happened, and how it happened.

The management of systems logs in large organizations is a complex process and is sometimes considered to be an art in itself. Unless the security (or systems) administrators are vigilant, the logs can pile up quickly, because systems are constantly writing the activity that occurs on them. Fortunately, automated tools known as log analyzers can consolidate systems logs, perform comparative analysis, and detect common occurrences or behavior that is of interest. The behavior of interest may include anomalous network activity (such as port scanning), malware signatures, hacking attempts, and illicit use of controlled network resources or computer systems. Log analyzers, a component of some IDPSs, can detect activities in real time. Each type of IDPS (host-, network-, and application-based) also create logs. These logs are invaluable records of events and should be archived and stored for future review as needed. It is not unheard of for systems intruders to attempt to cover their tracks by erasing entries in logs. To prepare for this, wise administrators configure their systems to create duplicate copies of the logs and to store these copies on sources that cannot be easily modified, like optical disk technologies such as CD-R and DVD-R. Many vendors offer log consolidation and analysis features that allow for the integration of log files from multiple products, such as firewalls and network equipment, even that of other vendors.

To assist organizations in meeting their reporting, the information security program assessment questionnaire shown in Table 12-4 provides questions on many of the areas typically required for inclusion in reports. The questionnaire contains organization-wide, program-level questions that are not found in NIST SP 800-53. The questionnaire can be customized with organization-specific, program-related questions and can be completed by the CIO, the CISO, or an independent assessor who is evaluating the agency information security program.

Each question should be answered for each level of IT security maturity.

- For the Policy maturity level, to answer "Yes," the topic should be documented in organization policy.

- For the Procedures maturity level, to answer "Yes," the topic should be documented in detailed procedures.

- For the Implemented maturity level, to answer "Yes," the implementation is verified by examining the procedures and program area documentation and interviewing key personnel to determine that the procedures are implemented.

- For the Tested maturity level, to answer "Yes," documents should be examined and interviews should be conducted to verify that the policies and procedures for the question are implemented and operating as intended and provide the desired level of security.

- For the Integrated maturity level, to answer "Yes," the policies, procedures, implementation, and testing are continually monitored and improvements are made as a normal business process of the organization.

11. Security Services and Products Acquisition

Information security services and products are essential elements of an organization's information security program.

Program Questions	Policy	Proce-dures	Imple-mented	Tested	Integrated
1. Security Control Review Process Does management ensure that corrective information security actions are tracked using the plan of action and milestones (POA&M) process?					
2. Capital Planning and Investment Control Does the agency require the use of a business case/Exhibit 300/Exhibit 53 to record the resources required for security at an acceptable level of risk for all programs and systems in the agency?					
3. Investment Review Board Is there an investment review board (or similar group) designated and empowered to ensure that all investment requests include the security resources needed or that all exceptions to this requirement are documented?					
4. Integrating Information Security and Critical Infrastructure Protection into Capital Planning and Investment Control Is there integration of information security and critical infrastructure protection (CIP) into the CPIC process?					
5. Budget and Resources Are information security resources (internal FTEs and funding) allocated to protect information and information systems in accordance with assessed risks?					
6. Systems and Projects Inventory Are IT projects and systems identified in an inventory and is the information about the IT projects and systems relevant to the investment management process? Is there an inventory of systems as required by FISMA?					
7. IT Security Metrics Are IT security metrics collected agency-wide and reported?					
8. Enterprise Architecture and the Federal Enterprise Architecture Security and Privacy Profile Are system- and enterprise-level information security and privacy requirements and capabilities documented within the agency's enterprise architecture? Is that information used to understand the current risks to the agency's mission? Is that information used to help program and agency executives select the best security and privacy solutions to enable the mission?					
9. Critical Infrastructure Protection Plan If required in your agency, is there a documented critical infrastructure and key resources protection plan that meets the requirements of HSPD-7?					
10. Life Cycle Management Is there a system life cycle management process that requires each system to be certified and accredited? Is each system officially approved to operate? Is the system LCM process communicated to appropriate persons?					

Table 12-4 Information Security Program Questions

Such products are widely available in the marketplace today and are frequently used by federal agencies. Security products and services should be selected and used to support the organization's overall program to manage the design, development, and maintenance of its information security infrastructure and to protect its mission-critical information. Agencies should apply risk management principles to aid in the identification and mitigation of risks associated with the acquisition.

When acquiring information security products, organizations are encouraged to conduct a cost benefit analysis—one that also includes the costs associated with risk mitigation. This cost benefit analysis should include a life cycle cost estimate for the status quo and one for each identified alternative while highlighting the benefits associated with each alternative. NIST SP 800-36, *Guide to Selecting Information Technology (IT) Security Products,* first defines broad security product categories and specifies product types, product characteristics, and environment considerations within those categories. The guide then provides a list of pertinent questions that agencies should ask when selecting products.

The acquisition of services also bears considerable risks that federal agencies must identify and mitigate. The importance of systematically managing the process for acquisition of information security services cannot be underestimated because of the potential impact associated with those risks. In selecting this type of services, agencies should employ risk management processes in the context of information security services life cycle, which provides an organizational framework for information security decision makers. NIST SP 800-35, *Guide to Information Technology Security Services,* provides assistance with the selection, implementation, and management of information security services by guiding the reader through the various phases of the information security services life cycle. Information security decision makers must consider the costs involved, the underlying security requirements, and the impact of their decisions on the organizational mission, operations, strategic functions, personnel, and service-provider arrangements.

The process of selecting information security products and services involves numerous people throughout an organization. Each person involved in the process, whether on an individual or group level, should understand the importance of security in the organization's information infrastructure and the security impacts of their decisions. Depending on its needs, an organization may include all of the personnel listed below or a combination of particular positions relevant to information security needs.

Just as the SDLC supports the development of products, the security services life cycle (SSLC) provides a framework to help security decision makers organize and coordinate their security efforts from initiation to completion. Figure 12-7 depicts the security services life cycle for obtaining security services at a high level. Table 12-5 provides a brief summary of each phase.

Vulnerabilities in IT products surface nearly every day, and many ready-to-use exploits are widely available on the Internet. Because IT products are often intended for a wide variety of audiences, restrictive security controls are usually not enabled by default, so many IT products are immediately vulnerable out of the box. Security program managers should review NIST SP 800-70, *Security Configuration Checklists Program for IT Products,* which helps to facilitate the development and dissemination of security checklists so that organizations and individual users can better secure their IT products. A security configuration checklist (sometimes called a lockdown or hardening guide or benchmark) is, in its simplest form, a series of instructions for configuring a product to a particular operating environment.

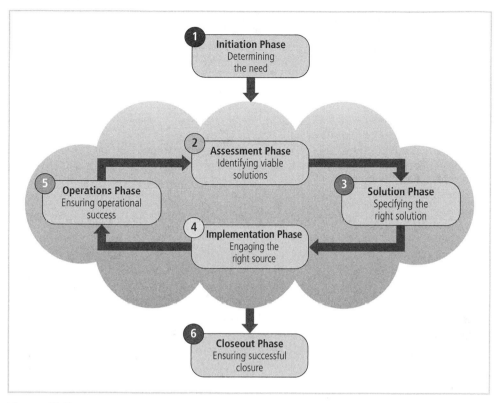

Figure 12-7 The Information Security Services Life Cycle

Source: Course Technology/Cengage Learning

Phase	Activity
Phase 1—Initiation	• Begins when the need to initiate the services life cycle is recognized • Consists of needs determination, security categorization, and the preliminary risk assessment
Phase 2—Assessment	• Involves developing an accurate portrait of the current environment before decision makers can implement a service and install a service provider • Baselines the existing environment; metrics creation, gathering, and analysis; total cost of ownership • Analyzes opportunities and barriers • Identifies options and risks
Phase 3—Solution	• Decision makers choose the appropriate solution from the viable options identified during the assessment phase • Develops the business case • Develops the service arrangement • Develops the implementation plan
Phase 4—Implementation	• Service providers are implemented during this phase • Identifies the service provider and develops the service agreement • Finalizes and executes the implementation plan • Manages expectations

Table 12-5 The Information Security Services Life Cycle

Phase	Activity
Phase 5—Operations	• The service's life cycle becomes iterative; the service is operational, the service provided is fully installed, and a constant assessment of the service level and source performance must be made • Monitors and measures organization performance • Evaluates and evolves
Phase 6—Closeout	• While unlikely, because of the iterative nature of the life cycle, the service and service provider could continue indefinitely • It is more likely that the environment will change such that information security program managers will identify triggers that initiate a new and replacement information security service • Selects the appropriate exit strategy • Implements the selected exit strategy

Table 12-5 The Information Security Services Life Cycle (*continued*)

12. Incident Response

As illustrated throughout this text, attacks on information systems and networks have become more numerous, sophisticated, and severe in recent years. While preventing such attacks would be the ideal course of action, not all information system security incidents can be prevented. Every organization that depends on information systems and networks should identify and assess the risks to its systems and its information and reduce those risks to an acceptable level. An important component of this risk management process is the trending analysis of past computer security incidents and the identification of effective ways to deal with them. A well-defined incident response capability helps the organization detect incidents rapidly, minimize loss and destruction, identify weaknesses, and restore IT operations rapidly.

NIST SP 800-61, *Computer Security Incident Handling Guide*, details a four-phase incident and formed the basis for the material in Chapter 5. This process is illustrated in Figure 12-8. This process is another critical ongoing effort as security managers struggle to prepare for and protect against, react to and recover from incidents.

As you learned in earlier chapters of this book, the first clue that an attack is underway often comes from reports by observant users. Similarly, the first clue that a security system has a fault or error may also come from user feedback. In many organizations, help desks handle these user reports as well as other system problems. If an organization does not have a help desk, it should probably consider establishing one or, at the very least, make other provisions to allow users to report suspicious systems behavior. The Offline titled "The Help Desk" discusses the function and organization of help desks.

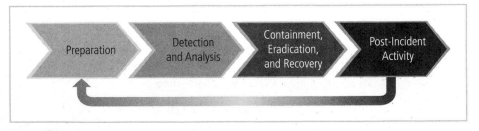

Figure 12-8 The Incident Response Life Cycle

Source: Course Technology/Cengage Learning

Help desk personnel must be trained to distinguish a security problem from other system problems. As help desk personnel screen problems, they must also track the activities involved in resolving each complaint in a help desk information system (a fictional help desk information system, the Information Status and Issues System, or ISIS, was described

Offline
The Help Desk

With a relatively small investment in an IT help desk, an organization can improve the quality of its IT support and information security functions. A small help desk with only a few call agents can provide good—perhaps excellent—service for an organization of several hundred users. Large organizations can also achieve strong improvements in customer service through the use of a help desk; those organizations must be sure to provide their help desks with adequate funding and professional management.

Although it may function differently in different organizations, a help desk commonly provides the following services:

- A single point of contact for service requests from users
- Initial screening of requests, answering common questions, solving common problems, and dispatching other types of calls to other units
- Entering all calls into a tracking system
- Dispatching service providers to respond to calls
- Reporting and analysis of call volumes, patterns, and process improvement

Other services that may be integrated into the help desk include:

- Deskside support for common IT applications such as Windows, end-user computing tools, and common applications
- New-user management
- Timely removal of users who no longer need system access
- Password management
- Smart card management
- Knowledge management for service requests and optimum resolutions
- Server configuration
- Network monitoring
- Server capacity monitoring
- Virus activity monitoring and virus pattern management

While each organization has its own approach to creating and growing a help desk solution, many help desks evolve, and alter the mix of services they offer over time.[1]

in Chapter 1's opening vignette). The tracking process is commonly implemented using a trouble ticket. A trouble ticket is opened when a user calls about an issue and is closed when help desk (or technical support) personnel resolve the issue. One key advantage to having formal help desk software is the ability to create and develop a knowledge base of common problems and solutions. This knowledge base can be searched when a user problem comes up; if the problem is similar to one that was already reported and resolved, the process of resolving complaints can be speeded up. This knowledge base can also generate statistics on the frequency of problems by type, by user, or by application, and thus can detect trends and patterns in the data. Incidentally, some user problems may actually be created or influenced by a security program because modifications to firewalls, implementations of IDPS rules, or new systems policies in the network can directly affect how users interact with the systems. A significant number of help desk trouble tickets are the result of user access issues involving passwords and other authentication, authorization, and accountability mechanisms. Proper user training and ongoing awareness campaigns can reduce these problems but not completely eliminate them.

To resolve a problem, a support technician may need to visit a user's office to examine equipment or observe the user's procedures, or interact with other departments or workgroups. It is not uncommon for the help desk team to include a dedicated security technician. In any case, the person working to resolve the trouble ticket must document not only the diagnosis but also the resolution, as both are invaluable components of the knowledge base. Once the problem has been resolved and the results documented, the ticket is closed.

13. Configuration (or Change) Management The purpose of configuration (or change) management (CM) is to manage the effects of changes or differences in configurations on an information system or network. In some organizations configuration management is the identification, inventory, and documentation of the current information systems status—hardware, software, and networking configurations. Change management is sometimes described as a separate function that only addresses the modifications to this base configuration. Here, we combine the two concepts to address the current and proposed states of the information systems and the management of any needed modifications.

Just as documents should have version numbers, revision dates, and other features designated to monitor and administer the changes made to them, so should the technical components of systems, such as software, hardware, and firmware. There are several terms used in the management of configuration and change in technical components, as follows:

- Configuration item: a hardware or software item that is to be modified and revised throughout its life cycle.
- Version: the recorded state of a particular revision of a software or hardware configuration item. The version number is often noted in a specific format: "M.N.b." In this notation, "M" is the major release number, and "N.b" can represent various minor releases or builds within that major release.
  - Major release: a significant revision of the version from its previous state.
  - Minor release (update or patch): a minor revision of the version from its previous state.
  - Build: a snapshot of a particular version of software assembled (or linked) from its various component modules.
- Build list: a list of the versions of components that make up a build.

- Configuration: a configuration is a collection of components that make up a configuration item.

- Revision date: the date associated with a particular version or build.

- Software library: a collection of configuration items that is usually controlled and that developers use to construct revisions and to issue new configuration items.

To make these definitions more concrete, consider the following hypothetical example: XYZ Security Solutions Corporation develops a new software application—Panacea, the Ultimate Security Solution. Panacea is the configuration item. Panacea's configuration consists of three major software components: See-all, Know-all, and Cure-all. Thus, Panacea is Version 1.0, and it is built from its three components. The build list is See-all 1.0, Know-all 1.0, and Cure-all 1.0, as this is the first major release of the overall application and its components. The revision date is the date associated with the first build. To create Panacea, the programmers at XYZ Security Solutions Corporation pulled information from their software library. Suppose now that while the application is being used in the field, the programmers discover a minor flaw in a subroutine. When they correct this flaw, they issue the minor release, Panacea 1.1. If at some point they need to make a major revision to the software to meet changing market needs or to fix more substantial problems with the subcomponents, they would issue a major release, Panacea 2.0.

CM assists in streamlining change management processes and prevents changes that could detrimentally affect the security posture of a system before they happen. In its entirety, the CM process reduces the risk that any changes made to a system (insertions/installations, deletions/uninstallations, and modifications) result in a compromise to system or data confidentiality, integrity, or availability in that it provides a repeatable mechanism for effecting system modifications in a controlled environment. In accordance with the CM process, system changes must be tested prior to implementation to observe the effects of the change, thereby minimizing the risk of adverse results.

Each organization must take into account the associated costs and expenses, the required planning and scheduling, and the necessary training associated with a thorough and effective CM process. However, because each general CM approach is universal, agencies can structure and implement a repeatable CM process to save organizational resources on future projects. Additionally, CM helps to eliminate the risk of confusion, problems, and unnecessary spending. The additional resources required to correct a problem that could have been prevented through sound CM practices is likely to far exceed the amount of resources required to develop and implement an effective enterprise CM process.

NIST Special Publication 800-64, *Security Considerations in the Information System Development Life Cycle*, states

> *Configuration management and control procedures are critical to establishing an initial baseline of hardware, software, and firmware components for the information system and subsequently to controlling and maintaining an accurate inventory of any changes to the system. Changes to the hardware, software, or firmware of a system can have a significant impact on the security of the system ... changes should be documented, and their potential impact on security should be assessed regularly.*

NIST SP 800-53, Revision 1, *Recommended Security Controls for Federal Information Systems*, defines seven CM controls that organizations are required to implement based on

12

Identifier	Title	Control
CM-1	Configuration Management Policy and Procedures	The organization develops, disseminates, and periodically reviews and updates (1) a formal, documented CM policy that addresses purpose, scope, roles, responsibilities, and compliance; and (2) formal, documented procedures to facilitate the implementation of the CM policy and associated CM controls.
CM-2	Baseline Configuration	The organization develops, documents, and maintains a current baseline configuration of the information system and an inventory of the system's constituent components.
CM-3	Configuration Change Control	The organization documents and controls changes to the information system. Appropriate organization officials approve information system changes in accordance with organizational policies and procedures.
CM-4	Monitoring Configuration Changes	The organization monitors changes to the information system and conducts security impact analyses to determine the effects of the changes.
CM-5	Access Restrictions for Change	The organization enforces access restrictions associated with changes to the information system.
CM-6	Configuration Settings	The organization configures the security settings of IT products to the most restrictive mode consistent with information system operational requirements.
CM-7	Least Functionality	The organization configures the information system to provide only essential capabilities and specifically prohibits and/or restricts the use of the following functions; ports, protocols, and/or services: [*Assignment: organization-defined list of prohibited and/or restricted functions, ports, protocols, and/or services*]. Information systems are capable of providing a wide variety of functions and services. Some of the functions and services provided by default may not be necessary to support essential organizational operations (e.g., key missions, functions). The functions and services provided by information systems should be carefully reviewed to determine which functions and services are candidates for elimination (e.g., voice over Internet protocol, instant messaging, file transfer protocol, hypertext transfer protocol, file sharing).

Table 12-6   NIST SP 800-53 Configuration Management Control Family

an information system's security categorization. The required CM controls are defined in Table 12-6.

The CM process identifies the steps required to ensure that all changes are properly requested, evaluated, and authorized. The CM process also provides a detailed, step-by-step procedure for identifying, processing, tracking, and documenting changes. An example CM process is depicted in Figure 12-9 and is described in the following sections.

Step 1: Identify Change   The first step of the CM process begins with a person or process associated with the information system identifying a need for a change. The change can be initiated by numerous individuals, such as users or system owners, or it may be identified by audit findings or other reviews. A change may consist of updating the fields or records of a database to upgrading the operating system with the latest security patches. Once the need for a change has been identified, a change request should be submitted to the appropriate decision-making body.

Figure 12-9 The Configuration Management Process

Source: Course Technology/Cengage Learning

Step 2: Evaluate Change Request After initiating a change request, the effects that the change may have on the system or other interrelated systems must be evaluated. An impact analysis of the change should be conducted using the following guidelines:

- Whether the change is viable and improves the performance or the security of the system
- Whether the change is technically correct, necessary, and feasible within the system constraints
- Whether system security will be affected by the change
- Whether associated costs for implementing the change were considered
- Whether security components are affected by the change

Step 3: Implementation Decision Once the change has been evaluated and tested, one of the following actions should be taken:

- Approve: Implementation is authorized and may occur at any time after the appropriate authorization signature has been documented.
- Deny: The request is immediately denied regardless of circumstances and information provided.
- Defer: Immediate decision is postponed until further notice. In this situation, additional testing or analysis may be needed before a final decision can be made.

Step 4: Implement Approved Change Request Once the decision to implement the change has been made, it should be moved from the test environment into production. If required, the personnel updating the production environment should be separate from those individuals who developed the change to provide a greater assurance that unapproved changes do not get implemented into production.

Step 5: Continuous Monitoring The CM process calls for continuous system monitoring to ensure that it is operating as intended and that implemented changes do not adversely impact either the performance or security posture of the system. Agencies can achieve the goals of continuous system monitoring by performing configuration verification tests to ensure that the selected configuration for a given system has not been altered outside of the established CM process. In addition to configuration verification tests, agencies can also perform system audits. Both configuration verification tests and system audits entail an examination of characteristics of the system and supporting documentation to verify that the configuration meets user needs and ensure that the current configuration is the approved system configuration baseline.

As part of the overall CM process, agencies should also perform patch management activities during this step. Patch management assists in the process of lowering the potential risk to a network by "patching" or repairing known vulnerabilities in any of the network or system

12

environments. Increasingly, vendors are proactive in developing and releasing to the public fixes (or antidotes) to known vulnerabilities, and agencies must remain vigilant to ensure that they capture all relevant fixes as they are released, test their implementation for adverse effects, and implement them if deemed appropriate after testing is concluded. Patching is associated with phase 4 in the life cycle as well as with phases 2 and 3. In phase 2, patch management relates to risk management to prevent any vulnerability from being exploited and compromised. Phase 3 contains the testing to ensure that any change (including the patching) does not negatively impact the system.

In general, configuration and change management should not interfere with the use of the technology. One person on the security team should be appointed as the configuration manager or change manager and made responsible for maintaining the appropriate data elements in the organization's cataloging mechanism, such as the specific version, revision date, and build associated with each piece of hardware and software implemented. In some cases, it may be better to have someone outside the implementation process document the process, so this person is not distracted by the installation, configuration, and troubleshooting of the new implementation. In the case of minor revisions, it may be simpler to have a procedure in place that involves documenting the machines on which a revision is installed, the date and time of the installation, and the name of the installer. While the documentation procedures required for the configuration and change management processes may seem onerous, they enable security teams to quickly and accurately determine exactly which systems are affected when a new vulnerability arises. When stored in a comprehensive database along with risk, threat, and attack information, configuration information enables organizations to respond quickly to new and rapidly changing threats and attacks.

The Security Maintenance Model

While a management model such as the 27000 series NIST SP 800-100 *Information Security Handbook: A Guide for Managers* deals with methods to *manage* and *operate* systems, a maintenance model is designed (in ways that complement the chosen management model) to focus organizational effort on *maintaining* systems. An approach that is recommended by this text for dealing with change caused by information security maintenance is presented in Figure 12-10. This figure diagrams a full maintenance program and serves as a framework for the discussion that follows.

The recommended maintenance model is based on five subject areas or domains:

- External monitoring
- Internal monitoring
- Planning and risk assessment
- Vulnerability assessment and remediation
- Readiness and review

In the sections that follow, each of these domains is explored and their interaction discussed.

Monitoring the External Environment

During the Cold War, the western alliance, led by the United States and Britain, confronted the Soviet Union and its allies. A key component of the Western alliance's defense was maintaining the ability to detect early warnings of attacks. The image of an ever-vigilant team of radar operators scanning the sky for incoming attacks using a global network of sensors

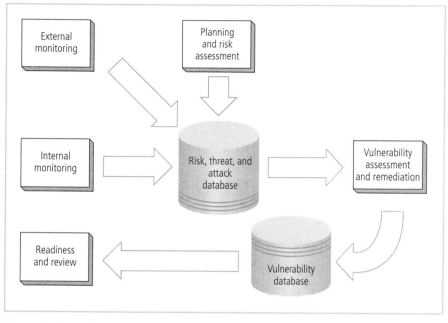

Figure 12-10 The Maintenance Model

Source: Course Technology/Cengage Learning

could also represent the current world of information security, where teams of information security personnel must guard their respective organizations against dangerous and debilitating threats. While the stakes for modern-day organizations are not equivalent (i.e., they do not typically involve the possibility of nuclear Armageddon), they are nevertheless very high—especially as organizations become more and more information dependent.

The objective of the **external monitoring domain** within the maintenance model is to provide the early awareness of new and emerging threats, threat agents, vulnerabilities, and attacks that the organization needs in order to mount an effective and timely defense. Figure 12-11 shows the primary components of the external monitoring process.

External monitoring entails collecting intelligence from various data sources and then giving that intelligence context and meaning for use by decision makers within the organization.

Data Sources Acquiring data about threats, threat agents, vulnerabilities, and attacks is not difficult. There are many sources of raw intelligence and relatively few costs associated with gathering the intelligence. What is challenging (and possibly expensive) is turning this flood of good and timely data into information that decision makers can use. For this reason, some organizations outsource this component of the maintenance model. Various service providers can provide a complete tailored supply of processed intelligence to organizations that can afford their subscription fees. Other providers supply varying levels of analysis and timeliness for their clients.

As shown in Figure 12-11, external intelligence can come from three classes of sources:

- Vendors: When an organization uses specific software products as part of its information security program, the vendor often provides either direct support or indirect tools

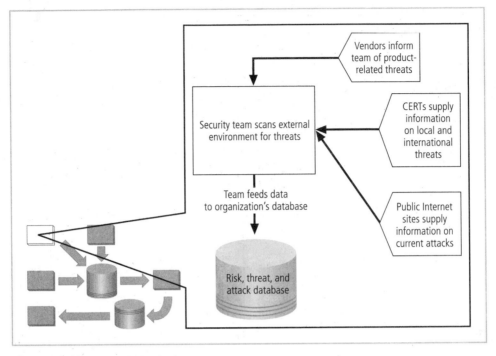

Figure 12-11 External Monitoring

Source: Course Technology/Cengage Learning

that allow user communities to support each other. This support often includes intelligence on emerging threats.

- CERT organizations: Computer emergency response teams (CERTs) exist in varying forms around the world. Often, US-CERT (*www.us-cert.gov*) is viewed as the definitive authority. Many states have CERT agencies, and many countries have CERT organizations to deal with specific national issues and threats. Your local, state, or national government may have a CERT outreach program to provide the notification services to you at no direct cost. The U.S. Department of Homeland Security works with the CERT/CC program at Carnegie Mellon to provide the services at US-CERT. More information about this joint program is available at www.us-cert.gov/aboutus.html.

- Public network sources: Many publicly accessible information sources, both mailing lists and Web sites, are freely available to those organizations and individuals who have the time and expertise to make use of them. Table 12-7 lists some of these information security intelligence sources.

Regardless of where or how external monitoring data is collected, in order to be useful it must be analyzed in the context of the organization's security environment. To perform this evaluation and take appropriate actions in a timely fashion, the CISO must:

- Staff the function with people who have the correct depth and breadth of technical information security knowledge, as well as a comprehensive understanding of the organization's complete IT infrastructure and a thorough grounding in the business operations of the organization

- Provide documented and repeatable procedures
- Train the primary and backup staff assigned to perform the monitoring tasks
- Equip assigned staff with proper access and tools to perform the monitoring function

Source Name	Type	Comments
Bugtraq	Mailing list	A set of moderated mailing lists, provided by SecurityFocus, full of detailed, full-disclosure discussions and announcements about computer security vulnerabilities (see descriptions of the individual mailing lists in the table entries that follow). The primary mailing list, called Bugtraq, provides time-sensitive coverage of emerging vulnerabilities, documenting how they are exploited, and reporting on how to remediate them. Individuals can register for the flagship mailing list or any one of the entire family of Bugtraq mailing lists at *www.securityfocus.com/archive*.
Bugtraq focus-ids	Mailing list	Contains information about intrusion detection systems vulnerabilities, and discusses both how to exploit them and how to use them in defending networks.
Bugtraq focus-ms	Mailing list	Discusses the inner workings and underlying software weaknesses of Microsoft software products. It includes detailed discussions on the various security mechanisms available to help assess, secure, and remediate Microsoft software products.
Bugtraq forensics	Mailing list	A discussion of technical and process methodologies for the application of computer forensics. The discussion is centered around technical methodology, audit trail analysis (technical procedures), general postmortem analysis (technical procedures), products and tools for use in this field (technical discussion), process methodology for evidence handling (technical discussion), search and seizure (nontechnical procedures and discussion), and evidence-handling policies (nontechnical procedures and discussion).
Bugtraq incidents	Mailing list	A lightly moderated mailing list that facilitates the quick exchange of security incident information. Topics include information about rootkits and back doors; new Trojan horses, viruses, and worms; sources of attacks; and telltale signs of intrusions.
Bugtraq pen-test	Mailing list	Allows people to converse about professional penetration testing. The list is not OS-specific and has discussions on many varieties of networks and devices.
Bugtraq vuln-dev	Mailing list	Contains reports of potential or undeveloped vulnerabilities. This is a full-disclosure list and can include exploit code.
Bugtraq focus-virus	Mailing list	Discusses the inner workings and underlying issues of the various products, tools, and techniques available that may help secure systems from virus threats.
CERT/CC and US-CERT	Web site	The CERT Coordination Center (CERT/CC) is a center of Internet security expertise and is located at the Software Engineering Institute, a federally funded research and development center operated by Carnegie Mellon University. CERT/CC and the U.S. Department of Homeland Security support the Web site, which is usually considered the definitive authority to be consulted when emerging threats become demonstrated vulnerabilities. See CERT/CC's home page at *www.cert.org*.
US-CERT Advisory Mailing List	Mailing list	The CERT/CC, in conjunction with the U.S. Department of Homeland Security, provides the National Cyber Alert System, which can send e-mail advisory and supporting information to registered organizations and individuals. You can select the type of notifications you need and register for the desired advisory list at *www.us-cert.gov/cas/index.html*.

Table 12-7 **External Intelligence Sources**

Source Name	Type	Comments
IBM Internet Security Systems (ISS)	Web site	A commercial site with a focus on the vendor's own commercial IDPS and other security products. The site also provides breaking news about emerging threats, and allows individuals to subscribe to alerts. See *www.iss.net*.
Insecure Mailing List Archive	Web site	*Insecure.org* is the creation of the well-known hacker Fyodor. He and his associates operate *www.insecure.org* and provide the Internet community with software (Nmap is the best known of the *www.insecure.org* tools) and information about vulnerabilities. Many topics are covered in the available lists at *www.seclists.org*.
NESSUS-DEVEL	Mailing list	Tenable's Web site dedicated to the Nessus vulnerability scanner. The Nessus Web site has information about emerging threats and how to test for them. It can be found at *www.nessus.org*.
Nmap-hackers	Mailing list	Intended to facilitate the development of Nmap, a free network exploration tool. Read the file at *seclists.org/about/nmap-hackers.txt* to learn how to subscribe.
Packet Storm	Web site	A commercial site focusing on current security tool resources. *www.packetstormsecurity.org*.
Security Focus Online	Web site	A commercial site providing general coverage and commentary on information security. *www.securityfocus.com*.
Snort-sigs	Mailing list	Includes announcements and discussion of Snort, an open-source IDPS. The list includes discussions and information about the program and its rule sets and signatures. It can be a useful source for information about detecting emerging threats. Individuals can register for this mailing list at *lists.sourceforge.net/ lists/listinfo/snort-sigs*.

Table 12-7   **External Intelligence Sources (***continued***)**

- Cultivate expertise among the monitoring analysts so they can perform analytic steps to cull meaningful summaries and actionable alerts from the vast flow of raw intelligence

- Develop suitable communications methods for moving processed intelligence to designated internal decision makers in all three communities of interest—that is, in IT, information security, and general management

- Integrate the incident response plan with the results of the external monitoring process to produce appropriate, timely responses

Monitoring, Escalation, and Incident Response The basic function of the external monitoring process is to monitor activity, report results, and escalate warnings. The optimum approach for escalation is based on a thorough integration of the monitoring process into the IRP (discussed in Chapter 5). The monitoring process has three primary deliverables:

- Specific warning bulletins issued when developing threats and specific attacks pose a measurable risk to the organization. The bulletins should assign a meaningful risk-level to the threat to help decision makers in the organization formulate the appropriate response.

- Periodic summaries of external information. The summaries present either statistical results (for example, the number of new or revised CERT advisories per month) or itemized lists of significant new vulnerabilities.

- Detailed intelligence on the highest risk warnings. This information prepares the way for the detection and remediation of vulnerabilities in the later steps of vulnerability assessment. This intelligence can include identifying which vendor updates apply to which vulnerabilities as well as which types of defenses have been found to work against the specific vulnerabilities reported.

Data Collection and Management Over time, the external monitoring processes should capture information about the external environment in a format that can be referenced both across the organization as threats emerge and for historical use. This can be accomplished using e-mail, Web pages, databases, or even paper-and-pencil recording methods, so long as the essential facts are communicated, stored, and can be used to make queries when needed. In the final analysis, external monitoring collects raw intelligence, filters it for relevance to the organization, assigns it a relative risk impact, and communicates these findings to the decision makers in time to make a difference. As an alternative view of the way data flows into the monitoring process, a data flow diagram (DFD) approach may prove useful. On the left-hand side of Figure 12-12, a level 0 data flow diagram for the entire maintenance process shows how data flows in the overall process. On the right-hand side, a Level 1 diagram for the external data collection process shows the sources of external monitoring data in more detail.

Monitoring the Internal Environment

The primary goal of the **internal monitoring domain** is to maintain an informed awareness of the state of all of the organization's networks, information systems, and information security defenses. This awareness must be communicated and documented, especially for components that are exposed to the external network. Internal monitoring is accomplished by:

- Building and maintaining an inventory of network devices and channels, IT infrastructure and applications, and information security infrastructure elements.

- Leading the IT governance process within the organization to integrate the inevitable changes found in all network, IT, and information security programs.

- Monitoring IT activity in real-time using IDPSs to detect and initiate responses to specific actions or trends of events that introduce risk to the organization's information assets.

- Monitoring the internal state of the organization's networks and systems. This recursive review of the network and system devices that are online at any given moment and of any changes to the services offered on the network is needed to maintain awareness of new and emerging threats. This can be accomplished through automated difference-detection methods that identify variances introduced to the network or system hardware and software.

The value of internal monitoring is high when the resulting knowledge of the network and systems configuration is fed into the vulnerability assessment and remediation maintenance domain. But this knowledge becomes invaluable when incident response processes are fully integrated with the monitoring processes.

Figure 12-13 shows the component processes of the internal monitoring domain, which are discussed in the sections that follow.

12

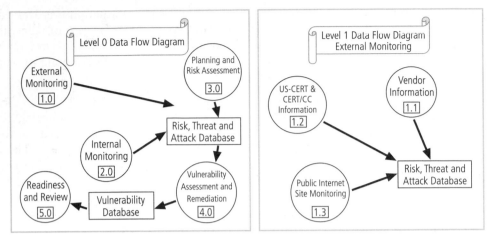

Figure 12-12 Data Flow Diagrams for External Data Collection

Source: Course Technology/Cengage Learning

Network Characterization and Inventory Organizations should have a carefully planned and fully populated inventory of all their network devices, communication channels, and computing devices. This inventory should certainly include servers, as well as desktop applications and *partner interconnections*—that is, network devices, communications channels, and applications that may not be owned by the organization but are essential to the continued operation of the organization's partnership with another company. The process of collecting this information is often referred to as *characterization*.

Once the characteristics of the network environment have been identified and collected as data, they must be carefully organized and stored using a manual or automated mechanism that allows for timely retrieval and rapid integration of disparate facts. For all but the smallest network environments, this requires a relational database. The attributes of the network devices (systems, switches, gateways, and the like) have been discussed in earlier chapters (namely, in the discussion on information asset identification in Chapter 4). In contrast to the attributes collected for risk management, which are concerned with economic and business value, the characteristics collected here—manufacturer and software versions—are about technical functionality, and they should be kept highly accurate and up-to-date. Also, the technology underpinning the storage of this data should be stand-alone and portable, because if this data is called into action to support incident responses and disaster recovery, server or network access may be unavailable.

Making Intrusion Detection and Prevention Systems Work To be put to the most effective use, the information that comes from an IDPS must be integrated into the maintenance process. An IDPS generates a seemingly endless flow of alert messages that often have little effect on the immediate operational effectiveness of the information security program. Except for an occasional real-time alert that is not a false positive, the IDPS is reporting events that have already occurred. Given this, the most important value of the raw intelligence provided by the IDPS is that it can be used to prevent future attacks by pointing to current or imminent vulnerabilities. Whether the organization outsources IDPS monitoring, staffs IDPS monitoring 24/7, staffs IDPS monitoring during business hours, or

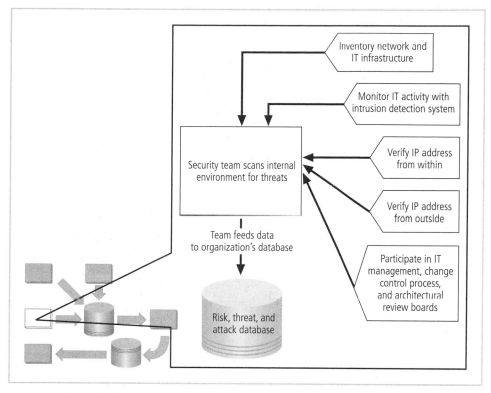

Figure 12-13 Internal Monitoring

Source: Course Technology/Cengage Learning

merely ignores the real-time alerts from IDPS, the log files from the IDPS engines can be mined for information that can be added to the internal monitoring knowledge base.

Another element of IDPS monitoring is traffic analysis. Analyzing the traffic that flows through a system and its associated devices can often be a critically important process, as it identifies the most frequently used devices. Also, analyzing attack signatures from unsuccessful system attacks can help identify weaknesses in various security efforts. An example of the type of vulnerability exposed via traffic analysis occurs when an organization is trying to determine if all its device signatures have been adequately masked. In general, the default configuration setting of many network devices allows the device to respond to any request with a device signature message that identifies the device's make and model and perhaps even its software version. In the interest of greater security, many organizations require that all devices be reconfigured to conceal their device signatures. Now suppose one such organization performs an analysis of unsuccessful attacks, and the analysis reveals that lesser-known UNIX attacks are being launched against one of its servers. This discovery might inform the organization that the server under attack is responding to requests for OS type with its device signature.

Detecting Differences One approach that can improve the situational awareness of the information security function uses a process known as difference analysis to quickly identify changes to the internal environment. **Difference analysis** is a procedure that compares the current state of a network segment (the systems and services it offers) against a known previous state of that same network segment (the baseline of systems and services).

Any unexpected differences between the current state and the baseline state could indicate trouble. Table 12-8 shows how several kinds of difference analyses can be used.

Note that Table 12-8 lists suggestions for *possible* difference analyses. Each organization should identify what differences it wants to measure and its criteria for action. The value of difference analysis depends on the quality of the baseline, which is the initial snapshot portion of the difference comparison. It also depends on the degree to which the notification of discovered differences can induce action.

Planning and Risk Assessment

As described in the previous section on the security management maintenance model, the primary objective of the **planning and risk assessment domain** is to keep a lookout over the entire information security program, in part by identifying and planning ongoing information security activities that further reduce risk. In fact, the bulk of the security management maintenance model could fit in this domain. Also, the risk assessment group identifies and documents risks introduced by both IT projects and information security projects. It also identifies and documents risks that may be latent in the present environment. The primary objectives of this domain are:

- Establishing a formal information security program review process that complements and supports both the IT planning process and strategic planning processes

Suggested Frequency	Method of Analysis	Data Source	Purpose
Quarterly	Manual	Firewall rules	To verify that new rules follow all risk assessment and procedural approvals; identify illicit rules; ensure removal of expired rules; and detect tampering
Quarterly	Manual	Edge router rules	To verify that new rules follow all risk assessment and procedural approvals; identify illicit rules; ensure removal of expired rules; and detect tampering
Quarterly	Manual	Internet footprint	To verify that public Internet presence (addresses registered to the organization) is accurate and complete
Monthly	Automated	Fingerprint all IP addresses	To verify that only known and authorized devices offering critical services can be reached from the internal network
Weekly	Automated	Fingerprint services on critical servers on the internal network	To verify that only known and approved services are offered from critical servers in the internal network
Daily	Automated	Fingerprint all IP addresses from the outside	To verify that only known and approved servers (and other devices) can be reached from the public network
Hourly	Automated	Fingerprint services on critical servers exposed to the Internet	To enable the e-mail notification of administrators if unexpected services become available on critical servers exposed to the Internet

Table 12-8 Types of Difference Analysis

- Instituting formal project identification, selection, planning, and management processes for information security follow-up activities that augment the current information security program

- Coordinating with IT project teams to introduce risk assessment and review for all IT projects, so that risks introduced by the launching of IT projects are identified, documented, and factored into decisions about the projects

- Integrating a mindset of risk assessment across the organization to encourage other departments to perform risk assessment activities when any technology system is implemented or modified

Figure 12-14 illustrates the relationships between the components of this maintenance domain. Note that there are two pivotal processes: the planning needed for the information security programs and evaluation of current risks using operational risk assessment.

Information Security Program Planning and Review Periodic review of an ongoing information security program coupled with planning for enhancements and extensions is a recommended practice for any organization. The strategic planning process should examine the future IT needs of the organization and the impact those needs have on information security.

A recommended approach is to take advantage of the fact that most larger organizations have annual capital budget planning cycles. Thus, the IT group would develop an annual list of project ideas for project planning and then prepare an estimate for the effort needed to

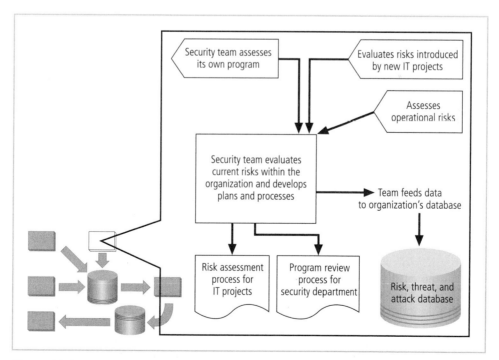

Figure 12-14 Planning and Risk Assessment

Source: Course Technology/Cengage Learning

complete it and the capital it might require, as well as a preliminary assessment of the risks associated with performing or not performing each project. These assessments become part of the organization's project-planning process. When capital and expense budgets are made final, the projects to be funded are chosen using the planning information already prepared. This allows executives to make informed decisions about which projects to fund. The IT group then follows up with quarterly reviews of progress, which include an updated project risk assessment. As each project nears completion, an operational risk assessment group reviews the impact of the project on the risk profile of the organization. The sponsors of the project, and perhaps other executives, then determine if the risk level is acceptable, if the project requires additional risk remediation, or if the project must be aborted.

Projects that organizations might fund to maintain, extend, or enhance the information security program will arise in almost every planning cycle. Larger information security projects should be broken into smaller, incremental projects. Doing this is important for several reasons:

- Smaller projects tend to have more manageable impacts on the networks and users.

- Larger projects tend to complicate the change control process in the implementation phase.

- Shorter planning, development, and implementation schedules reduce uncertainty for IT planners and financial sponsors.

- Most large projects can easily be broken down into smaller projects, giving the security team more opportunities to change direction and gain flexibility as events occur and circumstances change.

Security Risk Assessments A key component in the engine that drives change in the information security program is a relatively straightforward process called an **information security operational risk assessment** (RA). The RA is a method of identifying and documenting the risk that a project, process, or action introduces to the organization and may also involve offering suggestions for controls that can reduce that risk. The information security group is in the business of coordinating the preparation of many different types of RA documents, including:

- Network connectivity RA: Used to respond to network change requests and network architectural design proposals. May be part of or support a business partner's RA.

- Dialed modem RA: Used when a dial-up connection is requested for a system.

- Business partner RA: Used when a proposal for connectivity with business partners is being evaluated.

- Application RA: Used at various stages in the life cycle of a business application. Content depends on the project's position in the life cycle when the RA is prepared. Usually, multiple RA documents are prepared at different stages. The definitive version is prepared as the application is readied for conversion to production.

- Vulnerability RA: Used to assist in communicating the background, details, and proposed remediation as vulnerabilities emerge or change over time.

- Privacy RA: Used to document applications or systems that contain protected personal information that needs to be evaluated for compliance with privacy policies of the organization and relevant laws.

- Acquisition or divesture RA: Used when planning for reorganization as units of the organization are acquired, divested, or moved.

- Other RA: Used when a statement about risk is needed for any project, proposal, or fault that is not contained in the preceding list.

The RA process identifies risks and proposes controls. Most RA documents are structured to include the components shown in Table 12-9. Most training programs on information security include training sessions for the preparation of RA documents.

Component	Description	When and How Used
Introduction	A standard opening description to explain the RA to readers who are unfamiliar with the format. The exact text varies for each RA template. Here is an example: "The primary purpose of the security risk assessment is to identify computer and network security risks to information assets that may be introduced to the organization by the issue described in this risk assessment document. This security risk assessment is also used to help identify security controls planned or proposed. Further, the sections below may identify risks that are not adequately controlled by the planned controls."	Found in all RA document templates
Scope	A statement of the boundaries of the RA. Here is an example: "To define the security and control requirements associated with project X running application Y with access via Internet and the migration of that application into the organization's environment."	Found in all RA document templates
Disclaimer	A statement containing language that identifies limits in the risk assessment based on where in the project life cycle the report was developed. The information available at different times in the life of the project affects how comprehensive and accurate the report is. Often, risk assessments are the most imprecise at the earliest stages of a project, and it is important that decision makers are made aware of this lack of precision when it is based on incomplete information. This statement is sometimes removed in the final RA when all information about the project is available, but it may be left in order to provide awareness that some imprecision is inherent in the process. Here is an example: "The issues documented in this report should not be considered all inclusive. A number of strategic and tactical decisions will be made during the development and implementation stages of the project, and therefore the security control deliverables may change based on actual implementation. Any changes should be reassessed to ensure that proper controls will still be enacted."	Found in all draft RA document templates; some issues may remain in the disclaimer in some final RA templates

Table 12-9 Risk Assessment Documentation Components

Component	Description	When and How Used
Information security resources	A list of the names of the information security team members who collected information, analyzed risk, and documented the findings.	Found in all RA document templates
Other resources	A list of the names of the other organization members who provided information, assisted in analyzing risk, and documented the findings.	Found in all RA document templates
Background	A documentation of the proposed project, including network changes, application changes, and other issues or faults.	Found in all RA document templates
Planned controls	A documentation of all controls that are planned in the proposed project, including network changes, application changes, and other issues or faults.	Found in all RA document templates
IRP and DRP planning elements	A documentation of the incident response and disaster planning elements that have been or will be prepared for this proposed project, including network changes, application changes, and other issues or faults.	Recommended in all document templates
Opinion of risk	A summary statement of the risk to the organization introduced by the proposed project, network change, application, or other issue or fault. Here is an example: "This application as it currently exists is considered high risk. IMPORTANT NOTE: Because of the high risk of the current implementation and the potential for impact on the organization if system or data is compromised in any way, this notification needs to be escalated to the director or manager who would be held responsible for the added expense or loss of revenue associated with such a compromise. In addition, an acknowledgement of and signing off on the understanding of the nature of the risk and the urgency of correcting it must be returned to the CISO of the organization."	Found in all RA document templates
Recommenda-tions	A statement of what needs to be done to implement controls within the project to limit risk from the proposed project. Here is an example: "A project team should be formed to assist the operating unit and technical support team to create a comprehensive plan to address the security issues within application X. Specific areas of concern are authentication and authorization. The corrections of configuration errors found in the platform security validation process must continue. All user accounts need to be reviewed and scrubbed to determine whether the user or service account requires access. All user accounts need to be reviewed and assigned the appropriate privileges. Integrity: the Web server function of the application needs to be separated from the application and database server."	Found in all RA document templates

Table 12-9 Risk Assessment Documentation Components (*continued*)

Component	Description	When and How Used
Information security controls recommendations summary	A summary of the controls that are planned or needed, using the security architecture elements of the system as an organizing method. The following categories of information are recommended to be documented in tabular form: • Security architecture elements and what they provide: ◦ Authentication: the user is verified as authentic. ◦ Authorization: the user is allowed to use the facility or service. ◦ Confidentiality: content must be kept secret from unintended recipients. ◦ Integrity: data storage must be secure, accurate, and precise. ◦ Accountability: actions and data usage can be attributed to specific individuals. ◦ Availability and reliability: systems work when needed. ◦ Privacy: systems comply with organizational privacy policy. • Security requirement written for a general audience in terms of the organization's information security policies using the following core principles of information security: ◦ Authentication: must conform to organizational authentication policies. ◦ Authorization: must conform to organization authorization and usage policies. ◦ Confidentiality: must comply with the requirement to protect data in transit from interception and misuse by using hard encryption. ◦ Integrity: must process data with procedures that ensure freedom from corruption. ◦ Accountability: must track usage to allow actions to be audited at a later time for policy compliance. ◦ Availability and reliability: must be implemented to assure availability that measures up to current organizational expectations. ◦ Privacy: must process, store, and transmit data using procedures sufficient to meet legal privacy requirements. • Security controls planned or in place: identify controls for each architectural element. • Planned completion date when the control will be fully operational. • Who is responsible: which group or individuals are accountable for implementing the control? • Status: what is the status of the control implementation?	Recommended in all document templates

Table 12-9 **Risk Assessment Documentation Components (*continued*)**

A risk assessment's identification of the systemic or latent vulnerabilities that introduce risk to the organization can provide the opportunity to create a proposal for an information security project. When used as part of a complete risk management maintenance process, the RA can be a powerful and flexible tool that helps identify and document risk and remediate the underlying vulnerabilities that expose the organization to risks of loss.

Vulnerability Assessment and Remediation

The primary goal of the **vulnerability assessment and remediation domain** is to identify specific, documented vulnerabilities and remediate them in a timely fashion. This is accomplished by:

- Using documented vulnerability assessment procedures to collect intelligence about networks (internal and public-facing), platforms (servers, desktops, and process control), dial-in modems, and wireless network systems safely

- Documenting background information and providing tested remediation procedures for the reported vulnerabilities

- Tracking vulnerabilities from when they are identified until they are remediated or the risk of loss has been accepted by an authorized member of management

- Communicating vulnerability information including an estimate of the risk and detailed remediation plans to the owners of the vulnerable systems

- Reporting on the status of vulnerabilities that have been identified

- Ensuring that the proper level of management is involved in the decision to accept the risk of loss associated with unrepaired vulnerabilities

Figure 12-15 illustrates the process flow of the vulnerability assessment and remediation domain. Using the inventory of environment characteristics stored in the risk, threat, and attack database, the vulnerability assessment processes identify and document vulnerabilities. These vulnerabilities are stored, tracked, and reported within the vulnerability database until they are remediated.

The process of identifying and documenting specific and provable flaws in the organization's information asset environment is called **vulnerability assessment (VA)**. As shown in Figure 12-15, there are five common vulnerability assessment processes: internet VA, intranet VA, platform

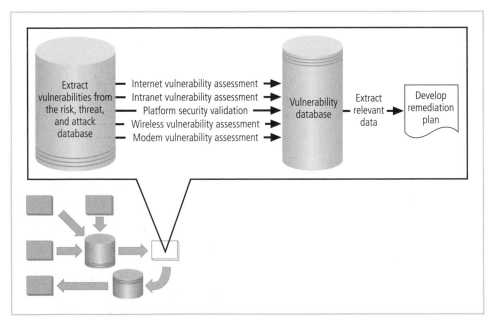

Figure 12-15 Vulnerability Assessment and Remediation

Source: Course Technology/Cengage Learning

security validation, wireless VA, and modem VA. While the exact procedures associated with each can vary, these five vulnerability assessment processes can serve many organizations as they attempt to balance the intrusiveness of vulnerability assessment with the need for a stable and effective production environment. Some organizations pursue a strategy of monthly vulnerability assessments that involve all five processes. Others perform an Internet vulnerability assessment weekly and choose from the other four processes on a rotating monthly or quarterly basis. These choices depend on the quantity and quality of the resources dedicated to vulnerability assessments.

Penetration Testing Penetration testing, a level beyond vulnerability testing, is a set of security tests and evaluations that simulate attacks by a malicious external source (hacker). A penetration test, or *pen test*, is usually performed periodically as part of a full security audit. While in most security tests, such as vulnerability assessments, great care is taken not to disrupt normal business operations, in pen testing the analyst tries to get as far as possible, simulating the actions of an attacker. Unlike the attacker, however, the pen tester's ultimate responsibility is to identify weaknesses in the security of the organization's systems and networks and then present findings to the system owners in a detailed report.

While vulnerability testing is usually performed inside the organization's security perimeter, with complete knowledge of the networks configuration and operations, pen testing can be conducted one of two ways—black box pen testing and white box pen testing. In black box pen testing, or blind testing, the "attacker" has no prior knowledge of the systems or network configurations and thus must investigate the organization's information infrastructure from scratch. In white box testing, also known as full disclosure testing, the organization provides information about the systems to be tested, allowing for a faster, more focused test. White box pen testing is usually used when a specific system or network segment is suspect and the organization wants the pen tester to focus on a particular aspect of the target. Variations of black and white box testing, known as grey box or partial disclosure tests, involve partial knowledge of the organization's infrastructure.

It is quite common for organizations to hire private security firms or consultants to perform penetration testing, for a number of reasons:

- The "attacker" would have little knowledge of the inner working and configuration of the systems and network other than that provided by the organization, resulting in a more realistic attack.

- Unlike vulnerability assessment testing, penetration testing is a highly skilled operation, requiring levels of expertise beyond that of the average security professional.

- Also unlike vulnerability assessment testing, penetration testing requires customized attacks, preventing the use of standard, preconfigured scripts and utilities.

- External consultants have no vested interests in the outcome of the testing and are thus in a position to offer more honest, critical reports.

A common methodology for pen testing is found in the Open Source Security Testing Methodology Manual. "The OSSTMM is a manual on security testing and analysis created by Pete Herzog and provided by ISECOM, the non-profit Institute for Security and Open Methodologies. The methodology itself that covers what, when, and where to test is free to use and distribute under the Open Methodology License (OML). The manual, the OSSTMM as a whole, is also free, released under the Creative Commons 2.5 Attribution-NonCommercial-NoDerivs license. The manual states, 'All things being interconnected, this methodology is free precisely because we prefer to be as well.'"[2] The manual can be accessed from *www.isecom.org/osstmm*.

There are a number of penetration testing certifications that people interested in this aspect of security testing can pursue. The Information Assurance Certification Review Board (IACRB) offers a pen testing certification known as the Certified Penetration Tester (CPT). The CPT requires that the applicant pass a multiple-choice exam as well as a take-home practical exam that requires the candidate to perform a penetration test against live servers. Subject areas on the multiple choice exam include:

- Penetration testing methodologies
- Network protocol attacks
- Network reconnaissance
- Vulnerability identification
- Windows exploits
- Unix/Linux exploits
- Covert Channels and rootkits
- Wireless security flaws
- Web application vulnerabilities

For more information on this certification visit *www.iacertification.org*.

There are other penetration testing exams and approaches that use the term *ethical hacking*. While these penetration testing certifications and efforts are valid, the use of the term *ethical hacking* is problematic, as described in the Offline "Ethical Hacking."

Offline
Ethical Hacking

An Etymological View of Ethical Hacking[3]

How we describe something defines it. A specific choice of words can cause irreparable damage to an idea or immortalize it. Part of the foundation of the field of information security is the expectation of ethical behavior. Most modern certifications and professional associations in information security, and to a lesser extent information technology in general, require their members to subscribe to codes of ethics. These canons ("a body of rules, principles, or standards accepted as axiomatic and universally binding in a field of study or art"[4]) provide guidance to the members and associates of an organization. They also represent an agreement between the members and their constituencies to provide ethical ("being in accordance with the rules or standards for right conduct or practice, esp. the standards of a profession"[5]) service.

If there is any doubt as to the validity of these ethical codes or to the actual conduct of those who subscribe to them, the entire discipline suffers. One such area which is gaining notoriety in the field of computing is the concept of the "hacker."

When the computer era began, *hacker* was a term used to describe a computer enthusiast, someone who enjoyed pushing the boundaries of computer technologies and who frequently had to apply unorthodox techniques to accomplish their desired goals. In the mid-1950s the term *hacker* was reportedly associated with members of the MIT Model Railroad Club—"one who works like a hack at writing and experimenting with software, one who enjoys computer programming for its own sake."[6] Today, the term has evolved into one with a much more sinister definition. According to the American Heritage Dictionary, to hack is:

a. "*Informal* To alter (a computer program)
b. To gain access to (a computer file or network) illegally or without authorization"[7]

The problem with hacking isn't merely the fact that some individuals actively seek to gain unauthorized access to others' information assets; rather, the problem is much, much deeper. The problem lies in the inexplicable fascination that society has with the disreputable. This phenomenon is widespread, and one has only to reflect on our own popular culture to find "felonious heroes" like Jesse James, Al Capone, Bonnie and Clyde, and those portrayed in the popular media. We are enthralled by the apparent disregard for authority exhibited by these individuals, many of whom are portrayed as wrongfully accused. Some argue that we live vicariously through those who display no apparent regard for proper behavior, allowing themselves to behave as the whim suits them, rather than by society's bonds. Others seek the public attention afforded those who are reported as "public enemies" and made notorious by the media. Whatever the psychological attraction, the end result is that some segments of our society choose to turn a blind eye on certain crimes, most notably in recent generations in the field of computers with the growing notoriety of computer hacking.

Computer hacking in the media is portrayed with a mixed message. Movies like *Ferris Beuller's Day Off*,[8] *WarGames*,[9] and *Hackers*[10] portray teenage hackers as idols and heroes. Unfortunately this mixed message is being perpetuated into the modern information security society. We as the stoic guardians of information assets should completely and totally condemn the entire hacker genre and culture.

This brings us to the point of this rant—the ethical hacker. The phrase *ethical hacker* is an oxymoron ("a figure of speech by which a locution produces an incongruous, seemingly self-contradictory effect"[11]). The MIT/Stanford "hacker ethic" written by Stephen Levy attempted to justify the actions of the hacker, stating that "access to computers should be unlimited and total; all information should be free; authority should be mistrusted," further promoting the concepts that hacking "promotes the belief of individual activity over any form of corporate authority or system of ideals."[12] Yet it is unlikely that Mr. Levy is willing to make his personal financial information "free" to everyone. This manifesto that "information wants to be free" seems to be encouraging an environment designed to promote and encourage illicit activity. Even in the information security community, there is some dissent over the true meaning of hacking; however, it is generally accepted that a hacker is not someone who truly intends to follow the policies, rules, and regulations associated with fair and responsible use of computer resources.

The actions taken by an information security professional to thoroughly test an organization's information assets and their security posture up to and including actually gaining access to the root information by bypassing security controls is not hacking, it is referred to as *penetration testing* (or simply *pen testing*). Most professional information security service organizations offer pen testing, and many information security professionals receive training in the craft.

Some will argue that the mindset of the penetration tester is sufficiently different from that of, say, the firewall administrator as to the skills needed to break into a server or network, as opposed to protecting it. They argue that those with the "hacker mentality" have a unique perspective on this activity, whether or not they have acted on their abilities illegally. This begs the question, "Are hackers the only ones who can master these skills?" Is it not possible to undergo professional training, building upon the ingenuity of the human psyche, to be naturally curious to investigate and solve these puzzles? Or must one "walk on the dark side" to gain this knowledge? There are far too many information security professionals tasked with penetration testing to claim that all are "reformed" or "converted" hackers.

The heart of the distinction between the pen tester and the hacker is really the issue of *authorization*. With authorization ("permission or power granted by an authority; sanction"[13]), pen testers are able to identify and recommend remediation for faults in the information protection strategy of the organization. They are able to determine the presence of vulnerabilities and exposures and demonstrate the techniques used by hackers to conduct attacks upon them. But at the day's end, the pen tester is responsible for documenting their actions and making recommendations as to the resolution of these flaws in the defense posture. The hacker, being irresponsible, has no expectation of obligation or responsibility, only motives that are dubious at best. Some will argue that this presents a futile semantic debate, that it's the intent, not the title, that defines the difference between the white hat and the black hat, the hacker and cracker. Yes, the business world judges harshly on the face value of a professional.

The Code of the (ISC)^2 is (ISC)^2's version of the Hippocratic oath ("I will prescribe regimens for the good of my patients according to my ability and my judgment and never do harm to anyone."[14]) for the information security professional and includes the following:

> *Safety of the commonwealth, duty to our principals, and to each other requires that we adhere, and be seen to adhere, to the highest ethical standards of behavior...*

Code of Ethics Canons:

- Protect society, the commonwealth, and the infrastructure.
- Act honorably, honestly, justly, responsibly, and legally.

- Provide diligent and competent service to principals.
- Advance and protect the profession.[15]

The code also calls for information security professionals to:

"discourage such behavior as ...:

- Professional association with non-professionals
- Professional recognition of or association with amateurs
- Associating or appearing to associate with criminals or criminal behavior[16]

The fundamental assertion of this discussion is that any group of professionals ("a person who belongs to one of the professions, esp. one of the learned professions; a person who is expert at his or her work"[17]) should be held to higher moral standards than the average employee. Take it for what you will, but information security professionals are expected to be above reproach as the true guardians of the organization's information assets. Any doubt as to our true beliefs, motives, and ethics undermines the efforts of us all. Adopting the juvenile moniker and attitude of a "hacker" is a cry for attention, to belong to a group of social outcasts. Even though an information security professional may not be a member of the (ISC)², the fundamental lesson is what is important. Above all else, do no harm...

Internet Vulnerability Assessment

The **Internet vulnerability assessment** process is designed to find and document the vulnerabilities that may be present in the public-facing network of the organization. Because attackers from this direction can take advantage of any flaw, this assessment is usually performed against all public-facing addresses, using every possible penetration testing approach. The steps in the process are as follows:

- Planning, scheduling, and notification of the penetration testing: To execute the data collection phase of this assessment, large organizations often need an entire month, using nights and weekends but avoiding change control blackout windows (i.e., periods when changes are not allowed on the organization's systems or networks). This yields vast quantities of test results and requires many hours of analysis (as explained in the section that follows). A rule of thumb is that every hour of scanning results in two to three hours of analysis. Therefore, scanning times should be spread out so that analysis is being performed on fresh scanning results over the course of the assessment period. Also, the various technical support communities should be given the detailed plan so that they know when each device is scheduled for testing and what tests are used. This makes disruptions caused by invasive penetration testing easier to diagnose and recover from.

- Target selection: Working from the network characterization database elements that are stored in the risk, threat, and attack database, the penetration targets are selected. As previously noted, most organizations choose to test every device that is exposed to the Internet.

- Test selection: This step involves using the external monitoring intelligence to configure a test engine (such as Nessus) for the tests to be performed. The selection of the test library to be employed usually evolves over time and matches the evolution of the threat environment. After the ground rules are established, there is usually little debate about the risk level of the tests used. After all, if a device is placed in a public-facing role, it must be able to take everything the Internet can send its way, including the most aggressive penetration test scripts.

- Scanning: The penetration test engine is unleashed at the scheduled time using the planned target list and test selection. The results of the entire test run are logged to text log files for analysis. This should be a monitored process, so that if an invasive penetration test causes a disruption to a targeted system, the outage can be reported immediately and recovery activities can be initiated. Note that the log files generated by this scanning, along with all of the data generated in the rest of this maintenance domain, must be treated as highly confidential.

- Analysis: A knowledgeable and experienced vulnerability analyst screens the test results for the **candidate vulnerabilities** logged during scanning. During this step, the analyst must perform three tasks:
  - Classify the risk level of the candidate vulnerability as needing attention or as an acceptable risk.
  - Validate the existence of the vulnerability when it is deemed to be a significant risk— that is, the risk is higher than the risk appetite of the organization. This validation is important because it establishes the *reality* of the risk; the analyst must therefore use manual testing, human judgment, and a large dose of discretion. The goal of this step is to tread lightly and cause as little disruption and damage as possible while removing false positive candidates from further investigation. These proven cases of real vulnerabilities can now be considered **vulnerability instances**.
  - Document the results of the verification by saving a **trophy** (usually a screenshot) that can be used to convince skeptical systems administrators that the vulnerability is real.

- Record keeping: In this phase, the organization must record the details of the documented vulnerability in the vulnerability database, identifying the logical and physical characteristics and assigning a response risk level to the vulnerability to differentiate the truly urgent from the merely critical. When coupled with the criticality level from the characteristics in the risk, threat, and attack database, these records can help the systems administrators decide which items they need to remediate first.

As the list of documented vulnerabilities is identified for the Internet information assets, these confirmed items are moved to the remediation stage.

Intranet Vulnerability Assessment

The **intranet vulnerability assessment** process is designed to find and document selected vulnerabilities that are likely to be present on the internal network of the organization. Intranets attackers are often internal members of the organization, affiliates of business partners, or automated attack vectors (such as viruses and worms). This assessment is usually performed against selected critical internal devices with a known, high value and thus requires the use of selective penetration testing. The steps in the process are almost identical to the steps in the Internet vulnerability assessment, except as noted below:

- Planning, scheduling, and notification of the penetration testing: Most organizations are amazed at how many devices exist inside even a moderately sized network. Bigger networks contain staggering numbers of networked devices. In order to plan a meaningful assessment process, the planner should be aware that any significant degree of scanning will yield vast quantities of test results and require many hours of analysis effort (see the description that follows). The same rule of thumb for Internet vulnerability assessment applies: every hour of scanning results in two to three hours of analysis, so organizations must plan accordingly. Just as in Internet scanning, the various technical support communities should be notified, but these are probably different individuals than those notified for Internet scanning. Like the Internet support teams, the intranet support teams use this information to make any disruptions caused by invasive penetration testing easier to diagnose and recover from. In contrast to Internet systems administrators who prefer the penetration testing to be performed at low-demand periods (such as nights and weekends for commercial operations), intranet administrators often prefer that penetration testing (both scanning and analysis) be performed during working hours. The best process takes the systems administrator's planning needs into account when the schedule is built.

- Target selection: Like the Internet vulnerability assessment process, the intranet scan starts with the network characterization database elements stored in the risk, threat, and attack database. Intranet testing has so many target possibilities, however, that a more selective approach is required. At first, the penetration test scanning and analysis should focus on testing only the highest value, most critical systems. As the configuration of these systems is improved and fewer candidate vulnerabilities are found in the scanning step, the target list can be expanded. The list of targeted intranet systems should eventually reach equilibrium so that it targets as many systems as can be scanned and analyzed with the resources dedicated to the process.

- Test selection: The testing for intranet vulnerability assessment usually uses different, less stringent criteria from Internet scanning. The selection of the tests to be performed usually evolves over time and matches the evolution of the perception of the intranet threat environment. Most organizations focus their intranet scanning efforts on a few very critical vulnerabilities at first, and then expand the test pool to include more test scripts to detect more vulnerabilities. The degree to which an organization is willing to accept risk while scanning and analyzing also affects the selection of test scripts. If the organization is unwilling to risk disruptions to critical internal systems, test scripts that pose such risks should be avoided and alternate means to confirm safety from those vulnerabilities should be pursued.

- Scanning: Intranet scanning is the same process used for Internet scanning. Just as in Internet scanning, the scanning process should be monitored so that if an invasive penetration test causes disruption, it can be reported for repair.

- Analysis: Despite the differences in targets and tested vulnerabilities, the intranet scan analysis is essentially identical to the Internet analysis. It follows the same three steps: classify, validate, and document.

- Record keeping: This process step is identical to the one followed in Internet vulnerability analysis. Organizations should use the similarities between the processes to their advantage by sharing the database, the reports, and the procedures used for record keeping, reporting, and follow-up.

By both leveraging the common assessment processes and using difference analysis on the data collected during the vulnerability assessment, an organization can identify a list of documented internal vulnerabilities, which are the essential pieces of information needed for the remediation stage.

Platform Security Validation The platform security validation (PSV) process is designed to find and document the vulnerabilities that may be present because there are misconfigured systems in use within the organization. These misconfigured systems fail to comply with company policy or standards as adopted by the IT governance groups and communicated in the information security and awareness program. Fortunately, automated measurement systems are available to help with the intensive process of validating the compliance of platform configuration with policy. Two products known to provide this function are Symantec Enterprise Security Manager and NetIQ VigilEnt Security Manager. Other products are also available, but the approach and terminology presented here are based on the NetIQ product.

- Product selection: Typically an organization implements a PSV solution in the information security program deployment. That solution serves for ongoing PSV compliance as well. If a product has not yet been selected, a separate information security project selects and deploys a PSV solution.

- Policy configuration: As organizational policy and standards evolve, the policy templates of the PSV tool must be changed to match. After all, the goal for any approach selected is to be able to measure how well the systems comply with policy.

- Deployment: All systems that are mission critical should be enrolled in PSV measurement. If the organization can afford the associated licensing and support costs and can dedicate sufficient resources to the PSV program, it should enroll all of its devices. Security personnel should remember that attackers often come into a network using the weakest link, which may not be a critical system itself but could be connected to critical systems.

- Measurement: Using the PSV tools, the organization should measure the compliance of each enrolled system against the policy templates. Deficiencies should be reported as vulnerabilities.

- Exclusion handling: Some provision should be made for the exclusion of specific policy or standard exceptions. For instance, one metric is to identify the user accounts that never expire. Some organizations have adopted practices that assume the risk of having service accounts that do not expire or that have change intervals that are longer than standard user accounts. If the proper organizational decision makers have made an informed decision to assume that risk, the automated PSV tool should be able to exclude the assumed risk factor from the compliance report.

- Reporting: Using the standard reporting components in the PSV tool, most organizations can inform the systems administrators of deficiencies that need remediation.

- Remediation: Systems out of compliance need to be updated with configurations that comply with policy. When the PSV process shows an outstanding configuration fault that has not been promptly remedied, the information about the vulnerable system should flow to the vulnerability database to assure remediation.

The ability of PSV software products to integrate with a custom vulnerability database is not a standard feature, but most PSV products on the market have the ability to provide data extracts that can be imported to the organization's vulnerability database for integrated use in the remediation phase. If this degree of integration is not needed or cannot be justified, the stand-alone reporting capabilities of the products can generate sufficient reports for the remediation functions of this maintenance domain.

Wireless Vulnerability Assessment The **wireless vulnerability assessment** process is designed to find and document the vulnerabilities that may be present in the wireless local area networks of the organization. Because attackers from this direction are likely to take advantage of any flaw, this assessment is usually performed against all publicly accessible areas using every possible wireless penetration testing approach. The steps in the process are as follows:

- Planning, scheduling, and notification of the wireless penetration testing: This is a noninvasive scanning process and can be done almost any time without notifying systems administrators. Even if company culture requires that administrators be notified, the organization should still consider scheduling some unannounced scans, as administrators have been known to turn off their wireless access points on scheduled test days to avoid detection and the resulting remediation effort. Times and days should be rotated over time to detect wireless devices that are used for intermittent projects.

- Target selection: All areas of the organization's premises should be scanned with a portable wireless network scanner, with special attention to the following: all areas that are publicly accessible; all areas in range of commonly available products (such as 802.11b); and areas where visitors might linger without attracting attention. Because the radio emissions of wireless network equipment can act in surprising ways, all locations should be tested periodically.

- Test selection: Wireless scanning tools should look for all wireless signals that do not meet the organization's minimum level of encryption strength.

- Scanning: The walking scan should survey the entire target area and identify all wireless local area network (WLAN) access points that are not cryptographically secure.

- Analysis: A knowledgeable and experienced vulnerability analyst should screen the test results for the WLANs that have been logged as previously described. During this step, the analyst should perform these steps:

  ○ Remove false positive candidates from further consideration as vulnerabilities while causing as little disruption or damage as possible.

  ○ Document the results of the verification by saving a screenshot or other documentary evidence (often called a trophy). This serves a double purpose. It can convince skeptical systems administrators that the vulnerability is real. It also documents those wireless access points that are transient devices and thus may be off the air at a later time.

- Record keeping: Good reporting makes the effort to communicate and follow-up much easier. Just as in earlier vulnerability assessment phases, effective reporting maximizes results.

At this stage in the process, the wireless vulnerabilities are documented and ready for remediation.

Modem Vulnerability Assessment The **modem vulnerability assessment** process is designed to find and document any vulnerability that is present on dial-up modems connected to the organization's networks. Because attackers from this direction take advantage of any flaw, this assessment is usually performed on all telephone numbers owned by the organization, using every possible penetration testing approach. One of the elements of this process involves using scripted dialing attacks against a pool of phone numbers; this is often called **war dialing**. The steps in the modem vulnerability assessment process are as follows:

- Planning, scheduling, and notification of the dial-up modem testing: Most organizations find that they need to run the dial-up modem-testing appliance (dedicated system and software, such as PhoneSweep) continuously. Because this is a 24/7 operation, planning of schedules and notification is not required.

- Target selection: All telephone numbers controlled by the organization should be in the test pool, unless the configuration of the phone equipment on premises can assure that no number can be dialed from the worldwide telephone system.

- Test selection: The entire set of tests in the testing product should be used, including tests for dial-in modems, callback modems, and facsimile machines.

- Scanning: This is a 24/7 process. The raw vulnerability reports should be prepared daily or weekly for the analysis steps that follow.

- Analysis: A knowledgeable and experienced modem vulnerability analyst should screen the test results to eliminate false positives and document the vulnerabilities using the process steps common to the Internet, intranet, and wireless vulnerability assessments already noted. The end result is a list of documented modem vulnerabilities ready for remediation.

Now that each group of vulnerability assessments has been described, a discussion of the record keeping process is in order.

Documenting Vulnerabilities The vulnerability database, like the risk, threat, and attack database, both stores and tracks information. It should provide details about the vulnerability being reported as well as a link to the information assets characterized in the risk, threat, and attack database. While this can be done through manual data storage, the low cost and ease of use associated with relational databases makes them a more realistic choice.

The data stored in the vulnerability database should include the following:

- A unique vulnerability ID number for reporting and tracking remediation actions

- Linkage to the risk, threat, and attack database based on the physical information asset underlying the vulnerability; the IP address is a good choice for this linkage

- Vulnerability details, usually based on the test script used for the scanning step of the process; if the Nessus scanner is used, each test script has an assigned code (NASL, or Nessus attack scripting language) that can identify the vulnerability effectively

- Dates and times of notification and remediation activities

- Current status of the vulnerability instance, such as *found*, *reported*, or *repaired*

- Comments are always useful to add to the vulnerability instance since they give the analyst the chance to provide the systems administrators with detailed and specific information about how to fix the vulnerability

- Other fields as needed to manage the reporting and tracking processes in the remediation phase

The vulnerability database is an essential part of effective remediation as it helps organizations avoid losing track of specific vulnerability instances as they are reported and remediated.

Remediating Vulnerabilities The final process in the vulnerability assessment and remediation domain is the remediation phase. The objective of remediation is to repair the flaw causing a vulnerability instance or remove the risk associated with the vulnerability. Alternatively, informed decision makers with the proper authority may, as a last resort, decide to accept this risk.

When approaching the remediation process, it is important to recognize that building relationships with those who control the information assets is the key to success. In other words, success depends on the organization adopting a team approach to remediation in place of cross-organizational push and pull.

Remediation of vulnerabilities can be accomplished by accepting or transferring the risk, removing the threat, or repairing the vulnerability.

Acceptance or Transference of Risk In some instances, risk must either simply be acknowledged as being part of an organization's business process, or else the organization should buy insurance to transfer the risk to another organization. The information security professional must assure the general management community that the decision to accept the risk or buy insurance was made by properly informed decision makers. Further, these decision makers must have the proper level of authority within the organization to assume the risk. In reality, however, many situations where risk is assumed violate these conditions, as described below:

- Decisions are made at the wrong level of the organization. Thus, for example, it is problematic when systems administrators decide to skip using passwords on a critical application server because it creates more work for them.

- Decisions are made by uninformed decision makers. Thus, for example, it is problematic when a project manager convinces an application sponsor that database-level security is not needed in an application and that all users need unlimited access to all data, because the sponsor may not realize all of the implications of this decision.

In the final analysis, the information security group must make sure the right people make risk assumption decisions and that these people are aware of both the potential impact of their decision and the cost of the available security controls.

Threat Removal In some circumstances, threats can be removed without requiring a repair of the vulnerability. For example, if an application can only run on an older desktop system that cannot support passwords, the older desktop system can be removed from the network and stored in a locked room or equipment rack to be used only as a stand-alone device. Other vulnerabilities may be mitigated by inexpensive controls, for example disabling the Web services on a server that provides other important services instead of taking the time to update the Web software on the server.

Vulnerability Repair The optimum solution in most cases is to repair the vulnerability. Applying patch software or implementing a workaround often accomplishes this. Many recent vulnerabilities have exploited Web servers on Windows operating systems, and simply updating the version of the installed Web server removes the vulnerability. Simple repairs are possible in other cases, too. For instance, if an account is flagged as a vulnerability because it has a password that has not been changed for longer than the specified interval, changing the password removes the vulnerability. Of course, the most common repair is the application of a software patch; this usually makes the system function in the expected fashion and removes the vulnerability.

Readiness and Review

The primary goal of the **readiness and review domain** is to keep the information security program functioning as designed and to keep it continuously improving over time. This is accomplished by the following:

- Policy review: Policy needs to be reviewed and refreshed from time to time to ensure that it's sound—in other words, that it provides a current foundation for the information security program.

- Program review: Major planning components should be reviewed on a periodic basis to ensure that they are current, accurate, and appropriate.

- Rehearsals: When possible, major plan elements should be rehearsed.

The relationships among the sectors of the readiness and review domain are shown in Figure 12-16. As the diagram indicates, policy review is the primary initiator of the readiness and review domain. As policy is revised or current policy is confirmed, the various planning elements are reviewed for compliance, the information security program is reviewed, and rehearsals are held to make sure all participants are capable of responding as needed.

Policy Review and Planning Review Policy needs to be reviewed periodically. The topic of policy management and policy review is covered in Chapter 5. The planning and review process for incident response, disaster recovery, and business continuity planning are also covered in Chapter 5.

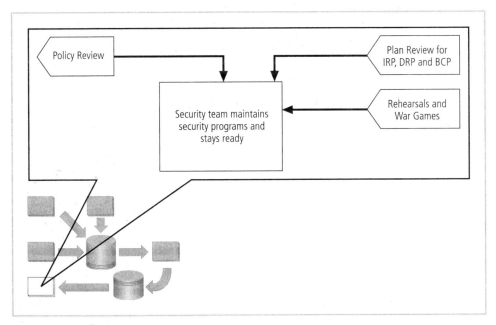

Figure 12-16 Readiness and Review

Source: Course Technology/Cengage Learning

Program Review As policy needs shift, a thorough and independent review of the entire information security program should be undertaken. While an exact timetable for review is not proposed here, many organizations find that the CISO should conduct a formal review annually. Earlier in this chapter, the role of the CISO in the maintenance process was discussed. The CISO uses the results of maintenance activities and the review of the information security program to determine if the status quo can adequately meet the threats at hand.

If the current information security program is not up to the challenges, the CISO must determine if incremental improvements are possible or if it is time to launch a new initiative to restructure the information security function within the organization.

Rehearsals and War Games Where possible, major planning elements should be rehearsed. Rehearsal adds value by exercising the procedures, identifying shortcomings, and providing security personnel the opportunity to improve the security plan before it is needed. In addition, rehearsals make people more effective when an actual event occurs.

Rehearsals that closely match reality are called **war games**. A war game or simulation puts a subset of plans in place to create a realistic test environment. This adds to the value of the rehearsal and can enhance training.

Digital Forensics

Whether due to a character flaw, a need for vengeance, curiosity, or some other reason, an employee, contractor, or outsider may attack a physical or information asset. When the asset attacked is in the purview of the CISO, that executive is expected to understand how policies and laws require the matter to be managed. In order to protect the organization, and to possibly assist law enforcement in the conduct of an investigation, they must act to document what happened and how. The investigation of what happened and how is **digital forensics**.

Digital forensics is based on the field of traditional forensics. Forensics is the coherent application of methodical investigatory techniques to present evidence of crimes in a court or court-like setting. Made popular by scientific detective shows focusing on crime scene investigations, forensics involves the use of science to investigate events. Not all events involve crimes; some involve natural events, accidents, or system malfunctions. Forensics allows investigators to determine what happened by examining the results of an event. It also allows them to determine how it happened by examining activities, individual actions, physical evidence, and testimony related to the event. What it may never do is figure out the why. Why did this event transpire? The *why* is the focus of psychological, sociological, and criminal justice studies. Here the focus is on the application of forensics techniques to the digital arena.

Digital forensics involves the preservation, identification, extraction, documentation, and interpretation of computer media for evidentiary and/or root cause analysis. Like traditional forensics, it follows clear, well-defined methodologies, but still tends to be as much art as science. This means the natural curiosity and personal skill of the investigator play a key role in discovering potential evidentiary material. **Evidentiary material (EM)**, also known as an item of potential evidentiary value, is any information that could potentially support the organization's legal or policy-based case against a suspect. An item does not become evidence until it is formally admitted to evidence by a judge or other ruling official.

Digital forensics investigators use a variety of tools to support their work, which you will learn about later in this chapter. However, the tools and methods used by attackers can be equally sophisticated. Digital forensics can be used for two key purposes:

1. To investigate allegations of digital malfeasance. A crime against or using digital media, computer technology, or related components (computer as source or object of crime) is referred to as **digital malfeasance**. To investigate digital malfeasance, you must use digital forensics to gather, analyze, and report the findings of an investigation. This is the primary mission of law enforcement in investigating crimes involving computer technologies or online information.

2. To perform root cause analysis. If an incident occurs and the organization suspects an attack was successful, digital forensics can be used to examine the path and methodology used to gain unauthorized access, as well as to determine how pervasive and successful the attack was. This is used primarily by IR teams to examine their equipment after an incident.

Some investigations are undertaken by organizational personnel, while others require immediate involvement of law enforcement. In general, whenever an investigator discovers evidence of the commission of a crime, they should immediately notify management and recommend contacting law enforcement. Failure to do so could result in unfavorable action against the investigator or organization.

The organization must choose one of two approaches when employing digital forensics:

1. Protect and forget. This approach, also known as patch and proceed, focuses on the defense of the data and the systems that house, use, and transmit it. An investigation that takes this approach focuses on the detection and analysis of events to determine how they happened, and to prevent reoccurrence. Once the current event is over, who caused it or why is almost immaterial.

2. Apprehend and prosecute. This approach, also known as pursue and prosecute, focuses on the identification and apprehension of responsible individuals, with additional attention on the collection and preservation of potential EM that might support administrative or criminal prosecution. This approach requires much more attention to detail to prevent contamination of evidence that might hinder prosecution.

An organization might find it impossible to retain enough data to successfully handle even administrative penalties, but should certainly adopt the latter approach if it wishes to pursue formal administrative penalties, especially if the employee is likely to challenge these penalties.

The Digital Forensics Team

Most organization cannot sustain a permanent digital forensics team. In most organizations, such expertise is so rarely called upon that it may be better to collect the data and then outsource the analysis component to a regional expert. The organization can then maintain an arm's-length distance from the case and have additional expertise to call upon in the event the process ends in court.

Even so, there should be people in the information security group trained to understand and manage the forensics process. Should a report of suspected misuse from an internal or external individual arise, this person or group must be familiar with digital forensics procedures in order to avoid contaminating potential EM.

This expertise can be obtained by sending staff members to a regional or national information security conference with a digital forensics track or to dedicated digital forensics training, as mentioned in Chapter 11. The organization should use caution in selecting the training for the team or specialist as many forensics training programs begin with the analysis process and promote a specific tool rather than teaching the management of the process.

Affidavits and Search Warrants

Most investigations begin with an allegation or an indication of an incident. Whether via the help desk, the organization's sexual harassment reporting channels, or direct report, someone makes an allegation that another worker is performing actions explicitly prohibited by the organization or that make another worker uncomfortable in the workplace. The organization's forensics team must then request permission to examine digital media for potential EM. In law enforcement, the investigating agent would create an affidavit requesting a search warrant. An **affidavit** is sworn testimony that certain facts are in the possession of the investigating officer that they feel warrant the examination of specific items located at a specific place. The facts, the items, and the place must be specified in this document. When an approving authority signs the affidavit or creates a synopsis form based on this document, it becomes a **search warrant**, or permission to search for EM at the specified location and/or to seize items to return to the investigator's lab for examination. In corporate environments, the names of these documents may change, and in many cases may be verbal in nature, but the process should be the same. Formal permission is obtained before an investigation occurs.

Digital Forensics Methodology

In digital forensics, all investigations follow the same basic methodology:

1. Identify relevant items of evidentiary value (EM)
2. Acquire (seize) the evidence without alteration or damage
3. Take steps to assure that the evidence is at every step verifiably authentic and is unchanged from the time it was seized
4. Analyze the data without risking modification or unauthorized access
5. Report the findings to the proper authority

This process is illustrated in Figure 12-17.

In order to support the selection and implementation of a methodology, the organization may wish to seek legal advice or consult with local or state law enforcement. Other sources which should become part of the organization team's library are:

- Electronic Crime Scene Investigation: A Guide for First Responders July 2001 (*www. ncjrs.gov/pdffiles1/nij/187736.pdf*)
- First Responders Guide to Computer Forensics (*www.cert.org/archive/pdf/ FRGCF_v1.3.pdf*)
- Searching and Seizing Computers and Obtaining Electronic Evidence in Criminal Investigations (*www.Cybercrime.gov/ssmanual/index.html*)
- Scientific Working Group on Digital Evidence: Best Practices for Computer Forensics *www.oas.org/juridico/spanish/cyb_best_pract.pdf*.

Identify Relevant Items The affidavit or warrant authorizing a search action must specifically identify what items of evidence can be seized. It is essential that only EM that

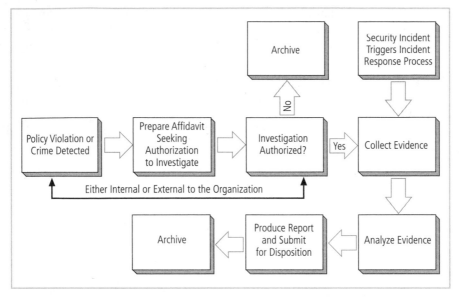

Figure 12-17 The Digital Forensics Process

Source: Course Technology/Cengage Learning

fits the description on the authorization is included in the acquisition process. Many times, the acquisition phase occurs under stressful circumstances and under strict time constraints; thorough item descriptions help this process function smoothly and ensure that critical evidence is not overlooked and that excluded items are not wrongly included as EM, which could jeopardize the investigation.

One of the crucial aspects of any digital forensic investigation is the process of identifying the potential EM and its probable location. Users have access to many online server locations, via free e-mail archives, ftp servers, video archives, and the like, and could have terabytes of information stored in offsite locations across the Web or on their local systems. Unless investigators have an idea of what to look for (that is, evidence that the accused has been selling intellectual property related to future product offerings or has been viewing objectionable or illegal content), they may never find it in such a vast array of possible locations.

Acquire the Evidence The principal responsibility of the response team is to acquire the information without altering it. Computers modify data constantly. Every time someone opens, modifies, or saves a file, or even opens a directory index to view the available files, they change the state of the system. Normal system file changes may be difficult to explain to a layperson (e.g., a jury member with little or no technical knowledge). A normal system consequence of the search for EM could be portrayed by a defense attorney as affecting the authenticity or integrity of the EM, which could lead a jury to suspect that the EM was planted or is otherwise suspect. The biggest challenge is to show that the person under investigation is the one who stored, used, and maintained the EM, or who conducted the unauthorized activity.

One of the most heated ongoing debates in digital forensics is the "to pull or not to pull" argument—that is, balancing the investigator's need to acquire the EM without modifying it against the possible loss of information in volatile memory. To "pull" means to pull the power cord on whatever computer technology is suspected of housing the EM. By removing the power source, the investigatory team can freeze the system in a known state. Pulling the plug is the only way to assure the system does not change before it can be imaged. Pulling the plug may also prevent any software defense mechanisms from destroying information. The problem is that pulling the plug can destroy information in volatile memory, such as temporary processes or threads. The system may also be critical to the ongoing operations of the organization, like an online file server for example, in which case management cannot afford to allow the system to be taken offline.

Online vs. Offline Data Acquisition   There are generally two methods of acquiring evidence from a system. The first is the offline model, in which the investigator removes the power source and then uses a utility or special device to make a bit-stream sector-by-sector copy of the hard drives contained in the system. By copying the drives at the sector level, you can ensure that any hidden or erased files are also captured. The copied drive then becomes the image that can be used in the analysis, and the original drive is stored for safekeeping as true EM (or possibly returned to service). For the purposes of this discussion, the term "copy" refers to a drive duplication technique, whereas an image is the file containing all of the information from the source drive.

This approach requires the use of read-only hardware known as write-blockers (or sound processes and techniques) to prevent the accidental overwriting of data on the source drive. The use of these tools also allows investigators to assert that the EM was not modified during acquisition. In another offline approach, the investigator can reboot the system with an alternate operating system or a specialty boot disk like Helix or Knoppix. Special tools contained on the boot CD or disk can be used to copy the drive to an image file. For optimal security, both write-blockers and alternate boot systems should be used together. Yet a third approach involves specialty hardware that connects directly to a powered-down hard drive and provides direct power and data connections to copy data to an internal drive. These devices avoid any contamination from use of the host system input/output devices, possible even with alternate operating systems.

In online or "live" data acquisition, investigators use network-based tools to acquire a protected copy of the information. The only real difference between the two methods is that the source system cannot be taken offline, and the tools must be sophisticated enough to avoid altering the system during the data acquisition. Table 12-10 shows these and other methods of acquiring data.

Note that the creation of a copy or image can take a substantial amount of time. Users who have made USB copies of their data know how much time it takes to back up several gigabytes of data. When dealing with networked server drives, the data acquisition phase can take many hours to complete. This is one reason why investigators prefer to seize drives and take them back to the lab to be imaged or copied.

Other Potential Evidence   Not all EM is on a suspect's computer hard drive. A technically savvy attacker is more likely to store incriminating evidence on other digital media, such as removable drives, CDs, DVDs, flash drives, memory chips or sticks, or on other computers accessed across the organization's networks or via the Internet. EM located outside the organization is particularly problematic, as the organization cannot legally search systems

Method	Advantages	Disadvantages
Use a dedicated forensic workstation to examine a write-protected hard drive or image of suspect hard drive.	No concern about the validity of either the software or hardware on the suspect host. Produces evidence most easily defended in court.	Inconvenient, time-consuming. May result in loss of volatile information.
Boot the system using a verified, write-protected floppy disk or CD with kernel and tools.	Convenient, quick. Evidence is defensible if suspect drives are mounted as read-only.	Assumes that hardware has not been compromised (which is rare). May result in loss of volatile information.
Build a new system containing an image of the suspect system and examine it.	Completely replicates operational environment of suspect computer without running the risk of changing its information.	Requires availability of hardware that is identical to suspect computer. May result in loss of volatile information.
Examine the system using external media with verified software on it.	Convenient, quick. Allows examination of volatile information.	If a kernel is compromised, results may be misleading. External media may not have every necessary utility on it.
Verify the software on the suspect system, and then use the verified local software to conduct examination.	Requires minimal preparation. Allows examination of volatile information. Can be performed remotely.	Lack of write protection for suspect drives makes evidence difficult to defend in court. Finding sources for hash values and verifying the local software requires a minimum of several hours, unless Tripwire was used ahead of time.
Examine the suspect system using the software on the suspect system (without verifying the software).	Requires least amount of preparation. Allows examination of volatile information. Can be performed remotely.	Least reliable method. This is exactly what cyber attackers are hoping you will do. Often a complete waste of time.

Table 12-10   **Summary of Methods Employed to Acquire Forensic Data**[18]

they don't own. However, the simple act of viewing EM on a system leaves clues about the location of the source material, and a skilled investigator can at least provides some assistance to law enforcement when conducting a preliminary investigation. Log files are another source of information about the access and location of EM, as well as what happened when.

Some evidence isn't electronic or digital in nature. Many suspects have been further incriminated when the passwords to their digital media were discovered in the margins of user manuals, in calendars and day planners, and even on notes attached to their systems.

EM Handling   Once the evidence is acquired, both the copy image and the original drive should be handled so as to avoid legal challenges based on authenticity and preservation of integrity. If the organization or law enforcement cannot demonstrate that no one had physical access to the evidence, they cannot provide strong assurances that it has not been altered. Once the evidence is in the possession of investigators, they must track its movement, storage, and access until the resolution of the event or case. This is typically accomplished by means of chain of evidence or chain of custody procedures. **Chain of evidence** or **chain of custody** is defined as the detailed documentation of the collection, storage, transfer, and ownership of collected evidence from the crime scene through its presentation in court. The evidence is

---

E V I D E N C E

AGENCY: _____

Agent: _____

Case #: _____ Item #: _____

Date: _____ Time: _____

Description: _____

_____

_____

Location: _____

_____

Remarks: _____

CHAIN OF CUSTODY

Received From: _____

By: _____

Date: _____ Time: _____

Received From: _____

By: _____

Date: _____ Time: _____

Received From: _____

By: _____

Date: _____ Time: _____

Received From: _____

By: _____

Date: _____ Time: _____

Figure 12-18 Evidence Form Used in Digital Forensics

Source: Course Technology/Cengage Learning

then tracked wherever it is located. When the evidence changes hands or is stored, the documentation is updated. Figures 12-18 and 12-19 show examples of evidence tags and chain of custody forms used in such an event.

Not all evidence handling requirements are met through the chain of custody process. Digital media must be stored in an environment designed for storage of digital media which can be secured to prevent unauthorized access. Individual items should be stored in ESD protective containers or bags, marked as sensitive to ESD and magnetic fields, and so forth. Additional details are provided in the Technical Details Box.

Authenticate the Recovered Evidence The copy or image is typically transferred to the laboratory for the next stage of authentication. The team must be able to demonstrate that any analyzed copy or image is a true and accurate replica of the source EM. This is accomplished by the use of cryptographic hash tools. As you learned in Chapter 8, the hash tool takes a variable-length file and creates a single numerical value, usually represented in hexadecimal notation, rather like a digital fingerprint. By hashing the source file and the

	Original Affidavit–Authorizing Manager 1st copy – CISO 2nd copy – Serve	Original warrant – Return 1st copy – CISO 2nd copy – Serve 3rd copy – Issuing Authority
Computer Gaming Technology	**SEARCH WARRANT**	**CASE NO:**
		Agency Report No.: _____

TO THE CHIEF INFORMATION SECURITY OFFICER OR DESIGNATED REPRESENTATIVE:

_____ , has sworn to the attached affidavit regarding the following:

1. The person, place, or thing to be searched is described as and is located at:

2. The PROPERTY to be searched and seized, if found, is specifically described as:

IN THE NAME OF ABC Company, INCORPORATED 1992: I have found that probable cause exists and you are directed to make the search and seize the described property. Leave a copy of this warrant with affidavit attached and a written inventory of all property with the person from whom the property was taken or at the premises. You are further directed to promptly return this warrant and inventory to me.

Issued: _____   _____
   Date   Authorizing Manager   Position

RETURN AND INVENTORY

Search was completed on _____ and the following property was seized:
                 Date

☐ Continued on inventory form no. _____

_____

Copy of affidavit, warrant, and inventory served by: _____ on: _____ .
                               Name   Date
Inventory compiled and placed into evidence by: _____ on: _____ .
                               Name   Date

Figure 12-19 Affidavit and Search Warrant

Source: Course Technology/Cengage Learning

copy, the investigator can assert that the copy is a true and accurate duplicate of the source. Should the defense desire copies of all seized materials for their own investigation, the investigators can create another copy from the source, provide evidence of the hash value, and return the source to custody.

Analyze the Data The most complex part of an investigation is the analysis of the copy or image for potential EM. While the process can be performed manually using simple utilities, two industry leading applications dominate the market for digital forensics:

- Guidance Software's EnCase (*www.guidancesoftware.com*)
- AccessData Forensics Tool Kit (FTK) (*www.accessdata.com*)

Each of these tools is designed to support a law enforcement investigation and assist in the management of the entire case. EnCase also has a sophisticated data acquisition component to simplify the data collection process, as well as the analysis. EnCase promotes the installation of its product on multiple systems—on laptops for field data acquisition, and on a

Technical Details:
General Procedures for Evidence Search and Seizure

In completing the affidavit:

1. Explain why it is believed that a crime or policy violation has been committed and identify any suspects.

2. Fully describe the person, place, or thing to be searched and give its exact location.

3. Explain why it is likely that digital evidence related to the crime or policy violation exists at the identified premises.

4. Fully describe the property that is to be searched and the types of items that are to be seized or imaged.

5. Present to forensics team leader for review if required.

6. Present the original of the affidavit and unsigned search warrant or authorization to the approving authority.

7. Swear to the contents of the affidavit and sign it before the approving authority.

8. Have the approving authority sign both the original of the affidavit and the search warrant or authorization.

9. Print names of the approving authority and investigator on all copies of the affidavit and/or search warrant. Make sure all copies of the affidavit and/or search warrant taken into the field are completed with original (not photocopied) signatures.

10. Leave original affidavit and copy of warrant with the approving authority.

11. Make sufficient copies to serve all individuals and leave at the scene.

12. Execute search warrant at location given.

13. Complete the tabulation (list) of property taken in the presence of the person(s) from whom it is seized, if present, or any other person (including another officer).

14. Have person before whom the tabulation is completed sign the tabulation as witness.

15. Leave a copy of the affidavit, search warrant, and completed tabulation with the person(s) from whom the property was taken, if present, or at the premises.

16. Return the original search warrant and complete tabulation to the court indicating the date returned and the name of the person(s) served.

At the crime scene, complete the following tasks:

1. Secure the crime scene by clearing all unauthorized personnel, delimit the scene with tape or other markers, and post a guard or other individual at the entrance.

2. Log into the crime scene by signing the entry/exit log.

3. Photograph the scene beginning at the doorway and covering the entire room in 360 degrees. Include specific photos of potential evidentiary material.

4. Sketch the layout for the room, including furniture and equipment.

5. Following proper procedure, begin searching for physical (documentary) evidence (papers, media such as CDs or flash memory devices, or other artifacts) that would support your case. Identify the location found with a marker or designator and cross reference it on the sketch. Photograph the item in situ to establish its location and state.

6. For each computer, first check for the presence of a screen saver by moving the mouse. Do not click the mouse or use the keyboard. If the screen is active photograph the screen. Pull the power on permitted systems. Document each computer by means of photography and a detailed written description of the manufacturer, model number, serial number, and so forth. Using sound processes, remove each disk drive and image it using the appropriate process and equipment. Document each source drive by photography and a detailed description of the manufacturer, serial number, and so forth. Package and secure the image.

7. For each object found complete the necessary evidence or chain of custody labels.

8. Log out of the crime scene by signing the entry/exit log.

9. Transfer all evidence to the lab for investigation or to a suitable evidence locker for storage. Store and transport all evidence items, documentation, and photographic materials in a locked field evidence locker.

Analyze the image:

1. Build the case file by entering background information including investigator, suspect, date, time, system analyzed, and so forth.

2. Load the image file (.img, .e01, .001 etc.) into the case file.

3. Index the image. Note that some systems use a database of known files to filter out files that are known to be applications, system files, or utilities. The use of this filter improves the quality and effectiveness of the indexing process.

4. Identify, export, and bookmark related text files by searching the index.

5. Identify, export, and bookmark related graphics by reviewing the images folder. Note: If the suspect is accused of viewing child pornography, do not directly view the images. Use the database of known images to compare hash values and tag as suspect. There are some things you can't "unsee."

6. Identify, export, and bookmark other evidence files

7. Integrate all exported and bookmarked material into the case report.

laboratory investigation system for analysis. The presence of a USB authentication token controls which system can be used for analysis at any specific moment.

The first component of the analysis phase is indexing. During indexing, many investigatory tools create an index of all text found on the drive. This includes data found in deleted files and in file slack space. This indexing is similar to the indexing performed by Google Desktop or Windows Desktop Search tools. The index itself can then be used by the investigator to locate specific documents or document fragments. While indexing, the tools typically organize files into categories, such as documents, images, executables, and so forth. Unfortunately, like imaging, indexing is a very time- and processor-consuming operation and could take days on large images (i.e., those larger than 20 gigabytes).

In some cases, the investigator may find password-protected files, used by the suspect to protect the data. There are several commercial password cracking tools that can assist the investigator. Some are sold in conjunction with forensics tools, like the AccessData Password Recovery Tool Kit.

Report the Findings As investigators examine the analyzed copies or images and identify potential EM, they can tag it and add it to their case files. Once they have found a suitable amount of information they can summarize their findings, along with a synopsis of their investigatory procedures, in a report and submit it to the appropriate authority. This authority could be law enforcement or management. The suitable amount of EM is a flexible determination made by the investigator. In certain cases, like child pornography, one file is sufficient to warrant turning the entire investigation over to law enforcement. On the other hand, a dismissal on the grounds of the unauthorized sale of intellectual property may require a substantial amount of information to support the organization's assertion. Reporting methods and formats vary from organization to organization and should be specified in the digital forensics policy. The general guideline for the report is that it should be sufficiently detailed to allow a similarly trained person to repeat the analysis and achieve similar results.

Evidentiary Procedures

In information security, most operations focus on policies—those documents which provide managerial guidance for ongoing implementation and operations. In digital forensics, however, the focus is on procedures. When investigating digital malfeasance or performing root cause analysis, keep in mind that the results and methods of the investigation may end up in criminal or civil court. For example, during a routine systems update, a technician finds objectionable material on an employee's computer. The employee is fired and promptly sues the organization for wrongful termination, and so the investigation of that objectionable material comes under scrutiny by the plaintiff's attorney, who will attempt to cast doubt on the ability of the investigator. While technically not illegal, the presence of the material may have been a clear violation of policy, thus prompting the dismissal of the employee, but if an attorney can convince a jury or judge that someone else could have placed the material on the plaintiff's system, then the employee could win the case and potentially a large financial settlement.

When the scenario involves criminal issues where an employee discovers evidence of a crime, the situation changes somewhat. The investigation, analysis, and report are typically performed by law enforcement personnel. However, if the defense attorney can cast reasonable doubt on whether organizational information security professionals compromised the digital evidentiary material, the employee might win the case.

How do you avoid these legal pitfalls? Strong procedures for the handling of potential evidentiary material can minimize the probability of an organization's losing a legal challenge.

Organizations should develop specific procedures, along with guidance on the use of these procedures. The policy document should specify the following:

- Who may conduct an investigation
- Who may authorized an investigation
- What affidavit-related documents are required

- What search warrant-related documents are required
- What digital media may be seized or taken offline
- What methodology should be followed
- What methods are required for chain of custody or chain of evidence
- What format the final report should take and to whom it should it be given

The policy document should be supported by a procedures manual, developed based on the documents discussed earlier, along with guidance from law enforcement or consultants. By creating and using these policies and procedures, an organization can best protect itself from challenges by employees who have been subject unfavorable action, administrative or legal, resulting from an investigation.

Selected Readings

- *Fighting Computer Crime: A New Framework for Protecting Information*, by Donn B. Parker. 1998. John Wiley and Sons.
- *Digital Evidence and Computer Crime, Second Edition*, by Eoghan Casey. 2004. Academic Press.
- *Guide to Computer Forensics and Investigations, Third Edition*, by Amelia Phillips, Bill Nelson, Frank Enfinger, and Christopher Steuart. 2009. Course Technology.

Chapter Summary

- Change is inevitable, so organizations should have procedures to deal with changes in the operation and maintenance of the information security program.
- The CISO decides whether the information security program can adapt to change as it is implemented or whether the macroscopic process of the SecSDLC must be started anew.
- The maintenance model recommended in this chapter is made up of five subject areas or domains. They are:
  - External monitoring
  - Internal monitoring
  - Planning and risk assessment
  - Vulnerability assessment and remediation
  - Readiness and review
- To stay current, the information security community of interest, led by the CISO, must constantly monitor the three components of the security triple—that is, threats, assets, and vulnerabilities.
- To assist the information security community in managing and operating the ongoing security program, the organization should adopt a security management maintenance model. These models are frameworks that are structured along the tasks of managing a particular set of activities or business functions.
- NIST SP 800-100 *Information Security Handbook: A Guide for Managers* outlines managerial tasks performed after the program is operational. For each of the thirteen

areas of information security management presented in SP 800-100, there are specific monitoring activities:

1. Information security governance
2. System development life cycle
3. Awareness and training
4. Capital planning and investment control
5. Interconnecting systems
6. Performance measures
7. Security planning
8. Information technology contingency planning
9. Risk management
10. Certification, accreditation, and security assessments
11. Security services and products acquisition
12. Incident response
13. Configuration (or change) management

- The objective of the external monitoring domain of the maintenance model is to provide early awareness of new and emerging threats, threat agents, vulnerabilities, and attacks so that an effective and timely defense can be mounted.

- The objective of the internal monitoring domain is to maintain an informed awareness of the state of all the organization's networks, information systems, and information security defenses. The security team documents and communicates this awareness, particularly when it concerns system components that face the external network.

- The primary objective of the planning and risk assessment domain is to keep an eye on the entire information security program.

- The primary objectives of the vulnerability assessment and remediation domain are to identify specific, documented vulnerabilities and to remediate them in a timely fashion.

- The primary objectives of the readiness and review domain are to keep the information security program functioning as designed and to keep improving it over time.

- The investigation of what happened and how in the arena of information security is digital forensics–the preservation, identification, extraction, documentation, and interpretation of computer media for evidentiary and/or root cause analysis.

Review Questions

1. List and define the factors that are likely to shift in an organization's information security environment.

2. Who decides if the information security program can adapt to change adequately?

3. List and briefly describe the five domains of the maintenance model.

4. What are the three primary aspects of information security risk management? Why is each important?

5. What is a management maintenance model? What does it accomplish?

6. What changes needed to be made to the model presented in SP 800-100 to adapt it for use in security management maintenance?

7. What are the ongoing responsibilities security managers have in securing the SDLC?

8. What is vulnerability assessment?

9. What is penetration testing?

10. What is the difference between configuration management and change management?

11. What is a performance baseline?

12. What is the difference between vulnerability assessment and penetration testing?

13. What are the objectives of the external monitoring domain of the maintenance model?

14. List and describe four vulnerability intelligence sources. Of those that you listed, which seems the most effective? Why?

15. What does CERT stand for? Is there more than one CERT? What is the purpose of a CERT?

16. What are the primary objectives of the internal monitoring domain?

17. What is the objective of the planning and risk assessment domain of the maintenance model? Why is this important?

18. What is the primary goal of the vulnerability assessment and remediation domain of the maintenance model? Is this important to an organization with an Internet presence? Why?

19. List and describe the five vulnerability assessment processes described in the text. Can you think of some other assessment processes that might exist?

20. What is digital forensics, and when is it used in a business setting?

Exercises

1. Search the Web for the Forum of Incident Response and Security Teams (FIRST). In your own words, what is the forum's mission?

2. Search the Web for two or more sites that discuss the ongoing responsibilities of the security manager. What other components of security management, as outlined by this model, can be adapted for use in the security management model?

3. This chapter lists five tools that can be used by security administrators, network administrators, and attackers alike. Search the World Wide Web for three to five other tools that fit this same description. Who do the sites promoting these tools claim to support?

4. Using the names of the tools you found in Exercise 3 and a browser on the World Wide Web, find a site that claims to be dedicated to supporting hackers. Do you find any references to any other hacker tools? If you do, create a list of the tools with their names and a short description of what they do and how they work.

5. Using the risk assessment documentation components presented in the chapter, draft a tentative risk assessment of one area (a lab, department, or office) of your university. Outline the critical risks you found and discuss these with your class.

Case Exercises

Remember from the beginning of this book how Amy's day started? Now imagine how it could have been:

For Amy, the day began like any other at the Sequential Label and Supply Company (SLS) help desk. Taking calls and helping the office workers with computer problems was not glamorous, but she enjoyed the work; it was challenging and paid pretty well. Some of her friends in the industry worked at bigger companies, some at cutting-edge tech companies, but they all agreed that technology jobs were a good way to pay the bills.

The phone rang, as it did on average about four times an hour, and about 28 times a day. The first call of the day, from a worried user hoping Amy could help him out of a jam, seemed typical. The call display on her monitor gave some of the facts: the user's name, his phone number, the department in which he worked, where his office was on the company campus, and a list of all the calls he'd made in the past. "Hi, Bob," Amy said. "Did you get that document formatting problem squared away?"

"Sure did, Amy. Hope we can figure out what's going on this time."

"We'll try, Bob. Tell me about it."

"Well, I need help setting a page break in this new spreadsheet template I'm working on," Bob said.

Amy smiled to herself. She knew spreadsheets well, so she would probably be able to close this call on the first contact. That would help her call statistics, which was one of the ways her job performance was measured.

Little did Amy know that roughly four minutes before Bob's phone call, a specially programmed computer out at the edge of the SLS network had made a programmed decision. This computer was generally known as postoffice.seqlbl.com, but it was called the "e-mail gateway" by the networking, messaging, and information security teams at SLS. The decision it had made was just like many thousands of other decisions it made in a typical day–that is, to block the transmission of a file that was attached to an e-mail addressed to Bob.Hulme@seqlbl.com. The gateway had determined that Bob didn't need an executable program that had been attached to that e-mail message, which (the gateway also determined) originated from somewhere on the Internet but contained a forged reply-to address from Davey Martinez at SLS. In other words, the gateway had delivered the e-mail to Bob Hulme, but not the attachment.

When Bob got the e-mail, all he saw was that another unsolicited commercial e-mail with an unwanted executable had been blocked. He had deleted the nuisance message without a second thought.

While she was talking to Bob, Amy looked up to see Charles Moody walking calmly down the hall. Charlie, as he liked to be called, was the senior manager of the server administration team and also the company's chief information security officer. Kelvin Urich and Iris Majwubu were trailing behind Charlie as he headed from his office to the door of the conference room. Amy thought, "It must be time for the weekly security status meeting."

She was the user representative on the company information security oversight committee, so she was due to attend this meeting. Amy continued talking Bob through the procedure for setting up a page break, and decided she would join the information security team for coffee and bagels as soon as she was finished.

Questions:

1. What area of the SP 800-100 management maintenance model addresses the actions of the content filter described here?

2. What recommendations would you give Sequential Label and Supply Company for how it might select a security management maintenance model?

Endnotes

1. Cuff, Jeanne. "Grow Up: How Mature Is Your Help Desk?" *Compass America, Inc.* Accessed 14 July 2007 from *www.compassme.com/destinations/white_papers/GrowUpWP.pdf.*

2. The Open Source Security Testing Methodology Manual. Accessed 29 March 2010 from *http://en.wikipedia.org/wiki/The_Open_Source_Security_Testing_Methodology_Manual.*

3. *Readings and Cases in the Management of Information Security: Legal and Ethical Issues.* 2010. Course Technology.

4. "Canon." Accessed 3 October 2008 from *http://dictionary.reference.com/browse/canon.*

5. "Ethical." Accessed 3 October 2008 from *http://dictionary.reference.com/browse/ethical.*

6. Multiple references including *www.edu-cyberpg.com/Technology/ethics.html.*

7. *http://dictionary.reference.com/search?q=hacking*

8. © 1986 Paramount Pictures.

9. © 1983 MGM/UA.

10. © 1995 MGM.

11. *http://dictionary.reference.com/browse/oxymoron.*

12. Levy, S. 1984. *Hackers: Heroes of the Computer Revolution.* Putnam, NY: Penguin.

13. *http://dictionary.reference.com/browse/authorization.*

14. *http://en.wikipedia.org/wiki/Hippocratic_Oath.*

15. (ISC)[2] Code of Ethics. Accessed 10 October 2008 from *www.isc2.org/cgibin/content.cgi?category=12.*

16. (ISC)[2] Code of Ethics. Accessed 10 October 2008 from *www.isc2.org/cgibin/content.cgi?category=12.*

17. *http://dictionary.reference.com/browse/professional.*

18. Kruse, W. G. & Heiser, J. G. *Computer Forensics Incident Response Essentials.* 2002. Boston: Addison Wesley Pearson Education, p. 7.

Glossary

accept control strategy The choice to do nothing to protect a vulnerability and to accept the outcome of its exploitation.

access The ability to use, manipulate, modify or affect an object.

access control Security measures such as a badge reader that admits or prohibits people from entering sensitive areas.

access control list (ACL) Consists of the user access lists, matrices, and capability tables that govern the rights and privileges of users.

access control matrix A combination of tables and lists, such that organizational assets are listed along the column headers, while users are listed along the row headers. The resulting matrix contains access control lists in columns for a particular device or asset, and capability tables in rows for a particular user.

access point and wireless switch locations Components that allow a wireless device to connect to a network.

accountability Synonymous with auditability. Ensures that all actions on a system, whether they are authorized or unauthorized, can be attributed to an authenticated identity.

accreditation Authorizes an IT system to process, store, or transmit information.

accuracy An attribute of information in which the data is free of errors and has the value that the user expects.

acquired value The value an asset gains over time within an organization.

active vulnerability scanner Devices that scan networks for highly detailed information. An "active" scanner is one that initiates traffic on the network in order to determine security holes.

address restrictions Rules designed to prohibit data packets with certain addresses or partial addresses from passing through devices.

Advanced Encryption Standard (AES) A Federal Information Processing Standard (FIPS) that specifies a cryptographic algorithm for use within the U.S. government to protect information in federal agencies that are not a part of the national defense infrastructure.

adware Any software program intended for marketing purposes such as those used to deliver and display advertising banners or popups to the user's screen or tracking the user's online usage or purchasing activity.

affidavit Sworn testimony that certain facts are in the possession of the investigating officer that they feel warrant the examination of specific items located at a specific place.

after-action review (AAR) A detailed examination of the events that occur from the first detection of a security breach to the final recovery.

aggregate information Information created by combining pieces of data that are not considered private in themselves, but raise privacy concerns when taken together.

Agreement on Trade-Related Aspects of Intellectual Property Rights (TRIPS) Created by the World Trade Organization to introduce intellectual property rules into the multilateral trade system. It is the first significant international effort to protect the intellectual property of both individuals and sovereign nations.

air-aspirating detectors Sophisticated systems that are used in high-sensitivity areas. They filter air by moving it through a chamber containing a detector.

alarm An indication, which may take the form of audible signals, e-mail messages, pager notifications, pop-up windows, or log entries, that a system has just been attacked and/or continues to be under attack. Synonymous with alert.

alarm clustering A consolidation of almost identical alarms into a single higher-level alarm to reduce the total number of alarms generated, thereby reducing administrative overhead, and also to indicate a relationship between the individual alarm elements.

alarm compaction A form of alarm clustering that is based on frequency, similarity in attack signature, similarity in attack target, or other similarities; it is also designed to reduce the total number of alarms generated, thereby reducing administrative overhead, and also to indicate a relationship between the individual alarm elements when they have specific similar attributes.

alarm filtering The process of classifying the attack alerts that an intrusion detection system produces in order to distinguish/sort false positives from actual attacks more efficiently.

alert An indication, which may take the form of audible signals, e-mail messages, pager notifications, pop-up windows, or log entries, that a system has just been attacked and/or continues to be under attack. Synonymous with alarm.

alert message A scripted description of the incident, usually just enough information so that each individual knows what portion of the IR plan to implement, and not enough to slow down the notification process.

alert roster A document containing contact information for the people to be notified in the event of an incident.

algorithm A set of steps or mathematical calculations used in solving a problem. In cryptography, it is the programmatic steps used to convert an unencrypted message into an encrypted sequence of bits that represent the message, or the programs that enable the cryptographic processes.

annualized cost of the safeguard (ACS) The total cost of owning and operating the specific control for each year of its expected operational life.

annualized loss expectancy (ALE) The overall loss an organization could incur from the specified threat over the course of an entire year.

annualized rate of occurrence (ARO) The anticipated rate of occurrence of a loss from the specified threat over one year.

application firewall Synonymous with application-level firewall. Frequently a dedicated computer, separate from the filtering router, but is commonly used in conjunction with a filtering router.

application gateway Synonymous with application firewall. Frequently a dedicated computer, separate from the filtering router, but is commonly used in conjunction with a filtering router.

application header (AH) protocol A feature of the IPSec protocol that provides system to system authentication and data integrity verification, but does not provide secrecy for the content of a network communication.

application-level firewall Synonymous with application firewall. Frequently a dedicated computer, separate from the filtering router, but is commonly used in conjunction with a filtering router.

application protocol verification A process in which higher-order protocols (e.g., HTTP, FTP, Telnet) are examined for unexpected packet behavior, or improper use.

asset The organizational resource that is being protected. An asset can be logical, such as a Web site or information owned or controlled by the organization; or an asset can be physical, such as a computer system, or other tangible object.

asset valuation The process of assigning financial value or worth to each information asset.

Association of Computing Machinery (ACM) An organization that focuses on the ethics of security professionals.

asymmetric encryption Synonymous with public key encryption. A method of communicating on a network using two different but related keys, one to encrypt and the other to decrypt messages.

asynchronous tokens Devices that use a challenge response method, in which a server challenges a user during login with a numerical sequence. The user places the sequence into a token, which generates a response that is entered to gain access.

attack An act that takes advantage of a vulnerability to compromise a controlled system.

attack profile A detailed description of the activities that occur during an attack.

attack protocol A series of steps or processes used by an attacker, in a logical sequence, to launch an attack against a target system or network.

attack scenario end case The summary that describes the attack, and the most likely outcome from the attack and associated costs from that outcome when assessing the impact to information assets from a specific attack profile.

auditability Synonymous with accountability. Ensures that all actions on a system, whether they are authorized or unauthorized, can be attributed to an authenticated identity.

auditing A process of reviewing the use of a system, not to check performance but rather to determine if misuse or malfeasance has occurred.

authentication The process of validating a supplicant's purported identity.

authentication factors Ways of validating a supplicant's purported identity. The three most common are something a supplicant knows, something a supplicant has or something a supplicant is.

authenticity A quality or state of information characterized by being genuine or original rather than reproduced or fabricated.

authorization The matching of an authenticated entity to a list of information assets and corresponding access levels.

availability A quality or state of information characterized by being accessible and correctly formatted for use without interference or obstruction.

availability disruption A situation in which a product or service is not delivered to the organization as expected.

back door Synonymous with trap door. An electronic hole in software that is left open by accident or intention that allows an attacker to access the system at will with special privileges. Can be installed by a virus, worm or by an attacker who takes control of a system.

back hack Hacking into a hacker's system to find out as much as possible about the hacker.

baseline A baseline is a "value or profile of a performance metric against which changes in the performance metric can be usefully compared.

baselining The analysis of measures against established internal standards. In information security, baselining is the comparison of current security activities and events against the organization's established expected levels of performance.

bastion host A dedicated server that receives screened network traffic. Usually prepared with extra attention to detail and hardened for use in an unsecured or limited security zone. Sometimes referred to as a sacrificial host.

behavioral feasibility Synonymous with operational feasibility. The examination of user acceptance and support, management acceptance and support, and the overall requirements of the organization's stakeholders.

behavior-based IDPS Synonymous with statistical anomaly-based IDS (stat IDPS). A device that collects data from normal traffic to establish a baseline. The IDS compares periodic data samples with the baseline to highlight irregularities.

benchmarking The process of seeking out and studying the practices used in other organizations that produce results you would like to duplicate in your organization.

benefit The value that an organization recognizes by using controls to prevent losses associated with a specific vulnerability.

best business practices Security efforts that seek to provide a superior level of performance in the protection of information are referred to as best business practices.

best practices Synonymous with best business practices and recommended practices. Procedures that provide a superior level of security for an organization's information.

biometric access control Access control based on the use of some measurable human characteristic or trait to authenticate the identity of a proposed systems user.

biometric locks Access-control devices that use a biometric detection device as a release mechanism.

blackout A lengthy loss of power.

Bluetooth The de facto industry standard for short-range wireless communications between devices.

boot virus A program that infects the key operating system files located in a computer's boot sector.

bot An abbreviation of "robot". An automated software program that executes certain commands when it receives a specific input.

bottom-up approach A method of establishing security policies that begins as a grassroots effort in which systems administrators attempt to improve the security of their systems.

brownout A prolonged drop in voltage.

brute force attack The application of computing and network resources to try every possible combination of options of a password.

buffer overflow Synonymous with buffer overrun. An application error that occurs when more data is sent to a buffer than it can handle.

bull's eye method A proven method for prioritizing a program of complex change whose fundamental concept is that issues are addressed from the general to the specific and that the focus is on systematic solutions instead of individual problems.

business continuity (BC) plan Ensures that critical business functions continue, if a catastrophic incident or disaster occurs.

business continuity planning Prepares an organization to reestablish critical business operations during a disaster that affects operations at the primary site.

business impact analysis (BIA) The first phase in the development of the continuity planning process. It extends the risk assessment process to determine the priority for risks in the area of information security.

C.I.A. triangle The industry standard for computer security since the development of the mainframe. It is based on three characteristics that describe the utility of information: confidentiality, integrity, and availability.

cache servers Servers used by proxy servers to temporarily store frequently accessed pages.

candidate vulnerabilities A possible vulnerability detected by an automated tool. Will be screened by an analyst to ascertain if it is an actual vulnerability.

capabilities table Synonymous with capability table. Specifies which subjects and objects users or groups can access.

centralized IDPS control strategy A control strategy for intrusion detection prevention systems (IDPSs) in which all IDPS control functions are implemented and managed in a central location.

certificate authority (CA) An organization which issues, manages, authenticates, signs, and revokes users' digital certificates.

certificate revocation list (CRL) A list distributed by the certificate authority that identifies all revoked certificates.

certification The comprehensive evaluation of the technical and nontechnical security controls of an IT system to support the accreditation process that establishes the extent to which a particular design and implementation meets a set of specified security requirements.

chain of custody Synonymous with chain of evidence. The detailed documentation of the collection, storage, transfer, and ownership of collected evidence from crime scene through its presentation in court.

chain of evidence Synonymous with chain of custody. The detailed documentation of the collection, storage, transfer, and ownership of collected evidence from crime scene through its presentation in court.

champion A senior executive who promotes a security project and ensures its support.

change control A process to assure an organization that changes to systems are managed and all parties that need to be informed are aware of the planned changes.

chief information officer (CIO) An executive-level position in which the person is in charge of the organization's computing technology, and strives to create efficiency in the processing and accessing of the organization's information.

chief information security officer (CISO) This position is typically considered the top information security officer in an organization. The CISO is usually not an executive-level position, and frequently the person in this role will report to the chief information officer (CIO).

cipher or cryptosystem An encryption method or process encompassing the algorithm, key(s) or cryptovariable(s), and procedures used to perform encryption and decryption.

ciphertext A message that is formed when plaintext data is encrypted.

circuit gateway firewall Prevent directions between one network and another by creating tunnels connecting specific processes or systems on each side of the firewall, and then allowing only authorized traffic, such as a specific type of TPC connection for only authorized users, in these tunnels.

civil law A wide variety of laws that govern a nation or state and deal with the relationships and conflicts between organizational entities and people.

Class A fires Those fires that involve ordinary combustible fuels such as wood, paper, textiles, rubber, cloth, and trash. They are extinguished by agents that interrupt the ability of the fuel to be ignited. Water and multipurpose dry chemical fire extinguishers are ideal for these types of fires.

Class B fires Those fires fueled by combustible liquids or gases, such as solvents, gasoline, paint, lacquer, and oil. They are extinguished by agents that remove oxygen from the fire. Carbon dioxide, multipurpose dry chemical, and Halon fire extinguishers are ideal for these types of fires.

Class C fires Those fires with energized electrical equipment or appliances. They are extinguished with agents that must be nonconducting. Carbon dioxide, multipurpose dry chemical, and Halon fire extinguishers are ideal for these types of fires. A water fire extinguisher must never be used on a Class C fire.

Class D fires Those fires fueled by combustible metals, such as magnesium, lithium, and sodium. Fires of this type require special extinguishing agents and techniques.

clean agent A fire suppression system active ingredient that leaves no residue after application, nor does it interfere with the operation of electrical or electronic equipment.

clean desk policy Rules that require each employee to secure all information in its appropriate storage container at the end of each day.

cleartext Synonymous with plaintext. The original unencrypted message, or a message that has been successfully decrypted.

clipping level As detected by an intrusion detection prevention system, the level of network activity that is established as a baseline and therefore activity volumes above that level are considered suspect.

closed-circuit television (CCT) An electronic monitoring system. Some of these systems can be made to collect constant video feeds, whereas others rotate input from a number of cameras, sampling each area in turn.

code The process of converting components (words or phrases) of an unencrypted message into encrypted components.

cold site An alternate site that can be used by an organization if a disaster occurs at the home site. Contains rudimentary services and facilities.

communications security Securing information in transit using tools such as cryptographic systems, as well as its associated media and technology.

community of interest A group of individuals united by shared interests or values within an organization and who share a common goal of helping the organization to meet its objectives.

competitive advantage The leverage gained by an organization that supplies superior products or services. Establishing a competitive business model, method, or technique allows an organization to provide a product or service that is superior to others in the marketplace.

competitive disadvantage The leverage lost by an organization that supplies products or services perceived to be inferior to other organizations.

competitive intelligence Information gained legally that gives an organization an advantage over its competition.

computer forensics The process of collecting, analyzing, and preserving computer-related evidence.

Computer Fraud and Abuse Act of 1986 (CFA Act) The cornerstone of many computer-related federal laws and enforcement efforts. Defines and formalizes laws to counter threats from computer-related acts and offenses.

computer security A term that in the early days of computers specified the need to secure the physical location of hardware from outside threats. This term later came to stand for all actions taken to preserve computer systems from losses. It has evolved into the current concept of information security as the scope of protecting information in the organization has expanded.

Computer Security Act of 1987 One of the first attempts to protect federal computer systems by establishing minimum acceptable security practices by following standards and guidelines created by the National Bureau of Standards and the National Security Agency.

confidence value A value associated with an intrusion detection system's ability to detect and identify an attack correctly.

confidentiality The quality or state of information that prevents disclosure or exposure to unauthorized individuals or systems.

configuration rule policies The specific instructions entered into a security system that govern how it reacts to the data it receives.

contact and weight sensors Alarm sensors that work when contact in the alarm device is either created due to pressure, or removed due to a door or window opening.

content filter Synonymous with reverse firewalls. A software device that allows administrators to work within a network to restrict accessibility to information.

contingency plan The program developed to anticipate, react to, and recover from events that threaten the security of information and information assets in the organization, and, subsequently, to restore the organization to normal modes of business operations.

control Synonymous with safeguard and countermeasure. A security mechanism, policy, or procedure that can counter system attack, reduce risks, and resolve vulnerabilities.

Convention on Cybercrime Adopted by the Council of Europe in 2001, it created an international task force to oversee a range of security functions associated with Internet activities for standardized technology laws across international borders, along with attempting to improve the effectiveness of international investigations into breaches of technology law.

corporate governance Guiding documents, such as corporate charters or partnership agreements, appointed or elected leaders or officers, and planning and operating procedures which combine to dictate how a company does business.

correlation attacks Attempts to deduce the statistical relationships of the structure of the key and the output of the cryptosystem.

cost The amount of money needed to implement intrusion and detection systems.

cost avoidance The process of avoiding the financial impact of an incident by implementing a control.

cost benefit analysis (CBA) Synonymous with economic feasibility study. The comparison of the cost of protecting an asset with the worth of the asset or the costs of the compromise of an asset.

cracker An individual who removes an application's software protection that is designed to prevent unauthorized duplication, or a criminal hacker.

cracking Attempting to reverse-calculate a password.

criminal law Laws that address violations harmful to society and that are actively enforced through prosecution by the state.

crisis management The actions taken during and after a disaster.

crossover error rate (CER) The level at which the number of false rejections equals the false acceptances, and is also known as the equal error rate.

cross-site scripting (XSS) Occurs when an application running on a Web server gathers data from a user in order to steal it.

cryptogram A message that is formed when plaintext data is encrypted.

cryptography From the Greek work *kryptos*, meaning hidden, and *graphein*, meaning to write. The process of making and using codes to secure the transmission of information.

cryptology The science of encryption. A field of study that encompasses cryptography and cryptanalysis.

cryptovariable Synonymous with key, the information used in conjunction with an algorithm to create the ciphertext from the plaintext or derive the plaintext from the ciphertext. This can be a series of bits used by a computer program, or it can be a passphrase used by humans.

cultural mores Fixed moral attitudes or customs of a particular group.

cyberactivist Synonymous with hacktivist. An individual who uses technology as a tool for civil disobedience.

cyberterrorism The act of hacking to conduct terrorist activities through network or Internet pathways.

data classification scheme A method of categorizing the levels of confidentiality of an organization's data.

data custodians Individuals who are responsible for the storage, maintenance, and protection of information.

Data Encryption Standard (DES) An algorithm that is federally approved for encryption. The algorithm is based on the Data Encryption Algorithm (DEA), which uses a 64-bit block size and a 56-bit key.

data owners Individuals who determine the level of classification associated with data.

data users Individuals who work with information to perform their daily jobs supporting the mission of the organization.

Database Right A United Kingdom version of the Directive 95/46/EC.

database shadowing A process that duplicates data in real-time using databases at a remote site or to multiple servers.

de facto standards Informal norms. Early Internet connections were based on de facto standards.

de jure standards Formally recognized norms. As the Internet developed, de jure standards were established for its connections.

decipher To decrypt or convert ciphertext into the equivalent plaintext.

decryption The process of converting the ciphertext message back into plaintext so it can be readily understood.

defend control strategy The preferred risk control strategy which attempts to prevent the exploitation of vulnerabilities.

defense in depth The multiple levels of security controls and safeguards that an intruder faces.

deliverable A completed document or program module that can serve either as the beginning point for a later task or as an element in the finished project.

deluge systems A sprinkler system that contains valves that are kept open, so that when the first phase of sprinkler heads are activated, the water is immediately applied to various areas without waiting for a second phase to trigger the individual sprinkler heads.

demilitarized zone (DMZ) An intermediate area between a trusted network and an untrusted network.

denial-of-service (DoS) attack An attack in which the attacker sends a large number of connection or information requests to overwhelm and cripple a target.

Department of Homeland Security (DHS) U.S. federal agencies created in 2003 through the Homeland Security Act of 2002, which was passed in response to the events of September 11, 2001. DHS is made up of five directorates, or divisions, through which it carries out its mission of protecting the people as well as the physical and informational assets of the United States.

diameter protocol Defines the minimum requirements for a system that provides Authentication, Authorization and Accounting (AAA) services and can go beyond these basics and add commands and/or object attributes.

dictionary attack A form of brute force attack on passwords that uses a list of commonly used passwords instead of random combinations. In cryptography, this is done by encrypting each entry in the dictionary with the same cryptosystem used by the target, then comparing the resulting ciphertext against the target's ciphertext.

difference analysis A procedure that compares the current state of a network segment (the systems and services it offers) against a known previous state of that same network segment (the baseline of systems and services).

differential backup The storage of all files that have been changed or added since the last full backup.

Diffie-Hellman key exchange A method for exchanging private keys using public key encryption.

digital certificates Public-key container files that allow computer programs to validate the key and identify to whom it belongs.

digital forensics A formalized, process-based investigation of a security incident, specifically what happened and how, that may help law enforcement and protect the organization.

digital malfeasance A crime against or using digital media, computer technology or related components (computer as source or object of crime).

Digital Millennium Copyright Act (DMCA) An American version of an international effort to reduce the impact of copyright, trademark, and privacy infringement, especially through the removal of technological copyright protection measures.

Digital Signature Standard (DSS) The basis for digital signatures that has been approved and endorsed by the U.S. federal government.

digital signatures Encrypted messages that can be mathematically proven authentic.

direct changeover A modification to work practices that involves stopping the old method and beginning the new.

Directive 95/46/EC A European Union act that regulated the processing of personal data and the transmittal of such data to protect individual rights.

disaster recovery (DR) plan Addresses the preparation for and recovery from a disaster, whether natural or man-made.

discretionary access controls (DACs) A type of data access control in which data users are allowed to grant access to their peers.

disk duplexing For backup purposes, the use of twin drives, each with its own drive controller. A variation of disk mirroring.

disk mirroring A backup and recovery technique that uses twin drives in a computer system. Also known as RAID Level 1.

disk striping For backup purposes, the creation of one large logical volume across several hard disk drives and the storage of data in segments, called stripes, across all the disk drives in an array.

distinguished name (DN) Used with digital certificates, a series of name-value pairs that uniquely identify a certificate entity to a user's public key.

distributed denial-of-service (DDoS) attack An attack in which a coordinated stream of connection requests is launched against a target from many locations at the same time.

DNS cache poisoning Changing a legitimate host entry in a domain name server (DNS) to point to an attacker's website.

dry-pipe system A sprinkler system that is designed to work in areas where electrical equipment is used by spraying pressurized air rather than water.

due care The actions that demonstrate that an organization makes sure that every employee knows what is acceptable or not acceptable behavior, and knows the consequences of illegal or unethical actions.

due diligence The actions that demonstrate that an organization is diligent in ensuring that the implemented standards continue to provide the required level of protection.

dumb cards ID cards or ATM cards with magnetic stripes containing the digital (and often encrypted) user personal identification number (PIN) against which a user input is compared.

dumpster diving The retrieval of information from refuse that could prove embarrassing to the company or could compromise the security of information.

dust contamination A threat to the hardware components of information systems that falls in the forces of nature or acts of God category because it is unexpected or can occur with very little warning. Dust contamination can shorten the life of information systems or disrupt normal operations, causing unplanned downtime.

dynamic packet-filtering firewall A firewall that allows only a particular packet with a particular source, destination, and port address to enter through the firewall.

earthquake A threat to the hardware components of information systems that falls in the forces of nature or acts of God category because it is unexpected or can occur with very little warning. As a sudden movement of the earth's crust caused by the release of stress accumulated along geologic faults, or by volcanic activity, earthquakes can cause direct damage to all or part of the information system or, more often, to the building that houses it.

Economic Espionage Act in 1996. A federal law which attempts to prevent trade secrets from being illegally shared.

economic feasibility study Synonymous with cost benefit analysis. The comparison of the cost of protecting an asset with the worth of the asset or the costs of the compromise of an asset.

electromagnetic radiation (EMR) The energy that radiates from man-made electronic systems.

electromechanical locks Locking devices that can accept a variety of inputs as keys, including magnetic strips on ID cards, radio signals from name badges, personal identification numbers (PINs) typed into a keypad, or some combination of these to activate an electrically powered servo to unlock the mechanism.

Electronic Communications Privacy Act of 1986 Synonymous with the Federal Wiretapping Act. A collection of statutes that regulate the interception of wire, electronic, and oral communication. These statutes work in conjunction with the Fourth Amendment of the U.S. Constitution, which provides protections from unlawful search and seizure.

electronic locks Locks that can be integrated into alarm systems and combined with other building management systems—specifically, these locks can be integrated with sensors to create a number of various combinations of locking behavior.

electronic vaulting The transfer of large batches of data to an off-site facility.

electrostatic discharge (ESD) A threat to the hardware components of information systems that falls in the forces of nature or acts of God category because it is unexpected or can occur with very little warning. A spark produced from a buildup of static electricity.

elite hacker Synonymous with expert hacker. An individual who develops software scripts and program exploits used by novice or unskilled hackers. This individual is also a master of several programming languages, networking protocols, and operating systems, who also exhibits a mastery of the technical environment of the targeted system.

e-mail spoofing The process of sending an e-mail with a modified field. The modified field is often the address of the originator.

encapsulating security payload (ESP) protocol A component of the IPSec protocol that provides secrecy for the contents of network communications as well as system-to-system authentication and data integrity verification.

encipher To encrypt or convert plaintext into the equivalent ciphertext.

encryption The process of converting an original message into a form that is unreadable by unauthorized individuals.

end user Synonymous with data user. An individual who uses computer applications for his daily work.

enterprise information security policy (EISP) Also known as a general security policy, IT security policy, or information security policy, this policy is based on and directly supports the mission, vision, and direction of the organization and sets the strategic direction, scope, and tone for all security efforts.

enticement The process of attracting attention to a system by placing tantalizing bits of information in key locations.

entrapment The act of luring an individual into committing a crime to get a conviction.

ethics The study of how members of a society ought to behave.

evasion Process by which an attacker changes the format and/or timing of their activities to avoid being detected by IPS or IDS.

evidence A physical object or documented information that proves an action occurred or identifies the intent of a perpetrator.

evidentiary material (EM) Any information that could potentially support the organization's legal or policy based case against the subject.

exclusive OR operation (XOR) A function of Boolean algebra in which two bits are compared, and if the two bits are identical, the result is a binary 0. If the two bits are not the same, the result is a binary 1.

exit interview A discussion at the end of employment that reminds an employee of contractual obligations, such as nondisclosure agreements and obtains feedback on the employee's tenure in the organization.

expert hacker Synonymous with elite hacker. An individual who develops software scripts and program exploits used by novice or unskilled hackers. This individual is also a master of several programming languages, networking protocols, and operating systems, who also exhibits a mastery of the technical environment of the targeted system.

exploit A technique used to compromise a system.

exposure A single instance of a system being open to damage.

exposure factor (EF) An element of a formula for calculating the value associated with the most likely loss from an attack, or single loss expectancy (SLE). In SLE = asset value x exposure factor (EF), exposure factor equals the expected percentage of loss that would occur from a particular attack.

external monitoring domain The sector of a maintenance model that provides early awareness of new and emerging threats, threat agents, vulnerabilities, and attacks that the organization needs in order to mount an effective and timely defense.

extranet A segment of the DMZ where additional authentication and authorization controls are put into place to provide services that are not available to the general public.

facilities management The operation of an organization's physical security commonly including access controls for a building.

fail-safe lock A lock that ensures ability to exit. When the lock of a door fails, the door becomes unlocked.

fail-secure lock A lock that ensures entrance is prohibited. When the lock of a door fails the door remains locked.

false accept rate The percentage of identification instances in which unauthorized users are allowed access to systems or areas as a result of a failure in the biometric device.

false attack stimulus An event that triggers alarms and causes a false positive when no actual attacks are in progress.

false negative The failure of an intrusion detection prevention system (IDPS) to react to an actual attack event. Of all failures, this is the most grievous, because the very purpose of an IDPS is to detect attacks.

false positive An alarm or alert that indicates that an attack is in progress or that an attack has successfully occurred when in fact there was no such attack.

false reject rate The percentage or value associated with the rate at which authentic users are denied or prevented access to authorized areas as a result of a failure in the biometric device.

fault The complete loss of power for a moment.

Federal Privacy Act of 1974 An act that regulates the government in the protection of individual privacy. Created to insure that government agencies protect the privacy of individual and business information and to hold those agencies responsible if any portion of this information is released without permission.

ferroresonant standby UPS A device that replaces a UPS transfer switch. The transformer provides power conditioning and line filtering to the primary power source, reducing the effect of power outages.

field change order (FCO) An authorization issued by an organization for the repair, modification, or update of a piece of equipment.

fifth generation firewall This firewall evaluates packets at multiple layers of the protocol stack by checking security in the kernel as data is passed up and down the stack.

file hashing Method for ensuring information validity. Involves a file being read by a special algorithm that uses the value of the bits in the file to compute a single large number called a hash value.

Financial Services Modernization Act of 1999 Synonymous with the Gramm-Leach-Bliley Act of 1999. This act contains provisions on facilitating affiliation among banks, securities firms, and insurance companies. The act has significant impact on the privacy of personal information used by these industries.

fingerprinting A data-gathering process that discovers the assets that can be accessed from a network. Usually performed in advance of a planned attack. This is the systematic examination of the entire set of Internet addresses of the organization.

fire A threat to the hardware components of information systems that falls in the forces of nature or acts of God category because it is unexpected or can occur with very little warning. In this context, this threat is usually a structural fire that damages the building housing the computing equipment that comprises all or part of the information system. Also encompasses smoke damage from a fire and/or water damage from sprinkler systems or firefighters.

fire suppression systems Devices installed and maintained to detect and respond to a fire, potential fire, or combustion danger situation.

firewall Synonymous with application firewall and application-level firewall. A device that selectively discriminates against information flowing into or out of the organization. In the context of physical security, a firewall is a wall that limits the spread of damage should a fire break out in an office.

firewall subnet Multiple firewalls that create a buffer between networks inside and outside an organization.

firewalls Walls that limit the spread of damage should a fire break out in an office.

first generation firewall A static packet-filtering firewall that filters packets according to their headers as the packets travel to and from the organization's networks.

fixed temperature A fire detection system that contains a sensor that detects when the ambient temperature in an area reaches a predetermined level.

flame detector A sensor that detects the infrared or ultraviolet light produced by an open flame.

flame point The temperature of ignition.

flood A threat to the hardware components of information systems that falls in the forces of nature or acts of God category because it is unexpected or can occur with very little warning. A flood usually involves an overflowing of water onto land that is normally dry, causing direct damage to all or part of the information system or to the building that houses all or part of the information system.

footprinting The identification of the Internet addresses that are owned or controlled by an organization.

Fourth Amendment of the U.S. Constitution U.S. law that protects from unlawful search and seizure, cited in various other laws such as Electronic Communications Privacy Act of 1986.

fourth generation firewall Also known as dynamic packet-filtering firewalls, these allow only a particular packet with a particular source, destination, and port address to enter.

Fraud and Related Activity in Connection with Identification Documents, Authentication Features, and Information A federal law which criminalizes creation, reproduction, transfer, possession, or use of unauthorized or false identification documents or document-making equipment.

Freedom of Information Act An act that provides every person the right to request access to federal agency records or information that are not matters of national security.

friendly departures Individuals leaving jobs due to resignation, retirement, promotion, or relocation.

full backup A full and complete backup of the entire system, including all applications, operating systems components, and data.

fully distributed IDPS control strategy An intrusion detection prevention system (IDPS) control strategy in which all control functions and sensors are applied at the physical location of each IDS component. Thus, each sensor/agent is best configured to deal with its own environment.

gateway router A device that is designed primarily to connect the organization's systems to the outside world.

Georgia Computer Systems Protection Act State regulation passed by the state of Georgia in 1991 that seeks to protect information and establishes penalties for the use of information technology to attack or exploit information systems.

gold standard A subcategory within best practices consisting of practices that are typically viewed as "the best of the best."

Gramm-Leach-Bliley Act of 1999 Synonymous with the Financial Services Modernization Act of 1999. This act contains provisions on facilitating affiliation among banks, securities firms, and insurance companies. The act has significant impact on the privacy of personal information used by these industries.

ground fault circuit interruption (GFCI) Special grounding equipment used when electrical equipment is situated where water can accumulate. GFCI can quickly identify and interrupt a ground fault.

hackers People who use and create computer software to gain access to information illegally.

hacktivist Synonymous with cyberactivist. An individual who uses technology as a tool for civil disobedience.

hash algorithms Public functions that create a hash value, also known as a message digest, by converting variable-length messages into a single fixed-length value.

hash functions Mathematical algorithms that generate a message summary or message digest that allows a hash algorithm to confirm that the content of a specific message has not been altered.

hash value A fingerprint of the author's message that is compared with the recipient's locally calculated hash of the same message.

Health Insurance Portability and Accountability Act Of 1996 (HIPAA) Synonymous with the Kennedy-Kassebaum Act. This act protects the confidentiality and security of health-care data by establishing and enforcing standards and by standardizing electronic data interchange.

hierarchical roster A list of names of people who are called in the case of an emergency. The first person calls a few other people on the roster, who in turn call a few other people.

honeynet A network or system subnet that is configured to misdirect hackers by resembling networks or system subsystems that are rich with information.

honeypot Decoy systems designed to lure potential attackers away from critical systems.

host-based IDPS An intrusion detection and prevention system that is installed on the machines they protect to monitor the status of various files stored on those machines.

hostile departures Individuals leaving jobs due to termination for cause, permanent downsizing, temporary lay-off, or some instances of quitting.

hot site Synonymous with business recovery site. A remote location with systems identical or similar to a home site for use after a disaster.

hot swapped Data drives that can be replaced without taking the entire system down.

humidity The amount of moisture in the air.

hurricane or typhoon A threat to the hardware components of information systems that falls in the forces of nature or acts of God category because it is unexpected or can occur with very little warning. In this context, these tropical cyclones, which typically originate in the equatorial regions of the Atlantic Ocean or Caribbean Sea or eastern regions of the Pacific Ocean and usually involve heavy rains, can directly damage all or part of the information system or, more likely, the building that houses it.

hybrid VPN A type of virtual private network (VPN) that combines trusted VPNs with secure VPNs, providing encrypted transmissions (as in secure VPN) over some or all of a trusted VPN network.

identification A mechanism whereby an unverified entity, called a supplicant, that seeks access to a resources proposes a label by which they are known to the system.

identification (ID) card A type of access control device that is typically concealed.

IDPS terrorists Individuals or groups who carry out attacks designed to trip an organization's IDPS, essentially causing the organization to conduct its own DoS attack by over-reacting to an actual, but insignificant, attack.

incident Any clearly identified attack on the organization's information assets that would threaten the assets' confidentiality, integrity, or availability.

incident candidate A potential incident or ambiguously identified attack that could be an actual attack.

incident classification The process of examining a potential incident.

incident damage assessment The determination of the scope of a breach of the confidentiality, integrity, and availability of information immediately following an incident.

incident reaction Actions outlined in an incident response plan for security information that guide an organization in attempting to stop an incident, mitigate the impact of an incident, and provide information for recovery.

incident response (IR) Activities taken to plan for, detect, and correct the impact of an incident on information assets.

incident response (IR) plan Addresses the identification, classification, response, and recovery from an incident.

incremental backup The archives of files that have been modified on a particular day.

industrial espionage Information gained illegally that gives an organization an advantage over its competition.

information security The protection of information and the systems and hardware that use, store, and transmit that information.

information security governance The application of the principles of corporate governance -- that is, executive management's responsibility to provide strategic direction, ensure the accomplishment of objectives, oversee that risks are appropriately managed, and validate the responsible resource utilization -- to the information security function.

information security operational risk assessment A method to identify and document the risk that a project, process, or action introduces to the organization and may also involve offering suggestions for controls that can reduce that risk.

information security policy An organization's rules for the protection of the information assets of the organization.

information system (IS) The entire set of software, hardware, data, people, procedures, and networks necessary to use information as a resource in the organization.

Information Systems Audit and Control Association (ISACA) A professional association focused on auditing, control, and security.

Information Systems Security Association (ISSA) A nonprofit society of information security professionals.

integer bugs A mathematical computing bug that is exploited indirectly by an attacker to corrupt other areas of memory in order to control an application.

integrity The quality or state of being whole, complete, and uncorrupted.

internal monitoring domain The sector of a maintenance model whose primary goal is to maintain an informed awareness of the state of all of the organization's networks, information systems, and information security defenses.

International Information Systems Security Certification Consortium, Inc. (ISC)2 An international consortium dedicated to improving the quality of security professionals.

Internet Protocol Security (IPSec) An open source protocol for securing communications across any IP-based network such as LANs, WANs, and the Internet.

Internet vulnerability assessment A process designed to find and document the vulnerabilities that may be present in the public-facing network of the organization.

intrinsic value The essential worth of an asset.

intrusion A type of attack on information assets in which the instigator attempts to gain entry into a system or disrupt the normal operations of a system with, almost always, the intent to do malicious harm.

intrusion detection and prevention systems (IDPSs) Devices that are a combination of intrusion detection systems and intrusion prevention systems.

intrusion detection systems (IDSs) Devices that detect unauthorized activity within the inner network or on individual machines.

intrusion prevention system (IPS) Devices that work to prevent unauthorized network access.

ionization sensor A smoke detection device that contains a small amount of a harmless radioactive material within a detection chamber. When certain by-products of combustion enter the chamber, they change the level of electrical conductivity with the chamber and activate the detector.

issue-specific security policy (ISSP) A program that addresses specific areas of technology and contains a statement on the organization's position on each specific issue.

job rotation Synonymous with task rotation. A security check that requires that every employee is trained to perform the work of another employee.

joint application development A way project managers can reduce resistance to change by involving employees in the project plan.

jurisdiction A court's right to hear a case because a wrong was committed in its territory or involving its citizenry.

Kennedy-Kassebaum Act Synonymous with the Health Insurance Portability and Accountability Act Of 1996. This act protects the confidentiality and security of health-care data by establishing and enforcing standards and by standardizing electronic data interchange.

Kerberos A cryptosystem that uses symmetric key encryption to validate an individual user to various network resources.

kernel proxy Fifth generation of specialized firewall that works under the Windows NT Executive kernel.

key Synonymous with cryptovariable, the information used in conjunction with an algorithm to create the ciphertext from the plaintext or derive the plaintext from the ciphertext. This can be a series of bits used by a computer program, or it can be a passphrase used by humans.

keyspace The entire range of values that can possibly be used to construct an individual key.

knowledge-based IDPS Synonymous with signature-based IDPS and misuse-detection IDPS. A device that examines data traffic for signature matches with predefined, preconfigured attack patterns.

known-plaintext attack A method of attacking a cryptosystem that relies on knowledge of some or all of the plaintext that was used to generate a ciphertext.

landslide or mudslide A threat to the hardware components of information systems that falls in the forces of nature or acts of God category because it is unexpected or can occur with very little warning. Specifically, this is the downward sliding of a mass of earth and rock that may directly damage all or part of an information system or, more likely, the building that houses it.

lattice-based access control A matrix of authorizations that control access to data.

laws Rules adopted for determining expected behavior in modern society and drawn from ethics.

least privilege A security measure by which employees are provided access to a minimal amount of information for a minimal amount of time necessary for them to perform their duties.

liability The legal obligation of an entity that includes responsibility for a wrongful act and the legal obligation to make restitution.

lightning A threat to the hardware components of information systems that falls in the forces of nature or acts of God category because it is unexpected or can occur with very little warning. An abrupt, discontinuous natural electric discharge in the atmosphere, lightning usually directly damages all or part of an information system an/or its power distribution components.

likelihood The overall rating of the probability that a specific vulnerability within an organization will be successfully attacked.

line-interactive UPS A type of uninterruptible power supply (UPS) in which the internal components of the standby models are replaced with a pair of inverters and converters.

link encryption A series of encryptions and decryptions between a number of systems, wherein each system in a network decrypts the message sent to it and then re-encrypts it using different keys and sends it to the next neighbor, and this process continues until the message reaches the final destination

log file monitor (LFM) An approach to intrusion detection systems that is similar to the one used for network-based intrusion detection systems (NIDPSs). Using LFM, the system reviews the log files generated by servers, network devices, and even other IDPSs.

long arm jurisdiction A law that reaches across the country or around the world to pull an accused individual into its court systems.

loss A single instance of an information asset suffering damage or unintended or unauthorized modification or disclosure.

macro virus A virus that is contained in a downloaded file attachment such as word processing documents, spread sheets, and database applications.

mail bomb A form of denial-of-service attack in which the abuser sends a large number of connection or information requests to overwhelm and cripple a target.

malicious code Synonymous with malware or malicious software. Software designed to damage, destroy, or deny service to the target system.

malicious software Synonymous with malicious code or malware. Software designed to damage, destroy, or deny service to the target system.

malware Synonymous with malicious code or malicious software. Software designed to damage, destroy, or deny service to the target system.

managerial controls Security processes that are designed by strategic planners and implemented by the security administration of an organization.

managerial guidance A document created by management to guide the implementation and configuration of technology as well as to address the behavior of people in the organization in ways that support the security of information.

mandatory access controls (MACs) The regulations that control access to information resources.

man-in-the-middle Synonymous with TCP hijacking. An attack in which the abuser records data packets from the

network, modifies them, and inserts them back into the network.

man-in-the-middle attack A method of attacking a cryptosystem that relies on knowledge of some or all of the plaintext that was used to generate a ciphertext.

mantrap A small physical enclosure that is used in secure facilities that has an entry point and a different exit point.

manual fire detection systems Human responses to fires, such as calling the fire department, as well as manually activated alarms, such as sprinklers and gaseous systems.

manual locks Locks that are often preset by the manufacturer and therefore unchangeable, thus once they are installed into doors, they can be changed only by highly trained locksmiths.

McCumber Cube A graphical representation of the architectural approach widely used in computer and information security.

mechanical lock Locks that rely on a key that is a carefully shaped piece of metal that a person rotates or a dial that causes the proper rotation of slotted discs to release secured loops of steel, aluminum, or brass.

message authentication code (MAC) A key-dependent, one-way hash function that allows only specific recipients to access the message digest.

message digest Synonymous with hash value. A fingerprint of the author's message that is compared with the recipient's locally calculated hash of the same message.

methodology A formal approach to solving a problem based on a structured sequence of procedures.

metrics-based measures Benchmarking comparisons based on numerical standards such as numbers of successful attacks; staff-hours spent on systems protection; dollars spent on protection; numbers of security personnel; estimated value in dollars of the information lost in successful attacks and loss in productivity hours associated with successful attacks.

milestone A specific point in the project plan when a task and its action steps are complete and have a noticeable impact on the progress of the project plan as a whole.

minutiae Used in biometrics, unique points of reference that are digitized and stored in an encrypted format for comparison with scanned human characteristics.

mission A written statement of an organization's purpose.

misuse-detection IDPS Synonymous with knowledge-based IDPS and signature-based IDPS. A device that examines data traffic for signature matches with predefined, preconfigured attack patterns.

mitigate control strategy Attempts to reduce the impact caused by the exploitation of vulnerability through planning and preparation.

modem vulnerability assessment The process of finding and documenting any vulnerability that is present on dial-up modems connected to an organization's networks.

monitoring port A specially configured connection on a network device that is capable of viewing all of the traffic that moves through the entire device. Also known as a switched port analysis (SPAN) port or mirror port.

monoalphabetic substitution In encryption, the substitution of one value for another using a single alphabet.

motion detectors Alarm systems that detect movement within a confined space, and are either active or passive.

mutual agreement A contract between two or more organizations that specifies how each assists the other in the event of a disaster.

name badge A form of identification that, unlike an ID card, is typically visible.

National Information Infrastructure Protection Act of 1996 An act that modified several sections of the Computer Fraud and Abuse Act and increased penalties for selected crimes.

National InfraGard Program A cooperative effort between the FBI and local technology professionals to protect critical national information. Each FBI field office has an InfraGard chapter.

National Security Agency (NSA) The organization responsible for signal intelligence and information system security.

need-to-know A category within a data classification structure that grants access to individuals based on the fact that they require the information to perform their jobs.

negative feedback loop Synonymous with cybernetic loop. A process to manage a project that ensures that progress is measured periodically and that measured results are compared to expected results.

network security The protection of the networks (systems and hardware) that use, store, and transmit an organization's information.

network-based IDPS (NIDPS) Devices that look at patterns of network traffic and attempt to detect unusual activity based on previous baselines.

noise Alarm events that are accurate and noteworthy but that do not pose a significant threat to information security. Noise can also refer to any interference in the normal pattern of an electrical current.

nondiscretionary controls Controls that are managed by a central authority in the organization and can be based on an individual's role—role-based controls—or a specified set of tasks the individual is assigned—task-based controls.

nonrepudiation The principle of cryptography that gives credence to the authentication mechanism collectively known as a digital signature. In this asymmetric cryptographic process, the sender's private key is used to encrypt a message, and the sender's public key must be used to decrypt the message—when the decryption happens successfully, it provides verification that the message was sent by the sender and cannot be refuted.

object A passive entity in an information system that receives or contains information.

object of an attack The object or entity being attacked.

offline UPS Synonymous with standby uninterruptible power supplies (UPS). An offline battery backup that detects the interruption of power to equipment.

operational controls Management and lower-level planning functions that deal with the operational functionality of security in an organization, such as disaster recovery and incident response planning.

operational feasibility Synonymous with behavioral feasibility. The examination of user acceptance and support, management acceptance and support, and the overall requirements of the organization's stakeholders.

operations security A process used by an organization to deny an adversary information (generally not confidential information) about its intentions and capabilities by identifying, controlling, and protecting the organization's planning processes or operations. OPSEC does not replace other security disciplines—it supplements them.

organizational culture The specific social and political atmosphere within a given organization that determines the organization's procedures and policies and willingness to adapt to changes.

organizational feasibility A comparison of how proposed information security alternatives contribute to the efficiency, effectiveness, and overall operation of an organization.

packet-filtering firewall Networking devices that filter data packets based on their headers as they travel in and out of an organization's network.

packet monkeys Hackers of limited skill (also known as script kiddies) who use automated exploits to engage in distributed denial-of-service attacks.

packet sniffer A network tool that collects copies of packets from the network and analyzes them.

padded cell A honeypot that has been protected so that that it cannot be easily compromised.

parallel operations A method of modifying work practices that involves using the new methods alongside the old methods.

partially distributed IDPS control strategy An intrusion detection prevention system (IDPS) control strategy in which individual agents can still analyze and respond to local threats, but they are required to report to a hierarchical central facility—which creates a blended approach that enables the organization to detect widespread attacks and also intelligent attackers who probe an organization through multiple points of entry before they launch a concerted attack.

passive vulnerability scanner A vulnerability scanner that listens in on the network and determines vulnerable versions of both server and client software.

passphrase A series of characters, typically longer than a password, from which a virtual password is derived.

password A private word or combination of characters that only the user knows.

password attack An attempt to repeatedly guess passwords to commonly used accounts.

penetration testing A level beyond vulnerability testing; a set of security tests and evaluations that simulate attacks by a malicious external source.

performance gap The difference between an organization's measures and those of others.

permutation cipher The rearranging of values within a block to create coded information.

personal identification numbers (PINs) A set of numbers that allow access or entrance.

personnel security To protect the individual or group of individuals who are authorized to access the organization and its operations.

pharming The redirection of legitimate web traffic to an illegitimate site for the purpose of obtaining private information.

phased implementation An approach to implementing new security systems that involves rolling out a piece of a new system across the entire organization.

phishing An attempt to obtain personal or financial information using fraudulent means, usually by posing as a legitimate entity.

photoelectric sensors A type of smoke detector that projects and detects an infrared beam across an area. If the beam is interrupted (presumably by smoke), the alarm or suppression system is activated.

phreaker A person who hacks the public telephone network to make free calls and disrupt services.

physical security An aspect of information security that addresses the design, implementation, and maintenance of countermeasures that protect the physical resources of an organization.

pilot implementation The changing of work practices that involves implementing all security improvements in a single office, department, or division, and resolving issues within that group before expanding to the rest of the organization.

plaintext Synonymous with cleartext. The original unencrypted message, or a message that has been successfully decrypted.

planning and risk assessment domain The domain of the security maintenance model concerned with keeping a lookout on the entire information security program by identifying and planning organization information security activities that further reduce risk.

platform security validation (PSV) A process designed to find and document the vulnerabilities that may be present because of misconfigured systems that are in use within an organization.

plenum In an office building the space above the ceiling, below the floor above.

policies A body of expectations that describes acceptable and unacceptable behaviors of employees in the workplace.

policy A plan or course of action used to convey instructions from an organization's senior-most management to those who make decisions, take actions, and perform other duties.

policy administrator The champion and manager of an information security policy.

political feasibility An analysis that defines what changes can and cannot occur within an organization based on the consensus and relationships between the communities of interest.

polyalphabetic substitutions In encryption, the substitution of one value for another, using two or more alphabets.

polymorphic threat A threat that changes its apparent shape over time, to become a new threat not detectable by techniques looking for a preconfigured signature.

port scanners The tools used to identify (or fingerprint) computers that are active on a network, as well as the ports and services active on those computers, the functions and roles the machines are fulfilling, and other useful information.

possession The quality or state of having ownership or control of some object or item.

pre-action system A sprinkler system that has a two-phase response to a fire.

predecessors In a project plan, the tasks or action steps that come before the specific task at hand.

Pretty Good Privacy (PGP) A hybrid cryptosystem that combines some of the best available cryptographic algorithms. PGP is the open source de facto standard for encryption and authentication of e-mail and file storage applications.

privacy The state of being free from unsanctioned intrusion.

Privacy Enhanced Mail (PEM) Standard proposed by the Internet Engineering Task Force (IETF) to function with the public key cryptosystems.

Privacy of Customer Information Section Part of the common carrier regulation that specifies that any proprietary information shall be used explicitly for providing service, and not for any marketing purposes, and that carriers cannot disclose this information except when necessary to provide their services, or when a customer requests the disclosure of information.

private key encryption Synonymous with symmetric encryption. Private key encryption is a method of communicating on a network using a single key to both encrypt and decrypt a message.

private law Laws that regulate the relationship between the individual and the organization, and that encompass family law, commercial law, and labor law.

process-based measures Benchmarking comparisons that are generally less focused on numbers and more strategic than metrics-based measures.

project plan A program that delivers instructions to individuals for carrying out the implementation stage of the security systems development life cycle.

project scope The amount of time and effort-hours needed to deliver the planned features and quality level of the project deliverables.

project team For information security, a group of individuals with experience in the requirements of both technical and nontechnical fields.

project wrap-up A procedural task assigned to a mid-level IT or information security manager where they collect documentation, finalize status reports, and deliver a final report and a presentation in order to resolve any pending issues, critique the overall project effort and draw conclusions about how to improve the process in the future.

projectitis The phenomenon of becoming so engrossed in project administration that the project itself suffers.

protocol stack verification A process in which a network-based intrusion detection prevention system (NIDPS) looks for invalid data packets—i.e., packets that are malformed under the rules of the TCP/IP protocol.

proximity reader A type of access control device that does not require keycard insertion.

proxy firewall Synonymous with proxy server. A server that is configured to look like a Web server and performs actions on behalf of that server to protect it from hacking.

proxy server Synonymous with proxy firewall. A server that is configured to look like a Web server and performs actions on behalf of that server to protect it from hacking.

public law A law that regulates the structure and administration of government agencies and their relationships with citizens, employees, and other governments.

public-key encryption Synonymous with asymmetric encryption. A method of communicating on a network using two different but related keys, one to encrypt and the other to decrypt messages.

Public-key Infrastructure (PKI) An integrated system of software, encryption methodologies, protocols, legal agreements, and third-party services that enables users to communicate securely.

qualitative assessment An evaluation process that is based on characteristics that do not use numerical measures.

quantitative assessment The evaluation of an organization's assets, estimated values, and formulas.

rate-of-rise A fire detection system in which a sensor detects an unusually rapid increase in the area temperature, within a relatively short period of time.

readiness and review domain The domain of the security maintenance model concerned with keeping the information security program functioning as designed and keeping it continuously improving over time.

recommended practices Security efforts that seek to provide a superior level of performance in the protection of information are referred to as best business practices.

redundancy The implementation of multiple types of technology that prevent the failure of one system from compromising the security of information.

redundant array of independent drives (RAID) A form of data backup for online usage that uses a number of hard drives to store information across multiple drive units, so as to minimize the impact of a single drive failure.

registration authority (RA) A component of a Public Key Infrastructure system that operates under the trusted collaboration of the certificate authority and can be delegated day-to-day certification functions, such as verifying registration information about new registrants, generating end-user keys, revoking certificates, and validating that users possess a valid certificate.

Remote Authentication Dial-In User Service (RADIUS) A system that authenticates the credentials of users who are trying to access an organization's network through a dial-up connection.

remote journaling The transfer of live transactions to an off-site facility.

replay attack An attack in which an abuser has successfully broken an encryption and attempts to resubmit the deciphered authentication to gain entry to a secure source.

request for proposal (RFP) An invitation for providers of a product or service to bid on the right to supply that product or service to the issuer of the RFP.

residual risk The risk that remains to an information asset after an existing control has been applied.

restitution The compensation for a misdeed.

reverse firewalls Synonymous with content filter. A software device that allows administrators to work within a network to restrict accessibility to information.

risk The probability that something can happen.

risk appetite The quantity and nature of risk that organizations are willing to accept.

risk assessment The analysis of a danger to assign a risk rating or score to an information asset.

risk assessment specialist An individual who understands financial risk assessment techniques, the value of organizational assets, and security methods.

risk control The process of applying controls to reduce the risks to an organization's data and information systems.

risk identification The formal process of examining and documenting the security posture of an organization's information technology and the risks it faces.

risk management The process of identifying vulnerabilities in an organization's information systems and taking carefully reasoned steps to ensure the confidentiality, integrity, and availability of all components in the organization's information system.

role-based controls A type of access control in which individuals are allowed to use data based on their positions in an organization.

RSA algorithm The *de facto* standard for public use encryption applications. The security of the algorithm is based on the computational difficulty of factoring large composite numbers and computing the *eth roots modulo*, a composite number for a specified odd integer *e*.

sacrificial host A dedicated server that receives screened network traffic. Usually prepared with extra attention to detail and hardened for use in an unsecured or limited security zone. Sometimes referred to as a bastion host.

sag A momentary incidence of low voltage.

salami theft Aggregation of information used with criminal intent.

Sarbanes-Oxley Act of 2002 A critical piece of legislation that affects the executive management of publicly traded corporations and public accounting firms.

screened subnet An entire network segment that protects the DMZ systems and information from outside threats by providing a network of intermediate security, and protects the internal networks by limiting how external connections can gain access to them.

script kiddies Hackers of limited skill who use expertly written software to exploit a system but do not fully understand or appreciate the systems they hack.

search warrant A legal document that grants permission to search for evidentiary material at the specified location and/or to seize items to return to the investigator's lab for examination. The basis for a search warrant is an affidavit.

second generation firewall Application-level firewalls or proxy servers, which are dedicated systems that are separate from the filtering router and that provide intermediate services for requestors.

secret key Password or passphrase used in private key or symmetric encryption.

Secure Electronic Transactions (SET) A means of securing Web transactions that was developed by MasterCard and VISA in 1997 to provide protection from electronic payment fraud.

secure facility A physical location that has been engineered with controls designed to minimize the risk of attacks from physical threats.

Secure Hash Standard (SHS) An encryption norm that specifies SHA-1 (Secure Hash Algorithm 1) as a secure algorithm for computing a condensed representation of a message or data file.

Secure HTTP (S-HTTP) A protocol designed to enable secure communications across the Internet. S-HTTP is the application of SSL over HTTP, which allows the encryption of all information passing between two computers through a protected and secure virtual connection.

Secure Multipurpose Internet Mail Extensions (S/MIME) A specification developed to increase the security of e-mail that adds encryption and user authentication.

Secure Sockets Layer (SSL) A protocol to use public key encryption to secure a channel over the internet.

secure VPN A type of private and secure network connection, or VPN, that uses security protocols and encrypts traffic transmitted across unsecured public networks like the Internet.

security To be protected from adversaries—from those who would do harm, intentionally or otherwise.

Security and Freedom through Encryption Act of 1999 An attempt by Congress to provide guidance on the use of encryption. Provided measures for public protection from government intervention.

security blueprint The basis for the design, selection and implementation of all security program elements including policy implementation, ongoing policy management, risk management programs, education and training programs, technological controls, and maintenance of the security program.

security clearance A level of authorization to classified material that an individual is granted after a formal evaluation process.

security domains Areas within a computer system in which users can safely communicate.

security education, training, and awareness (SETA) A control measure designed to reduce the incidences of accidental security breaches by employees.

security framework An outline of the overall information security strategy for the organization and a roadmap for planned changes to the information security environment of the organization.

security perimeter The edge between the outer limit of an organization's security and the beginning of the outside world.

security policy Synonymous with security program policy (SPP), a general security polity, IT security policy, and information security policy. A set of rules developed to protect an organization's assets.

security policy developer An individual who understands the organizational culture, existing policies, and requirements for developing and implementing security policies.

security posture Synonymous with protection profile. The implementation of an organization's security policies, procedures, and programs.

security professional A specialist in the technical and nontechnical aspects of security information.

security systems development life cycle (SecSDLC) A methodology for the design and implementation of security system.

selected-plaintext attack A crypto system attack in which the attackers send a target a section of plaintext they want encrypted and returned in order to reveal information about the target's encryption systems.

sensor range The distance a wireless device is able to connect to a network. It can be affected by atmospheric conditions, building construction, and the quality of both the wireless network card and access point.

separation of duties A control used to reduce the chance of an individual violating information security and breaching the confidentiality, integrity, or availability of the information.

sequential roster A list of people who are called by a single person in the case of an emergency.

server fault tolerance Technologies and techniques used to make a server computing system more resistant to failure. Will include designing server systems using redundant components (power supplies, disk drives, processors, and others) configured in ways that allow the system to continue operating even when one or more components fail.

service bureau A service agency that provides a service for a fee.

Service Level Agreement (SLA) The contract of a Web host provider covering responsibility for Internet services as well as for hardware and software used to operate the Web site.

session keys Limited-use symmetric keys for encrypting electronic communication.

shoulder surfing The act of observing information without authorization by looking over a shoulder or spotting information from a distance.

signature-based IDPS Synonymous with knowledge-based IDPS and misuse-detection IDPS. A device that examines data traffic for signature matches with predefined, preconfigured attack patterns.

signatures Preconfigured, predetermined attack patterns.

simple polyalphabetic A basic code used in substitution ciphers where one letter is replaced with another.

single loss expectancy (SLE) The calculation of the value associated with the most likely loss from an attack.

site policy The rules and configuration guidelines governing the implementation and operation of IDPSs within the organization.

site policy awareness The ability of intrusion detection prevention system to dynamically modify its site policies in reaction or response to environmental activity.

smart card A device that contains a computer chip that can verify and validate a number of pieces of information about an individual above and beyond a PIN.

smoke detection Systems that detect a potentially dangerous fire and are required by building codes in most residential dwellings and commercial buildings.

sniffer A program or device that can monitor data traveling over a network.

social engineering The process of using social skills to convince people to reveal access credentials or other valuable information to the attacker.

software piracy The unlawful use or duplication of software-based intellectual property.

spam Unsolicited commercial e-mail.

spear phishing A highly targeted phishing attack that usually appears to be from an employer, colleague, or other legitimate correspondent.

spoofing A technique used to gain unauthorized access to computers, wherein the intruder sends messages to a computer with an IP address indicating that the message is coming from a trusted host.

sprinkler systems Devices that are designed to apply liquid, usually water, to all areas in which a fire has been detected.

spyware Any technology that aids in gathering information about a person or organization without their knowledge.

SSL Record Protocol A protocol responsible for the fragmentation, compression, encryption, and attachment of an SSL header to the cleartext prior to transmission.

standard HTTP A protocol that provides the Internet communication services between client and host without consideration for encryption of the data that is communicated over the connection between client and server.

standard of due care A legal term that becomes relevant when organizations adopt levels of security for a legal defense and therefore might be required to show that they have done what any prudent organization would do in similar circumstances.

standard operating procedures (SOPs) Documentation provided to members of the organization that help them to act decisively in unfamiliar situations.

standards Detailed statements of actions that comply with policy.

standby UPS Synonymous with offline uninterruptible power supplies (UPS). An offline battery backup that detects the interruption of power to equipment.

state table A feature of stateful inspection firewalls that tracks the state and context of each packet in the conversation by recording which station sent what packet and when.

stateful inspection firewall Devices that track network connections that are established between internal and external systems.

stateful protocol analysis (SPA) The process of comparing predetermined profiles of generally accepted definitions of benign activity for each protocol state against observed events to identify deviations.

static electricity The spark that occurs when two materials are rubbed or touched and electrons are exchanged, resulting in one object becoming more positively charged and the other more negatively charged.

statistical anomaly-based IDPS (stat IDPS) Synonymous with behavior-based IDS. A device that collects data from normal traffic to establish a baseline. The IDS compares periodic data samples with the baseline to highlight irregularities.

steganography A method of hiding the existence of a secret message.

strong authentication In access control, security systems that use two or more authentication mechanisms.

subject An active entity that interacts with an information system and causes information to move through the system for a specific purpose. Examples include individuals, technical components, and computer processes.

subject of an attack An agent entity that is used as an active tool to conduct an attack.

substitution cipher In encryption, an encryption method that involves the substitution of one value for another.

successors In a project plan, the tasks or action steps that come after the task at hand.

sunset clause Prevents a temporary policy from becoming a permanent mistake by specifying a discontinuation date.

surge A prolonged increase in voltage.

symmetric encryption Synonymous with private key encryption. A method of communicating on a network using a single key to both encrypt and decrypt a message.

synchronous tokens Authentication devices that are synchronized with a server, so that each device (server and token) uses the time or a time-based database to generate a number that is entered during the user login phase.

System Administration, Networking, and Security Institute (SANS) A professional organization dedicated to the protection of information and systems.

system integrity verifiers Synonymous with host-based IDPSs. Resides on a particular computer or server, known as the host, and monitors activity only on that system.

systems administrator An individual responsible for administering information systems.

systems development life cycle (SDLC) A methodology for the design and implementation of an information system.

tailgating A security breach that occurs when an authorized individual gains admission to a secure area by presenting a badge or key and is directly followed into the area by an unauthorized individual.

task-based controls A type of data access control in which individuals are allowed to use data, based on their job responsibilities.

task rotation Synonymous with job rotation. A security check that requires that every employee is trained to perform the work of another employee.

TCP hijacking attack An attack in which the abuser records data packets from the network, modifies them, and inserts them back into the network.

team leader For information security, a project manager who understands project management, personnel management, and technical requirements.

technical controls Tactical and technical implementations of the security in the organization.

technical feasibility An analysis that examines whether or not the organization has or can acquire the technology necessary to implement and support the proposed control.

technical specifications A document created to translate the management intent for the technical control into an enforceable technical approach.

technology governance A complex process that an organization uses to manage the impacts and costs caused by technology implementation, innovation, and obsolescence.

telecommuting Offsite computing that uses Internet connections, dial-up connections, connections over leased point-to-point links between offices, and other connection mechanisms.

TEMPEST A program developed by the U.S. Government to reduce the risk of EMR monitoring.

Terminal Access Controller Access Control System (TACACS) A remote access system that validates a user's credentials.

terminate control strategy Directs the organization to avoid those business activities that introduce uncontrollable risks.

theft The illegal taking of another's property.

thermal detection systems Fire detection systems that contain a sophisticated heat sensor. There are two types, fixed temperature and rate-of-rise.

thermal detectors A type of alarm sensor for detecting intrusions that works by detecting rates of change in the ambient temperature in the room.

third generation firewall Stateful inspection firewalls which monitor network connections between internal and external systems using state tables.

threat An object, person, or other entity that represents a constant danger to an asset.

threat agent A specific instance or component that represents a danger to an organization's assets. Threats can be accidental or purposeful, for example lightning strikes or hackers.

threat assessment The examination of a danger to assess its potential to impact an organization.

time–memory tradeoff attack A method of attack in which attackers compare hashed text against a database of pre-computed hashes from sequentially calculated passwords.

time-share A site that is leased by an organization in conjunction with a business partner for use if a disaster occurs at the home site.

timing attack An attack in which an abuser explores the contents of a Web browser's cache. These attacks allow a Web designer to create a malicious form of cookie to store on the client's system.

top-down approach A methodology of establishing security policies that is initiated by upper management.

tornado or severe windstorm A threat to the hardware components of information systems that falls in the forces of nature or acts of God category because it is unexpected or can occur with very little warning. Because these storms are typically rotating columns of air whirling at destructively high speeds, they can directly damage all or part of an information system or, more likely, the building that houses it.

transport mode One of the two modes of operation of the IP Security Protocol. In transport mode, only the IP data is encrypted, not the IP headers.

transposition cipher Synonymous with permutation cipher. The rearranging of values within a block to create coded information.

trap-and-trace A combination of resources that detect an intrusion and trace it back to its source.

trap door In cryptography, a secret mechanism that enables you to easily accomplish the reverse function in a one-way mechanism. Also knows as a back door.

trespass The act of entering a premises or system without authorization.

triboelectrification A process that causes static electricity and occurs when two materials are rubbed together causing electrons to be exchanged and one object to become more positively charged and the other more negatively charged. When a third object with an opposite charge or ground is encountered, electrons flow again and a spark is produced.

triple DES (3DES) An enhancement to the Data Encryption Standard (DES). An algorithm that uses up to three keys to perform three different encryption operations.

Trojan horses Software programs that hide their true nature (usually destructive), and reveal their designed behavior only when activated.

trophy A piece of evidence (usually a screenshot) that can be used to convince skeptical system administrators that the vulnerability is real.

true attack stimulus An event that triggers alarms and causes an intrusion detection prevention system (IDPS) to react as if a real attack is in progress.

true online UPS A top-of-the-line, expensive type of uninterruptible power supply (UPS) that is capable of delivering a constant, smooth, conditioned power stream to computing systems.

trusted network A network that is inside an organization's firewall.

trusted VPN A type of private and secure network connection that uses leased circuits from a service provider and conducts packet switching over these leased circuits. Also known as a legacy VPN.

tsunami A threat to the hardware components of information systems that falls in the forces of nature or acts of God category because it is unexpected or can occur with very little warning. Specifically, this is a very large ocean wave caused by an underwater earthquake or volcanic eruption that can directly damage all or part of an information system or, more likely, the building that houses it.

tuning The process of adjusting an IDPS's ability to correctly detect and identify certain types of attacks.

tunnel mode One of the two modes of operation of the IP Security Protocol. In tunnel mode, the entire IP packet is encrypted and placed as payload into another IP packet.

two-person control A security check that requires that two individuals review and approve each other's work before a task is categorized as finished.

U.S. Secret Service A department within the Department of the Treasury. Provides protective services for key members of the U.S. government and detects and arrests any person committing a United States federal offense relating to computer fraud or false identification crimes.

unskilled hacker An individual who depends on the expertise of others to abuse systems.

untrusted network A network outside an organization's firewall, such as the Internet.

USA PATRIOT Act of 2001 This act modified a wide range of existing laws to provide law enforcement agencies with a broader latitude of actions to combat terrorism-related activities.

USA PATRIOT Improvement and Reauthorization Act Made permanent 14 of the 16 expanded powers of the Department of Homeland Security, and the FBI in investigating terrorist activity.

utility The quality or state of having value for an end purpose. Information has utility if it serves a purpose.

Vernam cipher An element of cryptosystems that was developed at AT&T and uses a set of characters only one

time for each encryption process. Also known as the one-time pad.

vibration sensors A type of alarm sensor for detecting intrusion that works by detecting minute movements of the sensor caused by the vibration of the structure shared with the object being protected.

Vigenère cipher An advanced type of substitution cipher that uses a simple polyalphabetic code and involves using the Vigenère Square, which is made up of 26 distinct cipher alphabets.

virtual organization A group of individuals brought together through electronic communication for a specific task, usually from different organizations, divisions, or departments.

virtual password A password calculated or extracted from a passphrase that meets system storage requirements.

virtual private network (VPN) A private and secure network connection between systems that uses the data communication capability of an unsecured and public network.

virus One of two forms of malicious code or malware. A virus requires a host software environment in which to execute and it cannot function without such a host.

virus hoax E-mail warning of a virus that is fictitious.

vision A written statement of the organization's goals.

vulnerability Weakness in a controlled system, where controls are not present or are no longer effective.

vulnerability assessment (VA) The process of identifying and documenting specific and provable flaws in the organization's information asset environment.

vulnerability assessment and remediation domain The identification of specific, documented vulnerabilities and their timely remediation.

vulnerability instances The existence of a vulnerability that is deemed a significant risk.

war dialer An automatic phone-dialing program that dials every number in a configured range (e.g., 555-1000 to 555-2000), and checks to see if a person, answering machine, or modem picks up.

war dialing An attack that uses scripted dialing against a pool of phone numbers.

war game A simulation of an attack on an organization's information assets.

warm site An alternate site that can be used by an organization if a disaster occurs at the home site. Frequently includes computing equipment and peripherals with servers but not client workstations.

water mist sprinklers A form of sprinkler system that produces an ultra fine mist instead of a shower of water characteristic of a traditional system.

waterfall model A methodology of the system development life cycle in which each phase of the process begins with the information gained in the previous phase.

wired network connections Network connection that eventually integrates wireless traffic with an organization's wired network.

wireless vulnerability assessment The process designed to find and document the vulnerabilities that may be present in wireless local area network.

work breakdown structure (WBS) A planning approach that breaks a project plan into specific action steps.

work factor The amount of effort (usually in hours) required to perform cryptanalysis on an encoded message so that it may be decrypted when the key or algorithm (or both) are unknown.

worm One of two forms of malicious code or malware. A virus that replicates itself on other machines without the need of another program environment.

zombie A computer that has been compromised and may later be used as an agent to be directed towards a target. The use as an agent is controlled remotely (usually by way of a transmitted command) by the attacker.

Index

Note: page numbers followed by f or t refer to Figures or Tables